Politics and the Histories of International Law

Legal History Library

VOLUME 50

Studies in the History of International Law

VOLUME 18

The titles published in this series are listed at *brill.com/shil*

Politics and the Histories of International Law

The Quest for Knowledge and Justice

Edited by

Raphael Schäfer and Anne Peters

BRILL
NIJHOFF

LEIDEN | BOSTON

The Introduction and Chapters 1, 3, 5–8, 11, 12, 14, 15 and 18 were originally published in *Journal of the History of International Law / Revue d'histoire du droit international*, Volume 22, Issue 2–3 (October 2020): Special Issue: Politics and the Histories of International Law. The page numbers in square brackets at the top of the pages in these chapters refer to the journal version.

The conference from which the book originates was funded by the Deutsche Forschungsgemeinschaft (DFG, German Research Foundation) – Project Number PE 631/6-1 and supported by Koninklijke Brill NV.

Cover illustration: Artemisia Gentileschi, "Clio", Proprietà della Fondazione Pisa/Palazzo Blu.

Library of Congress Cataloging-in-Publication Data

Names: Schäfer, Raphael, editor. | Peters, Anne (Editor of Politics and the histories of international law)
Title: Politics and the histories of international law : the quest for knowledge and justice / edited by Raphael Schäfer and Anne Peters.
Description: Leiden ; Boston : Brill/Nijhoff, 2021. | Series: Legal history library; volume 50 | Includes index.
Identifiers: LCCN 2021018091 (print) | LCCN 2021018092 (ebook) | ISBN 9789004461796 (hardback) | ISBN 9789004461802 (ebook)
Subjects: LCSH: International law—History. | International law—Historiography. | International law—Political aspects. | International relations.
Classification: LCC KZ1242 .P63 2021 (print) | LCC KZ1242 (ebook) | DDC 341.09—dc23
LC record available at https://lccn.loc.gov/2021018091
LC ebook record available at https://lccn.loc.gov/2021018092

Typeface for the Latin, Greek, and Cyrillic scripts: "Brill". See and download: brill.com/brill-typeface.

ISSN 1874-1793
ISBN 978-90-04-46179-6 (hardback)
ISBN 978-90-04-46180-2 (e-book)

This book is printed on acid-free paper and produced in a sustainable manner.

Contents

PART 5
New Methods and Approaches

Notes on Contributors

Raphael Schäfer
research fellow at the Max Planck Institute for Comparative Public Law and International Law, doctoral candidate at the Ruprecht-Karls-Universität Heidelberg, and the managing editor of the *Journal of the History of International Law*.

Anne Peters
director at the Max Planck Institute for Comparative Public Law and International Law, professor at Heidelberg, Freie Universität Berlin, and Basel, and L. Bates Lea Global Law Professor at the University of Michigan.

Jean d'Aspremont
professor of international law, Sciences Po School of Law Paris, and professor of public international law, University of Manchester.

Julia Bühner
PhD candidate and research assistant at the Department for the High and Late Middle Ages/Western European History, University of Münster.

Emiliano J. Buis
professor of public international law (Faculty of Law), professor of ancient Greek (Department of Classics), University of Buenos Aires, and permanent researcher at the National Scientific and Technical Research Council (CONICET), Argentina.

Maria Adele Carrai
assistant professor of global China studies, New York University Shanghai.

Jacob Katz Cogan
associate dean of academic affairs, Judge Joseph P. Kinneary Professor of Law and Faculty Director, Cincinnati Center for the Global Practice of Law, College of Law, University of Cincinnati.

Rián Derrig
postdoctoral research fellow, Center for Global Constitutionalism, WZB Berlin Social Science Center.

Angelo Dube
professor of international law, Department of Public, Constitutional and International Law, University of South Africa.

Michel Erpelding
PhD in law, visiting researcher at the Department of International Law and Dispute Resolution, Max Planck Institute Luxembourg for Procedural Law; independent academic expert, Bibliothèque nationale du Luxembourg; lecturer, Université Paris 1 Panthéon-Sorbonne/Cairo University.

Etienne Henry
PhD in law and lecturer, Faculty of Law, University of Neuchâtel.

Madeleine Herren
professor of modern history and director of the Institute for European Global Studies, University of Basel.

Randall Lesaffer
professor of legal history, KU Leuven and Tilburg University.

Anne-Charlotte Martineau
PhD in law, tenured researcher, French National Center for Scientific Research (CNRS); École Normale Supérieure Paris.

Parvathi Menon
doctoral researcher, Erik Castrén Institute of International Law and Human Rights and adjunct lecturer, Faculty of Law, University of Helsinki.

Lindelwa Mhlongo
PhD candidate in international economic law and lecturer, Department of Public, Constitutional and International Law, University of South Africa.

Momchil Milanov
PhD candidate and teaching assistant, University of Geneva, Global Studies Institute.

Hirofumi Oguri
senior assistant professor of international law, Okayama University.

José Gustavo Prieto Muñoz
postdoctoral researcher, Department of European, Public and International Law, Programme Human Rights in Context, Ghent University.

Hendrik Simon
associate fellow, Peace Research Institute Frankfurt, and lecturer, Institute of Political Science, Frankfurt University.

Sebastian M. Spitra
PhD in law, postdoctoral researcher, Department for Legal and Constitutional History, University of Vienna.

Deborah Whitehall
Institute for International Law and the Humanities, University of Melbourne.

Politics and the Histories of International Law: An Introduction

Anne Peters, Raphael Schäfer and Randall Lesaffer

•••

'L'histoire n'est pas une religion. L'historien n'accepte aucun dogme, ne respecte aucun interdit, ne connaît pas de tabous. Il peut être dérangeant.'[1]

∴

Almost all scholarship on the history of international law has political implications and repercussions. The putatively 'ideological nature' of international legal scholarship with 'political preferences remaining concealed',[2] the 'concern that legal scholarship could turn out to be nothing more than the pseudo-objective defence of ruling ideologies'[3] is acute not only when scholars examine contemporary international legal problems but also when they examine the history of international law.[4]

Famously, Hans Kelsen has denounced a 'tendency wide-spread among writers on international law' to produce 'political ideology'.[5] Kelsen sought to escape this by writing books of a 'purely juristic character'.[6] In his foreword to

1 'Liberté pour l'histoire' (L'appel du 12 décembre 2005), available at: http://www.lph-asso.fr/index34d1.html?option=com_content&view=article&id=2&Itemid=13&lang=fr (last accessed on 6 July 2020).

2 Feichtner, Isabel. 'Realizing Utopia through the Practice of International Law'. *European Journal of International Law* 23(4) (2012), 1143–1157, 1154.

3 Bernstorff, Jochen von. 'International Legal Scholarship as a Cooling Medium in International Law and Politics'. *European Journal of International Law* 25(4) (2014), 977–990, 977–978.

4 See on politics and ideology as a challenge for international legal scholarship Peters, Anne. 'International Legal Scholarship under Challenge', in *International Law as a Profession*, eds. Jean d'Aspremont, Tarcisio Gazzini, André Nollkaemper and Wouter Werner (Cambridge: Cambridge University Press, 2017), 117–159, 122–134.

5 Kelsen, Hans. 'Preface to the First Edition' (New York: Rinehart, 1952), in *Principles of International Law*, eds. Hans Kelsen and Robert Warren Tucker (New York: Holt, 2nd ed. 1967), ix.

6 Ibid.

the commentary on the UN Charter, he stressed that this work dealt 'with the law of the Organisation, not with its actual or desired role in the international play of powers. *Separation of law from politics* in the presentation of national or international problems is possible'.[7]

In contrast to what Kelsen believed and what he aspired to do, it is nowadays doubted that purging international legal scholarship of politics would work. Martti Koskenniemi at the opening conference of the European Society of International Law in Florence in 2004 put this as follows: 'The choice is not between law and politics but between one politics of law, and another. Everything is at stake, but not for everyone'.[8]

Historians of international law also have to make political choices. The question is not whether but why and in which ways international legal scholarship and, consequently, historical accounts of international law are 'political'.

To begin with, the object under investigation is itself a political matter. International law's content is to a large extent shaped by the political power of the parties which negotiated the treaties and who framed them according to their political values. And of course the historical personalities, the diplomats or scholars of the past, were likewise embedded in a political context. Their work we study now was driven by their personal beliefs, institutional allegiances and instrumental considerations which are difficult to disentangle. A case in point is Hugo Grotius' *Mare Liberum,* whose argument for an open sea was in line with the interests of the Dutch East India Company, a quasi-sovereign actor.[9] Or, the Dominican Friar Francisco de Vitoria issued a formal opinion ('parecer') on 'the education and conversion of the Indians to the holy faith' upon request by Emperor Charles V, King of Spain. That legal opinion today enjoys different, even contrary interpretations. While some read it as a defense of the *conquista*, others read it as a subtle critique of the enterprise.[10]

7 Kelsen, Hans. *The Law of the United Nations* (London: Stevens, 1950), viii (emphasis added).

8 Koskenniemi, Martti. 'International Law in Europe: Between Tradition and Renewal'. *European Journal of International Law* 16(1) (2005), 113–124, 123.

9 The Dutch East India Company had solicited *De jure praedae* in 1604 which remained unpublished. *Mare liberum* was a reworked version of its chapter 12 which Grotius published anonymously in 1609 in the context of the negotiations for the Twelve Years Truce with Spain, at the instigation of Oldenbarnevelt, the political leader of the Holland regents. Cf. Van Ittersum, Martine Julia. 'Hugo Grotius: The Making of a Founding Father of International Law', in *The Oxford Handbook of the Theory of International Law*, eds. Anne Orford and Florian Hoffmann (Oxford: Oxford University Press, 2016), 82–100.

10 See only Zapatero, Pablo. 'Legal Imagination in Vitoria. The Power of Ideas'. *Journal of the History of International Law* 11(2) (2009), 221–271, 248; Allemann, Daniel S. 'Empire and the Right to Preach the Gospel in the School of Salamanca'. *The Historical Journal* 62(1) (2019), 35–55, 36.

And this current reading again depends on the current political context by which the historian is inevitably influenced. As Richard Bourke reminds us, 'historical research usually engages the past under the influence of contemporary concerns', and consequently, 'relations between historical analysis and moral judgment' are 'often blurred'.[11]

Research on the history of international law is not only inherently political, but also specifically 'risk-prone'.[12] Writing on topics such as genocide, the state of exception, failed states, humanitarian intervention, asymmetrical war, or cyber-attacks is especially liable to being used and abused by participants in political controversies. In fact, when it comes to writing history, the fight over master narratives is usually fierce among competing political factions or governments.[13] This is notorious in territorial disputes. The 'historical evidence' presented in boundary disputes before the International Court of Justice has been famously dubbed as 'Foreign Office International Legal History'.[14] The governments normally seek to harness academia, to instrumentalise scholarship for their ends, and to 'seal' debates by decreeing an 'official' history.[15]

11 Bourke, Richard. 'European Empire and International Law from the Eighteenth Century to the Twentieth Century'. *The Historical Journal*, published online by Cambridge University Press on 16 June 2020, 1–10, 1.

12 Even if this is risk-prone in a different sense than the natural sciences' and life sciences' development of the atomic bomb, genetic engineering, bio-enhancement, and the like.

13 The elite's attempt to control history typically starts in the schoolbooks. See for the USA, e.g., Goldstein, Dana. 'Two States. Eight Textbooks. Two American Stories'. *New York Times* (12 January 2020), available at: https://www.nytimes.com/interactive/2020/01/12/us/texas-vs-california-history-textbooks.html (last accessed on 6 July 2020).

14 Bederman, David J. 'Foreign Office International Legal History', in *Time, History and International Law*, eds. Matthew Craven, Malgosia Fitzmaurice and Maria Vogiatzi (Leiden: Martinus Nijhoff, 2007), 43–63. Current examples are the invocation of 'historical titles' in the South China Sea dispute (Permanent Court of Arbitration, *The South China Sea Arbitration* (The Republic of Philippines v. The People's Republic of China), Case No. 2013-19 (Award on Jurisdiction and Admissibility of 29 October 2015; Merits of 12 July 2016). Another example is the quarrel over the name of the Former Yugoslav Republic Macedonia which was settled in the Prespas-Agreement of 12 June 2018 as 'Republic North Macedonia'.

15 A current example is furnished by the Russian and Ukrainian governing elites who are fighting over political history of the region. See the 'Open Letter from Scholars and Experts on Ukraine Re. the So-Called "Anti-Communist Law"', published in Krytika, April 2015, available at: https://krytyka.com/en/articles/open-letter-scholars-and-experts-ukraine-re-so-called-anti-communist-law (last accessed on 6 July 2020): 'Over the past 15 years, Vladimir Putin's Russia has invested enormous resources in the politicization of history. It would be ruinous if Ukraine went down the same road, however partially or tentatively. Any legal or "administrative" distortion of history is an assault on the most basic purpose of scholarly inquiry: pursuit of truth. Any official attack on historical memory is unjust. Difficult and contentious issues must remain matters of debate.'

The infamous example are memory laws which consecrate specific views on atrocities of the past (especially genocidal massacres) and which sometimes additionally criminalise the denial of those atrocities.[16] Some of these attempts to close historical debates by law have been criticised by historians, most famously in the petition 'Liberté pour l'histoire' by French historians reacting against various French memory laws.[17]

Battles over the 'correct' history are not only common among those who wield political positions but constantly go on in academic camps, even if inextricably bound up with the desire to generate knowledge. Maybe a blurry line between the two social systems (academia and politics) can be drawn along the primary purpose of the activity of the participants belonging to the respective systems, and the methods they employ.

Scholarly (and scientific) activity is normally understood to be a 'serious and systematic attempt to find out the truth', as the German Constitutional Court once put it.[18] This scholarly 'truth' is relative to the standpoint of the researcher and his or her research question, it is provisional, and subject to refutation.[19] This relativity notwithstanding, it is not the main objective of scholarship to make politics but to understand and explain, with help of steps (in the case of legal scholarship: with arguments) which are comprehensible and which can be replicated (at least intellectually) by others. Along this line, many scholars of history seek to uncover various aspects of past events and debates and to contextualise them, seeking to reach a modicum of objectivity and neutrality.[20] Of course, more context does not by itself lead to more objectivity. An over-contexualisation might do quite the opposite, as it suggests or even creates a 'context' which for the historical actors was of no importance.[21]

---

16 See the comparative study by Hennebel, Ludovic and Thomas Hochmann, eds. *Genocide Denials and the Law* (Oxford: Oxford University Press, 2011).

17 See above (n. 1).

18 BVerfGE 35, 79 (1 BvR 424/71 and 1 BvR 325/72), para. 128 (29 May 1973) 'alles, was nach Inhalt und Form als ernsthafter planmäßiger Versuch zur Ermittlung der Wahrheit anzusehen ist'; authors' translation.

19 Seminally on the 'situatedness' of the researcher: Haraway, Donna. 'Situated Knowledges: The Science Question in Feminism and the Privilege of Partial Perspective'. *Feminist Studies* 14(3) (1988), 575–599.

20 See, e.g., Lesaffer, Randall. 'International Law and Its History: The Story of an Unrequited Love', in *Time, History and International Law*, eds. Matthew Craven, Malgosia Fitzmaurice and Maria Vogiatzi (Leiden: Martinus Nijhoff, 2007), 27–41.

21 Zapf, Holger. *Methoden der Politischen Theorie: Eine Einführung* (Leverkusen-Opladen: Verlag Barbara Budrich, 2013), 77. See also Gaukroger, Stephen. 'Undercontextualization and Overcontextualization in the History of Science'. *Isis. A Journal of the History of Science Society* 107(2) (2016), 340–342.

And as far as evaluation is concerned, some scholars' strategies encompass conscious attempts to avoid judgment (as far as possible), while others are more prone to judging deliberately and to employing historical insights in contemporary political debates.[22] For example, Patrick Boucheron, in his inaugural lecture of 2015 at the Collège de France called for 'une réassurance scientifique du régime de vérité de la discipline historique que nous devons collectivement travailler'. In order to establish this 'regime of truth of the discipline of historiography' we need to reconcile 'l'érudition et l'imagination'. And the key objective of 'érudition' is, according to Boucheron, to 'faire front à l'entreprise pernicieuse de tout pouvoir injuste'.[23] With Boucheron, we might say that erudition is inextricably bound up with our sense of justice. Each and every scholar therefore walks somewhere in between the unattainable ideal of 'scholarly neutrality' on the one side, and partisan politics on the other side.[24] And it is a matter of personal inclination whether he or she errs more to the one or the other.

It is against this background that an international conference was held at the Max Planck Institute for Comparative Public Law and International Law in Heidelberg under the auspices of the *Journal of the History of International Law* on 16th and 17th February 2019. Unfortunately, one of the journal's editors, Emmanuelle Tourme Jouannet, could not join us. Scholars of different origin, background and training discussed the duties and responsibilities of those researching on the history of international law. Under the heading 'Politics and the Histories of International Law', presentations given at the conference illustrated some key historical manifestations of politics. The contributions not only reflected the 'plurality of visions of the history of international law' but also debated 'the methods, subjects and uses, as well as the bounds and dead-ends' of the discipline.[25]

22 No one today claims that scholarship can be 'value-free'. See Weber, Max. '"Objectivity" in Social Sciences', in *The Methodology of the Social Sciences*, eds. Edward Albert Shils and Henry A. Finch (New York: Free Press, 1949), 49–112; Maus, Heinz and Fürstenberg, Friedrich, eds. *Der Positivismusstreit in der deutschen Soziologie* (Berlin/Neuwied: Luchterhand, 1969). See the very useful exegesis of Max Weber by Dreier, Horst. 'Max Webers Postulat der Wertfreiheit in der Wissenschaft und die Politik', in *Wissenschaft und Politik*, eds. Horst Dreier and Dietmar Willoweit (Stuttgart: Franz Steiner Verlag, 2010), 35–70.

23 Boucheron, Patrick. 'Ce que peut l'histoire'. Collège de France, Leçon inaugurale prononcée le jeudi 17 décembre 2015, para. 67, available at: http://books.openedition.org/cdf/4507 (last accessed on 6 July 2020).

24 Engi, Lorenz. 'Wissenschaft und Werturteil – Wissenschaft und Politik'. *Ancilla iuris* 4 (2009), 25–33.

25 Tourme Jouannet, Emmanuelle and Anne Peters. 'The Journal of the History of International Law: A Forum for New Research'. *Journal of the History of International Law* 16(1) (2014), 1–8, 7–8.

Building on that conference, this book brings together contributions of nineteen authors from different legal systems and backgrounds. The *first part* addresses vulnerable groups in international law. MADELEINE HERREN shows how the concept of extraterritoriality privileged communities of foreigners, excluding the domestic population. ANNE-CHARLOTTE MARTINEAU addresses the role of politics and ideology in writing about the transatlantic slave trade and seeks to show how international law and the legacies of imperialism have contributed to the uneven distribution of freedom and wealth in the twenty-first century. PARVATHI MENON examines the impact of Edmund Burke's *Sketch of a Negro Code* (1780). The paternalistic idea of protecting slaves from planter brutality was invoked both by abolitionists and planters who relied in Burke's Code for attaining different ends. MOMCHIL MILANOV looks at the interplay between sovereignty and humanitarianism in the creation of the refugee status. The motivations of the actors involved cannot be simplistically divided into 'good' humanitarianism and bad 'politics'. Rather, the likewise political objectives of the humanitarians need to be examined closely.

The *second part* addresses the historiography on law of the use of force. HENDRIK SIMON considers the entanglement of both justification and critique of violence as a core phenomenon of this body of scholarship. ETIENNE HENRY argues that 'peaceful coexistence' was no inherent quest of Soviet foreign policy. Rather, it was primarily inspired by tactical necessities and only later forged into a doctrine. DEBORAH WHITEHALL analyses the wartime textbooks of international law by Hersch Lauterpacht, James Brierly and Georges Scelle, published between 1940 and 1945. The textbook genre became an unexpected, critical field which exposed the design flaws of interwar international law.

The *third part* deals with regional and cultural variations of international law. MARIA ADELE CARRAI discusses William A. P. Martin's translations of international law textbooks into Chinese. In that context, the theory of an Ancient Chinese international law matured, and Chinese scholars and officials sought to use Martin's work to universalise Confucianism and to modify international law for accommodating what they believed to be their own superior morality. GUSTAVO PRIETO MUÑOZ examines how the situation in Latin America shaped the development of mixed claims commissions. In that region, armed conflicts and revolutions generated legal conflicts over the property of foreigners, and new governments tried to restore the internal rule of law by engaging with international adjudication. ANGELO DUBE and LINDELWA MHLONGO identify pre-colonial African contributions to international law. They attribute the neglect of these contributions in mainstream legal thinking to the politics of the formative time of international law as we know it today and ask for a more inclusive approach. MICHEL ERPELDING deplores the lack of historical contextualisation in most accounts of EU law and EU institutions. The founders of the discipline were eager to provide a selective and partly decontextualised narrative which sought to describe EU law as unprecedented. They thereby constructed the 'supranational' and 'sui generis' character of their object of study and their nascent discipline.

The *fourth part* deals with the looming of the past over the present. SEBASTIAN SPITRA analyses the legal debates on the restitution of cultural objects. He reveals how the Eurocentric concept of civilisation catalysed the development of international norms on cultural heritage. RÍÁN DERRIG, drawing on archival material, re-assesses the New Haven School as an interwar, politically progressive project of engineering social order through law. The widespread preoccupation with psychology and science as formants of social order in early twentieth century and interwar legal theory has been neglected so far. JULIA BÜHNER examines the Spanish yearbook published by the Asociación Francisco de Vitoria and its political implications in the era of an international ostracism of the Francoist regime. She shows how the authors abused the Dominican friar for propagandistic purposes.

The *fifth part* presents new methods and approaches. JEAN D'ASPREMONT employs the image of turntablism to highlight that the engagement of international lawyers with history is still too wedded to the terms, vocabularies, and categories of the historical narratives they seek to disrupt or displace. EMILIANO J. BUIS considers the widespread negation of the existence of international legal rules in the pre-modern world to be a purely political move. By discarding the ancient precedents, most historiographers deny that hegemony and imperialism has always been part and parcel of international law. HIROFUMI OGURI seeks to unsettle the conviction that positivistic methods of international law are marred by a naïve faith in state practice and treatises without due regard for the historical context. He examines how historic authors identified customary international law in concrete cases, and argues that a well-equipped source criticism is a possible way to reduce such 'naïveté'. JACOB KATZ COGAN calls for a history of international law that focuses more on international law in action – the invocation, elaboration, and contestation of rules in and through their everyday application, not just by states, high-level state actors, legal theorists, and state-organized domestic and international institutions, but also by individuals, low-level officials, private groups, and nongovernmental actors and in places outside the usual forums. Such a history of international law 'in the vernacular' can make the story of international law both wider and deeper.

By examining the history writing on a wide range of issues from slavery over the use of force to extraterritorial jurisdiction, the book shows how historiography has often distorted or neglected regional cultures, and suggests alternative methods and approaches to history writing.

Acknowledgements

We wish to thank all colleagues who helped us in organising the conference, notably Anette Kreutzfeld, Richard Dören and Robert Stendel. Maren Körsmeier helped with editing and complementing references. The conference was funded by the Deutsche Forschungsgemeinschaft (DFG, German Research Foundation) – Project Number PE 631/6-1 and supported by Koninklijke Brill NV. We gratefully acknowledge these contributions. Twelve chapters of this book were also published as a special issue in JHIL 22 (2020), 197–496.

Bibliography

Allemann, Daniel S. 'Empire and the Right to Preach the Gospel in the School of Salamanca'. *The Historical Journal* 62(1) (2019), 35–55.

Bederman, David J. 'Foreign Office International Legal History', in *Time, History and International Law*, eds. Matthew Craven, Malgosia Fitzmaurice and Maria Vogiatzi (Leiden: Martinus Nijhoff, 2007), 43–63.

Bernstorff, Jochen von. 'International Legal Scholarship as a Cooling Medium in International Law and Politics'. *European Journal of International Law* 25(4) (2014) 977–990.

Boucheron, Patrick. 'Ce que peut l'histoire'. Collège de France, Leçon inaugurale prononcée le jeudi 17 décembre 2015, para. 67, available at: http://books.openedition.org/cdf/4507 (last accessed on 6 July 2020).

Bourke, Richard. 'European Empire and International Law from the Eighteenth Century to the Twentieth Century'. *The Historical Journal*, published online by Cambridge University Press on 16 June 2020, 1–10.

Dreier, Horst. 'Max Webers Postulat der Wertfreiheit in der Wissenschaft und die Politik', in *Wissenschaft und Politik*, eds. Horst Dreier and Dietmar Willoweit (Stuttgart: Franz Steiner Verlag, 2010), 35–70.

Engi, Lorenz. 'Wissenschaft und Werturteil – Wissenschaft und Politik'. *Ancilla iuris* 4 (2009), 25–33.

Feichtner, Isabel. 'Realizing Utopia through the Practice of International Law'. *European Journal of International Law* 23(4) (2012), 1143–1157.

Gaukroger, Stephen. 'Undercontextualization and Overcontextualization in the History of Science'. *Isis. A Journal of the History of Science Society* 107(2) (2016), 340–342.

Goldstein, Dana. 'Two States. Eight Textbooks. Two American Stories'. *New York Times* (12 January 2020).

Haraway, Donna. 'Situated Knowledges: The Science Question in Feminism and the Privilege of Partial Perspective'. *Feminist Studies* 14(3) (1988), 575–599.

Hennebel, Ludovic and Thomas Hochmann, eds. *Genocide Denials and the Law* (Oxford: Oxford University Press, 2011).

Van Ittersum, Martine Julia. 'Hugo Grotius: The Making of a Founding Father of International Law', in *The Oxford Handbook of the Theory of International Law*, eds. Anne Orford and Florian Hoffmann (Oxford: Oxford University Press, 2016), 82–100.

Kelsen, Hans. 'Preface to the First Edition' (New York: Rinehart, 1952), in *Principles of International Law*, eds. Hans Kelsen and Robert Warren Tucker (New York: Holt, 2nd ed., 1967).

Kelsen, Hans. *The Law of the United Nations* (London: Stevens, 1950).

Koskenniemi, Martti. 'International Law in Europe: Between Tradition and Renewal'. *European Journal of International Law* 16(1) (2005), 113–124.

Lesaffer, Randall. 'International Law and Its History: The Story of an Unrequited Love', in *Time, History and International Law*, eds. Matthew Craven, Malgosia Fitzmaurice and Maria Vogiatzi (Leiden: Martinus Nijhoff, 2007), 27–41.

Maus, Heinz and Friedrich Fürstenberg, eds. *Der Positivismusstreit in der deutschen Soziologie* (Berlin/Neuwied: Luchterhand, 1969).

Peters, Anne. 'International Legal Scholarship under Challenge', in *International Law as a Profession*, eds. Jean d'Aspremont, Tarcisio Gazzini, André Nollkaemper and Wouter Werner (Cambridge: Cambridge University Press, 2017), 117–159.

Tourme Jouannet, Emmanuelle and Anne Peters. 'The Journal of the History of International Law: A Forum for New Research'. *Journal of the History of International Law* 16(1) (2014), 1–8.

Weber, Max. '"Objectivity" in Social Sciences', in *The Methodology of the Social Sciences*, eds. Edward Albert Shils and Henry A. Finch (New York: Free Press, 1949), 49–112.

Zapatero, Pablo. 'Legal Imagination in Vitoria. The Power of Ideas'. *Journal of the History of International Law* 11(2) (2009), 221–271.

Zapf, Holger. *Methoden der Politischen Theorie: Eine Einführung* (Leverkusen-Opladen: Verlag Barbara Budrich, 2013).

PART 1

International Law and Vulnerable Groups

CHAPTER 1

Strength through Diversity? The Paradox of Extraterritoriality and the History of the Odd Ones Out

Madeleine Herren

Abstract

This contribution argues that the right of access to extraterritorial jurisdiction shaped privilege-based communities across national borders. It discusses extraterritoriality as a legal framework that enabled and shaped the building of communities of foreigners from many different backgrounds. Extraterritoriality – counterintuitively – amalgamated and strengthened a community through that very diversity. This was precisely why that community of foreigners – specified as the odd ones out – understood itself as a social unit across national boundaries, loosening and even contesting its affiliation to a specific nation and/or empire.

Keywords

global history – extraterritoriality – China – consular courts – imperialism – colonial justice – enemy aliens – citizenship

1 Introduction

The chapter's main claim is that extraterritoriality set in motion a colonial cosmopolitanism neither desired nor intended in the imperialist model of governance. Of even greater significance than colonial cosmopolitanism is the creation or amalgamation of a cohesive community from many diverse groups. This approach transcends the notion of foreignness defined by states as individual exemption from national and territorial belonging. Foreign communities are understood as independent actors rather than as objects of special regulations based on international treaties. However, the formation of such communities is tied to a paradox that is typical of 19th-century imperialism: Communities of foreigners – no matter how diverse – derive meaning,

 | DOI:10.1163/9789004461802_003

identity, and strength from privileges. These privileges are the result of complex international negotiations between states. Extraterritoriality is therefore at once a prerequisite for the strengthening of such communities *and* for their containment under state control. This approach presumes that legal debates about the controversial interpretation, use and implementation of extraterritorial privileges allow discussing the social coherence of diversity, giving foreign communities a voice through their legal claims as an indicator of asymmetrical power relations. In order to avoid denominations that are rarely self-attributed (e.g. 'those not living in their country of origin'), this chapter uses the non-specific metaphor of 'odd ones out' when describing the community of foreigners.

This contribution will present the social stratum of the legal staff both as a contested elite within the British Empire and as the founding fathers of their respective communities. By using the example of Hong Kong, we gain insight into how those concerned understood legal instruments as the delimitation of a social space. The approach presented strives for an interdisciplinary dialogue with legal history from the perspective of global history, focusing on contexts – that is, the extent to which legal institutions and experts played a major role in the constitutive legitimation of the respective society. Although the source material presented does not exclude legal texts, their reading and evaluation follow a specific historiographical approach. Through legal practice, colonial court cases render visible international careers and lives in the 19th century. At the same time, the approach used in this contribution examines how such amalgamated international communities further the understanding of a shared legal framework. The argument of creating a social space through the legal instrument of extraterritoriality intertwines three perspectives. First, the example of Sir Francis Piggott shows how a distinguished expert and internationally acclaimed researcher developed the concept of extraterritoriality and confronted determined resistance to his role as a colonial judge at the same time. The second historical perspective examines the way a community of foreigners constructed the history of Hong Kong. The third element of the argument examines the extent to which legal information had been requested by the expatriate community in a way that exceeds the political intentions of establishing extraterritorial rights. While the first perspective is based on contemporary legal literature, the empirical evidence for the second aspect consists of the earliest histories of Hong Kong. The third perspective relies on published and openly accessible material, due to the fact that legal decisions taken in colonial contexts were published in the local foreign-language press, just as specialised digests were becoming established. On the so-called Asia Directories, a Hong Kong-published reference work as an example among others, this chapter emphasizes the importance of the press for the publication of legal practices and sources.

These three elements show that extraterritoriality is more than a juridical instrument, and that claiming and exercising legal privileges represented a momentum of community-building that was highly contested in imperial governance.

2 Methods and Sources

It is not the aim of this chapter to discuss further the highly complex legal aspects of extraterritoriality.[1] Instead, it contributes to the (re)gained attention given to extraterritoriality in legal history.[2] This chapter benefits from case studies that derive potentially subversive, anti-colonial consequences from extraterritorial claims,[3] while espousing a global history approach, as e.g. in publications that connect global history to the idea of protection.[4] However, existing scholarship hardly says anything about extraterritoriality's capacity for community-building, about the characteristic of extraterritoriality as a multilayered and often contradictory system with elements from different origins, and with various actors involved. Almost every consul representing Western powers in Asia also presided over his own court.[5] And the British courts were not only accessible to Western foreigners but they also preserved the legal systems of former colonial powers and the legal representation of the indigenous population in a 'bewildering medley of systems'.[6] The resulting

1 The results presented in this chapter are partially an outcome of the research project 'The Divisive Power of Citizenship', financed by the Swiss National Science Foundation, available at: https://europa.unibas.ch/de/forschung/globalgeschichte-europas/the-divisive-power-of-citizenship/ (last accessed on 14 September 2020).

2 See, e.g., Kayaoglu, Turan. *Legal Imperialism: Sovereignty and Extraterritoriality in Japan, the Ottoman Empire, and China* (Cambridge: Cambridge University Press, 2010); Cassel, Pär Kristoffer. *Grounds of Judgment. Extraterritoriality and Imperial Power in Nineteenth-Century China and Japan* (Oxford: Oxford University Press, 2012); Margolies, Daniel S., Umut Özsu, Maia Pal and Nina Tzouvala, eds. *The Extraterritoriality of Law* (Abingdon: Routledge 2019).

3 Stephens, Julia. 'An Uncertain Inheritance: The Imperial Travels of Legal Migrants, From British India to Ottoman Iraq'. *Law and History Review* 32(4) (2014), 749–772.

4 Benton, Lauren, Adam Clulow and Bain Attwood, eds. *Protection and Empire. A Global History* (Cambridge: Cambridge University Press, 2018).

5 The consular jurisdiction offers examples of overcharged consuls. For the complexity of consular jurisdiction see the well-documented Swiss case: 'Politisches Departement, Besondere Fälle, Konsulargerichtsbarkeit: Bericht des Bundesrates an die Bundesversammlung über seine Geschäftsführung im Jahr 1897', *Schweizerisches Bundesblatt* (23 March 1898), 22.

6 Hall, Henry L. *The Colonial Office. A History* (London: Longmans, Green & Co., 1937), 137.

situation – 'shifting identities' and 'fluid jurisdictional realities' – has attracted scholarly interest in the inconsistencies of legal practices.[7] According to recent research, the apparently chaotic mess of existing legislations caused an almost hysterical 'rage for order' within the British empire, expressed in a continuous process of legal reform.[8]

There are therefore good reasons to look at the politics of ordering and the manifold contemporary activities aiming at a homogeneous and distinct understanding of legal competences. From the point of view of global history, incompatible legal systems with concomitant ambivalences and uncertainties developed their own historical patterns, which have not yet been adequately considered. Recent research on the interferences between Western and Chinese notions of law has revealed dynamics of a different understanding of law.[9] That research transcends the presumed divide between Chinese legal cruelties and Western progressiveness by recognising an ambivalent situation 'where orthodox notions of legality and justice from either the Chinese or Euro-American perspective could not be fully operative, and where everyday negotiations over law and jurisdiction came to transform the understanding of sovereignty and cultural boundary of both sides of the encounter', as Chen wrote.[10] Sharing Chen's criticism of an historiography that deepens the gap between China and the West in its narrative of the way necessary and useful extraterritorial rights existed in an allegedly barbarous environment, this contribution suggests shifting the focus to those who encountered different courts from different Western nations, all interfacing with existing Chinese legal frameworks. This legal quagmire gives us good reason to consider exactly who profited from uncertainties and ambivalences resulting from a multilayered and often contradictory legal situation. In this regard, I follow the excellent website of Australia's Macquarie University, which has set itself the goal of 'uncovering the hidden case law of the British empire's courts' and found that '(t)he more we study the case law of the empire's courts, the more we see that it was characterised by a pluralist web of influence rather than one way traffic from London downwards.'[11]

---

7 Fahmy, Ziad. 'Jurisdictional Borderlands: Extraterritoriality and 'Legal Chameleons', in Precolonial Alexandria, 1840–1870'. *Comparative Studies in Society and History* 55(2) (2013), 305–329.

8 Benton, Lauren and Lisa Ford. *Rage for Order. The British Empire and the Origins of International Law, 1800–1850* (Cambridge: Harvard University Press, 2016).

9 Kroll, Stefan. 'The Illiberality of Liberal International Law: Religion, Science, and the Peaceful Violence of Civilization', in *Paradoxes of Peace in Nineteenth Century Europe*, eds. Thomas Hippler and Miloš Vec (Oxford: Oxford University Press, 2015), 238–249.

10 Chen, Li. *Chinese Law in Imperial Eyes* (New York: Columbia University Press, 2016), 28.

11 Kercher, Bruce. 'Colonial Cases', available at: http://www.law.mq.edu.au/research/colonial_case_law/colonial_cases/site/cc_home/ (last accessed on 14 September 2020).

Besides addressing the colonial legal elites, still under-researched despite increasing interest in specific cases,[12] the following paragraphs will give a voice to those who took legal action and were accepted to approach the courts based on their claims of extraterritorial privileges. The chapter's key argument is that the right of access to extraterritorial jurisdiction shaped a community across national borders. What will be described as 'building community out of diversity' is based on those who claimed privileges in the purview of consular courts. For a better understanding of this process it is crucial to examine the extent to which this hybrid community invented its own tradition. Can we see the very existence of this community confirmed *ex negativo* – by provoking resistance against those who interpreted extraterritoriality in their function as judicial staff far from the control of the colonial office? The research rationale presented in this contribution tests and fleshes out what I describe as an inverse reading of community-building and belonging in two respects: Instead of sharing a common nationality, language, and cultural values, the communities described held a common stake in privileges. The question then is whether privilege-sharing also translated into an increase of social coherence among the privileged.

The study of the formation of community allows for an understanding of the foreigner in very different and inconsistent contemporary incarnations as alien, cosmopolitan, expat, refugee, and migrant. It critically questions a historical contextualisation of foreigners as individuals defined by qualities *missing* relative to the local environment: nationality, language, and religion, among others.[13] Instead, it presumes that extraterritorial privilege formed a community whose historical understanding as a model of building community from diversity describes a research desideratum both in global history and in the history of international law.[14] What can global history in particular contribute

12 For an overview see Brand, Paul and Joshua Getzler, eds. *Judges and Judging in the History of Common Law and Civil Law* (Cambridge: Cambridge University Press, 2012). For specific cases, e.g., the Bombay High Court, see Chandrachud, Abhinav. *An Independent Colonial Judiciary, A History of the Bombay High Court during the British Raj, 1862–1947* (Oxford: Oxford University Press, 2015).

13 Due to the shortcomings of clear-cut definitions of status in the migration discourse, the ICRC prefers broad descriptions of migrants not limited to their legal status. International Committee of the Red Cross. 'Note on Migration and the Principle of Non-Refoulement'. *International Review of the Red Cross* 99(1) (2017), 345–357, doi: 10.1017/S1816383118000152.

14 For the state of the art in global history, see Conrad, Sebastian. *What is Global History?* (Princeton: Princeton University Press, 2016); Hunt, Lynn. *Writing History in the Global Era* (New York: W. W. Norton & Company, 2014); Pomeranz, Kenneth. *The Great Divergence: China, Europe, and the Making of the Modern World Economy* (Princeton: Princeton University Press, 2000); Sachsenmaier, Dominic. *Global Perspectives on Global History: Theories and Approaches in a Connected World* (Cambridge: Cambridge University

to this question? With its focus on processes of transformations across borders, global history addresses the many shortcomings and limitations of analysing legal systems from an exclusive national and territorial point of view. By taking seriously the porosity of borders (a central issue of global history), this approach helps to clarify the social cohesiveness of diversity. Such cohesiveness created by no means a democratic, anti-imperial society but allows analysing a living model of a society built outside, beyond and sometimes even against the national paradigm at a point in time when the modern nation-state had become the master narrative of progress. Without romanticising the life of foreigners in Asia, such communities provide an interesting starting point for investigation of the odd ones out.

3 Shaping a Global Community from Legal Privileges: Piggott's Social Universe of Extraterritoriality

The following section elaborates in greater detail the concept of extraterritorial privileges, focusing on Hong Kong. It derives from an actor-centred debate that explicitly includes legal actors. Although not understood as specific legal rules but rather as a legally formalised social space, extraterritoriality also confirms the importance of law as an overarching normative value, a sort of legal 'commons' that transcends national, ideological and political differences. The building of community founded on the privileges of extraterritorial jurisdiction offers an approach based on sources heretofore not often considered in global history. They include the publications and biographies of legal actors, and cases published and commented on in foreign newspapers in Asia.[15] The cases in colonial and consular courts allow for a more precise understanding of how ex-territorial privileges manifested in everyday life and shaped a community of legally privileged outsiders.

In 1907, Sir Francis Piggott (1852–1925), the chief justice of Hong Kong, published an extended legal analysis of extraterritoriality from the perspective of

---

Press, 2011), doi: 10.1017/CBO9780511736544; Rosenberg, Emily S., ed. *A World Connecting* (Cambridge: Harvard University Press, 2012); Singaravélou, Pierre and Sylvain Venayre, eds. *Histoire du monde au XIXe siècle* (Paris: Fayard, 2017). However, the history of international law is not (yet) a point of reference in the debates about new directions in global history.

15 In contrast to the archives, the foreign newspapers have become increasingly accessible through large digitisation programs (e.g. National Library Board Singapore, https://eresources.nlb.gov.sg/newspapers/, and The Old Hongkong Newspapers Collection https://mmis.hkpl.gov.hk/old-hk-collection) (last accessed on 1 February 2020).

consular jurisdiction.[16] His considerations focus on the question of 'residence in Oriental countries' and follow – not surprisingly – the rationale of case studies, long established in English jurisdiction. Following this rationale for more than 300 pages, his book reveals the existence of a society that contradicts the prevalent narrative of differentiation in national, imperial and colonial entities, then as now the preferred perspective in global historiography. In the cases he quoted in his legal analysis mentioned above, the contested limitations of the legal framework afford insight into cosmopolitan lives: A widow petitioned the British Supreme Court in Constantinople in 1885 and later the Judicial Committee of the Privy Council in London in 1888, claiming that the distribution of assets had to follow British and not Ottoman law. The case provided the opportunity for a closer look into the biography of the testator and shows how a colonial subject gained a cosmopolitan afterlife: As explained in the legal sources, the Baghdad-born testator had started life under Ottoman law, spent his professional life in India under British rule, shifted his business to the port of Jeddah, and died in 1885 in Cairo, where British subjects could claim the privilege of extraterritoriality, notwithstanding that Egypt was under the suzerainty of the Ottoman empire. The question of whether this person should be considered a subject under extraterritorial privileges generated considerable legal debate, especially as the testator was a member of the Chaldean Catholic community.[17] Quoting such cases, Piggott developed a universe, where foreigners who did not fit into a territory-based legal framework shifted from being a marginal disturbance of rules to forming a community whose social coherence inhered in that they all shared the same extraterritorial privileges despite belonging to different nations, religions and regions. At first glance nothing more than an expression of Western imperialism, the structural framework of this privilege-based narrative was, however, much more than just another argument in the great divergence debate. In Piggott's reading, the concept of extraterritoriality merged Western privileges with the uncontested acceptance of sovereignty vis-à-vis Asian states. Even in the case of China, considered semi-colonial after 1900 by contemporary

16 Piggott, Sir Francis. *Exterritoriality: The Law Relating to Consular Jurisdiction and to Residence in Oriental Countries* (Hongkong: Kelly & Walsh, 1907).

17 For the case see Judicial Committee of the Privy Council, *Abd-ul-Messih v. Farra*, 17 March 1888. This case is accessible via a research project on colonial cases at Macquarie University, Sydney, available at: http://www.law.mq.edu.au/research/colonial_case_law/colonial_cases/less_developed/constantinople/abd-ul-messih_v_farra_1888/ (last accessed on 14 September 2020). Also quoted in Maas, Willem, ed. *Multilevel Citizenship* (Philadelphia: University of Pennsylvania Press, 2013).

literature and today's research alike,[18] this approach insisted that with the consular courts, the British king acted on behalf of the Chinese emperor in all cases where foreigners were involved.[19] In this reading, the Chinese sovereignty remained apparently untouched, and religion – e.g. the claimed superiority of Christianity – lost its legal importance. Even more importantly, the privilege presumed the existence of an explicitly foreign community: '[F]oreigners form part of the same exterritorial community,' as Piggott explained in the context of the bankruptcy jurisdiction of consular courts.[20]

With his deliberations, Piggott substantially enlarged the meaning of law in a global context. The usual contemporary assumption was that international law be understood as a distinction between civilised and non-civilised states, while those Western communities profiting from the distinction remained out of view. Following this assumption, to Georg Jellinek, China was clearly not a member of the international legal community.[21] In the aftermath of the Boxer uprising (1899–1901), even if the Chinese government were to accept the rules based on European and Christian traditions, the credibility of such an engagement seemed dubious to Western scholars like Jellinek. China remained entangled in a multi-layered system of international treaties, notably described after World War I as 'unequal treaties'.[22]

Through Piggott's writing, the position of China, fixed by a variety of multi- and bilateral treaties, provided an important but by no means exclusive lens for a better understanding of relations between East Asia and the Western Powers. Rather, the intergovernmental exchange interfered in the living conditions of foreign residents in complex ways. It enhanced the social dynamics of migration, all the more so as Western companies discovered China as the new

---

18 Osterhammel, Jürgen. 'Semi-Colonialism and Informal Empire in Twentieth-Century China: Towards a Framework of Analysis', in *Imperialism and After: Continuities and Discontinuities,* eds. Wolfgang J. Mommsen and Jürgen Osterhammel (London: Allen & Unwin, 1986), 290–314; Nuzzo, Luigi. 'International Legal Theory. The Birth of an Imperial Location: Comparative Perspectives on Western Colonialism in China'. *Leiden Journal of International Law* 31(3) (2018), 569–596.

19 Piggott, *Exterritoriality* 1907 (n. 16), 27.

20 Ibid., 209.

21 Jellinek, Georg. 'China und das Völkerrecht'. *Deutsche Juristen-Zeitung* 5(19) (1900), 401–403. However, Jellinek also concluded that the marginalisation of China was not a real option: 'Wie immer Chinas Geschicke sich gestalten mögen, es ist unmöglich, diese Riesenmacht aus der Reihe der selbständigen Staaten gänzlich zu streichen.' (Ibid., 403).

22 Peters, Anne. 'Treaties, Unequal'. *The Max Planck Encyclopedia of Public International Law,* ed. Rüdiger Wolfrum (Oxford: Oxford University Press, 2012), available at: https://opil.ouplaw.com/view/10.1093/law:epil/9780199231690/law-9780199231690-e1495 (last accessed on 14 September 2020). Chen, *Chinese Law* 2016 (n. 10); Bickers, Robert A. *Out of China: How the Chinese Ended the Era of Western Domination* (London: Penguin, 2018).

El Dorado for foreign investment following the Boxer uprising. While these activities depended on the privilege of extraterritoriality, a legal understanding of this concept not only blurred distinctions between international law, private law, national and civil rights among Western states, it also scrutinised colonial governance, since Western domination championed the promise of a legal order as the crucial expression of Western civilisation. Hong Kong – Piggott's bailiwick as Chief Justice – challenged this. As a British colony based on treaties signed in 1843 between the British empire and China, Hong Kong from the start combined a multiplicity of (global) actors with a notorious reputation. The 'Gibraltar of the East' turned into a highly conspicuous place due to the constricted territorial situation, the lack of raw materials, the small population of foreign residents, and the impossibility of reducing the dynamics of exchange without endangering profits gained from its status as a port. Here a legal system had to fight piracy, gambling, prostitution and slavery, among other sins, the existence of which on a British-controlled territory posed a significant challenge to the presumptive lofty standard of Western civilisation. In addition, Hong Kong was constantly the focus of armed attack – from the Taiping uprising, to pirate raids on the port, to the meddling of Western military forces. This situation strengthened the social cohesion of foreign residents, shaped the community of the odd ones out and piqued their interest in close cooperation with local communities described in contemporary literature as 'respectable Chinese'.[23] This group even came under British protection, and Chinese members were included in the colonial administration from an early stage.[24]

The situation in Hong Kong, while remaining famously chaotic into the 1860s, also gave an insight into the multi-layered claims balancing within legal frameworks.[25] To Piggott, the concept of extraterritoriality was indeed able to foster a community of diverse foreigners, even one with some transparency towards indigenous communities. He explained extraterritoriality as a hybrid system which 'recognizes the existence of two separate communities in the same country. Where one is savage and the other is civilized, the points of disturbance are few. But where the foreign community is a large one carrying on

23 Dennys, Nicholas B., Charles King and William Frederick Mayers. *The Treaty Ports of China and Japan. A Complete Guide to the Open Ports of those Countries, together with Peking, Yedo, Hongkong and Macao* (London: Trübner & Co., 1867), 77.

24 Ibid., 78.

25 From the 1860s onwards described as a 'bourgeois revolution' from the Chinese population's point of view, the social coherence started to improve. See Munn, Christopher. *Anglo-China. Chinese People and British Rule in Hong Kong 1841–1880* (Abingdon: Routledge, 2013).

a prosperous trade, and where the native community is also prosperous and busy, has its own laws, police, Courts, and the whole system of executive government, the points of disturbance are many, deepening in interest with every recurrence of them.'[26]

In the case of Hong Kong, reality was indeed far from a clear-cut differentiation between 'savage' and 'civilized'. British jurisdiction, rather than showcasing the virtues of Western civilisation, exposed both Western delinquency and a colonial government under suspicion of corruption. In Hong Kong, an American was found guilty of piracy in 1857.[27] In 1860 the 'respectable Chinese' businessman Tam Achoy was arrested after he used a hired vessel under British flag to feign a pirate attack on a group of Hakka Chinese.[28] Small (British) trading houses criticised the colonial government for favouring big companies such as Jardine & Matheson; and public debate from Hong Kong to London fomented suspicion about cooperation between pirates and the colonial government. This was subsequently investigated, validating suspicions of corruption within the empire and providing insight into the specific circumstances of the lives of those whose presence in Hong Kong stemmed from very different reasons.[29]

4 Community Building in a 'Difficult Dependency'?

With regard to tensions between Hong Kong and London, the colonial legal actors had indeed attained an ambivalent position. On the one hand, Hong Kong offered a formidable legal apparatus compared to other colonies, including a Supreme Court established in 1845, which also acted as a colonial court. On the other hand, legal actors had become suspicious of the Colonial Office due to its (alleged) incompetence in the early years. In Hall's history of the Colonial Office, published in 1937, Hong Kong was memorably mentioned in the category of 'difficult dependencies' and apparently had a bad reputation.[30]

---

26 Piggott, *Exterritoriality* 1907 (n. 16), 2.

27 Shavit, David. *The United States in Asia: A Historical Dictionary* (West Port: Greenwood Press, 1990), 51–52; Dennys, *Treaty Ports* 1867 (n. 23), 75.

28 Dennys, *Treaty Ports* 1867 (n. 23), 86; for the notion of the 'respectable Chinese' and the British strategy of accessing wealthy Chinese traders see Munn, *Anglo-China* 2013 (n. 25), 166.

29 Munn, Cristopher. 'Colonialism "in a Chinese Atmosphere": The Caldwell Affair and the Perils of Collaboration in Early Colonial Hong Kong', in *New Frontiers, Imperialism's New Communities in East Asia, 1842–1953*, eds. Robert Bickers and Christian Henriot (Manchester: Manchester University Press, 2000), 12–37.

30 Hall, *The Colonial Office* 1937 (n. 6), 237–249.

In addition, the Office was fully aware of the rather unwieldy variety of legal rules as well as the difficulties in appointing legal experts ready and willing to serve in the colonies.

As London eagerly followed the situation in Hong Kong, the comparatively small society of the odd ones out evolved a social identity shaped more by its distance from empire than by any support. Coming back to the question of the extent to which the privilege of extraterritoriality was key in establishing social cohesion, the development of a common history was crucial to a fragmented community of foreigners.

A social space under construction needs a shared past. Thanks to their community-building functions, such histories provide valuable information on social preferences in how they are composed, to whom they are addressed, and the way such histories are written. In looking at these questions, we go beyond established historiography, where early histories of Hong Kong published in the 19th century are seen as old-fashioned chronicles written by colonial civil servants, sometimes 'eccentric' and 'difficult to pin down'.[31] In the 19th century, contemporary authors had already addressed the difficulties resulting from the need to build a common history out of fragmented interests: Nicholas Belfield Dennys' historical sketch of Hong Kong concludes that 'there are few places of which the history (owing to the personal nature of the dissensions which have arisen amongst people still residents here) presents greater difficulties to the compiler….'[32] It is fitting that, due to the lack of a common past deriving from the foreign residents' backgrounds, the first attempts to write a history of Hong Kong referred to shared privileges and came from those legal actors, who were viewed with such suspicion in London.

In building a community out of diverse groups, crucial authors of 19th-century Hong Kong history preferred to establish a chronology where court cases shaped the narrative, as opposed to typhoons, wars, and visits from British dignitaries. Although far removed from a classical history of law, these publications contributed to the building of the community of foreigners in two respects: On the one hand, the histories made legal decisions accessible to the public, while on the other, decision-making arising from incompatibilities between extraterritorial privileges and nationally-based legal practices indirectly confirmed the community-building function of those privileges. Such an approach challenges the assumption that Hong Kong should be understood

31 Munn, *Anglo-China* 2013 (n. 25), 5; for the difficulties of a shared past across borders see Xu, Guoqui. *Chinese and Americans, a Shared History* (Cambridge: Harvard University Press, 2014).

32 Dennys, *Treaty Ports* 1867 (n. 23), 15.

as 'little Britain'.[33] It underscores the importance of a legal elite in the colonies at the expense of the colonial government should tensions result within the British Empire. In addition, the outcome of legal decision-making should be championed so that far-flung foreigners would come to understand themselves as a community, if not outside of, at least not identical to the British empire.

The evidence is sufficient for both assumptions. At turn of the century, James William Norton-Kyshe (1855–1920), at the time registrar of the Supreme Court of Hong Kong, published an extended *History of the Laws and Courts in Hongkong*. Here, the author developed the model of an extended and legally grounded history, offering in addition to parliamentary debates the 'tracing [of] consular jurisdiction in China and Japan.'[34] His *History* reflects the mistrust of the residents towards their British government by quoting the increasingly important local English-language press over the government Gazette. And indeed, after the publication of the *History*, Norton-Kyshe's career foundered. He was appointed registrar of the Supreme Court in 1895, over the following years systematically passed over from promotion, and eventually forced to retire in 1904.[35] Even to his biographer, it remains unclear whether Norton-Kyshe was correct in his own assessment that the publication of *History* destroyed his career, or whether he was the victim of an (anti-Semitic) intrigue, an unstable personality, or simply unable to make friends.[36] At almost the same moment, Ernest John Eitel (1838–1908), a German-born court translator, published another historical narrative focusing on the foreign community in Hong Kong. According to his book *Europe in China*, the opening of the Suez Canal substantially augmented Hong Kong's value to the West and turned the port colony into a central platform in a world increasingly shaped by Asia.[37] Again, the legal framework was crucial to both Eitel's book and the author personally.[38] He was originally a sinologist, employed as court translator, as well as a missionary interested in education and working as Inspector of schools. Although suffering fewer repercussions than Norton-Kyshe, his career as civil servant also came to a halt after he headed the translation

33 Munn, *Anglo-China* 2013 (n. 25), 22.

34 Norton-Kyshe, James William. *History of the Laws and Courts of Hongkong. Tracing Consular Jurisdiction in China and Japan and Including Parliamentary Debates, and the Rise, Progress, and Successive Changes in the Various Public Institutions of the Colony from the Earliest Period to the Present Time*, vol. 1 (London: T. Fisher Unwin, 1902).

35 Wesley-Smith, Peter. 'James William Norton-Kyshe'. *Hong Kong Law Journal* 2(3) (1972), 278–293.

36 Ibid.

37 Eitel, Ernest John. *Europe in China* (London: Luzac & Company, 1895).

38 Eitel especially mentioned the first Chinese admitted to the local bar. Ibid., 532.

service established by Governor Hennessy, whom he also served briefly as private secretary.[39] As with Piggott, the colonial administration in London clearly neither appreciated his magnum opus nor his meticulous elaboration on the dynamics of social coherence among foreigners benefitting from extraterritorial privilege. Piggott, too, was forced to retire as Chief Justice in 1912 and fight for his pension. After the end of his juridical career, he practised as a barrister in Hong Kong, constantly battling the insolvency that dogged him to his grave.[40] Notwithstanding, he was a well-known scholar and legal expert, contributing to international private law conferences.[41] Again, from a historiographical point of view, it remains unclear whether this individual with a 'tempestuous career' was merely an incompetent, uncontrollable and biased judge or, alternatively, an expert whose competence in analysing extraterritoriality transgressed the comfort threshold of the London colonial establishment, which then reacted with disciplinary measures.[42]

5 The Odd Ones Out as a Public: Constructing Communities beyond the Reach of British Administration?

In the histories mentioned above, the community described and addressed as a privilege-based entity transitioned from objects of law (albeit invested with certain privileges) into subjects demanding rights and thus claiming transparency both in jurisdiction and in ways accessible to the social space of which these foreigners were part. More than just a specificity of Hong Kong, the obligations to publish legal decision-making was closely associated with the growing presence of foreign newspapers in Asia.[43] Although research literature does mention the spectacular increase in the number of newspapers published in East Asia and the media are discussed as profiting from extraterritoriality, we

39 The local press considered this position as an unacceptable extension of the Governor's power. The China Mail of 4 April 1881. Hongkong Newspapers Collection (n. 15).

40 Wesley-Smith, Peter. 'Sir Francis Piggott: Chief Justice in His Own Cause'. *Hong Kong Law Journal* 12(3) (1982), 261–292.

41 His publications even reached the Paris Peace Conference in 1919: Payk, Marcus M. *Frieden durch Recht? Der Aufstieg des modernen Völkerrechts und der Friedensschluss nach dem Ersten Weltkrieg* (Berlin: De Gruyter, 2018), 304–305. His international reputation brought him as a constitutional advisor to Japan from 1887 to 1890, a position that took his career beyond the usual ambit of a colonial civil servant and fed his interest in Japanese music and art.

42 Wesley-Smith, 'Sir Francis Piggott' 1982 (n. 40), 260.

43 O'Connor, Peter. *The English-Language Press Networks of East Asia, 1918–1945* (Leiden/Kent: Global Oriental/Brill, 2010).

are still lacking the legal dimensions to the increasing importance of media as tools in forming diverse communities. In the case of Hong Kong, the political reforms of the 1860s found their expression in a request for more legal transparency on behalf of the public. To this end, Yorick Jones Murrow (1817–1884), the enigmatic owner of the Hong Kong-based newspaper *Daily Press*, initiated the publication of *The Directory & Chronicle of China, Japan, Korea, Indo-China, Straits Settlements, Malaya, Siam, Netherlands India, Borneo,* and *The Philippines*, among others.[44] Referenced here as Asia Directories and Chronicles, the serial appeared continuously until 1941. This publication voluminously documented the foreign residents, their social and commercial activities, and all information the editors deemed essential to survival for the foreigner in Asia. The Asia Directories clarified the community's conception of itself, which in many respects transcended the limits of British colony: In their eyes, Hong Kong was a paradigm for global exchange, more a global city than a Chinese territory under British lease and colonial governance.[45] This and similar publications spread throughout East Asia, specifying and substantiating those claiming extraterritorial privileges as a community based on an admittedly complex legal framework. Throughout their long-lasting period of publication of almost 80 years, the Asia Directories hewed closely to the aim Murrow presented in the preface of the first volume published in 1863: Lamenting the demise of the *Chinese Repository*,[46] the editor committed to publish the 'official documents of importance' going forward, arguing that 'there are not only the Treaties, but the laws made and enacted for carrying out those Treaties. All the Treaties contain the favored nation clause, and therefore a complete file is essential, because a concession in one regulates all. Some of the Treaties are totally abrogated, some partially so. Many of the laws affecting these treaties have been repealed, and some of them conflict.'[47] Indeed, foreigners had every reason to worry about the consequences of the 'most favoured nation' clause.

---

44 For an ongoing research project and ADC as digital resource see https://fr-benchmark.unibas.hasdai.org/, https://zenodo.org/record/2580998 (last accessed on 14 September 2020).

45 For the presentation of Hong Kong, see Colonial and Indian Exhibition, 1886. *Her Majesty's Colonies: A Series of Original Papers Issued under the Authority of the Royal Commission* (London: William Clowes and Sons, 1886), 483–505.

46 The Chinese Repository was printed in Canton from 1832 to 1851. Its editor Elijah Coleman Bridgman is usually mentioned as the first American protestant missionary in China. See Lazich, Michael. 'E. C. Bridgman (1801–1861) America's First Missionary to China'. *Studies in the History of Missions*, vol. 19 (Lewiston: Mellen, Lampeter, 2000); The Repository was more of a chronicle about the China mission and the spreading of Chinese protestant communities than a secular legal book or reference.

47 *The Chronicle & Directory of China, Japan & The Philippines for 1863* (Hongkong: The Hongkong Daily Press Office, 1863), vi.

This specific legal instrument connected the national diversity of foreigners indirectly, since commercial advantages fixed in a treaty needed to be shared with all future treaty partners. It also implied the respective documentation of almost every Western state. Favoured nation clauses thus constitute a topic the truly global extension of which has not yet found adequate reflection in global history debates.[48]

Colonial lawyers and courts shared the foreign residents' interest in proper documentation albeit for different reasons – namely, to build legal cases from the many existing treaties. A case law-based system without additional works of reference was increasingly difficult to handle – all the more because journalists and not legal experts prepared the judgements for publication.[49] In addition, the cases in question were spread widely among different issues of newspapers, which were occasionally no longer available, making cases difficult to cite or reference. When Piggott arrived in Hong Kong in 1905, he literally ended the Norton-Kyshe era by introducing formal law reporting, including an official stenographer and a barrister who edited the judgements to be printed in the newly-launched Hong Kong Law Reports.[50] However, foreign newspapers remained a crucial sounding board for extraterritorial privileges.

6 The Practice of Extraterritoriality and the Consequences of Being Privileged: The 'Most Favoured Nation' Treatment and the Foreign Jurisdiction Act

The issue of extraterritorial privilege remained a highly complex matter with not even remotely comprehensible repercussions. In his book, Piggott went well beyond covering the king's foreign jurisdiction as the framework upon which international law extraterritoriality was based. Besides criminal jurisdiction, he convincingly presented the influence of extraterritoriality on almost every aspect of a foreigner's life: bankruptcy, marriage, legacy, mortgage and others.[51] In order to build a community based on diversity it was crucial to understand

48 As a recently published example of an increasing interest in the most favoured nation clause as early form of multilateralism see Coutain, Bryan. 'The Unconditional Most-Favored-Nation Clause and the Maintenance of the Liberal Trade Regime in the Postwar 1870s'. *International Organization* 63(1) (2009), 139–179.

49 Wesley-Smith, 'Sir Francis Piggott' 1982 (n. 40), 267.

50 Ibid.

51 The colonial court cases provide a complex picture of the difficulties that arose in everyday life. Failure to keep promises of marriage are among the often cited problems. See Kercher, 'Colonial Cases' 2019 (n. 11).

that for all these topics, case law established a practice that differed from the national legislation. Colonial courts and consular jurisdiction therefore established a specific legal framework, the mechanics of which indirectly confirmed the existence of a specific foreign community. This community had a British imprint but was by no means identical with the Empire. Although based on the jurisdiction of (British) consular courts, such practices fit into a highly global context, since extraterritoriality offering a privilege-based community spread worldwide alongside colonial power settings. The constantly changing dynamics of extraterritoriality could be described as a sort of legal 'commons', forming its own rationale but also accessible to various actors at any moment in time.

The two examples of the most-favoured-nation treatment and the Foreign Jurisdiction Act offer a more precise insight into this entity by explaining why the metaphor is heuristically helpful and not merely hiding an unspecific approach of reducing complexity to 'anything goes'. The concept of the most-favoured-nation treatment – that is, British subjects will enjoy any privileges the Chinese emperor grants to subjects of any other nation – developed into a myriad of interfering Western legislations.[52] The concept, however, had a clear limitation differing from the commercial treaties from which the very model derived: In contrast to British commercial treaties, this treatment lacked reciprocity.[53] As a consequence, the building of community out of diversity remained a Western concept. To put it differently, the beginning of a global citizenship developed in Asia – but not in Europe. From an historical point of view, the dynamics of the legal framework help in sorting out the multilayered dynamics involved: Extraterritoriality did indeed blur the differentiation among nationalities. In the logic of the king's jurisdiction establishing foreign legal activities, British consular courts represented the Chinese emperor with regard to all foreigners. Qualifying in such activities as 'foreign and not consular courts, their functioning became thus independent from a formal, territory-based colonial possession.'[54] Moreover, the very definition of 'foreigner' underwent constant change, and the label 'European' gave reason to disputes: In terms of daily life, the question 'who lives where' went before the courts, because owners of houses classified as 'semi-European' had to pay higher insurance premiums.[55] A case of a disputed contract gave *The Canton*

52 The model for this argumentation was the Treaty of Tientsin in 1858, see Piggott, *Exterritoriality* 1907 (n. 16), 45.

53 Piggott mentioned Persia as one exception with a reciprocity clause, e.g. guaranteeing Persians in Europe the most favorite nation clause. Ibid., 46.

54 Ibid., 51.

55 Law reports, H. B: Supreme Court, Shanghai, Messrs. Glover, Dow & Co. v. F. Torckler, Colonial Case Law, (n. 11) 24 February 1870, available at: http://www.law.mq.edu.au/

Times every reason to ask 'What is a European?' Referring to a case in Calcutta, one Mr Meyer, who was born at Baghdad as Ottoman subject and naturalised in British India, was not granted permission to be addressed as European.[56] Even the most obvious definition in an extraterritorial context – namely the understanding of foreigners as subjects of a treaty power – became unclear due to the often used clause. At the end of the century, literally all persons under British protection were treated similar to British subjects. This approach crossed not only national but religious borders as well. And, as we saw from the example of the 'respectable Chinese',[57] even indigenous peoples could claim this specific sort of protection. In fact, foreign communities established a close relationship to rich Chinese trading families. In the case of Hong Kong, the specific interest of the foreign trading community in integrating at least some parts of the urban Chinese population found its expression in both the publication of growing numbers of Western newspapers translated into Chinese and an interest in standardising financial transactions.[58] If we take the porosity of borders seriously, even accounting for the fact that 'foreign jurisdiction depends in no wise upon allegiance', an adequate analysis should focus all the more on the absence of reciprocity.[59]

Turning our focus to the Western world, the picture there at the same point in the late 19th century clearly demonstrates that the main actors in world trade promoted the circulation of goods from Asia while limiting migration for racial reasons. The colour line was a clear presence in the migration and naturalisation laws of Western states, with many manifestations in various contexts. In 1884, for instance, the Amendment to the US Exclusion Act broadened restrictions on Chinese immigration, expanding the exclusion by using a racial as opposed to a national definition. Even in Piggott's work, which did not mention race at all, the discourse on naturalisation reflects the asymmetrical

research/colonial_case_law/colonial_cases/less_developed/china_and_japan/1870_decisions/glover_dow_and_co_v_torckler_1870/ (last accessed on 14 September 2020).

56 'What is a European?'. *The Canton Times* (15 April 1920), Colonial Case Law, (n. 11), Minor Cases Calcutta, http://www.law.mq.edu.au/research/colonial_case_law/colonial_cases/less_developed/calcutta/minor_cases_calcutta/ (last accessed on 5 August 2020).

57 See (n. 28).

58 See a Petition of Chinese Merchants about abstaining from the use of fictional names in commercial relationship. 'Petition of Chinese Merchants in Favour of Compulsory Registration of Partners', in *The Commercial Law Affecting Chinese; with Special Reference to Partnership, Registration and Bankruptcy Laws in Hongkong (Reprinted from the 'China Mail')* (Hongkong: Printed at the 'China Mail' Office, 1882), 37–39.

59 Piggott, *Exterritoriality* 1907 (n.16), 175.

acceptance of global communities in Asia and the West.[60] For an accurate historical analysis of community-building, it is important to follow neither an exclusively Asian nor a singular Western approach. Although the semi-colonial status of China is a well-introduced and accepted premise, the presumptive existence of weak states in the East does not fit into the extraterritoriality discourse. The theoretical cornerstone of extraterritoriality as a legal practice derived its relevance from the Foreign Jurisdiction Act, the years-long presence of which in non-legal publications such as the Asia Directories suggests that the communities of foreigners recognised its importance as well. While the Foreign Jurisdiction Act even extended the reach of British extraterritorial jurisdiction, the abolition of Western extraterritoriality in Japan as a consequence of the Aoki-Kimberley Treaty told another story. But again, within the international settlements, Japanese residents were increasingly part of those communities, and the very existence of a Japanese concession in Tientsin gives ample reason to reflect on whether the Eurocentric use of community-building out of diversity *but based on racial discrimination* was also useful for establishing supremacy in an Asian context.

7 Conclusion

Citizenship and belonging, migration and refugee crises dominate today's debates in the press and on social media, and there are very good reasons to understand the post-Cold War era as a complex interplay between the presumed economic benefits of a global market and the negative attitude toward human migrations. Scholarly debates rarely elaborate the multi-layered connections between the circulation of goods and of people, opting instead for discussions that differentiate human population movements into various forms, from displaced persons to expat communities. Within this approach, the scope of action depends on whether or not people have a national citizenship. This chapter has chosen a different approach by focusing on extraterritoriality, which it understands as a legal framework that shaped colonial dependencies between states but also offered opportunities for community-building. By terming those coming under the privilege of extraterritoriality as acting subjects, this approach questions well-established assumptions in

60 The case of Eitel gives an example that naturalization was limited in a colonial context. The official decision said that Eitel 'enjoy in this Colony and not elsewhere the rights and privileges of a British subject'; 'A Bill to Naturalise Re. E. J. Eitel'. *The China Mail*, (12 August 1880), Hongkong Newspapers Collection (n. 15).

several respects. First, extraterritorial privileges challenge the assumption that community-building has an undeniable connection to nation-building, at least since the 19th century. The privileges thus help to investigate the conditions and opportunities for building communities invigorated by diversity. Second, extraterritoriality opens up insights into a highly contested space. By taking as an example those living under the privilege of extraterritoriality in East Asian countries, we gain insights into the tensions between local claims and colonial politics as well as into struggles that developed between colonial governance and those using the legal framework of extraterritoriality to their own ends of self-organisation. Third, extraterritoriality established highly unstable conditions, all the more so as Western imperial powers insisted on safeguarding the principle of sovereignty. These dynamic conditions allow us to consider the changing historical conditions of foreigners living abroad and to incorporate them into the master narrative of the 19th and 20th centuries – namely, a territory-based form of national belonging. Fourth, this outside-the-box approach avoids the usual classification of persons on the move (e.g. expats, migrants, refugees) in using the metaphor of odd ones out. This rather unspecific concept allows to understand changing denominations as results as opposed to presumptions of the research rationale, and overcomes the tendency of narrowing down such communities to certain categories. This is especially true as extraterritorial privileges had a function of exclusion but also included local communities: They never exclusively addressed Western elites or Western institutions such as municipal councils. Fifth, using the lens of extraterritoriality implies a strong focus on legal frameworks. Both as a topic and as a method, it introduces a bipartite interplay between law and history. As a topic, extraterritoriality interfered with the building of legal instruments such as international treaties and colonial and consular courts. Those coming under the privilege were never just an object of court decisions but also established at least the pre-history to what Hannah Arendt later called the 'right to have rights'.[61] While Arendt's notion was attributed to (national) citizenship, and extraterritorial privileges were far from that, court decisions on the basis of extraterritorial privileges nevertheless had crucial consequences: In addition to their uncontested disciplinary functions, they enshrined the right to court access. In addition, the case law system made those invested with legal power crucial actors in measuring the distance between privilege and the national legislation. From a methodological point of view, the focus on legal frameworks unlocks access to colonial court cases and chronologies

61 Arendt, Hannah. *The Origins of Totalitarianism* (New York: Schocken Books, 1951).

based on legal decision making, in source material rarely used in global history to date. Presenting the local conditions of global connectivity, the legal cases offer insights into transcultural biographies that would otherwise be difficult to approach. Even more, the public accessibility of legal decisions became a highly contested field in the building of a public sphere for a community based on extraterritorial privileges. Scholarly investigations on extraterritorial privileges thus open up an opportunity to explore the conditions, opportunities, and failures of community-building beyond the national paradigm.

Acknowledgments

I would like to thank Anne Peters, Raphael Schäfer and Toshiki Mogami for their helpful support.

Bibliography

'A Bill to Naturalise Re. E. J. Eitel'. *The China Mail* (12 August 1880), Old Hongkong Newspapers Collection, available at: https://mmis.hkpl.gov.hk/old-hk-collection (last accessed on 14 September 2020).

Arendt, Hannah. *The Origins of Totalitarianism* (New York: Schocken Books, 1951).

Benton, Lauren and Lisa Ford. *Rage for Order. The British Empire and the Origins of International Law, 1800–1850* (Cambridge: Harvard University Press, 2016).

Benton, Lauren, Adam Clulow and Bain Attwood, eds. *Protection and Empire. A Global History* (Cambridge: Cambridge University Press, 2018).

Bickers, Robert A. *Out of China: How the Chinese Ended the Era of Western Domination* (London: Penguin, 2018).

Brand, Paul and Joshua Getzler, eds. *Judges and Judging in the History of Common Law and Civil Law* (Cambridge: Cambridge University Press, 2012).

Cassel, Pär Kristoffer. *Grounds of Judgment. Extraterritoriality and Imperial Power in Nineteenth-Century China and Japan* (Oxford: Oxford University Press, 2012)

Chandrachud, Abhinav. *An Independent Colonial Judiciary, A History of the Bombay High Court during the British Raj, 1862–1947* (Oxford: Oxford University Press, 2015).

Chen, Li. *Chinese Law in Imperial Eyes* (New York: Columbia University Press, 2016), doi: 10.7312/chen17374>.

Colonial and Indian Exhibition, 1886. *Her Majesty's Colonies: A Series of Original Papers Issued under the Authority of the Royal Commission* (London: William Clowes and Sons, 1886), 483–505.

Conrad, Sebastian. *What is Global History?* (Princeton: Princeton University Press, 2016).

Coutain, Bryan. 'The Unconditional Most-Favored-Nation Clause and the Maintenance of the Liberal Trade Regime in the Postwar 1870s'. *International Organization* 63(1) (2009), 139–179.

Dennys, Nicholas B., King, Charles and Mayers, William Frederick. *The Treaty Ports of China and Japan. A Complete Guide to the Open Ports of Those Countries, Together with Peking, Yedo, Hongkong and Macao* (London: Trübner & Co., 1867).

Eitel, Ernest John. *Europe in China* (London: Luzac & Company, 1895).

Fahmy, Ziad. 'Jurisdictional Borderlands: Extraterritoriality and 'Legal Chameleons', in Precolonial Alexandria, 1840–1870'. *Comparative Studies in Society and History* 55(2) (2013), 305–29.

Hall, Henry L. *The Colonial Office. A History* (London: Longmans, Green & Co., 1937).

Hunt, Lynn. *Writing History in the Global Era* (New York: W. W. Norton & Company, 2014).

International Committee of the Red Cross. 'Note on Migration and the Principle of Non-Refoulement'. *International Review of the Red Cross* 99(1) (2017), 345–357, doi: 10.1017/S1816383118000152.

Jellinek, Georg. 'China und das Völkerrecht'. *Deutsche Juristen-Zeitung* 5(19) (1900), 401–403.

Kayaoglu, Turan. *Legal Imperialism: Sovereignty and Extraterritoriality in Japan, the Ottoman Empire, and China* (Cambridge: Cambridge University Press, 2010).

Kercher, Bruce. 'Colonial Cases', available at: http://www.law.mq.edu.au/research/colonial_case_law/colonial_cases/site/cc_home/ (last accessed on 14 September 2020).

Kroll, Stefan. 'The Illiberality of Liberal International Law: Religion, Science, and the Peaceful Violence of Civilization', in *Paradoxes of Peace in Nineteenth Century Europe*, eds. Thomas Hippler and Miloš Vec (Oxford: Oxford University Press, 2015), 238–249.

Law Reports, H. B: Supreme Court, Shanghai, Messrs. Glover, Dow & Co. v. F. Torckler, Colonial Case Law, 24.2.1870, Macquarie Law School.

Lazich, Michael. 'E. C. Bridgman (1801–1861) America's First Missionary to China'. *Studies in the History of Missions*, vol. 19 (Lewiston: Mellen, Lampeter, 2000).

Maas, Willem, ed. *Multilevel Citizenship* (Philadelphia: University of Pennsylvania Press, 2013).

Margolies, Daniel S., Umut Özsu, Maia Pal and Nina Tzouvala, eds. *The Extraterritoriality of Law* (Abingdon: Routledge 2019).

Munn, Christopher. *Anglo-China. Chinese People and British Rule in Hong Kong 1841–1880* (Abingdon: Routledge, 2013).

Munn, Cristopher. 'Colonialism "in a Chinese Atmosphere": The Caldwell Affair and the Perils of Collaboration in Early Colonial Hong Kong', in *New Frontiers, Imperialism's*

New Communities in East Asia, 1842–1953, eds. Robert Bickers and Christian Henriot (Manchester: Manchester University Press, 2000), 12–37.

Norton-Kyshe, James William. *History of the Laws and Courts of Hongkong. Tracing Consular Jurisdiction in China and Japan and Including Parliamentary Debates, and the Rise, Progress, and Successive Changes in the Various Public Institutions of the Colony from the Earliest Period to the Present Time*, vol. 1 (London: T. Fisher Unwin, 1902).

Nuzzo, Luigi. 'International Legal Theory. The Birth of an Imperial Location: Comparative Perspectives on Western Colonialism in China'. *Leiden Journal of International Law* 31(3) (2018), 569–596.

O'Connor, Peter. *The English-Language Press Networks Of East Asia, 1918–1945* (Leiden/Kent: Global Oriental/Brill, 2010).

Osterhammel, Jürgen. 'Semi-Colonialism and Informal Empire in Twentieth-Century China: Towards a Framework of Analysis', in *Imperialism and After: Continuities and Discontinuities,* eds. Wolfgang J. Mommsen and Jürgen Osterhammel (London: Allen & Unwin, 1986), 290–314.

Payk, Marcus M. *Frieden durch Recht? Der Aufstieg des modernen Völkerrechts und der Friedensschluss nach dem Ersten Weltkrieg* (Berlin: De Gruyter, 2018).

Peters, Anne. 'Treaties, Unequal'. *The Max Planck Encyclopedia of Public International Law*, ed. Rüdiger Wolfrum (Oxford: Oxford University Press, 2012), available at: https://opil.ouplaw.com/view/10.1093/law:epil/9780199231690/law-9780199231690-e1495 (last accessed on 14 September 2020).

'Petition of Chinese Merchants in Favour of Compulsory Registration of Partners', in *The Commercial Law Affecting Chinese; with Special Reference to Partnership, Registration and Bankruptcy Laws in Hongkong (Reprinted from the 'China Mail')* (Hongkong: Printed at the 'China Mail' Office, 1882), 37–39.

Piggott, Sir Francis. *Exterritoriality: The Law Relating to Consular Jurisdiction and to Residence in Oriental Countries* (Hongkong: Kelly & Walsh, 1907).

'Politisches Departement, Besondere Fälle, Konsulargerichtsbarkeit: Bericht des Bundesrates an die Bundesversammlung über seine Geschäftsführung im Jahr 1897', *Schweizerisches Bundesblatt*, (23 March 1898), 22.

Pomeranz, Kenneth. *The Great Divergence: China, Europe, and the Making of the Modern World Economy* (Princeton: Princeton University Press, 2000).

Rosenberg, Emily S., ed. *A World Connecting* (Cambridge: Harvard University Press, 2012).

Sachsenmaier, Dominic. *Global Perspectives on Global History: Theories and Approaches in a Connected World* (Cambridge: Cambridge University Press, 2011), doi: 10.1017/CBO9780511736544.

Shavit, David. *The United States in Asia: A Historical Dictionary* (West Port: Greenwood Press, 1990).

Singaravélou, Pierre and Sylvain Venayre, eds. *Histoire du monde au XIXe siècle* (Paris: Fayard, 2017).

Stephens, Julia. 'An Uncertain Inheritance: The Imperial Travels of Legal Migrants, From British India to Ottoman Iraq'. *Law and History Review* 32(4) (2014), 749–772.

The Chronicle & Directory of China, Japan & The Philippines for 1863 (Hongkong: The Hongkong Daily Press Office, 1863).

Wesley-Smith, Peter. 'Sir Francis Piggott: Chief Justice in His Own Cause'. *Hongkong Law Journal* 12(3) (1982), 260–292.

Wesley-Smith, Peter. 'James William Norton-Kyshe'. *Hong Kong Law Journal* 2(3) (1972) 278–293.

'What is a European?'. *The Canton Times* (15 April 1920), Colonial Case Law, Macquarie Law School. Minor Cases Calcutta, available at: http://www.law.mq.edu.au/research/colonial_case_law/colonial_cases/less_developed/calcutta/minor_cases_calcutta/ (last accessed on 14 September 2020).

Xu, Guoqui. *Chinese and Americans, a Shared History* (Cambridge: Harvard University Press, 2014).

CHAPTER 2

The Politics of Writing on the History of Slavery in International Law

Anne-Charlotte Martineau

Abstract

This chapter engages with questions on the role of politics and ideology in the historiographies of international law through a case-study: slavery, and more specifically the slave trade. It argues that international lawyers tend to examine the history of their field in relation to slavery in either one of two ways. In the standard narrative, the point of departure is the slave trade abolition. The story that is told is narrow; it strengthens the thinking about slavery as an economic or socio-political phenomenon that exists in spite of international law. In the counterpoint narrative, the historical point of departure also revolves around the slave trade abolition. But the history that unfolds is different: light is shed on the intricate relationship between the legal abolition of slavery and European imperialism. At the end, it suggests a number of directions so as to go beyond the two narratives.

Keywords

Slavery – Slave Trade – Critical Approaches – Political Economy

1 Introduction

This chapter addresses the question of the role of politics and ideology in the historiographies of international law through a case-study: that of slavery, and more specifically the transatlantic slave trade. This choice is motivated by the fact that slavery is one of the very few issues that is indisputably and unanimously condemned by modern international lawyers. In fact, as Frederic Mégret rightly observed, 'few causes have marked the modern development of international law as much as the abolition of slavery.'[1] The prohibition against

1 Mégret, Frédéric. 'Droit international et esclavage: Pour une réévaluation'. *African Yearbook of International Law* 18(1) (2010), 121–183, 122.

 | DOI:10.1163/9789004461802_004

slavery is regularly cited as a ius cogens norm while the long campaign to abolish the transatlantic slave trade has been presented as 'the most successful episode ever' in the history of our discipline.[2] It has become common to present the involvement of international law on matters pertaining to slavery through a specific historical narrative –namely, one of humanitarian progress.[3] It is a 200-year long story of abolition that starts with the 1815 Declaration made at the Congress of Vienna by European powers, that continues with the anti-slavery commissions set up by the United Kingdom in the mid-19th century, and that triumphs with the adoption of the 1926 Slavery Convention, the 1930 Forced Labour Convention, and the 1956 Supplementary Convention.[4] Mention is then usually made of the progress achieved thanks to human rights mechanisms and the criminalisation of slavery through the Palermo Protocol and the Statute of the International Criminal Court (ICC).[5]

At the same time, however, a number of problems have emerged that have both challenged this narrative of progress and triggered a renewed interest in the history of slavery in international law. The first issue that international lawyers have been concerned about is the paradox that slavery has survived its own abolition and perhaps even thrived. Around 20 to 30 million people are estimated to be trapped in situations of modern slavery, forced labour, and

---

2 Martinez, Jenny. *The Slave Trade and the Origins of International Human Rights Law* (Oxford: Oxford University Press, 2012), 13.

3 This is a tendency on which international still operates. See Altwicker, Tilmann and Diggelmann, Oliver. 'How is Progress Constructed in International Legal Scholarship?'. *European Journal of International Law* 25(2) (2014), 425–444.

4 Nanda, Ved and M. Chief Bassiouni. 'Slavery and Slave Trade: Steps toward Eradication'. *Santa Clara Law Review* 12(2) (1972), 424–442. The same narrative can be found in international legal textbooks. See also Drescher, Seymour and Paul Finkelman. 'Slavery', in *The Oxford Handbook of the History of International Law*, eds. Bardo Fassbender and Anne Peters (Oxford: Oxford University Press, 2012), 890–916; Gaurier, Dominique. *Histoire du droit international. De l'antiquité à la création de l'ONU* (Rennes: Presses Universitaires de Rennes, 2014), 1058–1070; Daillier, Patrick and Alain Pellet. *Droit international public* (Paris: Libraire générale de droit et de jurisprudence, 7th ed. 2002), 707–708 ; Shaw, Malcolm N. *International Law* (Cambridge: Cambridge University Press, 2008), 270. Online encyclopedias tend to endorse the same narrative. See Scarpa, Silvia. 'Slavery'. *Oxford Bibliography on International Law*, available at: http://www.oxfordbibliographies.com/view/document/obo-9780199796953/obo-9780199796953-0097.xml (last accessed on 28 November 2020); Weissbrodt, David. 'Slavery'. *Max Planck Encyclopedia of Public International Law*, ed. Rüdiger Wolfrum (Oxford: Oxford University Press, 2014), available at: http://opil.ouplaw.com/view/10.1093/law:epil/9780199231690/law-9780199231690-e874 (last accessed on 28 November 2020).

5 For a survey of UN mechanisms such as the Special Rapporteur on Contemporary Forms of Slavery and the Human Rights Committee, see Stoyanova, Vladislava. 'United Nations against Slavery: Unravelling Concepts, Institutions and Obligations'. *Michigan Journal of International Law* 38(3) (2017), 359–454.

human trafficking.[6] How do international lawyers explain the tension between the legal prohibition of slavery and the reality of its existence? One way is to look at it as a problem of effectiveness.[7] That is to say, if slavery still exists, it is because international law can only do so much to enforce its rules. More recently, though, some scholars have attempted to deal with this problem by turning to history: perhaps there is a lesson to be learned that we have missed? This is how I understand Jenny Martinez's approach in her book *The Slave Trade and The Origins of International Human Rights Law* (Section 1).

The progressive narrative has suffered from a second critique. A number of scholars have shed light on the intricate relationship between the legal abolition of slavery and European imperialism. They have shown that the progressive narrative is problematic in both its teleological and European-driven nature, insofar as it suggests that abolition has been a process of expansion from ('enlightened') core to ('backward') periphery.[8] These historical studies have been particularly instructive and they have destabilised the discipline's self-conception as an anti-slavery champion. What will need to be explained, however, is why these studies cease to be enlightening when speaking about the present and debating which institutional arrangement should address modern forms of slavery (Section 2).

At the end of my chapter, for reasons I hope will have become clear, I will suggest a number of directions so as to move forward. One important step is to (re)introduce the history of political economy. Another is to understand that the slave trade was a legal system – thus, abolition did not arise as an effect of law but as a critique of law (Section 3).

---

6 See Batstone, David. *Not for Sale: The Return of the Global Slave Trade – and How We Can Fight It* (New York: Harper Collins, 2007); Bales, Kevin, Zoe Trodd and Alex Ken Williamson. *Modern Slavery: The Secret of 27 Million People* (Oxford: One World, 2009); Kara, Siddharth. *Sex Trafficking: Inside the Business of Modern Slavery* (New York: Columbia University Press, 2009). Some go as far as suggesting that 40 million people are enslaved today. See Nicholson, Andrea, Minh Dang and Zoe Trodd. 'A Full Freedom: Contemporary Survivors Definitions of Slavery'. *Human Rights Law Review* 18(4) (2018), 689–704. On the politics of such data, see Gallagher, Anne. 'Human Rights and Human Trafficking: Quagmire or Firm Ground? A Response to James Hathaway'. *Virginia Journal of International Law* 49(4) (2009), 789–848, 797.

7 'The gap … between the theoretical protection offered by international law, and the reality of non-enforcement … is wide and shocking.' Cockayne, James, Nick Grono and Kari Panaccione. 'Introduction'. *Journal of International Criminal Justice* 14(2) (2016), 253–267, 255.

8 Anghie, Anthony. 'Slavery and International Law: The Jurisprudence of Henry Richardson'. *Temple International and Comparative Law Journal* 31(1) (2017), 11–23.

2 History as Lesson: International Law's Role in the Slave Trade Abolition

'There is something especially baffling about the fact that slavery, outlawed since the nineteenth century and one of the first human rights violations to become the subject of an international convention, is still continuing to this day.'[9] That modern-day slavery exists despite the important legal apparatus set up to prohibit it is a puzzle ('baffling') that is often raised by those involved in current international law and policies against slavery. Many of them call for more international institutional involvement to get around national obstacles as well as social, political or economic power. 'Slavery is ... an extreme form of inequality. And while this may be recognized by the international community, state sovereignty limits both the bargaining power of states in the face of international capital, and the reach of international supervisory mechanisms (such as [the] ILO).'[10] This plea emanates from members of institutional mechanisms as well. Take the statement that David Weissbrodt and Anti-Slavery International made in 2002 on behalf of the UN Working Group on Contemporary Forms of Slavery: 'The right of all individuals to be free from slavery is a basic human right; yet this lack of an adequate implementation procedure does little to encourage States to establish safeguards against all contemporary forms of slavery. The mandate of the Working Group on Contemporary Forms of Slavery could be extended to incorporate such a function to provide for a systematic review procedure.'[11]

More recently, this well-rehearsed argument (opposing international mechanisms to sovereign will, law against social, political or economic power, public institutions against private actors, etc.) has been supported by an historical claim.[12] To have recourse to history is understandable: given the 'evils of global slavery'[13] today, it may be tempting to look back and enquire what happened in

9 Anker, Christien van den, ed. *The Political Economy of New Slavery* (London: Palgrave Macmillan, 2004), 1–12, 2. A similar statement can be found in Bales, Kevin and Robbins, Peter T. 'No One Shall Be Held in Slavery or Servitude: A Critical Analysis of International Slavery Conventions'. *Human Rights Review* 2(2) (2001), 18–45.

10 Cockayne/Grono/Panaccione, 'Introduction' 2016 (n. 7), 256.

11 Weissbrodt, David and Michael Dottridge. *Abolishing Slavery and Its Contemporary Forms* (Geneva: Office of the UN High Commissioner for Human Rights, HR/PUB/02/4, 2002), para. 188, available at: https://www.ohchr.org/Documents/Publications/slaveryen.pdf (last accessed on 28 November 2020).

12 On such dichotomies, see Kennedy, David. 'When Renewal Repeats: Thinking against the Box'. *New York University Journal of International Law and Politics* 32(2) (1999), 335–500.

13 Němcová, Tereza. 'Book Review: The Political Economy of New Slavery by Christien van den Anker'. *Perspectives* 26 (2006), 91–110, 93.

the 19th century when the transatlantic slave trade was actually abolished. The most famous example of this endeavour is Jenny Martinez's book, *The Slave Trade and The Origins of International Human Rights Law* published in 2012. Her starting point is that chattel slavery – i.e., a legal institution that had been commonplace worldwide– disappeared by the end of the 19th century. 'How did such a dramatic shift occur in disparate societies around the world in less than a century?'[14] To answer this question, Martinez examined in great details the workings of mixed commissions (or 'courts', as she generally refers to them) that Great Britain established with various treaty partners to hear cases involving slave ships. Most of the sized ships were captured by the British navy and the overwhelming majority of these were duly condemned, often at the end of summary proceedings. In light of this, Martinez argues that the abolition of the slave trade was made possible thanks to the establishment of institutional mechanisms that are still used today to enforce human rights –namely, a combination of treaties and courts supported by a civil-society movement.

Martinez's book rests on solid historical research into the mixed commissions established to determine the fate of ships seized that were suspected of involvement in the slave trade. As Philip Alston pointed out, 'Martinez does an excellent job of bringing alive the story of the mixed commissions, primarily through archival research that provides a real feel for the ways in which the commissions functioned. She offers fascinating vignettes of the lives of those involved, including the slaves themselves, the ships' captains and crews, the judicial officers, the slave owners and plantation managers, and the imperial bureaucrats.'[15] But Martinez did not limit herself to retrieving the number of cases (500), ships seized (225), and persons freed (more than 80,000). She wanted to make a stronger and bolder claim, namely that 19th century international efforts to end the slave trade formed 'the origins of our contemporary system of international legal protection for human rights.'[16] This claim was found to be problematic.[17] Renowned historian Samuel Moyn, for instance, criticised Martinez for having failed to bridge the past and the present in any convincing

14 Martinez, 'Slave Trade' 2012 (n. 2).

15 Alston, Philip. 'Does the Past Matter? On the Origins of Human Rights'. *Harvard Law Review* 126(7) (2013), 2043–2081, 2047.

16 Martinez, 'Slave Trade' 2012 (n. 2), 6.

17 Martinez left out conflicting interpretations of the abolition process, such as Lauren Benton's, for instance, who has argued that the British government shouldered the (costly) antislavery effort not out of a concern for humanity, but in order to cement its imperial control of the oceans. Benton, Lauren. 'Abolition and Imperial Law, 1790–1820'. *The Journal of Imperial and Commonwealth History* 39(3) (2011), 355–374. See also Benton, Lauren. 'The Slave Trade and the Origins of International Human Rights Law'. *Victorian Studies* 56(1) (2013), 127–129.

fashion. While it may be true that today's normative instruments and institutions look like those of yesterday, Martinez did not connect the dots between the 19th and 21st centuries in any meaningful way.[18] This proved to be particularly dangerous as Martinez did not hesitate to draw lessons from what she considered to be a successful episode.[19] Among others, she called upon the world's leading power, the United States, to get inspiration from the British Empire and 'foster democracy and human rights both through the use of force and through legal institutions.'[20] Alston's response to this imperial nostalgia is unequivocal: 'to the extent that major elements of the British approach were imperialistic, albeit partly in the pursuit of an admirable goal, it becomes all the more important to exercise caution and discernment in drawing lessons for the future.'[21]

Nonetheless, other international lawyers have picked up on Martinez's tendency to simplify and celebrate international law's involvement in ending the slave trade; they have redeployed that role in the present in order to promote some kind of humanitarian project.[22] One example is the special issue on slavery that was published in the *International Journal for Criminal Justice* in 2016. Although the issue was entitled 'Slavery and the Limits of International Criminal Justice', the whole point was to promote the role international criminal law could play in the fight against slavery. For this, the three organizers of the special issue –all of them being involved in international policy-making on slavery– argued that the origins of their field lay in the slave trade abolition process. In the words of James Cockayne, Nick Grono, and Kari Panaccione, 'slavery was arguably the spur that set the international criminal justice train in motion, 200 years ago.'[23] To support this argument about their field's origins, they relied explicitly on Martinez's thesis. They asserted that mixed commissions established by Great Britain through bilateral treaties in the 19th century played a catalysing role in the emergence of international criminal law. Granted, they said, these courts could not exact penalties against crews or owners of slave ships. But they had a deterrent effect insofar as they were authorised to confiscate vessels, equipment and merchandise, and also to

18 Moyn, Samuel. 'The Nation: Of Deserts and Promised Lands: The Dream of Global Justice'. The Nation (20 February 2012), available at: https://www.thenation.com/article/deserts-and-promised-lands-dream-global-justice/ (last accessed on 28 November 2020).

19 Martinez, 'Slave Trade' 2012 (n. 2), 15.

20 Ibid. While the United States could still do so, it should also project its 'economic and military power' into the future by supporting the International Criminal Court. Ibid., 170–171.

21 Alston, 'Origins of Human Rights' 2013 (n. 17), 2061.

22 As Anthony Anghie observed, slavery has become 'an abhorrence against which international law can demonstrate its commitment to protecting human dignity and furthering the cause of international law.' Anghie, 'Jurisprudence of Henry Richardson' 2017 (n. 8), 13.

23 Cockayne/Grono/Panaccione, 'Introduction' 2016 (n. 7), 258.

release captives. In addition, because courts had jurisdiction to arrest nationals of the States party to the treaties, who were then obliged to try them in their own courts, mixed commissions could –and should– be seen as a 'precursor to the modern system of complementarity'.[24]

International lawyers working in the field of human rights and criminal justice are not the only ones invoking international law's heroic role in the 'fight against slavery' to assert their field's authority. References to the past, and especially the slave trade, constitute a privileged discursive strategy in the context of competing knowledge communities and international legal regimes dealing with slavery. Over the last two decades, the fight against modern slavery has come to be chiefly understood in terms of 'fighting human trafficking'. This was triggered, in part, by the adoption of the UN Protocol to Prevent, Suppress and Publish Trafficking in Persons, Especially Women and Children in 2000 – otherwise known as the Palermo or Trafficking Protocol – which supplemented the UN Convention Against Transnational Organized Crimes. The fight against human trafficking has experienced a remarkable degree of success in terms of popular awareness, institutional leverage, and resource allocation. In 2005, the Council of Europe adopted its own Convention on Action against Trafficking in Human Beings.[25] References to the slave trade have been commonly used to frame the discourse on modern trafficking. Take the speech the then US President George W. Bush gave to the UN General Assembly on 23 September 23 2003:

> There's another humanitarian crisis spreading [beside famine], yet hidden from view. Each year, an estimated 800,000 to 900,000 human beings are bought, sold or forced across the world's borders. Among them are hundreds of thousands of teenage girls, and others as young as five, who fall victim to the sex trade. This commerce in human life generates billions of dollars each year – much of which is used to finance organized crime .... We must show new energy in fighting back an old evil. Nearly two centuries after the abolition of the transatlantic slave trade, and more than a century after slavery was officially ended in its last strongholds, the trade in human beings for any purpose must not be allowed to thrive in our time.[26]

24 Ibid.

25 For a 2016 survey of the (imposing) implementation apparatus, see Sousa Santos, Boaventura de. 'European Commission: The Fight against Trafficking in Human Beings in EU: Promoting Legal Cooperation and Victims' Protection', available at: http://www.transcrime.it/wp-content/uploads/2016/01/THB_CoopToFight.pdf (last accessed on 28 November 2020).

26 'Statement by His Excellency Mr George W. Bush, President of the United States of America. Address to the United Nations General Assembly, 23 September 2003', available

In comparison to Martinez's book or the special issue of the *International Journal of Criminal Justice*, the narrative here is meant to be realistic. Bush's tone is grave and the dangers are palatable. Did Bush, by presenting himself to the UN as the leader of a large-scale campaign to end human trafficking, seek to gain support for the rather intrusive monitoring measures that the United States had put in place (and are still in place today)?[27] In any case, Bush glided over the reality that United States' internal slavery did not end until the Civil War and the adoption of the Thirteenth Amendment to the American Constitution. He also made no mention of the slave-like conditions endured by former slaves and their descendants.[28] My point is that the so-called realism that characterises the anti-trafficking discourse depicts a highly selective 'reality' of the slave trade abolition and, in so doing, indicates the kind of law that will be privileged. The focus is no longer on the role played by courts and civil society, but on the punishment of deviant criminal behaviour and protection of 'vulnerable' people.[29]

3 History as Caution: The Prohibition of Slavery and European Imperialism

Over the last decade, a number of international lawyers have attempted to provide a more meticulous picture of the abolition of the slave trade and the role of international law therein. I am particularly appreciative of the work of Jean

at: http://www.un.org/webcast/ga/58/statements/usaeng030923.htm (last accessed on 28 November 2020).

27 The US has established an Office to Monitor and Combat Trafficking in Persons. The State Department also issues a 'Trafficking in Persons (TIP) Report' annually, one that monitors how countries are addressing the challenges of human trafficking. See https://www.state.gov/j/tip/rls/tiprpt/ (last accessed on 28 November 2020).

28 Bravo, Karen. 'The Role of the Transatlantic Slave Trade in Contemporary Anti-Human Trafficking Discourse'. *Seattle Journal for Social Justice* 9(2) (2011), 555–597, 562.

29 To say it differently, the anti-trafficking discourse presents a very narrow interpretation of the slave trade abolition, seeks to project that interpretation onto the present, and extrapolates an extremely limited set of legal lessons. Critical voices have pointed out that references in the passive voice to one's own country's abolition of slavery, followed by mention of the return of slavery today, reinforces the 'denial of any complicity … in the slavery's re-emergence' while condemning developing countries to be responsible for modern slavery. Bravo, Karen. 'Exploring the Analogy between Modern Trafficking in Humans and the Trans-Atlantic Slave Trade'. *Boston University International Law Journal* 25(2) (2007), 207–293, 221. See also Soderlund, Gretchen. 'Running from the Rescuers: New U.S. Crusades against Sex Trafficking and the Rhetoric of Abolition'. *The National Women's Studies Association Journal* 17(3) (2005), 64–87.

Allain,[30] Joel Quirk,[31] Karen Bravo,[32] and Michel Erpelding,[33] who have offered a sophisticated and nuanced reading.

Against Martinez *et al*, Quirk and Erpelding have shown that imperialism and colonialism were not side-issues in the 19th century but central to the law-making process on slavery. This also applies to the definitions of slavery and forced labour that were elaborated under the League of Nations.[34] These issues had become closely linked to European powers' colonial policies: how should they condemn slavery –after all, this had been one of the justifications for colonising Africa in the first place– without jeopardizing the need for a slavery-like labour force in their colonies?[35] This intricate balance was achieved by separating, in legal terms, the issue of slavery from that of forced labour, and by defining both terms narrowly. To start with, the drafters of the 1926 Slavery Convention agreed upon a formal definition of slavery as 'the status or condition of a person over whom any or all of the powers attaching to the right of ownership are exercised.'[36] From that moment onwards, the powers attached to the individual right of ownership as attributed by law became the *sine qua non* of slavery.[37] This definition made it easier for colonial authorities to close their eyes on African social mores such as domestic serfdom and servile marriage; these practices were considered either as 'soft or benevolent

30 Allain, Jean. *Slavery in International Law: Of Human Exploitation and Trafficking* (Leiden: Brill, 2012).

31 Quirk, Joel. *The Anti-Slavery Project: From the Slave Trade to Human Trafficking* (Philadelphia: University of Pennsylvania Press, 2011).

32 Bravo, 'Analogy' 2007 (n. 31).

33 Erpelding, Michel. *Le droit international antiesclavagiste des "Nations Civilisées" (1815–1945)* (Paris: Institut universitaire Varenne, 2017).

34 To give one example, the French maintained forced labour for public works (*prestations en nature*) in their colonies until 1946. Frimigacci, Jean. 'L'Etat colonial français, du discours mythique aux réalités (1880–1940)'. *Matériaux pour l'histoire de notre temps* 27 (1993), 27–35, 32–33.

35 In other words, European powers sought to abolish slavery (in the strict sense of chattel slavery) while ensuring the continuance of forced labour for public purposes in their colonies. Erpelding, Michel. 'L'Esclavage en droit international: Aux origines de la relecture actuelle de la définition conventionnelle de 1926'. *Journal of the History of International Law* 17(2) (2015), 170–220.

36 International Slavery Convention (1926), art. 1(1).

37 This concerned effort to restrict the definition of slavery did not apply in case a non-European government was the subject of inquiry (that is, Liberia). See Erpelding, *Le droit international antiesclavagiste* 2017 (n. 33), 508–517.

slavery'[38] or as falling outside the formal definition of slavery.[39] What is more, all major colonial Powers opposed the inclusion of forced labour in the Slavery Convention on grounds of an infringement of their national sovereignty. This led the drafters to transfer that 'problem' to the International Labour Organization (ILO). A specific treaty was concluded in 1930 under the auspices of the ILO; it was largely the work of a committee which included four former colonial governors and the official adviser on African mine labour in the Transvaal.[40] Parties to the Forced Labour Convention agreed to progressively abolish 'all work or service which is exacted from any person under the menace of any penalty and for which the said person has not offered himself voluntarily.'[41] Otherwise, the convention required little more than the restriction of forced labour to a limited range of public works. This, again, was not incidental: forced labour was deemed necessary to colonial Powers so that they could develop 'in the interests of humanity', no less, 'the riches and resources of those African countries placed under their sovereignty.'[42]

Likewise, against Bush *et al*, Bravo and Allain have shown that the genesis of the anti-trafficking project lies not in the transatlantic slave trade but in the white slave traffic. 'The regime of white slave traffic', argues Allain, is 'fundamental to understanding the evolution of what is today understood as human trafficking generally, and more specifically, trafficking related to sexual exploitation; and the dynamics which shaped its contemporary contours and the language used to define it.'[43] The white slave traffic arose in relation to the issue of venereal disease in the late 19th century and was grounded in Victorian

38 Queuneuil, Henry. 'Conférence anti-esclavagiste de Bruxelles. Acte général du 2 juillet 1890: Application et résultats'. *Revue générale de droit international public* 15 (1908), 131–146, 136.

39 See, for instance, Weidner, Fritz. *Die Haussklaverei in Ostafrica: Geschichtlich und politisch dargestellt* (Jena: Gustav Fischer, 1915).

40 See Miers, Suzanne. *Slavery in the Twentieth Century. The Evolution of a Global Problem* (Walnut Creek: Altamira Press, 2003), 121–130.

41 Forced Labour Convention (1930) (n. 29), art. 2(1).

42 League of Nations, Note Submitted to the First Sub-Committee of the Six Committee by the Portuguese Delegate, General Freire d'Andrade, 11 September 1925, AVI/S.C.1/2.1925, quoted by Allain, Jean. 'The Legal Definition of Slavery into the 21st Century', in *The Legal Understanding of Slavery. From the Historical to the Contemporary*, ed. Jean Allain (Oxford: Oxford University Press, 2012), 199–219, 202.

43 Allain, Jean. 'White Slave Traffic in International Law'. *Journal of Trafficking and Human Exploitation* 1(1) (2017), 1–40, 1; see also Allain, Jean. 'Genealogies of Human Trafficking and Slavery', in *Routledge Handbook of Human Trafficking*, eds. Ryszard Piotrowicz and Conny Rijken (Abingdon: Routledge, 2018), 3–12.

paternalism.[44] The question was how to control women in the face of communicable diseases which were playing havoc on troops destined to engage in Europe's colonial projects. Rumours had arisen of organized networks that procured and sent women abroad for prostitution. One of the fears was that white women were being sold into slavery to non-white males. In response, a number of international instruments were adopted by European countries and the United States. The first one was the 1904 International Agreement for the Suppression of the White Slave Trade.[45] An important point of disagreement during the negotiation had been the nature of the offence for women over the age of majority *vs.* women under the age of majority. Which offence should be given priority? Did it matter if women gave their consent? But at what age was a woman able to consent to sex?[46] These questions only found partial answers in the 1904 Agreement, and the latter proved ineffective due to the high number of reservations. In 1910, the same governments negotiated the International Convention for the Suppression of White Slave Traffic. This time, Europeans and Americans (male) diplomats agreed to criminalise, on the one side, the exploitation of the prostitution of women over the age of majority and, on the other side, the prostitution of those underage. Implementation was left to State Parties.

This genealogy is powerful in suggesting that today's anti-trafficking project has more to do with late 19th century European sexism and racism than with 'fighting an old evil'. 'Just as the spectre of involuntary sex and despoilment of innocent white maidens seized the Western world's attention in the late 1880s and early 1890s', comments Bravo, 'overtones of that appalled, fascinated, and condemnatory prurience continued to pervade public and institutional perceptions of the traffic in human beings into the early twenty-first century.'[47] The reminiscence of Victorian paternalism is not only politically conservative; it also has important distributional implications. Today's focus on 'innocent women and children and illicit sex foisted upon them'[48] draws both attention and resources away from other forms of human exploitation and structural inequalities. It has also been noted that not unlike yesterday's scandal, today's

44 Walkowitz, Judith. *Prostitution and Victorian Society: Women, Class, and the State* (Cambridge: Cambridge University Press, 1980).

45 On the racial component of the treaty, see Scully, Eileen. 'Pre-Cold War Traffic in Sexual Labour and Its Foes: Some Contemporary Lessons', in *Global Human Smuggling*, eds. David Kyle and Rey Koslowski (Baltimore: The Johns Hopkins University Press, 2nd ed. 2011), chapter 4.

46 Allain, 'White Slave Traffic' 2017 (n. 45), 16.

47 Bravo, 'The Role of the Transatlantic Slave Trade' 2011 (n. 30), 575.

48 Ibid.

global cause has been consolidated through the deployment of a series of dubious 'facts and figures' regarding the dimensions of human trafficking.[49]

In these examples, history is taken seriously and international legal scholars explore the long-rooted relationship between law, economy, and power. That said, I find their writings less convincing when discussing today's challenges. What are the latter? Much of the discussion revolves around the 'fragmentation' of the law on human exploitation.[50] That slavery is now regulated by different subfields of international law (such as the law of the sea, human rights law, international criminal law, international humanitarian law, international labour law, international refugee law, etc.) raises a number of concerns. The major concern is this: to what extent this state of affairs is giving rise to conflicting interpretations of slavery?[51] Fragmentation is depicted as a problem that could be resolved only if we were to identify more clearly what amounts to slavery in contrast to lesser forms of exploitation, such as forced labour. This explains why so much ink has been spilled on the relevance of the 1926 definition: should we keep article 1 of the 1926 Slavery Convention, which defines slavery in relation to ownership exclusively (as endorsed by the ICC and the anti-trafficking regime), or should we prefer an expansive definition which focuses on the degree of control and coercion (as promoted by the European Court of Human Rights)? As I have shown elsewhere, the turn to history loses

49 Bunting, Annie and Joel Quirk, eds. *Contemporary Slavery. Popular Rhetoric and Political Practice* (Vancouver: University of British Columbia Press, 2017). On the genesis of today's US anti-trafficking debate, see Lobasz, Jennifer. *Constructing Human Trafficking. Evangelicals, Feminists, and an Unexpected Alliance* (London: Palgrave Macmillan, 2018). On the previous scandal, see Chaumont, Jean-Michel. *Le mythe de la traite des blanches. Enquête sur la fabrication d'un fléau* (Paris: La Découverte, 2009).

50 Martineau, Anne-Charlotte. *Une analyse critique du débat sur la fragmentation du droit international* (Bruxelles: Bruylant, 2015).

51 See Scott, Rebecca. 'International Law and Contemporary Slavery: The Long View'. *Michigan Journal of International Law* 38(3) (2017), 349–357, 349; Cullen, Holly. 'Contemporary International Legal Norms on Slavery. Problems of Judicial Interpretation and Application', in *The Legal Understanding of Slavery: From Historical to the Contemporary*, ed. Jean Allain (Oxford: Oxford University Press, 2012), 304–321; McGeehan, Nicholas Lawrence. 'Misunderstood and Neglected: The Marginalisation of Slavery in International Law'. *The International Journal of Human Rights* 16(3) (2012), 436–460, 436; Rassam, Yasmine. 'International Law and Contemporary Forms of Slavery: An Economic and Social Rights-Based Approach'. *Penn State International Law Review* 23(4) (2005), 809–855; Cavallo, Michele. 'Formes contemporaines d'esclavage, servitude et travail forcé: Le TPIY et la CEDH entre passé et avenir'. *Droits fondamentaux* 6 (2006), 1–16; Duffy, Helen. 'Litigating Modern Day Slavery in Regional Courts. A Nascent Contribution'. *Journal of International Criminal Justice* 14(2) (2016), 375–403, 375; Stoyanova, Vladislava. 'Article 4 of the ECHR and the Obligation of Criminalising Slavery, Servitude, Forced Labour and Human Trafficking'. *Cambridge Journal of International and Comparative Law* 3(2) (2014), 407–443, 407.

here its critical bite.[52] There is no more analysis of the ways in which, in different time and space, international law has allowed the exploitation of men by men in the name of liberal and humanistic values. There is no re-interpretation of the past in terms of discontinuous or unexpected genealogies. Let me be clear: the problem is not that the counterpoint uses the past for present purposes.[53] The problem is that in today's debate on the legal definition of slavery, references to history end up justifying the choice of the regime or institution allowed to rule on it. In short, history has become caught up in the fragmentation of international law.

4 Moving Forward?

In light of these shortcomings, one may wonder: how to move forward? How to study slavery? I do not pretend to have all the answers. But I would like to suggest three directions for a renewed critical engagement with the history of international law and slavery.

First, we should prevent ourselves from falling into the trap of international law's reformist mission. I have shown earlier that international lawyers in the field of human rights, criminal justice, and human trafficking do not hesitate to harness the vocabulary and iconography of slavery in order to draw popular attention and capital investment to their programmatic solutions. I have argued that this instrumentalisation of the past is politically dubious and intellectually regressive. What I now want to underscore is the historical nexus between slavery and intervention. It is striking that today's international lawyers, regardless of their fields of expertise, are resolute to intervene in the same regions and 'protect' the same people. They typically are: 'Mauritanians born into hereditary or 'chattel' slavery, Indian children labouring in debt bondage in brick kilns, Thai fishermen trapped in servitude, workers trafficked to construction projects in Qatar, girls abducted into sexual slavery by Boko

52 Martineau, Anne-Charlotte. 'Contested Histories: Revisiting the Relationship between International Law and Slavery', in *International Law and the Humanities*, eds. Sundhya Pahuja and Shane Chalmers (Abingdon: Routledge, forthcoming 2021).

53 For theoretical reflexions on the relationship between past and present in international law, see Orford, Anne. 'The Past as Law or History? The Relevance of Imperialism for Modern International Law', in *Droit international et nouvelles approches sur le tiers-monde: Entre répétition et renouveau*, eds. Emmanuelle Jouannet, Mark Toufayan and Hélène Ruiz-Fabri (Paris: Société de législation comparée, 2013), 97–118; Koskenniemi, Martti. 'Why History of International Law Today?'. *Rechtsgeschichte – Legal History* 4 (2004), 61–66, 61; Craven, Matthew. 'Theorizing the Turn to History in International Law', in *The Oxford Handbook of the Theory of International Law*, eds. Anne Orford and Florian Hoffmann (Oxford: Oxford University Press, 2016), 21–37.

Haram and Islamic State of Iraq and the Levant (ISIL), and political prisoners enslaved in Democratic People's Republic of Korea (DPRK).'[54] Notwithstanding these people's plight, one may wonder about the imperialist dimensions of the latest projects to end slavery. Hasn't international law always 'presented itself as improving the lives of conquered peoples',[55] developing far-reaching mechanisms to govern the decolonized world?

This postcolonial reading is strengthened by the fact that the fight against slavery is a powerful precedent in the international legal discourse. Indeed, the impetus to abolish slavery and the slave trade is precisely what was invoked at the end of the 19th century to promote international law's 'mission to civilise Africa'.[56] That imperial European powers justified the colonisation of Africa on the grounds that they were furthering civilisation and ending slavery was formalised in the Berlin Act of 1885.[57] It is well-known that during the conference that led to the adoption of that Act, the fate of the Independent State of the Congo was closely intertwined with the impetus to suppress slavery and the slave trade in the Congo basin.[58] There is a lesson to be learned: whenever the slave trade abolition is invoked, it should come with a warning sign –making us attuned to the dangers (i.e., imperialism at play) when current international legal projects claiming to address human vulnerability are legitimized by reference to the role international law played in the abolition of slavery.[59]

Second, we should work on providing a more complex and more credible assessment of the role international law played in the abolition of the slave trade and slavery. This would include, for instance, a close examination of the work carried out by 'Offices of the Protector' throughout the 19th century. They were set up in various locations in the French and British Empires following the abolition of the slave trade and were meant to guarantee the amelioration

---

54 Cockayne/Grono/Panaccione, 'Introduction' 2016 (n. 7), 255.

55 Anghie, Anthony. 'On Critique and the Other', in *International Law and Its Others*, ed. Anne Orford (Cambridge: Cambridge University Press, 2008), 389–400, 394.

56 See, for instance, Montardy, Henry De. *La traite et le droit international* (Paris: Girard & Brière, 1906); Couvé, Edouard. *La traite au point de vue du droit des gens* (Paris: Rousseau, 1889); Lévy, Henri. *La traite des noirs et les puissances* (Nancy: Crépin-Leblond, 1894); Quéneuil, Henry. *De la traite des noirs et de l'esclavage. La conférence de Bruxelles et ses résultats* (Paris: Larose & Tenin, 1907); Sarrien, Michel-Louis-Ferdinand. *La traite des nègres et le droit de visite au cours du XIXe siècle dans les rapports de la France et de l'Angleterre* (Paris: Jouve et Cie, 1910); Gareis, Karl. *Der Sklavenhandel, das Völkerrecht und das deutsche Recht* (Berlin: Deutsche Zeit- und Streit-Fragen, 1885).

57 Linden, Mieke van der. *The Acquisition of Africa (1870–1914). The Nature of International Law* (Leiden: Brill 2016).

58 Anghie, 'Jurisprudence of Henry Richardson' 2017 (n. 8), 20.

59 See Emmanuelle Tourme Jouannet's insightful comments in her preface of Erpelding, *Le droit international antiesclavagiste* 2017 (n. 33).

of slaves' (and then freemen's) status. But these Offices also allowed the sovereign to exert control over the slaves to prevent resistance to authority.[60] As this example suggests, a more realistic account of the legal history of abolition implies a departure from two traditional dichotomies: national / international and abolition / freedom. If what we want is to gain a better understanding of how imperial power operated through time and space, then we need to look more closely at the ways in which intersecting laws (and not only classical law of nations) prompted new versions of unfreedom. The reason is, European Empires constantly and violently moved people around to some places as slaves, indentures, labourers, etc., thanks to a variety of laws –the law of the sea, colonial laws, commercial laws, domestic laws, etc. What is more, the abolition of chattel slavery in the 19th century was accompanied by the maintenance and/or creation of other forms of exploitation and movement of peoples. 'Yet', observes Renisa Mawani, 'we write histories of slavery, indenture, and so-called free migration as though they are discrete, separated by time and space, and in ways that assume we can easily distinguish between the freedom and unfreedom of movement.'[61]

This research avenue, I admit, remains Eurocentric. Given the canons of legal research and the standards of evidence, it is difficult to tell the story 'in a different language, one that makes the slave the center of her own history rather than an ancillary and subordinated figure in the triumphant story'[62] of Western-led abolition. One fruitful road scholars have taken to write the history of international law and slavery 'from below' is to look at the ways in which Indigenous peoples, African captives, indentured labourers, and other colonial subjects mobilized laws to fight for their own freedoms and self-determination.[63] Sometimes these strategies were successful, other times they were not – what would also be interesting is to investigate how these were

---

60 On the Office of the Protector in the British Colony of Trinidad, see Menon, Pavarthi. *Protecting Empire in Slave Colonies: The Politics of a Humanitarian Authoritarianism* (Helsinki: University of Helsinki, PhD Thesis, unpublished).

61 Dhillon, Hardeep. 'Borderlines: Genealogies of Law Across Land, Peoples & Sea: In Conversation with Renisa Mawani' (14 February 2009), available at: https://www.borderlines-cssaame.org/ (last accessed on 28 November 2020). See more generally Mawani, Renisa. *Across Oceans of Law. The Komagata Maru and Jurisdiction in the Time of Empire* (Durham: Duke University Press, 2018).

62 Anghie, 'Jurisprudence of Henry Richardson' 2017 (n.8), 15.

63 Henry Richardson has provided a detailed narrative of African-American claims to, interests in and appeals to international law over approximately two centuries spanning from the landing of the first African slaves at Jamestown in 1619 to the 1815 Treaty of Ghent (ending the War of 1812 between Britain and the United States). See Richardson, Henry. *The Origins of African-American Interests in International Law* (Durham: Carolina Academic Press, 2008).

absorbed into regimes of colonial power.[64] Another approach is to focus on the encounter between Europe and the 'New World' in order to complexify the (European-driven) abolitionist narrative. Non-European States did use anti-slavery in order to support their own particular projects –Brazilian responses to British interventions in the name of slave trade abolition, for instance, were not purely docile but also meant to assert Brazil's affinity with Europe and its distinctiveness from Africa.[65] A third way to deal with Eurocentrism would be to pay more attention to other slave trades (that is, other than the transatlantic one), which tend to appear in historiographies of international law only as justifications for European colonial intervention in the late 19th century. This is the case of the Arab slave trade, which Bismarck famously invoked during the 1884–1885 Berlin Conference to intervene in East Africa. The point of such studies would not be to show that 'they too had a slave trade', obviously, but rather 'to illuminate the diversity of human experience and to create critical distance towards the intuitive naturalness of stories we have learned.'[66]

This brings me to my third and last suggestion: we should move away from abolition altogether and pay more attention to questions of political economy.[67] I have shown that the overwhelming majority of international lawyers look at the field's involvement in slavery matters from the 19th century onwards. But international law was involved well before the 19th century, not in the abolition but in the actual establishment and upholding of various forms of human exploitation, including chattel slavery. This point was fundamental to the young Georges Scelle, whose post-doctoral work stands out from his later work. In his *thèse d'Etat* published in 1906, Scelle explored what he called 'the legal and political history of the slave trade to Spanish America'.[68] Instead of looking –like his peers did– at the relationship between international law

64 Renard Painter, Geneviewe. 'A Letter from the Haudenosaunee Confederacy to King George V: Writing and Reading Jurisdictions in International Legal History'. *London Review of International Law* 5(1) (2017), 7–48, 7.

65 This is the PhD topic of Adriane Sanctis at the University of Sao Paolo (unpublished chapter).

66 Koskenniemi, Martti. 'Histories of International Law: Dealing with Eurocentrism'. *Rechtsgeschichte – Legal History* 19 (2011), 152–176, 169.

67 On the 'turn to political economy' in international law, see Haskell, John and Akbar Rasulov. 'International Law and the Turn to Political Economy'. *Leiden Journal of International Law* 31(2) (2018), 243–250, 243.

68 The final product is a 1610-page long comprehensive analysis of the life and death of *asientos de negros*, that is to say, contracts by which the Spanish Crown granted an individual, a company or another state the privilege –and often the monopoly– to supply African slaves to Spanish colonies. Scelle, Georges. *Histoire politique de la traite négrière aux Indes de Castille. Contrats et traités d'assiento* (Paris: Sirey, 1906), Volume 1: *Les contrats (XVIe et XVIIe siècles)*, Volume 2: *L'assiento et la guerre de succession d'Espagne*.

and slavery through the abolition lens, he focused on what happened before the 19th century. He took it for granted that the enslavement of Africans was made possible, was commercialised, and was globalised through extensive legal work. This legal work is what constituted his object of inquiry. In short, Scelle's approach contrasts with the deep-seated tendency in our discipline to celebrate the role international law has played in ending slavery. On the backdrop of such ideological move, Scelle comes in to remind us that slavery was a global legal regime and that we have to deal with it as such.[69]

One way to think this through is to envisage slavery as a hybrid legal regime (public / private, national / international) that has varied greatly across contexts. International lawyers know little about the many different regimes that instituted slavery. Instead, the tendency in our discipline is to present slavery in a flat or sweeping manner as a socio-anthropological fact that has always existed until modern international law ought to have intervened.[70] Slavery may have been a practice deeply entrenched in most societies, but it was supported by various forms of authority and legal arguments, including natural law and *ius gentium*. For instance, what did 16th-century Spanish theologians and jurists –those we like to think of as 'founders of international law'[71] – say about black slavery?[72] In the 17th and 18th centuries, practically all European argumentation on slavery and the slave trade took place within the idiom of political economy. I think there is much to be learned by looking at these various arguments.[73]

---

69 Martineau, Anne-Charlotte.'Georges Scelle's Study of the Slave Trade: French Solidarism Revisited'. *European Journal of International Law* 27(4) (2016), 1131–1151, 1131.

70 To give one stirring example: 'With the exception of marriage, slavery may be humanity's oldest and must ubiquitous organized social institution. … [S]lavery has existed in almost every place and culture in the world. Like the mythical vampire, it always seems to be there, ready to pounce on the innocent and vulnerable, sucking out their blood for the benefit of their masters and the larger culture.' Finkelman, Paul and Seymour Drescher. 'The Eternal Problem of Slavery in International Law: Killing the Vampire of Human Culture'. *Michigan State Law Review* 87(1) (2017), 755–801, 756.

71 Shaw, Malcom. *International Law* (Cambridge: Cambridge University Press, 6th ed. 2008), 22. See also the contributions of Mechoulan, Henry and Peter Haggenmacher. *Actualité de la pensée juridique de Francisco de Vitoria* (Bruxelles: Bruylant, 1988).

72 While their views on the status and treatment of the 'Indians' are well-known, much less so are their reflections on the buying, transportation, and selling of the 'Ethiopians'. There are few exceptions among contemporary international lawyers. See Obregón, Lilliana. 'Criticas tempranas a la esclavización de los Africanos', in *Afrodescendientes en las Américas. Trayectorias sociales e identitarias*, eds. Claudia Mosquera, Mauricio Pardo and Odile Hoffmann (Bogotá: Universidad Nacional de Colombia, 2002), 2–45; Allain, *Slavery in International Law* 2012 (n. 32), 9–55.

73 On the relationship between slavery and capitalism, see Benot, Yves. *La modernité de l'esclavage. Essai sur la servitude au cœur du capitalisme* (Paris: Découverte, 2003).

Another issue that immediately comes to mind when thinking about slavery as a global legal regime is that of reparations. Ever since the Durban Conference, claims for reparations for slavery are in need of legal imagination. The inclusion in the 2001 Final Declaration of a clause stating that slavery is now a crime against humanity but that it was not in the past prevents, in the eyes of many commentators, the articulation of any legal claims for reparations.[74] How can international law be used to confront the enduring socio-political and economic legacies of slavery and racial discrimination? A good starting point may be Martha Biondi's suggestion that 'the philosophical and tactical brilliance of reparations lies in its synthesis of moral principles and political economy.'[75] The language of reparations brings to the fore the harsh reality that slave labour created modern states; it also changes the discursive image of slave descendants from victims to creditors. One does not need to be a fully-blown Marxist to see the paradox that emerges then between, on the one hand, the extreme reluctance of Western states to provide meaningful forms of redress for black slavery (including labour-as-property), and, on the other hand, previous measures taken by the same Western states to preserve the value of captive labour to former slave-owners via direct financial compensation. This paradox is drawn most sharply in the case of France and Haiti: not only did France compensate its own slave owners in Saint-Domingue, but it also obtained from Haiti a huge financial 'compensation' in return for statehood recognition.[76] In fact, Haiti is the major blindspot in the historiography of international law and slavery. The story of the world's most significant abolition, which took place as a result of a revolution by black slaves – and not by Europeans –, has yet to be told by international lawyers.[77]

---

74 See for instance Van Bueren, Geraldine. 'Slavery as Piracy: The Legal Case for Reparations for the Slave Trade', in *The Political Economy of New Slavery*, eds. Christien van den Anker (London: Palgrave Macmillan, 2004), 235–247. Some have even argued that international lawyers should stay away from such complicated and sensitive matter and leave philosophers deal with it. See Tourme Jouannet, Emmanuelle. 'Reparations for Historical Wrongs: The Lessons of Durban', in *What is a Fair International Society?*, eds. Emmanuelle Tourme Jouannet (Oxford: Hart Publishing, 2013), 187–201. I am of the opinion that silence, especially in slavery matters, has too often been an act of complicity and that there is *a priori* no 'better' language to deal with them.

75 Biondi, Martha. 'The Rise of the Reparations Movement', in *Redress for Historical Injustices in the United States: On Reparations for Slavery, Jim Crow, and Their Legacies*, eds. Michael T. Martin and Marilyn Yaquinto (Durham: Duke University Press, 2007), 255–275, 277.

76 In Britain and in France, millions were paid to slave owners 'in compensation' for the loss of their slaves after emancipation. See Araujo, Ana Lucia. *Reparations for Slavery and the Slave Trade: A Transnational and Comparative History* (London: Bloomsbury Academic, 2017).

77 Gainot, Bernard. *La révolution des esclaves. Haïti, 1763–1803* (Paris: Vendémiaire, 2017).

5 Conclusion

International lawyers interested in contemporary slavery issues often speak about the past. Mentioning the past usually serves the making of a point about the present, even if it is done metaphorically or in passing, as a way of opposing 'past' practices to 'present' ones.[78] This is not a problem *per se*. That the concern is a contemporary one is not in itself negative – on the contrary, the 'turn to history' is a move forward insofar as it helps us to understand the present.[79] What is problematic, in my view, is when history turns into ideology and ends up legitimizing current (human rights, criminal law, and/or anti-trafficking) regimes or projects.

In light of this, I have made three suggestions –namely, to be attentive to humanitarian actions carried out in the name of ending slavery; to provide a more contextualised account of the legal abolition of slavery; and to bring political economy in and envisage slavery as a global legal regime that has evolved over time and space. These suggestions have an effect on the *problématique* with which I started this chapter. Indeed, the contradiction between law ('prohibition of slavery') and reality ('persistence of slavery') is no longer the cliffhanger when we conceive slavery to be a legal regime whose contours have varied greatly across contexts. There is a shift in perspective. We can start thinking about how oppression operates in the world through the legal experience of slavery.[80] Do not get me wrong: there is an earnest element when international lawyers concerned with the tremendous scale of exploitative practices around the world speak of a definitional deficiency in law. But whatever the intention, seeking to unveil what slavery 'really' means in international law obscures more than it explains the practices that the concept is being used to denounce.[81] The challenge for international lawyers interested in studying the history of slavery is to understand why freedom and wealth remain so unevenly distributed in the twenty-first century, and what international law and the legacies of imperialism have to do with that.

---

78 The underlying argument is usually that 'new' and 'old' slavery display different characteristics and are driven by different dynamics so that 'old' slavery has little bearing upon ongoing problems that are now over a century removed from legal abolition. Gross, Ariela J. and Chantal Thomas. 'The New Abolitionism, International Law, and the Memory of Slavery'. *Law and History Review* 35(1) (2017), 99–119, 102.

79 Koskenniemi, Martti. 'Histories of International Law: Significance and Problems for a Critical View'. *Temple International and Comparative Law Journal* 27(2) (2013), 215–241.

80 For the argument that 'legal arrangements offer a privileged window onto political economic dynamics', see Kennedy, David. 'Law and the Political Economy of the World'. *Leiden Journal of International Law* 26(1) (2013), 7–49, 8.

81 I am inspired by Orford, Anne. 'In Praise of Description'. *Leiden Journal of International Law* 25(3) (2012), 609–625.

Bibliography

Allain, Jean. 'Genealogies of Human Trafficking and Slavery', in *Routledge Handbook of Human Trafficking*, eds. Ryszard Piotrowicz and Conny Rijken (Abingdon: Routledge, 2018), 3–12.

Allain, Jean. 'The Nineteenth Century Law of the Sea and the British Abolition of the Slave Trade'. *British Yearbook of International Law* 78(1) (2008), 342–348.

Allain, Jean. *Slavery in International Law: Of Human Exploitation and Trafficking* (Leiden: Brill, 2012).

Allain, Jean. 'The Legal Definition of Slavery into the 21st Century', in *The Legal Understanding of Slavery. From the Historical to the Contemporary*, ed. Jean Allain (Oxford: Oxford University Press, 2012), 199–219.

Allain, Jean, ed. *The Legal Understanding of Slavery. From the Historical to the Contemporary* (Oxford: Oxford University Press, 2012).

Allain, Jean. 'White Slave Traffic in International Law'. *Journal of Trafficking and Human Exploitation* 1(1) (2017), 1–40.

Alston, Philip. 'Does the Past Matter? On the Origins of Human Rights'. *Harvard Law Review* 126(7) (2013), 2043–2081.

Altwicker, Tilmann and Oliver Diggelmann. 'How is Progress Constructed in International Legal Scholarship?'. *European Journal of International Law* 25(2) (2014), 425–444.

Anghie, Anthony. 'Slavery and International Law: The Jurisprudence of Henry Richardson'. *Temple International and Comparative Law Journal* 31(1) (2017), 11–23.

Anker, Christien van den, ed. *The Political Economy of New Slavery* (London: Palgrave Macmillan, 2004).

Anghie, Anthony. 'On Critique and the Other', in *International Law and its Others*, ed. Anne Orford (Cambridge: Cambridge University Press, 2008), 389–400.

Araujo, Ana Lucia. *Reparations for Slavery and the Slave Trade: A Transnational and Comparative History* (London: Bloomsbury Academic, 2017).

Bales, Kevin and Peter T. Robbins. 'No One Shall Be Held in Slavery or Servitude: A Critical Analysis of International Slavery Conventions'. *Human Rights Review* 2(2) (2001), 18–45.

Bales, Kevin, Zoe Trodd and Alex Ken Williamson. *Modern Slavery: The Secret of 27 Million People* (Oxford: One World, 2009).

Batstone, David. *Not for Sale: The Return of the Global Slave Trade – and How We Can Fight It* (New York: Harper Collins, 2007).

Benot, Yves. *La modernité de l'esclavage. Essai sur la servitude au cœur du capitalisme* (Paris: Découverte, 2003).

Benton, Lauren. 'Abolition and Imperial Law, 1790–1820'. *The Journal of Imperial and Commonwealth History* 39(3) (2011), 355–374.

Benton, Lauren. 'The Slave Trade and the Origins of International Human Rights Law'. *Victorian Studies* 56(1) (2013), 127–129.

Biondi, Martha. 'The Rise of the Reparations Movement', in *Redress for Historical Injustices in the United States: On Reparations for Slavery, Jim Crow, and Their Legacies*, eds. Michael T. Martin and Marilyn Yaquinto (Durham: Duke University Press, 2007), 255–275.

Bravo, Karen. 'The Role of the Transatlantic Slave Trade in Contemporary Anti-Human Trafficking Discourse'. *Seattle Journal for Social Justice* 9(2) (2011), 555–597.

Bravo, Karen. 'Exploring the Analogy between Modern Trafficking in Humans and the Trans-Atlantic Slave Trade'. *Boston University International Law Journal* 25(2) (2007), 207–293.

Bunting, Annie and Quirk, Joel, eds. *Contemporary Slavery. Popular Rhetoric and Political Practice* (Vancouver: University of British Columbia Press, 2017).

Cavallo, Michele. 'Formes contemporaines d'esclavage, servitude et travail forcé: Le TPIY et la CEDH entre passé et avenir'. *Droits fondamentaux* 6 (2006), 1–16.

Chaumont, Jean-Michel. *Le mythe de la traite des blanches. Enquête sur la fabrication d'un fléau* (Paris: La découverte, 2009).

Cockayne, James, Grono, Nick and Panaccione, Kari. 'Introduction'. *Journal of International Criminal Justice* 14(2) (2016), 253–267.

Couvé, Edouard. *La traite au point de vue du droit des gens* (Paris: Rousseau, 1889).

Craven, Matthew. 'Theorizing the Turn to History in International Law', in *The Oxford Handbook of the Theory of International Law*, eds. Anne Orford and Florian Hoffmann (Oxford: Oxford University Press, 2016), 21–37.

Cullen, Holly. 'Contemporary International Legal Norms on Slavery. Problems of Judicial Interpretation and Application', in *The Legal Understanding of Slavery: From Historical to the Contemporary*, ed. Jean Allain (Oxford: Oxford University Press, 2012), 304–321.

Daillier, Patrick and Alain Pellet. *Droit international public* (Paris: Libraire générale de droit et de jurisprudence, 7th ed. 2002).

Dhillon, Hardeep. 'Borderlines: Genealogies of Law Across Land, Peoples & Sea: In Conversation with Renisa Mawani' (14 February 2009), available at: https://www.borderlines-cssaame.org/ (last accessed on 28 November 2020).

Drescher, Seymour and Finkelman, Paul. 'Slavery', in *The Oxford Handbook of the History of International Law*, eds. Bardo Fassbender and Anne Peters (Oxford: Oxford University Press, 2012), 890–916.

Duffy, Helen. 'Litigating Modern Day Slavery in Regional Courts. A Nascent Contribution'. *Journal of International Criminal Justice* 14(2) (2016), 375–403.

Erpelding, Michel. *Le droit international antiesclavagiste des "Nations Civilisées" (1815–1945)* (Paris: Institut universitaire Varenne, 2017).

Erpelding, Michel. 'L'Esclavage en droit international: Aux origines de la relecture actuelle de la définition conventionnelle de 1926'. *Journal of the History of International Law* 17(2) (2015), 170–220.

Finkelman, Paul and Seymour Drescher. 'The Eternal Problem of Slavery in International Law: Killing the Vampire of Human Culture'. *Michigan State Law Review* 17(4) (2017), 755–801.

Frimigacci, Jean. 'L'Etat colonial français, du discours mythique aux réalités (1880–1940)'. *Matériaux pour l'histoire de notre temps* 27 (1993), 27–35.

Gareis, Karl. *Der Sklavenhandel, das Völkerrecht und das deutsche Recht* (Berlin: Deutsche Zeit- und Streit-Fragen, 1885).

Gainot, Bernard. *La révolution des esclaves. Haïti, 1763–1803* (Paris: Vendémiaire, 2017).

Gallagher, Anne. 'Human Rights and Human Trafficking: Quagmire or Firm Ground? A Response to James Hathaway'. *Virginia Journal of International Law* 49(4) (2009), 789–846.

Gaurier, Dominique. *Histoire du droit international. De l'antiquité à la création de l'ONU* (Rennes: Presses Universitaires de Rennes, 2014).

Gross, Ariela J. and Chantal Thomas. 'The New Abolitionism, International Law, and the Memory of Slavery'. *Law and History Review* 35(1) (2017), 99–119.

Haskell, John and Akbar Rasulov. 'International Law and the Turn to Political Economy'. *Leiden Journal of International Law* 31(2) (2018), 243–250.

Kara, Siddharth. *Sex Trafficking: Inside the Business of Modern Slavery* (New York: Columbia University Press, 2009).

Kennedy, David. 'Law and the Political Economy of the World'. *Leiden Journal of International Law* 26(1) (2013), 7–48.

Kennedy, David. 'When Renewal Repeats: Thinking against the Box'. *New York University Journal of International Law and Politics* 32(2) (1999–2000), 335–500.

Koskenniemi, Martti. 'Why History of International Law Today?'. *Rechtsgeschichte – Legal History* 4 (2004), 61–66.

Koskenniemi, Martti. 'Histories of International Law: Dealing with Eurocentrism'. *Rechtsgeschichte – Legal History* 19 (2011), 152–176.

Koskenniemi, Martti. 'Histories of International Law: Significance and Problems for a Critical View'. *Temple International and Comparative Law Journal* 27(2) (2013), 215–240.

Kyle, David and Rey Koslowski, eds. *Global Human Smuggling* (Baltimore: The Johns Hopkins University Press, 2nd ed. 2011).

Lévy, Henri. *La Traite des Noirs et les Puissances* (Nancy: Crépin-Leblond, 1894).

Linden, Mieke van der. *The Acquisition of Africa (1870–1914). The Nature of International Law* (Leiden: Brill 2016).

Lobasz, Jennifer. *Constructing Human Trafficking. Evangelicals, Feminists, and an Unexpected Alliance* (London: Palgrave Macmillan, 2018).

Martin, Michael T. and Marilyn Yaquinto, eds. *Redress for Historical Injustices in the United States: On Reparations for Slavery, Jim Crow, and Their Legacies* (Durham: Duke University Press, 2007).

Martineau, Anne-Charlotte. *Une analyse critique du débat sur la fragmentation du droit international* (Bruxelles: Bruylant, 2015).

Martineau, Anne-Charlotte. 'Contested Histories: Revisiting the Relationship between International Law and Slavery', in *International Law and the Humanities*, eds. Sundhya Pahuja and Shane Chalmers (Abingdon: Routledge, forthcoming 2021).

Martineau, Anne-Charlotte. 'Georges Scelle's Study of the Slave Trade: French Solidarism Revisited'. *European Journal of International Law* 27(4) (2016), 1131–1151.

Martinez, Jenny. *The Slave Trade and the Origins of International Human Rights Law* (Oxford: Oxford University Press, 2012).

Mawani, Renisa. *Across Oceans of Law. The Komagata Maru and Jurisdiction in the Time of Empire* (Durham: Duke University Press, 2018).

McGeehan, Nicholas Lawrence. 'Misunderstood and Neglected: The Marginalisation of Slavery in International Law'. *The International Journal of Human Rights* 16(3) (2012), 436–460.

Mechoulan, Henry and Peter Haggenmacher. *Actualité de la pensée juridique de Francisco de Vitoria* (Bruxelles: Bruylant, 1988).

Mégret, Frédéric. 'Droit international et esclavage: Pour une réévaluation'. *African Yearbook of International Law* 18(1) (2010), 121–183.

Menon, Pavarthi. *Protecting Empire in Slave Colonies: The Politics of a Humanitarian Authoritarianism* (Helsinki: University of Helsinki, PhD Thesis, unpublished).

Miers, Suzanne. *Slavery in the Twentieth Century. The Evolution of a Global Problem* (Walnut Creek: Altamira Press, 2003).

Montardy, Henry De. *La traite et le droit international* (Paris: Girard & Brière, 1906).

Moyn, Samuel. 'The Nation: Of Deserts and Promised Lands: The Dream of Global Justice'. 20 February 2012, available at: https://www.thenation.com/article/deserts-and-promised-lands-dream-global-justice/ (last accessed on 28 November 2020).

Nanda, Ved and M. Cherif Bassouni. 'Slavery and Slave Trade: Steps toward Eradication'. *Santa Clara Law Review* 12(2) (1972), 424–442.

Němcova, Tereza. 'Book Review: The Political Economy of New Slavery by Christien van den Anker'. *Perspectives* 26 (2006), 91–110.

Nicholson, Andrea, Minh Dang and Zoe Trodd. 'A Full Freedom: Contemporary Survivors' Definitions of Slavery'. *Human Rights Law Review* 18(4) (2018), 689–704.

Obregón, Lilliana. 'Criticas tempranas a la esclavización de los Africanos', in *Afrodescendientes en las Américas. Trayectorias sociales e identitarias*, eds. Claudia Mosquera, Mauricio Pardo and Odile Hoffmann (Bogotá: Universidad Nacional de Colombia, 2002), 423–452.

Orford, Anne. 'The Past as Law or History? The Relevance of Imperialism for Modern International Law', in *Droit international et nouvelles approches sur le tiers-monde: Entre répétition et renouveau*, eds. Emmanuelle Jouannet, Mark Toufayan and Hélène Ruiz-Fabri (Pedone: Paris, 2013), 97–118.

Orford, Anne. 'In Praise of Description'. *Leiden Journal of International Law* 25(3) (2012), 609–625.

Piotrowicz, Ryszard and Conny Rijken, eds. *Routledge Handbook of Human Trafficking* (Abingdon: Routledge, 2018).

Queneuil, Henry. *De la traite des noirs et de l'esclavage. La conférence de Bruxelles et ses résultats* (Paris: Larose & Tenin, 1907).

Queuneuil, Henry. 'Conférence anti-esclavagiste de Bruxelles. Acte général du 2 juillet 1890: Application et résultats'. *Revue générale de droit international public* 15 (1908), 131–146.

Quirk, Joel. *The Anti-Slavery Project: From the Slave Trade to Human Trafficking* (Philadelphia: University of Pennsylvania Press, 2011).

Rassam, Yasmine. 'International Law and Contemporary Forms of Slavery: An Economic and Social Rights-Based Approach'. *Penn State International Law Review* 23(4) (2005), 809–855.

Renard Painter, Geneviewe. 'A Letter from the Haudenosaunee Confederacy to King George V: Writing and Reading Jurisdictions in International Legal History'. *London Review of International Law* 5(1) (2017), 7–48.

Richardson, Henry. *The Origins of African-American Interests in International Law* (Durham: Carolina Academic Press, 2008).

Sarrien, Michel-Louis-Ferdinand. *La traite des nègres et le droit de visite au cours du XIXe siècle dans les rapports de la France et de l'Angleterre* (Paris: Jouve et Cie, 1910).

Scarpa, Silvia. 'Slavery'. *Oxford Bibliography on International Law* (2 November 2017), available at: http://www.oxfordbibliographies.com/view/document/obo-9780199796953/obo-9780199796953-0097.xml (last accessed on 28 November 2020).

Scelle, Georges. *Histoire politique de la traite négrière aux Indes de Castille. Contrats et traités d'assiento* (Paris: Sirey, 1906), Volume 1: *Les contrats (XVIe et XVIIe siècles)*, Volume 2: *L'assiento et la guerre de succession d'Espagne*.

Scott, Rebecca. 'International Law and Contemporary Slavery: The Long View'. *Michigan Journal of International Law* 38(3) (2017), 349–357.

Scully, Eileen. 'Pre-Cold War Traffic in Sexual Labour and Its Foes: Some Contemporary Lessons', in *Global Human Smuggling*, eds. David Kyle and Rey Koslowski (Baltimore: The Johns Hopkins University Press, 2nd ed. 2011), chapter 4.

Shaw, Malcom. *International Law* (Cambridge: Cambridge University Press, 6th ed. 2008).

'Statement by His Excellency Mr George W. Bush, President of the United States of America. Address to the United Nations General Assembly, 23 September 2003', available at: http://www.un.org/webcast/ga/58/statements/usaeng030923.htm (last accessed on 28 November 2020).

Soderlund, Gretchen. 'Running from the Rescuers: New U.S. Crusades against Sex Trafficking and the Rhetoric of Abolition'. *The National Women's Studies Association Journal* 17(3) (2005), 64–87.

Sousa Santos, Boaventura de. 'European Commission: The Fight against Trafficking in Human Beings in EU: Promoting Legal Cooperation and Victims' Protection', available at: http://www.transcrime.it/wp-content/uploads/2016/01/THB_CoopToFight.pdf (last accessed on 28 November 2020).

Stoyanova, Vladislava. 'United Nations against Slavery: Unravelling Concepts, Institutions and Obligations'. *Michigan Journal of International Law* 38(3) (2017), 359–454.

Stoyanova, Vladislava. 'Article 4 of the ECHR and the Obligation of Criminalising Slavery, Servitude, Forced Labour and Human Trafficking'. *Cambridge Journal of International and Comparative Law* 3(2) (2014), 407–443.

Tourme Jouannet, Emmanuelle. 'Reparations for Historical Wrongs: The Lessons of Durban', in *What is a Fair International Society?*, eds. Emmanuelle Tourme Jouannet (Oxford: Hart Publishing, 2013), 187–201.

Tourme Jouannet, Emmanuelle. *What is a Fair International Society?* (Oxford: Hart Publishing, 2013).

Van Bueren, Geraldine. 'Slavery as Piracy: The Legal Case for Reparations for the Slave Trade', in *The Political Economy of New Slavery*, eds. Christien van den Anker (London: Palgrave Macmillan, 2004), 235–247.

Walkowitz, Judith. *Prostitution and Victorian Society: Women, Class, and the State* (Cambridge: Cambridge University Press, 1980).

Weidner, Fritz. *Die Haussklaverei in Ostafrica: Geschichtlich und politisch dargestellt* (Jena: Gustav Fischer, 1915).

Weissbrodt, David and Michael Dottridge. Abolishing Slavery and Its Contemporary Forms (Geneva: Office of the UN High Commissioner for Human Rights, HR/PUB/02/4, 2002), available at: https://www.ohchr.org/Documents/Publications/slaveryen.pdf (last accessed on 28 November 2020).

Weissbrodt, David. 'Slavery'. Max Planck Encyclopedia of Public International Law, ed. Rüdiger Wolfrum (Oxford: Oxford University Press, 2014), available at: http://opil.ouplaw.com/view/10.1093/law:epil/9780199231690/law-9780199231690-e874 (last accessed on 28 November 2020).

CHAPTER 3

Edmund Burke and the Ambivalence of Protection for Slaves: Between Humanity and Control

Parvathi Menon

Abstract

This chapter focuses on the period between 1812 and 1834, when the British Empire introduced protection measures to mitigate the suffering of slaves from planter brutality, but also to protect planters from slave rebellion. By examining the impact and influences wielded by Edmund Burke's *Sketch of a Negro Code* (1780), this chapter studies protection as an alliance between the abolitionists and planters who, despite contestations, found in Burke's Code a means to attain their separate ends. Through the workings of the Office of the Protector, instituted by the imperial authorities in the slave colony of Trinidad, this study examines how it granted slaves the humanity of 'rights' against their masters, while also protecting the right to property (in slaves) of the planters. I argue that the practice of protection was, as is in the present, at the center of the exploitation of subjugated groups.

Keywords

slavery – slave trade – plantation economy – amelioration – Office of the Protector – Crown Colony – Trinidad – slave emancipation

'All political power which is set over men ... ought to be some way or other exercised ultimately for their benefit ... as a trust', argued the Irish politician and philosopher Edmund Burke (1729–1797) in his critique of British rule in India. Contemporary scholars like Adom Getachew credit Burke with the creation of the trusteeship model as a limit to imperial rule, while arguing that it was later redeployed by the end of the 19th century to expand imperial power.[1] Alternatively, scholars such as Antony Anghie state that 'whereas the

1 Getachew, Adom. *Worldmaking after Empire: The Rise and Fall of Self-Determination* (Princeton: Princeton University Press, 2019), 81.

 | DOI:10.1163/9789004461802_005

positivist international law of the nineteenth century endorsed the conquest and exploitation of non-European peoples, the Mandate System, by contrast, sought to ensure their protection'.[2] My account departs from both these views. First, I argue that Burke's trusteeship ideas, albeit widely written about as limiting imperial rule (concerning his efforts in India, largely demonstrated by the Warren Hastings trial),[3] can also be described as a tool for imperial expansion in the early 19th century (as in the case of its redeployment in the Mandates model). To re-characterize Burke as neither radical nor conservative, but as a pragmatist who believed that one must 'allow an evil to correct it',[4] I examine the underlying meaning of what became his 'trusteeship model' from the perspective of his plan to protect slaves. Second, I claim that if we move past the strict international-national delineation present in international law today,[5] we can appreciate that the legal technique of protection was at the center of the exploitation of non-European peoples for much longer during the '*Pax Britannica*'. Thus counteracting the progressive narrative surrounding international institutions and international law, this chapter argues that the relationship between protection and humanitarianism has a longer history.[6]

---

2 Anghie, Antony. *Imperialism, Sovereignty and the Making of International Law* (Cambridge: Cambridge University Press, 2005), 116.

3 Marshall, Peter James. *The Impeachment of Warren Hastings* (Oxford: Oxford University Press, 1965); see also Mukherjee, Mithi. 'Justice, War, and the Imperium: India and Britain in Edmund Burke's Prosecutorial Speeches in the Impeachment Trial of Warren Hastings'. *Law and History Review* 23(3) (2005), 589–630.

4 Although I use the term pragmatism to denote a compromise between the radical and conservative approaches, I remain mindful that pragmatism itself functions on a political spectrum where Burke's ideas may be labelled as 'pragmatic conservative'. See Lacey, Robert J. *Pragmatic Conservatism: Edmund Burke and His American Heirs* (Basingstoke: Palgrave Macmillan, 2016).

5 Without thinking of the British Empire's colonies as mere extensions of its territories and therefore 'domestic law', international law historians like Wilhelm Grewe's describe it as a 'world-wide unorganised, interconnected State system that developed in the 19th century … [with a] universalistic way of thinking that extended such a geographically disparate world empire over the entire globe …'; Grewe, Wilhelm G. *The Epochs of International Law* (Berlin: De Gruyter, 2000), 461.

6 See Benton, Lauren and Adam Clulow, eds. *Protection and Empire: A Global History* (Cambridge: Cambridge University Press, 2018). This edited volume traces the history of different practices of protection across different Empires but surprisingly leaves out protection as a measure for slaves, which predated protection for aborigines in a chapter describing the case of New South Wales by Ford, Lisa. 'Protecting the Peace on the Edges of Empire: Commissioners of Crown Lands in New South Wales', in *Protection and Empire: A Global History*, eds. Lauren Benton and Adam Clulow (Cambridge: Cambridge University Press, 2018), 175–193. Aboriginal protection emanated after a Select Committee Meeting in 1837 that drew from the evangelical movements for slaves.

The 'Imperial Humanitarianism'[7] embodied in the language of protection already signified in the early 19th century that limits had to be set against authoritarianism in the colonies. Nevertheless, the language of protection also served the civilizational agenda that was key to advancing political and economic interests of the imperial powers. Protection measures existed in different iterations under the British Empire (also the French and the Spanish), perhaps best exemplified in anti-slavery humanitarianism.[8]

The study of British anti-slavery humanitarianism often starts with one of the two events, which are considered its milestones – abolition of the slave trade (1807) and the abolition of slavery (1833) in the British Empire. Whether as a celebration of international law's humanitarian causes or as vilification of its insufficient tackling of the issue, international law scholars rely on these milestones to carry out a progressive narrative of the history of humanity.[9] In this chapter, I shift the focus to a period that remains understudied by international legal scholars – the period of 'amelioration', from 1812 to 1833, during which the introduction of protection for slaves, to mitigate their suffering from enslavement, was central. Amelioration was considered merely an *interim* period awaiting abolition of slavery, the real emancipatory moment. However protection measures for slaves, by enforcing limits on planter brutality and granting slaves 'rights' against the authority of their masters, underscored an important political juncture which had an enduring import in the trajectory of the British Empire and the global legal order: A complex alliance – despite contestations – between the pro-slavery 'conservatives', the radical anti-slavery evangelists, and 'liberals'.[10] These alliances and contestations more often than not rendered the categorisation of the people behind them uncertain, or at the very least questioned any progressive or linear histories of the humanitarianism of protection for vulnerable groups thereafter. Protection projected humanity that put the welfare of slaves at the centre and yet, maintained the authorities' control over the slaves. The language of protection came with an ambivalence that was capable of portraying the protector as the benevolent

7 Barnett, Michael. *Empires of Humanity: A History of Humanitarianism* (New York: Cornell University Press, 2011), 9.

8 Mellor, George R. *British Imperial Trusteeship 1783–1850* (London: Faber & Faber, 1951).

9 See the chapter by Anne-Charlotte Martineau in this volume.

10 While it is anachronistic and imprecise to refer to the pro-slavery group as 'conservatives' in the late 18th and early 19th century, I use the term as a convenient conceptual shorthand for the defenders of the Crown, and 'liberals' for those who drew inspiration from the Glorious Revolution of 1688, of the supremacy of parliament over monarchy.

sovereign, i.e., as protecting the slaves from planter brutality (protection as *humanity*), but also one that allowed the sovereign to exert control over the protected to prevent resistance to authority (protection as *control*).[11] I will examine the politics behind protection for slaves in Trinidad in the early 19th century to show how protection, as a legal strategy, served these different ends in the British Empire, of humanity and control alike, and was influenced by the legacy of Edmund Burke. Although Burke died the same year Trinidad was captured, his views and elaborate plan for the slaves had its most notable impact in the amelioration program implemented in Trinidad in 1824.

In the following sections, I will examine the role played by the conservatives, the liberals, and the abolitionists in adding their ambivalences to the meaning of protection (section 1) and Burke's reformist agenda that shaped its politics (section 2). The suggested protections for slaves redefined the relationship between the Crown and the Colony (section 3), and was tested in one of its newly acquired colonies, Trinidad, to see whether competing aspects of humanity and control satisfied varied interests (section 4).

1 The Politics of Protection in the Metropole: Contestations and Alliances

The period of amelioration for slaves often pits the anti-slavery groups against the pro-slavery groups.[12] However, British imperial politics in the late 18th and early 19th century was far more complex and less categorical. It was a period that witnessed the revolutions in America, France, and Haiti, as well as the Napoleonic Wars. The fear of slave revolt and the maltreatment of slaves were both matters of concern to the British metropole and the colonies, and equally to the abolitionists and the planters. In the aftermath of the abolition of the slave trade in 1807 in the British Empire, the debates that ensued in the British

11 Ghachem, Malick. *The Old Regime and the Haitian Revolution* (Cambridge: Cambridge University Press, 2012).

12 Titus, Noel. *The Amelioration and Abolition of Slavery in Trinidad, 1812–1834: Experiments and Protests in a New Slave Colony* (Bloomington: Author House, 2009); cf. Spence, Caroline Q. *Ameliorating Empire: Slavery and Protection in the British Colonies, 1783–1865* (Harvard University, PhD Thesis, 2014), available at: http://nrs.harvard.edu/urn-3:HUL.InstRepos:13070043 (last accessed on 29 March 2021); and Dierksheide, Christa. *Amelioration and Empire: Progress and Slavery in the Plantation Americas* (Charlottesville: University of Virginia Press, 2014). Dierksheide uses the binary characterization of 'antislavery amelioration' and 'proslavery amelioration' as the two sets of ideas converging in the amelioration phase. While I agree with her premise, the purpose of my analysis is to show how neither of the groups could be restricted to their erstwhile categories.

Parliament struggled to come to terms with conflicting interests. The desire to maintain the lucrative plantation economy in the wake of a dwindling slave population meant, in the words of Burke, compelling the savages to order and civilization, or what I refer to as the *humanity-control* aspect of protection.[13] Prior to the enactment of amelioration measures, it was unclear whether free labour from emancipated slaves could yield a similar profitable model, or worse still, whether emancipated slaves would misuse their freedoms, i.e., rebel. These attitudes, therefore, impacted the period of amelioration and the politics of protection in Britain, manifesting as contestations *and* alliances between the conservatives, liberals, and a heterodox group of abolitionists.[14]

The introduction of the slave register in the year 1812, through an Order-in-Council, is considered the starting point of the period of amelioration.[15] However, the parliamentary discussions regarding protection for slaves began much earlier, in 1792, owing to public campaigns against slavery that occurred between 1787 and 1792. While the anti-slavery debates commenced in the parliament in 1792, the idea of protecting slaves from planter brutality was introduced by British West-Indian planters and members of the parliament like Charles Rose Ellis (1771–1845) and Bryan Edwards (1743–1800) in 1797 as a bargaining chip to maintain the 'necessary evil of slavery' and help sustain the plantations.[16] William Wilberforce (1759–1833), the leading voice of the abolitionist movement, with his single-minded focus on Evangelicalism, had initially concentrated merely on ending the slave trade, only later campaigning for slavery abolition when the former did not lead to the latter as hoped.[17] After the slave trade was abolished, many abolitionists such as Wilberforce and James Stephen (1789–1859), British Undersecretary of State for the Colonies, agreed to protection as a means to prepare the slaves for emancipation, and only a few like Elizabeth Heyrick (1769–1831) were committed to immediate emancipation. Therefore, the debates began with a more rudimentary

13 Burke, Edmund. 'Sketch of a Negro Code', in *The Writings and Speeches of Edmund Burke*, vol. III, ed. Paul Langford (Oxford: Oxford University Press, 1981), 562–581.

14 In this section, I use 'conservative' and 'liberal' stances not as all-encompassing ideologies, but more as a discrete set of conversations.

15 Titus, *Amelioration and Abolition* 2009 (n. 12).

16 This was uttered in the House of Commons by a planter, Bryan Edwards, who was considered William Wilberforce's arch opponent on the issue of slavery. He supported protection measures, which he claimed had worked successfully in Jamaica, Dominica, Antigua, and Grenada; and in Grenada, he said the appointment of Guardian of Slaves proved 'a measure of peculiar efficacy'. *The Parliamentary Register*, ser. 3, vol. 2 (1797).

17 See Borthwick, Peter. *Report of a Lecture on Colonial Slavery and Gradual Emancipation* (Edinburgh: W. Ritchie and Co., 1833), 19, where he accuses Wilberforce of 'goading the government ... into doing the most unjust and cruel act [of immediate emancipation]'.

positioning as either pro-abolition or anti-abolition, but later fused into a moderate 'gradualist' approach of amelioration. The Secretary of State, Henry Dundas (1742–1811), put forward such a motion of 'gradual' emancipation of slaves already in 1792, which was more of a pragmatic compromise between the conservative and radical approaches. While different factions had their own brand of protection, all of them turned back to refer to a meticulous plan penned by Burke in 1780, years before the slavery debates began among the British public or in the parliament.

Burke, considered the Father of Modern Conservatism,[18] was a member of the Whig party whose contribution to the legal strategies for protecting slaves has largely gone unheeded in the accounts that deal with amelioration.[19] He was not an abolitionist, but laid down a slave reform program in the *Sketch of a Negro Code* (1780). It was an elaborate document that had four parts, three of which dealt with the slave-trade and one with the 'regulations relative to the state and condition of slaves in West Indies, their manumission', i.e., amelioration. The foundation of Burke's slave code stood solely for neither the conservative nor the radical arguments made by certain planters and abolitionists, yet they all commended his work during the parliamentary debates as an example of how they wished for the motion regarding slavery to unfold. They saw in his code a means to attain their separate ends. This is perhaps where

18 The scholarship on Edmund Burke appears less definitive. Some have portrayed strands of liberalism in the man whose legacy is conservative. See especially Mehta, Uday Singh. *Liberalism and Empire* (Chicago: University of Chicago Press, 1999); and more recently Pitts, Jennifer. *A Turn to Empire: The Rise of Imperial Liberalism in Britain and France* (Princeton: Princeton University Press, 2006). Others have tried to bring down his anti-imperial hero image from the Warren Hastings trial by relying on his opinions about the West Indies and Americas. See Kohn, Margaret and Daniel O'Neill. 'A Tale of Two Indias: Burke and Mill on Empire and Slavery in the West Indies and America'. *Political Theory* 34(2) (2006), 192–228, where the authors argue that Burke was dismissive of Africans, evident from his embrace of the civilizing process. See also O' Neill, Daniel. *Edmund Burke and the Conservative Logic of Empire* (Oakland: University of California Press, 2016).

19 The exceptions are the two works on amelioration: Dierksheide, *Amelioration and Empire* 2014 (n. 12) and Spence, *Ameliorating Empire* 2014 (n. 12). Both refer to Burke's Negro Code, but without drawing much from the influence he had on abolitionists and planters alike. On the other hand, Christopher Brown's book on abolitionism and more recent works by Gregory Collins and P. J. Marshall evaluate in detail the influence and strategies of Burke's Code albeit not necessarily from the perspective of amelioration as a tool of imperial control. Brown, Christopher. *Moral Capital: Foundations of British Abolitionism* (Charlottesville: University of North Carolina Press, 2004); Collins, Gregory M. 'Edmund Burke on Slavery and the Slave Trade'. *Slavery & Abolition* 40(3) (2019), 494–521; Marshall, Peter James. *Edmund Burke and the British Empire in the West Indies: Wealth, Power, and Slavery* (Oxford: Oxford University Press, 2019).

Burke's ambivalence becomes most ostensible and the value of his plan most discernible.[20]

Burke's image in scholarship thus far has oscillated between *Reflections on the Revolution in France* (1790), which reinforced his 'affection for traditional hierarchies and aristocratic government',[21] and the Warren Hastings impeachment proceedings (1788–1795),[22] attesting to his anti-imperial image in the crusade against the oppression by the East India Company officials. In this chapter, by turning to Burke's earlier works on slavery and slave trade, I argue that the fluctuation of Burke's image between conservative and liberal, which authors largely based on two separate works, can be found in his single plan of slave amelioration. Burke's sympathies towards the slaves in the colonies and his universalist aspiration to apply similar standards both at home and abroad[23] is best understood by studying how he devised 'protection' as the bridge between the civilized and the uncivilized, preparing savages for emancipation.

Burke was a political and moral strategist, who embedded his reformist agenda without isolating the members of his constituency, Bristol, which was a major slave-trading port. Therefore, although his views condemned the poor condition of slaves, he also recognised the impossibility of slave-trade abolition.[24] At the same time, albeit writing about the slave trade, he wished for the African Company of Merchants, operating from 1752 to 1821 in the Gold Coast area of modern Ghana, to carry out a set of welfare functions to ameliorate the condition of slaves such as: building schools, hospitals, churches at trading posts; and also a set of administrative roles: appointing governors and counsellors to act as justices of peace. All of these, in Burke's plan, would be conducted following instructions from the African Company for Merchants, which was the successor of the Royal African Company since 1750, constituted

20 Scholars like Mehta and Pitts revived Burke's liberalism as a response to the mantle of conservatism that shrouded his reputation, yet being mindful of the limits to such a view. Pitts, *Turn to Empire* 2005 (n. 18); Mehta, *Liberalism and Empire* 1999 (n. 18). David Armitage, in contrast, recognised how the renewed interest in Burke has in no way helped classify him any better: 'whether he was a realist or an idealist, a rationalist or a revolutionist, has concluded variously that he was a "conservative crusader" or an "historical empiricist" … or a "proto-Marxist, or a proto-Gramscian" theorist of hegemony'. Armitage, David. 'Edmund Burke and Reason of State'. *Journal of the History of Ideas* 61(4) (2000) 617–634.

21 Pitts, *A Turn to Empire* 2005 (n. 18), 75.

22 Marshall, Peter James. *The Impeachment of Warren Hastings* (London: Oxford University Press, 1965).

23 In Clause 37 of the Sketch, Burke writes that the slaves must be afforded rights just like any British subject. See also Pitts, *Turn to Empire* 2005 (n. 18), 59–101.

24 Collins, 'Edmund Burke' 2019 (n. 19), 494–521.

by an Act of Parliament to manage English possessions on the coast of West Africa.[25] These functions were intended to help "civilize" the coast of Africa, which he believed the trade worsened. Burke had an innate vision, it appears, of bestowing upon the African Company welfare tasks, much like the East India Company, which not only advanced a belief in the benevolent power of the imperial regulatory state but also to recast the private enterprise in a humane light.[26] However, unlike intended in his plan, after the abolition of the slave trade in 1807, everything changed for the African Company.[27] Nevertheless, the amelioration plan for slaves in the last part of his *Sketch* had an enduring significance in the debates that ensued in the Parliament. The success of Burke's plan for slave protection lay in its quality of bringing together the 'proslavery ameliorationists' and the 'antislavery ameliorationists',[28] to use Dierksheide's categorisation; or in other words, planters and abolitionists.

Planters and abolitionists themselves were not of homogenous groups in any sense, although they each endorsed the humanity-control idea built into the protection strategy in their separate ways. West Indian planters like Charles Rose Ellis, who presented himself as more anti-slavery than Bryan Edwards did, found merit in Burke's plan, which advocated for protecting the slaves from cruel treatment at the hands of the masters. Ellis believed that when the supply of slaves reduces, it will become imperative to protect them so that they can continue working on the plantations. He also sensed that Burke's plan to enforce a better treatment of the slaves at the hands of the masters could help form an attachment between them: pivotal in the aftermath of the Haitian revolution, which had instilled in him and other planters a fear of slave revolt.

---

25 Parliament of Great Britain. *An Act for Extending and Improving the Trade to Africa* (Library Location: Schomburg Center for Research in Black Culture, Manuscripts, Archives and Rare Books Division, The New York Public Library, retrieved from http://digitalcollections.nypl.org/items/5b08efa0-c3ac-0133-5dd1-00505686a51c) (last accessed on 29 March 2021) (London: Assigns of Robert Baskett, 1750); *Company of Royal Adventurers of England Trading with Africa and Successors: Records*, T70, 1660–1833 (held by The National Archives, London). For a detailed study on the Royal African Company, see Pettigrew, William A. *Freedom's Debt: The Royal African Company and the Politics of the Atlantic Slave Trade, 1672–1752* (Chapel Hill: University of North Carolina Press, 2013).

26 See also Burke, Edmund. 'Speeches on African Slave Trade, 5 June 1777', in *The Writings and Speeches of Edmund Burke*, vol. 3, eds. Warren M. Elofson, John A. Woods and William B. Todd (Oxford: Oxford University Press, 1996).

27 For a detailed description of the African Company, see Adams, Charles Hansford, ed. *The Narrative of Robert Adams, a Barbary Captive: A Critical Edition* (Cambridge: Cambridge University Press, 2005).

28 On amelioration as the meeting place for proslavery advocates and antislavery advocates, see Dierksheide, *Amelioration and Empire* 2014 (n. 12).

2 'It Is Better to Allow the Evil, in Order to Correct It'

Burke's approach to slavery was first evidenced in his 1757 book co-authored with his cousin, William Burke, titled *An Account of the European Settlements in America.*[29] The Burkes carry out a cost-benefit analysis of allowing the slaves moderate labour to prevent their deaths and in the end garner better profits.[30] Asserting the need for the exercise of humanity towards the slaves, the Burkes remind us in their *Account* that 'those nations which have behaved with the greatest humanity to their slaves were always best served, and ran the least hazard from their rebellions.'[31] Many of the 'indulgences' suggested for the slaves in the *Account* are reflected in the reforms Burke enunciates in his *Sketch* later. Much of Burke's view on slavery and his plan for protecting slaves emerged from the sentiment that 'it is better to allow the evil, in order to correct it, than by endeavouring to forbid, what we cannot be able to wholly prevent, to leave it under an illegal, and therefore an unreformed existence'.[32] Despite sympathising with the abolitionists, he infused a pragmatism into their radicalism (of abolition). Burke described abolition as a 'chimerical project', a type of abstract idea, with no grounding in reality.[33] The choice between abolition and preservation of slavery was unrealistic to Burke; the middle-ground option of gradualism (through protection) was far more appealing and practical. One of the steps to correct the evil was to discard the absolute sovereignty of the master over the slave and replace it with a shared sovereignty between the master and the imperial administration through an imperially constituted officer. '[H]is Majesty's Attorney-General for the time being successively shall, by his office, exercise the trust and employment of Protector of Negroes'. Without arguing against slavery, Burke's plan was an appeal for oversight of the slave colonies.[34] Much like how he envisaged the role of the African Company for

29 Burke, Edmund and William Burke. *An Account of the European Settlements in America,* volumes I and II (London: J. Dodsley, 1770).

30 Ibid. vol. II, 126 et seq.

31 Ibid. vol. II, 128.

32 Burke, 'Sketch of a Negro Code' 1981 (n. 13).

33 This was very much in line with the *gradualist abolition* of slavery that Dundas pitched in the parliament, later accepted by the abolitionists as well. The gradualist approach signified how Condorcet, too, wished to tackle the evil of slavery in the French territories. See Condorcet, Marquis de. *Réflexions sur l'esclavage des nègres* (Paris: Editions Flammarion, 2009).

34 This was similar to the stance he took in the case of the East India Company: without arguing against empire, he instead argued against East India Company's rule and argued for parliamentary oversight of its territories. Agnani, Sunil. *Hating Empire Properly: The Two Indies and the Limits of Enlightenment Anticolonialism* (New York: Fordham University Press, 2013).

the coast of West Africa, he believed the Protector, as an agent of the British imperial government, would ameliorate the conditions of the slaves by no longer entrusting them under the 'sole guardianship of their masters'.[35]

The division between the 'private authority' of the masters and the 'public authority' of the Crown in no way undermined the masters in Burke's eyes.[36] This was not principally a humanitarian measure, and it is evident from his *Sketch* that it was neither the subordination to masters nor the social hierarchy that Burke was uncomfortable with, but merely the maltreatment of the slaves. At the same time, he was equally a proponent of keeping the slaves, even if free, under control. In fact, in his address to the British Colonists in America in 1777, he describes the 'barbarism and savagery' of the slaves as a cause for concern, something that he did not wish to 'let loose' upon the colonists. One of the duties he prescribed for the Protector was, understandably, to ensure that if a freed slave was found guilty of disorderly conduct or disobeying the law twice, he or she would be sold back into slavery. Therefore, to Burke, unless the slaves proved themselves worthy of freedom whilst 'free', it would not be theirs to enjoy. This contrast was representative of how he described his plan to Dundas: 'The planter you must at once restrain and support, and you must control at the same time that you ease the servant [slave]'. Moreover, this is equally telling why different sides of the debate relied on the plan to represent, at least in part, their interests.

In Burke's 1792 letter to Dundas, when he first revealed the contents of his *Sketch*, he favoured slow emancipation and an increased regulation (rather than abstract principles like 'abolition'). He hoped to 'civilize the Coast of Africa by the trade', in a 'more reputable, and, possibly, a more profitable, connection with it.'[37] When he thought the trade had turned the coast more barbarous, his letter sympathised with the condition of the slaves, desirous of imposing regulations on them, who could not do anything for themselves. Hence dismissing the notion of their consent to the regulations, Burke believed that the reforms must be an imposition on the slaves. His model of protection reflected exactly that – to submit the slaves to a regulated system where their 'capacities' would be rewarded. His *Sketch* was intended to regulate the slave trade and also in the bargain, to help civilize the natives by inculcating 'religion, order, morality and

35 Burke. 'Sketch of a Negro Code' 1981 (n. 13).

36 See Ghachem, *Old Regime* 2012 (n. 11) on the struggle for sovereignty between masters and the colonial officers. While the treatment of the public/private divide between the Crown and planters/masters is not new, I rely on Ghachem's articulation mainly because he derives it from Montesquieu's works, someone Burke was influenced by. See Loughlin, Martin. 'Burke on Law, Revolution and Constitution'. *Journal of Constitutional History / Giornale di storia costituzionale* 29(1) (2015), 49–60.

37 Burke, 'Sketch of a Negro Code' 1981 (n. 13), 562–581.

virtue … the elemental principles, and the knowledge of letters, arts and handicraft trades, the chief means of such civilization and improvement'.[38] Burke's plan, not unlike the *Code Noir* (albeit more concertedly), stressed heavily on the role he hoped religion would play in the lives of slaves. From insisting on marriages between eligible slaves, 'as a means of forming men to a fitness to freedom', Burke's plan also punished those who refused marriage.[39] Thus, the civilizational process and religious instruction for slaves was very much a part of the Burkean model, which was in line with the attitudes of the abolitionists.

Abolitionists like Wilberforce rejected the recourse prescribed for slaves against master brutality in Burke's plan (of exercising their 'rights' and registering complaints much like the result of subjecthood) but endorsed Burke's proposal to civilize them through religious instruction and prepare them for emancipation. Abolitionists like the Anglican priest and surgeon Reverend James Ramsay (1733–1789), in his *Essay on the Treatment and Conversion of African Slaves in the British Sugar Colonies* (1784), on the other hand, believed that slaves, just like other members of society, must be granted the protection of law.[40] Yet, abolitionists like Ramsay and Wilberforce agreed on what society could achieve through Christianity. Moreover, Ramsay thought that granting slaves the benefit of religious instruction could allow them a mutually dependent relationship with their masters, of a 'voluntary compact of service and fidelity on the one side, [and] of wages and protection on the other'.[41] Protection continued to be characterised as an end, of fidelity. The reforms purported by the abolitionists were radical as far as ending the trade, evidenced by the formation of the Society for Effecting the Abolition of Slave Trade in 1787 by Granville Sharp (1735–1813), Thomas Clarkson (1760–1846), and ten others, in response to the Zong massacre – a mass killing of 132 sick African slaves by the crew of the British slave ship Zong.[42]

While Wilberforce found it hard to describe the planters as humane, his unwillingness to ascribe to the slaves a recourse against their masters was a sign of his perception of the slaves as unready to differentiate between the unjust master and the just master. Wilberforce was not a champion of granting rights to the slaves until he felt they could discern wrong from right; 'to think,

38 Ibid.

39 Ibid., Clauses 21–23.

40 He further draws from the Athenian practice, where the laws gave the slaves protection and remedy in their names against injuries done unto them. See Ramsay, James. *Essay on the Treatment and Conversion of African Slaves in the British Sugar Colonies* (London: James Philip Printing, 1784), 22.

41 Ibid., 31.

42 Faubert, Michelle. 'Granville Sharp's Manuscript Letter to the Admiralty on the *Zong* Massacre: A New Discovery in the British Library'. *Slavery & Abolition* 38(1) (2017), 178–195.

act, feel and decide; to resent an injury; to reach a point when they would not tolerate the injustices done unto them'.[43] In the words of James Stephen, unlike the Indians, the slaves need to be 'taught how to walk'.[44] There was an ambiguity here: a moral opposition to slavery on the one hand and the empiricism that was concerned with the limits of the slaves' understanding, on the other.[45] For Wilberforce, Burke's *Sketch* to protect the slaves would garner more opposition from the planters than abolition itself; he felt that giving them rights would force civilization upon them without preparing them for it. On the other hand, for abolitionists like James Stephen, the Haitian revolution was evidence that the masters' safety must be protected through immediate reform, else resulting in a 'speedy loss of dominium'.[46] The abolitionists took to amelioration as a viable method to combat various signs of rebellion that could arise from either granting slaves agency much too quickly or by disregarding the untoward possibilities if their shackles were not loosened. Consequently, Burke's protection model would become the blueprint for the protection plans that eventually found their way to the British slave colonies. While the plan granted certain rights to slaves, it was more about bringing the masters under imperial control through an imperial officer, later instituted as the first *Protector of Slaves* in Trinidad during the peak of the British ameliorative phase (1824) and ensuring law and order amongst 'free Negroes' as well.[47]

---

43 Wilberforce, William. *A Letter on the Abolition of the Slave Trade: Addressed to the Freeholders and other Inhabitants of Yorkshire* (London: Luke Hansard and Sons, 1807), 237.

44 Stephen, James. *Crisis of the Sugar Colonies* (London: J. Hatchard, 1802), 54.

45 Claudius Fergus describes Wilberforce's understanding of humanity as being consistent with the predominant view of the time that it was an elitist sentiment. Fergus, Claudius. '"Dread of Insurrection": Abolitionism, Security, and Labor in Britain's West Indian Colonies, 1760–1823'. *The William and Mary Quarterly* 66(4) (2009), 757–780; see also Poliakov, Leon. *The Aryan Myth: A History of Racist and Nationalist Ideas in Europe* (London: Sussex University Press, 1975), 145–150. The author equates Lockean empiricism to underlying racism that came with the Enlightenment myth of white superiority. See also Glausser, Wayne. 'Three Approaches to Locke and the Slave Trade'. *Journal of the History of Ideas* 51(2) (1990), 199–216.

46 Stephen, *Sugar Colonies* 1802 (n. 44), 125.

47 There is no evidence to show from where Burke drew inspiration for his *Sketch* and he most certainly does not attribute his ideas to either the Spanish or the French practices. Spence finds an uncanny resemblance to the Spanish practices of *papel* whereby mistreated slaves were to be resold to alternate masters, Spence, *Ameliorating Empire* 2014 (n. 13), 66 et seq. On the other hand, historian Robert Smith attributes it to his associations with Robert Burke, a close friend and relative, who was a slave owner in Jamaica. Smith, Robert. 'Edmund Burke's Negro Code'. *History Today* 26(11) (1976), 715–723.

3 Crown or Colony: Who Is the Better Protector?

The 1824 Order in Council introduced protection measures in the slave colony of Trinidad. According to the Order, the Crown directly dictated how the slaves must be treated in the colony.[48] Disgruntled by the Spanish laws governing the colony, British merchants desired English laws and the old representative system.[49] While certain colonial officials favoured the merchants, knowing the majority of the free-coloureds were French became the basis for others to oppose any kind of representative form of government.[50] The opposition came mainly from the then Secretary of State for War and Colonies and later the Prime Minister, Robert Banks Jenkinson, Earl of Liverpool (1770–1828). Why risk the position of the English who were already in minority was his thought. At the same time, he was equally wary of antagonising the French and Spanish in Trinidad by introducing English laws. In 1810, Liverpool made his decision: the Spanish laws would remain, but the British Crown might delegate some of its prerogative power of legislation to the governor. In other words, Britain reserved control over the island in what John Manning Ward would later describe as the 'least liberal form of Crown colony government'.[51]

This was unique to Trinidad, given all the other colonies had been governed by their colonial legislatures. Colonies like Jamaica, Barbados, and the Leeward Islands, which had different iterations of the slave code pre-existing the Trinidad model, had promulgated them locally with no interference from the Crown. There were several points of view concerning who must carry out the implementation of amelioration rules. The West Indian planter, Charles Rose Ellis, had recommended in 1797 along with his Burkean plan, that the colonial legislatures were the only persons fit for the formation and execution of such a plan.[52] The colonies ignored Ellis' pleas, and not a single legislature adopted any part of his proposed reforms. James Stephen's pamphlet outlined clearly why the colonial legislatures, who comprised of men with a direct interest in the private relations between master and slave, must not be in charge

48 Burke was a member of the King's Council advising the King in 1782 after he lost his Bristol constituency in the election, which is also around the time when he wrote his Sketch. I thank Giuseppe Caruso for bringing this fact to my attention.

49 Ward, John Manning. *Colonial Self-Government: The British Experience, 1759–1856* (London: Macmillan, 1976), 89.

50 The National Archives (TNA), Colonial Office (CO) 296/3, 64–65.

51 Ward, *Colonial Self-Government* 1976 (n. 49), 91.

52 Parliament of Great Britain. *The Parliamentary Register: History of the Proceedings of the House of Commons during 1st session of the 14th Parliament of Great Britain* (London: J. Almon, 1775–1804), 235.

of introducing the law: 'the ulcer will be tenderly touched, when the incision knife is in the hand of the patient'.[53]

In 1823, Wilberforce pleaded in the parliament for the Crown to directly implement measures to ameliorate the slaves, citing the failure of Ellis' proposals in 1797 as his main justification. When Ellis made his proposal in 1797, the conditions put forward were far more impactful upon the planters, as ameliorating slaves was meant to prevent the parliament from sanctioning the abolition of the slave trade. In the aftermath of the slave trade abolition, Wilberforce and Stephen were not convinced that the colonial legislatures would act for the betterment of the slaves. However, they overlooked another reason why planters would want to ameliorate slaves: precisely because slave trade had been abolished and there was no means to procure more slave labour and the need to maintain the existing slaves was more crucial than before.[54] In other words, the British government had to find a way to cope with one of the milestones in international law it prided itself with creating: abolition of slave trade. Ellis extended this as one of the possible outcomes of amelioration when he made his proposal in 1797: 'the civilization of Negroes in the West Indian islands, to a degree, which, by obviating the causes of a decrease in the population will render the supply [of slaves] unnecessary'. This was precisely the approach Burke had intended when he suggested to allow the evil to correct it. Much of Wilberforce's insistence on the British parliament's direct involvement can be better understood through his perception of the trade itself: 'it was a trade in which the planters and their agents had the profit and the British Parliament the guilt'.[55] This was (quite rightly) countered by Edwards, the West Indian planter, who said, 'both profit and guilt centre in this country ... the British government not merely encouraged, but absolutely forced, by every means in its power, the colonists to purchase African slaves from the British merchants'.[56] The British government, thus, owing not merely to its complicity in the condition of the slaves in the colonies but also the mere desire to control the populations in the lands far away, decided to turn to the Crown Colony model.[57]

---

53 Stephen, *Sugar Colonies* 1802 (n. 44), 150.

54 The introduction of the slave registers in 1812 allows us to track the rate of slave mortality. It shows that the number of slaves reduced from 25,717 in 1813 to 23,227 by 1823.

55 *Amelioration of the Condition of the Negroes in the West Indies* (6 April 1797) Hansard XXXIII, p. 853.

56 Parliament of Great Britain, *The Parliamentary Register* 1775–1804 (n. 52), 253 et seq.

57 Although I do not go into the details of the Crown Colony model and its implications in this chapter, it must be noted that the direct supervision from the Crown was an important change in the way the imperial government governed the colonies during this period. While royal powers were not absolute, there was still a shift from granting the colonists powers to run their own affairs and centralising the regulation of colonial governance.

4 Protection in the Colony: The Trinidadian Experiment

The Order in Council passed on 10th March in 1824 was very much akin to a *Code Noir*, intended to improve the lives of the slaves and provide for their religious instruction, drawn from Spanish and French practices.[58] However, unlike the 1685 French *Code Noir*, the 1824 Order provided the slaves access to the legal system. Historians like Caroline Spence attribute this shift to inspirations from the Spanish system.[59] Whilst not disputing the influences, it seems problematic to discard the impact Burke's Code had, simply because it was not 'implemented', on the model finally implemented in Trinidad. In this section, I outline the underlying humanity-control aspects of slave protection as it played out in Trinidad, the first of many British West Indian slave colonies where the Crown adopted ameliorative measures.

The Burkean model did not subscribe to an abstract philosophical criticism of slavery. Planter absolutism was the reason for slavery becoming impossible to justify, despite being a 'necessary evil'. The most significant shift in the 1824 Order was the elimination of masters' absolute sovereignty and setting up of an imperial office for the slaves called the Office of the Protector. All the previous codes had entrusted the masters with the task of protecting their slaves, while the current Order made a clear distinction between the private authority of the masters and public authority of the Protector, and the extent of public intervention that was allowed.[60]

The Office of the Protector was instituted with two goals in mind: the 'maintenance of public peace and good order' and protection and guardianship for slaves.[61] The Protector was a magistrate for the island, with the commandants of the quarters serving as the Assistant Protectors (clause 7 of the Order). The Order allowed slaves to invoke the assistance of the protector when they were charged with any offence by the masters, or when an offence was committed against the person of any slave. In other words, the Protector was the advocate for the slave, but only as long as such protection did not hamper the maintenance of peace and order. The Order envisioned the dual role of the Protector would thwart the vicious cycle of crimes by the masters and retaliation-crimes by the slaves.

58 TNA, CO 295/72, 15 et seq.

59 Spence, *Ameliorating Empire* 2014 (n. 12), 42 et seq.

60 Here I rely on Ghachem's usage in relation to the Code Noir and the Haitian slave colony, even though the Crown did not use the exact phrases concerning Trinidad. Ghachem, *Old Regime* 2014 (n. 11).

61 House of Commons, Draught of an Order in Council for Improving the Condition of the Slaves in Trinidad, Hansard Papers (16 March 1824), Clause 6.

The first (and only) Protector of slaves for Trinidad, Henry Gloster, maintained very detailed records that noted the crimes committed by the slaves, crimes that were committed against the slaves, the record of manumissions and the punishments given.[62] He served as Protector from 1824 to 1834, until the British Government abolished slavery in the Empire.[63] Unlike in Burke's plan, the Protector here was not the Attorney General of the island and, was barred from owning slaves (plantation slaves, not domestic slaves), but it remained the case that 'His majesty's Attorney-General' engaged the Protector to represent the slaves in criminal prosecutions both against the slaves and their masters. Henry Gloster was a barrister who was practicing law and less dependent on slave labour than most of the others approached for the role. Gloster's reports were maintained bi-annually and spoke of an 'impartiality' despite his role as a slave-protector against master brutality. Such impartiality suggested that he could also find slaves guilty if they committed a wrong: a relationship resembling the Roman law principle of *patria potestas*, or 'power of a father' over his children.

The 1824 Order stipulated many reforms in the treatment of slaves – whips were no longer allowed for females,[64] neither was corporal punishment. Punishments like flogging were given upper limits in the cases of male slaves (of 25 blows)[65] and they were also expected to be recorded in books. The humanitarianism of such a limit was offset by the need to control the slaves in cases of disobedience. Penalising disobedience towards their masters, in turn, ensured the masters' sense of control over the slave, even if not directly. Therefore, the instances when the limitations were inapplicable were two-fold: in the case of judicial punishment inflicted upon male slaves for cases that ranged from absconding to causing bodily harm[66] and in cases where the person of the slave was free from any lacerations from previous whipping.[67] This signalled a shift from the authority of the planters to that of the judges, albeit the judges themselves were slave and plantation owners.[68] This was a type of

62 TNA, CO 300/19 to 300/33, Half-yearly Reports of the Protector, 1824–1834.

63 His last report was dated June 1834. TNA CO 300/33.

64 TNA, CO 295/84, Rule XXI, Order in Council, February 3, 1830. It is clarified that the whip must not be carried as a stimulus to labour but is permitted to be used to punish the slave for wrongdoing (like the disobedience of orders, to work in the field).

65 Hansard Papers, Draught of an Order in Council, 1824, Clause 12.

66 For example, in the case of a slave named Frank Jemmet, who was charged with causing bodily injury to a soldier of His Majesty's Regiment, the court's sentence allowed for 200 lashes to be given to the prisoner in the public view of the market place. TNA, CO 300/27, 1927.

67 Hansard Papers, Draught of an Order in Council, 1824, Clause 12.

68 See Spence, *Ameliorating Empire* 2014 (n. 12), 138.

utilitarian justice meted out to the slaves without compromising the efficiency of labour required in the plantations. Later, when the Order in Council 1830 was passed, clause 21 revised the regulation concerning whips and additionally prevented the usage of whips as a stimulus to labour on the fields unless as punishment for a previously committed offence. The judgments were pronounced by the *alcaldes* (chief magistrates) and the *asesor* (judicial advisor), and the adjudicatory procedures were governed by the Order in Council of 16th September 1822. Cases involving the flogging of female slaves, despite a categorical prohibition in the Order in Council, were rarely decided in favour of the female slave. When her master, Hilaire Surieux, flogged Rose Joseph, a female slave, the *alcaldes* were divided on the master's guilt; the *asesor* ruled the master not guilty, while the president of the court found him guilty. In cases of hung juries, the prisoner was discharged. It seemed that the *alcaldes* and *asesors* could rule any way they wished; the reasons extended were sometimes as unambiguous as 'it is not a violation of the 1830 Order in Council'. Although the evidence put forward by the slave herself was often compelling, the members of the jury had little to no trust in a slave who complained against her master. Such cases demonstrated how the protection for slaves underlined a bias against the slaves on very substantive grounds, which the procedures established in the Order in Council could not discard too easily.

Slaves took their complaints directly to the Protector, almost like they had 'rights' as envisioned by Burke. However, most slaves were not considered fit to provide evidence[69] unless they had received sufficient religious instruction; while it is true that the slaves were able to have their grievances (strict violations of the Order) heard in court via the Protector, those who did complain, and proved unsuccessful, were punished for failing to establish a complaint and where malice was suspected.[70] Thus, the slaves required a degree of civilisation, gauged by their religious education, in order to avail the benefits of their rights. Although the Protector's reports are an indication of complaints filed on behalf of slaves and against slaves, it similarly makes clear the vast

69 TNA, CO 300/19, 1824. A further discussion on this issue is found in the Commission of Inquiry Report, in which the commissioners note the inconsistencies in the responses given by the Chief Judge and the Judge of Criminal Inquiry, when it came to the question 'whether this court frequently exercised the discretion given to it by the order in council above referred to [1824], of admitting slave evidence'. The former answered 'frequently', whilst the latter acknowledged that no decision could be given by relying solely on slave evidence. The Parliamentary Papers, *His Majesty's Commissioners of Legal Inquiry on the Colony of Trinidad*, 1827.

70 To protect the slaves, by an Order in Council of February 1830, this malice had to be proved before punishment could be given. Verteuil, Anthony de. *Seven Slaves and Slavery: Trinidad 1777–1838* (Port of Spain: St. Mary's College, 1992), 45.

difference between the measure of punishments applied to the slaves and the free.[71] The cases against the slaves often resulted in punishments of flogging and extensive imprisonment (with hard labour) from three to ten years, whilst the violations by the overseers even in cases of assaulting and killing a slave went unpunished owing to absence of witnesses. In an instance of flogging a female slave (for example, in the case of the slave Mary Noel), the master was let off owing to a 'technical defect discovered in a clause of the Order in Council' of lack of jurisdiction.[72] These technicalities or material frustrations further upheld the rule of law. Contrary to the recurring appearances of procedural justifications, the core of the rulings were a substantive endorsement of the masters' sovereignty over the slave.

The main rationale behind the office of the protector was not only to protect the slaves, but to defend the law and to uphold it at any cost – the law which the imperial administration portrayed as being committed to the cause of humanity for the slaves. This led to a conflation of the law and humanitarianism writ large. Further, as mentioned above, through the course of the amelioration period the imperial administration and the owner shared the authority over the slaves. While the slaves' disobedience to the owner was earlier severely punished by the latter, under the amelioration laws an owner was liable for punishment if found 'illegally exhibiting a cart whip in the field as an emblem of authority';[73] in other words, the owner was punishable if found exceeding his authority. Even if in principle the owner and the slaves were now in fear of the Order, the owner was allowed to exercise his authority within limits.

5 Conclusion

The focus of the chapter was on the late 18th and early 19th century debates surrounding the use of protection measures to ameliorate the condition of slaves that also depoliticized the relationship between slaves and their masters. While the focus was on the past, I rely on it to provide a critique of the present. In the present, international law is rife with paternalistic protective measures for disenfranchised groups or weak states, whilst preparing them to partake in the 'civilized world' they otherwise cannot access.[74] Establishing

71 TNA, CO 300/22, Correspondence of Government with Trinidad.

72 Ibid.

73 TNA, CO 300/25, 282–285.

74 See Erpelding, Michel. *Le droit international antiesclavagiste des « Nations Civilisées » (1815–1945)* (Paris: Institut Universitaire Varenne, 2017) on the rise and fall of anti-slavery

legal institutions (like the Office of the Protector in this case, but also those that emerged later, such as the protectorates and the Mandates System) that 'protect' the weak, in the words of Anne Orford, also grounds authority through its capacity to protect and creates obedient subjects in return.[75] Can protection become a means to emancipation or does it merely reify the hierarchical structure between protectors and protected? This question is at the foundation of my critique. At the same time, it is also a critique of the separation of public and private power, represented in the chapter by the imperial authorities and the slave masters and planters respectively, the regulation of which is carried out through the instrumentality of international law today. While we assume that public authorities can govern private power, in reality they co-produce rules and regulations that balance out the powers and interests of each.[76] In this chapter, by focusing on slave protection, I demonstrate how the public authority's language of rights to protect slaves was always balanced with the right to property of the planters. By tracing back the history of protection to the slave colonies, it becomes clear that already by early 1800, as Martti Koskenniemi writes, 'a conception of British Empire had arisen where the exercise of sovereign power was clearly derivative from and supplementary to claims about private property.'[77]

The impression of the private being subsumed within the authority of the public was true in certain instances when the masters felt they no longer had absolute sovereignty over their slaves. However, the other side of the story tells us that public authority depended on the success of the private authority to sustain its own power – the imperial authorities needed the masters and plantation owners to carry out an efficient functioning of the slave-run economy. Much like what the Enlightenment thought proffered, the institution of protection allowed the imperial authorities to have their cake and eat it too. The limits to protection for slaves in the wake of their disorderliness or disobedience, evident from Burke's plan and the 1824 Order, indicated that the gift of emancipation shall remain, at best, a reward for choosing not to rebel against their cruel circumstances. And at worst, slaves would never achieve real emancipation, much like how Burke perceived the status of 'free slaves' who could

---

international law, where while upholding the illegality of slavery, he shows how international law blurred the lines between slavery and forced labour.

75 Orford, Anne. *International Authority and the Responsibility to Protect* (Cambridge: Cambridge University Press, 2011).

76 Baars, Grietje. *The Corporation, Law and Capitalism: A Radical Perspective on the Role of Law in the Global Political Economy* (Leiden: Brill, 2019), 8.

77 Koskenniemi, Martti. 'Sovereignty, Property and Empire: Early Modern English Contexts'. *Theoretical Inquiries in Law* 18(2) (2017), 355–389, 355.

be sent back to slavery for their disorderliness. As a result, granting the slaves 'rights', whilst requiring from them a level of orderliness that could earn them such benefits was an ideal way to challenge the status quo and maintain it at the same time.

Acknowledgements

I thank Martti Koskenniemi, Anne-Charlotte Martineau, Immi Tallgren, and Alain Zamaria for their comments on earlier drafts. My thanks to the organisers and participants of the conference on the Politics and Histories of International Law, February 15–16 2019, Max Planck Institute for Comparative Public Law and International Law, Heidelberg, for the opportunity to present and receive feedback on this chapter. Lastly, I thank the editors of this volume for their helpful comments. All errors remain mine.

Bibliography

Adams, Charles Hansford, ed. *The Narrative of Robert Adams, A Barbary Captive: A Critical Edition* (Cambridge: Cambridge University Press, 2005).

Agnani, Sunil. *Hating Empire Properly: The Two Indies and the Limits of Enlightenment Anticolonialism* (New York: Temple University Press, 2013).

Anghie, Antony. *Imperialism, Sovereignty and the Making of International Law* (Cambridge: Cambridge University Press, 2005).

Armitage, David. 'Edmund Burke and Reason of State'. *Journal of the History of Ideas* 61(4) (2000), 617–634.

Baars, Grietje. *The Corporation, Law and Capitalism: A Radical Perspective on the Role of Law in the Global Political Economy* (Leiden: Brill, 2019).

Barnett, Michael. *Empires of Humanity: A History of Humanitarianism* (New York: Cornell University Press, 2011).

Benton, Lauren and Lisa Ford. 'Island Despotism: Trinidad, the British Constitution, and the Global Legal Order'. *The Journal of Imperial and Commonwealth History* 46(1) (2018), 21–46.

Benton, Lauren and Adam Clulow, eds. *Protection and Empire: A Global History* (Cambridge: Cambridge University Press, 2018).

Benton, Lauren and Lisa Ford. *Rage for Order: The British Empire and the Origins of International Law 1800–1850* (Cambridge: Harvard University Press, 2016).

Borthwick, Peter. *Report of a Lecture on Colonial Slavery and Gradual Emancipation* (Edinburgh: W. Ritchie and Co., 1833).

Brown, Christopher. *Moral Capital: Foundations of British Abolitionism* (Charlottesville: University of North Carolina Press, 2004).

Browne, Randy M. *Surviving Slavery in the British Caribbean* (Pennsylvania: University of Pennsylvania Press, 2017).

Burke, Edmund. 'A Letter to the Right Hon. Henry Dundas, One of His Majesty's Principal Secretaries of State [with the Sketch of the Negro Code]', in *The Writing and Speeches of Edmund Burke*. Volume IV, eds. Peter James Marshall, Donald Bryant and Paul Langford (Oxford: Clarendon Press, 1991).

Burke, Edmund. 'Sketch of a Negro Code', in *The Writings and Speeches of Edmund Burke*, vol. III, ed. Paul Langford (Oxford: Oxford University Press, 1981), 562–581.

Burke, Edmund. 'Speeches on African Slave Trade, 5 June 1777', in *The Writings and Speeches of Edmund Burke*, vol. 3, eds. Warren M. Elofson, John A. Woods and William B. Todd (Oxford: Oxford University Press, 1996).

Burke, Edmund and William Burke. *An Account of the European Settlements in America* (London: J. Dodsley, 1770).

Candlin, Kit. *The Last Caribbean Frontier, 1795–1815* (Basingstoke: Palgrave Macmillan, 2012).

Collins, Gregory M. 'Edmund Burke on Slavery and the Slave Trade'. *Slavery & Abolition* 40(3) (2019), 494–521.

Condorcet, Marquis de. *Réflexions sur l'esclavage des nègres* (Paris: Editions Flammarion, 2009).

Dierksheide, Christa. *Amelioration and Empire: Progress and Slavery in the Plantation Americas* (Charlottesville: University of Virginia Press, 2014).

Epstein, James. *Scandal of Colonial Rule: Power and Subversion in the British Atlantic during the Age of Revolutions* (Cambridge: Cambridge University Press, 2012).

Erpelding, Michel. *Le droit international antiesclavagiste des « Nations Civilisées » (1815–1945)* (Paris: Institut Universitaire Varenne, 2017).

Faubert, Michelle. 'Granville Sharp's Manuscript Letter to the Admiralty on the *Zong* Massacre: A New Discovery in the British Library'. *Slavery & Abolition* 38(1) (2017), 178–195.

Fergus, Claudius. '"Dread of Insurrection": Abolitionism, Security, and Labor in Britain's West Indian Colonies, 1760–1823'. *The William and Mary Quarterly* 66(4) Third Series (2009), 757–780.

Ford, Lisa. 'Protecting the Peace on the Edges of Empire: Commissioners of Crown Lands in New South Wales', in *Protection and Empire: A Global History*, eds. Lauren Benton and Adam Clulow (Cambridge: Cambridge University Press, 2018), 175–193.

Getachew, Adom. *Worldmaking after Empire: The Rise and Fall of Self-Determination* (Princeton: Princeton University Press, 2019).

Ghachem, Malick. *The Old Regime and the Haitian Revolution* (Cambridge: Cambridge University Press, 2012).

Glausser, Wayne. 'Three Approaches to Locke and the Slave Trade'. *Journal of the History of Ideas* 51(2) (1990), 199–216.

Grewe, Wilhelm G. *The Epochs of International Law* (Berlin: De Gruyter, 2000).

Jones, Emily. *Edmund Burke and the Invention of Modern Conservatism 1830–1914* (Oxford: Oxford University Press, 2017).

Kohn, Margaret and Daniel I. O'Neill. 'A Tale of Two Indias: Burke and Mill on Empire and Slavery in the West Indies and America'. *Political Theory* 34(2) (2006), 192–228.

Koskenniemi, Martti. 'Sovereignty, Property and Empire: Early Modern English Contexts'. *Theoretical Inquiries in Law* 18(2) (2017), 355–389.

Lacey, Robert J. *Pragmatic Conservatism: Edmund Burke and His American Heirs* (Basingstoke: Palgrave Macmillan, 2016).

Loughlin, Martin. 'Burke on Law, Revolution and Constitution'. *Journal of Constitutional History/Giornale di storia costituzionale* 29(1) (2015), 49–60.

Marshall, Peter James. *Edmund Burke and the British Empire in the West Indies: Wealth, Power, and Slavery* (Oxford: Oxford University Press, 2019).

Marshall, Peter James. *The Impeachment of Warren Hastings* (Oxford: Oxford University Press, 1965).

Martineau, Anne-Charlotte. 'The Politics of Writing on Slavery and International Law', in *The Politics of the Histories of International Law*, eds. Raphael Schäfer and Anne Peters (Leiden: Brill, 2021), 36–58.

Mehta, Uday Singh. *Liberalism and Empire* (Chicago: University of Chicago Press, 1999).

Mellor, George R. *British Imperial Trusteeship 1783–1850* (London: Faber & Faber, 1951).

Mukherjee, Mithi. 'Justice, War, and the Imperium: India and Britain in Edmund Burke's Prosecutorial Speeches in the Impeachment Trial of Warren Hastings'. *Law and History Review* 23(3) (2005), 589–630.

Muthu, Sankar. *Enlightenment against Empire* (Princeton: Princeton University Press, 2003).

O'Neill, Daniel. *Edmund Burke and the Conservative Logic of Empire* (Oakland: University of California Press, 2016).

Orford, Anne. *International Authority and the Responsibility to Protect* (Cambridge: Cambridge University Press, 2011).

Parliament of Great Britain. *The Parliamentary Register: History of the Proceedings of the House of Commons during 1st session of the 14th Parliament of Great Britain* (London: J. Almon, 1775–1804).

Pettigrew, William A. *Freedom's Debt: The Royal African Company and the Politics of the Atlantic Slave Trade, 1672–1752* (Chapel Hill: University of North Carolina Press, 2013).

Pitts, Jennifer. *A Turn to Empire: The Rise of Imperial Liberalism in Britain and France* (Princeton: Princeton University Press, 2006).

Poliakov, Leon. *The Aryan Myth: A History of Racist and Nationalist Ideas in Europe* (London: Sussex University Press, 1975).

Ramsay, James. *Essay on the Treatment and Conversion of African Slaves in the British Sugar Colonies* (London: James Philip Printing, 1784).

Scott, David. *Conscripts of Modernity: The Tragedy of Colonial Enlightenment* (Durham: Duke University Press, 2004).

Smith, Robert. 'Edmund Burke's Negro Code'. *History Today* 26(11) (1976), 715–723.

Spence, Caroline Q. *Ameliorating Empire: Slavery and Protection in the British Slave Colonies, 1783–1865* (Cambridge: Harvard University, PhD Thesis, 2014), available at: http://nrs.harvard.edu/urn-3:HUL.InstRepos:13070043 (last accessed on 29 March 2021).

Stephen, James. *Crisis of the Sugar Colonies* (London: J. Hatchard, 1802).

The Parliamentary Papers, *His Majesty's Commissioners of Legal Inquiry on the Colony of Trinidad*, 1827.

Titus, Noel. *The Amelioration and Abolition of Slavery in Trinidad, 1812–1834: Experiments and Protests in a New Slave Colony* (Bloomington: Author House, 2009).

Verteuil, Anthony de. *Seven Slaves and Slavery: Trinidad 1777–1838* (Port of Spain: St. Mary's College, 1992).

Ward, John Manning. *Colonial Self-Government: The British Experience, 1759–1856* (London: Macmillan, 1976).

Wilberforce, William. *Slave Trade: Addressed to the Freeholders and other Inhabitants of Yorkshire* (London: Luke Hansard and Sons, 1807).

Archival Sources

Company of Royal Adventurers of England Trading with Africa and Successors: Records, T70, 1660–1833 (held by the National Archives at Kew).

Parliament of Great Britain. *An Act for Extending and Improving the Trade to Africa* (Library Location: Schomburg Center for Research in Black Culture, Manuscripts, Archives and Rare Books Division, The New York Public Library, retrieved from http://digitalcollections.nypl.org/items/5b08efa0-c3ac-0133-5dd1-00505686a51c) (London: Assigns of Robert Baskett, 1750).

The National Archives. Colonial Office Correspondences 295/72.

The National Archives. Colonial Office 295/84, Order in Council, February 3, 1830.

The National Archives. Colonial Office 300/19, Half-yearly reports by the Protector of Slaves, 1824.

The National Archives. Colonial Office 300/22, Correspondence of Government with Trinidad, 1826.

CHAPTER 4

One Hundred Years of Soli(dari)tude: The Creation of the Refugee Regime and the Politics of Humanitarianism

Momchil Milanov

Abstract

The transformation of the post-WWI legal order had an immense impact on the firmly established 19th century positivist triad of nationality, territory and rights which was simultaneously challenged by two interrelated phenomena – by the plight of a million Russian refugees and secondly, by the minorities in the newly created states in Central and Eastern Europe. The paper addresses critically some shared assumptions in the historiography about the motivation of the actors involved in the creation of the status of the refugees in the 1920s. It demonstrates that the motivation of the actors involved cannot be reduced to simplified dialectic of 'good' humanitarianism and bad 'politics'.

Keywords

refugees – solidarity – politics – charity – League of Nations – revolution – humanitarianism

•••

'Man consists of a body, a soul and a passport'
MARC VICHNIAC, Le Statut International des Apatrides

•••

'You have to make the good out of the bad
because that is all you have got to make it out of'
ROBERT PENN WARREN, All the King's Men

•••

 | DOI:10.1163/9789004461802_006

> 'No, not at all,' said K. 'I don't want any tokens of favour from the castle, I want my rights.'
>
> FRANZ KAFKA, The Castle

∴

1 Introduction

In Gabriel García Marquez's novel *One Hundred Years of Solitude*, the repetition of history is a dominant theme. The protagonists are frequently visited by ghosts, incarnating the tormented relationship with the past and the inability to deal with it. The hundredth anniversary of the establishment of the League of Nations produced a similarly uncanny encounter with the past, which, instead of critical distance, created mainly confusion: the commemoration took place in a context in which it was hard to distance ourselves from this significant historical event and to pretend that the page of the League is irrevocably turned. Instead, we found ourselves trapped in a time loop, caught in an eternal déjà vu, deprived of the possibility to construct a meaningful explanation of those events precisely because past and future have become interchangeable categories. On the one hand, drawing analogies between 1920 and 2020 might be superficial, but on the other, ignoring the similarities might be equally irresponsible – refugee and migration crisis, global pandemic, raging nationalism and economic collapse to name the most conspicuous parallels. One word is present in both times, it dominates the pandemic crisis in 2020 and it featured prominently in the political discourse a hundred years ago: solidarity. Revisiting the history of the creation of the refugee regime and the politics of humanitarianism in this moment will push and even require us to rethink the ways in which solidarity functions but also, in more general terms, it may put an end to the condescending attitude towards the era of the League of Nations as the 'bad old times'. In the circular chronotope of crisis talk, 'bad old times' simply does not exist if only because it may turn out that we have inherited more from the League than we are willing to recognise. The 1920s were 'a time of creativity and innovation, a time when much was accomplished with minimal resources; a time when millions of refugees were helped to start new lives.'[1] Those years had a lasting influence over the subsequent developments in refugees' international status. The irony is that despite the persistent denial of all the major stakeholders that the relief efforts could constitute a precedent, the League's contribution to human rights law was perhaps its longest lasting achievement.[2]

This chapter addresses critically some shared assumptions in historiography about the motivation of the actors involved in the creation of the refugee status by looking at the interplay between sovereignty and humanitarianism. It argues, firstly, that the intense interaction between states, international organisations, private organisations, the Holy See, refugees and minorities throughout the whole period demonstrates the competing visions of international law. Secondly, it shows how claims are gradually transformed into rights. Ultimately, it demonstrates that the motivation of the actors involved cannot be reduced to the simplified dialectic of 'good' humanitarianism and bad 'politics'. The study of the interplay between humanitarianism and sovereignty shows that the humanitarian and the political are not two separate avenues. On the contrary, they constantly overlap and intersect, showing that refugee work cannot be apolitical[3] and that humanitarian actions have intrinsic political significance.[4] The main question is not whether politics are at stake but precisely what kind of politics; whose interests do they serve, and whether they serve primarily *other* purposes in which the refugee is merely instrumental.[5] Humanitarianism *is* politics, at times, even *Realpolitik*.

The history of the creation of the refugee status is the history of those types of solidarity which received the positive sanction of international law and those which failed to obtain it. Solidarity is a multifaceted concept which resembles the Russian *Matryoshka* doll: instead of a single and indivisible whole, we can find layers of solidarities, competing, conflicting and clashing

1 Skran, Claudena. *Refugees in Inter-War Europe: The Emergence of a Regime* (Oxford: Oxford University Press, 1995), 9.

2 Pedersen, Susan. 'Back to the League of Nations'. *American Historical Review* 112(4) (2007), 1091–1117, quoted in Lowe, Kimberly. 'Reassessing the League of Nations' Humanitarian Assistance Regimes, 1918–1939', in *Decades of Reconstruction: Postwar Societies, State-Building, and International Relations from the Seven Years' War to the Cold War*, eds. Ute Planert and James Retallack (Cambridge: Cambridge University Press, 2017), 293–314, 293.

3 Goodwin-Gill, Guy. 'The Politics of Refugee Protection'. *Refugee Survey Quarterly* 27(1) (2008), 8–23, 8–9.

4 Piana, Francesca. *Towards the International Refugee Regime: Humanitarianism in the Wake of the First World War* (Geneva: Graduate Institute of International and Development Studies, PhD Dissertation 2013), 105.

5 See Goodwin-Gill, 'Refugee Protection' 2008 (n. 3), 9.

interests which question and deny each other's legitimate existence. Solidarity is relational, contextual and frequently, oppositional. Group solidarity has no meaning without the existence of a catalysing factor: another rival group, an event, or both. While international law cannot *per se* decide which solidarity is genuine, legitimate or acceptable, each of the actors involved was aware of the importance of couching political claims in legal arguments in order either to bolster their legitimacy or to score a point on the political field. In the current debate about the origins of human rights, the 1920s are arguably a very plausible candidate if only because the Russian émigrés aimed at transcending their statelessness by arguing for an international human rights law. For them, human rights was proposed as an overarching solution from the impasse of the conflicting solidarities – religious, national, international, without doing away with those solidarities. Moreover, since in Russian 'dar' (дар) means 'gift', 'solidarity' literally contains in itself the seeds of the tension of humanitarianism – as a duty and as charity – the 'rights-talk' and the 'gifts-talk'.

An important clarification is warranted before proceeding to the substance. The chapter focuses mainly but not exclusively on Russian refugees. Since they were the first group that was granted *ad hoc* protection, they inevitably represent a special interest. As pointed out by British Liberal politician Sir John Simpson: 'It is above all the Russian refugees who have developed since the War what may be called the jurisprudence of refugeedom and contributed to political philosophy and practice a concept of refugee as novel and creative as the concepts of minority and mandate.'[6] However, the fact that other groups whose situation also required protection obtained it at a later stage or failed to obtain at all, is equally important as it illustrates the complexity of the concept of solidarity.

The chapter is divided in five sections. Section 2 situates and contextualises the problem. Section 3 introduces the concept of solidarity as a useful tool to understand how humanitarianism(s) function(s). It argues that solidarity is a complex multi-layered concept permeating the relations between many different actors with their own agendas. Section 4 discusses the sources, the functioning and gives some examples for the interplay of humanitarianism and politics. The final section contains the conclusion.

6 Simpson, Sir John Hope. *The Refugee Problem: Report of a Survey* (Oxford/London: Oxford University Press/Royal Institute of International Affairs, 1939), 108, cited in Ginsburgs, George. 'The Soviet Union and the Problem of Refugees and Displaced Persons 1917–1956'. *American Journal of International Law* 51(2) (1957), 325–362, 342.

2 The Politics of Status

The arrival of the Russian refugees in Europe between 1917 and 1922 was mainly a result of the October revolution and the subsequent civil war. It must be seen, however, in the broader context of the end of the Great War and the permanent state of emergency which ensued. Characterised by rampant nationalism, revolutions, uprising and several inter- and intra-state conflicts, it arguably lasted until the conclusion of the Lausanne Treaty in 1923 and lead to 'the largest displacement of peoples in Europe in modern times.'[7] In the wake of the Great War, the socio-economic systems of the post-war European states could not endure the strain of such a significant mass of persons. European states and societies viewed these populations with a mixture of compassion and worry, and were confronted with the dilemma whether to protect themselves from the revolutionary germ or to help those who had to flee from the civil war in Russia.[8] Their arrival also set the scene for the emergence of the legal framework to address the refugee problem: for the first time in the modern history, there was a large group of persons dispersed in several states with no rights or obligations, and for whom no one could be held accountable.

The creation of the refugee regime was the result of a long process involving several actors with different agendas: the League, the International Committee of the Red Cross, the host states and refugees' organisations. The refugee status was accepted as a solution only after two other options, namely, naturalisation and repatriation proved to be either inadequate or impossible.[9] The issue was internationalised only after states realised the problem required a collective effort: acting in the context of an international regime is preferable than scattered individual solutions, and sharing the financial burden was in the states'

7 Loescher, Gil. *Beyond Charity: International Cooperation and the Global Refugee Crisis* (Oxford: Oxford University Press, 1996), 34–35.

8 Cabanes, Bruno. *The Great War and the Origins of Humanitarianism, 1918–1924* (Cambridge: Cambridge University Press, 2014), 182.

9 Vichniac, Marc. 'Le statut international des apatrides'. *Recueil des cours de l'académie de droit international* 43 (1933), 115–246, 195. On repatriation see Long, Katy. *The Point of No Return* (Oxford: Oxford University Press, 2013), 45: 'Repatriation allowed the reconstruction of the state and the reshaping of the nation: it was an explicitly political act.' See also ibid., 57: 'In fact repatriation has always been considered the international community's ideal solution to refugee crises. This is because organized repatriation emerged in the early twentieth century in parallel with the consolidation of the liberal nation-state. If refugees were evidence of the inherent flaws in this formula, repatriation offered an apparent formula through which liberalism and nationalism might, at least in theory, be reconciled.'

enlightened interest.[10] The awareness that they were facing an exceptional situation lead the actors to switch to a crisis-mode and to look for temporary, *ad hoc* solutions. The creation of a permanent status would be unnecessary since temporary problems do not need permanent solutions. This view was also initially shared by many refugees who believed that once the situation in Russia improved and the Bolshevik regime collapsed, they would be able to return.[11] The adoption of the denationalisation decree by the All Russian Central Executive Committee was a watershed moment, a *capitis deminutio maxima* ('civil death').[12] After 15 December 1921, hundreds of thousands of refugees became *de jure* stateless.[13] Denaturalisation and confiscation of property by the Bolshevik government rubberstamped their exile.

The stateless refugees and the host states found themselves in a truly Kafkaesque situation, characterised by three factors. First, the policy of non-recognition of the Bolshevik government, adopted by the majority of the European states had a most serious impact on the everyday lives of the stateless Russian refugees thus additionally exacerbating their situation.[14] Without the possibility to invoke bilateral treaties which granted certain privileged regimes under the condition of reciprocity and in the absence of a minimum standard of treatment of aliens,[15] hundreds of thousands of refugees found themselves in the situation of a 'least favoured nation'.[16] The host states handled the question of passports as well as of legal status in different ways which were determined

10 Haddad, Emma. *The Refugee in International Society* (Cambridge: Cambridge University Press, 2008), 118.

11 Holborn, Louise. 'The Legal Status of Political Refugees, 1920–1933'. *American Journal of International Law* 32(4) (1938), 680–703, 682.

12 Lipovano wrote in his book on statelessness that they could be compared to the slaves of Ancient Rome. Lipovano, I. G. *L'apatridie* (Paris: Les éditions internationales, 1935), 22.

13 Fischer Williams, John. 'Denationalization'. *British Yearbook of International Law* 8 (1927), 45–61.

14 In an early essay, the famous Russian émigré writer Teffi wrote about the hardships faced by the refugees in Constantinople. 'Although there were moneychangers on every block, they were unwilling to accept Russian currency: "What state stands behind your banknote?" they asked. "Russia? Ha-ha!"' See Haber, Edythe. *Teffi: A Life of Letters and of Laughter* (London: I. B. Tauris, 2019), 99.

15 See Castellanos-Jankiewicz, León. 'Nationality, Alienage and Early International Rights' (unpublished manuscript, on file with author), 9–10.

16 Quite ironically, after 1924, when several European states (e.g. Austria, France, Greece, Italy and the United Kingdom) established diplomatic relations with the Soviet Union, effectively ending the non-recognition policy, the refugees' situation in Europe deteriorated. As Soviet relations with other states improved, the USSR started pressuring governments to curb exile activities. Goodwin-Gill, 'Refugee Protection' 2008 (n. 3), 13.

largely by their political attitude and their relation to the Soviet Government.[17] Second, refugees were driven to enter a neighbouring State illicitly. 'Should the refugee refuse to do so, he was arrested, tried, and condemned to imprisonment; at the end of his term he is again arrested, tried and condemned; and that may go on for an indefinite length of time.'[18] Third, domestic courts in the host states which refused to recognise the Bolshevik government grappled with the question how to treat the citizens of the Russian empire which had ceased to exist.[19] Uncertainty persisted also regarding the question which law should be applied to them – the law of the state of origin, of the domicile or the residence in case of transfer? The solution adopted by some states was that so long the state of residence had not recognised Soviet Russia, it could rely on a fiction that the previous regime was still in force and apply the old Tsarist code *Svod Zakonov*.[20] Thus, the pre-revolutionary Tsarist law survived a couple of more years in several European states, allowing the refugees to benefit from this fiction, and to obtain passports, documents and other consular services. However, with the passing of time it became more and more difficult to galvanize this *cadavre législatif*, as the court of Genoa described this fiction.[21]

3 The Politics of Solidarity

What the history of the Russian émigrés' plight shows is that solidarity is a multifaceted concept with legal, political and ethical undertones ranging from a powerful political argument to a criminal act.[22] Its apparent simplicity and omnipresence obscure a rich and multi-layered edifice with deep foundations and eclectic history of uses (and abuses). To start with, solidarity belongs to a category of concepts (another example is security) whose invocation serves

17 Gemma, Scipione. 'Les gouvernements de fait'. *Recueil des cours de l'académie de droit international* 4 (1924), 293–414, 398–399.

18 Rubinstein, Jacob. 'The Refugee Problem'. *International Affairs* 15(5) (1936), 716–734, 723–724.

19 Gousseff, Catherine. *L'exil Russe: La fabrique du réfugié apatride (1920–1939)* (Paris: CNRS Éditions, 2008), 219.

20 Vichniac, 'Le statut international' 1933 (n.9), 179.

21 Ibid., 180.

22 Article 116 of the Swiss Foreign Nationals and Integration Act criminalises the help provided to undocumented migrants even if they are acting purely for humanitarian reasons (the so-called 'solidarity crime'). See also the decision of the French *Conseil Constitutionnel* of 6 July 2018 where it found that: 'Il découle du principe de fraternité la liberté d'aider autrui, dans un but humanitaire, sans considération de la régularité de son séjour sur le territoire national.'

to emphasise simultaneously the need for and its absence in a particular situation. We talk about solidarity only when we do not feel it. However, the task of this chapter is not to define the concept;[23] on the contrary, it argues that a single definition, something along the lines of the Rortyian 'solidarity, our recognition of one another's common humanity'[24] reflects only a fraction of the philosophical luggage of a political concept. Instead, the idea is to see how it functions in a particular context. Solidarity may be said to have two dimensions: internal and external – the former characterises the mobilising force of the argument of the bonds uniting the members of a certain group while the latter emphasises the existence of a mobilising external factor. The functioning of solidarity as a political concept is inherently relational and frequently confrontational. It cannot exist without an external mobilising factor be it a rival group in times of raging nationalism, or an ethnic majority in a nation state, or another refugee group. Solidarity permeates the relations between hosts states and refugees, between host-states (burden-sharing), between refugees and other groups (for instance minorities), between host states and the state of origin of refugees (characterised by non-reciprocity) and even among different refugee groups.[25] Thus, where we hear voices of concern and complaints for lack of solidarity, we might actually be in the presence of other, less visible solidarities.

23 For a general theory of solidarity, see Hechter, Michael. *Principles of Group Solidarity* (Berkeley: University of California Press, 1987).

24 Rorty, Richard. *Contingency, Irony, Solidarity* (Cambridge: Cambridge University Press, 1989), 189. Iğsız, Aslı. *Humanism in Ruins* (Stanford: Stanford University Press, 2018), 43: 'Liberal humanism … invites an act of solidarity via a shared notion of humanity, rather than a reconsideration of politics and history. In that respect, the liberal humanist emphasis on suffering tends to divorce the affect from its political and historical contexts and thus obscures modes of relationality other than human feelings to consider the palimpsests of segregative biopolitics.'

25 For instance, the authority of the Nansen certificate was disputed by Ukrainians and Caucasians which disagreed in particular with the designation 'person of Russian origin' as obliterating the nationalities under the former empire which were represented in the emigration. In 1927, the Union of the associations of the Ukrainian émigrés in France submitted to the Secretary General of the League a request for recognition of a distinct refugee status of Ukrainians. The request met the opposition of the participants from the Russian refugee organisations who used all available bureaucratic means to water it down. Thus, ironically, even between stateless, the reflexes of the national continued to function to the extent that the Russian representatives together with Jewish and Armenian refugees organized a common front against the Ukrainians asking either for the inclusion of Ukrainian members on the executive of the Nansen Office, or for the exclusion of 'Great Russians'. See Kévonian, Dzovinar. *Réfugiés et diplomatie préventive: Les acteurs européens et la scène proche-orientale pendant l'entre-geux-guerres* (Paris: Publications de la Sorbonne, 2004), 246–247.

While Nansen was travelling extensively in Europe with the objectives to raise public awareness for the refugee cause and to collect money for the people in hunger-ridden regions of Soviet Russia, in January 1922, the most influential conservative newspaper in Norway *Aftenposten* launched a fundraising campaign for the poor Norwegian fishermen with the ominous slogan 'Our own people first'.[26]

Thus, instead of a single overarching human solidarity, we observe a multitude of solidarities, clashing, competing, denying each other's legitimacy in the political field.[27] Some of them received the sanction of international law, (i.e. the beautiful indeterminacy of the Wilsonian/Leninist principle of self-determination, the minorities treaties, the burden-sharing in the EU refugee resettlement schemes), some of them did not. These two dimensions of solidarity resemble the concept of the Political, as developed by Carl Schmitt during the interwar period. The analogy is nonetheless superficial[28] and limited;[29] it serves only to unveil and expose a deeply fragmented landscape of groups, for which Schmitt did not exhibit a particular interest. Schmitt did not offer a theory of nationalism capable to explain the formation of group identities;[30]

26 See Vogt, Carl-Emil. 'Først vore egne!" Da Aftenposten Saboterte Nansens Nødhjelp til Russland'. *Historisk Tidsskrift* 87(1) (2008), 29–59, mentioned by Cabanes, *The Great War* 2014 (n.8), 192.

27 Ivan Krastev used the expression 'clash of solidarities' in his piece Krastev, Ivan. 'Eastern Europe's Compassion Deficit'. *The New York Times* (8 September 2015), available at: https://www.nytimes.com/2015/09/09/opinion/eastern-europes-compassion-deficit-refugees-migrants.html (last accessed on 29 November 2020).

28 The distinction proposed by Schmitt is fraught with uncertainties and despite its categorical character, does not provide clear answers to many questions, for instance on the question of intensity, the distinction between domestic and international and the key issue related to the importance of identity for the formation of the group.

29 It is limited because it gives primary to the 'enemy' aspect which predominates over the friend. See Botwinick, Aryeh. 'Same / Other versus Friend / Enemy: Levinas contra Schmitt', in *The Oxford Handbook of Carl Schmitt*, eds. Jens Meierhenrich and Oliver Simons (Oxford: Oxford University Press, 2016), 338–366, 350.

30 'Schmitt wilfully resists any moral assessment of the particular substance that brings a specific collectivity together or, conversely, of the particular grounds on which they fight other collectivities bound by some other organizing substance. Schmitt will not even supply an account of the mechanisms, moral or not, that bring such people together to begin with and that keep them together; that is, he ignores what we conventionally understand as politics. At a more abstract level, Schmitt promotes social solidarity through the invocation at some points of a quasi-Catholic, juridical notion of "representation," and at others of a quasi- irrational "myth of the nation" – and sometimes the two simultaneously.' It bears noting however, that '[i]n his 1923 book *The Crisis of Parliamentary Democracy*, Schmitt appears to be agnostic regarding the specific substance of democratic homogeneity. He suggests that an appropriately political way of life could be constituted by identities formed around the phenomena of class, language, religion, or ethnicity.' See McCormick, John. 'Teaching in Vain', in *The Oxford Handbook of Carl Schmitt*, eds. Jens

and he rejected in most radical terms the possibility of acting in the name of humanity (repeating Proudhon's 'whoever invokes humanity wants to cheat'). For Schmitt humanity could never become a political subject as there was nothing outside it against which it would exist.[31] With this concept, Schmitt postulated the primacy of politics (Moyn calls it 'the debate on political first')[32] but he could not control the legacy of that concept. Schmitt's distinction is only useful in most general terms; first, more as an organising principle and a general criterion;[33] second, as a recognition that politics 'derive its energy from the most varied human endeavours, from the religious, economic, moral, and other antitheses.'[34] And thirdly, much later, in 1944, Schmitt admitted: 'In a pluralistic world, only jurisprudence was left, representing the unity of the legal will as opposed to *the multiplicity of egoistic parties and factions*.'[35] But international lawyers turned their backs on Schmitt. According to Koskenniemi, '[i]n part, ..., this may also be explained by the predominantly technical and positivist orientation of the field. International lawyers do not see themselves as representatives of an intellectual discipline. Their humanitarian sensibilities are not based on any well-articulated theory but have been *imbibed practically unconsciously* with the profession's technical routines.'[36]

3.1 *On Propitious Soil: Solidarity and Solidarism*

The beginning of the twentieth century was marked by the influential 'solidarist' movement.[37] Already in 1898, the French professor Antoine Pillet postulated the interdependence of states as a basic feature of the international

Meierhenrich and Oliver Simons (Oxford: Oxford University Press, 2016), 269–290, 280–281.

31 Koskenniemi, Martti. 'Carl Schmitt and International Law', in *The Oxford Handbook of Carl Schmitt*, eds. Jens Meierhenrich and Oliver Simons (Oxford: Oxford University Press, 2016), 592–611, 606.

32 Moyn, Samuel. 'Concepts of the Political in Twentieth-Century European Though', in *The Oxford Handbook of Carl Schmitt*, eds. Jens Meierhenrich and Oliver Simons (Oxford: Oxford University Press, 2016), 291–311, 307.

33 Ibid., 298.

34 Ibid., 297.

35 Schmitt, Carl. 'The Plight of European Jurisprudence'. *Telos* 83 (1990), 35–70, 49, cited in Koskenniemi, 'Carl Schmitt' 2016 (n. 31), 592 (emphasis added).

36 Ibid., 593 (emphasis added).

37 On the sociological jurisprudence in France see Koskenniemi, Martti. *The Gentle Civilizer of Nations: The Rise and Fall of International Law 1870–1960* (Cambridge: Cambridge University Press, 2001), 266–353, in particular 297–316 and 327–338. Kolb, Robert. 'Politis and Sociological Jurisprudence of Inter-War International Law'. *European Journal of International Law* 23(1) (2012), 233–243, 235–236.

system;[38] in 1901, Albert de Lapradelle drew attention to a new principle of solidarity, whose advent was announced by Bourgeois and Durkheim. In the equation between sovereignty and human rights, Lapradelle postulated the protection of the latter as the basis of a new international law.[39] Solidarity equally played a role in the conceptualisation of both the 'nation' and 'minority'. Weber wrote that the concept of nation implies that we may 'expect from certain groups a specific sentiment of solidarity in the face of other groups.'[40] The term was also used by the Permanent Court of International Justice in the important advisory opinion on the *Greco-Bulgarian Communities* to define the meaning of 'community' in the bilateral Convention on reciprocal emigration. The Court stated that:

> By tradition, which plays so important a part in Eastern countries, the 'community' is a group of persons *living in a given country or locality*, having a race, religion, language and traditions of their own and united by this identity of race, religion, language and traditions in a *sentiment of solidarity*, with a view to preserving their traditions, maintaining their form of worship, ensuring the instruction and upbringing of their children in accordance with the spirit and traditions of their race and *rendering mutual assistance to each other*.[41]

A couple of pages further, the Court observed that 'the very nature of a community shows that these relations are bonds of solidarity uniting the individuals who are members of the community and involving mutual rights and obligations for these individuals.'[42] These pronouncements are extremely interesting because of the 'Court's recognition of the extraordinary importance of ethnic 'solidarity' and the kin-states in the Convention that makes its augmentation

---

38 Pillet, Antoine. 'Recherches sur les droits fondamentaux des etats dans l'ordre des rapports internationaux et sur la solution des conflits qu'ils font naître'. *Revue générale de droit international public* 5 (1898), 66–89, 89, cited in Mandelstam, André. *La protection internationale des minorités* (Paris: Sirey, 1931), 5.

39 Lapradelle, Albert G. de. 'La question chinoise'. *Revue générale de droit international public* 8 (1901), 272–340, 339. See also Peters, Anne. *Beyond Human Rights* (Cambridge: Cambridge University Press, 2016), 17.

40 Weber, Max. *Economy and Society: An Outline of Interpretive Sociology* (Berkeley: University of California Press, 1978), 922, cited in Robertson, Roland and Kathleen White. *Globalization: Critical Concepts in Sociology*, vol. II (Abingdon: Routledge, 2003), 116.

41 Permanent Court of International Justice. *Greco-Bulgarian Communities*, Advisory Opinion Ser. B, No. 17, 21 (emphasis added).

42 Ibid., 25.

of international authority and discretion in this case so striking.'[43] They also demonstrate that solidarity functions always in relation to something and third, because they show that a stable community is normally related to a particular territory.[44] Solidarity of ethnic groups is based on a sense of identity nourished by prejudices.[45] Some of these prejudices received the positive sanction of international law like in the *Greco-Bulgarian communities* case while others did not (the prohibition of discrimination). The protection of minorities and the massive number of refugees in the wake of the Great War challenged the well-established nineteenth century triad of territory, nationality and rights and showed that there could exist other solidarities than the broad liberal humanitarian or the Weberian concept of nation.

Solidarity in the context of refugee law is best defined by its practice. Its existence as a principle in many domestic legal systems and as a principle implying burden-sharing in the context of the European Union also leaves no doubts.[46] I am much more interested in the praxis of solidarity in the 1920s when paradoxically, despite the powerful presence of the sociological approach, the explicit references to solidarity in the context of the refugee relief efforts are very few. One reason which is well illustrated by the above-mentioned advisory opinion is that solidarity always comes in the cloak of a duty of a certain kind, a legal or ethical obligation; without it, it is meaningless. For instance, in his influential book *The Development of International Law after the World War*, the German-Swiss professor Otfried Nippold stated:

> If it was a characteristic of international law of the past that states, boastful of their sovereignty, claimed rights for themselves, it is characteristic of modern international law that the states, knowing the solidarity of

---

43 See Berman, Nathaniel. 'But the Alternative Is Despair: European Nationalism and the Modernist Renewal of International Law'. *Harvard Law Review* 106(8) (1993), 1792–1904, 1858–1859, cited in Shahabuddin, Mohammed. *Ethnicity and International Law* (Cambridge: Cambridge University Press, 2016), 117.

44 Brownlie, Ian. 'The Place of the Individual in International Law'. *Virginia Law Review* 50(3) (1964), 435–463, 446.

45 Senarclens, Pierre de. 'From Group Identity to Ethnic Violence', in *Emotions in International Politics*, eds. Yohan Ariffin, Jean-Marc Coicaud and Vesselin Popovski (Cambridge: Cambridge University Press, 2016), 299–314, 300.

46 The Court of Justice of the European Union made a clear pronouncement in the joined cases *Slovak Republic and Hungary v Council of the European Union* CJEU, Cases C-643/15 and C-647/15, (Grand Chamber) Judgment of 6 September 2017 ECLI:EU:C:2017:631. For a more recent confirmation of the solidarity principle, see CJEU, Cases C-715/17, C-718/17 and C-719/17 *Commission v Poland, Hungary and the Czech Republic*, Judgment of 2 April 2020 ECLI:EU:C:2020:257.

> their interests, recognize duties, both toward the other states and toward the community of nations. This surely does not sound as pleasant as the former. One would speak of sovereignty than of duties.[47]

Nippold postulated that: 'Solidarity and co-operation will, accordingly, have to be unreservedly the watchword of nations after this war.'[48] He did not, however, apply this concept in the context of refugees, in the explicit way that was done by Simpson in 1939,[49] Loewenfeld in 1941,[50] or Franz Krenz in his 1966 article.[51] Such an explicit statement would be hard to find in the 1920s. The 'solidarists' did not use the refugee case as an opportunity to insist on the importance of solidarity for the individual and his rights. Only Redslob noted it and he did so in passing.[52] Yet, while solidarity was absent on the surface, it was arguably always present on several levels of interaction – international, national and even interreligious.

3.2 *Solidarity as a (Synallagmatic) Obligation*

In 1936, the report of the Committee on International Assistance to Refugees, presented to the Council of the League of Nations in June 1936 stated: 'In view of the heavy burden placed on the countries of refuge, the Committee considers it an international duty for the countries of origin of the refugees at least to alleviate to some extent, the burdens imposed by the presence of refugees

---

47 Nippold, Otfried. *The Development of International Law after the World War* (Oxford: Clarendon Press, 1923), 17.

48 Ibid., 51.

49 Simpson, *Refugee Problem* 1939 (n. 6), 205, cited in Stoessinger, John G. *The Refugee and the World Community* (Minneapolis: University of Minnesota Press, 1956), 25. The stamp system was used effectively in most countries and 'apart from the material benefits it provided, the system embodied a very useful principle of organized selfhelp, and was a symbol of the solidarity existing in the refugee community.'

50 Loewenfeld, Erwin. 'Status of Stateless Person'. *Transactions of the Grotius Society* 27 (1941), 59–112, 67: 'The exaggerated nationalism that created the Russian statelessness has to a large amount been made good by the increasing development of international solidarity.'

51 Krenz, Frank. 'The Refugee as a Subject of International Law'. *International and Comparative Law Quarterly* 15(1) (1966), 90–117, 116. Krenz argued that: 'It is clear that no further headway is possible unless more inter-national solidarity is practised in the admission of persecutees, especially by countries possessing a high standard of living, and by virtue of their geographical position not immediately called upon to receive and sustain a regular influx.'

52 Redslob, Robert. *Principes du droit des gens moderne* (Paris: A. Rousseau, 1937), 178.

in the territory of other states.'[53] Sir Robert Jennings was among the first to note this possibility in an article published in the *British Yearbook* in 1939.[54] Much later Stanley Hoffmann argued that 'ethical action requires a cooperative effort of all but the poorest countries to rule out the degrading perpetuation of camps, and to provide for the resettlement of the refugees – who, in the past, have often contributed to the economic development of the countries that let them in. Should such an effort fail, it remains the duty of each country to open its own borders as widely as possible, without looking for excuses or waiting for others to act.'[55]

Throughout the whole 1920s, host states did not act under a strict legal obligation prescribing them to accept refugees.[56] While Luke Lee had argued in favour of the existence of a quasi-contractual relationship between the host states which provided refugees with goods and services and the state of origin,[57] the multilateral agreements concluded in 1922, 1924, 1926 and 1928 were non-binding (the 1951 Geneva Convention was the outcome of the long gestation of the interwar period's soft law). It is more plausible to argue that the host states 'thought' they were acting under a moral imperative, a duty of cosmopolitan hospitality, the traces of which could be found already in Pufendorf,[58]

53 League of Nations, Doc C.2 M.2 1936 XII, cited in Lee, Luke. 'The Right to Compensation: Refugees and Countries of Asylum'. *American Journal of International Law* 80(3) (1986), 532–568, 557–558.

54 Jennings, Sir Robert. 'Some International Law Aspects of the Refugee Question'. *British Yearbook of International Law* 20 (1939), 98–114, 102.

55 Hoffmann, Stanley. *Duties without Borders* (New York: Syracuse University Press, 1981), 224–225.

56 See the letter of the Swiss Confederation informing the Secretary-General of the League of Nations that it 'felt morally bound to take under its care necessitous Russian nationals and to grant them financial aid.' *League of Nations Official Journal* (July-August 1921), 496. In November 1921, Sir Samuel Hoare, a deputy of Nansen, was sent by the League to several countries in the Balkans to try to convince them to accept more refugees. Some months later, he requested money from the League for relief in Constantinople, stating that: 'I am aware that the League has never undertaken any financial obligation regarding the refugees. Indeed, it has expressly guarded itself against financial liabilities, and, as a result, is apparently without financial resources. None the less, I say that a year ago, when the High Commissariat for Russian Refugees was officially formed, the League undertook *some kind of obligation*.' Cited in Stoessinger, *The Refugee* 1956 (n. 49), 20 (emphasis added).

57 Lee, 'Right to Compensation' 1939 (n. 53), 557.

58 Pufendorf, Samuel. *De Jure Naturae et Gentium Libri Octo*, vol. 2, ed. Charles Henry Oldfather and William A. Oldfather (Oxford: Clarendon Press, 1934), I.7.7, 118–119, cited in Glanville, Luke. 'Hypocritical Inhospitality: The Global Refugee Crisis in the Light of History'. *Ethics & International Affairs* 34(1) (2020), 3–12: Pufendorf developed a notion of 'imperfect' duties – which he considered duties whose performance is rightly subject to

Vattel[59] and Kant.[60] Others traced the obligation to assist refugees to the Judaeo-Christian religious tradition.[61] Haddad pointed out that some Western states like Britain and France 'found themselves morally and financially responsible for Russian refugees, many of whom had been part of the White armies in the Russian Civil War that Britain and France had unsuccessfully supported.'[62] I prefer to avoid tracing the sources of the duty of hospitality as it would involve a 'the chicken or the egg' dilemma: Must the right to asylum be preceded by duty of hospitality? One thing is certain, the experience of the Russian émigrés problematised the broken correlation between the rights and duties of refugees. Having lost their citizenship, the refugees were a group of people without rights and without obligations.[63] At that time the two principal elements of the bond of nationality were the duty of loyalty (of the individual towards the state) and its corollary – the exercise of diplomatic protection by the state. In the case of the stateless refugees, this bond was non-existent and they was considered as 'outlaws' not 'worthy of sympathy': they were unable to offer loyalty to any state, including their host.[64] In his 1925 PhD thesis on statelessness Noël Vindry (a lawyer, judge and later on prolific author of crime novels) wrote:

> [t]here is something *immoral* in the position of an individual who takes advantage of the benefits of a civilized state without fulfilling any corresponding military duty, of someone who lives, so to speak, as a parasite. It is not pleasant to receive people in such an ambiguous situation who live

---

the discretion of the duty bearer and not enforceable – and he offered hospitality as an example.

59 Glanville, 'Hypocritical Inhospitality' 2020 (n. 58), 9.

60 For an exposition and critique of Kant's concept of cosmopolitan hospitality, see Brown, Garrett W. 'Laws of Hospitality, Asylum Seekers and Cosmopolitan Right: A Kantian Response to Jacques Derrida'. *European Journal of Political Theory* 9(3) (2010), 308–327.

61 Skran, *Refugees* 1995 (n. 1), 70.

62 Haddad, *The Refugee in International Society* 2008 (n. 10), 117–118. See also Macartney, Carlile. *Refugees. The Work of the League* (London: League of Nations Union, 1930), 19.

63 Cabanes, *Great War* 2014 (n. 8), 182.

64 Vindry, Noël. *L'apatridie* (Aix-en-Provence: Université d'Aix-Marseille, PhD Dissertation 1925), 54, cited in Kévonian, Dzovinar. 'André Mandelstam and the Internationalization of Human Rights (1869–1949)', in *Revisiting the Origins of Human Rights*, eds. Pamela Slotte and Miia Halme-Tuomisaari (Cambridge: Cambridge University Press, 2015), 239–266, 242.

> on the margins of society and whose loyalties whether enemy or neutral, are impossible to determine in wartime.[65]

That same year, the Russian Red Cross complained to the chief Russian refugee representative to France, Vassily Maklakov,[66] that Russians in France were being denied their rights of asylum.[67] Quite interestingly, Maklakov's reaction was in substance very close to the line of argument developed by Vindry. Maklakov understood the essence of the humanitarian action as cold state interest or at best, a gift, mere charity:

> *the right to asylum has no juridical significance* and *does not grant any specific rights ... you are mistaken when you claim that all the Russian refugees are here as emigrants with asylum rights granted by* France ... the overwhelming majority are here not as emigrants, but as labour forces and therefore subject to special control and regulation.[68]

This statement raises the important issue of the dialectics of rights and gifts. If solidarity equals charity, if it is merely a 'dar' ('gift' in Russian), the host state

65 Cabanes, *Great War* 2014 (n. 8), 138–139. Interestingly, in the case of France, this justification disappeared in 1923 when the new legislation on recruitment was passed according to which 'les jeunes gens qui ne justifiaient d'aucune nationalité, résidant en France, sont appelés avec leur classe d'âge et incorporés dans les régiments étrangers pour y accomplir le temps de service imposé par la loi.' Vichniac, 'Le statut international' 1933 (n. 9), 186.

66 Maklakov was an influential Russian politician and lawyer, one of the leaders of the liberal Constitutional Democratic Party (also known as Cadets from the abbreviation K-D of the party name). In October 1917, Maklakov was appointed as ambassador to France. A recently published biography is Williams, Stephen. *The Reformer: How One Liberal Fought to Preempt the Russian Revolution* (New York: Encounter Books, 2017) which unfortunately does not cover in detail his activities in the post-1917 period.

67 Ippolitov, Sergei. *Rossiiskaya Emigratsiya i Evropa: Nesostoyavshiisya al'yans* (Moscow: Izdatelstvo Ippolitova, 2004), 67, cited in White, Elizabeth. 'The Legal Status of Russian Refugees, 1921–1936'. *Comparativ. Zeitschrift für Globalgeschichte und vergleichende Gesellschaftsforschung* 1(1) (2017), 18–38, 28 (emphasis added).

68 Ibid. (emphasis added). See also Schaufuss, Tatiana. 'White Russian Refugees'. *Annals of the American Academy of Political and Social Science* 203 (1939), 45–54, 50. See also Watenpaugh, Keith D. 'Between Communal Survival and National Aspiration: Armenian Genocide Refugees, the League of Nations and the Practices of Interwar Humanitarianism', in *The Routledge Handbook of the History of the Middle East Mandates*, eds. Cyrus Schayegh and Andrew Arsan (Abingdon: Routledge, 2015), 41–61, 51: 'For the countries through which the refugees circulated, the documents constituted a de facto temporary residence permit – far less than citizenship – which meant, among other things, that refugees could be easily deported in times of economic stress or in the face of political upheaval.'

has the discretion to decide on the extent of its charity efforts. The problem with the 'gifts-talk' is that, as explained by Mauss in his seminal anthropological study, '[t]he gift not yet repaid debases the man who accepted it.'[69] In other words, the charity would deny the personhood, and by inference, the personality of the refugee. On the contrary, if humanitarianism is couched in the language of rights, refugees could lay claims and participate in the political process by virtue of which those claims would eventually be transformed into rights.[70] The statements of Maklakov and Vindry demonstrate that the study of the relationship between sovereignty and humanitarianism is more complex than a Manichean vision of 'good humanitarianism' and 'bad politics'. The following section will provide some examples from the 1920s in which humanitarianism and political objectives cannot be disentangled easily.

4 The Politics of Humanitarianism

There are at least two possible ways by which one should approach the interaction between humanitarianism and politics. The first one views humanitarian action as 'mere' charity. The refugee issue is brought down from the political agenda; states frame their actions as 'gifts' and the refugees are prevented from claiming them as 'rights'.[71] A French delegate in the League had also stated that 'l'oeuvre humanitaire recueillerait de la sorte l'adhésion de tous les pays civilisés et il serait manifeste par cette unanimité *qu'aucun intérêt politique ne*

69 Mauss, Marcel. *The Gift. Forms and Functions of Exchange in Archaic Societies* (London: Cohen and West, 1970), 63, cited in Lammers, Ellen. 'Researching Refugees: Preoccupations with Power and Questions of Giving'. *Refugee Survey Quarterly* 26(3) (2007), 72–81, 78.

70 Watenpaugh, 'Between Communal' 2015 (n. 68), 54: 'The Nansen Passport made no provision for the refugees to have any ability to act politically in any arena. It provided states with a reservoir of controllable workers deprived of any ability to claim political agency or civil rights.'

71 Ignatieff, Michael. 'Human Rights, Global Ethics, and the Ordinary Virtues'. *Journal of International Law & International Relations* 13(1) (2017), 1–9, 7: '[r]ights talk and gift talk are two very different languages. Gift talk is transactional, conditional, and selective. It is nonuniversal. You do not give gifts to everyone, you give gifts to a select few. In rights talk, I have an obligation to all of you irrespective of your characteristics. In gift talk, it is absolutely selective and conditional. Tolerance is granted only if the stranger recognizes the citizen as the gift giver. It is withheld if the stranger insists that the toleration is a right, and that the stranger sets the terms. And so the civic toleration that results in Queens, New York or South Central Los Angeles is a transactional, conditional, contextual negotiation based on the *recognition and mutual recognition of otherness*.' (emphasis added)

pourrait être poursuivi à cette occasion.'[72] In her detailed study on the treatment of refugees in the inter-war period Kévonian mentions that:

> un dernier élément du consensus autour de la question des réfugiés et apatrides est *l'indispensable distinction entre le domaine politique et le domaine technique*.... Aucun acteur étatique n'est sans ignorer les dimensions politiques que recèle la question des réfugiés mais le gage de toute solution internationale est la neutralisation de ces implications au profit de mesures humanitaires, spécialisées et *sans portée idéologique*.[73]

Skran and Loescher have made similar observations. Skran has pointed out that: 'the fulfilment of the humanitarianism principle required that the needs of refugees be met *in an apolitical*, non-discriminatory way.'[74] In his analysis of the politicisation of humanitarian aid in the inter-war period Loescher observed: '[g]overnments were more likely to aid refugees fleeing from their enemies than from their friends. Governments in Eastern Europe, for example, aided refugees from the Soviet Union but not those from Germany. Refugees fleeing important political states, on the other hand, were a source of embarrassment.'[75] A sentence later he adds that '[a]ll governments were more willing to act in a nonpolitical, nondiscriminatory fashion toward refugees when they needed immigrant labor'. The institutional setting in which the refugee question was discussed, also seem to support this view. The deliberations on the refugee question did not take place under the 'political' section of the Assembly's agenda until May 1933, being considered a 'Social and Humanitarian Question' prior to this date.[76] The refugees themselves have made a similar argument. For instance, in 1921 right after the debate on the project submitted by Lapradelle at the *Institut* Mandelstam stated that:

> I am convinced that, *without resorting to the political arena*, the Institute's duty is to raise its voice loudly and to proclaim without delay the great

72 Archives MAE série Russie-Europe, d.596, 65, cited in Gousseff, *L'exil russe* 2008 (n. 19), 51 (emphasis added).
73 Kévonian, *Diplomatie préventive* 2004 (n. 25), 246 (emphasis added).
74 Skran, *Refugees in Inter-War Europe* 1995 (n. 1), 68 (emphasis added).
75 Loescher, *Beyond Charity* 1996 (n. 7), 39.
76 Haddad, *The Refugee in International Society* 2008 (n. 10), 114.

> new principle ... : human rights exist, and it is the duty of each state to respect them.[77]

The description of humanitarianism as principled, while at the same time seeing politics as unprincipled[78] is a very appealing assumption, related to the instinctive pull to consider oneself as being 'outside' or 'above' politics. The explanation according to which there was a unanimous agreement among states to de-politicise the refugee issue and to treat it as a technical matter is *per se* also a political one.

According to the second view, throughout the entire interwar period refugees were tools of foreign policy.[79] The emerging refugee regime operated within a highly political context in which refugees reiterated and defended political claims while governments supported refugee assistance programs for security and foreign policy reasons as much as out of humanitarian concern.[80] For instance, Haddad has pointed out that 'states were of course more willing to extend protection and assistance to refugees when it coincided with their foreign or domestic policy objectives, when the refugees had been forced out of enemy states, when the refugees had similar ethnic backgrounds to the majority population, or when there was a need for immigrant labour. Similarly, states were more ready to help other host countries if they were allies or of strategic importance.'[81] Even though the sentence does not spell our explicitly the word solidarity, the Schmittian distinction is in full swing.

That humanitarian assistance can simultaneously be used in pursuit of concrete political objectives was recognised by Herbert Hoover, the director of American Relief Administration (ARA). Hoover was convinced that food can be used as a weapon against Bolshevism in Europe.[82] In January 1919, President Wilson had declared before the Congress: 'Bolshevism is steadily advancing westward ... and is poisoning Germany. It cannot be stopped by force but it can be stopped by food'.[83] His Soviet counterparts were equally aware of that.

77 André Mandelstam, Speech delivered to the IDI, 8 October 1921, *Yearbook of the IDI* 28 (1921), 222, cited in Cabanes, *Great War* 2014 (n. 8), 313.

78 Cutts, Mark. 'Politics and Humanitarianism'. *Refugee Survey Quarterly* 17(1) (1998), 1–15, 5.

79 Skran, *Refugees in Inter-War Europe* 1995 (n. 1), 27.

80 Loescher, *Beyond Charity* 1996 (n. 7), 39.

81 Haddad, *The Refugee in International Society* 2008 (n. 10), 119.

82 Radosh, Ronald. 'The Politics of Food: How America Kept Russia from Starving'. *Humanities* 32(2) (2011), 39–43.

83 Edmondson, Charles. 'The Politics of Hunger: The Soviet Response to Famine, 1921'. *Soviet Studies* 29(4) (1977), 506–518, 510. See also Vogt, Carl-Emil. 'Fridtjof Nansen et l'aide alimentaire européenne à la Russie et à l'Ukraine bolcheviques en 1921–1923'. *Matériaux pour l'histoire de notre temps* 95 (2009), 5–12.

During the Riga negotiations between ARA and the Soviet Union, the Deputy People's Commissar of Foreign Affairs Litvinov stated twice: 'Gentlemen, food is a weapon'.[84] Hoover's plan was to accomplish political ends in Russia not *under the guise* of humanitarian relief, but rather *by means of* it.[85]

In the brochure *L'aide pontificale aux enfants affamés en Russie* Michel d'Herbigny writes that: '[l]e Saint-Père entreprit donc des démarches, *non point politiques ni diplomatiques, mais de pure charité*, afin de pouvoir envoyer une Commission de secours au people russe, ou plus exactement, aux enfants affamés de la Russie.'[86] The Holy See clearly privileged hunger relief inside the country over refugee assistance in Europe. Throughout the whole 1920s the catholic authorities pursued one main objective: to bring Orthodox Russia back to 'l'unité catholique'.[87] D'Herbigny's belief that the Church can benefit from the exile of the Orthodox Russians, was to be proven dramatically wrong. A real scandal erupted in 1925–26 when Orthodox émigrés accused Catholics in 'buying souls and distributing relief against promises of conversion.'[88] Recognition played a key role in the foreign policy objectives of the Soviet leaders, who claimed that the Holy See had recognised their regime *de jure*. The Holy See immediately dismissed 'la fausse nouvelle'[89] and rejected any hypothesis of recognition: '*pas de mission politique ou diplomatique ou juridique, mais uniquement une œuvre de charité*.'[90]

The hundreds of thousands unemployed Russians in the outskirts of big European capitals represented a humanitarian emergency, a social challenge for the post-war European societies and were perceived as a potentially dangerous

84 Patenaude, Bertrand. 'Herbert Hoover's Brush with Bolshevism'. Woodrow Wilson International Center for Scholars, Kennan Institute Occasional Paper Series #248, 1992 noted that: '[i]t did not help matters that on the eve of the mission a series of articles appeared in the journal *World's Work* written by the former ARA chief in Hungary, who boasted that Hoover and the ARA had been responsible for the downfall of the short-lived Communist regime of Béla Kun in April 1919', available at: https://www.wilsoncenter.org/publication/herbert-hoovers-brush-bolshevism-1992 (last accessed on 29 November 2020).

85 Ibid. (emphasis added).

86 d'Herbigny, Michel. 'L'aide pontificale aux enfants affamés de Russie'. *Orientalia Christiana* 4(14) (1925), 1–80, 26. (emphasis added).

87 Expression used by cardinal Dubois, Archbishop of Paris, *La croix* (11 March 1922) and by Mgr. Chaptal, *Semaine réligieuse de Paris* (15 January 1924), cited in Schor, Ralph. 'Les Russes blancs devant l'opinion française (1919–1939)'. *Cahiers de la méditerranée* 48 (1994), 211–224, 223.

88 Ibid., 224.

89 d'Herbigny, 'L'aide pontificale' 1925 (n. 86), 27.

90 Ibid. (emphasis added).

political force.[91] The creation of the International Labour Organisation (ILO) was among everything an enlightened response aimed at showing workers that their interests could be met by something less radical than communist revolution.[92] Nansen believed that, by focusing assistance on the creation of employment opportunities for refugees, the international refugee regime would also contribute to solving Europe's economic problems.[93] Albert Thomas, the energetic first Director of the ILO, shared this vision: the refugee work should form the nucleus of transforming the organisation into an 'international employment agency.'[94] This however, was particularly resisted by the British who feared an 'immigration dictatorship' by the ILO and an attack on their sovereignty.[95] The employment of Russian refugees suffered considerably in Central and Eastern Europe but also in France, due to restrictive legislation protecting national labour markets.[96] In Bulgaria and Greece, the situation of the Russian refugees was exacerbated by the presence of large groups of newly arrived nationals, as a result of the exchange of populations which had taken place between 1919 and 1923.[97] The host governments confronted the dilemma whether to help their own newly arrived citizens or the stateless refugees. Another example of the same phenomenon, but on a wholly different level, occurred among the different refugee groups, quite ironically, on the basis of ethno-national belonging. The 1922 agreement which established the Nansen certificate served immediately as a pretext for Poland to operate a distinction

---

91 Even John Simpson who was a refugee advocate, warned that a politically uprooted refugee 'may sink into the underworld of terrorism and political crime.' Simpson, *The Refugee Problem* 1939 (n. 6), 9. See Robinson, Paul. 'Zemgor and the Russian Army in Exile'. *Cahiers du monde russe* 46(4) (2005), 719–737, 732.

92 Rodley, Nigel. 'International Human Rights Law', in *International Law*, ed. Malcolm D. Evans (Oxford: Oxford University Press, 4th ed. 2014), 786.

93 Loescher, *Beyond Charity* 1996 (n. 7), 38–39: 'All governments were more willing to act in a nonpolitical, nondiscriminatory fashion toward refugees when they needed immigrant labor.'

94 Johnson, Thomas. *International Tramps: From Chaos to Permanent World Peace* (London: Hutchinson & Co., 1938), 183, cited in White, 'Legal Status' 2017 (n. 67), 35.

95 Ibid.

96 White, 'The Legal Status' 2017 (n. 67), 27. In 1925 for instance, the Bulgarian government wrote to ILO to ask for assistance in connection with the problem of 'numerous refugees', whose arrival had caused high levels of unemployment and complaints by Bulgarian workers, and who were therefore seen as 'a source of danger to production and to social peace' in that country. Sinclair, Guy Fiti. 'A "Civilizing Task": The International Labour Organization, Social Reform, and the Genealogy of Development'. *Journal of the History of International Law* 20(2) (2018), 145–198, 163.

97 Simpson, *The Refugee Problem* 1939 (n. 6), 36.

between refugees and economic migrants and refused to accept persons entered after the date of the signature of the agreement.[98]

The politics of humanitarianism were particularly conspicuous in the (non) extension of the regime to other vulnerable groups. The restricted character and the exceptional nature of the protection, available only to particular groups had to serve as a guarantee against 'spill-over' of the regime and a sign for the respect of the sovereignty. In 1921, the Council decided not to assist approximately thirty million individuals threatened with starvation in Russia and the Ukraine, with League members agreeing that nothing should be done that may in any way help bolster Bolshevism.[99] At the Assembly debate of the issue in September 1921, delegates rejected humanitarian pleas from Nansen, (acting as the delegate from Norway), and sided with the delegate from Serbia, who argued that Bolshevism posed a greater threat to Russia than famine; therefore, the League should not do anything to help the Bolshevik government.[100] Nansen was 'extremely annoyed about the League of Nations' bureaucratic and heartless attitude to human suffering.'[101] When he was reproached for being naïve and with no understanding of *Realpolitik* he replied '*Charity is Realpolitik*'.[102] It was a matter of politics and Nansen witnessed it firsthand. During the negotiations leading to the compulsory exchange in January 1923 between Greece and Turkey, the parties agreed on one thing: the paternity of the idea of the compulsory exchange was attributed to Nansen who quickly had to write to inform Geneva and to exculpate himself.[103]

98 See Ginsburgs, 'Problem of Refugees' 1957 (n. 6), 327. This fact shows that, contrary to the position expressed by Professor Karatani, the beginnings of the different treatment of refugees and migrants could be traced to the period prior to the Second World War. See further Karatani, Rieko. 'How History Separated Refugee and Migrant Regimes: In Search of Their Institutional Origins'. *International Journal of Refugee Law* 17(3) (2005), 517–542, 518. For a study of the 'tangled history of refugees and migrants in the interwar period see Long, Katy. 'When Refugees Stopped being Migrants: Movement, Labour and Humanitarian Protection'. *Migration Studies* 1 (2013), 4–26.

99 Skran, *Refugees in Inter-War Europe* 1995 (n. 1), 86.

100 League of Nations, Records of the Second Assembly: Plenary Meetings, Geneva 1921, 552. Quoted by ibid., 86.

101 Fosse, Marit and John Fox. *Nansen: Explorer and Humanitarian* (London: Hamilton Books, 2016), 62.

102 Ibid. See also Chetail, Vincent. 'Fridtjof Nansen and the International Protection of Refugees: An Introduction'. *Refugee Survey Quarterly* 22(1) (2003), 1–6, 3.

103 Kévonian, *Diplomatie Préventive* 2004 (n. 25), 122–123.

5 Conclusion

This chapter argued that the creation of refugee status from the very beginning was a political process in which the concept of solidarity, directly and indirectly, played an important role: as a legal, political and ethical principle underlying the claims of all the actors involved. Arguments based on international law were used by different actors oscillating between sovereignty and humanitarianism, or attempting to accommodate both. Refugees argued for the creation of a special status which would fill the gap between resident stateless persons and citizens, thus diminishing the importance of citizenship as 'the right to have rights' in favour of an international human rights law. The Bolshevik government's main objective was the recognition of the European states. The reluctance of the host states to conclude legally binding instruments could be interpreted also as a sign of the importance of formal commitments. The history of the creation of the refugee status is the history of those types of solidarity which received the positive sanction of international law and those which failed to obtain it.

Analysing the origins of humanitarianism implies the duty to go beyond the easy separation between 'good' humanitarianism and 'bad' politics and the awareness of all the competing solidarities. International law plays a very important role in providing the platform for their struggle. 'International law is an important instrument for the realisation of valuable purposes and its formality offers a useful platform to channel disagreement. It is hard to see how it could be able to serve those objectives if the field remains in denial about its inflated expectations and occasional hypocrisy and if no light is allowed on the way it inevitably prefers some interests and players over others.'[104] Second and as a direct consequence from the first conclusion, international law speaks the language of universality and the dialects of particularity. Some dialects appear genuine, while others do not. International law 'operates as a polemical vocabulary that allows the indictment of those in power; without its idealism we could not even begin to distinguish between false and genuine universality.'[105] Frequently, it is a matter of imposition of hegemonic preferences; at times it is about persuasion. In any case, it is crucial to study the functioning of solidarity in context. Otherwise we run the risk of seeing the history of international law only as a chain of successes or failures, a rather simplistic Manichean imagery; in short, of relying on received ideas. The refugee problem is cyclical, ever-recurring and it will remain so as long as international refugee law is

104 Koskennieimi, 'Carl Schmitt' 2016 (n. 31), 607.

105 Ibid., 608.

premised on the 'crisis – need for urgent palliative response – normalisation' paradigm in order to find a compromise between the two conflicting positions. The Russian refugees understood this and wanted to go beyond the 'solidarity-humanitarianism' paradigm towards the normalcy offered by a generalised human rights law, beyond sovereignty to a position where the only important factors would be the human being as such and his/her legal status as a resident in a given territory.

At the end of March 2020, the Portuguese government decided to grant full access to the state's healthcare system to all migrants and asylum seekers by which they became full citizens in the social dimension.[106] Although the measure was temporary and would last only for the duration of the pandemic, it was an important sign of solidarity. The shift from such temporary measures to the recognition of this lowest common denominator will crown with success the efforts of the Russian refugees. Until then, we will live from one disaster to the next and from one crisis to the next, trapped in the gaze of the Benjamin's angel of history. Trapped in the past which is not dead. Which 'is not even past'.

Acknowledgements

The author would like to thank Teresa Mafalda Cabrita and Raphael Schäfer for their valuable comments and suggestions. All the views expressed in the chapter are personal and should not be attributed to any other person or organisation. All errors or omissions are my sole responsibility.

Bibliography

Alberti, Mia and Vasco Cotovio. 'Portugal Gives Migrants and Asylum-Seekers Full Citizenship Rights during Coronavirus Outbreak'. *CNN* (31 March 2020), available at: https://edition.cnn.com/2020/03/30/europe/portugal-migrants-citizenship-rights-coronavirus-intl/index.html (last accessed on 29 November 2020).

Berman, Nathaniel. 'But the Alternative Is Despair: European Nationalism and the Modernist Renewal of International Law'. *Harvard Law Review* 106(8) (1993), 1792–1904.

106 Alberti, Mia and Vasco Cotovio. 'Portugal Gives Migrants and Asylum-Seekers Full Citizenship Rights during Coronavirus Outbreak'. CNN (31 March 2020), available at: https://edition.cnn.com/2020/03/30/europe/portugal-migrants-citizenship-rights-coronavirus-intl/index.html (last accessed on 29 November 2020).

Botwinick, Aryeh. 'Same / Other versus Friend / Enemy: Levinas contra Schmitt', in *The Oxford Handbook of Carl Schmitt*, eds. Jens Meierhenrich and Oliver Simons (Oxford: Oxford University Press, 2016), 338–366.

Brown, Garrett W. 'Laws of Hospitality, Asylum Seekers and Cosmopolitan Right: A Kantian Response to Jacques Derrida'. *European Journal of Political Theory* 9(3) (2010), 308–327.

Brownlie, Ian. 'The Place of the Individual in International Law'. *Virginia Law Review* 50(3) (1964), 435–463.

Cabanes, Bruno. *The Great War and the Origins of Humanitarianism, 1918–1924* (Cambridge: Cambridge University Press, 2014).

Castellanos-Jankiewicz, León. 'Nationality, Alienage and Early International Rights' (unpublished manuscript, on file with author).

Chetail, Vincent. 'Fridtjof Nansen and the International Protection of Refugees: An Introduction'. *Refugee Survey Quarterly* 22(1) (2003), 1–6.

Cutts, Mark. 'Politics and Humanitarianism'. *Refugee Survey Quarterly* 17(1) (1998), 1–15.

Edmondson, Charles. 'The Politics of Hunger: The Soviet Response to Famine, 1921'. *Soviet Studies* 29(4) (1977), 506–518.

Fischer Williams, John. 'Denationalization'. *British Yearbook of International Law* 8 (1927), 45–61.

Fosse, Marit and John Fox. *Nansen: Explorer and Humanitarian* (London: Hamilton Books, 2016).

Gemma, Scipione. 'Les gouvernements de fait'. *Recueil des cours de l'académie de droit international* 4 (1924), 293–414.

Ginsburgs, George. 'The Soviet Union and the Problem of Refugees and Displaced Persons 1917–1956'. *American Journal of International Law* 51(2) (1957), 325–362.

Glanville, Luke. 'Hypocritical Inhospitality: The Global Refugee Crisis in the Light of History'. *Ethics & International Affairs* 34(1) (2020), 3–12.

Goodwin-Gill, Guy. 'The Politics of Refugee Protection'. *Refugee Survey Quarterly* 27(1) (2008), 8–23.

Gousseff, Catherine. *L'exil russe: La fabrique du réfugié apatride (1920–1939)* (Paris: CNRS Éditions, 2008).

Haber, Edythe. *Teffi: A Life of Letters and of Laughter* (London: I. B. Tauris, 2019).

Haddad, Emma. *The Refugee in International Society* (Cambridge: Cambridge University Press, 2008).

Hechter, Michael. *Principles of Group Solidarity* (Berkeley: University of California Press, 1987).

d'Herbigny, Michel. 'L'aide pontificale aux enfants affamés de Russie'. *Orientalia Christiana* 4(14) (1925), 1–80.

Hoffman, Stanley. *Duties without Borders* (New York: Syracuse University Press, 1981).

Holborn, Louise. 'The Legal Status of Political Refugees, 1920–1933'. *American Journal of International Law* 32(4) (1938), 680–703.

Ignatieff, Michael. 'Human Rights, Global Ethics, and the Ordinary Virtues'. *Journal of International Law & International Relations* 13(1) (2017), 1–9.

Iğsız, Aslı. *Humanism in Ruins* (Stanford: Stanford University Press, 2018).

Ippolitov, Sergei. *Rossiskaya Emigratsiya i Evropa: Nesostoyavshiisya al'yans* (Moscow: Izdatelstvo Ippolitova, 2004).

Jennings, Sir Robert. 'Some International Law Aspects of the Refugee Question'. *British Yearbook of International Law* 20 (1939), 98–114.

Johnson, Thomas. *International Tramps: From Chaos to Permanent World Peace* (London: Hutchinson & Co., 1938).

Karatani, Rieko. 'How History Separated Refugee and Migrant Regimes: In Search of Their Institutional Origins'. *International Journal of Refugee Law* 17(3) (2005), 517–542.

Kévonian, Dzovinar. *Réfugiés et diplomatie préventive: Les acteurs européens et la scène proche-orientale pendant l'entre-deux-guerres* (Paris: Publications de la Sorbonne, 2004).

Kévonian, Dzovinar. 'André Mandelstam and the Internationalization of Human Rights', in *Revisiting the Origins of Human Rights*, eds. Pamela Slotte and Miia Halme (Cambridge: Cambridge University Press, 2015), 239–266.

Kolb, Robert. 'Politis and Sociological Jurisprudence of Inter-War International Law'. *European Journal of International Law* 23(1) (2012), 233–243.

Koskenniemi, Martti. *The Gentle Civilizer of Nations: The Rise and Fall of International Law 1870–1960* (Cambridge: Cambridge University Press, 2001).

Koskenniemi, Martti. 'Carl Schmitt and International Law', in *The Oxford Handbook of Carl Schmitt*, eds. Jens Meierhenrich and Oliver Simons (Oxford: Oxford University Press, 2016), 592–611.

Krastev, Ivan. 'Eastern Europe's Compassion Deficit'. *The New York Times* (8 September 2015), available at: https://www.nytimes.com/2015/09/09/opinion/eastern-europes-compassion-deficit-refugees-migrants.html (last accessed on 29 November 2020).

Krenz, Frank. 'The Refugee as a Subject of International Law'. *International and Comparative Law Quarterly* 15(1) (1966), 90–117.

Lammers, Ellen. 'Researching Refugees: Preoccupations with Power and Questions of Giving'. *Refugee Survey Quarterly* 26(3) (2007), 72–81.

Lapradelle, Albert G. de. 'La question chinoise'. *Revue générale de droit international public* 8 (1901), 272–340.

Lee, Luke. 'The Right to Compensation: Refugees and Countries of Asylum'. *American Journal of International Law* 80(3) (1986), 532–568.

Lipovano, I. G. *L'apatridie* (Paris: Les éditions internationales, 1935).

Loescher, Gil. *Beyond Charity: International Cooperation and the Global Refugee Crisis* (Oxford: Oxford University Press, 1996).

Loewenfeld, Erwin. 'Status of Stateless Person'. *Transactions of the Grotius Society* 27 (1941), 59–112.

Long, Katy. *The Point of No Return* (Oxford: Oxford University Press, 2013).

Long, Katy. 'When Refugees Stopped being Migrants: Movement, Labour and Humanitarian Protection'. *Migration Studies* 1 (2013), 4–26.

Lowe, Kimberly. 'Reassessing the League of Nations' Humanitarian Assistance Regimes, 1918–1939', in *Decades of Reconstruction: Postwar Societies, State-Building, and International Relations from the Seven Years' War to the Cold War*, eds. Ute Planert and James Retallack (Cambridge: Cambridge University Press, 2017), 293–314.

Macartney, Carlile. Refugees. *The Work of the League* (London: League of Nations Union, 1930).

Mandelstam, André. *La Protection Internationale des Droits de l'Homme* (Paris: Les Editions Internationales, 1931).

Mandelstam, André. *La protection internationale des minorités* (Paris: Sirey, 1931).

Mauss, Marcel. *The Gift. Forms and Functions of Exchange in Archaic Societies* (London: Cohen and West, 1970).

McCormick, John. 'Teaching in Vain', in *The Oxford Handbook of Carl Schmitt*, eds. Jens Meierhenrich and Oliver Simons (Oxford: Oxford University Press, 2016), 269–290.

Moyn, Samuel. 'Concepts of the Political in Twentieth-Century European Though', in *The Oxford Handbook of Carl Schmitt*, eds. Jens Meierhenrich and Oliver Simons (Oxford: Oxford University Press, 2016), 291–311.

Nippold, Otfried. *The Development of International Law after the World War* (Oxford: Clarendon Press, 1923).

Patenaude, Bertrand. 'Herbert Hoover's Brush with Bolshevism'. Woodrow Wilson International Center for Scholars, Kennan Institute Occasional Paper Series #248, 1992.

Pedersen, Susan. 'Back to the League of Nations'. *American Historical Review* 112(4) (2007), 1091–1117.

Peters, Anne. *Beyond Human Rights* (Cambridge: Cambridge University Press, 2016).

Piana, Francesca. *Towards the International Refugee Regime: Humanitarianism in the Wake of the First World War* (Geneva: Graduate Institute of International and Development Studies, PhD Dissertation, 2013).

Pillet, Antoine. 'Recherches sur les droits fondamentaux des etats dans l'ordre des rapports internationaux et sur la solution des conflits qu'ils font naître'. *Revue générale de droit international public* 5 (1898), 66–89.

Pufendorf, Samuel. *De Jure Naturae et Gentium Libri Octo*, vol. 2, ed. Charles Henry Oldfather and William A. Oldfather (Oxford: Clarendon Press, 1934).

Radosh, Ronald. 'The Politics of Food: How America Kept Russia from Starving'. *Humanities* 32(2) (2011), 39–43.

Redslob, Robert. *Principes du droit des gens moderne* (Paris: A. Rousseau, 1937).

Robertson, Roland and Kathleen White. *Globalization: Critical Concepts in Sociology*, vol. II (Abingdon: Routledge, 2003).

Robinson, Paul. 'Zemgor and the Russian Army in Exile'. *Cahiers du monde russe* 46(4) (2005), 719–737.

Rodley, Nigel. 'International Human Rights Law', in *International Law*, ed. Malcolm D. Evans (Oxford: Oxford University Press, 4th ed. 2014).

Rorty, Richard. *Contingency, Irony, Solidarity* (Cambridge: Cambridge University Press, 1989).

Rubinstein, Jacob. 'The Refugee Problem'. *International Affairs* 15(5) (1936), 716–734.

Schaufuss, Tatiana. 'White Russian Refugees'. *Annals of the American Academy of Political and Social Science* 203 (1939), 45–54.

Schmitt, Carl. 'The Plight of European Jurisprudence'. *Telos* 83 (1990), 35–70.

Schor, Ralph. 'Les Russes Blancs devant l'opinion française (1919–1939)'. *Cahiers de la méditerranée* 48 (1994), 211–224.

Senarclens, Pierre de. 'From Group Identity to Ethnic Violence', in *Emotions in International Politics*, eds. Yohan Ariffin, Jean-Marc Coicaud and Vesselin Popovski (Cambridge: Cambridge University Press, 2016), 299–314.

Shahabuddin, Mohammed. *Ethnicity and International Law* (Cambridge: Cambridge University Press, 2016).

Simpson, Sir John Hope. *The Refugee Problem: Report of a Survey* (Oxford/London: Oxford/Royal Institute of International Affairs, 1939).

Sinclair, Guy Fiti. '"A Civilizing Task": The International Labour Organization, Social Reform, and the Genealogy of Development'. *Journal of the History of International Law* 20(2) (2018), 145–198.

Skran, Claudena. *Refugees in Inter-War Europe: The Emergence of a Regime* (Oxford: Oxford University Press, 1995).

Stoessinger, John G. *The Refugee and the World Community* (Minneapolis: University of Minnesota Press, 1956).

Vichniac, Marc. 'Le statut international des apatrides'. *Recueil des cours de l'académie de droit international* 43 (1933), 115–246.

Vindry, Noël. *L'apatridie* (Aix-en-Provence: Université d'Aix-Marseille, PhD Dissertation 1925).

Vogt, Carl-Emil. 'Først vore egne!" Da Aftenposten Saboterte Nansens Nødhjelp til Russland'. *Historisk Tidsskrift* 87(1) (2008), 29–59.

Vogt, Carl-Emil. 'Fridtjof Nansen et l'aide alimentaire européenne à la Russie et à l'Ukraine bolcheviques en 1921–1923'. *Matériaux pour l'histoire de notre temps* 95 (2009), 5–12.

Watenpaugh, Keith D. 'Between Communal Survival and National Aspiration: Armenian Genocide Refugees, the League of Nations and the Practices of Interwar Humanitarianism', in *The Routledge Handbook of the History of the Middle East Mandates*, eds. Cyrus Schayegh and Andrew Arsan (Abingdon: Routledge, 2015), 41–61.

Weber, Max. *Economy and Society: An Outline of Interpretive Sociology* (Berkeley: University of California Press, 1978).

White, Elizabeth. 'The Legal Status of Russian Refugees, 1921–1936'. *Comparativ. Zeitschrift für Globalgeschichte und vergleichende Gesellschaftsforschung* 1(1) (2017), 18–38.

Williams, Stephen. *The Reformer: How One Liberal Fought to Preempt the Russian Revolution* (New York: Encounter Books, 2017).

PART 2

The Use of Force Discourse in a Historical Perspective

CHAPTER 5

Theorising Order in the Shadow of War: The Politics of International Legal Knowledge and the Justification of Force in Modernity

Hendrik Simon

Abstract

The History of International Law lacks systematic studies on the link between legal scholars and practices of justifying war. This missing analytical link has for a long time given the impression that legal scholars describe 'state practice' in an 'objective', unpolitical way. Contradicting this impression, the chapter turns to the politics of legal scholars in the genesis of the modern war discourse. It reflects on the fateful entanglement of violence, law and politics, but nevertheless distinguishes between 'objective' and 'political' scholarship on the basis of Hans Kelsen's work. Furthermore, the chapter illustrates the politicisability of legal scholars in selected historical cases of the 'long 19th century' (1789–1918). In all cases, two hearts pounded in lawyers' chests: one scientific, the other political. As will be shown, the modern war discourse is shaped by a phenomenon that enables scholars to expand the intrinsic limits to the political instrumentalisation of law: 'multi-normativity'.

Keywords

politics and law – International Legal Scholarship – modern war discourse – Ius ad Bellum – 'long 19th Century' – multi-normativity – nationalism – Kelsen

1 Introduction: The Politics of Legal Knowledge – A Missing Link in the History of War Justifications

Paradoxically or not, at the core of the discipline of (the History of) International Law lies a phenomenon of a highly *political* nature: the entanglement

DOI:10.1163/9789004461802_007

of the justification and the critique of violence.[1] Hence, the historical reconstructions of war discourses have been constitutive for the emergence of international law as a scientific discipline.[2] However, an analytical imbalance in favour of doctrinal histories can clearly be identified. To fill the gap between practice and theory is highly important for the further orientation of the History of International Law in its own right.[3] As part of such an endeavour, the present chapter focusses on a specific aspect of the analytical gap between theory and practice: It reflects on the *politics* of legal knowledge in historical war discourses.

The History of International Law is not only lacking insights into the role of norms in political practices of justifying war[4] – it also lacks systematic and comparative studies on the link between legal scholars and politics in this particular policy field.[5] Legal scholars are the primary authors of writing legal histories – and at the same time, they are their primary historical sources. For a long time, this dual role has given the impression that doctrine describes and systematises 'state practice' in an 'objective' way.[6] But instead, the resulting doctrinal histories and narratives largely miss reflection on what Reinhart Koselleck has called a scholar's personal *Standpunkt* ('viewpoint') and its influence on the way scholars 'observe' international law.[7]

If legal scholars' *preferences* are to be taken more seriously in the policy field of war and peace, a couple of fundamental questions arise: Firstly and

1 Brock, Lothar and Hendrik Simon, eds. *The Justification of War and International Order. From Past to Present* (Oxford: Oxford University Press, 2021).

2 Neff, Stephen C. *War and the Law of Nations: A General History* (Cambridge: Cambridge University Press, 2005).

3 Tischer, Anuschka. *Offizielle Kriegsbegründungen in der Frühen Neuzeit: Herrscherkommunikation in Europa zwischen Souveränität und korporativem Selbstverständnis* (Berlin: LIT-Verlag, 2012); Payk, Marcus M. *Frieden durch Recht? Der Aufstieg des modernen Völkerrechts und der Friedensschluss nach dem Ersten Weltkrieg* (Berlin: De Gruyter, 2018); Benton, Lauren. 'Beyond Anachronism: Histories of International Law and Global Legal Politics'. *Journal of the History of International Law* 21(1) (2019), 7–40, doi: 10.1163/15718050-12340100.

4 Brock/Simon, *Justification of War* 2021 (n. 1).

5 A textbook example is Grotius' work for the Dutch East India Company in the 17th century, see Van Ittersum, Martine Julia. 'The Long Goodbye: Hugo Grotius' Justification of Dutch Expansion Overseas, 1615–1645'. *History of European Ideas* 36(4) (2010), 386–411; and Hathaway, Oona A. and Scott Shapiro. *The Internationalists: How a Radical Plan to Outlaw War Remade the World* (New York: Simon & Schuster, 2017), chapter 1.

6 See also the critique in Carty, Anthony. 'Doctrine versus State Practice', in *Oxford Handbook of the History of International Law*, eds. Bardo Fassbender and Anne Peters (Oxford: Oxford University Press, 2012), 972–996.

7 Koselleck, Reinhart. *Vergangene Zukunft: Zur Semantik geschichtlicher Zeiten* (Frankfurt am Main: Suhrkamp, 10th ed. 2017).

fundamentally, which role do politics play in the shaping of discourses on war and international order by legal scholars? Secondly, do scholars 'objectively' anticipate, accompany or synthesise[8] the debates? Or are they themselves political actors in their legal interpretation of certain cases – and if so: for what reason? Thirdly, which normative concepts shape their political agenda of justifying or criticising the use of force? Do they refer to law or do they try to by-pass it?

Reflecting on these questions in historical context seems decisive for the investigation of perhaps 'the most difficult problem of the scientific treatment of international law in its history',[9] the relationship between political practice and international legal doctrine or, in other words: the 'power-knowledge nexus'[10] in the legal history of war discourses. Far from being able to offer general or even final answers to this problem here, the chapter addresses this nexus, and it does so in the following way: It first develops a distinction between 'objective' and 'political' scholars on the basis of Hans Kelsen's work (section 2). It then turns to concrete case studies of the 'long 19th century' (section 3) (3.1: French Revolutionary Wars; 3.2: German Unification Wars; 3.3: Russo-Turkish Wars), before some conclusions from these case studies are summarised in a broader historical outlook (section 4).

The chapter's central thesis is that throughout modernity (1789 onwards), international lawyers have been exposed to a tension between the values and norms of the *international* legal community and *national* political interests. This has tended to politicise legal scholarship. How this tension came about will be illustrated with historical examples: To the extent that it corresponded to their political aims, the lawyers in the focus of this chapter referred to positive law and tried to interpret it according to their political preferences. However, where it appeared useful, they referred to different normative orders, which competed for authority in debates on the legitimacy of force.

As will be argued, this 'multi-normativity'[11] shapes the entire modern war discourse down to the present day, thus providing a useful political instrument

---

8 Janssen, Wilhelm. *Die Anfänge des modernen Völkerrechts und der neuzeitlichen Diplomatie: Ein Forschungsbericht* (Stuttgart: Metzler, 1965).

9 Steiger, Heinhard. 'Ius belli in der Völkerrechtsgeschichte – Universelle Geltung oder Beschränkung auf „anerkannte Kulturvölker"?', in *Legalität, Legitimität und Moral. Können Gerechtigkeitspostulate Kriege rechtfertigen?*, eds. Thomas Bruha, Sebastian Heselhaus and Thilo Marauhn (Tübingen: Mohr Siebeck, 2008), 59–98, 62.

10 Foucault, Michel. *L'archéologie du savoir* (Paris: Gallimard, 1969).

11 Vec, Miloš. 'Multinormativität in der Rechtsgeschichte', in *Jahrbuch 2008* (Berlin: Berlin-Brandenburgische Akademie der Wissenschaften, 2009), 155–166; Duve, Thomas. 'Was ist "Multinormativität"? Einführende Bemerkungen'. *Rechtsgeschichte – Legal History* 25 (2017), 88–101.

for jurists to circumvent the authority of law if deemed necessary. How did the ambivalence between legal scholarship and politics develop in the 'long 19th century' (1789–1918), the birth era of both modern war discourse and modern international order? This question is at the heart of the present chapter.

2 Legal Scholarship as a Political Vocation? Ordering War between Scientific Impartiality and 'National' Interests

In 1951, Hans Kelsen published an article in *The American Political Science Review* entitled 'Science and Politics' (the dichotomy is already revealing). Kelsen stated 'that the search for truth, which is the essential function of science, should not be influenced by political interests'; he characterised the latter as 'a function of will'.[12] Echoing Immanuel Kant's normative telos of positive law and thus positioning himself in the liberal tradition of *ius contra bellum*,[13] Kelsen argued that avoiding 'the mingling of these two heterogeneous spheres [– the legal and the political –] is as essential for the preservation of the scientific character of jurisprudence as the separation of science from politics is a vital condition for the existence of all independent science'; Kelsen concluded that the

> postulation of the separation of the science of positive law from politics means that the legal scientist, in describing his object, must refrain from political value judgments as judgments referring to norms other than norms of positive law, especially from evaluating his object as just or unjust.[14]

This is a textbook definition of the positivist legal scientist in the spirit of Kant's legal philosophy: Accordingly, the emergence of positive law is not only the best evidence for the emergence of 'objective' truth,[15] the reference to positive law is also the best evidence for an 'objective' legal scientist.

---

12 Kelsen, Hans. 'Science and Politics'. *The American Political Science Review* 45(3) (1951), 641–661, 641.

13 Kelsen, Hans. *Peace through Law* (Chapel Hill: The University of North Carolina Press, 1944).

14 Kelsen, *Science* 1951 (n. 12), 661.

15 Kleingeld, Pauline. 'What do the Virtuous Hope for? Re-reading Kant's Doctrine of the Highest Good', in *Proceedings of the Eighth International Kant Congress: Memphis, 1995*, eds. Hoke Robinson (Milwaukee: Marquette University Press, 1995). On Kelsen's project of positivism, see also García-Salmones Rovira, Mónica. *The Project of Positivism in International Law* (Oxford: Oxford University Press, 2013), chapters 4–6.

However, in an earlier article published in the *Juristische Wochenschrift* in 1929, Kelsen had expressed scepticism about legal scholars' actual political independence. He feared that public law scholarship provided 'the 'objectivity' that no politics is able to generate on its own'. Kelsen assumed that international legal scholarship in his time acted as a mouthpiece for the powerful by presenting political interests 'as what is objectively right'.[16] With this, Kelsen had developed a real-typical photonegative of the ideal-typical, positivist legal scholar characterised in his later article of 1951. With his deep concern for the politicisability of international legal scholarship as a political instrument of scientific justification, Kelsen proved that he was by no means a utopian, whose pure doctrine of law existed only beyond the realities of the political world. Rather, by pointing to the politicisability of legal scholarship, Kelsen anticipated a core statement of current critical legal theory:[17] Norms and lawyers 'both justify and enable the critique of established practices.'[18]

Here, an important caveat to Kant's project of international legalisation was voiced through Kelsen's criticism: More law is not necessarily better law. Legalisation is not necessarily an evidence for an objective 'progress' in the sense of Kant's telos. Rather, law is always politicisable, part of political projects – even a political project itself (demanded by reason), as Walter Benjamin put it.[19] The professional lawyer is ultimately always political. This does not only apply to *'first order' scholars* in close proximity to political or legal practice, but also to *'second order' scholars* who keep their critical academic distance from practice.[20] For neither are universities or academic institutes

16 Kelsen, Hans. 'Juristischer Formalismus und Reine Rechtslehre'. *Juristische Wochenschrift* 58(3) (1929), 1723–1726, 1723; see also Bernstorff, Jochen von. 'International Legal Scholarship as a Cooling Medium in International Law and Politics'. *European Journal of International Law* 25(4) (2014), 977–990, 977, doi: 10.1093/ejil/chu073.

17 Carty, Anthony. 'Critical International Law: Recent Trends in the Theory of International Law'. *European Journal of International Law* 2(1) (1991), 1–27; Singh, Prabhakar and Benoît Mayer, eds. *Critical International Law. Postrealism, Postcolonialism, and Transnationalism* (Oxford: Oxford University Press, 2014).

18 Koskenniemi, Martti. 'What is Critical Research in International Law? Celebrating Structuralism'. *Leiden Journal of International Law* 29(3) (2016), 727–735, 731.

19 Benjamin, Walter. 'Critique of Violence', in *Walter Benjamin, Reflections: Essays, Aphorisms, Autobiographical Writings*, ed. Peter Demetz (Boston: Harcourt, 1978), 277. See also Brock, Lothar and Hendrik Simon. 'Die Selbstbehauptung und Selbstgefährdung des Friedens als Herrschaft des Rechts'. *Politische Vierteljahresschrift* 59(2) (2018), 269–291.

20 For the distinction between 'first order' and 'second order' scholarship see Bernstorff, *Cooling Medium* 2014 (n. 16), 990.

apolitical spaces, nor can scholars isolate themselves from the historical, socio-political, or economic contexts in which they think and act.[21]

Much in this vein, Anne Peters has stated convincingly that a 'complete value-free academic activity appears impossible, because any kind of statement and any interpretation are pre-structured by the speaker's *Vorverständnis*' (preliminary understanding).[22] Even legal positivism may be regarded as a political project. As Benedict Kingsbury has argued with reference to Lassa Oppenheim, it is supported normatively 'as being the best conception of law for the realization of higher normative goals relating to peace, order, certain forms of justice, and the legal control of violence.'[23] Or, in Oppenheim's own words: 'The science of international law ... is merely a means to certain ends outside itself.'[24]

Accordingly, Martti Koskenniemi concludes: 'The choice is not between law and politics, but between one politics of law, and another. Everything is at stake, but not for everyone.'[25] This is also due to the fact that the decision on what is scholarly 'objective' and which legal theories and sources are accepted depends – like everything created by humans – on historical context.[26] The very existence of different theoretical schools,[27] the rise and fall of scholarly authority, of *mainstreams* and *orthodoxies*, foster Foucauldian scepticism towards an impartial genesis of knowledge in underlining the inner and outer 'politics of expertise'.[28] There is no escape from politics in the science of law.

---

21 Koselleck, *Vergangene Zukunft* 2017 (n. 7); Foucault, *L'archéologie* 1969 (n. 10); Weber, Max. 'Wissenschaft als Beruf', in *Max Weber, Gesamtausgabe*, vol. 1, eds. Birgit Morgenbrod, Wolfgang J. Mommsen and Wolfgang Schluchter (Tübingen: Mohr Siebeck, 1992); Horkheimer, Max. *Traditionelle und kritische Theorie: Fünf Aufsätze* (Frankfurt am Main: Fischer, 1992).

22 Peters, Anne. 'International Legal Scholarship under Challenge', in *International Law as a Profession*, eds. Jean d'Aspremont, Tarcisio Gazzini, André Nollkaemper and Wouter Werner (Cambridge: Cambridge University Press, 2017), 117–159, 129.

23 Kingsbury, Benedict. 'Legal Positivism as Normative Politics: International Society, Balance of Power and Lassa Oppenheim's Positive International Law'. *European Journal of International Law* 13(2) (2002), 401–436. On Oppenheim's project of positivism, see also García-Salmones, *Project of Positivism* 2013 (n. 15), chapter 2.

24 Oppenheim, Lassa. 'The Science of International Law: Its Tasks and Method'. *American Journal of International Law* 2(2) (1908), 313–356, 314, quoted after Kingsbury, *Legal Positivism* 2002 (n. 23), 403.

25 Koskenniemi, Martti. 'International Law in Europe: Between Tradition and Renewal'. *European Journal of International Law* 16(1) (2005), 113–124, 123.

26 Peters, *Scholarship* 2017 (n. 22), 134.

27 For an overview, see Orford, Anne and Florian Hoffmann, eds. *The Oxford Handbook of the Theory of International Law* (Oxford: Oxford University Press, 2016).

28 Kennedy, David W. 'The Politics of the Invisible College: International Governance and the Politics of Expertise'. *European Human Rights Law Review* 463(5) (2001), 463–497.

So, does that mean that law – perhaps not in its inner logic, but rather through the politicisability of legal knowledge – in the end is only politics, as *Realists* and critical legal scholars tell us?[29] After all, researching 'politicisation' – defined as 'making previously unpolitical matters political'[30] – in an already highly politicised field of knowledge might seem useless at best. For a theoretical answer, insights from *constructivist* norm research might help. According to these insides, law is indeed politics, and legal knowledge is always also political knowledge, but not *only*: Law possesses a certain logic of its own, which eludes too crude manipulation and abuse of law – something, which Lothar Brock has referred to as the intrinsic limits of the political instrumentalisation of law. Following Brock, the essential unavailability (*Unverfügbarkeit*) of law results from the fact that law can only serve as a political instrument as long as a relevant audience is acknowledging its normative meaning as law:[31] 'Those who use the language of law submit to the logic of law, because otherwise the reference to law would remain politically ineffective. Every reference to law is therefore an act of self-binding to law.'[32] Accordingly, despite its highly political nature, law is more than a mere continuation of politics by other means. Instead, the *politics of legal knowledge*, as I grasp them here, are defined as a scholar's *deliberate* ignorance, avoidance or selective application of international legal normativity because of extra-legal, i.e. political preferences.

Thus, the critical analysis proposed here aims at deconstructing these deliberate scholars' subordinations of law under politics and the justificatory strategy behind them. For this, I propose a reflexive analysis of historical discourses on war, politics and the histories of international law in the sense of Reinhart Koselleck: As Koselleck described it, writing history scientifically is simply impossible without theory formation on 'possible histories'. It depends on the historian's *Standpunkt*, his ideological biases. At the same time, however, the scholar's *Standpunkt* is limited by the fact that historical (and legal)

---

29 See, e. g., Hurd, Ian. *How to Do Things with International Law. A Provocative Reassessment of the Rule of Law in World Politics* (Princeton: Princeton University Press, 2017).

30 Zürn, Michael. 'The Politicization of World Politics and its Effects: Eight Propositions'. *European Political Science Review* 6(1) (2014), 47–71, 50.

31 Brock, Lothar. 'Frieden durch Recht. Anmerkungen zum Thema im historischen Kontext', in *Frieden durch Recht?*, eds. Peter Becker, Reiner Braun and Dieter Deiseroth (Berlin: Berliner Wissenschafts-Verlag, 2010), 15–34. See also Brock/Simon, *Selbstbehauptung* 2018 (n. 19) and Forst, Rainer. *Normativity and Power: Analyzing Social Orders of Justification* (Oxford: Oxford University Press, 2017).

32 Brock, Lothar. 'Frieden durch Recht. Zur Verteidigung einer Idee gegen die "harten Tatsachen" der internationalen Politik'. *Hessische Stiftung Friedens- und Konfliktforschung Standpunkte* 18(3) (2004), 8; Brock, *Frieden durch Recht* 2010 (n. 31).

sources have a *Vetorecht* (veto power).[33] It describes the possibility of (other) scholars to reject obviously wrong, i.e. untenable historical (or legal) interpretations and theories through source criticism. The task of a critical science of (the politics of) international law could therefore be to recognise the political character of law as well as its essential political unavailability, and to take on a mediating position of law as political *and* apolitical: In Anne Peters' words, 'scholars might acknowledge that an ambivalence between normative and positive analysis characterises international legal scholarship, and that this ambivalence embodies a tension which can be productive.'[34]

Even more: In writing histories of international law and its politics, these ambivalences increase, as we are not only confronted with our own *standpoints*, but also with those of the authors we write about. Nonetheless, reconstructing these *Standpunkte* developed by lawyers in specific historical contexts may help us to better understand not only the role of legal scholars in the field of tension between objective impartiality and political interests, but also the authority, politicisability and essential political unavailability of law. In order to stimulate such political-sociological perspectives on legal knowledge and modern justifications of war, the next section develops a short genealogy of the formation of (parts of) the modern war discourse and investigates the role of international legal knowledge in this genesis. For this, I turn to 19th-century Europe.

3 Politics, 19th-Century Legal Scholarship and the Birth of the Modern War Discourse

Liberal histories of legal progress classically recognise the 19th century war discourses as pre-modern and anarchical, followed by a 'New World Order' in the 20th century. In *The Internationalists*, Oona A. Hathaway und Scott J. Shapiro claim that in the 'Old World Order' prior to the legal prohibition of war in 1928, war was 'simply a continuation of politics by other means' – 'might was right'.[35] However, as I have argued elsewhere, the widespread positivist thesis of a 'free right to go to war' (*liberum ius ad bellum*) does not stand up to a closer examination of 19th-century legal theory and political practice; it constitutes a *Clausewitzian* myth (or fallacy) in the History of International Law.[36]

33 Koselleck, *Vergangene Zukunft* 2017 (n. 7).

34 Peters, *Scholarship* 2017 (n. 22), 134.

35 Hathaway/Shapiro, *The Internationalists* 2017 (n. 5), xv.

36 Simon, Hendrik. 'The Myth of *Liberum Ius ad Bellum*: Justifying War in 19th-Century Legal Theory and Political Practice'. *European Journal of International Law* 29(1) (2018), 113–136, doi: 10.1093/ejil/chy009. I have developed this argument in more detail in Simon,

In terms of the international normative order governing the use of force, the 19th century was not a century of anarchy. Instead, following the French Revolution(ary Wars), the long 19th century witnessed the birth of the modern discourse of war, normativity and international order.[37] While there existed no general legal prohibition of war, 'the preservation of the peace of Europe' became a desired norm both in legal theory and political practice. Although wars of aggression (if in different definitions of the term) have been regarded as illegitimate throughout human history,[38] now – in the 19th century – political and theoretical efforts to achieve a positive *ius contra bellum* were made for the first time.

However, in addition to legalisation, non-legal spheres also kept their discursive power in 19th century war discourses: *inter alia* morality, politics, social custom, economics, and, to an increasing extent, nationalism. My thesis is therefore that to this day the modern discourse of war is shaped by 'multinormativity'[39] and that for lawyers, this normative plurality poses both scientific challenges and political opportunities. Accordingly, the 19th-century legal-political debates on the use of force in the ambivalent interplay between nationalism[40] and internationalism are closer to the present than usually assumed. This makes it an ideal starting point for reflecting on the politics of legal knowledge and the justification of force in modernity.

3.1 *Revolutionary Mind-Sets: International Legal Scholarship at the Dawn of the 'Long 19th Century'*

When in 1796 German legal scholar Georg Friedrich Martens was commenting on recent developments in international law, he recognised the dialectic liaison between violence and (international) order: The war discourse in Revolutionary France had been radicalised. It challenged the acceptance of shared practices, sources and principles of international law. Nationalism was spreading. Martens through his close connections with the Hanover Electorate was a legal *and* political representative of the old international order in one

Hendrik. *Der Mythos vom „freien Recht zum Krieg". Zu einer Genealogie der modernen Kriegslegitimation* (forthcoming).

37 Ibid.

38 Ibid.; Tischer, *Herrschaftskommunikation* 2012 (n. 3); Lesaffer, Randall. 'Aggression before Versailles'. *European Journal of International Law* 29(3) (2018), 773–808, doi: 10.1093/ejil/chy038. See also the contributions in Brock/Simon, *Justification of War* 2021 (n. 1).

39 Vec, *Multinormativität* 2009 (n. 11).

40 Berman, Nathaniel. *Passion and Ambivalence: Colonialism, Nationalism, and International Law* (Leiden: Martinus Nijhoff, 2012).

way or another.[41] To him, the revolution and its natural-law principles seemed to endanger the society of sovereign states.[42] From Martens' conservative and positivist point of view, the revolutionary thinkers could not be taken seriously. Their natural law principles were developed essentially along concrete conflicts, not in abstract treatises: The justification of violence against the first of seven enemy coalitions (1792–1815) was debated in the French National Assembly. As many delegates were lawyers or philosophers – some of them publishing on politics and law –, political practice and legal/political theory were to some extent interwoven in these debates. Although widely ignored in the History of International Law,[43] the legal ideas of French Revolutionaries shaped the modern war discourse significantly.

While the revolutionary discourse on the use of force was pacifist in its early phase, this peaceful mantle was quickly thrown off. Now a narrative became central, which would challenge the international order for the entire 19th century: the principle of popular sovereignty.[44] In April 1792, revolutionaries both scandalised the alleged threat of a military intervention by Austria and Prussia and at the same time justified their 'counter violence' *au nom de la Nation*. After the Declaration of Pillnitz, the French nation was to be protected from monarchical interference. For this, the doctrine of 'just war' was modified: In 1792, this meant to justify preventive self-defence.

Particularly interesting for the French legal war discourse is Philippe Antoine Merlin de Douai, *un jurist en politique* experienced both in legal theory and practice.[45] In 1790, he justified an early case of French annexations, the case of Alsace: After having interpreted old international treaty law in favour of France, Merlin de Douai rejected this very treaty law as an 'old language' not to be used anymore. 'The law of nations is not founded on the treaties of princes'. Instead, he referred to the 'sovereignty of the people' in Alsace and the

41 Koskenniemi, Martti. 'Into Positivism: Georg Friedrich von Martens (1756–1821) and Modern International Law'. *Constellations* 15(2) (2008), 189–207.

42 Martens, Georg Friedrich von. *Einleitung in das positive Europäische Völkerrecht auf Verträge und Herkommen gegründet* (Göttingen: Dieterich, 1796), 297.

43 Lesaffer, Randall. 'In the Embrace of France. An Introduction', in *In the Embrace of France: The Law of Nations and Constitutional Law in the French Satellite States of the Revolutionary and Napoleonic Age (1789–1815)*, eds. Beatrix Jacobs, Raymund Kubben and Randall Lesaffer (Baden-Baden: Nomos, 2008), 7–14, 1, 7–14.

44 Yack, Bernard. 'Popular Sovereignty and Nationalism'. *Political Theory* 29(4) (2011), 517–536; Kolla, Edward J. *Sovereignty, International Law, and the French Revolution* (Cambridge: Cambridge University Press, 2017).

45 Leuwers, Hervé. *Un juriste en politique: Merlin de Douai, 1754–1838* (Arras: Artois Presses Université, 1996).

will of the Alsatian people to unite with the French.[46] As Hervé Leuwers and Edward J. Kolla have shown, Merlin de Douai argued as a politicised lawyer, not only in so far, as he adopted the normative language of the French Revolution – but also because of the fact that he was willing to propose to the German princes indemnities for Alsace instead of insisting on a consequent, 'objective' application of revolutionary law.

Another important example of the French Revolution's impact on theoretical war discourses is Immanuel Kant as a modern thinker on 'peace through legal progress': From a *Königsberger* distance, Kant witnessed the unfolding of the revolution with mixed feelings. On the one hand, he hoped for democratisation and legalisation of human relations through the proliferation of reason in open discourse. The telos of his normative project was a republican constitution. Thus, Kant had sympathies for the revolutionary ideas of prohibiting wars of aggression, which seemed to indicate the emergence of a peaceful republic. This meant that Kant was hostile to a forceful spread of the revolution via conquest.[47] He neither accepted wars justified by natural law nor by political interests.

On the other hand, however, recent studies argue that Kant was not only enthusiastic about the revolution and indifferent to the execution of King Louis XVI,[48] but – while denying a right to resistance against a self-determined and liberal legislation – he also assumed a right to resist tyrants and despots acting against the law.[49] The latter assumption is plausible insofar as Kant tolerated revolutionary violence if it resulted in an adequate constitution.[50] Kant's idea of law was that it would overcome violence – but at the same time he accepted political violence embedded in legal emancipation. The dialectics of the Enlightenment become plainly apparent here. If even the legal-theoretical thinking of Kant was not entirely free of the politics of his time, it is reasonable to assume that multi-normativity would prevail in 19th century legal thinking on war and peace: With Kant, positive law became the new theology of the

---

46 Kolla, *Sovereignty* 2017 (n. 44), 64–66.

47 Kant, Immanuel. *Project for a Perpetual Peace: A Philosophical Essay* (London: Couchman, 1796).

48 Paula Oliveira, Maria Lúcia de. 'Compatibility of the Moral Foundation of Law in Kant with the Theory of Reflective Judgment and with the Kantian Theory of Revolution', in *Kant's Theory of Law*, eds. Jean-Christophe Merle and Alexandre Trivisonno (Stuttgart: Franz Steiner Verlag, 2015), 35–44.

49 Pfordten, Dietmar von der. 'Kant on the Right of Resistance', in *Kant's Theory of Law*, eds. Jean-Christophe Merle and Alexandre Trivisonno (Stuttgart: Franz Steiner Verlag, 2015), 101–119.

50 Eberl, Oliver and Peter Niesen. *Immanuel Kant. Zum ewigen Frieden und Auszüge aus der Rechtslehre – Kommentare* (Frankfurt am Main: Suhrkamp, 2011), 291.

normative discourse of modernity[51] – and legal scholars became its priests. However, convinced as they may have been – these priests always had other gods beside them. Nationalism was one of them.

3.2 *The (Dis-)Unity of Law: Nationalism, War and Legal Scholarship in the 19th Century*

When the principle of self-determination underpinning the French Revolutionary Wars shook up Europe's international order, the Great Powers aimed at restoring order at the Congress of Vienna. 'Vienna 1814/15' became a 'decisive turning point' of international history:[52] From now on, multilateral diplomacy was to guarantee a general European peace between the Great Powers. Political conflicts were to be judged in 'perfect concert';[53] unilateral warfare beyond the consensus of the Great Powers became inacceptable. Of course, the use of force remained the object of a highly political discourse, but at the same time, legal rules and behavioural norms played an important role – and lawyers became central actors in ordering this discourse.[54]

Perhaps the Concert's central construction error was its mismanagement of social conflicts: The Great Powers nullified the revolutionary legal principle of self-determination. Yet, they could not expel it from the *Zeitgeist*.[55] Social conflicts did not simply disappear. As Jürgen Osterhammel has put it: The 19th century may not have been a century of nation states (instead of empires), but it was a century of *nationalism* as an emerging political mythology.[56] Nationalism both delegitimised the existing legal order of empires and promoted an international order based on the nation state.[57] This becomes apparent in the fact that war was the first instrument of choice for achieving nationalist unification as in the German Unification Wars and the Italian

51 Habermas, Jürgen. *The Philosophical Discourse of Modernity: Twelve Lectures* (Cambridge: Massachusetts Institute of Technology Press, 1990).

52 Schroeder, Paul W. *The Transformation of European Politics. 1763–1848* (Oxford: Oxford University Press, 1994), vii.

53 Schulz, Matthias. *Normen und Praxis. Das Europäische Konzert der Großmächte als Sicherheitsrat, 1815–1860* (Berlin: De Gruyter, 2009), 4.

54 Simon, *Myth* 2018 (n. 36); Payk, *Frieden durch Recht?* 2018 (n. 3).

55 Fisch, Jörg. *A History of the Self-Determination of Peoples: The Domestication of an Illusion* (Cambridge: Cambridge University Press, 2015), 105.

56 Osterhammel, Jürgen. *The Transformation of the World: A Global History of the Nineteenth Century* (Princeton: Princeton University Press, 2014).

57 Summers, James. *Peoples and International Law: How Nationalism and Self-Determination Shape a Contemporary Law of Nations* (Leiden: Martinus Nijhoff, 2007).

Risorgimento, and that nationalism finally devastated the European Concert in the Great War.

Starting from this contribution's core thesis that legal scholarship is open to politicisation, it comes as no surprise that especially in the German and Italian territories legal doctrines referred to the principles of self-determination and nationalism. An important theoretical source was Friedrich Carl von Savigny's historical school of law and its 'supranational historicism'.[58] Savigny, a German conservative and cosmopolitan lawyer, believed in the lawyer's task to reflect on the 'legal conscience' of a national culture (*Volksgeist*).[59] Accordingly, *Völker* should become the prime actors in international law.

This historical school was influential particularly among 19th-century liberal nationalist legal scholars like Mancini, Bluntschli or Lieber.[60] While Savigny himself was sceptical about German nationalism at his time, his followers more and more reconciled liberalism and (moderate) nationalism. This liaison between liberalism and nationalism seems contradictory from a later point of view and the collective memory of two World Wars. Already in 1910, Westlake would warn that nationalities, 'though often important in politics, must be kept outside of international law'.[61] Yet the liaison was logically plausible in the mid-19th century as multinational empires were at the time the most illiberal states and nationalism could be seen as an emancipatory mission.[62]

Accordingly, the appeal that European 'civilised' peoples had the right to unite had an anti-imperial impetus. The Italian Pasquale Stanislao Mancini referred to the French Revolution and argued in favour of peoples' moral and legal right to unite in a state.[63] In fact, liberal lawyers usually did not understand nationalism and internationalism as contradicting, but as consecutive principles. But the lawyers' 'reflexive relationship' with the *Volk*,[64] as Savigny had described it, also made liberal lawyers become more and more committed to national, and, with this, to political projects. From now on, it made a political difference whether someone was a *German*, *French* or *Russian* international lawyer.

58 Koskenniemi, Martti. *The Gentle Civilizer of Nations: The Rise and Fall of International Law, 1870–1960* (Cambridge: Cambridge University Press, 2002), 45; Shahabuddin, Mohammad. *Ethnicity and International Law. Histories, Politics and Practices* (Cambridge: Cambridge University Press, 2016), 53.

59 Koskenniemi, *Gentle Civilizer* 2002 (n. 58), 45.

60 Summers, *Peoples and International Law* 2007 (n. 57), 112.

61 Ibid., 157.

62 Ibid.

63 Kolla, *Sovereignty* 2017 (n. 44), 294.

64 Koskenniemi, *Gentle Civilizer* 2002 (n. 58), 43.

Furthermore, liberal scholars began to accept political violence as a means of legal progress. With this, Kelsen's boundaries between law and politics became blurred. Particularly revealing are the writings of German (speaking) liberal lawyers in the context of the German Wars of Unification. An important example is Swiss lawyer Johann Caspar Bluntschli, professor in Heidelberg and later one of the founding members of the *Institut de Droit International*: Bluntschli wrote in Kant's legal pacifist tradition. Accordingly, he strove for a complete legalisation of war in the sense of a positive *ius contra bellum*. Bluntschli became a main opponent of those German legal scholars who would recognise war as a *Clausewitzian* political instrument.[65] A war for political reasons was to be rejected, wrote Bluntschli: 'The mere interest of the state in itself does not justify war.'[66] In *this* respect, he perfectly corresponded to Kelsen's ideal type of a legal scholar advocating the de-politicisation of law.

However, Bluntschli not only sympathised with Bismarck's unification policy from a scholarly distance, he also justified it as a member of the Baden Parliament. In *this* respect, he corresponded to Kelsen's real type of a politicisable legal scholar. Even if Bluntschli rejected Rousseau's *Contrat Social* as the basis of state theory, the analogy of his justification of Prussia's wars to those of French revolutionary legal scholar Merlin de Douai is astonishing: Bluntschli wrote of the 'holy, natural and important right' of a *Volk* as a political community. The necessity of a contemporary reorganisation of the state was to be recognised and carried out. At the same time, the existence of the historically evolved law had to be protected as long as it was viable and contemporary, argued Bluntschli.[67] Obviously, however, this also meant that positive law should not be regarded as sacrosanct. Rather, the Concert's norms of restraint were to be abandoned when they proved to be out of date. According to Bluntschli, contesting emerging law (*werdendes Recht*) meant disregarding the 'vital nature of right' (*lebendige Natur des Rechts*) and, thus, the further development of law as a means of 'self-fulfilment of peoples' (*Entwicklung der Völker*). In this understanding of law as a living body, Savigny's impact on Bluntschli's thinking becomes clear.

But Bluntschli also left Savigny clearly behind, as he was referring to nationalism and self-determination as narratives for the justification of the German Wars of Unification. This is remarkable: It is clear not only to subsequent

65 Lueder, Karl. 'Krieg und Kriegsrecht im Allgemeinen', in *Handbuch des Völkerrechts*, ed. Franz von Holtzendorff (Berlin: Haber, 1889), 169–397, 169, 180–184. See also Simon, *Myth* 2018 (n. 36).

66 Bluntschli, Johann Caspar. *Das moderne Völkerrecht der civilisirten Staten: als Rechtsbuch dargestellt* (Nördlingen: C.H. Beck, 1868), 290–291.

67 Ibid.

historians, but it was also recognised by some contemporaries that Bismarck had planned the wars for a considerable time and unleashed them for purely political reasons – even though Bismarck tried to bring his policies into line with the norms of the European Concert. Bismarck tried to justify the war against France as a defensive war[68] when Bismarck's *Realpolitik* had already become obvious in the war of 1866, which had begun without a declaration of war.

Nevertheless, Bluntschli followed Bismarck in declaring the Franco-Prussian War as a defensive war.[69] Furthermore, Bluntschli described Bismarck as one of the two most brilliant statesmen in German history – alongside Frederic the Great. What a curious admiration of a liberal lawyer for two of the most explicit representatives of Prussian *Realpolitik*! Bluntschli justified the violent integration of Schleswig and Holstein into the German Confederation (1864) as well as the 1866 war against Austria as an emancipatory act of a German nation that 'defends its right and honour' (*seine Ehre zu wahren, und daher sein Recht*).[70]

Bluntschli's justification was clearly based on an understanding of nations as catalysts for legal progress. While for Bluntschli a state did not have to be ethnically homogeneous, it had to have a certain status of power and 'civilization'.[71] As a cosmopolitan, Bluntschli sought to reconcile law, nationalism and liberalism. In this context, violence was acceptable for the liberal cosmopolitan – if it served the right national purpose. With this, the analogies in Bluntschli's and Merlin de Douai's thinking become clear: Both delegitimised 'old', dynastic international law in favour of a nation's unity derived from natural law. According to Bluntschli, people had the right 'to take the state-form necessary to develop its natural capacity, to fulfil its destiny, to ensure its security and to preserve its honour, and therefore the right to resort to arms if necessary.' In his view, this was 'a much more sacred, natural and important right than any dynastic law'.[72] Like Merlin de Douai in 1790, Bluntschli advocated progress *de lege ferenda*, based on natural law, nationalism and political convictions. As becomes evident here, multi-normativity was still alive in the war discourse of the so-called 'positivist century'.[73]

68 Simon, *Myth* 2018 (n. 36).

69 Bluntschli, Johann Caspar. *Das moderne Völkerrecht in dem Kriege 1870: Rede zum Geburtsfeste des höchstseligen Grossherzogs Karl Friedrich von Baden und zur akademischen Preisvertheilung am 22. November 1870* (Heidelberg: Mohr, 1870).

70 Bluntschli, *Das moderne Völkerrecht* 1868 (n. 66), 291.

71 Bluntschli, Johann Caspar. *The Theory of the State* (Kitchener: Batoche Books, 1875), 94.

72 Bluntschli, *Das moderne Völkerrecht* 1868 (n. 66), 291.

73 Vec, Miloš. 'Sources in the 19th Century European Tradition: The Myth of Positivism', in *The Oxford Handbook of the Sources of International Law*, eds. Samantha Besson and Jean d'Aspremont (Oxford: Oxford University Press, 2017), 121–145.

Similarly – but from a different legal-theoretical perspective – liberal lawyer Rudolf von Jhering expressed sympathy for the German unification in private correspondences.[74] What is remarkable here is Rudolf von Jhering's inner conflict emerging from the tension between law, morality and his political sympathy for Prussian nationalism, as expressed in a letter to Austrian lawyer Julius Glaser of 1 May 1866: Jhering, who described himself in the letter as an opponent of the Austrian political system – 'but not of the Austrians' –, wrote that perhaps no war had ever been started with a 'shamelessness' (*Schamlosigkeit*), 'a horrible frivolity' (*grauenhaften Frivolität*), as the one Bismarck was trying to drum up against Austria at that time. Jhering was outraged at such 'an offence against all the principles of law and morality'. However, he felt a contradiction between law and politics in himself: His sense of law (*Rechtsgefühl*) and his political interests had come into 'a tragic conflict', as he reported to Glaser. From a legal perspective, Jhering felt the duty to wish Austria luck in war. However, for political reasons, he felt the need to wish the 'unjust cause' – Prussia's victory – success in the battlefield.

Obviously, there were two hearts pounding in Jhering's chest, one political and one legal: Finally, Jhering's political heart was to beat faster, as he informed Leipzig legal scholar Bernhard Joseph Hubert Windscheid in a letter of 15 June 1866:[75] He bowed to the genius of Bismarck, who had 'delivered a political masterpiece'. And Jhering even mocked the powerless honesty and scientific objectivity of legal scholars: Full of national pride, Jhering concluded, for a political genius like Bismarck, he would give a hundred of liberals of powerless honesty. What a triumph of politics over law! Of course, these were private correspondences, not scientific treatises. And it is also true that Jhering was very open and reflective about his initial discomfort with his own euphoria about Prussia's wars. Nevertheless, Jhering weighed between law and politics, and made a clear decision: Politics was it.

The arguments of Jhering and Bluntschli – two of the most important German liberal lawyers at their times – demonstrate that Kelsen would be right in his concern that legal scholars could become the mouthpiece of nationalist power politics. The devastating potentials of nationalism as a source of war justification became even clearer at the end of the century. As I have shown elsewhere,[76] the unification of Germany – praised by liberal legal

74 Quoted according to Faber, Karl-Georg. 'Realpolitik als Ideologie. Die Bedeutung des Jahres 1866 für das politische Denken in Deutschland'. *Historische Zeitschrift* 203(1) (1966), 1–45.

75 Ibid.

76 Simon, *Myth* 2018 (n. 36).

scholars – enabled the development of a German legal doctrine oriented towards a *Clausewitzian* understanding of war, which placed *Realpolitik* above the need to contain war. This became obvious in German justifications of violence in the contexts of the Herero and Nama Genocide and the First World War.[77] Of course, in the latter, lawyers of all nations succumbed to nationalism. But particularly in German political and legal discourse, militarism and nationalism had now at last outdone liberalism – politics had won over law, Clausewitz over Kant.

3.3 *Inventing Intervention, Circumventing Law: Another Normative Telos of Modernity*

The prime instrument of the European Great Powers to counter emerging nationalism was military intervention. What distinguished it from war was that a military intervention should not be conducted in the name of unilateral interests, but in the name of the 'international community'.[78] Interventions thus were to enforce the norms of the Concert. In view of its highly political character, however, intervention was also repeatedly a test for Concert diplomacy. Particularly in legal doctrine, intervention became one of the most debated issues of the 19th century.[79] It was poorly regulated not to stand in the way of the Concert's interests: The vocabulary of positive law was not to become a language barrier for politics.

In the course of the 19th century, a new type of intervention emerged as part of dealing with the *Oriental Question*: 'humanitarian intervention'.[80] According to Russian lawyer Fedor Fedorovich Martens, a military intervention was justifiable following the 'commonality of religious interests and the commandments of humanity, that is the principles of natural law'. The Eurocentric focus of intervention came to light when Martens added that an

---

77 Hull, Isabel V. *Absolute Destruction. Military Culture and the Practices of War in Imperial Germany* (Ithaca: Cornell University Press, 2005); Hull, Isabel V. *A Scrap of Paper: Breaking and Making International Law during the Great War* (Ithaca: Cornell University Press, 2014).

78 Schulz, *Normen und Praxis* 2009 (n. 53).

79 Vec, Miloš. 'Intervention / Nichtintervention, Verrechtlichung der Politik und Politisierung des Völkerrechts im 19. Jahrhundert', in *Macht und Recht. Völkerrecht in den internationalen Beziehungen*, eds. Ulrich Lappenküper and Reiner Marcowitz (Paderborn: Schöningh, 2010), 135–160.

80 Rougier, Antoine. 'La théorie de l'intervention d'humanité'. *Revue génerale de droit international public* 17 (1910), 468–526.

intervention was explicitly legitimate 'in Turkey, China, Japan and other Asian states' if the Christian population was subjected to persecution or 'slaughter'.[81]

In the debates on 'humanitarian interventions', international lawyers played a central role, as can be illustrated with a view to the Russo-Turkish War of 1877/78: With the Crimean War of 1853–56, the Oriental Question had interrupted, but not destroyed the Vienna Peace Order. The defeat of the Russians against the alliance of the Ottoman Empire, England, France and Piedmont-Sardinia was clearly expressed in the Peace Treaty of 1856. Article 9 of the treaty prohibited intervention in the territory of the Ottoman Empire; this was backed by the assurance on the part of the Ottoman Sultan to improve the situation of the Christian population in the Balkan regions. Article 7 formally granted the Ottoman Empire participation in the European community of international law and in the Concert of the Great Powers, although it did not *de facto* grant it the status of a European Great Power. These provisions of the Treaty of Paris amounted to a regional ban on intervention which was clearly directed against Russian war policies. According to the peace treaty, positive international law denied Russia the right to intervene into what was to be considered as the internal affairs of the Ottoman Empire. Nevertheless, on 24 April 1877, Russian Tsar Alexander II declared war on the Sublime Porte after Turkish armed forces had suppressed uprisings in their Balkan areas in the spring of 1876 using extensive force and killing numerous civilians in the so-called *Bulgarian Horrors*.

It is not surprising that the legal ban on intervention formulated in the treaty as positive law was invoked as a normative obstacle to the justification of the Russian use of force. Russian Foreign Minister Alexander Gorchakov summed up the Russian denial of the norm by claiming that 'the European action in Turkey has been reduced to impotency by the stipulations of 1856'.[82] According to Gorchakov, Turkey's independence had to be subordinated to 'interests of humanity, the Christian community and general peace'.[83] Russia was successful with its strategy to invalidate Article 9 of the Peace of 1856 after the victorious war against the Ottomans: In the Berlin Treaty of 1878, the norm of non-intervention into the internal affairs of the Ottoman Empire was abandoned. This was the political side of the matter.

---

81 Martens, Friedrich von. *Völkerrecht. Das internationale Recht der civilisirten Nationen* (Berlin: Weidmann, 1883), 302.

82 Gortschakow, 19th November 1876, in *The Map of Europe by Treaty. Showing the Various Political and Territorial Changes which Have Taken Place since the General Peace of 1814. With Numerous Maps and Notes*, vol. 4: 1875–1891, ed. Edward Hertslet (London: Butterworths, 1891), 2523.

83 Gortschakow, 19th November 1877, in Hertslet, *Map of Europe* 1891 (n. 82), 2524.

As to the academic side, Fedor Fedorovich Martens, law professor and diplomat in St. Petersburg, was entrusted with the task of investigating Russian politics scientifically – or, rather, with justifying it? Martens' dual professional role[84] is particularly interesting here: On the one hand, he was a legal scholar highly respected throughout Europe. On the other hand, Martens was crown jurist of the Russian Tsar as well as diplomat of the Russian Foreign Ministry. Thus, he was recognised as 'the most legal-minded of diplomats and the most expert diplomat among lawyers'.[85] In a 46-page 'historical study' published in West and Central European journals in 1877, Martens examined the Russian 'intervention' in the Ottoman Empire. In his study, Martens argued that the protection of Christians in Turkey was a pan-European responsibility. However, since the Great Powers were disunited, Russia had a '*moral* and *legal* right to intervene in Turkey's internal affairs'.[86] With this argument, Martens attempted to disguise Russia's political interests in the Balkans by referring to the humanitarian task of the international community.

Like Gorchakov, Martens referred in particular to Article 9 of the 1856 peace treaty and the Sultan's voluntary concessions therein to improve the lot of the Christian population: According to Martens, Russia had only signed the treaty in 1856 because the European Concert had assumed the right of collective intervention in Russia's place. Thus, in Martens' view the Treaty of Paris had neither left Christians to 'Muslim fanaticism' nor abolished 'Europe's right to intervene'.[87] If Europe did not exert its right, the powers particularly involved in the Oriental question were free to intervene – the article could not be interpreted differently, Martens argued.[88] Martens constructed a Russian right and obligation to intervene in the Ottoman Empire, for which he combined historical law – in particular the Treaty of Kütschük-Kainardschi of 1774 – and religious rights of Christians.

What is striking, however, is that Martens did not fully discuss Article 9 of the Treaty of Paris in his essay. He simply ignored its ban of interventions. Moreover, a comparison of Martens' argumentation in his 'historical study' and his scientific textbook on international law of 1883 reveals an interesting

---

84 Mälksoo, Lauri. 'F. F. Martens and His Time: When Russia Was an Integral Part of the European Tradition of International Law'. *European Journal of International Law* 25(3) (2014), 811–829.

85 Eyffinger, Arthur. *The 1907 Hague Peace Conference: 'The Conscience of the Civilized World'* (The Hague: Judicap, 2007), 29.

86 Martens, Friedrich von. *Die russische Politik in der Orientalischen Frage. Eine historische Studie* (St. Petersburg: H. Schmitzdorff, 1877), 45 et seq. (italics in the original).

87 Ibid., 19.

88 Ibid., 15.

self-contradiction: In 1877, Martens denied the fact that the treaty of 1856 had established a legal prohibition of unilateral intervention into the Ottoman Empire. In the second volume of his 1883 textbook, however, Martens criticised the 1856 treaty precisely for having abolished the right both of collective and unilateral intervention.[89] This criticism presupposes, of course, that Martens recognised the non-intervention norm set out in 1856 as legally binding. Even Martens' observation that Europe had turned to illegal politics of intervention in the Orient before with the French occupation of Syria in 1860, on closer examination turns into an argument against his own reasoning: The intervention of 1860 was preceded by negotiations between the Great Powers and the Ottoman Empire, in which – as Martens himself admitted – the Ottoman Empire agreed to an intervention.[90] Moreover, the accusation that Europe had broken the non-intervention norm of 1856 in 1860 seems downright absurd in view of the fact that Martens himself ignored this prohibition of military intervention in his study of 1877.

In any case, Martens' remarks were incompatible with the positive law of the normative sub-order of 1856. Martens simply became an apologist of Alexander's II politics of war: In his argumentation, international law and politics are inseparable. Martens' study can be understood as a justification for the offensive Russian policy towards the Orient. Instead of a legal scientific study of positive law, Martens presented a political treatise. Martens even opposed the attempt of other members of the *Institut de Droit* to publicly protest Russian excesses of violence and its violations of positive law during the campaign – ironically, he did so in the name of 'scientific neutrality'.[91] Even though, from a methodological perspective, Martens' argumentation is highly interesting: He mixed alleged historical law (customs) and natural law in order to delegitimise the treaty law of 1856. At the same time, the new positive legal norm of 1878 was scientifically fleshed out with reference to natural law and historical customs of civilised states.

Martens' claim that his study was not 'to influence the judgment of our readers'[92] seems hardly credible – for the true intentions of Martens' study were revealed in the introduction to the German translation in the *Russische Revue*: Accordingly, the aim of the publication was 'to eliminate the still widespread misconceptions about Russia's oriental politics and its goals in the Orient.'[93] In

89 Martens, *Völkerrecht* 1883 (n. 81), 127.
90 Martens, *Russische Politik* 1877 (n. 86), 21.
91 Koskenniemi, *International Law in Europe* 2005 (n. 25), 124.
92 Martens, *Russische Politik* 1877 (n. 86), 2.
93 Ibid., 1.

fact, politics had triumphed over scholarly 'objectivity' here. Again, natural law had become the most important instrument to enforce political goals and to circumvent positive law. In the 19th century, it remained a substitute religion for the priests of positive law.

4 Conclusion and Outlook: The Multi-Normativity of Legal Knowledge in the Modern War Discourse

The starting point of this chapter was a distinction between 'objective' and 'political' scholars developed based on some of Hans Kelsen's works. The politicisability of legal scholars was first discussed at a theoretical level and then illustrated by analysing discursive fragments from the modern discourse of war and international order in its epoch of birth, the 'long 19th century'. This was done without any claim to provide the last word on the issue, but rather to (re-)open this exciting field of research by demonstrating the fuzziness of the borderlines between legal and political discourse. Of course, I could only address individual examples as 'illustrations' of the politicisability of international legal scholars here; however, these illustrations refer to lawyers/ legal thinkers who were particularly respected in their times.

Thus, what can be concluded here is quite remarkable: *Firstly*, all legal scholars examined in this chapter were politicisable in the sense of Hans Kelsen's real type. Some of them confessed their political projects, if with a certain uneasiness: During the German Wars of Unification, Jhering felt both a legal and a political heart beating in his chest. In contrast, Fedor Fedorovich Martens tried to disguise his political objectives by claiming 'scientific objectivity'. The misuse of the latter helped to suppress the intrinsic value of law and even to marginalise scientific opponents in the name of scientific neutrality – just as Kelsen would criticise.

Secondly, there is an astonishing similarity in the justification strategies of the legal scholars examined: Merlin de Douai, Bluntschli, Jhering and Martens all justified breaches of positive law in accord with their political programs by pointing to a plurality of normative arguments, be it natural law, nationalism, self-determination, custom, honour, or even openly formulated political interests. Furthermore, *lege ferenda* was played out against *lege lata*. As can be clearly observed here, the modern war discourse, which emerged in the so-called 'positivist 19th century',[94] is characterised by multi-normativity. This has considerable effects on legal scholarship and its politicisability.

94 Critically on this term Vec, *Sources* 2017 (n. 73).

In order to return to the starting point of this symposium: What do these paradoxes tell us about the relationship between law and politics? *Firstly*, that law is politically contested,[95] and that legal scholars are political actors in the struggle for law (Jhering). Lawyers are not only affected by the shadow of war, it is also lawyers who turn this shadow into a smokescreen. *Secondly*, it is worth looking twice at who is speaking in legal discourse, from which *Standpunkt* and with what arguments, and how law is dealt with as a political instrument *and* as a politically unavailable phenomenon.[96] Deconstructing the frequent political projects behind legal knowledge helps us to better grasp the fateful liaison between violence, politics and law.[97]

Thus, a broader comparison of historical case studies in the sense of a *political sociology of international legal knowledge* in the field of justifying force could provide us with patterns about when and why scholars throughout modernity were susceptible to politicisation (or not). Perhaps it could even help us to answer the question whether we are 'better off than those colleagues who set up the profession of international law' 147 years ago'[98] – insofar as the reference to expanding positive law and particularly the legal prohibition of force in Art. 2 (4) UN Charter might enable 'us' to oppose arbitrary politicisation of legal knowledge more effectively and in the sense of Koselleck's *Vetorecht*.[99]

But then again, would not this reference to positivism be politically motivated itself, as Lassa Oppenheim admitted? So, are we moving in circles in our attempt to do justice to Kelsen's ideal of an apolitical researcher – and should we possibly abandon this ideal altogether? Or is it worth bearing this ambivalence of science and politics – and if so, for whom?

Part of my argument in this chapter with its focus on the 19th century was that narratives of progress or the impossibility of progress in the face of eternal anarchy are always deceptive. As could only be indicated here, in light of the fact that the 19th century is not an anarchic mirror-image of the modern

95 For the concept of 'contestation' in the Theory of International Relations, see Wiener, Antje. *Contestation and Constitution of Norms in Global International Relations* (Cambridge: Cambridge University Press, 2018).

96 Brock, *Frieden durch Recht* 2010 (n. 31).

97 Benjamin, *Critique* 1978 (n. 19); Foucault, *L'archéologie* 1969 (n. 10); Brock/Simon, *Selbstbehauptung* 2018 (n. 19).

98 Koskenniemi, *International Law in Europe* 2005 (n. 25),

99 Critically on this issue Peevers, Charlotte. *The Politics of Justifying Force. The Suez Crisis, the Iraq War, and International Law* (Oxford: Oxford University Press, 2013); see also Marauhn, Thilo. 'How Many Deaths Can Art 2 (4) UN Charter Die?', in *The Justification of War and International Order. From Past to Present*, eds. Lothar Brock and Hendrik Simon (Oxford: Oxford University Press, 2021).

discourse of war and international order, but rather marks its beginning,[100] the 'radical' plans to outlaw war[101] of 1920, 1928 or 1945 appear much less radical seen from a perspective of *longue durée*.[102] Thus, the cases described here are more than anecdotes – in their logic of justification of war they appear as part of our present. Nationalism and multi-normativity are still with us. A glance at more recent scholarly justifications of the use of force – regarding the NATO-intervention in Kosovo (1999), the Iraq War (2003) or the Russian annexation of the Crimea (2014) – seems to confirm Kelsen's concern: Legal scholars can always be the mouthpieces of the powerful – and thus not only gentle civilisers, but at the same time gentle justifiers of violence.

Acknowledgments

I am grateful to Lothar Brock, Anthony Carty, Anne Peters, Miloš Vec and the anonymous reviewers for helpful comments and advice. A first draft of this text was presented at the stimulating JHIL-symposium on 'Politics and the Histories of International Law' in Heidelberg on 15 February 2019.

Bibliography

Benjamin, Walter. 'Critique of Violence', in *Walter Benjamin, Reflections: Essays, Aphorisms, Autobiographical Writings*, ed. Peter Demetz (Boston: Harcourt, 1978).

Benton, Lauren. 'Beyond Anachronism: Histories of International Law and Global Legal Politics'. *Journal of the History of International Law* 21(1) (2019), 7–40, doi .org/10.1163/15718050-12340100.

Berman, Nathaniel. *Passion and Ambivalence: Colonialism, Nationalism, and International Law* (Leiden: Martinus Nijhoff, 2012).

Bernstorff, Jochen von. 'International Legal Scholarship as a Cooling Medium in International Law and Politics'. *European Journal of International Law* 25(4) (2014), 977–990, doi.org/10.1093/ejil/chu073.

Bluntschli, Johann Caspar. *Das moderne Völkerrecht der civilisirten Staten: als Rechtsbuch dargestellt* (Nördlingen: C. H. Beck, 1868).

100 Simon, *Myth* 2018 (n. 36).

101 Hathaway/Shapiro, *The Internationalists* 2017 (n. 5).

102 For such a perspective of *longue durée* see Brock/Simon, *Justification of War* 2021 (n. 1).

Bluntschli, Johann Caspar. *Das moderne Völkerrecht in dem Kriege 1870: Rede zum Geburtsfeste des höchstseligen Grossherzogs Karl Friedrich von Baden und zur akademischen Preisvertheilung am 22. November 1870* (Heidelberg: Mohr, 1870).

Bluntschli, Johann Caspar. *The Theory of the State* (Kitchener: Batoche Books, 1875).

Brock, Lothar. 'Frieden durch Recht. Zur Verteidigung einer Idee gegen "die harten Tatsachen" der internationalen Politik'. *Hessische Stiftung Friedens- und Konfliktforschung Standpunkte* 18(3) (2004).

Brock, Lothar. 'Frieden durch Recht. Anmerkungen zum Thema im historischen Kontext', in *Frieden durch Recht?*, eds. Peter Becker, Reiner Braun and Dieter Deiseroth (Berlin: Berliner Wissenschafts-Verlag, 2010), 15–34.

Brock, Lothar and Hendrik Simon. 'Die Selbstbehauptung und Selbstgefährdung des Friedens als Herrschaft des Rechts'. *Politische Vierteljahresschrift* 59(2) (2018), 269–291.

Brock, Lothar and Hendrik Simon, eds. *The Justification of War and International Order. From Past to Present* (Oxford: Oxford University Press, 2021).

Carty, Anthony. 'Critical International Law: Recent Trends in the Theory of International Law'. *European Journal of International Law* 2(1) (1991), 1–27.

Carty, Anthony. 'Doctrine versus State Practice', in *Oxford Handbook of the History of International Law*, eds. Bardo Fassbender and Anne Peters (Oxford: Oxford University Press, 2012), 972–996.

Duve, Thomas. 'Was ist "Multinormativität"? – Einführende Bemerkungen'. *Rechtsgeschichte – Legal History* 25 (2017), 88–101.

Eberl, Oliver and Peter Niesen. *Immanuel Kant. Zum ewigen Frieden und Auszüge aus der Rechtslehre – Kommentare* (Frankfurt am Main: Suhrkamp, 2011).

Eyffinger, Arthur. *The 1907 Hague Peace Conference: 'The Conscience of the Civilized World'* (The Hague: Judicap, 2007).

Faber, Karl-Georg. 'Realpolitik als Ideologie. Die Bedeutung des Jahres 1866 für das politische Denken in Deutschland'. *Historische Zeitschrift* 203(1) (1966), 1–45.

Fisch, Jörg. *A History of the Self-Determination of Peoples: The Domestication of an Illusion* (Cambridge: Cambridge University Press, 2015).

Forst, Rainer. *Normativity and Power: Analyzing Social Orders of Justification* (Oxford: Oxford University Press, 2017).

Foucault, Michel. *L'archéologie du savoir* (Paris: Gallimard, 1969).

García-Salmones Rovira, Mónica. *The Project of Positivism in International Law* (Oxford: Oxford University Press, 2013).

Habermas, Jürgen. *The Philosophical Discourse of Modernity: Twelve Lectures* (Cambridge: Massachusetts Institute of Technology Press, 1990).

Hathaway, Oona A. and Scott Shapiro. *The Internationalists: How a Radical Plan to Outlaw War Remade the World* (New York: Simon & Schuster, 2017).

Hertslet, Edward, ed. *The Map of Europe by Treaty. Showing the Various Political and Territorial Changes which Have Taken Place since the General Peace of 1814. With Numerous Maps and Notes*, vol. 4 (London: Butterworths, 1891).

Horkheimer, Max. *Traditionelle und kritische Theorie: Fünf Aufsätze* (Frankfurt am Main: Fischer, 1992).

Hull, Isabel V. *Absolute Destruction. Military Culture and the Practices of War in Imperial Germany* (Ithaca: Cornell University Press, 2005).

Hull, Isabel V. *A Scrap of Paper: Breaking and Making International Law during the Great War* (Ithaca: Cornell University Press, 2014).

Hurd, Ian. *How to Do Things with International Law. A Provocative Reassessment of the Rule of Law in World Politics* (Princeton: Princeton University Press, 2017).

Janssen, Wilhelm. *Die Anfänge des modernen Völkerrechts und der neuzeitlichen Diplomatie: Ein Forschungsbericht* (Stuttgart: Metzler, 1965).

Kant, Immanuel. *Project for a Perpetual Peace: A Philosophical Essay* (London: Couchman, 1796).

Kelsen, Hans. 'Juristischer Formalismus und Reine Rechtslehre'. *Juristische Wochenschrift* 58(3) (1929), 1723–1726.

Kelsen, Hans. *Peace through Law* (Chapel Hill: The University of North Carolina Press, 1944).

Kelsen, Hans. 'Science and Politics'. *The American Political Science Review* 45(3) (1951), 641–661.

Kennedy, David W. 'The Politics of the Invisible College: International Governance and the Politics of Expertise'. *European Human Rights Law Review* 463(5) (2001), 463–497.

Kingsbury, Benedict. 'Legal Positivism as Normative Politics: International Society, Balance of Power and Lassa Oppenheim's Positive International Law'. *European Journal of International Law* 13(2) (2002), 401–436.

Kleingeld, Pauline. 'What do the Virtuous Hope for? Re-reading Kant's Doctrine of the Highest Good', in *Proceedings of the Eighth International Kant Congress: Memphis, 1995*, eds. Hoke Robinson (Milwaukee: Marquette University Press, 1995).

Kolla, Edward J. *Sovereignty, International Law, and the French Revolution* (Cambridge: Cambridge University Press, 2017).

Koselleck, Reinhart. *Vergangene Zukunft: Zur Semantik geschichtlicher Zeiten* (Frankfurt am Main: Suhrkamp, 10th ed. 2017).

Koskenniemi, Martti. *The Gentle Civilizer of Nations: The Rise and Fall of International Law, 1870–1960* (Cambridge: Cambridge University Press, 2002).

Koskenniemi, Martti. 'International Law in Europe: Between Tradition and Renewal'. *European Journal of International Law* 16(1) (2005), 113–124.

Koskenniemi, Martti. 'Into Positivism: Georg Friedrich von Martens (1756–1821) and Modern International Law'. *Constellations* 15(2) (2008), 189–207.

Koskenniemi, Martti. 'What is Critical Research in International Law? Celebrating Structuralism'. *Leiden Journal of International Law* 29(3) (2016), 727–735.

Leuwers, Hervé. *Un juriste en politique: Merlin de Douai, 1754–1838* (Arras: Artois Presses Université, 1996).

Lesaffer, Randall. 'In the Embrace of France. An Introduction', in *In the Embrace of France: The Law of Nations and Constitutional Law in the French Satellite States of the Revolutionary and Napoleonic Age (1789–1815)*, eds. Beatrix Jacobs, Raymund Kubben and Randall Lesaffer (Baden-Baden: Nomos, 2008), 7–14.

Lesaffer, Randall. 'Aggression before Versailles'. *European Journal of International Law* 29(3) (2018), 773–808, doi: 10.1093/ejil/chy038

Lueder, Karl. 'Krieg und Kriegsrecht im Allgemeinen', in *Handbuch des Völkerrechts*, ed. Franz von Holtzendorff (Berlin: Haber, 1889), 169–397.

Mälksoo, Lauri. 'F. F. Martens and His Time: When Russia Was an Integral Part of the European Tradition of International Law'. *European Journal of International Law* 25(3) (2014), 811–829.

Marauhn, Thilo. 'How Many Deaths Can Art 2 (4) UN Charter Die?', in *The Justification of War and International Order. From Past to Present*, eds. Lothar Brock and Hendrik Simon (Oxford: Oxford University Press, 2021).

Martens, Friedrich von. *Die russische Politik in der Orientalischen Frage. Eine historische Studie* (St. Petersburg: H. Schmitzdorff, 1877).

Martens, Friedrich von. *Völkerrecht. Das internationale Recht der civilisirten Nationen* (Berlin: Weidmann, 1883).

Martens, Georg Friedrich von. *Einleitung in das positive Europäische Völkerrecht auf Verträge und Herkommen gegründet* (Göttingen: Dieterich, 1796).

Neff, Stephen C. *War and the Law of Nations: A General History* (Cambridge: Cambridge University Press, 2005).

Oppenheim, Lassa. 'The Science of International Law: Its Tasks and Method'. *American Journal of International Law* 2(2) (1908), 313–356.

Orford, Anne and Florian Hoffmann, eds. *The Oxford Handbook of the Theory of International Law* (Oxford: Oxford University Press, 2016).

Osterhammel, Jürgen. *The Transformation of the World: A Global History of the Nineteenth Century* (Princeton: Princeton University Press, 2014).

Paula Oliveira, Maria Lúcia de. 'Compatibility of the Moral Foundation of Law in Kant with the Theory of Reflective Judgment and with the Kantian Theory of Revolution', in *Kant's Theory of Law*, eds. Jean-Christophe Merle and Alexandre Trivisonno (Stuttgart: Franz Steiner Verlag, 2015), 35–44.

Payk, Marcus M. *Frieden durch Recht? Der Aufstieg des modernen Völkerrechts und der Friedensschluss nach dem Ersten Weltkrieg* (Berlin: De Gruyter, 2018).

Peevers, Charlotte. *The Politics of Justifying Force. The Suez Crisis, the Iraq War, and International Law* (Oxford: Oxford University Press, 2013).

Peters, Anne. 'International Legal Scholarship under Challenge', in *International Law as a Profession*, eds. Jean d'Aspremont, Tarcisio Gazzini, André Nollkaemper and Wouter Werner (Cambridge: Cambridge University Press, 2017), 117–159.

Pfordten, Dietmar von der. 'Kant on the Right of Resistance', in *Kant's Theory of Law*, eds. Jean-Christophe Merle and Alexandre Trivisonno (Stuttgart: Franz Steiner Verlag, 2015), 101–119.

Rougier, Antoine. 'La théorie de l'intervention d'humanité'. *Revue génerale de droit international public* 17 (1910), 468–526.

Schroeder, Paul W. *The Transformation of European Politics. 1763–1848* (Oxford: Oxford University Press, 1994).

Schulz, Matthias. *Normen und Praxis. Das Europäische Konzert der Großmächte als Sicherheitsrat, 1815–1860* (Berlin: De Gruyter, 2009).

Shahabuddin, Mohammad. *Ethnicity and International Law. Histories, Politics and Practices* (Cambridge: Cambridge University Press, 2016).

Simon, Hendrik. 'The Myth of *Liberum Ius ad Bellum*: Justifying War in 19th-Century Legal Theory and Political Practice'. *European Journal of International Law* 29(1) (2018), 113–136, https://doi.org/10.1093/ejil/chy009.

Simon, Hendrik. *Der Mythos vom „freien Recht zum Krieg". Zu einer Genealogie der modernen Kriegslegitimation* (forthcoming).

Singh, Prabhakar and Benoît Mayer, eds. *Critical International Law. Postrealism, Postcolonialism, and Transnationalism* (Oxford: Oxford University Press, 2014).

Summers, James. *Peoples and International Law: How Nationalism and Self-Determination Shape a Contemporary Law of Nations* (Leiden: Martinus Nijhoff, 2007).

Steiger, Heinhard. 'Ius belli in der Völkerrechtsgeschichte – Universelle Geltung oder Beschränkung auf „anerkannte Kulturvölker"?', in *Legalität, Legitimität und Moral. Können Gerechtigkeitspostulate Kriege rechtfertigen?*, eds. Thomas Bruha, Sebastian Heselhaus and Thilo Marauhn (Tübingen: Mohr Siebeck, 2008), 59–98.

Tischer, Anuschka. *Offizielle Kriegsbegründungen in der Frühen Neuzeit: Herrscherkommunikation in Europa zwischen Souveränität und korporativem Selbstverständnis* (Berlin: LIT-Verlag, 2012).

Van Ittersum, Martine Julia. 'The Long Goodbye: Hugo Grotius' Justification of Dutch Expansion Overseas, 1615–1645'. *History of European Ideas* 36(4) (2010), 386–411.

Vec, Miloš. 'Multinormativität in der Rechtsgeschichte', in *Jahrbuch 2008* (Berlin: Berlin-Brandenburgische Akademie der Wissenschaften, 2009), 155–166.

Vec, Miloš. 'Intervention/Nichtintervention, Verrechtlichung der Politik und Politisierung des Völkerrechts im 19. Jahrhundert', in *Macht und Recht. Völkerrecht in den internationalen Beziehungen*, eds. Ulrich Lappenküper and Reiner Marcowitz (Paderborn: Schöningh, 2010), 135–160.

Vec, Miloš. 'Sources in the 19th Century European Tradition: The Myth of Positivism', in *The Oxford Handbook of the Sources of International Law*, eds. Samantha Besson and Jean d'Aspremont (Oxford: Oxford University Press, 2017), 121–145.

Weber, Max. 'Wissenschaft als Beruf', in *Max Weber, Gesamtausgabe*, vol. 1, eds. Birgit Morgenbrod, Wolfgang J. Mommsen and Wolfgang Schluchter (Tübingen: Mohr Siebeck, 1992).

Wiener, Antje. *Contestation and Constitution of Norms in Global International Relations* (Cambridge: Cambridge University Press, 2018).

Yack, Bernard. 'Popular Sovereignty and Nationalism'. *Political Theory* 29(4) (2011), 517–536.

Zürn, Michael. 'The Politicization of World Politics and its Effects: Eight Propositions'. *European Political Science Review* 6(1) (2014), 47–71.

CHAPTER 6

The Road to Collective Security: Soviet Russia, the League of Nations, and the Emergence of the *ius contra bellum* in the Aftermath of the Russian Revolution (1917–1934)

Etienne Henry

Abstract

This chapter argues that the quest for 'peaceful coexistence', sometimes depicted as an inherent quality of Soviet foreign policy, rather reflects a re-interpretation of actual practice in the light of subsequent developments – in connection with the emergence of Joseph Stalin's doctrine of Socialism in one country. The latter was primarily inspired by tactical necessities rather than doctrinal dogmas. Even though Soviet Russia was perceived and sometimes acted as an outsider, if not a disrupting agent, until the accession of the USSR to membership in the League of Nations in 1934, Soviet foreign legal policy discourse in the 1920s and early 1930s, with its increasing focus on 'peaceful coexistence' and collective security rather than world proletarian revolution, contributed substantively to the emergence and development of modern *ius contra bellum*.

Keywords

League of Nations – collective security – *ius ad bellum* – aggression – USSR – Russia – Disarmament Conference – self-defence

1 Introduction

The prohibition of the use of force under Article 2(4) of the United Nations Charter has sometimes been envisaged as an exclusive legacy of Western – or even US – legal thought and diplomacy.[1] The post-Cold War historiography has

1 See, e.g., Hathaway, Oona A. and Scott J. Shapiro. *The Internationalists: How a Radical Plan to Outlaw War Remade the World* (New York: Simon & Schuster, 2017); and the criticism of

 | DOI:10.1163/9789004461802_008

indeed largely ignored the role played by Soviet Russia in the context of the progressive emergence of *ius contra bellum* in the 1920s and early 1930s. As noted by Bill Bowring, '[t]oday the Soviet theory and practice of international law … [is] [m]ost often … ignored.'[2]

Soviet legal doctrine, however, often placed the foreign policy of the Russian Socialist Federative Soviet Republic (RSFSR) and subsequently the USSR in the field of the use of force and non-intervention under the catchphrase of 'peaceful coexistence' (*мирное сосуществование*). This concept attracted substantial attention, especially during the Cold War.[3] According to one of the leading Soviet scholars, Grigory Ivanovich Tunkin (1906–1993), the principle of peaceful coexistence was one of the major contributions to international legal thought brought about by the October Revolution.[4]

This chapter intends to fill the gap between the somewhat idealistic depiction of Soviet scholarship and the more recent historiography of *ius contra bellum*, by identifying and providing a critical assessment of Soviet Russia's contribution. In doing so, it relies both on Soviet and Western sources while attempting to situate the legal issues in their broader historical context. Hopefully, this chapter will contribute to a better understanding of the role played by the USSR in the emergence of modern *ius contra bellum* in the period that immediately precedes the increase in tensions leading up to World War II. As is well known, to this day, the role of the USSR at the outbreak and during that conflict remains a subject of heightened political controversy.

Bradley, Anna S. 'The Internationalists: How A Radical Plan to Outlaw War Remade the World. By Oona A. Hathaway and Scott J. Shapiro'. *American Journal of International Law* 112(2) (2018), 330–335, 334.

2 Bowring, Bill. *Law, Rights and Ideology in Russia: Landmarks in the Destiny of a Great Power* (Abingdon: Routledge, 2014), 80.

3 See, e.g., Lerner, Warren. 'The Historical Origins of the Soviet Doctrine of Peaceful Coexistence'. *Law and Contemporary Problems* 29(4) (1964), 865–870; Lipson, Leon. 'Peaceful Coexistence'. *Law and Contemporary Problems* 29(4) (1964), 871–881; Meissner, Boris. 'Die sowjetische Auffassung von der „friedlichen Koexistenz"', in *Aussenpolitik und Völkerrecht der Sowjetunion: Ausgewählte Beiträge*, ed. Boris Meissner (Cologne: Verlag Wissenschaft und Politik, 1987), 63–82.

4 Tunkin, Grigory Ivanovich. 'Международно-правовые идеи Великой Октябрьской социалистической революции [International Legal Ideas of the Great October Socialist Revolution]'. *Советский ежегодник международного права* [*Soviet Yearbook of International Law*] (1966–1967), 15–29, 15; see also Durdenevskiĭ, Vsevolod Nikolaevich and M. I. Lazarev. *Пять принципов мирного сосуществования* [*Five Principles of Peaceful Coexistence*] (Moscow: State Editions of Legal Literature, 1957), 5–6; Karpov, Victor P. 'The Soviet Concept of Peaceful Coexistence and its Implications for International Law'. *Law and Contemporary Problems* 29(4) (1964), 858–864, 859; Ushakov, Nikolaĭ Aleksandrovich. *Невмешательство во внутренние дела государств* [*Non-Intervention in Domestic State Affairs*] (Moscow: International Relations, 1971), 16–18.

Six tendencies, roughly corresponding to distinct historic stages, can be distinguished in the evolution of Soviet foreign policy up to the adhesion of the USSR to the League of Nations (LoN) in 1934. Each of them will be the object of the following sections of this chapter. Accordingly, Section 2 deals with the *bellum iustum* discourse in early revolutionary documents and the aggressive revolutionary interventionism reflected in early Soviet foreign policy discourse. Section 3 then scrutinizes the progressive transition from such revolutionary propaganda to the doctrine of 'socialism in one country', resulting in the increasing use of the term 'peaceful coexistence' as a defining element of Soviet foreign policy. Section 4 continues with a description of the first encounters between the RSFSR and the LoN, characterized by overt reciprocal hostility. Section 5 analyses some of the provisions of bilateral treaties concluded by Soviet Russia prohibiting foreign intervention. Section 6 examines the provisions of some of the latter as well as later treaties aimed at preventing external aggression. Finally, Sections 7 and 8, describe the eventual adhesion of the USSR to collective security and the outlawing of war.

2 Revolutionary Russia and the Great War: The Marxist-Leninist Ideological Contribution to the Modern *ius contra bellum*

Terms commonly associated with the just war doctrine (*bellum iustum*) were relatively common in the writings of Vladimir Lenin (1870–1924), even though he did not apply them with doctrinal rigour.[5] Lenin saw World War I as an 'unjust' and even a 'criminal war'.[6] However, his views can be characterized neither as pacifist nor even as peace-loving. In his opinion, class struggle, turned into civil war, amounted to 'the only war that is legitimate, just and sacred – not in the clerical but in the human sense – the sacred war of the oppressed to overthrow the oppressors and liberate the working people from all oppression.'[7] In the end, the justice of the war was dependent on who wages it rather than on who attacked first.[8] Drawing lessons from the crushing of the

5 See also, stressing that there is no continuation of the classical *bellum iustum* theories but 'some interesting similarities' in the writings of Lenin, Socher, Johannes. 'Lenin, (Just) Wars of National Liberation, and the Soviet Doctrine on the Use of Force'. *Journal of the History of International Law* 19(2) (2017), 219–245, 226–227, doi: 10.1163/15718050-19231018.

6 'For Bread and Peace (14 (27) December 1917)', in Lenin, *Collected Works*, vol. 26 (Moscow: Progress Publishers, 1964; Digital Reprints, 2011), 386–387, 386, available at: https://www.marxists.org/archive/lenin/works/cw/index.htm (last accessed on 14 September 2020).

7 'Fear of the Collapse of the Old and the Fight for the New (24–27 December 1917 (6–9 January 1918))', in Lenin, *Collected Works* 1964 (n. 6), vol. 26, 400–403, 401.

8 See Meissner, Boris. 'Außenpolitische Theorie und Völkerrechtsdoktrin der Sowjetunion', in Aussenpolitik und Völkerrecht der Sowjetunion: Ausgewählte Beiträge, ed. Boris Meissner (Cologne: Verlag Wissenschaft und Politik, 1987), 13–33, 27.

Paris Commune of 1871, he argued, in connection with his concept of 'dictatorship of the proletariat', that 'violence is always the midwife of the old society', facilitating the transition from the bourgeois to the socialist society.[9]

Manifesting an outright optimism, Lenin asserted the inevitability of the oncoming proletariat revolutions in Europe.[10] Given the economic, military and moral situation in Russia, the immediate priority was, however, to put a halt to the war with the Central Powers. With the *Decree on Peace*, adopted by the Second Congress of the Soviet of Workers', Soldiers', and Peasants' Deputies on 26 October (8 November) 1917, Russia thus offered a 'just or democratic peace' that could only be accepted by the proletariat masses of the bourgeois and imperialist states. According to the *Decree*,

> [b]y a just or democratic peace … the government means an immediate peace without annexations (i.e., without the seizure of foreign lands, without the forcible incorporation of foreign nations) and without indemnities.[11]

The *Decree* thus contained an early expression of the rejection of coercion and annexation of territory that would crystalize internationally only in the 1930s, most notably as a result of the adoption of the Kellogg-Briand Pact,[12] the so-called Stimson policy of non-recognition, adopted in 1932 in reaction to the creation of the puppet-state Manchukuo by Japan, as well as the 'Saavedra-Lamas Pact'.[13]

In the same vein, the Decree of the All-Russian Central Executive Committee of 13 November 1918 on the annulation of the Treaty of Brest-Litovsk emphasized the inadmissibility of the recourse to coercion.[14] The unilateral character of the decree buttresses this interpretation, even though by the fifteenth condition of the Convention of Armistice of 11 November 1918, later confirmed in Article 116 of the Versailles Treaty, Germany had already renounced to benefit from the terms of the Treaty of Brest-Litovsk.[15] When the Allied and Associated

9 'Fear of the Collapse of the Old and the Fight for the New (24–27 December 1917 (6–9 January 1918))', in Lenin, *Collected Works* 1964 (n. 6), vol. 26, 400–403, 401.

10 'The Russian Revolution and Civil War: They Are Trying to Frighten us with Civil War (29 (16) September 1917)', in Lenin, *Collected Works* 1964 (n. 6), vol. 26, 28–42, 40.

11 'Decree on peace (25–26 October (7–8 November) 1917)', in ibid., 249–252, 249.

12 94 LNTS 57.

13 163 LNTS 393, 405, art. II.

14 *Документы Внешней Политики СССР* [*Documents of the Foreign Policy of the USSR*], vol. 1 (Moscow: Politicheskoĭ Literatury, 1959–1970), 565–567, 565.

15 Convention d'Armistice, 11 Novembre 1918, available at: http://www.servicehistorique.sga.defense.gouv.fr/sites/default/files/LaConventionDarmistice.pdf (last accessed on 14 September 2020).

Powers replied to the comments by the German delegation on the terms of the Versailles Treaty, they implicitly endorsed the Soviet view.[16] This early rejection of coercion was reaffirmed in Article I of the Treaty of 16 March 1921 between the RSFSR and Turkey[17] and in the framework of a treaty of friendship with Persia, concluded on 26 February 1921, where Russia rejected the 'policy of usurpation of the Tsarist Government', with an implicit reference to the principle *ex iniuria ius non oritur*.[18]

Soviet and contemporary Russian authors have argued that the principle of 'peaceful coexistence' as well as the prohibition – and indeed the criminalization – of aggressive wars were already fully expressed in the *Decree on Peace*.[19] In the light of the abovementioned examples, it is certain that early revolutionary documents contain germs of future developments in the field of *ius contra bellum*.[20] The reality was, however, more nuanced than the utopian depiction of a peace-loving Russia, sometimes conveyed by Soviet authors.

3 From World Revolution to Peaceful Coexistence

Very quickly, a tension emerged between revolutionary propaganda and diplomatic discourse. The latter was aimed at reinsuring foreign powers and facilitating renewed economic cooperation, based on 'peaceful coexistence'. As will be shown in this section, as far as the international legal discourse is

16 See 'Reply of the Allied and Associated Powers to the Observations of the German Delegation on the Conditions of Peace'. *International Conciliation* 6 (Doc. No. 141) (1919) 1341–1426, 1401.

17 *Documents of the Foreign Policy of the USSR* 1959–1970 (n. 14), vol. 3, 597–604, 597–598; see also Treaty of Kars, 13 October 1921, in ibid., vol. 4, art. 2.

18 9 LNTS 383, 403, art. 3(2).

19 See Tunkin, Grigory I. 'Co-Existence and International Law'. *Recueil des cours de l'académie de droit international de La Haye* 95 (1958-III), 1–81, 14 and 64; see also Il͡ukhina, Ruzanna Mikhaĭlovna. *Лига Наций: 1919–1934* [*League of Nations: 1919–1934*] (Moscow: Science Publisher, 1982), 182; Ashavskiĭ, Boris Matveevich. 'Октябрь 1917 Года и Международное Право [October 1917 and International Law]'. *Вестник Московского университета имени С. Ю. Витте. Серия 2. Юридические науки* [*Herald of the University of Moscow named after S. Yu. Vitte. Series 2. Legal sciences*] 13(4) (2017), 23–29, 25, doi: 10.21777/2587-9472-2017-4-23-29.

20 See, in this sense, Kuznet͡sov, Valeriĭ Ivanovich, Raĭs Abdulkhakovich Tuzmukhamedov and Nikolaĭ Aleksandrovich Ushakov. *От Декрета о мире к Декларации мира* [*From the Decree on Peace to the Friendly Relations Declaration*] (Moscow: International Relations Publisher, 1972), 4.

concerned, this tension was soon resolved in favour of a classical conception of international law, attached to the protection of sovereignty.

Indeed, a radically innovative idea underpinned the *Decree on Peace*: anticipating as much as fostering oncoming political changes, its authors were speaking not (only) to the legally recognized representatives of all belligerent States, but to their workers and soldiers and more broadly to their people. The *Decree* thus showed the willingness of Soviet authorities to bypass, if necessary, the usual canals of diplomatic relations.[21] This amounted to a challenge to the classical law on recognition of states and government that was deeply grounded on the principle of effectivity, irrespectively of the political merits of each government. After all, would not professional diplomats necessarily wither away alongside with states themselves, with the advent of communism?[22]

In a decree of 13 (26) December 1917, the Soviet of People's Commissaries affirmed the necessity to provide assistance to 'the left, internationalist, wing of the workers' movement' and allocated two million roubles for this purpose.[23] The *Declaration of Rights of the Working and Exploited People*, adopted on 3 (16) January 1918 by the Constituent Assembly also made clear that democratic peace must be attained 'at all costs, by revolutionary means.'[24]

It is, therefore, hardly surprising that political authorities of 'bourgeois' and 'imperialist' states saw the advent of communist rule in Russia as a great danger and accused the Soviet government of mischievous intentions.[25] Such inflammatory rhetoric could indeed only instil mistrust and provide arguments to the advocates of military intervention and to those opposed to the recognition of the Bolsheviks.[26]

The Soviet government would however soon be confronted with the evolution of the military and economic situation inside Russia as well as the intransigence of Germany, leading them, on 3 March 1918, to agree to the terms of the

---

21 See Mälksoo, Lauri. 'Russia-Europe', in *The Oxford Handbook of the History of International Law*, eds. Bardo Fassbender and Anne Peters (Oxford: Oxford University Press, 2012), 764–786, 783.

22 See Lenin. *The State and Revolution. The Marxist Theory of the State and the Tasks of the Proletariat in the Revolution*, vol. 25 (first published in 1918), in Lenin, *Collected Works* 1964 (n. 6), 385–497, 467–469.

23 See English translation in Committee on the Judiciary of the US Senate. *Bolshevik Propaganda* (Washington: Government Printing Office, 1919), 1185.

24 Lenin, *Collected Works* 1964 (n. 6), vol. 26, 423–425, 424.

25 See, e.g., Dewar, George A. B. 'Britain's Recognition of the Soviet Government'. *Foreign Affairs* 3(2) (1924), 313–319.

26 See, e.g., Report of 30 July 1919 quoted in 'Certain Aspects of the Bolshevist Movement in Russia: Part II: Bolshevist Program of World Revolution'. *International Conciliation* 7 (Doc. No. 149) (1920), 159–200, 163.

Brest-Litovsk Peace Treaty, that resulted in the dismemberment of the former Russian Empire. By Article II of the Treaty, the parties undertook to cease all their 'agitation' activities. The Soviet regime was thus assuming a formal obligation to renounce its ambitions of World Proletarian Revolution. This radical turn was obviously not inspired by ideological considerations but motivated by a realistic calculus of the forces in presence and the resulting unlikeliness of a military victory over the German Empire. However, the retreat from World Revolution was operated in diplomatic and legal discourse rather than in actual practice. This was made evident by statements of Soviet leaders at the time of ratification of the treaty and subsequent actions of Soviet Russia in Germany,[27] or the active – though often covert – Soviet support to communist factions in the Finnish, Estonian and Latvian civil wars as well as the attempted Communist *Coup d'État* in 1924 in Estonia.[28]

One of the leading Soviet international lawyer of the time, Evgeny Alexandrovich Korovin (1892–1964) even wrote, in 1924, that the support systematically provided to revolutionary movements in the Baltic States and in the Caucasus proved that Russia would readily resort to intervention for 'progressive' purposes.[29] Intervention was sometimes justified on the basis of self-determination, as occurred with the invasion of Georgia of February 1921, even though the event was depicted primarily as a an uprising followed by a request for intervention by the newly-established Bolshevik government,[30] but no coherent legal doctrine of revolutionary interventionism was ever officially promulgated. On the contrary, the 1920 peace treaty with Georgia contained a mutual undertaking of non-intervention.[31] Soviet historiography is reported

27 Ibid., 163–164.

28 See Trotsky, Leon. *The Revolution Betrayed* (London: Faber & Faber, 1937), 193–194; Karandashov, Innokenty and Ksenia Shestakova. 'The Principle of Equality of States in the Wake of the Russian Revolution'. *Russian Law Journal* 5(4) (2017), 8–42, 35, doi: 10.17589/2309-8678-2017-5-4-8-42; Mälksoo, Lauri. 'The Soviet Approach to the Right of Peoples to Self-Determination: Russia's Farewell to *Jus Publicum Europaeum*'. *Journal of the History of International Law* 19(2) (2017), 200–218, 211, doi: 10.1163/15718050-19231035.

29 Korovin, Evgeniĭ Aleksandrovich. *Международное право переходного времени* [*International Law of the Transition Time*] (Petrograd: State Publisher, 1924), 59–60. See, for a critical reading of Korovin's theses, Mirkine-Guetzévitch, Boris. 'La doctrine soviétique du droit international'. *Revue générale de droit international public* 32 (1925), 313–337, 322–323.

30 See, e.g., 'Speech of V. I. Lenin at a meeting of the Plenum of the Moscow Council of Workers and Peasants' Deputies, 28 Feburary 1921', in *Documents of the Foreign Policy of the USSR* 1959–1970 (n. 14), vol. 3, 547–550, 549–550; see also Mälksoo, 'The Soviet Approach' 2017 (n. 28), 208 and 211.

31 English translation reproduced in Graham, Malbone W. 'The Soviet Security System'. *International Conciliation* 12 (Doc. No. 252) (1928–1929), 345–430, 382.

to have insisted on alleged violations of the treaty by the Georgian Menshevik government in the form of support allegedly provided to anti-communist forces, even though such reports were likely manufactured.[32]

However, the evolution of the international situation in 1919, with the crushing of the German communist uprising as well as the inability of the Hungarian Soviet Republic to establish itself durably, would soon temper the hopes of Bolshevik leaders. The defeat against Poland put a halt to the hopes placed in a policy of revolutionary interventionism.[33] As later noted by Leon Trotsky (1879–1940) '[t]he "theory" of socialism in one country ... signalized an effort to liberate Soviet foreign policy from the programme of international revolution.'[34] In legal literature, revolutionary interventionism was largely confined to the doctrinal writings of a few authors.[35] Indeed, Korovin would soon align with the 'orthodox' views of Evgeny Pashukanis (1891–1937) – more consonant with classical international legal scholarship[36] – and renege on his own earlier views.[37] He would even affirm, a decade later, that 'the U.S.S.R. is in principle opposed to all intervention and has never proposed to propagate socialism in other countries by means of Soviet bayonets, since it considers the exportation of revolution nonsense.'[38]

However, the notion of 'peaceful coexistence' was not immediately turned into a *leitmotif* of Soviet propaganda. Lenin used such terms on few occasions, mainly in interviews given to Western journalists, after 1920.[39] Lenin's intentions related to the necessity of reinsuring Western public opinion of the pacific intentions of the RSFSR at a time when the survival of the regime in the

---

32 See Blank, Stephen. 'The Soviet Conquest of Georgia'. *Central Asian Survey* 12 (1993), 33–46, doi: 10.1080/02634939308400798.

33 Engelstein, Laura. *Russia in Flames: War, Revolution, Civil War, 1914–1921* (Oxford: Oxford University Press, 2018), 628–629; Lerner, 'The Historical' 1964 (n. 3), 868.

34 Trotsky, *The Revolution* 1937 (n. 28), 178.

35 See Bowring, Bill. *The Degradation of the International Legal Order? The Rehabilitation of Law and the Possibility of Politics* (Abingdon: Routledge, 2008), 27–29.

36 See Pashukanis, Evgeniĭ Bronislavovich. *Очерки по международному праву* [*Essays in International Law*] (Moscow: Soviet Law, 1935), 111. See also, affirming that Pashukanis, 'as an international legal practitioner ... was comfortable with orthodox conceptions of international law', Bowring, *Law* 2014 (n. 2), 67.

37 See Korovin, Evgeniĭ Aleksandrovich. *Международное право переходного времени* [*International Law of the Transition Time*] (Moscow: State Publisher, 2nd ed. 1925), 61, where the abovementioned passage was removed.

38 Korovine, Eugene A. 'Review of *The Soviet Union and International Law*'. *Harvard Law Review* 49(8) (1936), 1392–1395, 1394.

39 See, 'In Reply to Questions Put by Karl Wiegand, Berlin Correspondent of Universal Service (February 18, 1920)', in Lenin, *Collected Works* 1964 (n. 6), vol. 30, 365–367, 365; see also infra, note 56 and related text.

long-term was still not ensured and the need to re-establish regular economic relations with 'bourgeois' states was acutely felt. It was therefore a tactical rhetorical move, not grounded in any deeply held ideological conceptions.[40]

The contradiction between discourse and practice subsisted through a division of tasks between Soviet authorities and the, formally autonomous, Third International (Comintern). The former rarely provided open support for revolutionary movements. The Comintern, however, used incendiary rhetoric, encouraging World Revolution and manifesting outright opposition to the LoN, peaceful settlement of dispute or reduction of armaments.[41]

Notwithstanding their notorious control over the Comintern, Soviet authorities insisted on the distinct identity and the absence of any organic link between the two entities.[42] Well into the 1920s, Stalin sometimes indulged in such aggressive revolutionary propaganda.[43] Diplomatic practice, however, especially after the acceptance of Stalin's theory of socialism in one country, increasingly revolved around the catchphrase 'peaceful coexistence',[44] conceived as a logical corollary of the former theory.[45]

40 See Freeman, Alwyn V. 'Some Aspects of Soviet Influence on International Law.' *American Journal of International Law* 62(3) (1968), 710–722, 713.

41 See 'The Terms of Admission into the Communist International (published in July 1920)', in Lenin, *Collected Works* 1964 (n. 6), vol. 31, 206–211, 208.

42 See 'Note of 4 February 1921 of the Government of the RSFSR to the Government of Great-Britain', in *Documents of the Foreign Policy of the USSR* 1959–1970 (n. 14), vol. 3, 501–506, 503. But see Note of the US Secretary of State of 10 August 1920 to the Ambassador of Italy, reproduced in 'Notes Exchanged on the Russian-Polish Situation by the United States, France and Poland'. *International Conciliation* 7 (Doc. No. 155) (1920), 459–478, 466.

43 See, e.g., Stalin, Joseph. *Problems of Leninism* (Moscow: Foreign Languages Publishing House, 1954; transl. from the 11th ed.), 237–246, 242.

44 See, e.g., 'Report of the People's Commissar for Foreign Affairs of the RSFSR G. V. Chicherin at a meeting of the All-Russian Central Executive Committee on June 17, 1920'. *Documents of the Foreign Policy of the USSR* 1959–1970 (n. 14), vol. 2, 638–661, 638; see also, 'Instructions from the People's Commissar of Foreign Affairs of the RSFSR to the Plenipotentiary Representative of the RSFSR in Lithuania, S. I. Aralov, 28 April 1921', in ibid., vol. 4, 84–88, 84; 'Speech by the Chairman of the Soviet delegation V. V. Osinsky at the eleventh plenary meeting of the International Economic Conference in Geneva, 23 May 1927', in ibid., vol. 10, 221–224, 222–223.

45 See 'Interview with the People's Commissar of Foreign Affairs of the USSR M. M. Litvinov to representatives of foreign press, 26 July 1930', in ibid., vol. 13, 424–427, 425.

4 First Encounters with the League of Nations

The dissolution of the Russian Empire and the resulting blossoming of newly independent states, that often opted for a 'bourgeois' type of government and quickly fell under the influence of Western powers, left the RSFSR in a precarious geopolitical situation. In this context, the relationships with the LoN, designed as a purposely 'universal' organisation aimed towards the maintenance of the territorial *status quo* resulting from the Paris peace conference proved difficult.

In fact, on each side, the revolutionary ambitions of the new regime were perceived as an unsurmountable obstacle to Russia's adhesion to the LoN and to the restoration of 'normal' international relations.[46] Certainly, US President Woodrow Wilson (1856–1924) ambitioned to include Russia in his planned 'League of Nations' and he called for a conciliatory attitude towards the newly established Bolshevik authorities.[47] However, as a result of the October Revolution, Western policymakers would soon see Russia as a dangerous source of subversion. The official policy was eventually to achieve universal membership in the LoN, as was provided for in Article 1 of the Covenant.[48] However, the dominant view was that the adhesion of Russia could only happen after the overthrow of the Bolsheviks and return to liberal democracy.[49]

These views were sometimes reflected in legal literature. The legal historian and Russian *émigré* Paul Vinogradoff (1854–1925), comparing the League to a sort of enlightened Holy Alliance, suggested that the (purposely humanitarian) intervention of the Entente Powers in Russia would be a typical task for the League.[50]

---

46 See, e.g., Mirkine-Guetzévitch, 'La doctrine' 1925 (n. 29), 315; Korovin, Evgeniĭ Aleksandrovich. 'Лига наций и ее эволюция [The League of Nations and Its Evolution]'. *Советское право* [*Soviet Law*] No. 1 (1923), 36–43, 43.

47 Wilson, Woodrow. 'Address to a Joint Session of Congress on the Conditions of Peace, January 8, 1918'. 1918, available at: https://www.presidency.ucsb.edu/documents/address-joint-session-congress-the-conditions-peace (last accessed on 29 March 2021).

48 See 'Procès-Verbal of the Eighth Session of the Council of the League of Nations'. *League of Nations Official Journal* 1(6) (1920), 304–346, 309 (Italy, M. Tittoni); Oppenheim, Lassa. 'Du caractére essentiel de la Société des Nations'. *Revue générale de droit international public* 26 (1919), 234–244.

49 See 'Appendix I to C.F. 37 – Despatch to Admiral Kolchak, Paris 26th May 1919', in *Papers Relating to the Foreign Relations of the United States, 1919, Russia*, ed. Joseph V. Fuller (Washington: US Government Printing Office, 1937), Document 390, 367–370, 369, available at: https://history.state.gov/historicaldocuments/frus1919Russia/d390 (last accessed on 29 March 2021).

50 Vinogradoff, Paul. 'The Legal and the Political Aspects of the League of Nations', in *On the History of International Law and International Organization: Collected Papers of Sir Paul Vinogradoff*, ed. William Elliott Butler (Clark: Lawbook Exchange, 2009), 37–43, 43.

Soviet authors did not fail to stress the blatant gap between the universalistic aspirations of the LoN and its actual nature as a particular compact between a limited number of 'bourgeois', 'capitalist' and 'imperialist' states.[51] They also compared the League with the Holy Alliance,[52] and sometimes depicted it as a centre of coordination of anti-Bolshevik policies.[53] Allegedly, according to Lenin, the League, 'that contemptible agency of imperialism'[54] – 'ha[d] become one of England's diplomatic offices.'[55] He declared that the League was 'marked by the absence of anything resembling the establishment of the real equality of rights between nations [and] anything resembling a real chance of their peaceful coexistence.'[56]

There was some exaggeration in such statements, since the members of the Entente proved unable to agree on a common policy towards Soviet Russia,[57] not to mention the LoN itself; a point that was indeed not lost on Lenin.[58]

The People's Commissar for Foreign Affairs Georgy Vasilyevich Chicherin (1872–1936) wrote to Lenin that the League 'is simply a tool of the Entente.'[59] He further stated his general views on international organization and collective security, stressing the inanity of the idea of an international army and the inherent risk of abuse.[60] Lenin wholeheartedly approved of Chicherin's views.[61] In short, Lenin and other Soviet leaders were wary of what they perceived as naive 'liberal pacifism.'

Some authors rather saw the League as a direct concurrent to the project of a future World Soviet Federation, and therefore as an enemy. Tellingly, the title of a

51 See, e.g., Korovin, 'The League' 1923 (n. 46), 43; Korovin, *International Law* 1924 (n. 29), 56–57.

52 See Vodovozov, Vasiliĭ Vasil'evich. *Версальский мир и Лига наций* [*The Peace of Versailles and the League of Nations*] (Petrograd: Mysl', 1922), 41; Korovin, 'The League' 1923 (n. 46), 36.

53 See Xorvatskiĭ, Vladimir L'vovich. *Лига наций* [*The League of Nations*] (Moscow: Sot͡sėkgiz, 1937), 8.

54 *Manifesto of the Communist International* (Chicago: C.E.C. Communist Party of America, 1920), 30, available at: https://www.marxists.org/history/international/comintern/2nd-congress/2-Manifesto-2nd-Congress-CI-1920.pdf (last accessed on 14 September 2020).

55 Ibid., 6.

56 'Interview Given to Michael Farbman, *Observer* and *Manchester Guardian* Correspondent (October 27, 1922)', in Lenin, *Collected Works* 1964 (n. 6), vol. 33, 383–389, 387.

57 See Zimmern, Alfred. *The League of Nations and the Rule of Law: 1918–1935* (London: Macmillan, 1936), 293–294.

58 See, e.g., 'Ninth Congress of the R.C.P.(B.), March 29–April 5, 1920: Report of the Central Committee, March 29', in Lenin, *Collected Works* 1964 (n. 6), vol. 30, 443–462, 447.

59 'Letter to G. V. Chicherin (March 14, 1922)', in ibid., vol. 45, 506–512, 508.

60 Ibid., 510.

61 Ibid. (marginal note by Lenin): 'Correct!'

book published in Baku in 1920 was *League of Nations or World Soviet Republic?*[62] This sense of a concurrence between the two projects was also acutely felt at the Paris Peace Conference.[63] In 1923, Korovin pointed out that the League had already failed to act as a superior arbiter and had become nothing more than a big administrative union and an alliance of 'bourgeois' democracies.[64]

However, despite the interventions of Japan, France, the USA and the United Kingdom at various stages and locations of the Russian Civil War,[65] the League *itself* did never openly act with the overt aim to intervene in Russian internal affairs. The British delegate at the first Assembly submitted a draft resolution asking explanations to the Council for its inaction in the context of the Polish-Soviet War, despite the clear wording of Article 11, that proclaimed any war to be 'a matter of concern to the whole League'.[66] The French delegate, Léon Bourgeois (1851–1925) reported that the Council had decided not to intervene because of the reticence of Russia.

Hoping to foster the reestablishment of economic relationships with the RSFSR, the Council had created a Commission of Enquiry to report on the latter's policies.[67] The Russian reply to a request for an onsite visit was positive, but it requested that no Polish nationals or any national of a state that was assisting Poland in the ongoing war would be appointed to such commission.[68] Such conditions were regarded as unacceptable by the Council, which, absent Russian consent, finally renounced to dispatch the commission.[69] This attitude of non-intervention would be confirmed by the Permanent Court of

62 Nurin, *Лига наций или Всемирная республика Советов* [*League of Nations or World Soviet Republic*] (Baku: Azerf͡sentropechat', 1920); see also Mirkine-Guetzévitch, 'La doctrine' 1925 (n. 29), 318.

63 See Miller, David Hunter. *The Drafting of the Covenant*, vol. 2 (New York: G. P. Putnam's Sons, 1928), 202.

64 Korovin, 'The League' 1923 (n. 46), 43; see also Kotli͡arevskiĭ, Sergeĭ Andreevich. 'Кризис международного права [The Crisis of International Law]'. *Право и Жизнь* [*Law and Life*] 1 (1922), 80–182, 81.

65 See, e.g., Moulis, Émile and Eugène Bergonier. *La guerre entre les alliés et la Russie (1918–1920)* (Paris: Librairie générale de droit et la jurisprudence, 1937); Wood, Alan. *Russia's Frozen Frontier: A History of Siberia and the Russian Far East 1581–1991* (London: Bloomsbury, 2011), 175–190.

66 See Rougier, Antoine. 'La première assemblée de la Société des Nations (Genève, novembre–décembre 1920)'. *Revue générale de droit international public* 28 (1921), 197–412, 381–382.

67 'Procès-Verbal of the Third Session of the Council of the League of Nations'. *League of Nations Official Journal* 1(2) (1920), 60–64, 62.

68 See 'Procès-Verbal of the Fifth Session of the Council of the League of Nations'. *League of Nations Official Journal* 1(4) (1920) 115–156, 149–150.

69 'Procès-Verbal of the Sixth Session of the Council of the League of Nations'. *League of Nations Official Journal* 1(5) (1920), 213–226, 221.

International Justice in the *Eastern Carelia* case, the Court refusing to give an opinion on a dispute between Finland and the RSFSR as a result of the opposition of the latter.[70]

The hostility between the League and the RSFSR on matters of high politics did not prevent mutual cooperation on 'apolitical' humanitarian and sanitary questions such as the prevention of epidemics, the repatriation of prisoners of war, or the fight against famine.[71] In the latter case, however, the RSFSR carefully ensured that the decision to grant access to the High Commissioner for Relief to Russia, Fridtjof Nansen (1861–1930), could not serve as a disguised means for intervention in Russian domestic affairs.[72]

In several cases, however, the League's attitude manifested an anti-Soviet bias, as attested by the policy of non-recognition of the RSFSR well into the 1920s, despite the consolidation of Soviet rule, as became apparent in the treatment by the Council of the question of the Åland Islands.[73] In the case of Bessarabia, the signatories of the Paris Peace Treaty of 28 October 1920, had recognized the Romanian absorption and unilaterally endowed the Council with the task of drawing the border between Romania and Soviet Russia.[74] In 1920, a Soviet naval operation against the White Fleet of Admiral Anton Denikin in the Persian town of Enzeli (now Bandar-e Anzali) was qualified by the Council as an act of aggression. The Council acted without hearing the views of the RSFSR, thus disregarding completely the principle *audiatur et altera pars*.[75]

70 See PCIJ, *Status of Eastern Carelia*, Advisory Opinion, 23 July 1923, Series B, No. 5, 7–29, 27–28.

71 See Hudson, Manley O. 'Membership in the League of Nations'. *American Journal of International Law* 18(3) (1924), 436–458, 452–453.

72 'Conventions entre le Dr. Nansen et G. Tchitcherine'. *Revue internationale de la croix-rouge* 3(33) (1921), 910–918, 916.

73 See the Report on the Aaland Islands Question, adopted by the Council on September 20, 1920, reproduced in 'Procès-Verbal of the Ninth Session of the Council of the League of Nations'. *League of Nations Official Journal* 1(7) (1920), 391–414, 395.

74 Rodgers, William L. 'Suggestions as to Changes in the International Law for Maritime War'. *American Journal of International Law* 17(1) (1923), 3–17, 7–11, arts. 1–2. For the Soviet position, see the note of the Soviet Ambassador in Rome, sent at the occasion of the ratification of the treaty by Italy, on 17 March 1927, reproduced in *Revue de droit international* 1 (1927), 442–443.

75 See 'Procès-Verbal of the Sixth Session' 1920 (n. 69), 217–218.

5 Ensuring the Internal Security of the Soviet State against Intervention through Bilateral Treaties

As a result of the political isolation of Soviet Russia, Soviet diplomacy would aim at the conclusion of bilateral treaties intended to ensure the external security of the RSFSR (and then the USSR) and its counterparts against foreign armed intervention in domestic affairs.[76] Incidents occurred during the civil war such as the dispute between Persia and Russia arising from the alleged 'safe harbour' provided to the Caspian fleet of Denikin's white army were certainly a direct source of inspiration for provisions containing a prohibition of intervention and, more specifically, of provision of support to revolutionary movements. In the treaty of friendship with Persia, signed a few months after the incident, both states committed 'to abstain from any intervention in the internal affairs of the other.'[77]

Article 7(5) of the 1920 Tartu Treaty of Peace between Russia and Estonia – the first of a long series of bilateral treaties – contained a commitment

> to forbid the formation, and the presence in their territory, of any organisations or groups whatsoever claiming to govern all or part of the territory of the other contracting Party, and the presence of representatives or officials of organisations or groups whose object is to overthrow the Government of the other Party to the Treaty.[78]

According to Article 7(6), both governments undertook to mutually exchange information on the presence on their respective territories of military and paramilitary organizations and their military equipment.

Treaties concluded with Lithuania (1920),[79] Latvia (1920),[80] Poland (1920 and 1921),[81] Turkey (1921),[82] Mongolia (1921),[83] China (1924),[84] Japan (1925),[85]

---

76 See Korovin, Eugene A. 'Soviet Treaties and International Law'. *American Journal of International Law* 22(4) (1928), 753–763, 753; Graham, Malbone W. 'The Soviet Security Treaties'. *American Journal of International Law* 23(2) (1929), 336–350, 339–340.

77 9 LNTS 383, art. 4.

78 11 LNTS 30.

79 3 LNTS 105, 126, art. 4(1).

80 2 LNTS 195, 215–216, art. 4.

81 4 LNTS 7, 35–36, art. 2; see also 6 LNTS 51, 131, art. 5.

82 Treaty between Russia and Turkey, 1921 (n. 17), art. VIII, first paragraph.

83 *Documents of the Foreign Policy of the USSR* 1959–1970 (n. 14), vol. 3, 476–480, 477, art. III.

84 37 LNTS 175, 178, art. VI(1).

85 34 LNTS 31, 35, art. V.

Afghanistan (1931),[86] and France (1932)[87] comprise equally unequivocal, provisions in this regard. In a study on revolutionary activities by private persons against foreign states, Hersch Lauterpacht argued that all these provisions on the prohibition of intervention in domestic affairs were exorbitant of general international law.[88] In his view, 'the Soviets [we]re not prepared to enter into such engagements with other Powers.' However, it seems that Soviet authorities were indeed willing to enter into reciprocal commitments of non-intervention with whatever third states would agree. Thus, Korovin stressed that Soviet Russia, as a reason of her political isolation, soon turned into a 'champion of sovereign equality'.[89]

6 Protecting the USSR against External Aggression

In an ensuing phase (which in fact partially coincided with the former), Soviet foreign policy laid more emphasis on the prevention of the risk of wars of aggression rather than on foreign intervention aimed at regime change. Bilateral treaties, contained either commitments of non-aggression or neutrality or both – mutual assistance in case of aggression not being envisaged at this stage –, as in the treaties with Turkey (1925),[90] Lithuania (1926),[91] Germany (1926),[92] Afghanistan (1931),[93] Finland (1932),[94] Latvia (1932),[95] Estonia (1932),[96] Poland (1932),[97] France (1932),[98] Italy (1933),[99] and China (1937).[100]

In Soviet circles, the existence of the League itself was perceived as comporting a risk of aggression. Some of the bilateral treaties even contained

86 157 LNTS 371, 379–380, art. 3.
87 157 LNTS 411, 419, art. V.
88 Lauterpacht, Hersch. 'Revolutionary Activities by Private Persons against Foreign States'. *American Journal of International Law* 22(1) (1928), 105–130, 121.
89 Korovin, *International Law* 1924 (n. 29), 43–45.
90 157 LNTS 353, 355, arts. 1 and 2.
91 60 LNTS 145, 153, art. 3.
92 53 LNTS 387, 393, art. 2.
93 157 LNTS 371, 379–380, arts. 1 and 2.
94 157 LNTS 393, 395 and 397, art. 1(1).
95 148 LNTS 113, 125, art. 2.
96 131 LNTS 297, 305, art. 1.
97 136 LNTS 41, 49 and 51, arts. 1–3.
98 157 LNTS 411, 418, arts. I and II.
99 148 LNTS 319, 327, arts. 1 and 2.
100 181 LNTS 101, 102, arts. 1 and 2.

provisions that would work as a juridical shield against intervention by the LoN. Thus, according to Article 3 of a 1927 treaty of guarantee and neutrality with Persia, the parties

> agree[d] to take no part, whether *de facto* or *de jure*, in political alliances or agreements directed against the safety of the territory or territorial waters of the other Contracting Party or against its integrity, independence or sovereignty.[101]

Furthermore, they 'likewise agree[d] to take no part in any economic boycotts or blockades organised by third Powers against one of the Contracting Parties.'[102] The latter was an obvious reference to economic sanctions under Article 16 of the Covenant. Other treaties concluded with Germany (1926),[103] Lithuania (1926)[104] and Estonia (1932)[105] contained similar clauses.

The conformity of such undertakings with the LoN Covenant was disputable, as they could potentially have the effect of precluding the parties' participation in measures adopted against Covenant-breakers.[106] According to Article 20, first paragraph of the Covenant, '[t]he Members of the League … solemnly undertake that they will not hereafter enter into any engagements inconsistent with the terms [of the Covenant].' Of course, as a result of the relative binding force of treaties, Article 20 had no bearing on the USSR until its accession in 1934.[107] The treaty partners of the USSR sometimes specifically reserved their obligations as members of the League,[108] at least as far as their fulfilment would not amount to an act of aggression.[109]

101 112 LNTS 275, 292.
102 Ibid., 293.
103 53 LNTS 387, 393, art. 3.
104 60 LNTS 145, 153, art. 4.
105 131 LNTS 297, 305, art. 2.
106 See, e.g., Rutenberg, Gregory. 'The Baltic States and the Soviet Union'. *American Journal of International Law* 29(4) (1935), 598–615.
107 See, in this sense, Rousseau, Charles. 'De la compatibilité des normes juridiques contradictoires dans l'ordre international'. *Revue générale de droit international public* 39 (1932), 133–192, 162.
108 See, e.g., Exchange of Notes related to the 1827 Treaty of Guarantee and Neutrality between Persia and the USSR, 112 LNTS 275, 295; see also the Exchange of notes related to the 1926 Treaty of nonaggression between Lithuania and the USSR, 60 LNTS 145, 155–157.
109 See Treaty of Non-Aggression between Estonia and the USSR, 1932, 131 LNTS 297, 305, art 3; see also Treaty of Non-Aggression between Latvia and the USSR, 1932, 148 LNTS 113, 125, art. 3.

However, a German note was attached to the treaty between Germany and the USSR, containing an interpretation of Article 16 of the Covenant that almost amounted to a nullification of its effects in case of sanctions against the USSR.[110]

The issue of compatibility of the provision contained in the 1925 treaty with Turkey[111] arose in 1932, with the accession of Turkey to the LoN. Turkey addressed Soviet concerns by guaranteeing that, as a LoN member, it would oppose any tendencies 'inconsistent with the principles of peace' directed against the USSR. It also stressed the weakness of the obligations entailed by Articles 16 and 17 of the Covenant.[112]

7 Embracing Collective Security

The debates surrounding disarmament manifested an acute awareness of the links between collective security and disarmament. Disarmament and security, national or collective, were, in turns, both seen as results and as preconditions for one another.[113] One of the effects of this correlation – alongside with other factors, such as the rejection of the 1923 Draft Treaty of Mutual Guarantee and the 1924 Geneva Protocol[114] – was to place disarmament issues at the centre of attention of the League's activities. This is also the reason why questions belonging to collective security and *ius contra bellum* have been dealt with in this context. Complete disarmament was, however, seen as a utopic endeavour by most stakeholders.[115]

However, the Soviet delegation, led by Deputy Commissar for Foreign Affairs Maxim Maximovich Litvinov (1876–1951), chose exactly this path when it first attended the Preparatory Commission, during its fourth session, in December 1927, renewing the call made four years earlier by Chicherin at

110 53 LNTS 387, 394–395.

111 157 LNTS 353, 355, Art. 2.

112 See Güçlü, Yücel. 'Turkey's Entrance into the League of Nations'. *Middle Eastern Studies* 39(1) (2003), 186–206, 200, doi:10.1080/00263200412331301637.

113 See, e.g., Il͡iukhina, *League of Nations* 1982 (n. 19), 183–184.

114 See Guieu, Jean-Michel. 'L'"Insécurité collective". L'Europe et la Société des Nations dans l'entre-deux-guerres'. *Bulletin de l'Institut Pierre Renouvin* 30(2) (2009), 21–43, doi:10.3917/bipr.030.0021.

115 See, e.g., 'First Meeting, November 30th, 1927, at 11 a.m.', in *League of Nations*, Documents of the Preparatory Commission for the Disarmament Conference, Series V, Doc. C. 667. M. 225. 1927 IX [C.P.D. 1 (d)] (16 January 1928), 6–12, 6.

the Genoa Conference.[116] Litvinov denounced the 'frenzied piling-up of armaments' that, in his opinion, would inevitably lead to renewed major confrontations between European powers, regardless of the intentions of policy-makers. He thus, unsuccessfully proposed to take a radical turn towards *complete disarmament* through the immediate abolition of all standing armies and destruction of military equipment rather than *partial reduction* of armaments.[117]

In Litvinov's view, the disarmament question was intimately linked with the ongoing discussions on the abolition of war as an instrument of national policy. He therefore addressed the US delegate, affirming that he expected support from the US Government.[118] In his view, only the acceptance of his proposal of complete disarmament would lead to the 'abolition of the possibility of war'.[119] Outlawing war without proceeding to immediate disarmament would prove pointless and amounted to hypocrisy.[120] At a conference gathered in Moscow on 2 December 1922 for the limitation of armament, Litvinov had relied on similar arguments in order to reject a draft pact of non-aggression submitted by Poland.[121] This time, however, the USSR soon converted to one of the most fervent adherents to the Kellogg-Briand Pact, becoming the first state to adhere to the Pact, on 27 September 1928.[122]

In the view of the USSR, the purpose of the Pact aligned perfectly with Soviet foreign policy since 1917.[123] In some ways, the USSR was arguably even more committed to the spirit of the Pact than its authors. Thus Litvinov

---

116 See Chicherin's declaration on 10 April 1922, reproduced in Korovin, Evgeniĭ Aleksandrovich, ed. *Международные договоры и акты нового времени* [*International Treaties and Acts of the New Time*] (Moscow/Leningrad: State Publisher, 1924), 147–151, 149. Had this earlier call for disarmament call received a warmer reception at the Genoa Conference, the RSFSR might perhaps have adopted a different policy towards Germany and would perhaps not have concluded the secret military protocol to the Rapallo Treaty. See, in this regard, Bowring, Bill. 'Yevgeniy Pashukanis, His *Law and Marxism: A General Theory*, and the 1922 Treaty of Rapallo between Soviet Russia and Germany'. *Journal of the History of International Law* 19(2) (2017), 274–295, 288–291, doi: 10.1163/15718050-19231033.

117 See 'First Meeting' 1928 (n. 115), 9–12.

118 'Third Meeting (Public), held on Monday, March 19th, 1928, at 3.30 p.m.', in ibid., 237–243, 241.

119 Ibid.

120 See Xorvatskiĭ, *The League* 1937 (n. 53), 47–50.

121 See Graham, 'The Soviet Security Treaties' 1929 (n. 76), 350.

122 94 LNTS 57, 59.

123 Text of note sent, August 31, 1928, by the Soviet Government to the French Ambassador at Moscow, reproduced in 'Text of the General Pact [*sic*] for the Renunciation of War, Signed in Paris, August 27, 1928'. *International Conciliation* 12 (Doc. No. 243) (1928), 521–536, 528.

criticized the declarations by France, the USA, and the United Kingdom.[124] These declarations asserted the self-judging character of the right of self-defence[125] and reserved the 'Monroe Doctrine'[126] or an unfettered British right of intervention.[127] According to Article III, first paragraph of the Pact, the latter would enter into force only after the ratification by all the signatory parties.[128] Frustrated by the slowness of the process, the USSR initiated negotiations with some of its neighbours of a treaty providing for the immediate entry into force of the Pact, the so-called 'Litvinov Protocol'.[129] Further states, including Lithuania, Persia and Turkey, soon acceded to the protocol.

The USSR soon became one of the first states suspected of a breach of the Kellogg-Briand Pact, with the outbreak of the Sino-Soviet Conflict of 1929, originating in the seizure, by Chinese forces, of the premises and personnel of the Chinese Eastern Railway,[130] soon followed by successful Soviet military operations in Manchuria. The Chinese government of Nanking claimed that the USSR, through its actions in Manchuria, had violated its commitment not to engage in communist propaganda activities, under the Peking Agreement of 1924.[131] When US Secretary of State Henry L. Stimson (1867–1950) called on both parties to respect their undertakings,[132] the USSR argued, substantially,

124 League of Nations, *Records of the Conference for the Reduction and Limitation of Armaments, Series B. Minutes of the General Commission*, vol. II, 236–237; for further criticism, see, e.g., Borchard, Edwin M. 'The Kellogg Treaties Sanction War'. *Zeitschrift für ausländisches öffentliches Recht und Völkerrecht* 1 (1929), 126–131, 128–129; Lauterpacht, Hersch. 'The Pact of Paris and the Budapest Articles of Interpretation'. *Transactions of the Grotius Society* 20 (1934), 178–204, 198–199; Mandelstam, André. 'L'interprétation du pacte Briand-Kellogg'. *Revue générale de droit international public* 40 (1933), 537–605, 604.

125 Letter of the French Minister of Foreign Affairs (Briand) to the American Ambassador (Herrick), Paris, 14 July 1928, reproduced in Shotwell, James T. 'The Pact of Paris with Historical Commentary'. *International Conciliation* 12 (Doc. No. 243) (1928), 447–520, 503–505.

126 Kellogg, Frank B. 'Address at the Annual Dinner'. *Proceedings of the American Society of International Law at its Annual Meeting* 22 (1928), 141–145.

127 Shotwell, 'The Pact of Paris' 1928 (n. 125), 508–509.

128 94 LNTS 57, 63.

129 89 LNTS 369.

130 See Yoshitomi, M. 'L'affaire de la perquisition de l'ambassade soviétique à Pékin par les autorités chinoises'. *Revue générale de droit international public* 35 (1929), 184–192.

131 'Manifesto of the Chinese Government on the Sino-Soviet Situation (Nanking, 25 October 1929)', in Fuller, *Papers* 1943 (n. 49), Document 244, 333–336, available at: https://history.state.gov/historicaldocuments/frus1929v02/d244 (last accessed on 14 September 2020).

132 'The Secretary of State to Certain Diplomatic Representatives (Washington, December 1, 1929)', in ibid., Document 298, 371–373, available at: https://history.state.gov/historicaldocuments/frus1929v02/d298 (last accessed on 14 September 2020).

that Soviet actions could be justified as self-defence, even though it stressed that it was not willing to invoke the abovementioned declarations.[133] The Soviet note further denied any legal standing to the USA to complain of an alleged violation of the Pact in a dispute between third parties.[134] The USSR was thus far from accepting *avant la lettre* the *erga omnes* character of *ius contra bellum* obligations. Stimson, however, went on and publicly criticized the USSR for adopting a rather retrograde and legally unwarranted view on the nature of such friendly communications.[135] A critical assessment of the Soviet claim of self-defence would be conjectural given both the lack of a reliable factual record and the indeterminacy of the concept of self-defence at the time, resulting primarily from the US and British reticence to agree on a definition.[136]

By banning 'war', the Kellogg-Briand Pact notoriously left a lacuna, in that previously tolerated uses of force 'short of war' – including armed reprisals – remained, at least arguably, untouched.[137] On ratification, the USSR underlined this major shortcoming.[138] In some bilateral treaties, the USSR and its counterparts included provisions *complementing* the material scope of application of the Pact. Thus, in Article 1 of the 1932 treaty of non-aggression with Estonia, the parties undertook not only to refrain from acts of aggression, but also

> from any acts of violence directed against the territorial integrity and inviolability or the political independence of the other Contracting Party, regardless of whether such aggression or such acts are committed separately or together with other Powers, with or without a declaration of war.[139]

---

133 See Soviet note of 3 December 1929, in 'The Chargé in France (Armour) to the Secretary of State (Paris, December 7, 1929)', in ibid., Document 355, 404–406, 405, available at: https://history.state.gov/historicaldocuments/frus1929v02/d355 (last accessed on 14 September 2020).

134 Ibid., 406.

135 'Statement by the Secretary of State Issued to the Press on December 4, 1929', in Fuller, *Papers* 1943 (n. 49), Document 327, 388–389, available at: https://history.state.gov/historicaldocuments/frus1929v02/d327 (last accessed on 14 September 2020).

136 See, in this sense, Vandy, François. 'Le pacte Kellogg'. *Revue générale de droit international public* 37 (1930), 5–18, 11.

137 Ibid., 13–14; Korovin, Evgeniĭ Aleksandrovich. 'Пакт Келлога и присоединение к нему СССР [Pact Kellogg and Accession of the USSR]'. *Советское право* [*Soviet Law*] No. 6 (1928), 26–48. It could be argued, however, that by undertaking to settle their disputes exclusively by 'pacific means' (art. II), the Kellogg-Briand pact entailed the prohibition of the use of force beyond war.

138 See 'General Pact' 1928 (n. 123), 530.

139 131 LNTS 297, 305.

The preamble of the treaty made clear that the shared intention was to confirm and supplement the Pact. Provisions of the treaties concluded with Latvia (1932),[140] Poland (1932),[141] Finland (1932),[142] France,[143] and China (1937)[144] contained analogous provisions. As Korovin stressed, these provisions effected a complete renunciation to war and force, without any exception.[145]

At the Conference for the Reduction and Limitation of Armament, the Soviet delegation submitted a draft definition of aggression based on a list of acts qualifying as aggression. These included declaration of war, invasion even without previous declaration of war, bombardment by land, naval or air, unconsented introduction or use of forces located on a third state's territory and naval blockade.[146] The proposed definition sanctified the so-called principle of anteriority – today reflected in Article 2 of the UN General Assembly's definition of aggression annexed to resolution 3314 (XXIX) of 1974: a state that was the first to commit any of the listed act was to be considered the aggressor. An annex made clear that a series of potential excuses, including 'alleged maladministration', or any other political motive, could never justify the commission of an act of aggression.[147]

The USSR did not include so-called 'indirect aggression' amongst the actions listed in its proposal.[148] After discussion in the Committee on Security Questions the list of acts was completed, in the so-called 'Politis Report', by the addition of the

> provision of support to armed bands formed in its territory which have invaded the territory of another State, or refusal, notwithstanding the request of the invaded State, to take in its own territory all the measures in its power to deprive those bands of all assistance or protection.[149]

140 148 LNTS 113, 123, art. 1.

141 136 LNTS 41, 49, art. 1(2).

142 157 LNTS 393, 395, preamble, sixth paragraph.

143 157 LNTS 411, 418, art. I.

144 181 LNTS 101, 103, art. 1.

145 Korovine, Eugene A. 'The U.S.S.R. and Disarmament'. *International Conciliation* 15 (Doc. No. 292) (1932–1933), 293–358, 305.

146 See Definition of 'Aggressor': Draft Declaration, Doc. Conf.D/C.G.38., in League of Nations, *Records of the Conference for the Reduction and Limitation of Armaments, Series B. Minutes of the General Commission*, vol. II, 1933, 237–238.

147 Ibid.

148 Ibid., 237–238.

149 'Report of the Committee on Security Questions, Annex I: Draft Act relating to the definition of the aggressor', 24 May 1933, Doc. Conf.D./C.G./108, in Conference for the Reduction

Although no consensus was reached on the definition – mainly as a result of the opposition of the advocates of an elastic definition, including Italy, Spain and the United Kingdom –, the 'Litvinov-Politis formula' received support from a majority of the participants – including Poland, Chile, Turkey, Persia, Rumania, Yugoslavia, and Czechoslovakia. It was soon incorporated into a series of conventions defining aggression concluded in July 1933.[150] At the time of the adoption of the conventions, Litvinov regretted the fact that the conference had proved unable to adopt a universal convention and affirmed the will of the USSR to conclude such an undertaking with any other state.[151] The automatism of the definition as well as the extension of the scope of the prohibition of the Kellogg-Briand Pact to any use of force that it entailed, were acclaimed as important developments by numerous authors – some of them even comparing its importance to the conclusion of the Kellogg-Briand Pact.[152] In fact, even the USA and the United Kingdom later relied on the Litvinov-Politis formula at the London International Conference on Military Trials.[153] However, this time the Soviet delegate opposed any reference to these conventions.[154]

and Limitation of Armaments, *Conference Documents*, vol. II, Geneva, 1934, Doc. IX. Disarmament 1935.IX.4, 683–684.

150 See Convention signed at London, for the Definition of Aggression, 3 July 1933, 147 LNTS 67 (Afghanistan, Estonia, Latvia, Persia, Poland, Rumania, Turkey, and the USSR; later accessed by Finland); Convention for the Definition of Aggression between Roumania, the USSR, Czechoslovakia, Turkey and Yugoslavia, signed at London, 4 July 1933, 148 LNTS 211 (open to accession by any state, per art. IV); Convention between Lithuania and the USSR for the Definition of Aggression, signed at London, 5 July 1933, 148 LNTS 79.

151 *Documents of the Foreign Policy of the USSR* 1959–1970 (n. 14), vol. 16, 393–395.

152 See Donnedieu de Vabres, Henri. 'Un traité multilatéral pour la définition de « l'agresseur »'. *L'année politique francaise et étrangère* 8 (1933) 400–404; Sibert, Marcel. 'À propos des conventions signées à Londres le 3 juillet 1933'. *Revue générale de droit international public* 40 (1933), 529–536; Brière, Yves de la. 'Un nouveau progrès sur la route du droit : La définition de l'agresseur'. *Esprit international* 7(28) (1933), 616–625, 619–625; Friede, Wilhelm. 'Die Ostpakte über die Definition des Angreifers'. *Zeitschrift für Ostrecht* 7(8/9) (1933), 719–723; Le Fur, Louis. 'Les conventions de Londres (1933) et la définition de l'agresseur'. *Revue de droit international, de sciences diplomatiques et politiques* 11 (1933), 179–191; Lapradelle, Albert de. '"Sécurité collective" ou "sûreté sociale"?'. *Revue de droit international* 14 (1934), 9–13, 13; Camille-Jordan, Augustin. 'La définition de l'agresseur'. *Revue de droit international* 14 (1934), 111–128; Kopelmanas, Lazare. 'The Problem of Aggression and the Prevention of War'. *American Journal of International Law* 31(2) (1937), 244–257, 248.

153 See Report of Robert H. Jackson, US Representative to the International Conference on Military Trials – London, 1945, US Department of State, 1949, 273–274, 294 and 302.

154 Ibid., 298.

8 Concluding Remarks

The progressive amelioration of the relationships between the LoN and the USSR, finally led to the latter's adhesion to the League. This was made possible by the internal consolidation of the Soviet regime – meaning the end of its extreme vulnerability to foreign intervention – and by the realization on behalf of Soviet decision-makers that an all-out hostile policy towards 'bourgeois' States, was bound to fail and could even threaten the survival of the USSR, as it could be used as a pretext for further Western interventions. Once the USSR had secured its immediate surroundings through the conclusion of a series of bilateral conventions that included mutual guarantees of non-hostile behaviour within the LoN, the USSR could be ensured that the latter could no longer serve exclusively as an instrument of the Entente.

Germany's and Japan's withdrawals from the LoN made a *rapprochement* with Western states strategically desirable. In 1933, Stalin expressed the view that membership could become an option if it was proven that that organization could contribute to reduce the risk of war.[155] The LoN was by then no longer considered as a potential tool for the union of anti-Soviet forces.[156]

It is undeniable that the outcomes of this early policy of peaceful coexistence, such as the rejection of coercion and annexation have coincided (and sometimes preceded) the emergence of modern *ius contra bellum*, even though their actual implementation was in some cases subordinated to the defence of Soviet national interest. Another example is the definition of aggression officially adopted in Soviet practice in the 1930s. Strikingly, the core elements of the current definition of aggression in international law are based on the Soviet draft as amended in the 'Politis report'.[157]

Arguably, Tunkin and other Soviet authors have participated in the construction of a mythology of 'peaceful coexistence' as one of the constitutive elements of the ideological bases of the October Revolution. More realistically, the increasing commitment of Soviet authorities towards non-intervention and international peace was mainly inspired by military, economic and political realities, rather than axiological principles.[158] As a distinguished analyst of Soviet foreign policy would later observe, 'every human society inevitably adopts and develops

155 Interview published in the *Pravda*, quoted in Xorvatskiĭ, *The League* 1937 (n. 53), 9.

156 Ibid., 10–12.

157 See Tsagourias, Nicholas. 'Nicolas Politis' Initiatives to Outlaw War and Define Aggression, and the Narrative of Progress in International Law'. *European Journal of International Law* 23(1) (2012), 255–266, 259–260, doi: 10.1093/ejil/chr109.

158 See Lerner, 'The Historical' 1964 (n. 3), 870; Lipson, 'Peaceful Coexistence' 1964 (n. 3), 877; Cherviatsova, Alina and Oleksandr Yarmysh. 'Soviet International Law: Between

those ideas that are, at a given moment, best suited to maintaining and expanding the conditions of its existence.'[159] However, this should not obliterate the fact that Soviet foreign legal policy in the interwar period, with its affirmation of 'peaceful coexistence' and collective security, was indeed the source of a significant contribution to the development of modern *ius contra bellum*. From a legal-positivist point of view, the fact that Soviet commitments have sometimes been breached does not remove anything from their historical significance as a contribution to the development of *ius contra bellum*: violations of the law do not deprive it of its legal force. Of course, such violations are susceptible to raise serious doubts as to the sincerity of at least some of the Soviet decision-makers' commitments in the field of collective security.[160]

This story is a welcome illustration of the claim that foreign security policy is best guided by pursuing the defence of concrete and legitimate interests rather than by an inflexible and exclusive reference to values or ideological dogmas.[161] Indeed, the softening of Soviet positions in the field of revolutionary interventionism was reflected in the abandonment, on behalf of the USA of their liberal democratic interventionism. It also made the *rapprochement* with the LoN and the eventual Soviet accession possible. This lesson remains highly relevant in our times of allegedly 'humanitarian' and 'democratic' interventions.

Acknowledgements

I would like to thank the organizers of the conference 'Politics and the Histories of International Law' for giving me the opportunity to present and discuss an early version of this chapter. My gratitude also goes to Bill Bowring and Bakhtiyar Tuzmukhamedov for having agreed to discuss the subject of this chapter. Their advices and encouragements were precious. Of course, I am exclusively responsible for the views expressed therein.

Slogans and Practice'. *Journal of the History of International Law* 19(2) (2017), 296–237, doi: 10.1163/15718050-19231034.

159 Djilas, Milovan. *Conversations with Stalin* (London: Penguin, 2014), 34.

160 See, e.g., Hochman, Jiří. *The Soviet Union and the Failure of Collective Security, 1934–1938* (Ithaca: Cornell University Press, 1984), 172–173. For the view that Litvinov acted in good faith (as opposed to Stalin), see Haslam, Jonathan. *The Soviet Union and the Struggle for Collective Security in Europe, 1933–39* (London: MacMillan, 1984), 230; Graebner, Norman A. and Edward M. Bennett. *The Versailles Treaty and Its Legacy: The Failure of the Wilsonian Vision* (Cambridge: Cambridge University Press, 2011), 211 and 215–220.

161 See, in this sense, Graf Vitzthum, Wolfgang. 'Russland und das Völkerrecht'. *Archiv des Völkerrechts* 54(3) (2016), 239–260, 257; Tunkin, 'Co-Existence' 1958 (n. 19), 78.

Bibliography

'Certain Aspects of the Bolshevist Movement in Russia: Part II: Bolshevist Program of World Revolution'. *International Conciliation* 7 (Doc. No. 149) (1920), 159–200.

'Conventions entre le Dr. Nansen et G. Tchitcherine'. *Revue internationale de la croix-rouge* 3(33) (1921), 910–918.

Документы Внешней Политики СССР [*Documents of the Foreign Policy of the USSR*] (Moscow: Politicheskoĭ Literatury, 1959–1970).

'Notes Exchanged on the Russian-Polish Situation by the United States, France and Poland'. *International Conciliation* 7 (Doc. No. 155) (1920) 459–478.

'Procès-Verbal of the Eighth Session of the Council of the League of Nations'. *League of Nations Official Journal* 1(6) (1920), 304–346.

'Procès-Verbal of the Fifth Session of the Council of the League of Nations'. *League of Nations Official Journal* 1(4) (1920), 115–156.

'Procès-Verbal of the Ninth Session of the Council of the League of Nations'. *League of Nations Official Journal* 1(7) (1920), 391–414.

'Procès-Verbal of the Sixth Session of the Council of the League of Nations'. *League of Nations Official Journal* 1(5) (1920), 213–226.

'Procès-Verbal of the Third Session of the Council of the League of Nations'. *League of Nations Official Journal* 1(2) (1920), 60–64.

'Reply of the Allied and Associated Powers to the Observations of the German Delegation on the Conditions of Peace'. *International Conciliation* 6 (Doc. No. 141) (1919), 1341–1426.

Ashavskiĭ, Boris Matveevich. 'Октябрь 1917 Года и Международное Право [October 1917 and International Law]'. *Вестник Московского университета имени С. Ю. Витте. Серия 2. Юридические науки* [*Herald of the University of Moscow named after S. Yu. Vitte. Series 2. Legal sciences*] 13(4) (2017), 23–29, 25, doi: 10.21777/2587-9472-2017-4-23-29.

Blank, Stephen. 'The Soviet Conquest of Georgia'. *Central Asian Survey* 12 (1993), 33–46, doi: 10.1080/02634939308400798.

Borchard, Edwin M. 'The Kellogg Treaties Sanction War'. *Zeitschrift für ausländisches öffentliches Recht und Völkerrecht* 1 (1929), 126–131.

Bowring, Bill. *The Degradation of the International Legal Order? The Rehabilitation of Law and the Possibility of Politics* (Abingdon: Routledge, 2008).

Bowring, Bill. *Law, Rights and Ideology in Russia: Landmarks in the Destiny of a Great Power* (Abingdon: Routledge, 2014).

Bowring, Bill. 'Yevgeniy Pashukanis, His *Law and Marxism: A General Theory*, and the 1922 Treaty of Rapallo between Soviet Russia and Germany'. *Journal of the History of International Law* 19(2) (2017), 274–295, doi: 10.1163/15718050-19231033.

Bradley, Anna S. 'The Internationalists: How A Radical Plan to Outlaw War Remade the World. By Oona A. Hathaway and Scott J. Shapiro'. *American Journal of International Law* 112(2) (2018), 330–335.

Brière, Yves de la. 'Un nouveau progrès sur la roite du droit: La définition de l'agresseur'. *Esprit international* 7(28) (1933), 616–625.

Camille-Jordan, Augustin. 'La définition de l'agression'. *Revue de droit international* 14 (1934), 111–128.

Cherviatsova, Alina and Oleksandr Yarmysh. 'Soviet International Law: Between Slogans and Practice'. *Journal of the History of International Law* 19(2) (2017), 296–237, doi: 10.1163/15718050-19231034.

Committee on the Judiciary of the US Senate. *Bolshevik Propaganda* (Washington: Government Printing Office, 1919).

Dewar, George A. B. 'Britain's Recognition of the Soviet Government'. *Foreign Affairs* 3(2) (1924), 313–319.

Djilas, Milovan. *Conversations with Stalin* (London: Penguin, 2014).

Donnedieu de Vabres, Henri. 'Un traité multilatéral pour la définition de "l'agresseur"'. *L'année politique et étrangère* 8 (1933), 400–404.

Durdenevskiĭ, Vsevolod Nikolaevich and M. I. Lazarev. *Пять принципов мирного сосуществования* [*Five Principles of Peaceful Coexistence*] (Moscow: State Editions of Legal Literature, 1957).

Engelstein, Laura. *Russia in Flames: War, Revolution, Civil War, 1914–1921* (Oxford: Oxford University Press, 2018).

Freeman, Alwyn V. 'Some Aspects of Soviet Influence on International Law'. *American Journal of International Law* 62(3) (1968), 710–722.

Friede, Wilhelm. 'Die Ostpakte über die Definition des Angreifers'. *Zeitschrift für Ostrecht* 7(8/9) (1933), 719–723.

Graebner, Norman A. and Edward M. Bennett. *The Versailles Treaty and Its Legacy: The Failure of the Wilsonian Vision* (Cambridge: Cambridge University Press, 2011).

Graham, Malbone W. 'The Soviet Security System'. *International Conciliation* 12 (Doc. No. 252) (1928–1929), 345–430.

Graham, Malbone W. 'The Soviet Security Treaties'. *American Journal of International Law* 23(2) (1929), 336–350.

Güçlü, Yücel. 'Turkey's Entrance into the League of Nations'. *Middle Eastern Studies* 39(1) (2003), 186–206, doi: 10.1080/00263200412331301637.

Guieu, Jean-Michel. 'L'"Insécurité collective". L'Europe et la Société des Nations dans l'entre-deux-guerres'. *Bulletin de l'Institut Pierre Renouvin* 30(2) (2009), 21–43, doi: 10.3917/bipr.030.0021.

Haslam, Jonathan. *The Soviet Union and the Struggle for Collective Security in Europe, 1933–39* (London: MacMillan, 1984).

Hathaway, Oona A. and Scott J. Shapiro. *The Internationalists: How a Radical Plan to Outlaw War Remade the World* (New York: Simon & Schuster, 2017).

Hochman, Jiří. *The Soviet Union and the Failure of Collective Security, 1934–1938* (Ithaca: Cornell University Press, 1984).

Hudson, Manley O. 'Membership in the League of Nations'. *American Journal of International Law* 18(3) (1924), 436–458.

Il͡ukhina, Ruzanna Mikhaĭlovna. *Лига Наций: 1919–1934* [*League of Nations: 1919–1934*] (Moscow: Science Publisher, 1982).

Karandashov, Innokenty and Ksenia Shestakova. 'The Principle of Equality of States in the Wake of the Russian Revolution'. *Russian Law Journal* 5(4) (2017), 8–42, 35, doi: 10.17589/2309-8678-2017-5-4-8-42.

Karpov, Victor P. 'The Soviet Concept of Peaceful Coexistence and Its Implications for International Law'. *Law and Contemporary Problems* 29(4) (1964), 858–864.

Kellogg, Frank B. 'Address at the Annual Dinner'. *Proceedings of the American Society of International Law at Its Annual Meeting* 22 (1928), 141–145.

Kopelmanas, Lazare. 'The Problem of Aggression and the Prevention of War'. *American Journal of International Law* 31(2) (1937), 244–257.

Korovin, Evgeniĭ Aleksandrovich. 'Лига наций и ее эволюция [The League of Nations and Its Evolution]'. *Советское право* [*Soviet Law*] No. 1 (1923), 36–43.

Korovin, Evgeniĭ Aleksandrovich. *Международное право переходного времени* [*International Law of the Transition Time*] (Petrograd: State Publisher, 1924).

Korovin, Evgeniĭ Aleksandrovich, ed. *Международные договоры и акты нового времени* [*International Treaties and Acts of the New Time*] (Moscow/Leningrad: State Publisher, 1924).

Korovin, Evgeniĭ Aleksandrovich. *Международное право переходного времени* [*International Law of the Transition Time*] (Moscow: State Publisher, 2nd ed. 1925).

Korovin, Eugene A. 'Soviet Treaties and International Law'. *American Journal of International Law* 22(4) (1928), 753–763.

Korovin, Evgeniĭ Aleksandrovich. 'Пакт Келлога и присоединение к нему СССР [Pact Kellogg and accession of the USSR]'. *Советское право* [*Soviet Law*] No. 6 (1928), 26–48.

Korovine, Eugene A. 'The U.S.S.R. and Disarmament'. *International Conciliation* 15 (Doc. No. 292) (1932–1933), 293–358.

Korovine, Eugene A. 'Review of *The Soviet Union and International Law*'. *Harvard Law Review* 49(8) (1936), 1392–1395.

Kotl͡arevskiĭ, Sergeĭ Andreevich. 'Кризис международного права [The Crisis of International Law]'. *Право и Жизнь* [*Law and Life*] 1 (1922), 80–82.

Kuznet͡sov, Valeriĭ Ivanovich, Raĭs Abdulkhakovich Tuzmukhamedov and Nikolaĭ Aleksandrovich Ushakov. *От Декрета о мире к Декларации мира* [*From the Decree on Peace to the Friendly Relations Declaration*] (Moscow: International Relations Publisher, 1972).

Lapradelle, Albert de. '"Sécurité collective" ou "sureté sociale"?'. *Revue de droit international* 14 (1934), 9–13.

Lauterpacht, Hersch. 'Revolutionary Activities by Private Persons against Foreign States'. *American Journal of International Law* 22(1) (1928), 105–130.

Lauterpacht, Hersch. 'The Pact of Paris and the Budapest Articles of Interpretation'. *Transactions of the Grotius Society* 20 (1934), 178–204.

League of Nations, *Records of the Conference for the Reduction and Limitation of Armaments, Series B. Minutes of the General Commission*, vol. II.

Le Fur, Louis. 'Les conventions de Londres (1933) et la définition de l'agresseur'. *Revue de droit international, de sciences diplomatiques et politiques* 11 (1933), 179–191.

Lenin. *Collected Works* (Moscow: Progress Publishers, 1964; Digital Reprints, 2011), available at: https://www.marxists.org/archive/lenin/works/cw/index.htm (last accessed on 14 September 2020).

Lerner, Warren. 'The Historical Origins of the Soviet Doctrine of Peaceful Coexistence'. *Law and Contemporary Problems* 29(4) (1964), 865–870.

Lipson, Leon. 'Peaceful Coexistence'. *Law and Contemporary Problems* 29(4) (1964), 871–881.

Mälksoo, Lauri. 'Russia-Europe', in *The Oxford Handbook of the History of International Law*, eds. Bardo Fassbender and Anne Peters (Oxford: Oxford University Press, 2012), 764–786.

Mälksoo, Lauri. 'The Soviet Approach to the Right of Peoples to Self-Determination: Russia's Farewell to *Jus Publicum Europaeum*'. *Journal of the History of International Law* 19(2) (2017), 200–218, doi: 10.1163/15718050-19231035.

Mandelstam, André. 'L'interprétation du pacte Briand-Kellogg'. *Revue générale de droit international public* 40 (1933), 537–605.

Meissner, Boris. 'Außenpolitische Theorie und Völkerrechtsdoktrin der Sowjetunion', in *Aussenpolitik und Völkerrecht der Sowjetunion: Ausgewählte Beiträge*, ed. Boris Meissner (Cologne: Verlag Wissenschaft und Politik, 1987), 13–33.

Meissner, Boris. 'Die sowjetische Auffassung von der "friedlichen Koexistenz"', in *Aussenpolitik und Völkerrecht der Sowjetunion: Ausgewählte Beiträge*, ed. Boris Meissner (Cologne: Verlag Wissenschaft und Politik, 1987), 63–82.

Miller, David Hunter. *The Drafting of the Covenant* (New York: G. P. Putnam's Sons, 1928).

Mirkine-Guetzévitch, Boris. 'La doctrine soviétique du droit international'. *Revue générale de droit international public* 32 (1925), 313–337.

Moulis, Émile and Eugène Bergonier. *La guerre entre et la Russie et les alliés (1918–1920)* (Paris: Librairie générale de droit et de jurisprudence, 1937).

Oppenheim, Lassa. 'Du caractère essentiel de la Société des Nations'. *Revue générale de droit international public* 26 (1919), 234–244.

Pashukanis, Evgeniĭ Bronislavovich. *Очерки по международному праву* [*Essays in International Law*] (Moscow: Soviet Law, 1935).

Rougier, Antoine. 'La première assemblée de la Société des Nations (Genève, Novembre–Décembre 1920)'. *Revue générale de droit international public* 28 (1921), 197–412.

Rousseau, Charles. 'De la compatibilité des normes jurisdiques contradictoires dans l'ordre international'. *Revue générale de droit international public* 39 (1932), 133–192.

Rutenberg, Gregory. 'The Baltic States and the Soviet Union'. *American Journal of International Law* 29(4) (1935), 598–615.

Shotwell, James T. 'The Pact of Paris with Historical Commentary'. *International Conciliation* 12 (Doc. No. 243) (1928), 447–520.

Sibert, Marcel. 'À propos des conventions signées à Londres le 3 juillet 1933'. *Revue générale de droit international public* 40 (1933), 529–536.

Socher, Johannes. 'Lenin, (Just) Wars of National Liberation, and the Soviet Doctrine on the Use of Force'. *Journal of the History of International Law* 19(2) (2017), 219–245, doi: 10.1163/15718050-19231018.

Stalin, Joseph. *Problems of Leninism* (Moscow: Foreign Languages Publishing House, 1954; transl. from the 11th ed.).

Trotsky, Leon. *The Revolution Betrayed* (London: Faber & Faber, 1937).

Tsagourias, Nicholas. 'Nicolas Politis' Initiatives to Outlaw War and Define Aggression, and the Narrative of Progress in International Law'. *European Journal of International Law* 23(1) (2012), 255–266, doi: 10.1093/ejil/chr109.

Tunkin, Grigory I. 'Co-Existence and International Law'. *Recueil des cours de l'académie de droit international de La Haye* 95 (1958-III), 1–81.

Tunkin, Grigory Ivanovich. 'Международно-правовые идеи Великой Октябрьской социалистической революции [International Legal Ideas of the Great October Socialist Revolution]'. *Советский ежегодник международного права* [*Soviet Yearbook of International Law*] (1966–1967), 15–29.

Ushakov, Nikolaĭ Aleksandrovich. *Невмешательство во внутренние дела государств* [*Non-Intervention in Domestic State Affairs*] (Moscow: International Relations, 1971).

Vandy, François. 'Le pacte Kellogg'. *Revue générale de droit international public* 37 (1930), 5–18.

Vinogradoff, Paul. 'The Legal and the Political Aspects of the League of Nations', in *On the History of International Law and International Organization: Collected Papers of Sir Paul Vinogradoff*, ed. William E. Butler (Clark: Lawbook Exchange, 2009), 37–43.

Vitzthum, Wolfgang Graf. 'Russland und das Völkerrecht'. *Archiv des Völkerrechts* 54(3) (2016), 239–260.

Vodovozov, Vasiliĭ Vasil'evich. *Версальский мир и Лига наций* [*The Peace of Versailles and the League of Nations*] (Petrograd: Mysl', 1922).

Wilson, Woodrow. 'Address to a Joint Session of Congress on the Conditions of Peace, January 8, 1918'. 1918, available at: https://www.presidency.ucsb.edu/documents/address-joint-session-congress-the-conditions-peace (last accessed on 14 September 2020).

Wood, Alan. *Russia's Frozen Frontier: A History of Siberia and the Russian Far East 1581–1991* (London: Bloomsbury, 2011).

Xorvatskiĭ, Vladimir L'vovich. *Лига наций* [*The League of Nations*] (Moscow: Sotsėkgiz, 1937).

Yoshitomi, M. 'L'affaire de la perquisition de l'ambassade soviétique à Pékin par les autorités chinoises'. *Revue générale de droit international public* 35 (1929), 184–192.

Zimmern, Alfred. *The League of Nations and the Rule of Law: 1918–1935* (London: Macmillan, 1936).

CHAPTER 7

Three Wartime Textbooks of International Law

Deborah Whitehall

Abstract

Three wartime textbooks of international law published and then reissued by Hersch Lauterpacht, James Brierly and Georges Scelle between 1940 and 1945 present a collective argument against the politics of war by analysing the design flaws of interwar international law. Though the criticism was not new, its repetition in textbooks during war highlights the strategic significance of using basic principles to defend the pacifistic function of international law when lawlessness reigned the global imaginary. The textbook genre became an unexpected, critical field which enlivened when its first readers found the past of international law in their present, conditioned by crisis. There, against the scene of first reading and writing, the texts became counter texts which side-stepped diplomatic controversy to critically examine the reasons for the breakdown of order and remind internationalists about the continuity of law despite war, the political limits on legal function, and the tasks for their diligent, expert attention.

Keywords

World War Two – textbooks – wartime – Lauterpacht – Brierly – Scelle

1 Introduction

Hersch Lauterpacht's revised, sixth edition of Lassa Oppenheim's *Disputes, War and Neutrality*, went to press simultaneously with the fall of France in June 1940. The wartime revisions to the classic handbook annotated the unfolding crisis indirectly by analysing the flaws of interwar international law for readers to register and draw their own conclusions.[1] Almost simultaneous publication of other textbooks by eminent international lawyers compounded the strategic effects of using history to expound the basic principles of international law concerning the legal status of war. The third edition of James Brierly's *The Law*

1 Oppenheim, Lassa. *International Law. A Treatise*, vol II, ed. Hersch Lauterpacht (London: Longmans, 6th ed. 1940).

 | DOI:10.1163/9789004461802_009

of Nations appeared in 1942 after the formal extension of the European war into Asia, and preceded the 1943 publication of *Manuel Élémentaire de Droit International Public* by Georges Scelle.[2] Each author explained how war survived as a legally and/or politically permissible category despite the initiatives of the Covenant of the League in the *1919 Treaty of Peace* and the *1928 Pact of Paris*.[3] Though the criticism was not new, its repetition in textbooks during war highlights the strategic utility of using basic principles to advance arguments about the continuity and function of law when crisis overwhelmed the global imaginary. The effect refigures the textbook genre as an unexpected critical field about the politics of law which the routine substitutions by updated editions leave behind as the truth of another generation.

The suggestion shared by the three wartime textbooks makes visible the critical rise among the privileged ranks of liberal international law that concentrates during intervals of crisis through explanations of basic principles. Other polemics published by liberal international lawyers during war, including by Brierly and Scelle, contained similar messages about the legal significance of war or the author's hopes for new principles to guarantee a more peaceful future.[4] The radical aspect of the textbook genre followed from its systematic emphasis on legal and diplomatic history to explain disciplinary truths relevant to war for amateur readers.[5] Historical analysis, especially of key interwar situations and the juridical framework for mediating international disputes

---

2 Brierly, James L. *The Law of Nations* (Oxford: Oxford University Press, 3rd ed. 1942); and Scelle, Georges. *Manuel élémentaire de droit international public <avec les textes essentiel>* (Paris: Domat-Montchrestien, 1943).

3 Treaty of Peace between the Allied and Associated Powers and Germany (signed 28 June 1919, entered into force 10 January 1920) (1919) 226 CTS (1919 Treaty of Peace) and Treaty between the United States and other Powers Providing for the Renunciation of War as an Instrument of National Policy (signed 27 August 1928, entered into force 24 July 1929) (1929) 94 LNTS 57 (1928 Pact of Paris).

4 For examples, see Scelle, Georges. *Le sens international* (Paris: Presses Universitaires de France, 1942); Brierly, James. *The Outlook for International Law* (Oxford: Oxford University Press, 1944); Lauterpacht, Hersch. 'The Law of Nations, the Law of Nature and the Rights of Man'. *Transactions of the Grotius Society* 29 (1943), 1–33; Kelsen, Hans. *Law and Peace in International Relations* (Cambridge: Harvard University Press, 1942); Schwarzenberger, Georg. *Power Politics: A Study of International Society* (London: Stevens & Sons, 1941); Schwarzenberger, Georg and George Keeton. *Making International Law Work* (London: Stevens & Sons Ltd, 1939); Schwarzenberger, Georg. *International Law and Totalitarian Lawlessness* (London: Stevens & Sons, 1943); and Wright, Quincy. *A Study of War* (Chicago: University of Chicago Press, 1942).

5 The difference between the textbooks examined in this chapter and other polemics published by jurists during war, including those addressing the foundations of international law and the problem of war, related to the methods of the latter. Other scholarship pursued sophisticated, complex and direct arguments for the future that went beyond exposition of

overseen by the League of Nations, insulated the textbooks from controversy by directing questions about the war to the preceding generation. The textbook genre utilised explication of the existing and consequently, non-controversial foundations of the present law as a persuasive technique to further arguments concerning the continuity of law, the dangers of sovereignty for peace and the function of all internationalists with legal expertise. Authority to define the foundations of a field of knowledge followed from the reputed expertise of the author, the relative naïveté of readers or their different professional standing, the systematic organization and straightforward tone of explanations, the motivation of the reader to learn and the absence of a clear contradictor. For the international lawyer, the articulation of legal principles also sets the authoritative standards for assessing risk, solving disputes and advising clients of their options in legal practice. These factors give the pedagogical genre especial persuasive significance for the authors' polemic by allowing existing legal phenomena to expose, as objective facts, the reasons why law fails to prevent war when war was also part of the wartime reader's present reality.

Attention to the critical element of the textbooks adds another layer to contemporary scholarly debates about the bias that defines and narrows the history of international law by privileging the activities of certain states and internationalists. Complaints about Eurocentrism typify this debate and urge the expansion of conventional historiographies beyond the familiar compass set by geography, war, market domination and other forms of exploitation by the nation-state.[6] Lauterpacht, Scelle and Brierly represent cliché examples of the elite targeted by scholarly efforts to uncover plural histories and diversify the meaning of international law.[7] Their textbooks outlined the field for the

---

existing or basic principles of war and peace and engaged more directly with the political significance of international law. See, e.g., Brierly, *Outlook for International Law* 1944 (n. 4), 91–94.

6 Fassbender, Bardo and Anne Peters. 'Introduction: Towards a Global History of International Law', in *The Oxford Handbook of the History of International Law*, eds. Bardo Fassbender and Anne Peters (Oxford: Oxford University Press, 2012), 1–24, 2.

7 Efforts to categorise or separate historical and legal methods with analytical precision also accompany the plurality of practices that contribute to the production of historical and normative meanings that can and do mobilise without categorical allegiance to or by exclusion of alternative methodological options. Historians reflect on the dynamic exchanges between text and textual setting that produce contingent meaning encouraged, not fixed, by a combination of factors. Those factors may hold political charge depending on what or whose past is identifiable as history according to numerous variables relevant to the material or temporal setting. Innovative historical scholarship flourishes, as Lauren Benton suggests, alongside urging for methodical precision or truth and, as this study of the wartime textbooks also indicates, often generates meaning reflexively, fluidly and even, intuitively, according to the preferences of the author of an historical text and its reader. A study of the

war-generation of English and French students of international law as well as for interested amateurs and the international legal profession. The international law of the European nation-state sets the relevant parameters for their reflections to the exclusion of other protagonists, legalities or histories. The detail sometimes neglected by present-day concerns to complete international legal history beyond that frame relates to the critical work by internal contradictors such as Lauterpacht, Scelle and Brierly who were the unmistakable beneficiaries of their birthplace, culture and privileges and knew only the international law of their Europe and its ancestors. Rereading their texts reveals the critical projects which exist at the traditional centre of liberal international law and the polemics which unravel there by those who trust its authority and demand its revision.

Attention to both the texts and the context of reading and writing the wartime textbooks of international law exposes how the authors' strategic project progressed as basic lessons. Part 2 begins by considering the experience of the first, wartime reader of the textbooks to elucidate the methods of the author's polemic, the likely persuasiveness of the polemic, and the author's diligent avoidance of diplomatic controversy. Part 3 examines the political and historical context which conditioned the experience of reading and writing foundational texts in the shadow of war and which conditioned how the author's message took shape. Part 4 reads the texts as counter-texts by reference to the substance of the authors' explications. Part 5 draws three reminders from the preceding textual and contextual analysis before concluding, in Part 6, with reflections on the critical rise within privileged ranks of disciplinary knowledge which exploits such privilege to shape the discipline's past and its future.

2 The Wartime Reader

The legibility of the critical project shared by the wartime textbooks depends in part on the experience of its first readers who read during war as students, with

wartime textbooks which pays attention to the scene of first writing and reading exemplifies the interconnectedness between methods and the potential depth and reach of the critical yield that follows, as contingent meaning. For details of the methodological debates relevant to international legal history and reactions to calls for methodological precision, see comments and references in Benton, Lauren. 'Beyond Anachronism: Histories of International Law and Global Legal Politics'. *Journal of the History of International Law* 21(1) (2019), 1–34, see esp., reflections on the multiple, fluid and creative techniques by which historical actors shape legal discourses without compromising the integrity of alternatives, at 6, and the plurality (and interconnectedness) of research agendas, repertoires and techniques available to legal and historical thinkers that thicken scholarly insight and debate, and therefore, historical understanding e.g., 11–22 and 23.

professional aspirations, or experts. Focussing on the reader acknowledges its part in shaping textual meaning and its experience of war as integral to the scene of reading. Though reader-response dominates traditional conceptions of textuality, textual theorists now disagree about how far hermeneutics govern textuality or textual meaning and more often emphasise the relativity of reading, writing and historicising texts.[8]

The importance of relativity among methodological approaches is helpful to understanding all types of texts irrespective of genre. Putting the reader at the centre of textuality is not wrong but rather requires attention to what Jeremy McGann refers to the 'material constitutions' which make reading a 'phenomenal event' and substantiate the background against which a text enters the world. This approach is sympathetic to historical methods which highlight the significance of text and textual setting for the production of contingent meanings which are always responsive to a myriad of factors and perspectives but which always remember the 'determinate sociohistorical conditions' of writing.[9] Historians also regard that horizon when they valorise the plurality of stories which can arise from alternative methodologies. The helpful insight from textual studies relates to the special status of informational or historical texts which, like the wartime textbooks of international law, assume a certain social dynamic between the author and reader which highlights meaning as a message or instruction and consequently identifies the reader as a receiver or listener. Although the 'material constitutions' or noises that the reader hears when he or she encounters text matter, including vital historicising details which thicken textual meaning, those contextual noises take shape in informational texts with the help of authorial intervention. The textbook genre automatically gives the author's explications 'informational' stature which the wartime experts of international law exploited for strategic effect.

The identity of the reader is visible in the three textbooks in different ways and in each case, its presence as an amateur with little or basic knowledge

---

8 See, e.g., McGann, Jerome. *The Textual Condition* (Princeton: Princeton University Press, 1991), 4–5. Such approaches frequently take account of the distinction, drawn by French literary theorist Rolande Barthes in early 1970s, between readerly and writerly texts, the first leaves little room for interpretative initiative by readers and the second demands effort by the reader such that reading becomes part of the process of writing or constructing textual meaning: Barthes, Roland. *S/Z* (New York: Farrar, Straus & Giroux, 1991 ed. [1970]); and Buchanan, Ian. *Oxford Dictionary of Critical Theory* (Oxford: Oxford University Press, 2010), 399. A hybrid approach that takes account of the combined contribution of reader and writer in broader historical-political context is helpful for understanding the meaning of the wartime textbooks. For recent explication of debates about the relationship between textual and contextual methods relevant to the history of international law see e.g. n. 7.

9 McGann, *Textual Condition* 1991 (n. 8), 9.

of international law, or as an expert, reinforces the writer's authority and the reliability of his straightforward explications. Though experts used each of the texts, Hersch Lauterpacht's *Disputes* (1940) is exceptional among the three textbooks insofar as Oppenheim's renowned text, first published in 1906 and long-reputed as a leading professional manual, directly addressed practitioners and military personnel, including those employed in the British civil service or military forces during the Second World War.[10] The textbook defended for those readers, for example, the seemingly incompatible British practices of arming merchant ships, on the one hand, and forcing neutral merchant vessels into port for examination, on the other, or as with the other texts, included other signposts to the breakdown of international order and the unworkability of the interwar system administered by the League.[11] Though Lauterpacht does not identify his reader directly, his Preface acknowledges the assistance and advice of leading international lawyers who advised the British government during the war including Sir William Malkin, James Spaight and Arnold McNair.[12] In personal correspondence dated 23 November 1943, Lauterpacht also identifies American military personnel as readers, noting:

> [F]inally, I have received a peremptory request from Longmans to prepare as soon as possible a revised edition of the War Volume of Oppenheim. The present stock is exhausted – one reason being that practically every new American warship has it in its Library! If the American navy grows at the present rate, we shall have to have yet another edition in 1945![13]

---

10 Early reviews of Oppenheim, *Disputes* 1940 (n. 1) and Brierly, *Law of Nations* 1942 (n. 2) note the usefulness of the text for experts and students: e.g., Davies, J. 'Oppenheim's International Law, Vol. II: Disputes, War and Neutrality. Sixth edition. By H. Lauterpacht. London: Longmans, Green & Co., Ltd 1940 xliv and 766 pp.'. *Law Quarterly Review* 57(3) (1941), 429–430; Dunn, Frederick S. 'Oppenheim's International Law. Sixth Edition. Vol. II: Disputes, War, and Neutrality. Edited by H. Lauterpacht. (London: Longmans, Green and Company. 1940. Pp. xliv, 766. $17.50.)'. *American Political Science Review* 35(4) (1941), 779–780; P. H. W. 'The Law of Nations. By J. L. Brierly. Third edition. Oxford University Press 1942. Viii+272pp. (5s.)'. *British Yearbook of International Law* 21 (1944), 235–236; and F. M. G. 'The Law of Nations by J. L. Brierly'. *Journal of Comparative Legislation and International Law* 26(3/4) (1944), 86.

11 Oppenheim, *Disputes* 1940 (n. 1).

12 Ibid., vi.

13 Lauterpacht, Elihu. *The Life of Sir Hersch Lauterpacht, QC, FBA, LLD* (Cambridge: Cambridge University Press, 2010), 239.

The usefulness of the 1940 volume was 'indispensable', in the view of one wartime reviewer, 'for any serious inquiry, whether practical or academic, into the Law of War and Neutrality'.[14]

Although experts also turned to Brierly and Scelle during war, their textbooks contemplate a different reader who is either an intelligent amateur with interest in international affairs or a student. Scelle's Manuel addresses students in their 'troisième année de licence' and proposes to 'décrire' or 'expose' the field in 'un manuel élémentaire' which he intended to be 'une base pour des études' or written supplement to 'le cours oral'.[15] Straightforward descriptions, whether addressing the amateur or not, exemplify 'une intention didactique' that obliges readers, if only by the temporal and thematic provocations of Scelle's elementary explanations, to recognise the properly legal character of international law and deploy 'une gymnastique juridique dans des domaines particulièrement importants'.[16] Such 'juridical gymnastics' was also critical, in an ethical, social and political sense, because each author defended the system of international law by explicating existing rules relevant to international relations and the capacity of law, properly conceived, to restore order.

Brierly did not address a particular category of reader directly in 1942 but identifies both laymen and students in the preceding (1935) and subsequent (1949) editions and confirms his well-known commitment, which Scelle shared, for the inclusion of public international law in legal education.[17] Brierly noted in 1949 that,

> the purpose of the book remains what it was when it was first published ... it is not intended as a substitute for the standard text-books on the subject, but as an introduction either for students who are beginning their law courses, or, I hope, for laymen who wish to form some idea of the part that law plays, or that we may reasonably hope that it will play, in the relations of states.[18]

---

14 Davies, 'Disputes' 1941 (n. 10), 430.

15 Scelle, *Manuel* 1943 (n. 2), 7–9. The student readers studied international law in their 'third year' of studying for their professional licence and read Scelle's text as 'an elementary manual' which described or expounded relevant topics as the 'foundation for study' and as a supplement to lectures or classes.

16 Ibid. Brierly says the textbook's intention is to 'teach' students and expects the reader to be flexible in its study of various fields of international law.

17 Brierly, James L. 'International Law in the Education of a Lawyer'. *Michigan State Bar Journal* 27(10) (1948), 5; and Brierly, James L. 'International Law as a Subject of Education'. *Journal of the Society of Public Teachers of Law* (1926), 1–5.

18 Brierly, James L. 'Preface to Fourth Edition', in *The Law of Nations*, ed. James L. Brierly, (Oxford: Oxford University Press, 4th ed. 1949); see similar remarks: Brierly, *Law of*

The same anticipatory gesture to intelligent, political alert readers applied in 1935 when his Preface addressed 'the layman whose interests in international affairs may lead him to inquire what part law is capable of playing in that field'.[19] In 1942, as with the earlier and subsequent editions of *Law of Nations*, Brierly presented an argument defending the pacifist function of international law and dedicated his 'small book' to helping his readers work out how law might assist the 'building up of a saner international order'.[20] Reviewers of the wartime edition confirm the continuing success of Brierly's practical ambition for the broad use of his book by interested readers.[21]

Each of the textbooks was self-conscious of its historical placement on the cusp of radical normative change when existing law would undergo important revisions and reminded readers of the purpose of understanding the laws relevant to war. The identity of the reader of the textbooks elucidates how textual meaning arises from reading texts as much as from authorial choices about style and substance as well as the diplomatic setting. The persuasiveness of the author's polemic for its intended reader depended on the elementary format and style that typifies the genre and its use of historical methods.[22] This meant communicating arguments *against* the political and social restrictions on the pacifist function of law and *for* the rule of law with simplicity. The past provided authority for the irrefutability of existing rules and exposed the juridical design to critical comment which did not, at least directly, disturb the present politics or legal challenges of conducting the present war. The three wartime textbooks of international law present an example of how the numerous contingencies relevant to textual meaning interrelate to produce layers of meaning to progress a strategic project, presented as exposition of basic principles set in the past.[23] An elementary manual, a treatise or the suggestiveness of

---

Nations 1942 (n. 2), v–vi; Brierly, James L. *The Law of Nations* (Oxford: Clarendon Press, 2nd ed. 1928, 1930), v–vi; and Brierly, James L. *The Law of Nations* (Oxford: Clarendon Press, 1936, 1938), v–vi.

19 Brierly, *The Law of Nations*, 2nd ed. 1936, 1938 (n. 18), *vi.*

20 Scelle, *Manuel* 1943 (n. 2), 24; and Brierly, *Law of Nations*, 3rd ed., 1942 (n. 2), vi.

21 K. L. 'The Law of Nations. By J. L. Brierly. Third Edition. 1942. London: Humphrey Milford, Oxford University Press, viii and 272 pp. (6s. net.)'. *Cambridge Law Journal* 8(3) (1944), 340.

22 For empirical analyses of the international law textbook, as a specific genre, focussed on contemporary or nineteenth century examples see e.g., Roberts, Anthea. *Is International Law International?* (Oxford: Oxford University Press, 2017), 129–208; and Carty, John Antony. *19th Century Textbooks and International Law* (Cambridge: Jesus College Doctoral Dissertation, 1972). This chapter approaches the textbooks differently in order to elucidate relevant critical projects pursued in the textbooks and which depended on the interrelationship between various textual and contextual details.

23 See references at n. 7 and n. 8.

titles purporting to articulate all principles relevant to the field, indicate that there was little room for interpretative independence by readers. The textbook genre was a technique for disguising the author's polemical intention so as to avoid controversy and maximise its persuasive effect.

For readers of the three wartime textbooks, there was a double effect. Text and textual setting meant historical errors, recounted as normative permissions for war, enlivened against the reader's consciousness of the existing crisis, and further, alerted amateurs and experts to the political choices which lead to war and the responsibility of all readers for the proper functioning of law. The critical effect remained imprecise, as it always does, until the reader encounters the text under the material conditions that shaped the experience of reading new texts about war during war.

3 The Scene of Writing and Reading the Textbooks for the First Time

War conditioned the scene of writing and first reading of the textbooks and, for some readers, even prompted them to read. For an early reviewer of Lauterpacht's 5th edition of Oppenheim's Disputes, which was completed in June 1935 and before the effects of the arms embargo imposed by Britain on Italy and Ethiopia in July were clear, there was 'at this time ... a certain feeling of unreality' in reading a treatise on wars and neutrality.[24] How could a textbook name a crime and then elucidate the rules governing the conduct of states during its next, increasingly likely, commission? By 1940, the unreality of speculation about the next war and the efficacy of laws relevant to its conduct, became the new reality of international rupture and the dramatic reshaping of existing rules of neutrality. The textbooks did not criticise the diplomatic or military progress of war against Germany or question the legitimacy of the initiating declarations by France and Great Britain in September 1939. Each downplayed the impact of war on juridical principles, including those relevant to neutrality and the conduct of war, without contesting Allied choices and in several cases, confirmed the legality of Allied action. Nevertheless, consecutive publication of the three textbooks during war, the disciplinary stature of each author, their professional and diplomatic experience, and analysis of rules relevant to war and neutrality and the breakdown of legal regime established by the Covenant of the League in the *1919 Treaty of Peace* and *1928 Pact of Paris*,

24 G. 'Oppenheim's International Law, Vol. II, Disputes, War and Neutrality, 5th Edition by H. Lauterpacht. Longmans, Green & Co. ii+782pp (45s. net)'. *British Yearbook of International Law* 17 (1936), 234.

amplified their critical message. Contextual details, spoken or otherwise evident to the textbook readers, gave force to the authors' criticism of the political choices of states which allow war and frustrate the ordering potential of international law and the League's pacifistic functions. The collective message against war was also, unsurprisingly, a pledge for the continuity of international law and its future.

Lauterpacht, Brierly and Scelle wrote about war in general with a specific war at the hem of their analyses. Several reviewers of Lauterpacht's *Disputes* (1940) note the coalescence between the collapse of France and the publication of the treatise. One suggested the result ignored the convention that *inter arma silent leges* (among arms, laws are silent). The reviewer approved, finding it 'encouraging to see competent men, amidst wanton efforts to destroy civilization, devoting themselves to scholarly pursuits in the field of international law, undisturbed by the low esteem in which law is held today'.[25] Lauterpacht encouraged such judgments by introducing his text with a reminder of the world situation and the continuing relevance of the 'existing' rules of international law:

> The present volume goes to press in June 1940 – at a time of an anxious phase of a war whose outcome is bound to influence decisively the substance and the structure of International Law in the coming generation. In the meantime the exposition of the existing law must disregard the possibility or the prospects of its changes in the future or the fact of its violations in the past.[26]

Both Scelle and Brierly, also gestured to the existing crisis as part of the broader context of writing about international law and war or referred to pertinent interwar details which exposed the weaknesses of that system and prompted critical reflection on the causes of political rupture.[27] Scelle reminded his student reader, consistent with Lauterpacht's interest in espousing existing principles, that 'nous avons laissé de côté délibérément les développements

---

25 The aphorism conveys the suggestion that states do not observe the rule of law though the municipal origins of the maxim explain the deference of local laws to the national interest during times of military emergency: Fellmeth, Aaron and Maurice Horwitz. *Guide to Latin in International Law* (Oxford: Oxford University Press, 2009); for the review see Deák, Francis. 'International Law. By L. Oppenheim. Vol. II. Disputes, War and Neutrality. 6th ed. Edited by H. Lauterpacht. New York, London and Toronto: Longmans, Green & Co., 1940. Pp. xliv, 766. Index $17.50'. *American Journal of International Law* 35(2) (1941), 403–404, 403–404.

26 Oppenheim, *Disputes* 1940 (n. 1), v.

27 Brierly, *Law of Nations* 1942 (n. 2), vi; and Scelle, *Manuel* 1943 (n. 2), 7–9.

d'histoire diplomatique. Il importe que l'étudiant se convainque que le cours de Droit public international est, lui aussi, un cours de Droit'.[28] His promise to ignore the present diplomatic crisis was only partially true and contradicted his continuous efforts to evaluate the international situation against which the textbook issued. The *Manuel* concludes with a less subtle gesture to the possibilities of 'une nouvelle guerre revolutionnaire dont l'enjeu, certes, est d'ordre économique et social, mais dont le règlement exige une construction d'ordre juridique et instutionnel'.[29] Brierly referred directly to the 'difficulties of publication in war-time' as the reason for not updating certain passages which 'now appear to me to have been mistaken'.[30] His reminder, that law changes and that writing happens in context, elucidates the strategic entry of all texts as historically situated reflections about the continuity and possibilities of law. All authors presented law as a historically contingent phenomenon that exists and continues despite the widespread uncertainty about the end of law after 1939.

The disciplinary and professional repute of Lauterpacht, Brierly and Scelle reinforced the likely influence of their textbooks among a broad circle of interested readers. At the time of publication, each author was a renowned expert on the legal principles and theoretical debates relevant to the use of force and, importantly, had professional experience of the practical challenges for pacific solution in the absence of enforceable procedures or any satisfactory regime to protect reasonable state interests.[31] Hersch Lauterpacht held the Whewell

28 '... we have deliberately left aside developments of diplomatic history. It is important for the student to understand that the study of International Law is, for him also, the study of Law': Scelle, *Manuel* 1943 (n. 2), 9.

29 Ibid., 660 and 726: 'a new revolutionary war, the stakes of which, certainly, are the economic and social order, but of which settlement requires the construction of legal and institutional order'.

30 Brierly, *Law of Nations* 1942 (n. 2), *vi*.

31 See, e.g., Scelle, *Manuel* 1943 (n. 2), 726; Scelle, Georges. *Précis de droit des gens (principes et systématique)*, Vols. I & II (Paris: Recueil Sirey, 1932 and 1934); Scelle, Georges. 'Preface', in *Carl Strupp, Legal Machinery for Change* (London: Constable & Co., 1937). Lauterpacht, Brierly and Scelle published, lectured and engaged in diplomatic and advisory work in both languages and were well known to each other and in diplomatic circles. The assumed authoritative status of the revised, English textbooks follows not least from the availability of earlier editions in translation, including French for readers in diplomatic circles including Scelle, and the likelihood that both Brierly and Lauterpacht were familiar with Scelle's *Précis de Droit* which confirmed his intellectual preferences for his own idiosyncratic version of monism and views about the social function of law and which underpin international law, Scelle, *Manuel* 1943 (n. 2), e.g., 11–14, 726. For a brief appraisal of Scelle's historical and political methods, his monism and his social theory of international law see, e.g., Koskenniemi, Martti. *The Gentle Civilizer of Nations: The Rise and Fall of International Law* 1870–1960 (Cambridge: Cambridge University Press, 2001), 327–338.

Chair of International Law at the University of Cambridge (1938–1955); James Brierly held the Chichele Chair of Public International Law in Oxford (1922–1947); and Georges Scelle was Professor at the Faculté de Droit de Paris (1933–1948).[32] Brierly and Scelle also served as lieutenants in the First World War and all three were active in government or diplomatic service during the interwar or war period, either as legal advisers or counsel (Lauterpacht) or as legal members of committees or other delegations to the League of Nations and other international organizations for either the United Kingdom or France (Brierly and Scelle).

Those experiences helped shape the distinctive theoretical position developed by each author about the role of law as an ordering technique and which established their scholarly reputations in the 1920s and 1930s.[33] Each believed in the existing science of international law and its pacifist function though from varying theoretical angles and with varying degrees of optimism about the effectiveness of law against unruly states.[34] Scelle understood international law to be the organic effect or product of social cohesion, among a society of individuals and among various societies administered by those individuals. According to him, the rule of law, being the mirror of societal health, is anathema to unchecked state sovereignty and the privileging of national interests which lead to war. Lauterpacht, an ardent critic of orthodox positivism, understood the rule of law rather than social solidarity was the basis of international

---

32 For general biographical and bibliographical details see, e.g., Hamson, Charles J. 'Sir Hersch Lauterpacht (1897–1960)', in *Oxford Dictionary of National Biography* (Oxford: Oxford University Press, 2019 ed. [2004]); Jenks, Clarence W. 'Hersch Lauterpacht: The Scholar as Prophet'. *British Yearbook of International Law* 36 (1960), 1–103; Lauterpacht, *Life of Sir Hersch Lauterpacht* 2010 (n. 13); Waldock, Humphrey. 'James Leslie Brierly', in *Oxford Dictionary of National Biography* (Oxford: Oxford University Press, 2019 ed. [2004]); Tanca, Antonio. 'Georges Scelle (1878–1961): Biographical Note with Bibliography'. *European Journal of International Law* 1(1) (1990), 240–249.

33 On the interdependence of teaching and theory in Scelle see, e.g., Hubert, Thierry. 'The European Tradition in International Law: Georges Scelle: The Thought of Georges Scelle'. *European Journal of International Law* 1(1) (1990), 193, 195.

34 See, e.g., Brierly, James L. 'Relation of International Law to International Peace'. *Cornell Law Quarterly* 13(1) (1927), 385–398; Brierly, James L. 'Le fondement du caractère obligatoire du droit international'. *Recueil des cours de l'academie de droit international de La Haye* 3 (1928), 482; Brierly, James L. 'The Shortcomings of International Law'. *British Yearbook of International Law* 5 (1924), 4–16, 15; Lauterpacht, Hersch and Humphrey Waldock, eds. *The Basis of Obligation in International Law and other Papers by the Late James Leslie Brierly* (Oxford: Clarendon Press, 1958); Lauterpacht, Hersch. 'Brierly's Contribution to International Law'. *British Yearbook of International Law* 32 (1955–56), 1–19; Scelle, *Précis de Droit* 1932 and 1934 (n. 31); and Lauterpacht, Hersch. *The Function of Law in the International Community* (Oxford: Oxford University Press, 2011 ed. [1933]).

order and criticised state sovereignty as the reason for legal violations or for the weaknesses built into the legal system. Brierly's political realism tracked a path between doctrine and social cohesion by suggesting the rule of law was the key to order but its effectiveness required states to trust its capacity to satisfy sovereign interests and deliver justice. Each understood law was an ordering technique but that regulatory success depended on the ethical and psychological attitudes of states which were, in the end, not merely subjects but the agents and designers of rules.

The effect of each author's prior writings and renown – as a theorist, teacher and practitioner of the law – put the textbooks into conversation and reinforced the publications as authoritative and theoretically motivated statements of the existing field.[35] Each author was bilingual and shared scholarly and professional circles.[36] Each author continued to teach and write at his home institution despite changes to daily life in Britain and France, including the German occupation of Paris from June 1940.[37] Lauterpacht and Brierly also provided strategic advice to allied governments on questions of international law, including laws of war and neutrality or other matters of relevant to British and or American defence.[38] It is unsurprising in those circumstances – of timing and the professional and scholarly repute of each author – that the textbooks were in demand and reissued during or immediately after war despite paper shortages.[39]

---

35 Wartime reviews of each textbook noted the esteem of the author and the authority of their explanations of interwar international law, e.g., Davies, 'Oppenheim's International Law' 1940 (n. 9), 429, 430; Deák, *International Law* 1941 (n. 25); Friedmann, Wolfgang 'Textbook Myth on International Law'. *Modern Law Review* 4(4) (1940–1941), 299; K. L., '*The Law of Nations*' 1944 (n. 21).

36 Cf. n. 31 and n. 32.

37 See the biographical and professional details of each scholar, provided in n. 32.

38 None were engaged in active military service during World War Two. Scelle continued to write and teach at the Law Faculty at Paris throughout the Second World War which remained opened despite German occupation: Whitton, John. 'Public International Law in France since the War'. *American Journal of International Law* 2(43) (1949), 340–343, 341; Dupuy, René-Jean. 'Images de Georges Scelle'. *European Journal of International Law* 1(1) (1990), 235–239; Tanca, 'Georges Scelle' 1990 (n. 32), see esp. list of courses offered by Scelle, 248–249. Brierly served in various governmental Committees during war, though not with the same strategic energy or publicity of Lauterpacht who provided important strategic advice to the British and American administrations: Lauterpacht, *Life of Sir Hersch Lauterpacht* 2010 (n. 13), 104–250; Waldock, 'James Leslie Brierly' 2004 (n. 32). For Scelle, war represented a hiatus in his contributions to government and international organization and reflected the limitations of his employment by the University of Paris throughout war. Tanca, 'Georges Scelle' 1990 (n. 32) 240, 240.

39 The successive issue and reissue of their textbooks in 1940/1944 (Lauterpacht), 1942/1946 (Brierly) and 1943/1944 (Scelle) confirmed interest in the views of disciplinary leaders

Only Lauterpacht, who was Jewish and with family still in Poland, left Europe for America during the war following an invitation from the Carnegie Endowment for International Peace and with the help of the British Foreign Office and Ministry of Information.[40] His activities in America clearly enhanced the influence of his textbook and widened its readership. Lauterpacht arrived in New York with his wife and son in early October 1940 (some months after the sixth edition of *Disputes* appeared in June) and immediately commenced an extensive lecture tour to promote his understanding of international law and war and respond to questions about the international situation relevant to Anglo-British relations.[41] He also advised the U.S. government on numerous matters which helped it rationalise its war-contributions to Great Britain before formalising its status as a belligerent in 1942.[42] Key memorandums included the legality of the transfer of U.S. destroyers to Great Britain or the wide powers conferred on the President in the Lend-Lease Act to give various forms of aid to governments whose defence he deemed as vital to the defence of the United States.[43] In a letter to Stephen Gaselee at the British Foreign Office in early 1941, for example, Lauterpacht relayed details of his American activities and explained his flexible approach to the laws of neutrality. He could provide the American administration with sympathetic advice 'conscientiously and without any imputation of special pleading, for I have for many years held the view that neutral duties are not immutable and they are determined by the legal position of war at any given period.'[44] Relevant textbook passages echo the views expressed in his lectures and advice to both governments, repeating his case for what he called the 'reality' or continuity of international law and the role of international organization in securing order despite its violations and strategic adaptions of settled principles after 1939.[45] His criticism, as with Brierly and Scelle, was never against international law or

employed at three prestigious law faculties in the two states comprising Europe's most significant liberal alliance against Germany before the fall of France in 1940. Longmans first proposed reprinting the sixth edition of *Disputes* (1940) as soon as 1941, for example, but delayed due to paper shortages and adequacy of existing stocks in England and the U.S.: Lauterpacht, *Life of Sir Hersch Lauterpacht* 2010 (n. 13), 186.

40 Ibid., 104–137.

41 Ibid., 116–117.

42 Ibid., 135–136, 142 and 187–188.

43 Ibid., 142 and 187–188. For a contemporaneous American analysis of the controversial Lend-Lease Act, including the constitutional issues relevant to the President's wide powers see e.g., Wright, Quincy. 'The Lend-Lease Bill and International Law'. *American Journal of International Law* 35(2) (1941), 305–314, esp. at 308.

44 Lauterpacht, *Life of Sir Hersch Lauterpacht* 2010 (n. 13), 142.

45 Ibid., 165.

international organization per se but rather, against the politics of states which frustrate the effectiveness of those structures.

As a collective intervention, the textbooks use historical analysis to criticise the priority for state interests above the collective interests of peace and to defend the rule of law and the continuity of international law during crisis. A variation of the same message underpins each textbook though Lauterpacht's *Disputes* is, consistent with his strategic role during war, the more moderate in its critical observations about collective responsibility for the viability of the rule of law and the breakdown of international order. His conservativism after 1939 departs from earlier comments encouraging international lawyers to adopt a more critical attitude toward rules which make peaceful dispute resolution voluntary.[46] The differences between each text, methodological and substantive, and the sequence of publication puts the authors into a strategic and spontaneous conversation (despite the absence of direct address by cross-referencing or comparison) that restates and deepens arguments previously put directly about the responsibility of states (not law) for war.[47] The unfolding political crisis amplified the critical effect of their shared project by making the textbooks historically and politically pertinent. Pertinence also ensured the collective argument's audibility.

German-American law professor Wolfgang Friedman's 1941 review of Lauterpacht's *Disputes* claims the author's historical methods ignore the juridical effects of the war.[48] Friedman says the textbook presents a recent history of international law rather than its present, wartime meaning which was unknowable because all familiar legal categories were undergoing transition if not, revolution. Lauterpacht presents, for example, a non-controversial explication of developments until publication reflecting matters including the effort of liberal states, including the United States, 'to safeguard their neutrality,'[49] or otherwise safeguard the territorial boundaries of neutrality or the neutral status

46 Lauterpacht, *Function of Law* 1933 (n. 34), esp. 442–446, and citing Brierly in agreement, e.g., 431 and 442.

47 The classic interwar monographs of each author setting out their theoretical positions about the social and political function of international law and the challenges encountered by it as a consequence of state practice include, e.g., Scelle, *Précis de droit* 1932 and 1934 (n. 31); Scelle, 'Preface' 1937 (n. 31); Lauterpacht, *Function of Law* 1933 (n. 34). Brierly's defence of law's pacifist function and his wish for its extension is clear from earlier editions of *The Law of Nations* and clarified in other shorter contributions: see e.g., Brierly, 'International Peace' 1927–1928 (n. 34); Brierly, 'Shortcomings' 1924 (n. 34), and Brierly, James L. *The Law of Nations* (Oxford: Clarendon Press, 1st ed. 1928, 1930); and Brierly, James L. *The Law of Nations* (Oxford: Clarendon Press, 2nd ed. 1936).

48 Friedmann, 'Textbook Myth' 1941 (n. 35), 299.

49 Oppenheim, *Disputes* 1940 (n. 1), 502–505.

of traders after 1939 by interpretation and application of existing principles.[50] Entirely absent from the treatise is criticism of the resort to force by Britain and France against Germany, though Lauterpacht confirms the legality of the formal declarations of war issued in early September 1939, or the circumstances caused by the invasion of France in the weeks before publication.[51] It is difficult, even many decades later, to read Lauterpacht's *Disputes* (1940) without remembering the author's wartime role as a legal advisor to government on important strategic questions and the fact that the British Foreign Office approved publication of his textbook manuscript without addendum.[52] His efforts to avoid political controversy or reinforce the legality of Allied decisions were successful. His textbook also highlighted by its analysis of interwar principles another, more critical comment to experienced internationalists, including those active in the Foreign Office, about why their international law does not always guard international order.

The practical challenges of publishing an elementary text during war about a legal system which was evidently in crisis, alluded to by all three authors, highlights the urgency of the more subtle agendas shared by the three textbooks about the weaknesses of international law and the responsibility of international lawyers for its reinforcement. Practical obstacles to speaking and publishing did not prevent Lauterpacht and Scelle publishing and reissuing manuscripts of almost eight hundred pages. Nor did Brierly hesitate to approve two printings of his shorter edition.[53] The depletion of undergraduate class sizes in English and French universities due to military service also highlights the perceived significance of publishing elementary texts and the political and juridical significance, even urgency, of returning to the juridical conception of war.[54] The overtly critical tone and substance of Scelle's text and his teaching

---

50 See, e.g., Lauterpacht's discussion of the application by Britain and France of existing principles of reprisals in response to German submarine warfare and mine-laying in Norwegian territorial waters or the practice of sinking merchantmen, ibid. 385 and 542.

51 Oppenheim, *Disputes* 1940 (n. 1), 150.

52 Lauterpacht, *Life of Sir Hersch Lauterpacht* 2010 (n. 13), 103–104; and for details of Lauterpacht's contributions to the British 'war-effort' as a volunteer in the British Home Guard see generally, 100–140.

53 Lauterpacht, *Life of Sir Hersch Lauterpacht* 2010 (n. 13), 104–11; Brierly, *Law of Nations* 1942 (n. 2); and more generally on the challenges for the publishing industry during World War Two see, e.g., Holman, Valerie. *Book Publishing in England 1939–1945* (London: British Library, 2008); and Thomson, Zoe. 'How Did Publishers Respond to the Restrictions Placed on Them by the Outbreak of World War Two?'. *The Journal of Publishing Culture* 5 (2016), 1–10.

54 For details about the operation of the law schools in England and France, including the temporary closure of professional associations and journals of international

commitments in Paris during the war, characterise his textbook as the most passionate among the three textbooks and arguably, the most courageous. His efforts to explain his disagreement with the decisions of influential states (including his own) by reference to the weaknesses or abuse of basic norms, and publish his views in occupied France, highlights the transformation of the textbook into a critical field when direct comment was controversial.

4 Texts and Counter-texts

The textbooks spoke to the post-1939 crisis indirectly by analysing how the system of international governance designed by the preceding generation failed to prevent war. Each focussed on the language, meaning and operation of the *1919 Treaty of Peace* and the *1928 Pact of Paris* against the escalating tensions of the 1930s. Repeated remarks made in the context of analysing those conventions separated the legal conception of war from its causes and refused, in each case to elevate violence as a legal right. The effect was a strategically timed critique of the dangers of state sovereignty which were manifest at the time of writing. The textbooks agreed that war was a legal category insofar as it exists for the purposes of international regulation but also that war frustrates the pacifist function of law and resort to invasive force is illegal. Lauterpacht explains, for example, 'war is not inconsistent with, but a condition regulated by International Law' and further, that war is not a legal remedy for self-help for political or legal violations, but rather 'a fact recognised.... but not established by International Law'.[55] The status of war as a legal category meant that international law regulated the conduct of interstate conflicts, including by rules of neutrality or the treatment of persons affected by war, despite beginning as a violation. The catch for the textbook authors related to the opportunities for war that continued under the Covenant of the League in the *1919 Treaty of Peace* and the *1928 Pact of Paris*. Those options structure their analyses of

law in London during war see, e.g., Cassin, René. *Les hommes partis de rien : Le réveil de la France abattue* (Paris: Plon, 1975 ed. [1940–1941]), 1; Falconieri, Silvia. 'Situation at French Universities: Le « droit de la race ». Apprendre l'antisémitisme à la faculté de droit de Paris (1940–1944)'. *Histoire societe: Dieu me pardonne c'est son métier*. 10 April 2014, available at: https://histoireetsociete.wordpress.com/2014/04/10/le-droit-de-la-race-apprendre-lantisemitisme-a-la-faculte-de-droit-de-paris-1940-1944-par-silvia-falconieri/ (last accessed on 14 September 2020).

55 See Oppenheim, *Disputes* 1940 (n. 1), 166; and Brierly, *Law of Nations* 1942 (n. 2), 255; and Scelle, *Manuel* 1943 (n. 2), 638.

existing principles to highlight how legal design frustrated the pacifistic potential of law by facilitating the extra-legal and sometimes, illegal choices of states.

4.1 *The 1919 Treaty of Peace*

According to the textbooks, understanding the weaknesses of interwar international law begins by studying the design deficits of the League's control of emergency situations under Articles 10–16 of the *1919 Treaty of Peace*. Article 10 reminded member states to 'respect and preserve as against external aggression' in circumstances where the manner and effectiveness of institutional intervention was contingent on the balance of interests within the League and the voluntary cooperation of affected states. The existence of 'any war or threatened war' affecting any state triggered, for example, the authority of the League under Article 11 to 'take any action that may be deemed wise and effectual to safeguard the peace of nations'.[56] Despite the generality of the discretion and the extension to non-member states, the textbooks observed that stewardship of the institutional function concentrated in states of influence and limited how and for what ends the League's advice would mobilise, authoritatively in context.[57]

Each author stressed the non-compulsive character of any resolution undermined the League's capacity to prevent war alongside various technical hurdles which excused institutional hesitation in certain cases.[58] There was no legal requirement, as Brierly noticed, to take 'necessary' action to implement the Council's recommendations 'whatever the cost of fulfilling' the new duty to 'respect' and 'preserve' territorial sovereignty or otherwise heed the Council's 'advice'.[59] The risk of non-compliance escalated in parallel to the escalating danger of belligerence between the same states, whether the parties to a

56 Pursuant to Article 11, states which were members of the League of Nations possessed a 'friendly right' to initiate the advisory process by alerting the Council or Assembly to threatening situations.

57 On the successful application of Article 11 in the practice of the League as against the numerous challenges for giving the Council's recommendations practical effect see, e.g., Brierly, *Law of Nations* 1942 (n. 2), 230–231; Oppenheim, *Disputes* 1940 (n. 1), 84–86; and Scelle, *Manuel* 1943 (n. 2), 560.

58 All authors comment on the 'elasticity' of the potential range of advisory options available to the League, including for Lauterpacht, the potential to advise compulsory methods of dispute resolution: Brierly, *Law of Nations* 1942 (n. 2), 231–232; and Oppenheim, *Disputes* 1940 (n. 1), 85. Nevertheless, the lack of compulsive means of arbitral resolution limited the capacity of the League to prevent war: Brierly, *Law of Nations* 1942 (n. 2), 230–231; Oppenheim, *Disputes* 1940 (n. 1), 125–143; and Scelle, *Manuel* 1943 (n. 2), 622 and 633–634.

59 Brierly, *Law of Nations* 1942 (n. 2), 229.

dispute chose to recognise the authority of a resolution and, as was always open in the absence of any formal declaration of war, if the emergency or threat qualified as a proper trigger for institutional concern.[60] Scelle remarked that Article 11, 'n'a jamais donné les résultats qu'on en espérait' because the Council applied a strict 'règle de l'unanimité' which it extended to all parties or interested states by *ad hoc* inclusion in the decision-making process.[61] Affected states could, in effect, 'paralyser toute l'action conciliatrice' by disagreeing or abandoning the Council's advice.[62] In other cases, the democratisation of voting privileges permitted members of the League Council to question the legality of non-unanimous resolutions.[63]

For all three texts, Japan's invasion of Manchuria in September 1931 exemplified the reliance on technicalities by the League and by belligerent states to justify, resist or avoid responsibility for aggression.[64] It also highlights the history lesson that tethers legal meaning to its diplomatic context. Japan voted against a Council resolution calling for its withdrawal, prompting prominent members of the permanent quorum to doubt the legality of the direction on the basis of the principle of unanimity.[65] Such hesitation contradicted the relaxation of the voting regime in earlier cases where the absence of unanimity did not affect the validity of the Council's directives.[66] Interpretative inconsistency followed a predictable pattern where states with influence adjusted legal meaning according to the political expediency of institutional intervention. Japan and China did not act unpredictably, in those

60 Ibid., 230. Lauterpacht also notes that emergencies on the cusp of war without a clarifying 'intention' or 'initiation' proved by a declaration of war or evidence of resort to force escaped the technical meaning of 'war' necessary to prompt institutional scrutiny under Article 11: Oppenheim, *Disputes* 1940 (n. 1), 126.

61 Scelle explains that the provision 'never delivered the hoped-for results' due to respect for unanimity of support for Council resolutions which extended rights of veto beyond members of the League Council to parties to the dispute and due to the non-enforceability of resolutions: Scelle, *Manuel* 1943 (n. 2), 560. Membership of the League Council comprised representatives of the 'Principal Allied and Associated Powers' and four other nominated, and subsequently elected, member states: Article 4 of the *1919 Treaty of Peace*. The voting privileges of members, including the possibility of veto contrary to representations made by non-member states, reflected the undemocratic aspect of the advisory regime under Article 11 and increased the likelihood of non-compliance by states which disagreed with the Council's resolution: Article 15 of the *1919 Treaty of Peace*.

62 States possessed power to 'paralyse the conciliatory action': Ibid.

63 Oppenheim, *Disputes* 1940 (n. 1), 85–86.

64 Ibid. and 127–129; Brierly, *Law of Nations* 1942 (n. 2), 255 and 259; and Scelle, *Manuel* 1943 (n. 2), 653.

65 Oppenheim, *Disputes* 1940 (n. 1), 85–86.

66 Ibid.

circumstances, by not issuing a formal declaration of war when the legal category determined institutional obligations and the law was notoriously vague.[67] Invasion and annexation of territory was, however, clearly a qualifying act of war under Article 11 according to the League Assembly even if it declined to announce that the situation comprised a relevant rupture. The Assembly's 1933 report unanimously evaluated the invasion and 'forced' seizure of 'a large area of what was indisputably the Chinese territory' was not an act of self-defence by Japan but led to the creation of a newly independent zone. The report also repeated the Council's call to withdraw Japanese troops to restore Chinese sovereignty.[68] There being no formal finding of 'war', however, meant there was no imperative for the League to mobilise collective action against one of its members under Article 11. If the category of war was 'elastic' and presented opportunities for recalcitrant states to evade unwanted institutional attention, as the historical narrative proved, its flexibility also created opportunities for the League to not exercise its pacifistic functions.[69]

Analysis of how the Covenant of the League allowed the political priorities of members to inhibit collective intervention against belligerent states repeated in the context of Article 16.[70] The provision transforms the 'resort to war' by a League member into an act of war against every member and triggers a series of extreme consequences, beginning with expulsion from the League and boycott obligations enforceable against non-members. In the Manchurian situation, for example, the absence of a formal declaration of war by China or Japan relieved the League of the uncomfortable and politically inexpedient question of how to enforce the *1919 Treaty of Peace* against two of its original members.[71] It is unsurprising that some members took advantage of the pro-

67 The existence of a threatened or existing rupture was necessary to trigger institutional oversight, scrutiny and or interference (including the possibility of collective military action) pursuant to Articles 11, 12 and/or 16 of the *1919 Treaty of Peace*.

68 Related events proximate to Shanghai similarly escaped formal legal classification as 'war' by the League or affected states: Oppenheim, *Disputes* 1940 (n. 1), 127–129.

69 Lauterpacht says the 'elasticity' of the phrase 'resort to war' undermines the League's effectiveness but 'is not altogether destructive of the legal value of the Covenant' and proved to have utility in other instances, involving influential states, where the League Council or Assembly recognised and responded to an actual or threatened rupture without a formal declaration of war (e.g., wars between Bolivia and Paraguay (1934–1935); Italian invasion of Abyssinia (1935); Japanese invasion of China (1937); and Russian invasion of Finland (1939)): 129–130.

70 For discussion see Oppenheim, *Disputes* 1940 (n. 1), 137–142; Brierly, *Law of Nations* 1942 (n. 2), 231–234 and 240–244; and Scelle, *Manuel* 1943 (n. 2), 651–653.

71 Both Japan and China were original members of the League and continued as such until Japan's dramatic exit on 24 February 1933 following the adoption of the Assembly's report; see also, details of Japanese delegation's dramatic exit from the Assembly in

cedural requirements of the *1919 Treaty of Peace* by not formally declaring war after invasion. The League only invoked Article 16 once, when Italy invaded Abyssinia without, again, clarifying the legal status of its belligerent act by a formal declaration. Brierly gives extended attention to the brittleness of the Article 16 regime caused by the unwillingness of the League to escalate emergencies by antagonising a belligerent state.[72] He says, '[i]nternational lawyers as such are not concerned with the political reasons for this drawing back; they are concerned, however, with the lessons that the incident may have to teach with regard to the practicability of a scheme of sanctions such as that of the Covenant'.[73] The institutional habit of using legal technicalities as a pretext for inaction turned on political choices permitted by the gaps international lawyers helped design. Brierly speaks of historical lessons that for the international lawyer are also compelling reasons for his or her professional self-reflection about how juridical categories and drafting decisions facilitate the practical possibility of war as a political option.

The limitations of Articles 10 and 11 of the *1919 Treaty of Peace* crystallised for the textbook writers in the elaborate procedures outlined by Articles 12 to 15 and 17 for dealing with disputes.[74] Article 12 commits members to pacifist resolution of disputes likely to lead to rupture by arbitration (Article 13), judicial settlement (Article 14) or inquiry by the Council (Article 15). The regime delays rather than eliminates war by 'legalising' conflicts commenced at least three months after performance of settlement procedures.[75] Wars initiated without peaceful settlement (Article 12) or before the expiry of the three month period (Article 16) risked sanctions enforceable by a duty of member states to apply economic pressure and subject to further recommendation by the League

---

Brown, Stewart. 'Japan Stuns World, Withdraws from League'. *United Press International* (24 February 1933), available at: https://www.upi.com/Archives/1933/02/24/Japan-stuns-world-withdraws-from-league/2231840119817/ (last accessed on 14 September 2020).

72 Brierly, *Law of Nations* 1942 (n. 2), 243–246a.

73 Ibid., 245.

74 Brierly characterises Articles 12–17 as independent of, and in certain respects 'alternative', to the League's advisory obligations in Articles 10 and 11: Brierly, *Law of Nations* 1942 (n. 2), 232–233.

75 Article 12 provides that there should be no war until at least three months after the failure of peaceful attempts at settlement of disputes likely to escalate either by arbitration, adjudication, or an inquiry by the League council. Articles 13–15 elaborate or create the juridical machinery for the settlement procedure identified in Article 12, including making provision for the Permanent Court of Justice in Article 15. See Brierly, *Law of Nations* 1942 (n. 2), 239–240.

about 'effective' collective military action.[76] Brierly reflected that if 'Article 11 gives scope to the tact and discretion of the statesman; these articles rely on the technique of the lawyer' though with the same effect resulting from the absence of practical enforcement measures.[77] Lauterpacht says the absence of a binding regime for pacific settlement 'constitutes one of the principal defects of the Pact from the point of view of its ultimate effectiveness' and 'signifies a fundamental gap in the international legal system'.[78]

For Scelle, the flexibility of the phrases 'war' and 'resort to war' in Articles 10–12 and 16 represented deliberate design flaws which simultaneously outlawed and legalised war. States exposed the disingenuity of the collective pledge 'against external aggression' after the First World War by creating a double-conception of war that Scelle describes as 'la guerre-duel et la guerre-révision'.[79] Article 10 outlaws war and Articles 12–15 outline procedural requirements designed to delay and consequently, legalise war. He explains the contradiction in a critical tone which is typical of his textbook style and exaggerates its polemical effect:

> L'article changea le Droit. Il a une double portée, par quoi il prohibe l'agression dans son but et dans ses moyens. D'une part, l'agression, *en soi*, est interdit ; d'autre part, la *nouvelle procédure* de guerre doit la rendre impossible, parce qu'elle exige, avant de recourir à la force, l'épuisement des recours pacifiques.[80]

He concludes that the legality of war survived by the new procedure for war and reinforced by 'fissures' built into the procedural regime which preserved the right of states to 'take action as they shall consider necessary' under Article 15 where the Council did not unanimously agree or the dispute concerned a question of domestic law. Article 15 revives the Council's oversight of emergencies where there is no voluntary submission of disputes to arbitral or juridical decision under Articles 12–14.

---

76 Clause 16. Further, states violating covenants of the *1919 Treaty of Peace* could be subject to expulsion from the league. Wars relating to non-signatories escaped the obligation of the procedural rigours and could only face the sanctions regime under article 16 by agreement: Article 17 *1919 Treaty of Peace*.

77 Brierly, *Law of Nations* 1942 (n. 2), 233.

78 Oppenheim, *Disputes* 1940 (n. 1), 151; also see, Lauterpacht, *Function of Law* 1933 (n. 34).

79 Scelle, *Manuel* 1943 (n. 2), 635.

80 Ibid., 633: Scelle explained Article 10 changed the law in two respects, substantive and procedural. On one hand, aggression, itself, is forbidden; on the other hand, the new procedure for war makes the prohibition impossible, because it requires, before resorting to force, the exhaustion of peaceful remedy.

Scelle's textbook deploys close textual analysis to focus the attention of his readers on the juridical techniques by which war survives as a technical and material legal category. He de-emphasises, as Lauterpacht and Brierly do not, relevant interwar examples. His interest is to explain that war was predictable as a juridical fact after 1919 because of the deliberate contradictions built into the declaratory and procedural scope of the relevant provisions. He focusses his readers on the problem of a split or double concept of war that allows states to 'conserve sa compétence de guerre, sans égard au caractère abusive ou injuste que sa prétention peut revêtir, et le défendeur garde également la sienne, quelqu'abusif que puisse être son refus.'[81] The duality reflects the '"fissures du Pacte", fissures par òu peut se réintroduire la guerre,'[82] by allowing sovereign states to continue to act according to political expediency, in every situation.

4.2 *The 1928 Pact of Paris*

The textbooks agree that the weaknesses of the *1919 Treaty of Peace* did not disappear despite the reforms introduced by the *1928 Pact of Paris*.[83] Germany, the United States, France, Great Britain, Japan, Poland and Czechoslavkia famously agreed in 1928 to 'condemn recourse to war for the solution of international controversies, and renounce it, as an instrument of national policy' and further, to settle all disputes 'by pacific means'.[84] The same states returned as the

81 Ibid., 635–636: 'The contradictory concept of war permitted states to preserve the ability to go to war, regardless of any abuse or injustice, and permitted the same privilege to states in defence, irrespective of the character of the claim'.

82 Ibid., 635: 'The fissures or gaps in the Pact can reintroduce war'.

83 See Brierly, *Law of Nations* 1942 (n. 2), 232–253, esp. at 242; Oppenheim, *Disputes* 1940 (n. 1), 148–149; and *vi*; and Scelle, *Manuel* 1943 (n. 2), 638–641. The terms of Articles I and II admonished war but did not expressly prohibit it: Article I The High Contracting Parties solemnly declare … that they condemn recourse to war for the solution of international controversies and *renounce it as an instrument of national policy in their relations with another*. Article II The High Contracting Parties agree that the settlement of solution of all disputes or conflicts, of whatever nature or whatever origin they may be, which may arise among them, shall never be sought except by pacific means. For a more recent analysis of the Paris Pact 1928 see, e.g., Lesaffer, Randall. 'Kellogg-Briand Pact', in *Max Planck Encylopedia of Public International Law*, ed. Rüdiger Wolfrum (Oxford: Oxford University Press, 2010), available at: http://opil.ouplaw.com/view/10.1093/law:epil/9780199231690/law-9780199231690-e320 (last accessed on 14 September 2020); and Hathaway, Oona and Scott J. Shapiro. *The Internationalists. How a Radical Plan to Outlaw War Remade the World* (New York: Simon & Schuster, 2017).

84 Oppenheim, *Disputes* 1940 (n. 1), 148–151; Scelle, *Manuel* 1943 (n. 2), 638–643; Brierly, *Law of Nations* 1942 (n. 2), 125, 242, 263. Note: the practical insignificance of the Paris initiatives for 'outlawing' war account for the relatively minor attention to it in Brierly's text in contrast to his extensive analysis of the *1919 Treaty of Peace*.

protagonists of World War Two. If nothing more, that coincidence exposes the weak links in the juridical chain that leads the past of international law to subsequent crisis by highlighting why war continues despite the commitment of each generation to reforms designed to secure peace. For the textbook writers, the observation demonstrates the continuing responsibility of the international lawyer to critically examine the fault-lines that frustrate the rule of law.

There is general agreement among the textbook writers that the new vocabulary of 'renunciation' or 'condemnation' changed the law but also preserved the legal right to resort to force in certain circumstances. After 1928, only wars waged in furtherance of national policy were illegal, leaving belligerent states with numerous opportunities for the legal use of war. The legal category of war survived the 1928 reforms by the continuation of customary norms legitimising the resort to force for permissible self-defence, by collective action for the enforcement of international obligations or agreements such as those under Article 16 of the *1919 Treaty of Peace*, for disputes relating to non-signatories of the *1928 Pact of Paris*, or when a signatory to the *1928 Pact of Paris* violated its provisions.[85] The effect ensured the survival of war as a legal category in situations of actual or likely rupture, relegating the meaningful work of the reforms to uncontroversial cases.

Lauterpacht explained, for example, that there was no legal impropriety resulting from the declaration of war against Germany by Great Britain or France in 1939 after Germany invaded Poland in violation of the *1928 Pact of Paris*.[86] Invasion activated Articles 11 and 16 of the *1919 Treaty of Peace*. As such, the illegal act of war by Germany transformed into an act of war against all members of the League and triggered new individual and collective rights and obligations, including resort to military solution. Lauterpacht confirms:

> These exceptions are in themselves sufficient to show that, even for its signatories, the Paris Pact has not abolished the institution of war.[87]

Lauterpacht adds a strategic footnote which separates the design flaws of the interwar regime from the pacifistic potential of law:

---

85 Ibid.

86 Oppenheim, *Disputes* 1940 (n. 1), 150. See also n. 50–51 above. Article 16 of the *1919 Treaty of Peace* provided the technical reason for the legality of war against Germany by categorising its invasion of Poland as initiating a war against an existing member of the League. Poland was an original member of the League from 1920 though German membership (from 1926) ceased in 1933.

87 Ibid.

> [f]or these and other reasons the law of war must continue to be a legitimate object of the science of International Law. While a legal system can prohibit recourse to unlawful force, it cannot always prevent it; neither can it renounce physical compulsion for the purpose of enforcing the law.[88]

Lauterpacht's annotation reminds his readers that international law continues despite its violation; that states are responsible for abolishing war or its continuing viability. His perspective uses treaty analysis to elucidate state responsibility for war and confirm the escalation of situations by reactive or unruly states without antagonising Allied states. Simple explanations of existing rules, a technique also used by Brierly in his briefer remarks about the *1928 Pact of Paris*, protects Lauterpacht's analysis from political controversy.[89]

The different theoretical perspectives of the textbook authors shaped how each described the attempt to outlaw war. Lauterpacht and Brierly read the *1928 Pact of Paris* as abolishing the general right of states to go to war. Scelle identifies the abolition of war with Article 10 of the *1919 Treaty of Peace* and reads 'renunciation' as reproducing the same flawed prohibition by a new normative vocabulary. In the end, the textbooks arrive at the same substantive conclusion irrespective of the varied descriptions of the 1928 reforms: war remained a permissible legal category without reliable organizational control. Brierly evaluated the *1928 Pact of Paris*, for example, as an important juridical development by obliging states to 'distinguish between legal and illegal occasions of making war' and by attempting to formulate a law of intervention or rather by 'stigmatising as illegal' interventions before attempting pacific resolution.[90] Lauterpacht is emphatic that the 'Pact constitutes a radical change in International Law and a removal of the principal objection to its recognition as a system of law … . War cannot now legally, as it could be prior to the conclusion of the Pact, be resorted to either as a legal remedy or as an instrument for changing the law'.[91] War did change the juridical significance of the Pact: '[t]he fact that within a short period after the conclusion of the Pact its provisions were repeatedly violated cannot properly be regarded as detracting from its legal significance' or the 'magnitude of the change effected by the Pact in the system of International Law'.[92] For Lauterpacht, acts of aggression

88 Ibid., see para. § 52, at n. 4.
89 Brierly, *Law of Nations* 1942 (n. 2), 125, 242, 263.
90 Ibid., 248–249.
91 Oppenheim, *Disputes* 1940 (n. 1), 161.
92 Ibid.

after 1928 did not detract from the 'magnitude of the change effected by the Pact in the system of International Law' but rather, exposed its political limits which always determine the success or failure of the rule of law.

Scelle's critique of the sovereign state is less subtle. His *Manuel* explains how the design and interpretation of legal norms by sovereign states facilitates the belligerent choices of the same states. He notes the irony of generating 'une norme nouvelle' by which 'toute compétence de guerre est désormais absente de l'ordre juridique' when it did not apply to all states and was unenforceable.[93] For him, outlawry was a romantic label that did not correspond to juridical reality.[94] Scelle explains the weaknesses of the *1928 Pact of Paris* depended not on the sovereign state in general, nor the signatories to the twin agreements, but rather on the reservations made by the Allied powers and to the interpretative statement issued by the American government immediately before the conclusion of the 1928 negotiations.[95] France, Britain and the United States were directly responsible for the final ruptures after September 1939 because each assumed peace could follow from their paper renunciation of force when each also expected the legal exceptions discussed by Lauterpacht to continue.[96] Of these, the rights and interests of states that activated under Article 16 and the particular responsibilities concentrating in the Council, the Executive organ controlled by Great Britain and France and through them, by their strategic alliance with the U.S., cancelled the authenticity of the renunciation of war by those states. The balance of strategic influence in the League organs guarded the privileges of the three influential states to choose war where it was expedient and in circumstances not otherwise available to the other states which agreed to renounce war. Scelle says:

> [e]n fait, les deux grandes Puissances anglo-saxonnes réservaient leur droit d'intervention dans leurs sphères politiques respectives, – comme la France, en faisant spécifier le maintien du système sanctionnateur du

93 Scelle, *Manuel* 1943 (n. 2), 639; Scelle gave particular attention to the difficulties reconciling the 1919 and 1928 treaties due to different interpretations among states about the effect of the *1928 Pact of Paris* and a lack of uniform application of both agreements to all states by uniform signature and ratification. See, e.g., Scelle, *Manuel* 1943 (n. 2), 642–643.

94 Ibid., 639.

95 France and Great Britain made reservations on 19 May 1928 confirming the legality of force for the purposes of self-defence, and for acts consistent with Articles 15 and 16 of the *1919 Treaty of Peace*; supplemented by interpretative notes issued by the U.S. on 23 June 1928 similarly reserving the imperative of self-defence. Scelle, *Manuel* 1943 (n. 2), 640; also see, Lesaffer, 'Kellogg-Briand Pact' 2010 (n. 83), 10–11.

96 Ibid., and n. 83 above, esp., Oppenheim, *Disputes* 1940 (n. 1), 149–151; Scelle, *Manuel* 1943 (n. 2), 638–643; and Brierly, *Law of Nations* 1942 (n. 2), 125, 242, 263.

> Pacte ... Cela signifiait-il que les trois Puissances entendaient ainsi monopoliser la fonction exécutive que le Pact retirait en principe aux autres signataires ? Cette interprétation serait sans doute un peu grossie, mais non tout à fait fausse.[97]

Scelle's attitude was 'scientific' or technical in a different sense than Lauterpacht or Brierly. He examines basic rules to uncover the sociological and political factors at play in the processes and operation of treaty design. He reads the reservations of the American, French and English governments as proof of 'la logique sociologique internationale' that concentrates 'la compétence soveraine de guerre' by 'une sorte de cristallisation naturelle, aux mains des gouvernements les plus forts'.[98]

A French student reading and discussing the principles of war for the first time during war encountered a teacher and text with a passionate subtext that expanded against the political reality beyond the classroom and in the minds of everyone in France and abroad. A variation of the same message proceeded more cautiously in the English textbooks and for good reason. There, the political contest for the survival of the state was far from over. However faulty interwar international law, it continued. Whatever problems the sovereign state presented for the viability of the rule of law, war continued. In the early 1940s, war was a technical legal question and also, more urgently, a question of political survival.

5 Three Reminders

By selective, historical exposition of general principles, the textbooks presented a juridical landscape in which war was possible and which interwar events prefigured as increasingly likely, especially after 1931. Part of the reason for war, according to the textbook writers, related to the weaknesses of the rule of law against the political interests of sovereign states. International history

97 Scelle, *Manuel* 1943 (n. 2), 640: 'In fact, the two great Anglo-Saxon Powers reserved their right of intervention in their respective political spheres, – like France, in having specified the maintenance of the sanctioning system of the Covenant ... Did this mean that the three great Powers intended to monopolise the executive function that the Pact withdrew in principle from the other signatories? This interpretation will be without doubt a little exaggerated but not all false.'

98 Ibid.: 'The international sociological logic ... [that concentrates].... the sovereign war competence ... [by] a kind of natural crystallisation, in the hands of more powerful governments.'

proved the meagreness of the interwar design by demonstrating the multiple instances in which state interest prevailed over the opportunities for international intervention provided to the League under Articles 11 and 16 of the *1919 Treaty of Peace*. The textbook analyses of key provisions and historical situations did not, however, absolve international law of its pacifistic function or mark law as a 'failure'. Events after 1939 crystallised the more pertinent suggestions of the textbook for its first readers. For each textbook author, war highlights the unfortunate limits imposed on the rule of law by sovereign states and presented an occasion to reflect on the durability of law in the midst of political crisis. The limitations on the pacifistic function of law include not only belligerent contravention but equally, the politics underpinning juridical design and institutional administration. The positive suggestion of the textbooks for wartime readers was to understand why war happens despite legal plans for peace and then, to make a case for maintaining professional faith in the rule of law and in the role of the internationalist as an expert and agent of change as much as the witness of crisis. That case depended on three interrelated reminders: that law continues despite war; about the challenge for international law presented by state sovereignty; and about the role of the international lawyer.

5.1 *The Continuity of Law*

The textbooks share certain assumptions about the international law of war post-1939: that there was and could be an 'existing law' derived from the pre-1939 legal order; that violations or weaknesses of that 'existing' law did not affect its validity; and, that any change to the existing law was in the future. Lauterpacht, Brierly and Scelle did not, at least directly or in detail, speculate about future developments but rather examined existing rules and basic, irrefutable principles of international law. The effect, however, convinces readers about the utility of law as an objective thing which remains relevant to international relations despite war and consequently, remains relevant to the student, lawyer and internationalist as a tool for stabilising the contests between states.

The textbook assurance about the reality of international law contradicted the widespread despair among internationalists after 1939 which identified war with the end of law.[99] When the three volumes appeared, in relatively rapid succession, the professional and academic field of international law was in a state of anxiety, focussed on questions about the future of international law and interrupted by unusual pauses in the disciplinary exchange ordinarily

99 Friedmann, 'Textbook Myth' 1941 (n. 35), 302.

possible via publication and professional gatherings.[100] From the outbreak of war, emotional references to the sudden 'end of law' and the 'lawlessness' of German belligerency circulated among international lawyers.[101] Prominent or influential international lawyers and international law societies in England and the United States responded by defending the everyday regulatory function of international law during war and by professional projects dedicated to the future of international law.[102] The insertion of the three textbooks into *this* conversation presented a challenge to perceptions about the end of law when controversial agendas were politically inexpedient, the future uncertain and paper rationing restricted publication. One review of the *Law of Nations* (1942) noted the 'mischief' done to the repute of international law by pessimistic writers who forget that every system of law 'has, in the course of its history, to fight for its life against powerful antagonists'.[103] Against such mischief, Brierly's book (along with Lauterpacht's and Scelle's) provided an 'antidote'

100 See, e.g., Lauterpacht, Hersch. 'Resumption of the Publication of the British Yearbook of International Law'. *British Yearbook of International Law* 21 (1944), iii; Keeton, George W. 'International Law and the Future (A Plea for a Functional Approach)'. *Transactions of the Grotius Society* 27 (1941), 31–58; Keen, F. N., et al. 'International Law in Development: Discussion on the Re-Drafted Report of the Committee'. *Transactions of the Grotius Society* 27 (1941), 252–288; Keen, F. N., et al. 'The Future of International Law: Final Report by the Committee Appointed to Consider the Sources of International Law'. *Transactions of the Grotius Society* 27 (1941), 289–312; see also Carnegie Endowment for International Peace (Division of International Law). *The International Law of the Future: Postulates, Principles and Proposals* (Oxford: Oxford University Press, 1944); Brierly, *Outlook for International Law* 1944 (n. 4); and Lauterpacht, Hersch. *An International Bill of the Rights of Man* (Oxford: Oxford University Press, 2013 ed. [1945]).

101 Multiple observers expressed dismay about the destruction of the laws of warfare and neutrality by German ambivalence to codes governing belligerency, e.g., Friedmann, Wolfgang 'International Law and the Present War'. (Lecture to Grotius Society, 21 November 1940) *Transactions of the Grotius Society* 26 (1940), 211–233, 211, 216–227; Warren, Charles. 'Lawless Maritime Warfare'. *Foreign Affairs* 18(3) (1940), 424–441.

102 See, e.g., Jessup, Philip C. 'In Support of International Law'. *American Journal of International Law* 34(3) (1940), 505–508, at 505; Friedmann, 'Textbook Myth' 1941 (n. 35), 302; and Keen, 'The Future of International Law' 1941 (ibid.), 289, 291 and 302; and Brown, Philip Marshall. 'Changing Concepts of International Law'. *American Journal of International Law* 34(3) (1940), 503–505, at 504–505. The allusion to the transitional state of international legal doctrine is clear from the introductory remarks of all three texts, including notably, Brierly's brief note that 'there are some passages in this book which I hope to rewrite at a future date, but the difficulties of publication in war-time have prevented me from making a thorough revision of it in this edition'. Brierly, *Law of Nations*, 3rd ed. 1942 (n. 2) vi; see also similar remarks suggestive of future, unknown developments requiring further editorial revisions in Oppenheim, *Disputes* (1940) (n. 1), v; and Scelle, *Manuel* 1943 (n. 2) 9.

103 P. H. W., 'Law of Nations' 1944 (n. 10).

as a consequence of its steadying and balanced reminders of basic rules. The more admirable aspect of the textbook 'antidote', assumed by the reviewer, was its implicit assurance that international law continues despite the undoubted difficulties it must overcome. That each of the textbook writers went back to the basics during war intervened in debate about the end of law with the simple, yet bold, reminder that law exists as part of international life and survives societal rupture.

5.2 *The Sovereign State*

According to the textbooks, the principal challenge posed for the international rule of law was the sovereign state and not the inherent viability of the rule of law. The textbook reminder was controversial insofar as it implicated all states in the design and administration of interwar international law and whether the rules work as a guide for state behaviour. Legal history, a familiar technique for explicating legal principle, softened the controversy of the reminder about state responsibility for war.

The interwar system of international law revealed the weakness of rules against sovereign self-interest.[104] Scelle explains that war arises from 'la psychologie internationale' which constantly balances the collective interests of order against the political interests of states. For states, disputes concerning vital national interests are always political and leave only matters of lesser concern subject to law. He says:

> les gouvernements ont toujours la volonté de ne considérer comme « juridiques » que les litiges qui sont pour eux d'intérêt mineur et de qualifier de « politiques » ceux qui, à un moment donné et dans circonstances données, leur paraissent d' intérêt vital.[105]

History repeatedly demonstrated to Scelle, but also to Lauterpacht and Brierly, that laws which seek to restrict belligerent action are unlikely to be effective in cases most likely to antagonise vital interests, the life, security or prosperity of the nation state, and consequently, most likely to lead to war.[106] The same states which ask for peace design juridical routes to war by leaving gaps for political decision which more readily close in cases which states consider to be

104 See, e.g., Lauterpacht, *Life of Sir Hersch Lauterpacht* 2010 (n. 13), 303–304; Koskenniemi, *Gentle Civilizer* 2001 (n. 31), 356.

105 Scelle, *Manuel* 1943 (n. 2), 553: 'the governments can always consider as "legal" only those disputes which are for them of minor interest and type as "political" those which, at a given moment and in given circumstances, seem to them of vital interest.'

106 Brierly, James L. 'Vital Interests and the Law'. *British Yearbook of International Law* 21 (1944), 51–57.

less important and so, less likely to escalate into international situations. The sovereign state is always the potential enemy of the rule of law and becomes the real enemy, at least for Brierly and Scelle, when cohesion is missing in international society and the state feels its interests unprotected by law.[107] Consistent with the political realism which orientates his thought, Brierly reflects that the myriad of anti-social acts of states occur not because law is or is not an effective instrument of order but rather because it is not, at its present stage of development, accepted by enough states as a 'way of life'.[108]

Lauterpacht's rejection of orthodox positivism, and its emphasis on the pre-eminence of the sovereign state, leads him toward a juridical rather than socio-legal solution for stabilising the international political field. He agrees with Scelle and Brierly that sovereign states are responsible for war (its causes and purposes and its conduct) *and* for the weaknesses of the rule of law. The inter-war initiatives associated with the League introduced important changes, limiting the general right of war as the prerogative of national sovereignty, without addressing the likelihood of belligerency in situations affecting a state's vital interests. Lauterpacht suggests the problem presented by states for the rule of law continues because '[s]tatemen and Governments are not yet prepared to proceed on the view that, as within the State, there must exist avenues for effecting changes in existing rights by way not of force but of legislative action of the international community'.[109] Peace depends on sovereigns perfecting the rules of international organization and acceding to the authority of law. His wartime textbook reiterated his view, expressed in 1933, that the rule of law will succeed only when states agree to a general obligation of judicial settlement, to effective restraints on the recourse to force and to provide a working machinery for peaceful change of the existing law. If the problem for the rule of law was the sovereign state, the solution was to recognize the wholeness of law and its proper function did not depend on state will and not, as Brierly and Scelle emphasise, the strengthening of community sensibility among nations.

107 For reference to the sociological, natural law dimension of Brierly's position see, e.g., Brierly, *Outlook for International Law* 1944 (n. 4). This text included republication, with amendment, of Brierly's practical observations about the social function of international law and the requirement that it be responsive to the 'vital interests' of states. See also, Brierly, James L. 'The Essential Nature of International Disputes'. *Virginia Law Review* 16(6) (1930), 537–545, 538 and 542. For consideration of the complexities of Lauterpacht's 'progressive' and not merely 'naturalistic' or anti positivist approach to international law see, e.g., Koskenniemi, *Gentle Civilizer* (2001) (n. 31), 353–412.

108 Brierly, *Law of Nations* 1942 (n. 2), 222–223.

109 Oppenheim, *Disputes* 1940 (n. 1), 176.

5.3 *The Reader*

Despite theoretical differences, each textbook writer put the problems of international order to the reader as a potential designer or practitioner of the rule of law. Lauterpacht's provocation to readers distils in the suggestiveness of his analysis of the design and revision of the interwar system. Those insights, shared in many respects by Brierly and Scelle, reinforce earlier commentary about the responsibility of the international lawyer to maintain a critical perspective when interpreting and applying law. In *The Function of Law*, Lauterpacht identified the distinction international lawyers draw between justiciable and non-justiciable disputes as imposing an obstacle to legal progress. Though international lawyers were increasingly conscious of the difficulty 'their attitude on this question creates the impression of a passive acquiescence in an inherited evil' and insists their resignation is 'embarrassing' and evades 'the duty incumbent on the lawyer to adopt a critical attitude' toward unworkable doctrines.[110] The same position underpins Lauterpacht's discussion of the voluntary system of settlement overseen by the League in *Disputes* (1940) though without the directness of the earlier demand.[111]

Brierly and Scelle lead readers towards the solutions which depend on their critical perspective and their sensitivity to the sociological conditions of law. Scelle concludes his volume by reminding the reader that it is impossible to learn about international law without understanding its sociological challenges which condition its ability to keep the peace. The lesson is important because it implicates individual efforts in the material struggle for solidarity within nations and among nations and upon which the international rule of law depends. He says, '[c]'est cette lutte caractérisée du passionnel et du juridique qui est la clef de l'étude technique du Droit international' before concluding his text with a reminder about the unwritten solution that awaits the reader's further attention.[112] 'Quelle sera la solution?', was his rhetorical question because the reason for the new 'revolutionary' war was clear from his preceding analysis about the failure of the interwar prohibitions. New laws, newly adapted to the social and political pressures on international cooperation, were necessary even if the details were still uncertain and did not yet, during war, organise as an unequivocal guide for peace. Announcing the tasks of international law via rational analysis of the problem during the crisis of war was not merely opportunistic but urgent for the future of international peace. For

---

110 Lauterpacht, *Function of Law* 1933 (n. 34), 443–444.

111 Oppenheim, *Disputes* 1940 (n. 1), 143.

112 Scelle, *Manuel* 1943 (n. 2), 725–726: 'It is this characteristic struggle of passion and law which is the key to the study of international law'.

Scelle, the problem exists for the student as the fundamental question for their study of international law and which guides their future professional contribution. The problems do not dissolve as intellectual questions but required, in his view, that the international lawyer pay attention to the practical functions of international law for the international community. How international law works and can work better requires adjusting law and juridical practice.

Brierly repeated Scelle's suggestion. He implicates his readers in the tasks for the future by referring to the desires, practices and tasks of the international lawyer. He informs the future international lawyer, for example, that

> [n]o international lawyer is likely to doubt the desirability of ... states ... to accept the settlement of their disputes on the basis of law but more is needed than doctrinal change. Legal practice must take account of the dynamic element, which the international, like every other, system of law reveals as soon as it ceases to be a merely academic study and begins to be applied to factual situations by the accepted processes of judicial reasons.[113]

How courts or tribunals resolve international disputes was important. If judges could make decisions not on the basis of existing law but rather *ex aequo et bono*, justice and compliance was likely to follow. The adaptability of doctrine to its political environment was the key, for Brierly, not merely to the study of international law but also, more importantly, to its practice.

6 The Scene That Exists after Reading

Generation after generation of students and lawyers use textbooks to understand the foundations of international law. Such knowledge anchors professional training in a common set of principles and orientates the practice of the international lawyer in their everyday interactions as the starting point for identifying relevant issues and providing strategic advice to governments. The distinctiveness of the three wartime textbooks of international law by Lauterpacht, Brierly and Scelle for the usual progression and renewal of general principles that is typical of the textbook genre related to the strategic lessons presented to their first readers, reading between June 1940 and 1945, about the weaknesses of the existing system, how disaster unfolds as a historical, political and legal question, and the complexity of the design tasks ahead.

113 Brierly, *Law of Nations*, 3rd ed. 1942 (n. 2), 224–225.

Pedagogical methods also facilitated the progression of the author's theoretical projects about the legal concept of war or rather, cautiously advanced relevant strategic arguments at a time when diplomatic sensitivities complicated the tasks of scholarly critique.

Irrespective of their theoretical differences, Lauterpacht, Brierly and Scelle pursued those agendas about the past, present and future of international order with optimism about the continuity of international law during crisis and the pacifistic potential of the rule of law. Their returning reminder to the international lawyer was not merely about the reality of law as an objective fact but also about the reality of the social field with which law interacts and seeks to stabilise. International law belongs to sovereign states as a community and exists to better organise and bring stability and predictability to international relations. Textbook explanations offered wartime readers assurance about the potential for peace and the part played by the rule of law in ensuring world order. Brierly clarified that the dilemma of state sovereignty untangles with each step toward better understanding how the state co-exists and can better co-exist with law. He says,

> We have accepted a false idea of the state as a personality with a life and a will of its own … The truth is that states are not persons … they are merely *institutions*, that is to say, organizations which men establish among themselves for securing certain objects, of which the most fundamental is a system of order within which the activities of their common life can be carried on…. Their subjection to law is as yet imperfect, though it is real as far as it goes; the problem of extending it is one of great practical difficulty, but it is not one of intrinsic impossibility.[114]

Brierly's reflection reflects the sobering optimism of the international lawyer who finds his own discipline paling yet surviving the trials of war and awaits its end by offering, in the guise of a history lesson, a guidebook of future options. States are not persons and law is *real* as far as it goes.

Bibliography

Benton, Lauren. 'Beyond Anachronism: Histories of International Law and Global Legal Politics'. *Journal of the History of International Law* 21(1) (2019), 1–34.

114 Ibid., 45.

Brierly, James L. 'International Law in the Education of a Lawyer'. *Michigan State Bar Journal* 27(10) (1948), 5.

Brierly, James L. 'International Law as a Subject of Education'. *Journal of the Society of Public Teachers of Law* (1926), 1–5.

Brierly, James L. 'Relation of International Law to International Peace'. *Cornell Law Quarterly* 13(1) (1927), 385–398.

Brierly, James L. 'Le fondement du caractére obligatoire du droite international'. *Recueil des cours de l'academie de droit international de La Haye* 3 (1928), 482.

Brierly, James L. 'The Shortcomings of International Law'. *British Yearbook of International Law* 5 (1924), 4–16.

Brierly, James L. 'The Essential Nature of International Disputes'. *Virginia Law Review* 16(6) (1930), 537–545.

Brierly, James L. *The Law of Nations* (Oxford: Clarendon Press, 1928, 1930).

Brierly, James L. *The Law of Nations* (Oxford: Clarendon Press, 2nd ed. 1936).

Brierly, James L. *The Outlook for International Law* (Oxford: Clarendon Press, 1944).

Brierly, James L. *The Law of Nations* (Oxford: Oxford University Press, 3rd ed. 1942.

Brierly, James L. *The Law of Nations* (Oxford: Oxford University Press, 4th ed. 1949).

Brown, Philip Marshall. 'Changing Concepts of International Law'. *American Journal of International Law* 34(3) (1940), 503–505.

Brown, Stewart. 'Japan Stuns World, Withdraws from League'. *United Press International* (24 February 1933), available at: https://www.upi.com/Archives/1933/02/24/Japan-stuns-world-withdraws-from-league/2231840119817/ (last accessed on 14 September 2020).

Carnegie Endowment for International Peace (Division of International Law). *The International Law of the Future: Postulates, Principles and Proposals* (Oxford: Oxford University Press, 1944).

Cassin, René. *Les hommes partis de rien: Le réveil de la France abattue* (Paris: Plon, 1975 ed. [1940–1941]).

Deak, Francis. 'International Law. By L. Oppenheim. Vol. II. Disputes, War and Neutrality. 6th ed. Edited by H. Lauterpacht. New York, London and Toronto: Longmans, Green & Co., 1940. Pp. xliv, 766. Index $17.50'. *American Journal of International Law* 35(2) (1941), 403–404.

Falconieri, Silvia. 'Situation at French Universities: Le « droit de la race ». Apprendre l'antisémitisme á la faculté de droit de Paris (1940–1944)'. *Histoire societe: Dieu me pardonne c'est son métier.* 10 April 2014, available at: https://histoireetsociete.wordpress.com/2014/04/10/le-droit-de-la-race-apprendre-lantisemitisme-a-la-faculte-de-droit-de-paris-1940-1944-par-silvia-falconieri/ (last accessed on 14 September 2020).

Fellmeth, Aaron and Maurice Horwitz. *Guide to Latin in International Law* (Oxford: Oxford University Press, 2009).

Friedmann, Friedmann 'International Law and the Present War'. (Lecture to Grotius Society, 21 November 1940) *Transactions of the Grotius Society* 26 (1940), 211–233.

Hamson, Charles J. 'Sir Hersch Lauterpacht (1897–1960)', in *Oxford Dictionary of National Biography* (Oxford: Oxford University Press, 2004).

Holman, Valerie. *Book Publishing in England 1939–1945* (London: British Library, 2008).

Jenks, Clarence W. 'Hersch Lauterpacht: The Scholar as Prophet'. *British Yearbook of International Law* 36 (1960), 1–103.

Jessup, Philip C. 'In Support of International Law'. *American Journal of International Law* 34(3) (1940), 505–508.

Keen, F. N., et al. 'International Law in Development: Discussion on the Re-Drafted Report of the Committee'. *Transactions of the Grotius Society* 27 (1941), 252–288.

Keen, F. N., et al. 'The Future of International Law: Final Report by the Committee Appointed to Consider the Sources of International Law'. *Transactions of the Grotius Society* 27 (1941), 289–312.

Keeton, George W. 'International Law and the Future (A Plea for a Functional Approach)'. *Transactions of the Grotius Society* 27 (1941), 31–58.

Koskenniemi, Martti. *The Gentle Civilizer of Nations: The Rise and Fall of International Law* 1870–1960 (Cambridge: Cambridge University Press, 2001).

Lauterpacht, Elihu. *The Life of Sir Hersch Lauterpacht, QC, FBA, LLD* (Cambridge: Cambridge University Pess, 2010).

Lauterpacht, Hersch and Humphrey Waldock, eds. *The Basis of Obligation in International Law and other Papers by the Late James Leslie Brierly* (Oxford: Clarendon Press, 1958).

Lauterpacht, Hersch. 'Brierly's Contribution to International Law'. *British Yearbook of International Law* 32 (1955–56), 1–19.

Lauterpacht, Hersch. *The Function of Law in the International Community* (Oxford: Oxford University Press, 2011 [1933]).

Lauterpacht, Hersch. 'Resumption of the Publication of the British Yearbook of International Law'. *British Yearbook of Internatinal Law* 21 (1944).

Lauterpacht, Hersch. *An International Bill of the Rights of Man* (Oxford: Oxford University Press, 2013 [1945]).

Lesaffer, Randall. 'Kellogg-Briand Pact', in *Max Planck Encylopedia of Public International Law*, ed. Rüdiger Wolfrum (Oxford: Oxford University Press, 2010), available at: http://opil.ouplaw.com/view/10.1093/law:epil/9780199231690/law-9780199231690-e320 (last accessed on 14 September 2020).

Oppenheim, Lassa Francis Lawrence. *International Law. A Treatise,* vol. I, ed. Hersch Lauterpacht, (London: Longmans, 6th ed., 1940).

Roberts, Anthea. *Is International Law International?* (Oxford: Oxford University Press, 2017).

Scelle, Georges. *Le sens international* (Paris: Presses Universitaires de France, 1942).

Scelle, Georges. *Manuel élémentaire de droit international public <avec les textes essentiels>* (Paris: Domat-Montchrestien, 1943, reprinted 1944).

Scelle, Georges. *Précis de droit des gens (principes et systématique)*, vols. I & II (Paris: Recueil Sirey, 1932 and 1934).

Scelle, Georges. 'Preface', in *Carl Strupp, Legal Machinery for Change* (London: Constable & Co., 1937).

Tanca, Antonio. 'Georges Scelle (1878–1961): Biographical Note with Bibliography'. *European Journal of International Law* 1(1) (1990), 240–249.

Thomson, Zoe. 'How Did Publishers Respond to the Restrictions Placed on Them by the Outbreak of World War Two?'. *The Journal of Publishing Culture* 5 (2016), 1–10.

Warren, Charles. 'Lawless Maritime Warfare'. *Foreign Affairs* 18(3) (1940), 424–441.

Waldock, Humphrey. 'James Leslie Brierly', in *Oxford Dictionary of National Biography* (Oxford: Oxford University Press, 2004).

PART 3

Regional and Cultural Variations of International Law

CHAPTER 8

The Politics of History in the Late Qing Era: William A. P. Martin and a History of International Law for China

Maria Adele Carrai

Abstract

In the light of 19th-century attempts to universalize history and international law, the purpose of this chapter is to show how the theory of an Ancient Chinese international law matured and disseminated within one politics of history and helped generate another at the end of the Qing Dynasty. On the one hand, the middleman William Alexander Parsons Martin, who as part of his Christian mission and in order to make international law more acceptable to the Chinese, translated systematically international law into Chinese and attempted to universalize it by finding a proto-international law in Ancient China. On the other hand, Chinese scholars and officials sought to use Martin's theory to universalize Confucianism and rectify international law according to what they believed to be their own superior morality and history.

Keywords

international law – W. A. P. Martin – translation – Confucianism – history – politics – China

1 Introduction

More than neutral descriptions of past events, histories of international law are often normative reconstructions responding to contemporary necessities. In the 19th century, Western powers' expansion forced them into contact with cultures and civilizations that shared little in common with Christianity. These encounters often prompted intellectuals, historians, and jurists in the Western world to rethink the historical and philosophical underpinnings of their normative constructs. Equally, intellectuals of countries whose normative orders had been forcefully shaken by Western powers' civilizing missions

 | DOI:10.1163/9789004461802_010

had to rethink their histories to make sense of and accommodate the fact that the international legal order was expanding at the expense of their own. Before the Opium Wars (1839–1860), the Qing normative order was grounded on the *Tianxia* worldview that implied the orchestrated and symbolic superiority of the Chinese emperors over the entire world. Yet despite its millennium-old civilization, China was seen by Westerners as part of a backward, sleepy Orient. After defeat in the Opium Wars, the Chinese Empire slowly entered the Western normative orbit. Translations into Chinese of modern international law had already begun, but it was still far from replacing China's vision of the world. For Chinese officials and scholars, international law belonged to inferior foreigners; reformists saw the practical value of Western learning and international law to deal with foreigners and ward off encroachment, but they believed in the superiority of their value system.[1]

As part of his Christian mission and in order to make international law more acceptable to the Chinese while encouraging China's recognition within the family of nations, the author of the first systematic translation into Chinese of international law, US missionary William Alexander Parsons Martin, attempted to universalize it by finding a proto-international law in Ancient China. This involved opposing most late-19th century histories of international law, which relegated the Chinese and the Orient to the margins of the 'family of nations' and their history.[2] While much literature has discussed the introduction of western international law in China,[3] this chapter, considering Chinese intellectuals' earliest analogies between the contemporary international situation and

---

1 For instance the Self-Strengthening Movement of the 1860s was formed by those Confucian intellectuals and officials like Feng Guifen 馮桂芬 (1809–1874), Prince Gong 恭亲王 (1833–1898), Zeng Guofang 曾國藩 (1811–1872), Li Hongzhang 李鴻章 (1823–1901), and Zuo Zongtang 左宗棠 (1812–1885), who, while aware of and intrigued by Western science, were still dedicated to restoring imperial universal authority as the sole form of coherence and order. The restoration was led by the maxim of the famous official of the late Qing dynasty Zhang Zhidong (张之洞, 1837–1909): zhongxue weiti, xixue weiyong 中學為體， 西學為用 (Traditional learning at the core, Western learning as an instrument). Discussed in Carrai, Maria Adele. *Sovereignty in China. A Genealogy of a Concept since 1840* (Cambridge: Cambridge University Press, 2019), 58.

2 See Ruskola, Teemu. *Legal Orientalism: China, the United States, and Modern Law* (Cambridge: Harvard University Press, 2013), chapter 1; Hsü, Immanuel C. *China's Entrance into the Family of Nations: The Diplomatic Phase; 1858–1880* (Cambridge: Harvard University Press, 1968).

3 Svarverud, Rune. *International Law as World Order in Late Imperial China: Translation, Reception and Discourse, 1847–1911* (Leiden: Brill, 2007); Hsü, *China's Entrance* 1968 (n. 2); Chiu, Hungdah. 'The Development of Chinese International Terms and the Problem of Their Translation into English'. *Journal of Asian Studies* 27(3) (1967), 485–501; Liu, Lydia. 'Legislating the Universal: The Circulation of International Law in the Nineteenth Century', in *Tokens of Exchange: The Problem of Translation in Global Circulations*, ed. Lydia Liu (Durham: Duke University Press, 1999), 127–164; Masini, Federico. *The Formation of Modern Chinese Lexicon*

the Warring States period investigates how the theory of an Ancient Chinese international law was matured and disseminated within one politics of history and helped generate another at the end of the Qing Dynasty. On the one hand the middleman Martin wanted to universalize international law, seen as part of his religious toolkit, and make it acceptable to the Chinese. He wanted also to promote the emancipation in international society of the country that gave him, from 1869, a steady income and recognition. On the other hand, Chinese scholars and officials used Martin's theory to universalize Confucianism and rectify international law according to what they believed to be their own superior morality and history.

This chapter is composed of four sections. The first, *The Emerging International Order and a Search for Analogies in China's Past*, introduces the situation of China in the mid-19th century and Qing intellectuals' earliest analogies between the contemporary international situation and the Ancient Warring States period. These theories are the ones on which Martin's theory on the existence of international law in Ancient China relied. *W. A. P. Martin as God's Agent to Open China to the Gospel and International Law* presents Martin and his role in introducing religion blended with international law to China. The third part, *Ancient China's International Law: Expanding International Law's Spatial and Temporal Dimensions*, explores the genesis of Martin's theory about the existence of international law in Ancient China in light of debates at the Institut de Droit International and the reasons behind his attempts to universalize international law. The fourth section, *Universalizing Confucianism through the History of International Law: A Chinese Response*, looks at the debates that Martin's theory engendered within Chinese circles and the rationale of Chinese scholars in adopting it. The conclusion discusses the legacy of Martin's theory in light of current attempts at global histories of international law.

2 The Emerging International Order and a Search for Analogies in China's Past

International law came to be conceived as 'universal' only in the 18th and 19th centuries, shifting from *ius publicum europaeum* to *ius publicum universale*.[4]

---

and Its Evolution toward a National Language: The Period from 1840 to 1898 (Berkeley: Project on Linguistic Analysis, 1993).

4 Vec, Miloš. 'Universalization, Particularization, and Discrimination. European Perspectives on a Cultural History of the 19th Century International Law'. *InterDisciplines* 3(2) (2012), 79–101, 79, 82.

This new sense of universality justified and fueled colonial and imperial expansion in the 19th and 20th century.[5] The 19th century was the period in which modern international law's doctrine and practice largely developed, contributing to what has been defined as the birth of the modern world and international society.[6] For 19th-century internationalists, such as Fedor Fedorovitch Martens, Henry Wheaton, François-André Isambert, Johann Kaspar Bluntschli, Augusto Pierantoni or Ernest Nys, who imagined a progressive history of international law governed by an evolutionary principle capable of naturally leading them toward a pragmatic, cosmopolitan, humanitarian, and liberal international law in the 20th century, history was on their side.[7] As European expansion reached its peak in the 1880s and 1890s, international lawyers such as Johann Kaspar Bluntschli, Pasquale Fiore and Charles Salomon, started to use the theory of 'degrees of civilization' to explore its legal, historical, and philosophical underpinning.[8] Debates about the applicability of international law to 'the Orient' started to animate international lawyers' circles. According to the statutes of the Institute du Droit International, founded in 1873, the only object of its attention was the 'civilized world', but the location of that world's borders came under scrutiny in the early decades of its existence and gave rise to the 'The Oriental Question'.[9]

---

5 Vec, Miloš. 'From the Congress of Vienna to the Paris Peace Treaties of 1919', in *The Oxford Handbook of the History of International Law*, eds. Bardo Fassbender and Anne Peters (Oxford: Oxford University Press, 2012), 654–678.

6 International law was institutionalized in the 19th century, as can be seen by the great powers' large production of treaties, protocols, and declarations, and international law doctrine emerged in the 19th century. See Macalister-Smith, Peter and Joachim Schwietzke. 'Bibliography of the Textbooks and Comprehensive Treaties in Positive International Law in the 19th Century'. *Journal of the History of International Law* 3(1) (2001), 75–142; Vec, 'From the Congress of Vienna' 2012 (n. 5), 674.

7 Vec, 'European Perspectives' 2012 (n. 4), 79; Koskenniemi, Martti. *The Gentle Civilizer of Nations: The Rise and Fall of International Law 1870–1960* (Cambridge: Cambridge University Press, 2009), chapter 2; Kennedy, David. 'International Law and the Nineteenth Century: History of an Illusion'. *Nordic Journal of International Law* 65(3–4) (1990), 385–420, 387.

8 Koskenniemi, *Gentle Civilizer* 2009 (n. 7), 103.

9 Anghie, Antony. *Imperialism, Sovereignty and the Making of International Law* (Cambridge: Cambridge University Press, 2005), 59–63; The question of international law's universality and applicability to the Orient was addressed at the 1875 Hague Conference, prompting further discussions in the following years. In 1877 the Institute du Droit International sent a questionnaire to experts on the region and its legal systems about the 'Applicability of the European Law of Nations to the Oriental Nations', asking whether, given 'such radical differences' between Oriental and European nations, it was possible to admit them to the general international law community. *Annuaire de l'institut de droit international* (Gand, 1877), 123, 141. Because the questions could not be answered in general terms, the questionnaire was reformulated in 1879 under the chairmanship of Sir Travis Twiss with the title 'The Oriental

While European jurists already thought of international law as a universal order by the beginning of the 19th century, it was still far from the universally recognized system we know today. The Qing Empire, for instance, thought of itself as at the center of the universe, and together with its many vassals in East Asia ignored the existence of Wester international law. When the Western normative order encountered China, Western nations felt that 'the form of relationship specific to the Qing and imperial court was in some ways a transgression of an acceptable international norm', particularly its isolationism and Sinocentric, hierarchical world order.[10] In fact, the diplomatic protocol of the tribute system that left European diplomats puzzled in the 18th and 19th centuries was no more fictional than that of the modern international law conceived of as a science.[11] The need to include the 'otherness' of non-European

Question'. It addressed more technical aspects, such as the differences between 'less civilized' countries, and what kinds of reforms the Orient should implement to be civilized enough for admission. See Section H entitled 'Current Issues dealt from an international law perspective' in *Annuaire de l'institut de droit international* (Gand, 1878), 335. Within a few years, with the First Rapport of M. de Martens, admissibility came to depend on Western jurists' examination of East Asian countries' institutional and judicial reforms. See 'Examiner quelles réformes sont désirables dans les institutions judiciaires actuellement en vigueur dans les pays Orient, par rapport ause procès où est engagée une personne ressortissant à une puissance chrétienne d'Europe d'Amérique,' and 'Premier rapport de M. de Martens. Comme il a été dit plus haut', at 13, 26 and 27; 'La réforme des institutions judiciaires en Orient,' in *Annuaire de l'institut de droit international* (Gand, 1880–1882), 223, 229. In 1887 the question led to the creation of the Institute's twelfth commission, devoted to laying out the desirable reforms to the judicial institutions in Eastern countries. The commission was terminated in 1895–1896, after several states concluded bilateral treaties with Japan, negotiations had been conducted with other Oriental countries, and Japan had been admitted into the family of nations; it was noted that 'in these circumstances, our mandate has no longer reason to exist'. *Annuaire de l'institut de droit international* (Gand, 1895/96).

10 Hevia, James L. 'Sovereignty and Subject: Constituting Relationships of Power in Qing Guest Ritual', in *Body, Subject and Power in China*, eds. Angela Zito and Tani E. Barlow (Chicago: University of Chicago Press, 1994), 181–200, 182.

11 This was for instance the case of the famous British McCartney Embassy and its failure in 1793. Sponsored by the British East India Company, Lord George Macartney went to the Qing court as a representative of a sovereign nation, willing to perform the rituals required but without humiliating his country. The mission aimed to renegotiate British relations with China on new, more equal terms, establish permanent diplomatic missions, open up China to trade with Britain, and receive privileges to help rebalance Britain's trade deficit caused largely by tea imports. While Macartney did recognize the omnipotence of the emperor 'in China' and had banners inscribed 'The English Ambassador Bringing Tribute to the Emperor of China' in Chinese, when it came to ritual practices whose performance was not required in front of his own king, and that he felt would have implied recognition of the supreme authority of the Chinese emperor over her Britannic majesty, Macartney refused to kowtow, and this was tolerated by the Qing court. The letter Qianlong sent in

countries in the *ius publicum universale* led to the creation of states of exceptions in which sovereignty was suspended.[12] One of the clearest manifestations of this legal exceptionality here was the unequal treaties system, which brought China into the conceptual framework of international law, but as a semi-civilized country that lacked full rights.[13] In a sense international law, despite aspiring universality, has remained parochially European and a reflection of its politics.

As Europe's expansion peaked in the last two decades of the century, their 'uncivilized counterparts', as further discussed below, began seeking historical foundations in their own traditions to make sense of the new international order, facilitate their entrance into the family of nations, and ultimately rectify international law. At this point, amid Institute de Droit International debates about the possibility of applying customary international law to the Orient, Presbyterian missionary and long-time Institute member William Alexander Parsons Martin (Ding Weiliang 丁韙良, 1827–1916) ambitiously attempted to universalize it by expanding its origins to Ancient China. Indeed, he was the first historian of international law in China to explicitly posit, by manipulating original legal texts and constructing new historiographies, that in its antiquity China must have had a code of proto-international law. Martin with his translations created also a lexicon that would remain stable for over forty years; some of it is still used now in Chinese legal language.[14] Although his contribution to the Institute was modest, his theory not only had huge repercussions among China's newly trained jurists, but also has a strong legacy in today's histories of international law as Chinese jurists and international lawyers continue to refer to his theory about the existence of an Ancient Chinese international law.

Before China was accepted into the family of nations, it managed its foreign relations through the so-called tribute system.[15] Although the analytical

---

response to George III was deemed disappointing as it basically rejected all the requests; Qianlong remarked that China possessed all things and 'set no value on objects strange or ingenious and have no use for your country's manufactures.' Britain felt scorned by both the failure of its envoys to expand trade in China according to the rules of international law and the unequal treatment it received. Carrai, *Sovereignty in China* 2019 (n. 1), 44–45.

12 Nuzzo, Luigi. *Origini di una scienza. Diritto internazionale e colonialismo nel XIX secolo* (Frankfurt am Main: Vittorio Klostermann, 2012).

13 Wang, Dong. *China's Unequal Treaties: Narrating National History* (New York: Lexington Books, 2008), 25.

14 Masini, *Modern Chinese Lexicon* 1993 (n. 3); Svarverud, Rune. *International Law as World Order in Late Imperial China: Translation, Reception and Discourse, 1847–1911* (Leiden: Brill, 2007).

15 Although it has been heavily criticized and is in many ways outdated today, an important study of the Chinese tribute system was that of historian of China John K. Fairbank,

framework provided by this system, *chaogong tixi* 朝貢體系, is too simplistic and it does not do justice to the complex and differentiated set of rules regulating relations between the Middle Kingdom and its neighboring countries, it does highlight differences between the pre-20th century China normative system and that of the West. Before Martin's systematic translation, passages of codes of international law were introduced into China during the First Opium War (1839–1842), when Lin Zexu (林則徐), the Guangdong governor appointed by the Qing Government to negotiate opium-trade-related controversies with Britain, asked imperial interpreter Yuan Dehui (袁德輝) to translate passages from Emer de Vattel's *Le droit des gens* (1758). Yuan's final version, *Geguo lüli* 《各國律例》, in which de Vattel's name is translated as Hua Daer 滑達爾, was published in 1847 in Wei Yuan's sixty-chapter geographical work *An Illustrated Gazetteer of Maritime Countries* (*Haiguo Tuzhi* 《海國圖志》).[16] It was only after the Second Opium War (1856–1860), in 1864, that Martin's more comprehensive translation of works of international law was introduced. At this point Chinese diplomats started to adopt its conceptual and linguistic framework as a reference.[17]

---

whose scholarship has strongly influenced studies of Chinese foreign relations. See Fairbank, John K. and Ssu-yü Têng. 'On the Ch'ing Tributary System'. *Harvard Journal of Asiatic Studies* 6(2), 135–246; Fairbank, John K., ed. *The Chinese World Order, Traditional China's Foreign Relations.* (Cambridge: Harvard University Press, 1968), 196. See also Rossabi, Morris. *China among Equals: The Middle Kingdom and its Neighbors* (Berkeley: University of California Press, 1982); Mancall, Mark. *China at the Center: 300 Years of Foreign Policy* (New York: Free Press, 1984); For more recent and discursive interpretations of the tribute system, see Kang, David C. *East Asia before the West: Five Centuries of Trade and Tribute* (New York: Columbia University Press, 2010); Wright, David Curtis. *From War to Diplomatic Parity in Eleventh-Century China, Sung's Foreign Relations with Kitan Liao* (Leiden: Brill, 2005); Suzuki, Shogo. *Civilization and Empire: China and Japan's Encounter with European International Society* (Abingdon: Routledge, 2009); Hamashita, Takeshi. *China, East Asia and the Global Economy: Regional and Historical Perspectives* (Abingdon: Routledge, 2008).

16 Yuan's translation was based on Joseph Chitty's 1833 English translation of de Vattel as *Law of Nations, or Principles of the Law of Nature, Applied to the Conduct of and Affairs Nations and Sovereigns*. Lam Hok-Chung 林學忠. *Cong wanguo gongfa dao gongfa waijiao* 《從萬國公法到公法外交》 [From the Law of Nations to International Diplomacy] (Shanghai: Shanghai Guji Chubanshe, 2009), 44–48. The translation is also discussed in Hsü, *China's Entrance* 1960 (n. 2), 123–125; Liu, Lydia. *The Clash of Empires: The Invention of China in Modern World Making* (Cambridge: Harvard University Press, 2004), 118–119; Masini, *Modern Chinese Lexicon* 1993 (n. 3), 21–28; Svarverud, *International Law as World Order* 2007 (n. 14), 75–87.

17 Wheaton, Henry and William A. P. Martin. *Wan guo gong fa* 《萬國公法》 (Taibei: Zhongguo guo ji fa xue hui, 1998). Before Yuan Dehui's translation of Vattel, the missionary Martino Martini (1641–1661) translated passages from the international law work of

Martin's translation was prompted by the defeats in the two Opium Wars, after which Qing intellectuals gradually realized that they were facing issues that could not be properly addressed through the more traditional conceptual and normative system. The world had changed, and the Qing had to find new words and theoretical framework to deal with it. This is apparent in the work of Qing intellectual and geographer Xu Jiyu (徐繼畬) (1795–1873), a high-ranking official.[18] Appointed to the coastal prefecture of Fujian, he came in direct contact with foreigners and witnessed the defeat of the first Opium War firsthand. In his *A Short Account of the Maritime Circuit* (Yinghuan zhilüe, 《瀛環志略》), written in 1847 but not circulated because of conservative opposition until the 1860s, Xu provided a new geography of the world, in which China itself is re-dimensioned according to Western measurements and geographical representations. While in traditional maps China was represented as the world and at the center of universe, with no clear defined boundaries that separated it from the rest of the world, in the map of Xu Jiyu there are four continents and China is part of the Asian continent, although China rules supreme over its dependencies within that continent.[19] Moreover, Xu was the first scholar to initiate analogies between the contemporary international system and the Warring States period (475–249 BC), giving rise to what has been defined as the 'Spring and Autumn, Warring States theory' (*Chunqiu Zhanguo Lun* 《春秋戰國論》). According to the theory the current state of international relations and situation were analogous to the one in the Spring and Autumns Warring States Period, the era of division in ancient China characterized by the existence of various states that were at war before the Qin state conquered them all in 221 BC and reunited the territory under the Qin Dynasty (221 to 206 BC).[20]

---

the Salamanca School renown jurist Francisco Suarez (1548–1617), and in 1689 the missionaries Tomas Pereira (1645–1703) and Jean Francois Gerbillon (1654–1707) served as interpreters and negotiators for the China-Russia Treaty of Nerchinsk, pointing out the usefulness of international law. See Sebes, Joseph. *The Jesuits and the Sino-Russian Treaty of Nerchinsk (1689): The Diary of Thomas Pereira* (Rome: Institutum Historicum SI, 1961).

18 See Lutz, Jessie G. 'China's View of the West, A Comparison of the Historical Geographies of Wei Yuan and Xu Jiyu'. *Social Sciences and Mission* 25(1–2) (2012), 35–52.

19 Drake, Fred. *China Charts the World: Hsu Chi-Yu and His Geography of 1848* (Cambridge Harvard University Press, 1975), 68.

20 Among the scholars that have discussed the Qing intellectuals that have created a parallel between the international situation of the late 19th century and the Warring States Period see Zeng Tao 曾涛. 'Jindai Zhongguo de guojifa fuhui lun 近代中国的国际法附会论'. *Fashi xue kan* 法史学刊 (2007) available at: http://cesl.cupl.edu.cn/upload/201103224076038.pdf; (last accessed on 14 September 2020) Zhang Weiming 张卫明. 'Yangwu shiqi guoren dui jindai guji jushi yu guojifa de bifu 洋务时期国人对近代国际局势与国际公法的比附'. *Shijie Jingji yu Zhengzhi* 世界经济与政治 6 (2010), 81–83; Xiao Yonghong 萧永宏. 'Lun Yangwu shiqi Zhongguoren

The Eastern Zhou (770–256 BC), that comprises both the Spring and Autumns (771–476 BC) and the Warring States Period (475–221 BC), is the period in which the Zhou royal authority over the various feudal states started to erode. In the Warring States period, in particular, the various states of Qin, Chu, Zhao, Wei, Han, Yan, and Qi declared independence from the Zhou Dynasty and competed for power. In Chinese dynastic tradition the Eastern Zhou period is a significant one. Not only it was one of the key moments of disunity and fights for hegemony among the different states before the establishment of the first unified and long-lasting Chinese Empire in 221 BC. It was also a time in which many great philosophical schools emerged together with governmental structure and tenants of political culture. The crucial issue of rulership gave rise to the so-called Hundred Schools of Thoughts (including Confucianism, Legalism, Taoism, Mohism, the School of Yin-yang, the Logicians etc.). In the traditional political culture of China that favors the unity of the empire, it was not considered as a positive example. However, in the 19th and 20th centuries its legacy has generated much interest among political figures and academics as it was used as a repository of strategies and multi-state experiences for finding both analogies for the new international situation and remedies to the turmoil of the 19th and 20th centuries.[21]

Xu compared European countries and their relations to the Warring States period; specifically, Britain, Russia and France became identified with the some of the Warring States.[22] By providing a more realistic account of the contemporary world and dividing it into states, Xu's work was not only the first to create an analogy with Chinese history that would become essential for Qing intellectuals and for Martin; it also had implications for the perceived primacy of Chinese civilization.[23] Although Europe was geographically far from China and not transformed by Chinese rituals and music, Xu wrote, its civilization was still admirable and should have almost equal status with the Middle

de guoji zhengzhi guannian 论洋务时期中国人的国际政治观念'. *Xueshu yuekan* 学术月刊 12 (1997), 83–90; Wang Ermin 王尔敏. *Zhongguo Jindai sixiang shi lun*《中国近代思想史论》(Beijing: Shehui kexue wexian chuban, 2003); Tian Tao 田涛. *Guojifa shuru wanqing Zhongguo*《国际法输入与晚清中国》(Jinan: Jinan chubanshe, 2001).

21 Pines, Yuri. *Envisioning Eternal Empire, Chinese Political Thought of the Warring States Era* (Honolulu: University of Hawai'i Press, 2009), 1–4, 219–222.

22 "法国， 英国， 俄罗斯 '比权量力，不过齐秦普，楚相为敌已耳"葡萄牙则'不过滕", discussed in Zeng Tao 曾涛 , 'Jindai Zhongguo de guojifa fuhui lun 近代中国的国际法附会论' (2007); Zhang Weiming 张卫明. 'Yangwu shiqi guoren dui jindai guji jushi yu guojifa de bifu 洋务时期国人对近代国际局势与国际公法的比附'. *Shijie Jingji yu Zhengzhi* 世界经济与政治 6 (2010), 81–83.

23 Drake, *China Charts the World* 1975 (n. 19), 149.

Kingdom. *Zhongguo* 中国, the old name for China as it was considered the kingdom at the center of the world, hence, according to the Chinese cosmology, superior to other kingdoms.[24] Yet while the secular model of sovereign states with its ideology of the balance of power and equality may resemble China's ancient Warring States, for Xu it was not a valid alternative to the Chinese sacral imperial order; it was merely important to gain knowledge of it in order to become stronger and thus resist Western incursions. Nevertheless, by presenting a new image of the world, in which China was increasingly individualized as a sovereign state, the geographies Xu considered indirectly constituted a first autochthonous challenge to the idea of cosmic kinship, which was already threatened by pressures from foreign powers such as the unequal treaties. After the Second Opium War, the general inertia with which his works were received at court was replaced by a new attitude that prompted Martin's translations and a different approach to the West.[25]

Another important intellectual to further develop the analogy with the Warring States was Feng Guifen, who greatly contributed to the philosophy of the Self-Strengthening Movement (1861–72). In his 1861 *Petitions from Jiaobinlu* 《校邠廬抗議》, he wrote:

> Are not today's overseas barbarians and the countries of the Spring and Autumn Period in a similar situation and is not the context the same? When the level of power is high, it must be justified.... In the same way as in the Warring States period [in the current situation] the great country invades the small, the strong buries the weak, but there must be an excuse regardless of one's beliefs and it does not matter if it's unreasonable.[26]

This analogy had significant repercussions on Chinese scholars in the late Qing period. Using the analogy with the multi-states system of the Spring and Autumn and the Warring States periods, helped Chinese establishing a

---

24 For instance, the Prussian king is praised because he is able to connect the people to his government, and Germany is deemed to be the China of Europe not only for its geographical centrality but its sophisticated culture. Ibid., 145–146.

25 Schoppa, R. Keith. *Revolution and Its Past: Identities and Change in Modern Chinese History* (Upper Saddle River: Prentice Hall, 3rd ed. 2011), 92.

26 "今海外诸夷,一春秋时之列国也，不特形势同，即风气亦相近焉。势力相高而言必称理，谲诈相尚而口必道信，两军交战，不废通使，一旦渝平，居然与国。亦复大侵小、强陵弱，而必有其藉口之端，不闻有不论理、不论信，如战国时事者." Feng Guifen 冯桂芬, *Jiaobin lu Kangyi* 校邠庐抗议, vol. 2, available at: https://ctext.org/wiki.pl?if=gb&res=551265&searchu=%E4%BB%8A%E6%B5%B7%E5%A4%96&remap=gb (last accessed on 1 April 2021).

broader understanding of the world that by the end of the 19th century was characterized by a multinational system. By suggesting that China was not a central kingdom but a country among equal countries, it indirectly helped abolish Chinese centralism and bring the country into the new global context. It had also important repercussions on China's modern diplomatic thinking and practice, because it called for referencing ancient experience, especially in relation to the way the Western powers maintained international peace.[27] Moreover, it was on the basis of this analogy and reinterpretation of history that Martin's widely disseminated theory of the existence of international law in Ancient China would form.

3 W. A. P. Martin as God's Agent to Open China to the Gospel and International Law

China's defeat in the Second Opium War, in 1860, made manifest its incapacity to resist Western powers on its territory, either by force or conciliation. The 1858 Tianjin Treaty and the 1860 Beijing Convention put an end to the war and brought to maturity the unequal treaties system, which legalized Western encroachment of Chinese sovereignty.[28] China's weakness, the growing interference of Western powers, and the general internal discontent that exploded in the Taiping Rebellion (1850–1864) prompted a national sense of crisis among Chinese intellectuals, which encouraged a renewed interest in Western technology and science, seen as indispensable tools for recovering strength. Among the ruling class the change of attitude toward Western institutions and knowledge was sealed by the New Foreign Policy memorial submitted in January 1861 by three figures: Prince Gong, imperial commissioner and brother of the Emperor Xianfeng; Guiliang, grand secretary; and Wenxiang, assistant

27 Wang Ermin王尔敏. *Zhongguo Jindai sixiang shi lun* 《中国近代思想史论》 (Beijing: Shehui kexue wenxian chuban, 2003), 156–166.

28 While the 1942 Treaty of Nanjing had opened China only to Britain, France, and the US, the Treaty of Tianjin and the Convention of Beijing opened it to most Western powers: Russia, Belgium, Germany, Portugal, Denmark, the Netherlands, Spain, Italy, Austria-Hungary, Japan, Peru and Brazil: France (Treaty of Tianjin 1858, Convention of Beijing 1860), United States of America (Treaty of Tianjin 1858, Convention of Beijing 1868), Russia (Treaty of Tianjin 1858, Convention of Beijing 1860), Germany (Treaty of Tianjin 1861), Belgium (Treaty of Beijing 1865), Denmark (Treaty of Beijing 1863), Holland (Treaty of Tianjin 1863), Portugal (Treaty of Tianjin 1862), Spain (Treaty of Tianjin 1864), Italy (Treaty of Tianjin 1866), Austria-Hungary (Treaty of Beijing 1869), Japan (Treaty of Tianjin 1871), Peru (Treaty of Tianjin 1874). *Treaty, Convention, etc. between China and Foreign* States, vol. 1, 2 (Shanghai: Department of the Inspector General of the Customs, 1917).

secretary of the Board of Revenue. The first of the six regulations it contained established a new foreign affairs body, the Zongli Waiguo shiwu Yamen 總理外國事務衙門, launched in March 1861.[29] The fifth regulation ruled that delegates from Canton and Shanghai, who understood written and spoken foreign languages, must be sent to Beijing for consultation in what would later be known as the Tongwenguan 同文館, an institute dedicated to Western learning and the translation of Western texts founded in Beijing in 1862.[30]

It is within the Tongwenguan that Martin produced the first systematic translation of international law into Chinese.[31] It was printed by the Chinese

29 *New Foreign Policy memorial* of 1861 in John K. Fairbank and Ssu-yü Têng, *China's Response to the West: A Documentary Survey 1839–1923, with E-Tu Zen Su, Chao Yingfang & others, Cambridge, Mass.: Harvard University Press* (New York: Athenum, 1965), 47–49, 48–49.

30 See translation of *New Foreign Policy memorial* of 1861 in ibid. 48.

31 Martin was born in 1827 in Livonia, Indiana, and completed his theological studies at the McCormick Theological Seminary (later called the New Albany Theological Seminary) in 1849. He was appointed a missionary to China that same year and arrived in Ningbo with his wife in April 1850. In 1865 the Chinese government invited Martin to teach English two hours a day in the Tongwenguan. In 1867, as the language school was being reorganized and gradually expanded around a curriculum that included multiple aspects of Western learning, he was appointed professor of international law and political economy. He then took a second short but intense furlough in the US: 'I committed the interests of the mission to other hands and went for special studies prior to entering on the duties of my chair.'; Martin, William A. P. *A Cycle of Cathay: Or, China, South and North, with Personal Reminiscences* (New York: Fleming H. Revell, 1900), 241. He obtained a Doctor of Law from New York University (to be followed up by one from Princeton University in 1899) and came into contact with influential international law professor Theodore Dwight Woolsey at Yale University through his sons Pascal and Winfred, who were students there. Martin would translate Woolsey's 1860 book *Introduction to the Study of International Law: Designed as an Aid in Teaching, and in Historical Studies* into Chinese as *Gongfa bianlan* 《公法便览》; after its publication in 1875 it became the central text for training students at the Tongwen Guan. See Svarverud, *International Law as World Order* 2007 (n. 14), 96; Martin, *Cycle of Cathay* 1900 (n. 31), 235. For his achievements and aid to the Chinese government, in 1885 Martin was given the rank of Mandarin of Third Class, and in 1898, when the government founded the Imperial University of China (later Peking University), Guangxu Emperor made him its president and ranked him Mandarin of Second Class. The Boxer Rebellion of 1900 disrupted the institution's development and Martin's presidency, and he returned to the US for almost a year. Toward the end of 1901 the governor general, Zhang Zhidong, appointed him president of a new government university at Wuchang for a three-year term, but on arrival Martin found that the university was not yet established and instead spent 1902 to 1905 as president of the Hubei Mandarin Institute (Hubei Shixueyuan 湖北仕學院) and the Hubei Jimei Xuetang (湖北濟美学堂), teaching international law, diplomacy and geography to Zhang Zhidong's officials. Ding Weiliang 丁韪良, *Bangjiao Tiyao* 《邦交提要》 (廣學會清光緒三十年刻本, 1904), 2; Martin, William A. P. *The Awakening of China* (New York: Doubleday, Page & Company, 1910), 230. After his three-year mandate he returned briefly to the US

central government and widely circulated among modern Chinese politicians, diplomats, and intellectuals. No international law expert, Martin was a Presbyterian missionary from Indiana sent to Ningbo in 1849 who became acquainted with the subject as an interpreter for the US legation to the 1858 Tianjin Treaty negotiations.[32] Missionaries due to their knowledge of local languages and culture, they were often invited by merchants and diplomats to serve in communication and business. In the 19th and early 20th centuries, among Westerners in China, it was missionaries that were the most numerous and invested. Committed to learning the Chinese culture and language, they view Chinese people very differently from merchants and diplomats. They emphasized Chinese people 'welfare' and believed in their gradual conversion to Christianity.[33] Martin developed the idea of translating international law into Chinese and creating a high-grade school to train Chinese Christians in Western learning, in the belief such a translation would help expose the 'superiority of Christian Civilization' and ultimately spread Christianity in China.[34] Having come up with the idea during a 1859–1862 furlough, he initially considered de Vattel as a starting point; when he visited Shanghai in 1862, John E. Ward, US minister to China during the 1860 Dagu Crisis, recommended Henry Wheaton as 'more modern and equally authoritative'.[35] With the help of some Chinese translators and the support of new US Minister to China Anson Burlingame, new British Inspector-General of China's Imperial Maritime Custom Service Robert Hart, and the Zongli Yamen, he completed the translation of Wheaton's 1836 book *Elements of International Law* as *Wanguo Gongfa* in 1864.[36] Overall, *Wanguo Gongfa* is a very meaningful book, not only because

---

and was appointed honorary member of the North China Mission; he returned to Beijing in 1905 and died there in 1916. Wang Lixin 王立新, *Meiguo Chuanjiao shi yu wan qing zhongguo xiandaihua* 《美国传教士与晚清中国现代化》(天津: 天津人民出版社, 1997): Wang Weijian 王维俭, 'Dingzheng ruogan zhongwai ci shu zhong Ding Weiliang ci mu sheji de shishi 订正若干中外词书中'丁韪良'词目涉及的史实' *Zhongshan daxue Xuebao* 中山大学学报 2 (1987), 68–76.

32 Martin applied for the post with the US delegation. See Martin, *Cycle of Cathay* 1900 (n. 31), 147.

33 Wang, Jing. 'The Image of China Shaped by American Missionaries and Its Impact on the Early Twentieth Century'. *Journal of Cultural Interaction in East Asia* 6 (2015), 31–45.

34 Covell, Ralph R. *W. A. P. Martin, Pioneer of Progress in China* (Christian University Press, 1978), 133; Harris, Paul. 'Cultural Imperialism and American Protestant Missionaries: Collaboration and Dependency in Mid-Nineteenth-Century China'. *Pacific Historical Review* 60 (1991), 309–338.

35 Martin, *Cycle of Cathay* 1900 (n. 31), 221–222.

36 Ibid., 234–235; The translation was divided into four chapters (1. 釋公法之義，明其本源，題其大旨，2. 論諸國自然之權，3. 論諸國平時往來之權，4. 論交戰條規).

it is the first systematic translation of international law, but it also meant the approval and gradual acceptance of a different world order.

Scholars have given various motivations for Martin's translation of the book. For some, Martin, Burlingame, and Hart supported the translation to open up the closed-door policy of the Qing government and bring its diplomacy within the orbit of Western international law, its practices, and ultimately its religious and normative underpinnings: Their mission thus reflected a civilizing mission to conquer China religiously and normatively.[37] This reflects also Latourette's reading of missionaries 'work', for whom 'the primary motives back of the missionary movement were unselfish. Selfish ones were undoubtedly there: the increase of the glory and power of a Western nation or of an order or a society, the desire for personal renown, and the urge to adventure. Missionaries were pioneers and were impelled in part, as are all pioneers, by a passion for achievement in a fresh environment. In the great majority of missionaries, however, the dominant motive had little of self: it was a feeling of obligation to share with others a message, a salvation, a way of life which the missionary believed of supreme importance.'[38] For others, Martin's work was beneficial for China but simultaneously helped justify and legalize Western powers' invasion.[39] Other scholars, such as Norma J. Burns, Lin Zhiping and Wu Sumin, believe that the main motivation was the fact that the translation would be useful to China for its diplomatic interactions after the Second Opium War.[40] For Tian Tao, Zhang Yanqing, and Gao Liping, Martin sought to promote colonialism, but also, more importantly, to serve his religious commitment to introduce a standard of justice grounded on the Christian God. For them, Martin was

37 Wang Weijian 王伟检. 'Pu dan dazhankou chuanbo shijian he xifang guojifa chuanru zhongguo 普丹大沽口船舶事件和西方国际法传入中国'. *Xueshu yanjiu* 学术研究 5 (1985), 84–90.

38 Latourette, Kenneth S. *A History of Christian Missions in China* (London: Society for Promoting Christian Knowledge, 1929), 824.

39 Zhang Jingcao 张劲草, Qiu Zaijue 邱在珏. 'Lun guojifa zhi chuanru Zhongguo 论国际法之传入中国,' *Hebei Daxue Xuebao* 河北大学学报 2 (1984), 126–133.

40 Lin Zhiping 林治平，*Kexue yu jiu en-Jidujiao yu huaren xiandaihua meijie renwu de yanjiu* 《科學與救恩：基督教與華人現代化媒介人物的研究》(Taibei: Taibei Yuzhou guang chubanshe 1993), 251–252; Wu Suming 吴素敏，*Ding Weiliang zhi yanjiu (1827–1916)* 《丁韪良之研究 (*1827–1916*)》(Taibei Donghai Daxue Shuoshi lunwen, 1987) 158–159; Burns, Norma J. *W. A. P. Martin and the Westernization of China* (Indiana University, MA Thesis Mar. 1954), 218. See also Fu Deyuan, 傅德元, 'Ding Weiliang wanguo gong fa fanyi lanben ji yitu xin tan 丁韪良'万国公法'翻译蓝本及意图新探'. *Anhui Shixue* 安徽史学 1 (2008), 52–53.

devoted to promoting China's acceptance of such standards but also to ensure that it was accepted into the family of nations.[41]

Martin's motivations, of course, were multiple. While his first motivation was to spread Christianity and supporting his evangelic work, indeed, his motivations intersected and sometimes even clashed with each other, reflecting the complex personality and delicate position of a mediator between two world orders. As Fu Deyuan has observed, Martin's translation had to do with advancing his own career as well as spreading Christianity, and secondly, allowing Chinese to understand international law for use in diplomatic affairs.[42] China was the country that gave Martin much higher salary than the Mission and prestigious position, especially from 1869, when he resigned from the Presbyterian mission and became a Chinese government employee at the newly established Tongwenguan. The latter consulted him on questions of international law when political and legal disputes with European powers arose.[43] He had officially become an agent of God's providence in opening China to international law – with a salary almost ten times his previous one. He justified his new position thus: 'The college is secular, and it cannot be otherwise, but in my hands by the blessing of God it will be at least less anti-Christian than it would be otherwise'.[44]

---

41 Tian Tao 田涛. 'Wan qing guojifa shu shu lun 晚清国际法输述论,' *Tianjin shehui kexue* 天津社会科学 6 (1999), 99–103; Tian Tao 田涛，*Guojifa shuru wan qing Zhongguo* 《国际法输入与晚清中国》 2001, 49–50.

42 Fu Deyuan. 傅德元, 'Ding Weiliang wanguo gong fa fanyi lanben ji yitu xin tan 丁韪良'万国公法'翻译蓝本及意图新探,' *Anhui Shixue* 安徽史学 1 (2008), 45–53, 52–53.

43 'Rev. W. A. P. Martin, D. D., of China.' *The Missionary Review of the World* (March 1917), 198; Appendix F, Dr. W. A. P. Martin – Its First President 'The Tongwen College', in H.B. Morse, *The International Relations of the Chinese Empire,* vol. 3 (New York: Longmans, Green & Co., 1910).

44 'Peking, Martin to Board, 169, December 1, 1869', in *Presbyterian Church in the U.S.A. Board of Foreign Missions Correspondence and Reports*, 1833–1911. With Martin as president the Tongwen Guan became an important center for training top officials in the art of diplomacy, history, and international law. Many of its alumni were dispatched as interpreters and ministers, such as Ching Chang, as minister to France; 'Appendix F, Dr. W. A. P. Martin – Its First President "The Tongwen College"', in Hosea B. Morse, *The International Relations of the Chinese Empire,* vol. 3 (London: Longmans, Green & Co., 1910), 471–472; Martin, William A. P. *The Lore of Cathay, or, the Intellect of China* (New York: F. H. Revell, 1901). During Martin's presidency, the school translated several international law books, including Charles de Martens' *Guide Diplomatique* as Xingyao Zhigang 星轺指掌; Johann Caspar Bluntschli's *Das moderne Völkerrecht der civilisirten Staten als Rechtsbuch dargestellt* as *Gongfa huitong* 《公法汇通》 (1879); the Institute de Droit International's manual on rules on war, *Les Lois de la Guerre sur Terre*, as *Ludi zhanli xinxuan* 《陆地战例新选》 (1882); and William Edward Halland's *A Treatise on International Law* as *Gongfa xinbian* 《公法新编》 (1903).

Reflecting his evangelical work, there is no doubt that for Martin *Wanguo Gongfa* was part of his Christian mission in China: 'I was led to undertake it … providentially … as a work which might bring this atheistic government to the recognition of God and his Eternal Justice and perhaps impart to them something of the spirit of Christianity'.[45] He justified the translation in the English preface, saying that to international law's 'fundamental principle, the Chinese mind is prepared to yield a ready assent', that it was inscribed in human hearts and was thus universal.[46] Martin's view of international law as a complementary tool for recruiting new Christians could already be seen in 1857, when, due to his Chinese language skills, he was called on to assist Rev. Dr. Samuel Wells Williams as interpreter and adviser to US Minister William B. Reed. Justifying his decision to accept to the Presbyterian Church, he wrote that in helping with the treaty he especially hoped to promote liberty of conscience and missionary labor and to secure a missionary location in Beijing, as he believed a city residence would be useful to spread the faith.[47] Missionaries were not allowed in the capital, and previous years had seen debates in missionary circles on how to revise existing treaties to extract more privileges and Beijing access.[48] While Martin thought that 'in the dispensation of Providence it seems to be necessary that these conceited Asiatics should be humbled by the Sword, before they are exalted by the Gospel' and that force instead of religion or international law was the only way to deal with 'perfidious' Chinese, he also partly understood Chinese resentment toward the missionaries, who were seen as facilitators of opium smuggling. A critic of opium, Martin remarked that 'if the early missionaries had done more in pointing out the enormity of the opium evil, a curse might have been averted from China and a mountainous obstacle out of the way of Christian Mission'.[49] While in drafting the Treaty of 1858, Reed was 'not disposed' to include the article regarding religious

45 'CL VII, Martin to the Board, n. 44, October 1, 1863' in *Presbyterian Church in the U.S.A. Board of Foreign Missions Correspondence and Reports*, 1833–1911.

46 Martin, William A. P. *Wan guo gong fa* 《万国公法》 (Taibei: Zhongguo guo ji fa xue hui, 1998), 1.

47 'W. A. P. Martin, Shanghai June 3, 1859' and 'W. A. P. Martin, June 18, 1858,' in *Presbyterian Church in the U.S.A. Board of Foreign Missions Correspondence and Reports*, 1833–1911; see also W. A. P. Martin? Papers, 1869–1887, Record Group 357, Mr. Ward's Embassy; see also CL IV Ningbo, Martin to Board, 45. 1854 (letter that accompanied the annual report), *Presbyterian Church in the U.S.A. Board of Foreign Missions Correspondence and Reports*, 1833–1911.

48 Covell, *W. A. P. Martin* 1978 (n. 34), 240.

49 The first quotation is from an unpublished work at the Presbyterian Historical Society, *Two American Embassies*, I, 111, I, 32. CL IV, NINGBO, Martin to the Board, m. 86, May 22, 1859.

freedom, it was the missionary interpreters Williams and Martin who 'persisted' in having the clause included and eventually the paragraph on religious freedom was included. Article 29 in the American Treaty of Tianjin granted religious liberty to all Christians and opened the door for missionaries to enter China in droves.[50] The foreign powers were granted most-favored-nation clauses, and helped the missionary cause by opening China not only to further trade but to the Gospel and 'civilization', which, Martin increasingly thought, included international law.[51] Martin thus became not only an agent of God, but of the broader civilizing mission of the West that included the universalization of international law, seen as instrumental to his evangelical mission. 'All barriers are withdrawn', he wrote to the church after the Treaty's negotiations' success. 'The chief nations of the earth should thus conspire to advance the cause of Christ is a glorious harbinger of his universal sway'.[52] For Martin international law was a universalization tool that presupposed the existence of God. In order to find commensurability between China's system and international law, in his English preface to *Wanguo Gongfa*, Martin moralized and universalized the latter on the basis of a natural law inscribed by God in the heart of every human. Moreover, the translated title itself was an effort to show China that international law was not simply a regional (Western) rule system but had universal value. He translated the title of Wheaton's *Elements of International Law* into 'the law of the nations', implying its universal applicability to the international community. *Wanguo Gongfa* was thus accompanied by universalization both in its title and in its moralization in terms of natural

---

50 Latourette, Kenneth S. *A History of Christian Missions in China* (London: Society for Promoting Christian Knowledge, 1929), 275. The treaty would be signed by the US, Russia, England, and France, who each acquired a new right to station legations in Beijing. It also opened up more ports to trade, and allowed foreigners to travel, trade, and proselytize in China's interior. Moreover, it stipulated: 'The principles of the Christian religion, as professed by the Protestant and Roman Catholic churches, are recognized as teaching men to do good, and to do to others as they would have others do to them. Hereafter those who quietly profess and teach these doctrines shall not be harassed or persecuted on account of their faith. Any person, whether citizen of the United States or Chinese convert, who, according to these tenets, peaceably teach and practice the principles of Christianity, shall in no case be interfered with or molested'. 'The Treaty Of Tianjin (Tien-Tsin), 1858', in Department of the Inspector General of the Customs, *Treaty, Convention, etc. between China and Foreign States*, vols. 1–2 (Shanghai, 1917); see also Martin, *Two American Embassies* 1859 (n. 49), I, 197.

51 'Ningbo, E. B. Inslee to the Board, July 30, 1858', in *Presbyterian Church in the U.S.A. Board of Foreign Missions Correspondence and Reports*, 1833–1911.

52 'Ningbo, Martin to Board, n. 156, July 9, 1858'1858', in *Presbyterian Church in the U.S.A. Board of Foreign Missions Correspondence and Reports*, 1833–1911.

law, understood as a supranational restraint over states' ambitions and egotistic aspirations.[53]

Martin's approach to translation was far from rigid. Just as he believed it was important not just to translate the Bible into the local language, but to adapt and stretch or select its meanings to make it more acceptable and meaningful within local cultural heritage and symbols, Martin changed and manipulated Wheaton and the other texts to make them more palatable and comprehensible to Chinese. He thought that changing meaning was necessary to adapt the texts to the wants of China in its new foreign relations.[54] As Yang Zhuo has argued, this attitude led Martin to a real 're-writing of the text[s]' (*gaixie* 改寫).[55] A comparison of the original Wheaton text and *Wanguo Gongfa* makes clear that Martin rewrote and shortened parts. James Li has described how the intent to universalize is obvious in various passages: Martin used a semi-classical linguistic style to appeal to Chinese literati, but also paraphrased and interpreted Wheaton according to his own vision and politics of international law's history, especially when he wanted to convey the discipline's universality.[56] One salient example of Martin's changes, as discussed by Immanuel C. Y. Hsu, Yang Zhuo, and Li, comes when Wheaton, after quoting Grotius, Bynkershoek, Leibnitz, and Montesquieu, writes: 'There is then, according to these writers, no universal law of nations, such as Cicero describes in his treatise *De Republica*, binding upon the whole human race – which all mankind in all ages and countries, ancient and modern, savage and civilized, Christian and Pagan, have recognized in theory or in practice, have professed to obey, or have in fact obeyed'.[57] Martin's rendition of this paragraph, when retranslated literally, reads: 'Judging from them there is no universally practiced law as is said in Te-li [*De Republica*], for there has never been a case that is accepted by all nations

53 According to Carl Schmitt, when the state becomes the *justus hostis* and the equality of states replaces the religious authority of the pope, each state is the judge of its own affairs, and is bound only by its own treaties and its own interpretations of them. Because each is as sovereign as the other, each has the same *jus ad bellum*, and thus what is just is defined individually and subjectively. Schmitt, Carl. *The Nomos of the Earth* (New York: Telos Press, 2003), 143–147.

54 Martin, *Cycle of Cathay* 1900 (n. 31), 222.

55 Yang Zhuo 杨焯, *Ding shi 'wanguo gongfa' yanjiu* 《丁译'万国公法公法'研究》, (Hong Kong: The Hong Kong Polytechnic University, PhD Thesis, 2013), 18.

56 Li, Zhaojie (James). 'The Impact of International Law on the Transformation of China's Perception of the World: A Lesson from History'. *Maryland Journal of International Law* 27 (1) (2012), 128–153.

57 Hsü, *China's Entrance* 1960 (n. 2), 129; Wheaton, Henry. *Elements of International Law* (Lea and Blanchard, 1863), 17; Li, 'China's Perception of the World' 2012 (n. 56), 134.

at all times, barbarian or civilized, within or without the Church'.[58] Hsu, Yang Zhuo, and Li show that such imprecise translations run through the book.[59]

Martin also saw the introduction of international law as good for China, and in *New York Times* articles written under the pseudonym 'Perry Plus', suggested that China's acceptance of Western diplomatic modes, such as the Burlingame mission, was not only positive for cooperation between the two countries but also a sign of China adopting liberal attitudes.[60] His optimism and belief that China deserved better treatment from Western powers was opposed by Burlingame's successor, who claimed that Martin had 'materially contributed to the formation in the United States of an erroneous estimate of Chinese progress'.[61] Overall, the general sentiment in the West was still quite negative toward China progress within international society.

4 Ancient China's International Law: Expanding International Law's Spatial and Temporal Dimensions

Martin aimed to make international law more acceptable to Chinese intellectuals, who were disillusioned about it. He also tried to help China become a member of international society when the West considered it to be at an eternal standstill and Western jurists were just starting to debate the idea of applying international law to the Orient. If Martin was supported by the Chinese Government, Burlingame, and Hart, and in a first moment international law was welcomed with interest by Chinese, there was also opposition from both the international community and within China. Wheaton's text itself suggests that '[China] lacks certain attributes essential to regular and complete membership of the family of States, governed by, and enjoying the privileges of, the system of general international law.... [A]nd the refusal or inability of China to adopt the rules of war prescribed by the rules of civilized States for some time formed a grave if not an insuperable bar to her full recognition as a subject of international law.'[62] If Wheaton and others felt there were inescapable

58 Li, 'China's Perception of the World' 2012 (n. 56), 134; Martin, *Wangguo Gongfa*, 61; Hsü. *China's Entrance* 1960 (n. 2), 129.

59 Hsü, *China's Entrance* 1960 (n. 2), 129; Wheaton, *Elements of International Law* 1863 (n. 57), 17; Li, 'China's Perception of the World' 2012 (n. 56); Yang Zhuo 杨焯. *Ding shi 'wanguo gongfa' yanjiu* 《丁译'万国公法公法'研究》 (Fal lü Chubanshe 法律出版社, 2015).

60 Martin, William A. P. 'The Chinese Embassy'. *New York Times* (18 February 1868), 1–2.

61 Covell, *W. A. P. Martin* 1978 (n. 34), 155.

62 Wheaton, Henry and Coleman Phillipson. *Wheaton's Elements of International Law* (New York: Baker, Voorhis, 5th ed. 1916).

differences of civilization, some even opposed Martin attempting a translation. Michel Klecskowsky, the French charge d'affaires, said to Burlingame: 'Who is this man who is going to give the Chinese an insight into our European international law? Kill him – choke him off; he'll make us endless trouble.'[63] The US linguist, missionary and Sinologist Samuel Wells Williams believed that if China learned to understand how Western international law works, it would be able to justify the elimination of some aspects of the unequal treaties.[64] Martin, who would become a member of the Institut de Droit International in 1882, was familiar with both the debates taking place among leading international jurists about the Oriental Question, and the general sentiments in the West about China. Despite his conflicting views, he saw China's past as characterized by constant transformation in political, intellectual and religious ideas and practices, which disproved the popular Western belief that China had been passive and immobile for millennia.[65]

Meanwhile, the Chinese court was still quite conservative and continue to see with suspicion Western techniques and learning, and Martin's translation was not warmly welcomed by the Zongli Yamen, which in theory should have been more open to Western ideas. A 1864 memorandum from Prince Gong and Zongli Yamen officials to the emperor explains that while Martin's effort to translate Western law was appreciated, he had been told that 'China has her own laws and institutions and that it is inconvenient to consult foreign books'.[66] Martin was aware that international law was found suspect, 'as the Trojans did the gifts of the Greeks'.[67] While the first systematic translation of international law was received with some enthusiasm among Chinese elites,[68] the reality of power politics and the continuous encroachment of Qing territorial integrity by Western powers, which clearly considered China an outsider,

63 Martin, *Cycle of Cathay* 1900 (n. 31), 234.

64 'Diplomatic Dispatches from China, XXII, S. Wells Williams to William Seward, November 23, 1865', in *Presbyterian Church in the U.S.A. Board of Foreign Missions Correspondence and Reports*, 1833–1911.

65 Martin, *The Lore of Cathay* 1901, 2.

66 'Doc. 26 Prince Kung's Discovery of International Law', in Ssu-yü Têng, John K. Fairbank, et al., *China's Response to the West: A Documentary Survey 1829–1923* (Cambridge: Harvard University Press, 1954), 98.

67 Martin, *Cycle of Cathay* 1900 (n. 31), 235.

68 See for instance Xiao Yonghong 萧永宏. 'Lun Yangwu shiqi Zhongguoren de guoji zhengzhi guannian 论洋务时期中国人的国际政治观念', *Xueshu yuekan* 学术月刊 12 (1997), 86.

disappointed them.[69] International law, while increasingly necessary, was not enough to rescue China from its lowly international position.[70]

In response, in 1881 Martin elaborated the theory of the existence of international law in Ancient China. This could help convince the West that China was not uncivilized, and that it had many more similarities to the West than commonly believed.[71] It could also encourage Chinese acceptance of a normative system and worldview that seemed completely foreign. Martin elaborated on his theory when invited to talk at the Congress of Orientalists in Berlin on September 13, 1881. A condensed outline of his paper, 'Traces of International Law in Ancient China', was published in *Congrès des Orientalists* (no. 22, section 2, pp. 71–78) in 1882.[72] A Chinese version by Wang Fengzao was published by the Tongwen Guan as *Zhongguo gushi gongfa lunlüe* in 1884, and a Japanese version 1886.[73] It was also translated into French for *Revue de droit international* (no. 14, pp. 227–242) in 1882.[74] According to the paper presented in 1881:

> Chinese statesmen have pointed out the analogy of their own country at that epoch with the political division of modern Europe. In their own records they find usages, words and ideas corresponding to the terms

69 See Carrai, Sovereignty in China 2019 (n. 1), 66–73, 82–94.

70 Xiao Yonghong 萧永宏. 'Lun Yangwu shiqi Zhongguoren de guoji zhengzhi guannian 论洋务时期中国人的国际政治观念', *Xueshu yuekan* 学术月刊 12 (1997), 87.

71 *Annuaire de l'institut de droit international* (Gand, etc., 1878), 105; 'Applicabilité du droit des gens européen à la Chine. P. D. I. IX,' 387–401. *Annuaire de l'institut de droit international* (Gand, 1879–80); see also 'Rapport on China and oriental Nations: Administration of Justice and Christianity missionaries'. *Annuaire de l'institut de droit international* (Gand, 1879–80), 301–303, 306. 'Mais, en général, dans nos rapports avec l'humanité non chrétienne, l'Europe ne voit que son intérêt. L'ailairo de l'opium (1) et plus encore la façon brutale dont la Russie a exterminé ou expulsé les tribus du Caucase, suilisent pour prouver l'infériorité du point de vue auquel se placent les Etats civilisés. Ils ont forcé la Chine à leur ouvrir sons ports : était-ce dans l'intérêt do la Chine? Tout ce qui se fait en Égypte est uniquement au profit des créanciers européens. Et dans la question meme qui nous occupe maintenant, à quoi pensons-nous surtout, sinon à sauvegarder les intérêts de nous nationaux?', ibid., 306.

72 A revised version was published in the 'Traces of International Law in Ancient China', International Review 14(1), (1883), (63–77) in New York in January 1883 and reprinted in the *Chinese Recorder* (no. 14, 380–393) in Shanghai in September–October 1883. It was then further revised and included as 'International Law in Ancient China' in Martin's *Hanlin Papers* (second series, chapter 5) in Shanghai in 1894 and in his *The Lore of Cathay* (chapter 22) in New York in 1901.

73 Svarverud, *International Law as World Order* 2007 (n. 14), 100.

74 For further references to non-Chinese editions of Martin's paper, see Walker, Richard Louis. *The Multi-State System of Ancient China* (Westport: Greenwood Press, 1971), 129–130; Covell, *W. A. P. Martin* 1978 (n. 34), 194 n. 85, 232.

> of our modern international law, and they are by that fact the more disposed to accept the international code of Christendom, which it is no utopian vision to believe will one day become a bond of peace and justice between all the nations of the earth.[75]

Indeed, the idea relied on the analogy proposed by Xu Jiyu, as discussed above, and took up Martin's friend Zhang Sigui's original suggestion that there was an international law in Ancient China. Zhang had looked the preliminary version of *Wanguo Gongfa* and understood its relevance; his preface to the first edition suggests that the Warring States in many ways resembled the current European state system.[76] Zhang's rationale was similar to that of Feng Guifen, also discussed above, and further developed Xu's analogy, but he analyzed the configuration of European countries in more detail: Russia would be Qin, Britain and France Chu and Jin, Austria and Prussia Lu and Wei, Turkey and Italy Song and Zheng, and so on. However, although it is obvious that he believed in China's superiority, it is interesting to note that Zhang did not directly compare the Qing to any other country.[77] This no doubt reflected the influence of traditional thoughts in facing new problems.[78]

Martin's paper argues that during the period of chaos and disunity of the Warring States period, that was already considered by Xu Jiyu as the perfect analogy to better understand in Chinese terms the chaotic current international situation, the preconditions for international law existed: '1. The existence of a group of independent states, so situated as to require or favour the maintenance of friendly intercourse; 2. That those states should be so related

75 Martin, William A. P. 'Traces of International Law in Ancient China (1881)'. *Chinese Recorder and Missionary Journal*, vol. 13–14 (Charleston: Nabu Press, 2012), 393.

76 Martin, *Cycle of Cathay* 1900 (n. 31), 205.

77 "间尝观天下大局，中华为首善之区，四海会同，万国来王。遐哉勿可及已。此外诸国，一春秋时大列国也，。。。在昔春秋之世，秦并歧丰之地，守关中之险，东面而临诸侯，俄罗斯似之。楚国方城汉水，虽众无用，晋则表里山河，亦必无害，英、法两国似之。齐表东海，富甲天下，美利坚似之。至若奥地利、普鲁斯，亦欧罗巴洲中两大国，犹鲁、卫之政，兄弟也。土耳其、意大利，犹宋与郑，介与大国之间也。瑞士、比利时，国小而固，足以自守。丹尼、荷兰、西班牙、葡萄牙等国，昔为大国，后渐陵夷，然于会盟友、征伐诸事，亦能有　恃无恐，而不至疲于奔命。其间蕞尔国，不过如江、黄、州、蓼，降为附庸，夷于邱县，或割地而请和，或要盟以结信，不祀忽诸，可胜道哉" see Zhang Sigui's preface in Wheaton, Henry and W. A. P. Martin, Wan guo gong fa 《万国公法》 (Taibei: Zhongguo guo ji fa xue hui, 1998). Also discussed by Tian Tao 田涛, *Guojifa shuru wanqing Zhongguo* 《国际法输入与晚清中国》(Jinan: Jinan chubanshe, 2001), 55.

78 Wang Ermin 王尔敏. *Zhongguo Jindai sixiang shi lun xuji*《中国近代思想史论》(Beijing: Shehui kexue wexian chuban, 2003), 97.

as to conduct their intercourse on a basis of equality'.[79] The twelve Warring States developed a 'common code' that implied a basis of public law because it was recognized in times both of peace and war: a. In the conduct of war, the persons and property of non-combatants were required to be respected; b. In legitimate warfare, an enemy was not to be attacked without first sounding the drum and was to be given time to prepare for defence; c. A war was not to be undertaken without a decent pretext. d. A cause always recognized as just was the preservation of the balance of power; e. The right of existence was in general held sacred for the greater states which were held in fief from the imperial throne; f. The rights of neutrals were admitted, and to a certain extent respected.[80] He concludes both Ancient Greece and China of the Spring and Autumn period had a rudimentary international legal code and that it is 'quite possible that text-books on the subject of international relations may have existed in ancient China, without coming down to our times, just as the Greeks had books on that subject, of which nothing now survives but their titles'. For Martin, when the Roman Empire disintegrated, the rudimentary Greek code developed into a practice of international intercourse between independent and equal states in Europe. His conclusion that China had an international code analogous to the Western system bolstered Chinese arguments that modern international law in the West had its antecedents in Ancient China. Yet Martin wrote that because the Chinese Empire disintegrated and was later re-established as a unified entity, a code of intercourse between equal, independent states based on a balance of power did not develop there. A tributary system of unequal and dependent states developed instead, and the Western legal model was only introduced through the Opium Wars and foreign trade on Chinese soil.

Martin saw that for a country like China with a long history and civilization and its own development logic, accepting the Western worldview and international law would not be an easy or natural process. The two defeats of the Opium Wars did not eradicate China's confidence in its civilization, and the Tongzhi Restoration of that same period involved a quest to find its own path for regaining strength through its own cultural and philosophical traditions. Chinese scholars and officials initially took a utilitarian attitude toward the *Wanguo Gongfa* as a mere tool for dealing with foreign powers; China was after all outside public law and superior to it. Investigating Ancient China helped show that principles of international law were not lacking in Chinese history, thus persuading China to accept international law as something that already

79 Martin, 'Traces of International Law' 2012 (n. 75), 64.
80 Ibid., 74–77.

existed and belonged to it, and was not foreign.[81] One of Martin's purposes was thus to present the case that international law and diplomacy were not so much imposed on China by Europeans, as they were Chinese traditions resurrected for a new era; pre-Qing history was used to prove international law's universalism.[82]

Arguing for international law's existence in Ancient China reflected Martin's missionary flexibility, his idea that 'a good native pastor is indispensable to the prosperity of the little flock',[83] and his belief that Buddhism and Confucian ethics in particular could be related to Christian faith, preparing the soil for 'the cultivation of our Christian epoch'.[84] In the same way, China's past had prepared it for accepting Christianity and international law. His missionary approach was also reflected in the way he had preached international law in his very influential book *Tiandao suyuan* 天道溯源 (Evidences of Christianity), published in 1854 in China.[85] This book extensively refers to traditional Chinese views as a starting point for the integration of Western Christianity. When Martin arrived in China, he became open to listening and learning from Chinese culture, such as the classics *Book of Changes* (or *Yi Jing*) and *Spring and Autumn*, borrowing concepts to spread Christianity from the traditional Chinese viewpoint. For example, he associated the goodness of Confucianism with the spirit of Jesus. This kind of thinking suffused his academic efforts throughout his life. The purpose of his research in Sinology was to promote mutual understanding between East and West, but a prerequisite for this understanding was that China join the family of the world's civilized countries. For this purpose, he believed that China must overcome its prejudice against the world. When translating international law, he adopted *Evidences of Christianity* to his newer mission.

Martin's thesis has been criticized, and his arguments certainly contain flaws.[86] For some scholars, the relationship between vassal states during the Zhou Dynasty was not equivalent to that between modern sovereign states,

81 Zeng Tao 曾涛, 'Jindai Zhongguo de guojifa fuhui lun 近代中国的国际法附会论' (2007).

82 Wang Hui王晖，*Xiandai Zhongguo Sixiang de xingqi*《现代中国思想的兴起》(Beijing: Sheng huo du shu xin zhi san lian shu dian, 2008), 713.

83 'W. A. P. Martin, Shanghai, October 24, 1862', in *Presbyterian Church in the U.S.A. Board of Foreign Missions Correspondence and Reports* 1833–1911.

84 Martin, William A. P. 'Buddhism, A Preparation for Christianity'. *Chinese Recorder* (May, 1889), 193–203; Martin, William A. P. *Hanlin Papers: Or Essays on the Intellectual Life of the Chinese* (New York: Harper, 1880), 278–303; Martin, *The Lore of Cathay* 1901, 249–63.

85 Martin, William A. P. *Tiandao suyuan*《天道溯源》(Shanghai: Meihua shuguan, 1872).

86 Hao, Yen-p'ing and Erh-min Wang. 'Changing Chinese Views of Western Relations, 1840–95', in *The Cambridge History of China*, vol. 11 part 2, eds. John K. Fairbank and

as the vassal state did not have the same international legal subjectivity. For the sake of universalizing international law, moreover, Martin abstracted the idea of modern nations so as to find them in the Confucian classics *Zhou Li* (Rites of Zhou) and *Spring and Autumn Annals*, thereby dismissing the historical context in which this idea emerged. Martin's strategy relativized the meaning of international law.[87] It becomes a label defining the principles and laws governing relations between political entities in general. Martin forced it to become universal through a lack of historical accuracy, projecting into different times and spaces categories that were largely specific to European history. This was partly in opposition to the general view of jurists in Europe, for whom international law was a markedly European product; Martin was attempting to validate China's role in the history of a normative order that was until quite recently foreign to it – and initially imposed on it. The cost of this strategy appears to be a wholesale rewriting of history and a forceful imposition of Western categories onto China's complex history and pre-modern norms without questioning those categories, thus validating them and assuming them to be necessary. The idea, as pointed out by Wang Hui, was essentially to have the Chinese accept the legitimacy of European international law under the premise of its correspondence to universal principles, and then integrate China within the expanding Christian world order.[88] Yet despite its flows, Martin's idea became extremely popular not only in China but in the US and Europe, and its legacy is still alive today.

5 Universalizing Confucianism through the History of International Law: A Chinese Response

Martin might have not had much direct influence at the Institute du droit International, but after his 1881 presentation the idea that China had a system of interstate regulation resembling Western international law in the Zhou

Kwang-Ching Liu (Cambridge: Cambridge University Press, 1980), 142–201; Walker, *The Multi-State System of Ancient China* 1971 (n. 74).

87 See for example Hong Junpei 洪鈞培. *Chun qiu guo ji gong fa*《春秋國際公法》(Shanghai, Zhonghua shu ju, 1939); Sun Yurong 孙玉荣. *Gu dai Zhongguo guo ji fa yan jiu*《古代中国国际法研究》(Beijing Shi, Zhongguo zheng fa da xue chu ban she, 1999); Huai Xiaofeng and Sun Yurong 懷效鋒, 孫玉. *Gu dai Zhongguo guo ji fa shi liao*《古代中國國際法史料》(Beijing, Zhongguo zheng fa da xue chu ban she, 2000); Xu Chuanbao 徐傳寶, *Xian Qin guo ji fa zhi yi ji*《先秦國際法之遺跡》(Shanghai, Xu Chuanbao, 1931); Mu, He. 'The View of Early 20th Century Chinese Intellectuals on Ancient China's International Law'. *Peking University Law Journal* 2(2) (2014), 487–517.

88 Wang Hui. *Xiandai Zhongguo Sixiang de xingqi*《现代中国思想的兴起》.

era, before 3rd-century-BC unification, became a point of reference. In China many scholars started studying Ancient Chinese international law.[89] The concept of 'pre-Qing international law' flourished, and scholars directly compared international law with *Spring and Autumn* and *Zhou Li*; some compared Dutch jurist Hugo Grotius with Confucius.[90] It had a huge impact on Chinese intellectuals and the jurists who studied under him, and contributed to the universalization of international law, becoming the basis for new Chinese foreign policy. It spread in Europe and the US and inspired several publications in Western languages and in Japanese.[91]

As Rune Svarverud has noted, 'the very fact that an indigenous system of international law may be identified in these sacred writings, at the time of Confucius himself, and in the sacred tradition of the golden age of the ancient

89 The results included Hu Weiyuan's 'Guide to Public Law' (1899), Liu Renxi's 'The Spring and Autumn Annals of the Spring and Autumn Law' (1911), and 'The Spring and Autumn Annals of the Public Law' (1912); Zhang Xinzheng's 'Spring and Autumn International Public Law' (1924); Xu Chuanbao's 'International Law and Ancient China, Part I: Thoughts' (1926); 'The Relics of Ancient China's International Law' (1931); Chen Guyuan's 'China's International Law Tracing' (1931), Ning Xiewan's 'Current International Law' (1933); Hong Yupei's 'Spring and Autumn International Public Law' (1937); Lei Haizong's 'Ancient Chinese Diplomacy' (1941); and Liu Bojun's 'Spring and Autumn League Politics' (1962). More recent works include Wang Tieya's speech at the Hague Academy of International Law, 'China and International Law – In History and Contemporary Times' (1990); Chen Shicai's 'The Source of Chinese International Law' (1994); Wang Tieya's 'Introduction to International Law' (1998); Sun Yurong's 'Ancient Chinese International Law Research' (1999); and Zhao Yanchang's 'Spring and Autumn Period International Law Research' (2004). For references see Zeng Tao 曾涛, 'Jindai Zhongguo de guojifa fuhui lun 近代中国的国际法附会论' (2007). Many postgraduate theses by overseas Chinese students also discussed this issue, such as Xu Chuanbao and Hong Yupei, as well as Ma Derun, a doctoral thesis written by Ma Derun at the University of Berlin in Germany. Later, the paper was published in 1908 in Chinese by the Shanghai Commercial Press in the book 'China is in line with international public law.' He Bingsong wrote a master's thesis on 'Ancient Chinese International Law' in Princeton in 1916. In 1920, he published an article entitled 'Ancient Chinese International Law' in the *Journal of Law and Politics*, which was based on his master's thesis. See Zeng Tao 曾涛, 'Jindai Zhongguo de guojifa fuhui lun 近代中国的国际法附会论' (2007).

90 Svarverud, *International Law as World Order* 2007 (n. 34).

91 Foreign literature that uses the analogy includes, inter alia, Cheng Yude's *International Law of Early China* (1927); Breton's 'Inter-State Relations of China before 700 AD' (1935); Frank Russell's *Theories of International Relations* (New York: Appleton-Century-Croft, 1936); Ku Shicai's 'National Equality of Ancient China' (1941); Kalevi Jaakko Holsti's, *International Politics: A Framework for Analysis* (Englewood Cliffs: Prentice-Hall, 1992); Sato Shinichi's *Modern Chinese Intellectuals and Civilization* (1996); Lydia H. Liu's *The Clash of Empires* (Cambridge: Harvard University Press, 2004); Brière, M. Yves de la. *Le droit des gens et la chine antique* (Paris: Librairie de jurisprudence ancienne et moderne, 1926).

Zhou, has given these ideas high prestige in Confucian circles in China and in East Asia'.[92] It served to create a sense of self-confidence for Chinese diplomats and intellectuals in international affairs, going well beyond Martin's intentions. While he thought that a system that worked well for China was useful as a way to find commensurability with international law and deserved study, he did not advocate export of Ancient Chinese legal institutions abroad.[93] Chinese intellectuals, however, used Martin's idea not only to frame China's emerging international identity, but also to universalize Confucius in order to enlighten and correct the limits and hypocrisies of international law as translated from Western languages.

By the end of the 19th century, Chinese elites' acceptance of the framework of international law became a necessity. While even after the Second Opium War many conservatives at court saw international law as an instrument to handle inferior Western countries, the First Sino-Japanese War (1894–95) changed Chinese elites' self-understanding and permanently scattered the Chinese world order. Chinese scholar-officials had to reach a new understanding of themselves and their country's role in a world embracing international law, and emancipate themselves from the idea of Chinese civilization's uniqueness if they wanted to preserve their cultural traditions.[94] Finding resources in Chinese tradition to understand the new reality facilitated this. The theory of international law's existence in Ancient China was adopted by many Chinese intellectuals and diplomats.[95] For instance, in an 1884 article, the scholar and politician Liang Qichao (梁啟超) asked: 'Why should [we] have to be based upon a European book on international law for the principles of inter-state affairs?'[96] Liang and other scholars looked into their own traditions, in particular the Spring and Autumn period, to understand the contemporary international situation and find resources to confront it. In their description, England became Chu, France that of Qi, Germany became Jin, Russia became Qin, and the US the vassal Yan. Russia, given its increasing encroachment on Chinese territorial sovereignty, particularly in the northeast, was perceived as the greatest threat. The international society of the Spring and Autumn period,

92 Svarverud, *International Law as World Order* 2007 (n. 34); Fu Deyuan 傅德元, *Ding Weiliang yu jin dai Zhong xi wen hua jiao liu* 丁韙良與近代中西文化交流 (Taibei Shi: Guo li Taiwan da xue chu ban zhong xin, 2013).

93 Covell, *W. A. P. Martin* 1978 (n. 34), 233.

94 Wang Hui 王晖, *Xiandai Zhongguo Sixiang de xingqi* 《现代中国思想的兴起》, 726.

95 These included Tang Caichang (唐才常), Feng Guifen (馮桂芬), Wang Tao (王韜), Xue Fucheng (薛福成), Xu Keqin (許克勤), Zheng Guanying (鄭觀應), Ma Jianzhong (馬建忠), Zeng Jize (曾紀澤), and Zhang Zhidong (張之洞).

96 Svarverud, *International Law as World Order* 2007 (n. 34), 60.

and the law regulating states then, was assimilated for analogy to the current state of international affairs and to the newly introduced *gongfa*, thus promoting its universalization in Chinese terms and broader acceptance in China.

Chinese scholar-officials were not simply trying to regain cultural confidence by demonstrating that international public law existed in China 2,000 years before the West. They knew that international law was being used by Western powers to justify gunboat diplomacy and encroachment of sovereignty. The introduction of social Darwinism in China in the 1890s and the country's critical situation at that time made Chinese intellectuals particularly aware of the empty morality of an international law that had forcefully opened the country to Western exploitation through the unequal treaties. Not only did they compare Confucian classics such as *Spring and Autumn* and *Zhou Li* to international law, but they also found in these texts authoritative justification for criticizing the essence of existing international relationships and attempting to reshape international law's spirit. Therefore, although many late Qing scholars and diplomats complained that China had various disadvantages outside of public international law and called on the country to accept this, they did not propose that China accept the legitimacy of a system that was the historical result of Western powers' interactions. In other words, the international law China accepted became an extension of *Spring and Autumn* and the law generated by the international relations of the Warring States period.

For instance, Zheng Guanying, a supporter of Western learning and international law, did not abandon the Chinese traditional worldview even when he conceived of China as a sovereign state. Zheng did recognize that there was no longer a central hemisphere in the globe which China occupied, and that 'all the countries are under the same heaven and on the same earth', but he believed China was the only country that truly followed the *wangdao* 王道, characterized by the primacy of morality (and opposed to the hegemonic *badao* 霸道). He felt this might one day spread among the barbarians, who would finally learn to respect the benevolence of which China was the ultimate embodiment.[97] He envisioned a world in which all religions would merge into Confucianism, and in which the Four Seas would be united in a central land, *Zhongtu* 中土. The intellectual Wang Tao also believed China would sooner or later re-acquire its imperial primacy. In his essay 'China's Enduring Superiority', he wrote that China was the historical embodiment of *dao* and that its superior civilization was a constant, while the West and its sovereign states system

97 Translation of Zheng Guanying in *Renditions* 53–54 (Spring and Autumn 2000), 44, 48.

were doomed to destruction.[98] For him the West's technology and international legal apparatus, including sovereignty, were simply instruments: 'they cannot be called the basis for governing the state and pacifying the world. The way of Confucius is the human way. As long as humankind exists, the way will remain unchanged'. This way was that of the three bonds and five relationships (the ruler to ruled, father to son, husband to wife, elder brother to younger brother, friend to friend) – that is, of hierarchy, not equality.[99] International law and sovereignty were to be used temporarily in order to deal with foreigners, but soon the natural order of things would be restored. It is clear then that while Chinese scholars' arguments were similar to Martin's, their intentions were different. Martin was trying to universalize international law, clear the obstacles in the way Chinese acceptance of it, and promote China's recognition in international society among his colleagues at home. Late Qing Dynasty scholars, on the other hand, were attempting to create a new world order that, through reinterpretation of Confucian classics, embraced international law but through its Confucianization and the universalization of Chinese moral tradition.

After Chinese scholar-officials launched the reform movement in 1895, many intellectuals linked international law to the Spring and Autumn Period. Kang Youwei and Liang Qichao advocated for updating Confucius and made theoretical arguments for their political reforms. They interpreted history according to the Ancient Three Kingdoms (or *Sanguo*, used to refer to the period between 220–280 AD and the trio of warring Chinese states that followed the fall of the Han dynasty (206 BC–AD 220), namely the Cao-Wei Empire 曹魏 (220–265), the Shu-Han Empire 蜀漢 (221–263) and the Wu Empire 吳 (222–280)) and divided the human history into three periods: the chaotic world, the rising world, and the peaceful world, Taiping. Since human beings had not yet entered the Taiping, for Kang the international law that originated in the Spring and Autumn period had become the axiom of public justice in the world.[100] For Liang and other intellectuals, if Grotius' work could be applied to competing nation-states of the Warring States Period as 'public law', then *Spring and Autumn* could be used as the basic law of the new era of national competition, and Confucius' 'Great Harmony' thinking could

98 Cohen, Paul A. 'Wang T'ao's Perspective on a Changing World', in *Approaches to Modern Chinese History*, eds. Rhoads Murphey and Mary C. Wright (Berkeley: University of California Press, 1967), 15–162.

99 Cohen, 'Wang T'ao's Perspective' 1967 (n. 98).

100 Kang Youwei 康有为, *Kang Youwei Quanji*, 《康有为全集》 (Shanghai: Shanghai guji shudian, 1987), 574–575. Discussed in Zeng Tao, 'Jindai Zhongguo de guojifa fuhui lun'.

be used as a universal law that goes beyond competition for power.[101] Spring and Autumn international law could make up for the shortcomings of current international law. It was therefore imperative to not emphasize the uniqueness of the Chinese tradition, but to restructure a new world picture, using the internal context of Confucianism as a basis to establish a universalist worldview and public law. Without this kind of conceptual transformation, China would have to succumb to external rule.[102]

6 Conclusion

Politics of history continue to inform the historical constructions of international law. Normative reconstructions responding to contemporary necessities seem almost inescapable. This was the case in late-Qing China, where the histories of international law in Ancient China elaborated within one politics of history helped generate another: Martin, in keeping with his background, wanted to universalize international law as a way to bring about a 'Christian epoch', making it acceptable to the Chinese so that they would enter the family of civilized, Christian nations. Yet Chinese intellectuals took up Martin's idea not only to frame China's emerging international and sovereign identity, but also to universalize Confucius in order to use an autochthonous knowledge system to improve and reshape international law as translated from Western languages. By the 1890s the theory of the Spring and Autumn and Warring States was consolidated and used as a framework for understanding the new international situation and the Qing empire within it. Yet through the end of the Qing Dynasty and during the Republic of China (1911–1949), as it became increasingly enmeshed within international law and foreign powers, an acceptance of international law became the starting point of China's diplomacy and emergence as an equal and then great power over the past century. The universal quest around Confucian texts lacked broader appeal and, crucially, China lacked the military or any other type of power to promote it universally. Unable to universalize Confucius, China's pursuit of equal status in the family of nations within the expanding Western international law system became the most realistic diplomatic choice – and an urgent one.

---

101 See Liang Qichao 梁启超, *Liang Qichao quanji* 《梁启超全集》 (Beijing: Beijing chubanshe 1999), 153–154.

102 Zeng Tao 曾涛 and Wang Hui 汪晖, *Xiandai Zhongguo Sixiang de xingqi* 《现代中国思想的兴起》 vol. 1 (Hong Kong shudian, 2004), 726–727.

Nevertheless, the idea that Martin promoted, building on Chinese scholars' work, has continued to spark debates both within and outside China. In Japan, for instance, international law professor Keishiro Iriye wrote in 1967 that although there had been a system of quasi-sovereign equal states, a system of rituals characterized their relationships rather than international law.[103] In China many republican scholars, such as Chen Guyuan and Zhou Gengsheng, did trace international law back to Confucius.[104] Scholars like Wang Tieya and Xue Hanqin, although critical, have continued to rely on the idea that Ancient China had international law.[105] A 1991 article titled 'China and International Law – In History and Contemporary Times' by Wang Tieya, one of China's most influential recent international law scholars, criticized Martin but did not dismiss the idea that the Ancient Chinese inter-state system was similar to that of Ancient Greece, and may have generated a proto-international law.[106] More recently, legal historian Stephen Neff, in his *Justice among Nations: A History of International Law* (2014), embraced Martin's idea. In attempting to write a global history of international law, Neff ascribes its origins to China's Warring States period, arguing that the first systematic writing of international relations occurred then, meaning international law's first appearance as an intellectual discipline.[107] Just like Martin and many other scholars, especially in recent global histories of international law, in doing so Neff is required to force categories that are not necessarily universal into other histories. Ultimately, various Chinese scholars continue to use traditional resources to construct a vision of the Chinese world integrated within a universal one dominated by

---

103 Iriye, Keishiro. 'The Principles of International Law in the Light of Confucian Doctrine'. *Recueil des cours de l'académie de droit international de La Haye* 120 (1967), 1–59.

104 Chen Guyuan 陈顾远, Zhongguo guojifa suyuan 《中国国际法溯源》 (Shanghai: Shanghai shu dian, 1991); Zhou Gengsheng 周鲠生, *Guo ji fa* 《國際法》 [International Law] (Beijing: Shang wu yin shu guan, 1976); Zhou Gengsheng 周鲠生, *Guojifa dagang* 《國際法大綱》 [A manual of international law] (Shanghai: Shangwu yinshuguan faxing, 1929).

105 Wang Tieya 王铁崖, *Guojifa* 《国际法》 [International Law] (Beijing, Falü Chuban she, 1995); Wang Tieya. 'International Law in China: Historical and Contemporary Perspectives'. *Recueil des cours de l'académie de droit international de La Haye* 221 (1990), 195–237; Xue, Hanqin. 'Chinese Contemporary Perspectives on International Law: History, Culture and International Law'. *Recueil des cours de l'académie de droit international de La Haye* 355 (2011), 41–234.

106 Wang Tieya, 'Zhongguo yu guojifa – lishi yu dangdai' in *Zhongguo guojifa niankan* (Beijing: Zhongguo duiwai fanyi chubanshe, 1991), 5–115.

107 Neff, Stephen C. *Justice among Nations. A History of International Law* (Cambridge: Harvard University Press, 2014).

what was once Western international law, which has become in the course of the 20th century a globalized reality. However, there are also Chinese scholars that have started to look once again at the normative history of China beyond international law, in support of the country great rejuvenation. If in the 19th century the universal quest around Confucian texts lacked broader appeal and China lacked the military or any other type of power to promote it universally, today the situation might be different.

Acknowledgements

This chapter was first presented at the Conference 'Politics and the Histories of International Law' organized at the Max Planck Institute for Comparative Public Law and International Law under the auspices of the Journal of the History of International Law on 16 February 2019. I am thankful to the American Presbyterian Society in Philadelphia for allowing me to use W. A. P. Martin's archival material and for the valuable comments of the reviewers and Dr. Stephen V. Crowder.

Bibliography

Anghie, Antony. *Imperialism, Sovereignty and the Making of International Law* (Cambridge: Cambridge University Press, 2005).

Briere, M. Yves de la. *Le droit des gens et la chine antique* (Paris: Librairie de jurisprudence ancienne et moderne, 1926).

Burns, Norma J. *W. A. P. Martin and the Westernization of China* (Indiana University, M.A. Thesis, March 1954).

Carrai, Maria Adele. *Sovereignty in China. A Genealogy of a Concept Since 1840* (Cambridge: Cambridge University Press, 2019).

Chiu, Hungdah. 'The Development of Chinese International Terms and the Problem of Their Translation into English.' *Journal of Asian Studies* 27(3) (1967), 485–501.

Cohen, Paul A. 'Wang T'ao's Perspective on a Changing World', in *Approaches to Modern Chinese History*, eds. Rhoads Murphey and Mary C. Wright (Berkeley: University of California Press, 1967), 158–162.

Covell, Ralph R. *W. A. P. Martin, Pioneer of Progress in China* (Christian University Press, 1978).

Deyuan, Fu 傅德元, Ding Weiliang yu jin dai Zhong xi wen hua jiao liu 《丁韙良與近代中西文化交流》 (Taibei Shi: Guo li Taiwan da xue chu ban zhong xin, 2013).

Ding, Weiliang 丁韪良, *Bangjiao Tiyao* 《邦交提要》 (廣學會清光緒三十年刻本, 1904).

Drake, Fred. *China Charts the World: Hsu Chi-Yu and His Geography of 1848* (Cambridge: Harvard University Press, 1975).

Fairbank, John K. and Ssu-yü Têng. *China's Response to the West: A Documentary Survey 1839–1923, with E-Tu Zen Su, Chao Yingfang & others, Cambridge, Mass.: Harvard University Press* (New York: Athenum, 1965).

Fairbank, John K. and Ssu-yü Têng. 'On the Ch'ing Tributary System'. *Harvard Journal of Asiatic Studies* 6(2), 135–246.

Fairbank, John K., ed. *The Chinese World Order, Traditional China's Foreign Relations* (Cambridge: Harvard University Press, 1968).

Feng, Guifen 冯桂芬, *Jiaobin lu Kangyi* 《校邠庐抗议》, vol. 2, available at: https://ctext.org/wiki.pl?if=gb&res=551265&searchu=%E4%BB%8A%E6%B5%B7%E5%A4%96&remap=gb (last accessed on 14 September 2020).

Fu, Deyuan, 傅德元, 'Ding Weiliang wanguo gong fa fanyi lanben ji yitu xin tan 丁韪良'万国公法'翻译蓝本及意图新探,' *Anhui Shixue* 安徽史学 1 (2008), 45–53.

Guyuan, Chen 陈顾远, *Zhongguo guojifa suyuan* 《中国国际法溯源》 (Shanghai: Shanghai shu dian, 1991).

Hamashita, Takeshi. *China, East Asia and the Global Economy: Regional and Historical Perspectives* (Abingdon: Routledge, 2008).

Hao, Yen-p'ing and Erh-min Wang. 'Changing Chinese Views of Western relations, 1840–95', in *The Cambridge History of China*, vol. 11, part 2, eds. John K. Fairbank and Kwang-Ching Liu (Cambridge: Cambridge University Press, 1980), 142–201.

Harris, Paul. 'Cultural Imperialism and American Protestant Missionaries: Collaboration and Dependency in Mid-Nineteenth-Century China'. *Pacific Historical Review* 60(5) (1991), 309–338.

Hevia, James L. 'Sovereignty and Subject: Constituting Relationships of Power in Qing Guest Ritual', in *Body, Subject and Power in China*, eds. Angela Zito and Tani E. Barlow (Chicago: University of Chicago Press, 1994), 181–200.

Hong, Junpei 洪鈞培, *Chun qiu guo ji gong fa* 《春秋國際公法》 (Shanghai, Zhonghua shu ju, 1939).

Hsü, Immanuel C. *China's Entrance into the Family of Nations: The Diplomatic Phase; 1858–1880* (Cambridge: Harvard University Press, 1968).

Huai, Xiaofeng and Sun Yurong 懷效鋒, 孫玉, *Gu dai Zhongguo guo ji fa shi liao* 《古代中國國際法史料》 (Beijing: Zhongguo zheng fa da xue chu ban she, 2000).

Iriye, Keishiro. 'The Principles of International Law in the Light of Confucian Doctrine'. *Recueil des Cours de l'académie de droit international de La Haye* 120 (1967), 1–59.

Kang, David C. *East Asia before the West: Five Centuries of Trade and Tribute* (New York: Columbia University Press, 2010).

Kang, Youwei 康有为, *Kang Youwei Quanji* 《康有为全集》 (Shanghai: Shanghai guji shudian, 1987).

Kennedy, David. 'International Law and the Nineteenth Century: History of an Illusion'. *Nordic Journal of International Law* 65 (1990), 385–420.

Koskenniemi, Martti. *The Gentle Civilizer of Nations: The Rise and Fall of International Law 1870–1960* (Cambridge: Cambridge University Press, 2009).

Lam, Hok-Chung 林學忠, *Cong wanguo gongfa dao gongfa waijiao* 《從萬國公法到公法外交》 [From the Law of Nations to International Diplomacy] (Shanghai: Shanghai Guji Chubanshe, 2009).

Latourette, Kenneth S. *A History of Christian Missions in China* (London: Society for Promoting Christian Knowledge, 1929).

Li, Zhaojie (James). 'The Impact of International Law on the Transformation of China's Perception of the World: A Lesson from History'. *Maryland Journal of International Law* 27(1) (2012), 128–153.

Liang, Qichao 梁启超, *Liang Qichao quanji* 《梁启超全集》 (Beijing: Beijing chubanshe 1999).

Lin, Zhiping 林治平, *Kexue yu jiu en-Jidujiao yu huaren xiandaihua meijie renwu de yanjiu* 《科學與救恩：基督教與華人現代化媒介人物的研究》 (Taibei: Taibei Yuzhou guang chubanshe 1993).

Liu, Lydia. 'Legislating the Universal: The Circulation of International Law in the Nineteenth Century', in *Tokens of Exchange: The Problem of Translation in Global Circulations*, ed. Lydia Liu (Duke University Press, 1999), 127–164.

Liu, Lydia. *The Clash of Empires: The Invention of China in Modern World Making* (Cambridge: Harvard University Press, 2004).

Lutz, Jessie G. 'China's View of the West, A Comparison of the Historical Geographies of Wei Yuan and Xu Jiyu'. *Social Sciences and Mission* 25 (2012).

Macalister-Smith, Peter and Joachim Schwietzke. 'Bibliography of the Textbooks and Comprehensive Treaties in Positive International Law in the 19th Century'. *Journal of the History of International Law* 3(1) (2001), 75–142.

Mancall, Mark. *China at the Center: 300 Years of Foreign Policy* (New York: Free Press, 1984).

Martin, William A. P. *A Cycle of Cathay: Or, China, South and North, with Personal Reminiscences* (New York: Fleming H. Revell, 1900).

Martin, William A. P. 'Buddhism, A Preparation for Christianity'. *Chinese Recorder* (May, 1889), 193–203.

Martin, William A. P. *Hanlin Papers: Or Essays on the Intellectual Life of the Chinese* (London/New York: Trübner/Harper, 1880).

Martin, William A. P. *Tiandao suyuan* 《天道溯原》 (Shanghai: Meihua shuguan, 1872).

Martin, William A. P. *The Awakening of China* (New York: Doubleday, Page & Company, 1910).

Martin, William A. P. 'The Chinese Embassy'. *New York Times* (18 February 1868), 1–2.

Martin, William A. P. 'Traces of International Law in Ancient China' (1881). *Chinese Recorder and Missionary Journal*, vol. 13–14 (Nabu Press, 2012).

Martin, William A. P. *Wan guo gong fa* 《萬國公法》 (Taibei: Zhongguo guo ji fa xue hui, 1998).

Masini, Federico. *The Formation of Modern Chinese Lexicon and its Evolution toward a National Language: The Period from 1840 to 1898* (Berkeley: Project on Linguistic Analysis, 1993).

Morse, H. B. *The International Relations of the Chinese Empire* vol. 3 (London: Longmans, Green & Co., 1910).

Mu, He. 'The View of Early 20th Century Chinese Intellectuals on Ancient China's International Law'. *Peking University Law Journal* 2(2) (2014), 487–517.

Neff, Stephen C. *Justice among Nations. A History of International Law* (Cambridge: Harvard University Press, 2014).

Nuzzo, Luigi. *Origini di una Scienza. Diritto Internazionale e Colonialismo nel XIX secolo* (Frankfurt am Main: Vittorio Klostermann, 2012).

Pines, Yuri. *Envisioning Eternal Empire, Chinese Political Thought of the Warring States Era* (Honolulu: University of Hawai'i Press, 2009).

Presbyterian Church in the U.S.A. Board of Foreign Missions Correspondence and Reports, 1833–1911.

Presbyterian Historical Society, *Two American Embassies*, I, III, I, 32. CL IV, NINGBO, Martin to the Board, m. 86, May 22, 1859.

Renditions 53–54 (Spring and Autumn 2000).

Rossabi, Morris. *China among Equals: The Middle Kingdom and its Neighbors* (Berkeley: University of California Press, 1982).

Ruskola, Teemu. *Legal Orientalism: China, the United States, and Modern Law* (Cambridge: Harvard University Press, 2013).

Schmitt, Carl. *The Nomos of the Earth* (New York: Telos Press, 2003).

Schoppa, R. Keith. *Revolution and Its Past: Identities and Change in Modern Chinese History* (Upper Saddle River: Prentice Hall, 3rd ed. 2011).

Sebes, Joseph. *The Jesuits and the Sino-Russian Treaty of Nerchinsk (1689): The Diary of Thomas Pereira* (Rome: Institutum Historicum SI, 1961).

Sun, Yurong 孙玉荣, *Gu dai Zhongguo guo ji fa yan jiu* 《古代中国国际法研究》 (Beijing: Shi, Zhongguo zheng fa da xue chu ban she, 1999).

Suzuki, Shogo. *Civilization and Empire: China and Japan's Encounter with European International Society* (Abingdon: Routledge, 2009).

Svarverud, Rune. *International Law as World Order in Late Imperial China: Translation, Reception and Discourse, 1847–1911* (Leiden: Brill, 2007).

The Missionary Review of the World (March 1917).

Tian, Tao 田涛, *Guojifa shuru wanqing Zhongguo* 《国际法输入与晚清中国》 (Jinan: Jinan chubanshe, 2001).

Tian, Tao 田涛, 'Wan qing guojifa shu shu lun 晚清国际法输述论,' *Tianjin shehui kexue* 天津社会科学 6 (1999), 99–103.

Treaty, Convention, etc. between China and Foreign States, vol. 1 & 2 (Shanghai: Department of the Inspector General of the Customs, 1917).

Vec, Miloš. 'From the Congress of Vienna to the Paris Peace Treaties of 1919', in *The Oxford Handbook of the History of International Law*, eds. Bardo Fassbender and Anne Peters (Oxford: Oxford University Press, 2012), 654–678.

Vec, Miloš. 'Universalization, Particularization, and Discrimination. European Perspectives on a Cultural History of the 19th Century International Law'. *Inter-Disciplines* 3(2) (2012), 79–101.

Walker, Richard Louis. *The Multi-State System of Ancient China* (Westport: Greenwood Press, 1971).

Wang, Ermin 王尔敏, *Zhongguo Jindai sixiang shi lun* 《中国近代思想史论》 (Beijing: Shehui kexue wexian chuban, 2003).

Wang, Jing. 'The Image of China Shaped by American Missionaries and Its Impact on the Early Twentieth Century'. *Journal of Cultural Interaction in East Asia* 6 (2015), 31–45.

Wang, Dong. *China's Unequal Treaties: Narrating National History* (New York: Lexington Books, 2008).

Wang, Hui 王晖, *Xiandai Zhongguo Sixiang de xingqi* 《现代中国思想的兴起》. 1 (Beijing: Sheng huo du shu xin zhi san lian shu dian, 2008).

Wang, Lixin 王立新, *Meiguo Chanjiao shi yu wan qing zhongguo xiandaihua* 《美国传教士与晚清中国现代化》 (天津: 天津人民出版社, 1997).

Wang, Tieya 王铁崖, *Guojifa* 《国际法》 [International Law] (Beijing, Falü Chuban she, 1995).

Wang, Tieya. 'International Law in China: Historical and Contemporary Perspectives'. *Recueil des cours de l'académie de droit international de La Haye* 221 (1990), 195–370.

Wang, Weijian 王维俭, 'Dingzheng ruogan zhongwai ci shu zhong Ding Weiliang ci mu sheji de shishi 订正若干中外词书中'丁韪良'词目涉及的史实' *Zhongshan daxuebao* 中山大学学报 2 (1987) 68–76.

Wang, Weijian 王维俭, 'Pu dan da zhan kou chuanbo shijian he xifang guojifa chuanru zhongguo 普丹大沽口船舶事件和西方国际法传入中国,' *Xueshu yanjiu* 学术研究 5 (1985), 84–90.

Wheaton, Henry. *Elements of International Law* (Lea and Blanchard, 1863).

Wheaton, Henry and Coleman Phillipson. *Wheaton's Elements of International Law* (New York: Baker, Voorhis, 5th ed. 1916).

Wheaton, Henry and William A. P. Martin. *Wan guo gong fa* 《万国公法》 (Taibei: Zhongguo guo ji fa xue hui, 1998).

Wright, David Curtis. *From War to Diplomatic Parity in Eleventh-century China, Sung's Foreign Relations with Kitan Liao* (Leiden: Brill, 2005).

Wu, Suming 吴素敏, *Ding Weiliang zhi yanjiu (1827–1916)* 《丁韪良之研究 (1827–1916)》 (Taibei Donghai Daxue Zhuoshi lunwen, 1987).

Xiao, Yonghong 萧永宏, 'Lun Yangwu shiqi Zhongguoren de guoji zhengzhi guannian 论洋务时期中国人的国际政治观念,' *Xueshu yuekan* 学术月刊 12 (1997), 83–90.

Xu, Chuanbao 徐傳寶, *Xian Qin guo ji fa zhi yi ji* 《先秦國際法之遺跡》 (Shanghai: Xu Chuanbao, 1931).

Xue, Hanqin. 'Chinese Contemporary Perspectives on International Law: History, Culture and International Law'. *Recueil des cours de l'académie de droit international de La Haye* 221 (1990), 41–234.

Yang, Zhuo 杨焯, *Ding shi 'wanguo gongfa' yanjiu* 《丁译'万国公法公法'研究》 (Falü Chubanshe 法律出版社, 2015).

Yang, Zhuo 杨焯, *Ding shi 'wanguo gongfa' yanjiu* 《丁译'万国公法公法'研究》, (Hong Kong: The Hong Kong Polytechnic University, PhD Dissertation 2013).

Zeng, Tao 曾涛, 'Jindai Zhongguo de guojifa fuhui lun 近代中国的国际法附会论,' *Fashi xue kan 法史学刊* (2007), available at http://cesl.cupl.edu.cn/upload/201103224076038.pdf (last accessed on 1 April 2021).

Zeng, Tao 曾涛 and Wang Hui 汪晖, *Xiandai Zhongguo Sixiang de xingqi* 《现代中国思想的兴起》 vol. 1 (Sanlian shudian, 2004).

Zhang, Jingcao 张劲草, Qiu Zaijue 邱在珏, 'Lun guojifa zhi chuanru Zhongguo 论国际法之传入中国,' *Hebei Daxue Xuebao* 河北大学学报 2 (1984), 126–133.

Zhang, Weiming 张卫明, 'Yangwu shiqi guoren dui jindai guji jushi yu guojifa de bifu 洋务时期国人对近代国际局势与国际公法的比附,' *Shijie Jingji yu Zhengzhi* 世界经济与政治 6 (2010), 81–83.

Zhou, Gengsheng 周鲠生, *Guojifa dagang* 《國際法大綱》 [A manual of international law] (Shanghai: Shangwu yinshuguan faxing, 1929).

Zhou, Gengsheng 周鲠生, *Guo ji fa* 《國際法》 [International Law] (Beijing: Shang wu yin shu guan, 1976).

CHAPTER 9

Mixed Claims Commissions in Latin America during the 19th and 20th Centuries: The Development of International Law in between Caudillos and Revolutions

José Gustavo Prieto Muñoz

Abstract

This chapter examines the impact of Latin America on the development of 'mixed claims commissions', adjudication bodies founded in an ad hoc fashion by international agreements. It argues that these bodies are best understood in the context of their development during periods of crisis in Latin American nations, the majority of which were presidential states. Armed conflicts and internal revolutions led to the rise of strong executives and legal conflicts over the property of foreigners. As new governments tried to restore the internal rule of law, they engaged with international adjudication. The first part of this chapter examines the notion of 'Latin America' in the history of international law. I take an internal perspective on the legitimation of public authority in Latin American countries, instead of the usual external geopolitical perspective, which sees the region as largely defined by its relations with the United States and Europe. The second part analyzes the concrete evolution of 'mixed claims commissions', examining the first wave of such bodies, especially the Venezuelan claims commissions established after Cipriano Castro's Revolution (1899–1908) in the 20th century.

Keywords

Rule of Law – populism – mixed claims commissions – Latin America – international law

1 Introduction

The Jay Treaty of 19 November 1794, concluded between the United States and Great Britain, is frequently referred to as having created the first mixed commission: an international adjudicative body with the task to settle the

 | DOI:10.1163/9789004461802_011

differences between these two States. From that time up until 1938,[1] records attest to the existence of at least 409 adjudicative bodies with similar characteristics, created to resolve different kinds of international disputes. Among these, 193 bodies included a Latin American nation, one of the first known resulting in a treaty between Argentina and France of 1840.[2]

This means that, for over a century, almost half of all adjudicative process around the globe were related to Latin America. Accordingly, this region was keen to use international mechanisms to resolve its conflicts with foreigners. In this sense, it can also be inferred that, in the 19th and 20th centuries, the region served as a sort of 'laboratory' for international law. Here, the notion of laboratory implies that for brief periods of time there were sufficient levels of political agreement and financial resources to conduct a process of international adjudication. But time and resource constraints contributed to a process of 'trial and error'[3] experimentation with international law. For example, the rules that determine a state's responsibility for damages suffered by foreigners were developed during various cases adjudicated in Latin America.[4] In this context, there are still some questions worth addressing: What was the role that Latin American states played in the functioning of 'claims commissions' in the 19th and early 20th centuries? How did the internal political situation influence decisions and approaches taken by different claims commissions? How did the understanding and evaluation of these commissions change over time? Why does the influence of Latin Americans on claims commissions belong to the unwritten pages of the history of international law?

Questions about the history of international law in Latin America are usually answered from a geopolitical perspective that focuses on the influence that Europe and the United States had on the Latin-American region. While

---

1 Information on the known cases cited in this chapter comes from Stuyt, Alexander M. *Survey of International Arbitrations 1794–1938* (Berlin: Springer-Science & Business Media, 1939) and Moore, John Bassett. *History and Digest of the International Arbitrations to Which the United States Has Been a Party* (Washington: Government Printing Office, 1898), two collections covering international jurisprudence from 1794 to 1902. From 1902 to the present day such jurisprudence can only be found across diverse books and papers.

2 Stuyt, *International Arbitrations* 1939 (n. 1), 31.

3 Viñuales, Jorge E. 'Experiments in International Adjudication – Past and Present', in *Experiments in International Adjudication: Historical Accounts*, eds. Ignacio de la Rasilla and Jorge E. Viñuales (Cambridge: Cambridge University Press, 2019), 11–31, 11.

4 See Greenman, Kathryn. 'Aliens in Latin America: Intervention, Arbitration and State Responsibility for Rebels'. *Leiden Journal of International Law* 31(3) (2018), 617–639, 624; Koskenniemi, Martti. 'The Ideology of International Adjudication and the 1907 Hague Conference', in *Colloques/Workshop Series*, ed. Académie de droit international de La Haye (Leiden: Brill, 2008), 127–152, 149.

this geopolitical perspective is important, it tends to reduce the role of claims commissions to 'gun boat diplomacy', obscuring the internal dimensions of the countries involved and the contributions that Latin American citizens have made to the development of international law. Therefore, I address these questions by focusing on the internal political characteristics of the Latin American countries that engaged in the development of international law, as practiced by claims commissions, during the periods of relative political stability that occurred in the aftermath of armed conflicts, that is in between *caudillos* and revolutions. In concrete, I argue that when Latin American nations – the majority of which were presidential states which contributed to further concentration of power – experienced a crisis in the rule of law due to an armed conflict or internal revolution, strong executives emerged creating conflicts related to the property of foreigners. As new governments tried to restore the internal rule of law or sought political and financial resources to create a new type of autocracy, they tended to engage with international adjudication processes.

In this vein, the history of International Law in Latin America since the 19th century was written alongside the emergence of new independent states with presidential systems, strong leaders that become the political center of a country, usually referred to as *caudillos*,[5] and political instability in the form of revolutions. As pointed out by Pierson and Gil, some countries in the region, such as México, Guatemala, Paraguay and Venezuela, were governed by different forms of dictatorships for most of the 19th and 20th centuries.[6]

Among those Latin American states, Venezuela was particularly important for the development of international adjudication. In 1902, three European states – the United Kingdom, Germany and Italy – established a blockade in the Venezuelan ports as an attempt to resolve previous disputes between nationals of their countries and the state of Venezuela. As a result of the blockade, ten claims commissions were created between Venezuela and ten European countries in 1903.[7] While this period of history has been studied as an example of 'gun boat diplomacy', a closer look at the political situation in Venezuela shows how the conflict and later agreements resulted from the internal collapse of the rule of law and the emergence of Cipriano Castro, a leader that has been categorized as a 'caudillo' or an 'autocrat'.

5 See Carrancá y Trujillo, Raul. *La evolución política de Iberoamérica* (Madrid: Editorial Pérez, 1925), 181.

6 Pierson, William Whatley and Federico G. Gil. *Governments of Latin America* (New York: McGraw-Hill, 1957), 135.

7 Bray, Heather. 'Venezuelan Claims Commissions', in *Max Planck Encyclopedia of International Procedural Law*, ed. Hélène Ruiz Fabri (Oxford: Oxford University Press, 2018).

The argument of this chapter runs as follows: Section 2 explores the notion of 'Latin America' in the history of international law, stressing the need to take an internal perspective on the legitimation of public authority rather than an external geopolitical perspective in which the region is largely defined by its relations with the United States and Europe. Section 3 analyzes and gives some context for understanding Latin American 'mixed claims commissions', separating them into two periods: early war-related commissions, and later commission arising in response to internal crises in the rule of law. Section 4 argues that more recent commissions were established in periods where Latin American nations experienced a crisis in the rule of law due to an internal revolution, as caudillos emerged creating conflicts related to the property of foreigners. When the caudillo needed political and financial resources to stay in power, or a new government was forming, they tended to engage with international adjudication processes. In particular, I analyze the case of the Venezuelan claims commissions established during the rule of Cipriano Castro's Revolution.

2 An Internal Perspective on the Concept of 'Latin America' in the History of International Law

The term 'Latin America' was coined in the 19th century in France but has been used on the continent to resist interventions by the United States and Great Britan in the region[8] at least since 1856.[9] The term was employed to distinguish a group of countries belonging to a specific geographical region that share similar cultural-historical roots, but is worth mention that the notion of dividing conceptually 'America' in two, was documented in the Webster's 1828 American Dictionary, wich divided the continent at the Darien Gap (Panama) in 'north' and 'south' America.[10]

Most attempts to describe the role of this 'Latin' America in the development of international law have taken an external perspective that tends to focus on its relations with Europe and the United States. For instance,

8 See Obregón, Liliana. 'Between Civilisation and Barbarism: Creole Interventions in International Law'. *Third World Quarterly* 27(5) (2006), 815–832, 815.

9 This origin of the term is discussed by Gobat, Michel. 'The Invention of Latin America: A Transnational History of Anti-Imperialism, Democracy, and Race'. *American Historical Review* 118(5) (2013), 1345–1375.

10 See Grandin, Greg. 'The Liberal Traditions in the Americas: Rights, Sovereignty, and the Origins of Liberal Multilateralism'. *American Historical Review* 117(1) (2012), 68–91, 68, 80.

Alejandro Alvarez, in his classic 1909 piece 'Latin America and International Law', defines Latin America as a region that first, shares 'constituent elements', that is, physical, ethnic and social characteristics and second, has been shaped by the influence of western nations.[11]

In this same vein, most 19th century accounts related to the notion of 'Latin America' in international law have been characterized by a constant tension between two narratives: On the one hand, 'particularism', which argues in one way or another for the existence of a distinguishable legal latinoamerican tradition in international law. On the other hand, 'universalism', which denies the existence of 'Latin American International Law' as a category distinct from international public law in the development of law. The debates reflecting these two competing narratives can be traced back to Argentina in 1882, when Vicente Quesada, a jurist and diplomat, published an article in *Nueva Revista de Buenos Aires.* While speaking about the history of diplomacy, he referred to the notion of 'international latinoamerican law',[12] an idea that would lead to a series of arguments between supporters of these two narratives.[13]

However, neither of these perspectives can contribute much to the study of the phenomenon of claims comissions, which cannot per se be explained either by the 'universal' or 'particular' views that preoccupied international law professors at the time. Put in another way, the decisions taken by politicians in charge of Latin American nations regarding whether or not to enter into international adjudication processes such as claims comissions did not follow from any self-concept on the part of Latin America as a region, but were taken for concrete political reasons specific to each state. For this reason, it may be more useful to examine the claims commisions from an internal perspective, by trying to understand their political causes in a comparative historical public law framework, rather than attempting a reconstruction of Latin American

---

11 See Alvarez, Alejandro. 'Latin America and International Law'. *American Journal of International Law* 3(2) (1909), 269–354.

12 See Quesada, Vicente. 'Derecho international latino-americano'. *Nueva Revista de Buenos Aires* 22(5) (1882), 15. See also Scarfi, Juan Pablo. 'La emergencia de un imaginario latinoamericanista y antiestadounidense del orden hemisférico: De la Unión Panamericana a la Unión Latinoamericana (1880–1913)'. *Revista Complutense de Historia de América* 39 (2013), 81–104, 85; Scarfi, Juan Pablo. *The Hidden History of International Law in the Americas: Empire and Legal Networks* (Oxford: Oxford University Press, 2017).

13 Becker Lorca, Arnulf. 'International Law in Latin America or Latin American International Law? Rise, Fall, and Retrieval of a Tradition of Legal Thinking and Political Imagination'. *Harvard International Law Journal* 47(1) (2006), 283–307, 299; Becker Lorca, Arnulf. *Mestizo International Law: A Global Intellectual History 1842–1933* (Cambridge: Cambridge University Press, 2014).

history in international terms based only on its relations with Europe and the United States.

Here, I frame the concept 'Latin America' as describing a group of countries that, in addition to having similar cultural-historical roots, also share features in terms of their internal organization, legitimation of power and constitutional practice over more than 200 years as independent states. In this regard, the notion of 'Latin America', entails three common additional elements that are more or less present in each of the nations of this geographical region: (i) The existence of presidential systems (*presidencialismo*) as the dominant model to structure power; (ii) An emphasis on the sovereignty of the people (*el pueblo*), a concept linked more closely to social inequality than with national identity as a critical legitimator of authority; and (iii) the existence of continual transformative constitutional processes (*revoluciones*), which has resulted in the adoption of multiple constitutional texts in each country over the last 200 years.

First, over the last two centuries, the president has played a dominant role, a phenomenon known in the region as *presidencialismo*, which in many cases also leads to the emergence of a strong charismatic leader (*caudillo*). *Presidencialismo* is characterized by a constitutional architecture where the executive has a predominant position compared to the other branches of the state, and in practice or *de facto* the president is transformed into the political center of the state.[14] In addition, a presidential system may challenge the internal rule of law in a state, especially when the executive branch is led by a strong president or *caudillo*. The notion of caudillo is linked to a concentration of power that leads to autocracy and arbitrariness.[15] A caudillo generally emerges within a presidential state following a three-phase process: (a) capturing the imagination of the people in a given territory, (b) pursuing political domination, often including by force or self-proclaimed 'revolutions', and, finally, (c) consolidating her/his power by seeking unlimited rule.[16] While not every presidential state has generated *caudillos*, in the history of Latin America the two are in many cases closely related.

14 Gros Espiell, Hector. 'El predominio del poder ejecutivo en america latina', in *El predominio del poder ejecutivo en Latinoamérica*, ed. Barquín Alvarez Manuel (Ciudad de Mexico: Universidad Nacional Autónoma México, 1977), 9–25, 16.

15 Salcedo-Bastardo, José Luis. *Historia fundamental de Venezuela* (Caracas: Universidad Central de Venezuela, 1970), 399–406.

16 Carranca y Trujillo, Raul. *Panorama crítico de nuestra America*, quoted by Pierson, William W. and Federico G. Gil. *Governments of Latin America* (New York: McGraw-Hill, 1957), 139.

The strong presidential state is considered to be a 'native species' of the American continent, much as parliamentary systems are typical for Europe.[17] This tradition started with the United States constitution in 1787 and later expanded to the south where it acquired particular characteristics.[18] In practical terms, the existence of presidential states has resulted in parliaments playing a marginal role when making important decisions.

Second, in 'Latin American' countries the primary factor in legitimizing power and the exercise of public authority is placing sovereignty in the people (*el pueblo*). Throughout the constitutional history of Latin America, this means vesting authority in the 'people' rather than in other concepts such as 'the nation'. This notion was also imported from US constitutionalism by both liberal and conservative goverments.[19] For instance, Article 39 of the Mexican Constitution of 1857 reads as follows:

> National sovereignty resides essentially and originally in the people. All public power emanates from the people and is instituted for their benefit. The people have at all times the inalienable right to alter or modify the form of their government.[20]

The text of this article was maintained in the Queretaro constitution of 1917, and similar formulations can be found across Latin American constitutional texts during the 19th century. To a lesser extent, there were some provisions in the region that reference the 'nation'[21] as the source of authority, such as the Venezuelean constituion of 1857. These two features – presidential states and the idea of 'the people' – taken from US constitutionalism took a particular turn in a region that, because of historical social inequalities, had left many people outside major political and social systems, such as education and health. In this context, populist narratives used by leaders seek to potray foreigners as one of the 'enemies' of the 'people'.

Once the justification for authority over the nation rests with the people and the executive branch is both legally and *de facto* stronger than the legislative

---

17 Luiz Pinto Ferreira uses the term 'planta nativa' to describe this phenomenon in 'El Predominio del poder ejecutivo en America Latina' in Pablo Alegría, Jorge Carpizo Alonso and José Luis Stein V. *El Predominio del poder ejecutivo en Latinoamérica*, Serie B (13), Estudios comparativos de derecho latinoamericano (México: Instituto de investigaciones jurídicas UNAM, 1977), 25–64.

18 Ibid.

19 Ibid.

20 Art. 39 Constitución Política de la República Mexicana 1857.

21 Art. 2 Constitucion Politica del Estado de Venezuela 18 de abril de 1857.

branch, then the will of the president, without the proper checks and balances, is transformed into absolute will. Thus, presidents during this period became a sort of 'pater familias' of 'the people'; the 'primus solus' of the land.

In this context, international law and its agreements run the risk of being reduced to contracts and relations with other strong leaders 'primus solus', harking back to the Vattelian idea of international law from the 18th and 19th centuries.[22] The Vattelian idea implies the existence of a political setting or configuration for international law, where one nation possesses only one exclusive public authority over a defined territory which in turn can be engaged in agreements [the positive law of nations].[23] If a caudillo takes over the political system of the state, his personal conflicts with foreigners could cause conflicts that are relevant for international law.

Third, the sheer number of constitutional processes and constitutional texts has made it difficult to consolidate strong institutions in Latin American history. As a consequence, some branches of the state have experienced difficulties establishing legitimacy, which also explains the lack of equilibrium in the balance of power between the various branches of government – to the benefit of the executive branch. At the same time, the lack of strong institutions made it very difficult for the rule of law to withstand the emergence of strong leaders who tried to control the system. As a result, there have been many examples during political processes of self-proclaimed 'revolutions', which in the end amounted to a re-construction of elites and changes to constitutional texts.

For this reason, after more than 200 years of constitutional history, there is not a single constitution put in place during the 19th century that is still in force in its original form. This political instability should provide a guide to help track the moments when Latin America has been relevant to international law, as there is usually a period of political resistance after a '*revolución*' in one of the Latin American states. One example was the '*Revolucion Liberal Restauradora*' in Venezuela that brought Cipriano Castro to power. Castro mistreated foreigners leading to a disproportionate response from European nations who used force and introduced an embargo on shipments from Venezuelan ports. After this incident, the famous 'Drago Doctrine' was developed with the intention of preventing the use of force in the collection of debts.

22 For a development of international law from this perspective see Domingo, Rafael. 'Gaius, Vattel, and the New Global Law Paradigm'. *European Journal of International Law* 22(3) (2011), 627–647, 627, 637.

23 Vattel, Emer de. *The Law of Nations or Principles of the Law of Nature Applied to the Conduct and Affairs of Nations and Sovereigns* (London: Clarke, 1811), lxvi.

In sum, throughout Latin American history we find a link between strong leaders in presidential systems, *'revoluciones'*, crises in the rule of law, and the abuse of individuals, both nationals and foreigners. The difference is that foreigners could ask for redress for grievances at the international level, creating tensions between their states of origin and the host state. In turn, because of adjudication in these conflicts, international law had the opportunity to develop itself as a discipline.

If claims comissions are seen under this prism, it may help us look beyond the geopolitical narrative of Latin American as a region of resistance to the imperial expansion of the 'west'. Alternatively, the recurrent use of 'claims commissions' indicates that different countries in the region were keen to use international mechanisms after a conflict was over or a caudillo had lost power and they either needed to negotiate with foreign states or a new government needed some political and financial stability to rule.

What lay beneath financial conflicts with foreigners were weak moments in the rule of law in Latin America that affected both nationals and foreigners. After the internal crisis in the rule of law was overcome, new governments embraced solutions for disputes with foreigners using international adjudication. Therefore, in the 19th and early 20th centuries, there was never a clear 'Latin American approach' to creating claims commissions. However, these conflicts provided an opportunity for the development of peremptory norms of international law, such as the prohibition on war as a means to solve disputes.

3 Claims Commissions in Latin America in the 19th Century

Since the Jay Treaty between the USA and Great Britain in 1794, the term 'mixed commission' (*commission mixte*) has been used to describe a type of judicial body involved in ad hoc bilateral inter-State dispute settlements.[24] The term 'mixed claims commissions' (or just 'claims commissions') more specifically references a type of body founded in an ad hoc fashion on the basis of international agreements with the goal of 'settling claims which have arisen between citizens of different States, between citizens of one State and the other State, or between the States themselves in formal and final proceedings'.[25]

24 Boisson de Chazournes, Laurence and Danio Campanelli. 'Mixed Commissions', in *Max Planck Encyclopedia of Public International Law*, ed. Rüdiger Wolfrum (Oxford: Oxford University Press, 2006), para. 1.

25 Dolzer, Rudolf. 'Mixed Claims Commissions', in *Max Planck Encyclopedia of Public International Law*, ed. Rüdiger Wolfrum (Oxford: Oxford University Press, 2011), para. 1.

This conceptualization allows us to differentiate such bodies from similar ones, such as the 'compensation commissions' which did not emerge until the second half of the 20th century. The main distinguishing characteristic of 'compensation commissions' is that their legal basis is other than the will of the parties involved. For instance, the United Nations Compensation Commission of 1991 was a subsidiary organ of the Security Council that processed claims for losses suffered during the Iraq-Kuwait War.[26]

On the other hand, the term 'arbitral mixed commissions' or 'Mixed Arbitral Tribunals' has also been used to refer to specific bodies composed of an even number of adjudicators appointed by the States that are party to the dispute – the difference being that if a resolution cannot be reached in a specific case, a final decision will be taken by an arbitrator or a 'neutral umpire.'[27] This term was used to refer to adjudicative bodies created to process the enormous litigation born out of World War I or as a mean to compensate the harmful effects caused by the war measures during that period.[28]

Taking into account that the difference between the claims commission or arbitral is whether or not there is a 'neutral umpire', here I use the term 'claims commission' to refer to both the 'mixed' and 'arbitral' types, as long as their legal basis is the consent of the parties of an international agreement.

After the Jay Treaty, from 1794 to 1938, there were at least 409 known claims commissions. However, there was no central register for these earlier cases, making an historical analysis difficult. Most of the information available comes from private collections, notably, Herstlet's collection on Great Britain's treaties (1841),[29] Henri La Fontaine's *Pasicrisie Internationale* (1902),[30] John B. Moore's *History and digest of the international arbitrations (1898)*,[31] and the more complete collection of Alexander Stuy's *Survey of International Arbitrations (1939)*.[32]

26 See Mensah, Thomas A. 'United Nations Compensation Commission (UNCC)', in *Max Planck Encyclopedia of Public International Law*, ed. Rüdiger Wolfrum (Oxford: Oxford University Press, 2011).

27 Campanelli, 'Mixed Commissions' 2006 (n. 25).

28 Carabiber, Charles. *Les juridictions internationales de droit privé de l'arbitrage international à l'expérience des tribunaux arbitraux mixtes et à l'institution de juridictions internationales permanentes de droit privé* (Neuchâtel: de la Baconnière 1947), 161

29 Hertslet, Lewis. *A Complete Collection of the Treaties and Conventions and Reciprocal Regulations at Present Subsisting between Great Britain and Foreign Powers and of the Laws, Decrees, Orders in Council* (London: Butterworth, 1827).

30 La Fontaine, Henri. *Pasicrisie internationale 1794–1900 histoire documentaire des arbitrages internationaux* (Leiden: Martinus Nijhoff, 1997).

31 Moore, *Digest of the International Arbitrations* 1898 (n. 1).

32 Stuyt, *Survey of International Arbitration* 1939 (n. 1).

Among these 409 cases, 193 were decided by Latin American commissions – here I use the term to describe a body where at least one of the States involved was a country from the Latin American region. These commissions were set up to resolve all types of disputes, but most were principally concerned with compensating foreigners for loss of property, categorized later, in the 20th century, as 'investment'.[33] Among these Latin American cases, it is possible to distinguish between two clusters of claims commissions: those that arose in the aftermath of armed conflicts, usually related to wars of independence; and a second cluster that handled cases related to internal crises in the rule of law in new nations.

First, like the commissions created by the Jay Treaty, the first Latin-American commissions in the 19th century were related to wars of independence and the subsequent armed conflicts that arose between new nations fighting over territories. Out of 193 Latin-American commissions, at least 26 exclusively involved boundary disputes between countries in the region, while many others were related to damages suffered by European or US nationals that occurred during hostilities. One of the armed conflicts that provoked this type of adjudicative mechanism was the *Saltpeter War* (*Guerra del Guano y el Salitre*)[34] between Chile, Peru and Bolivia. The fact that not only was a commission set up between the warring parties, but several others comprising Chile and other nations such as Belgium and Great Britain were also established,[35] shows that there was political will to settle disputes with foreigners in the aftermath of hostilities.

The first mention of a Latin-American commission agreement can be found in the treaty between Brazil and Great Britain of 1829, which dealt with the capture of British ships in Brazilian waters.[36] This commission was designed to be composed of 4 members, 2 selected by each of the parties to solve disputes

33 See also Leiter, Andrea. 'The Silent Impact of the 1917 Revolutions on International Investment Law and What It Tells us about Reforming the System'. *European Society of International Law Reflections* 6(10) (2017).

34 For a complete account of the conflict, see Lopez, Jacinto. *Historia de la guerra del guano y el salitre* (Lopez: Editorial Milla Batres, 1979).

35 Bolivia- Chile, Commission, 1884; c) Belgium- Chile, Commission, Award 1884 in favour of Chile, Belgium claims rejected; d) Austria-Hungary – Chile, Commission, Settlement by Protocol Santiago, 1887; e) Argentine Republic – Chile, Edward VII, King of Great Britain and Ireland Arbitrator, Award 1902, Accepted by both parties. A Delimitation Commission was appointed to mark out the frontier; f) Argentine Republic – Chile, Commission, Settlement by verbal process, 1899; g) Bolivia – Chile, British Minister at Santiago, 1900.

36 Agreement between Great Britain and Brazil, relative to the settlement of British claims, signed at Rio de Janeiro, 5 May 1829. Império do Brasil Memorandum entered into between Lord Ponsonhy and the Brazilian Government, relative to the Capture of British

within a period of 8 months. Given its institutional design, decisions needed to be taken by a majority of commissioners and, if a majority was not possible, they needed to send communications to their respective sovereigns. However, there is no further information on this commission.

Later, the claims commission between Argentina and France in 1840 became the first to record that it had been created in order to decide claims remaining after France imposed a blockade on the ports of the Province of Buenos Aires.[37] This claims commission was established in a treaty between France and the Buenos Aires Province.[38] This treaty was signed on 29 October 1840 on board a French military ship (the *Boulnaise*), setting the tone for the content of the treaty, which was really a capitulation to French interests, involving the recognition of responsibility for a grave mistreatment of French nationals by locals. The result was the draft of an article where Argentina undertook responsibility for its actions and accepted that the French would retain control in the choice of an arbitrator if disputes between the representative commissioners could not be resolved.[39]

The fact that the treaty was signed inside the very same naval ship that was participating in the blockade might suggest that this commission simply used force to pressure the Buenos Aires government of Juan Manuel de Rosas. However, other documents point in the direction of a genuine intention on the side of the French to pursue 'justice' due to the mistreatment of French nationals during Rosas' internal struggles for power with other Argentine provinces. French interests were more specifically summarized in a letter signed by the French Consul in Montevideo on 22 February 1839, months before the Treaty was signed. In the last years of the 19th century, after the Chilean commissions related to the Saltpeter War, and thereafter, in the beginning of the 20th century, most of the conflicts over independence, including those arising over boundary disputes among the same Latin-American nations, had been settled. From this period onwards, the creation of claims commissions was more strongly related to crises in the internal rule of law. Thus, in this period, political and

---

ships in 1826 and 1827. See La Fontaine, Henri. *Pasicrisie internationale 1794–1900* (Leiden: Brill, 1997), 91; Stuyt, *International Arbitrations* 1939 (n. 1), 30.

37 Stuyt, *International Arbitrations* 1939 (n. 1), 36.

38 The treaty was signed by the Commander of the French forces, Rene Armand de Mackau, and the Foreign Affairs Minister for the Province, Felipe Arana. See Varela, Florencio. *Sobre la convencion de 29 de octubre de 1840 desarrollo y desenlace de la cuestión francesa en el Rio De La Plata.* (Montevideo: Imprenta de la Caridad, 1840), i.

39 Author's translation from the original, Varela, *La convencion de 29 de octubre de 1840* 1840 (n. 38), ii.

constitutional instability becomes a guide to help track the moments when Latin America was relevant to international law.

4 Crises in the Rule of Law and Claims Commissions in the 20th Century

The 20th century saw remarkable progress in adjudications, starting with the claims commissions of Venezuela and continuing with those in Mexico. In the case of Venezuela, 10 different commissions were established in 1903 with Germany, Great Britain, Italy, France, the United States, Belgium, Spain, Mexico, Sweden-Norway, and the Netherlands.[40]

The Venezuelan commissions were usually explained using a geopolitical narrative.[41] In that perspective, the commissions were presented as the conclusion of a geopolitical chess game between the US and European nations that lead first to the blockade of Venezuelan ports and later to the establishment of the commissions.[42] While this perspective is widely described in the literature,[43] it can also hide internal factors that also contributed to the conflict and the nature of the work of the commissions.

40 1) Protocol between Great Britain and Venezuela for the Settlement of British Claims etc., signed at Washington, 13 February 1903; 2) Protocol between Italy and Venezuela for the Settlement of Italian Claims, signed at Washington, 13 February 1903; 3) Protocol between the United States and Venezuela for the Arbitration of Claims, signed at Washington, 17 February 1903 (1903) IX RIAA 115; 4) Protocol between Mexico and Venezuela for the Arbitration of Claims, signed at Washington, 26 February 1903 (1903) X RIAA 694; 5) Protocol between France and Venezuela for the Arbitration of Claims, signed at Washington, 27 February 1903 (1903) X RIAA 6; 6) Protocol between the Netherlands and Venezuela for the Arbitration of Claims, signed at Washington, 28 February 1903 (1903) X RIAA 709; 7) Protocol between Belgium and Venezuela for the Arbitration of Claims, signed at Washington, 7 March 1903 (1903) IX RIAA 321; 8) Protocol respecting the Arbitration of Claims between Sweden and Norway and Venezuela, signed at Washington, 10 March 1903 (1903) X RIAA 763; 9) Protocol between Spain and Venezuela for the Arbitration of Claims, signed at Washington, 2 April 1903 (1903) X RIAA 737; 10) Protocol between Germany and Venezuela for the Arbitration of German Claims, signed at Washington, 7 May 1903. See also Bray, 'Venezuelan Claims Commissions' 2018 (n. 7), para 2.

41 See Castellanos, Rafael, Roberto Palacios, Elba Mata Kolster, Domingo Irwin, Yolanda Dovale and Helena Bauza eds.), *Documentos britanicos relacionados con el bloqueo de las costas venezolanas* (Instituto autonomo biblioteca nacional/Fundación para el rescate del acervo documental venezolano, 1982) 11–15.

42 See ibid., 10–11.

43 See Bray, 'Venezuelan Claims Commissions' 2018 (n. 7); Castellanos et al., *Documentos britanicos* 1982 (n. 41), 11–15; Salcedo-Bastardo, *Historia fundamental de venezuela* 1970 (n. 15); Scarfi, *International Law* 2017 (n. 12).

A closer look at the internal political causes of these developments shows a strong relationship between periods of weak rule of law and subsequent engagement with international adjudication. In the case of Venezuela, a revolution took Cipriano Castro to power from 1899 to 1908. Castro was a general who used strong anti-imperialist rhetoric, and continually compared himself with Simon Bolivar, the hero of independence. Castro favored integration with other Latin American nations and fell perfectly into the category of a *caudillo*. Many accounts acknowledge the role of Castro in the events that lead to the blockade, usually referred to as 'mistreatment' of foreigners.

However, the situation in Venezuela during those years involved more than mistreatment of foreigners; it represented the collapse of the rule of law in Venezuela. This included the elimination of limits to public power through legal reforms, disrespect for private property in general, the closure of universities, and the persecution of dissent. To sum up, the moral and economic decay of Venezuela.[44]

In other words, Castro's Venezuela exhibited several of the elements needed for the consolidation of power and common to Latin America described in the previous section. First, a strong executive branch that was both legally and *de facto* stronger than the legislative branch transformed the will of Castro into a quasi-divine mandate that made him the *'pater familias'* that at the end would lead Venezuela to confront European nations. Second, the transformative constitutional process that resulted in the enactment of a new constitution (*Constitucion de los Estados Unidos de Venezuela 1901*) followed the presidentialist tradition of the region. Third, it adopted the notion that legitimation of authority lies in the concept of the 'people', a concept expressly included in the 1901 constitution (*Artículo 21.- La Soberanía reside esencialmente en el pueblo*). This also included rhetoric portraying foreigners as the 'enemy' of the people, especially during the blockade in 1902.

In this scenario, many violations of rights of individuals occurred during Castro's rule. The difference was that foreigners could redress grievances and infringements of their rights within the institution of diplomatic protection, that lead to creation of the 10 Commissions. In total, those commissions decided upon 885 individual claims,[45] a case load that provided an opportunity for the development of international law as a discipline.

For example, one of the most important cases decided during this time was the Orinoco Shipping and Trading Company (*Orinoco Shipping*), a corporation

44 Salcedo-Bastardo, *Historia fundamental de Venezuela* 1970 (n. 15), 542–552.

45 Cases obtained from the account in Ralston, Jackson H. *Venezuelan Arbitrations of 1903* (Washington: Government Printing Office, 1904).

incorporated in Great Britain but owned almost entirely by citizens of the United States. *Orinoco Shipping* had been awarded navigation privileges on the Orinoco river by previous Venezuelan governments. However, Castro's regime cancelled via decrees[46] both their monopoly on the river and the contractual rights of the company. The case was later adjudicated by a claims commission.[47]

In the *Orinoco Shipping* claim, the decision was submitted to the designated umpire, Harry Barge, who dismissed several claims by the company and ordered the payment of a discrete sum. This decision, despite being agreed on in the original Protocol as 'final', became a topic of discussion and diplomatic issue by the United States until the year 1909 when Castro's rule ended, and General Juan Vicente Gomez was left in charge of the Government. Furthermore, in this year Gomez delegated his foreign affair minister to negotiate a second Protocol, one that submitted umpire Barge's decision to a second international tribunal, an arbitral body composed of three arbitrators from the Permanent Court of Arbitration in The Hague.[48]

The arbitral tribunal rendered an award on 25 October 1910,[49] increasing the amount originally granted as compensation. The second case of the *Orinoco Shipping* allowed for the development of two important procedural advances in international law. First, it introduced a prohibition (Article IV of Protocol 1909) on nationals of the interested parties being members of the arbitral tribunal and other members of the Court appearing as counsel for either nation, thereby reinforcing the objectivity of the tribunal. Second, for the first time, a judgment of an international tribunal was 'annulled and revised' by a second international tribunal on exceptional grounds of 'essential error'.[50] Until this award, any decision taken by a claims commission was considered to be final; the *Orinoco Shipping* case started along the path of institutionalizing setting aside proceedings, a path that would lead to some of the current alternatives, such as the ad-hoc ICSID annulment committees.

The *Orinoco Shipping* is just an example of the hundreds of claims adjudicated by the Venezuelan Commissions, were lawyers were confronted with multiple legal questions, with little time for answer, and scarce financial

46 Decree, 5 October 1900, Venezuelan government destroys the monopoly created in favor of *Orinoco Shipping Co. December 14, 1901* and terminated contractual benefits.

47 Article 1, Protocol Mixed Claims Commission United States-Venezuela (1903).

48 Protocol of an Agreement between the United States of America and the United States of Venezuela for the Decision and Adjustment of Certain Claims (1909).

49 *Orinoco Steamship Company Case United States of America v. Venezuela*, Award of the Tribunal (1910).

50 Dennis, W. Cullen. 'The Orinoco Steamship Company Case before the Hague Tribunal'. *American Journal of International Law* 5(1) (1911), 35–64, 36.

resources to allocate. However, if these efforts are perceived within the crisis of the rule of law in the Venezuelan state, the commissions were not only a mere continuation of 'gunboat diplomacy' as it is usually portrait within geopolitical accounts, but a space – a true laboratory for lawyers – for the development of international law. There are at least two reasons for this claim: The considerable number of cases that composed the universe of claims that had to be adjudicated; and the formation of a legal community that run the commission, which was composed in great number by Latin American lawyers whose contribution has been erased from the accounts of the region.

First, the Commissions had a legal capacity conferred by their foundational treaties to determine 'whether an injury took place' or whether a 'seizure was wrongful'.[51] If the considerable number of claims is taken into account (885) it means that the jurisdiction of the commissions could be compared to a sort of self-contained judicial branch which had to define its own procedural rules and standards of revision in a very short time during 1903. Second, the adjudication process was not executed only by a European state, but in reality, was the common effort of an international community of lawyers that was composed also by many Latin Americans. To be concrete, at least 14 individuals from the region participated in the functioning of the commissions, either as secretaries or commissioners itself.[52] This group of lawyers have been forgotten from any account of the contribution of Latin Americans to the development of international law.

Those two elements are absent from geopolitical accounts of history that stress the imperialist background of the creation of the commission. Acknowledging the internal collapse of the rule of law in countries like Venezuela in 1902, implies accepting part of the historical responsibility of these nations for violating the individual rights of locals and foreigners, as well as their inability to create functional states that protected their own citizens. Second, it renders the contribution of Latin Americans to the development of

51 Art III. Protocol between Great Britain and Venezuela (n. 41).

52 F. Arroyo-Parejo, Agent in 5 Commissions; Carlos F. Grisanti, Commissioner in 3 Commissions; Delicio Abzueta, Secretary in 2 Commissions; J. Padròn- Ustariz, Secretary in 2 Commssion; Emilio de las Casas, Secretary in 2 Commission; Segundo Antonio Mendoza, Secretary in 2 Commisions; José de Jesùs Paul, Commissioner in 2 Commission; Jose Vicente Iribarren, Commissioner in 2 Commissions; Nicomedes Zuluaga, Commissioner in 2 Commissions; Pedro Vicente Azpurùa Commissioner in 2 Commissions; José I. Arnal, Agent and Assistant Agent in 2 Commissions; Eduardo Calcaño-Sanabria, Secretary in 1 Commission; F. N. Guzmán Alfaro, Commissioner in 1 Comission; Luis Julio Blanco, Secretary in 1 Commission.

international law – from within the system, not only in the form of resistance – nearly invisible.

5 Conclusion

Looking back, the period of Castro's rule generated conflicts that later, during the process of adjudication, became a space for the creation of new developments in international law. On the one hand, this led to the idea of forbidding war as a mechanism for solving disputes between nations, the Drago doctrine. On the other hand, it allowed for other significant developments, such as revisions of international judgments by other international tribunals and rules regarding the impartiality of adjudicators.

These pages in the history of international law are usually portrayed within a narrative of 'Latin American resistance' to the imperial expansion of United States and European powers in the region.[53] However, the constant recourse (at least 193 times) to claims commissions and the recognition of arbitration in constitutional texts, such as the Castrist constitution of 1901, point in a different direction: Political factors – *caudillos*, populist discourses and constitutional changes – generated several moments in Latin American history where the power of the state became concentrated in one person, increasing the likelihood of conflicts with foreigners. These deficiencies in the internal rule of law in Latin American and the need for Latin American states to reactivate their economies together provided an opportunity to create provisional institutions that could adjudicate previous conflicts.

These developments in the history of the region are usually overlooked in narratives that focus on the imperial expansion of western states. Such narratives are constructed in one of three ways: First, by portraying Latin American individuals that were involved in the creation or functioning of a claim commission as 'traitors'. Second, by softening the real impact that certain individuals had on the collapse of internal institutions in Latin American states. Finally, by simply removing any reference to the contributions made by Latin American commissioners to the development of International Law.

By contrast, if the development of claims commissions is studied from a perspective that goes beyond this vision of Latin America as a space for the expansion of western imperial powers, it is possible to recognize the contribution of the region to the development of international law adjudication during periods of relative political stability in between caudillos and revolutions.

53 Castellanos et al., *Documentos britanicos* 1982 (n. 41).

When Latin American nations, the majority of which were presidential states, experienced a crisis in the rule of law, strong executives emerged creating conflicts related to the property of foreigners. As new governments tried to sustain their economies, they engaged with international law in an effort to increase the flow of capital into the region.[54]

The narrative that constructs a notion of 'Latin America' based on its resistance to imperialism has been used to transfer blame to the region for its inability to create functional states for more than two hundred years. In contrast, the study of claims commissions from the internal perspective of the rule of law provides two advantages. On the one hand, it allows us to see the specific contribution of individuals to the construction of international law through the drafting and functioning of claims commissions. On the other, it allows us to gain a better understanding of the concept of 'Latin America' in international law in the 19th and 20th centuries, as a hybrid historical construction between the tensions of particularism and universalism.

Bibliography

Alvarez, Alejandro. 'Latin America and International Law'. *American Journal of International Law* 3(2) (1909), 269–353.

Becker Lorca, Arnulf. 'International Law in Latin America or Latin American International Law? Rise, Fall, and Retrieval of a Tradition of Legal Thinking and Political Imagination'. *Harvard International Law Journal* 47(1) (2006), 283–306.

Becker Lorca, Arnulf. *Mestizo International Law a Global Intellectual History, 1842–1933* (Cambridge: Cambridge University Press, 2014).

Boisson de Chazournes, Laurence and Danio Campanelli. 'Mixed Commissions', in *Max Planck Encyclopedia of Public International Law*, ed. Rüdiger Wolfrum (Oxford: Oxford University Press, 2006), available at: https://opil.ouplaw.com/view/10.1093/law:epil/9780199231690/law-9780199231690-e65?rskey=IUmQGN&result=1&prd=MPIL (last accessed on 10 May 2021).

Bray, Heather. 'Venezuelan Claims Commissions', in *Max Planck Encyclopedia of International Procedural Law*, ed. Hélène Ruiz Fabri (Oxford: Oxford University Press, 2018).

54 One of the few reflections in the literature in that sense can be found in Nissel, Tzvika Alan. *History of State Responsibility: The Struggle for International Standards (1870–1960)* (Helsinki: University of Helsinki, PhD Thesis, 2016), cited in Greenman, Kathryn. 'Aliens in Latin America: Intervention, Arbitration and State Responsibility for Rebels'. *Leiden Journal of International Law* 31(3) (2018), 617–639, 626.

Carrancá y Trujillo, Raul. *La evolución política de Iberoamérica* (Madrid: Editorial Pérez, 1925).

Carabiber, Charles. *Les juridictions internationales de droit privé de l'arbitrage international à l'expérience des tribunaux arbitraux mixtes et à l'institution de juridictions internationales permanentes de droit privé* (Neuchatel: de la Baconniere 1947)

Castellanos, Rafael, Roberto Palacios, Elba Mata Kolster, Domingo Irwin, Yolanda Dovale and Helena Bauza, eds. *Documentos britanicos relacionados con el bloqueo de las costas venezolanas* (Instituto autonomo biblioteca nacional/Fundación para el rescate del acervo documental venezolano, 1982).

Dennis, William C. 'The Orinoco Steamship Company Case before the Hague Tribunal'. *American Journal of International Law* 5(1) (1911), 35–65.

Dolzer, Rudolf. 'Mixed Claims Commissions', in *Max Planck Encyclopedia of Public International Law*, ed. Rüdiger Wolfrum (Oxford: Oxford University Press, 2011), available at: https://opil.ouplaw.com/view/10.1093/law:epil/9780199231690/law-9780199231690-e64?rskey=BFOZHT&result=1&prd=MPIL (last accessed on 10 May 2021).

Domingo, Rafael. 'Gaius, Vattel, and the New Global Law Paradigm'. *European Journal of International Law* 22 (3) (2011), 627–647.

La Fontaine, Henri. *Pasicrisie Internationale 1794–1900 – Histoire documentaire des arbitrages internationaux* (Leiden: Martinus Nijhoff, 1997).

Gargarella, Roberto. *Latin American Constitutionalism, 1810–2010 – The Engine Room of the Constitution* (Oxford: Oxford University Press, 2013).

Gobat, Michel. 'The Invention of Latin America: A Transnational History of Anti-Imperialism, Democracy, and Race'. *American Historical Review* 118(5) (2013), 1345–1375.

Grandin, Greg. 'The Liberal Traditions in the Americas: Rights, Sovereignty, and the Origins of Liberal Multilateralism'. *American Historical Review* 117(1) (2012), 68–91.

Greenman, Kathryn. 'Aliens in Latin America: Intervention, Arbitration and State Responsibility for Rebels'. *Leiden Journal of International Law* 31(3) (2018), 617–639.

Gros Espiell, Hector. 'El predominio del poder ejecutivo en america latina', in *El predominio del poder ejecutivo en Latinoamérica*, ed. Barquín Alvarez Manuel (Ciudad de México: Universidad Nacional Autónoma México, 1977).

Hertslet, Lewis. *A Complete Collection of the Treaties and Conventions and Reciprocal Regulations at Present Subsisting between Great Britain and Foreign Powers and of the Laws, Decrees, Orders in Council* (London: Butterworth, 1827).

Koskenniemi, Martti. 'The Ideology of International Adjudication and the 1907 Hague Conference', in *Colloques/Workshop Series*, ed. Académie de droit international de La Haye (Leiden: Brill, 2008), 127–152.

Leiter, Andrea. 'The Silent Impact of the 1917 Revolutions on International Investment Law', *European Society of International Law Reflections* 6(10) (2017).

Lopez, Jacinto. *Historia de la guerra del guano y el salitre* (Lima: Editorial Milla Batres, 1979).

Mensah, Thomas A. 'United Nations Compensation Commission (UNCC)', in *Max Planck Encyclopedia of Public International Law*, ed. Rüdiger Wolfrum (Oxford: Oxford University Press, 2011), available at: https://opil.ouplaw.com/view/10.1093/law:epil/9780199231690/law-9780199231690-e424?rskey=oCDaMK&result=1&prd=MPIL (last accessed on 10 May 2021).

Moore, John Bassett. *History and Digest of the International Arbitrations to Which the United States Has Been a Party* (Washington: Government Printing Office, 1898).

Nissel, Tzvika A. *History of State Responsibility: The Struggle for International Standards (1870–1960)* (Helsinki: University of Helsinki, PhD Thesis, 2016).

Obregón, Liliana. 'Between Civilisation and Barbarism: Creole Interventions in International Law'. *Third World Quarterly* 27(5) (2006), 815–832.

Pierson, William Whatley and Federico G. Gil. *Governments of Latin America* (New York: McGraw-Hill, 1957).

Pinto Ferreira, Luiz. 'El predominio del poder ejecutivo en America Latina', in *El predominio del poder ejecutivo en Latinoamérica*, Serie B (13), Estudios comparativos de derecho latinoamericano, eds. Pablo Alegría, Jorge Carpizo Alonso and José Luis Stein. (Ciudad de México: Instituto de Investigaciones Jurídicas UNAM, 1977).

Quesada, Vicente. 'Derecho international latino-americano'. *Nueva Revista de Buenos Aires* 2(5) (1882), 15.

Ralston, Jackson H. *Venezuelan Arbitrations of 1903* (Washington: Government Printing Office, 1904).

Salcedo-Bastardo, José Luis. *Historia fundamental de Venezuela* (Caracas: Universidad Central de Venezuela, 1970).

Scarfi, Juan Pablo. 'La emergencia de un imaginario latinoamericanista y antiestadounidense del orden hemisférico: De la Unión Panamericana a la Unión Latinoamericana (1880–1913)'. *Revista Complutense de Historia de América* 39 (2013), 81–104.

Scarfi, Juan Pablo. *The Hidden History of International Law in the Americas: Empire and Legal Networks* (Oxford: Oxford University Press, 2017).

Stuyt, Alexander M. *Survey of International Arbitrations 1794–1938* (Berlin: Springer-Science+Business Media, 1939).

Varela, Florencio. *Sobre la convencion de 29 de octubre de 1840: Desarrollo y desenlace de la cuestión francesa en El Rio de la Plata* (Montevideo: Imprenta de la Caridad, 1840).

Vattel, Emer de. *The Law of Nations, Or, Principles of the Law of Nature, Applied to the Conduct and Affairs of Nations and Sovereigns* (London: Clarke, 1811).

Viñuales, Jorge E. 'Experiments in International Adjudication – Past and Present', in *Experiments in International Adjudication: Historical Accounts*, eds. Ignacio de la Rasilla and Jorge E. Viñuales (Cambridge: Cambridge University Press, 2019), 11–31.

CHAPTER 10

The Forgotten Continent? A South African Perspective on the Development of African International Legal Thought

Angelo Dube and Lindelwa Mhlongo

Abstract

There is a thin line between law and politics, both at the domestic and international levels. Quite often this tends to conflate law properly so called and elements of politics. This tension is not necessarily new and has always featured in the development of international law. The field of international law as it stands today cannot be divorced from the politics prevailing at the time of its initial development. So potent is the tension that international law as we know it today developed in a somewhat skewed manner. Many commentators have decried the omission of the contributions of marginalised geographic regions in the recording of the development of international law. It is trite that traditional writers in this field, such as Hugo Grotius, Alberico Gentili, Cornelius van Bynkershoek and others, wrote from a European perspective. However, this approach also meant that they were not able to take into account how other regions such as Africa, the Americas, and Asia contributed to the unfolding of international law. As a result, international law is to some extent regarded as portraying only the histories of European states and how they influenced this branch of law. Even eminent African authors on the subject follow this approach to the evolution of international law. In light of the above, the question that begs an answer is: What, if any, was Africa's contribution to the history of international law? This chapter seeks to identify selected pre-colonial contributions to the various branches international law from the African continent, as well as interrogate the causes of the existing gaps in capturing this contribution in mainstream legal thinking. The chapter further seeks to look at the impact of the politics of the time in shaping international law as we know it today.

Keywords

legal history – decolonisation – international law – Africa – Eurocentrism

 | DOI:10.1163/9789004461802_012

1 A Brief Outline of the Prevailing Ideas on the History of International Law

International law can be understood as a body of rules, regulations and principles, written or unwritten, that regulate the interactions between and the affairs of states and other international legal persons. Both the historical and ideological origins of international law are a matter of dispute among scholars. The prevailing view in academic circles is that this branch of law emerged in Europe after the conclusion of the Peace Treaty of Westphalia in 1648,[1] which resolved the Thirty Years' War.[2]

However, it would be incorrect and misleading to assume that international law has evolved only during the last four or five hundred years and only in Europe, or that Christian civilization has enjoyed a monopoly in prescribing rules to govern inter-state relations.[3] This is largely because the tendency was for each civilisation to develop within itself a community of political entities or a family of nations. These entities would then interact with each other as regulated by a set of customary rules and practices, rather than being a single nation governed by a single authority and a single system of law.[4]

---

1 The Peace of Westphalia, which signalled the end of the Thirty Years' War was concluded between feuding European nations in 1648 in Münster, Germany. Fassbender states that the Peace of Westphalia consisted of two separate treaties that were both signed at Münster, Germany. The first Treaty of Peace was between the Holy Roman Empire and France; whilst the second was between the Holy Roman Empire and Sweden. Both instruments were concluded on 24 October 1648. The treaties are sometimes referred to as the 'Peace of Münster' and the 'Peace of Osnabrück', the towns in which they were negotiated. See Fassbender, Bardo. 'Westphalia, Peace of (1648)', in *Max Planck Encyclopedia of Public International Law*, ed. Rüdiger Wolfrum (Oxford: Oxford University Press, 2011).

2 The so-called 'Thirty Years' War' is a central feature of European history. It was characterised by a series of wars fought by various European nations between 1618 and 1648. It is worth noting that religion played a huge role in these wars, and that the Peace of Westphalia is hailed as having brought the Thirty Years' War to an end. This could partly explain why most European scholars such as Malcolm Shaw extol Christianity and the Peace of Westphalia as the two defining elements of international law. See Malcom, Shaw. *International Law* (Cambridge: Cambridge University Press, 8th ed. 2017). See also Encyclopaedia Britannica. 'Thirty-Years' War', available at: https://www.britannica.com/event/Thirty-Years-War (last accessed on 29 January 2019).

3 Anand, Ram P. 'The Influence of History on the Literature of International Law', in *The Structure and Process of International Law*, eds. Ronald Macdonald and Douglas Johnston (Leiden: Martinus Nijhoff, 1983), 341–380, 342.

4 Ibid.

Culture, religion and racism were used to justify the exclusion of non-European states from participating fully in the international law regime at the time.[5] Whilst Europeans could and did assert their sovereignty and therefore the protection by international law, the ambiguous 'standard of civilisation' was used to prevent people of Africa, Asia, the Americas and the Pacific from asserting that same sovereignty and benefiting from international law.[6] They were subjected to political subordination and could not determine their own political fate.[7]

There is an inconsistency in the application of the term 'civilisation', particularly in the 19th century. 'Civilisation' was described and measured by arbitrary parametres or criteria. Countries were qualified as 'civilised' when Latin was studied there, when they possessed firearms and a printing press, or a certain mileage of electric telegraph and a large quantity of daily newspapers.[8]

Recent literature on the development of modern international law overlooks input from the Global South. Some contemporary scholars firmly assert that the South contributed only after World War II. However, there is ample evidence that African peoples and kingdoms played an active role in the development of international law long before World War II. It is for this reason that this chapter seeks to interrogate whether and how the participation of African peoples or kingdoms in international relations added to the development of modern international law. This chapter therefore intends to contribute to the rectification of the prevailing Eurocentric approach to international law and to clarify that the development of international rules and principles was not a purely European matter only. The chapter does not seek to review how each and every state in Africa took part, but it only addresses certain meaningful interventions from a selected few.

2 Beyond Western Traditions: Why It Is Overdue to Decolonize the Curriculum

The nationwide student protests that gripped South Africa in 2015/2016 under the banner of the Fees Must Fall Movement (#FeesMustFall) called for decolonised, Afro-centred education. Student formations rose to reject European and

5 Chesterman, Simon. 'Asia's Ambivalence about International Law and Institutions: Past, Present and Futures'. *European Journal of International Law* 24(4) (2017), 945–978, 947.

6 Ibid., 948.

7 Rodney, Walter. *How Europe Underdeveloped Africa* (Dar es-Salaam: Bogle – L'Ouveture Publications, 1973), 40.

8 Ibid.

western epistemologies, and demanded a transformation of the curriculum to suitably cater for the South African students of today.[9] These students started by calling for an end of domination by 'white, male, Western, capitalist, heterosexual, and European worldviews' in higher education and the incorporation of South African, African and global 'perspectives, experiences and epistemologies' as the central tenets of the curriculum, teaching, learning and research in the country.[10] The #FeesMustFall movement was preceded by a localised student protest at the University of Cape Town (UCT).

In March 2015, students from UCT embarked on class boycotts under the auspices of the Rhodes Must Fall movement (#RhodesMustFall) which was directed against a statue erected at the University that commemorated the colonialist Cecil John Rhodes.[11] The #RhodesMustFall movement was an attack on colonial symbols on campus that are physical reminders of white supremacy and black subjugation and oppression that is rooted in South Africa.[12] Du Preez *et al* assert that these movements and protests reflect the ways in which students and academics use their agency to think and act on societal matters that concern all citizens.[13] The protests highlighted in the South African context that no meaningful changes had been done to the higher education sector since the democratic government took power in 1994. The curriculum still largely resembled the racially prejudiced designs that the apartheid regime had introduced. For instance, despite the existence of African philosophers, jurisprudence students in most South African universities are still taught a curriculum based on the writings of European philosophers, such as Jeremy Bentham or Thomas Aquinas. This was a concern shared by most South Africans, a concern that Eurocentric knowledge is still canvassed as the 'regime of truth', ignoring other knowledge systems that exist elsewhere in the world.[14]

The protests were also aimed at decolonising the higher education space, transforming the curriculum and ensuring that institutional memory at UCT is

9 AOSIS Publishing. 'Transformation in Higher Education', available at: https://thejournal.org.za/index.php/thejournal/article/%20view/9%20/31 (last accessed on 16 December 2018).

10 Ibid.

11 South African History Online. 'Chumani Maxwele Ignites #RhodesMustFall Movement', available at: https://www.sahistory.org.za/dated-event/chumani-maxwele-ignites-rhodes mustfall-movement-uct (last accessed 17 December 2018).

12 Ibid.

13 Du Preez, Petro, Simmonds, Shan and Chetty, John. 'Ethical Reflections on #MustFall movements and Concomitant Gender-Based Violence'. *South African Journal of Higher Education* 31(6) (2017), 96–112, 97.

14 Heleta, Savo. 'Decolonising Knowledge in South Africa: Dismantling the "Pedagogy of Big Lies"'. *Ufahamu* 40(2) (2018), 47–65, 48.

inclusive and representative. In other words, students were calling for a curriculum that included lived South African and African experiences. Rekgotsofetse Chikane asserts that these protests and disruptions were not necessarily new. South African history is awash with similar protests over the years.[15] Yet these #FeesMustFall protests resonated with society, and signalled a significant change in youth politics.[16]

If international law has been around for about 500 years, as international law scholars claim, the question is why are we only now enquiring about the contribution of African states to the development of international law? Already in the 1960s and 1970s, similar questions were raised by authors writing from a Global South perspective, such as Graham Irwin and Robert Smith.[17] Their research was motivated by, for example, the attainment of independence and the glaring lack of equal participation of states in institutions such as the United Nations (UN). Although South Africa gained its freedom from the apartheid regime in 1994, decolonisation and transformation have gained renewed currency at the national level, buoyed by student activism.

Even though these campaigns and movements were not supported by everyone, they have forcefully asserted the importance of concrete transformation and decolonisation in South African universities. They have raised awareness amongst legal scholars and have helped kick-start the conversation regarding the place of Africans in the global social, economic and political space. They have made the enquiries into the origins of international law become even more pertinent in the South African higher education sector at this juncture. It is against this backdrop that we write this chapter. Furthermore, such daring calls from students indicate that the current curriculum has not been addressing their needs and is instead omitting the lived experiences of

15 Student activism and protest action were rife in the pre-democracy days, where young people fought against apartheid. See South African History Online. 'Student Protests in Democratic South Africa', available at: https://www.sahistory.org.za/article/student-protests-democratic-south-africa (last accessed on 16 December 2019).

16 Rekgotsofetse, Chikane. *Breaking a Rainbow, Building a Nation: The Politics Behind #MustFall Movements*. (Johannesburg: Picador Africa, 2018), 22.

17 Irwin, Graham. 'Precolonial African Diplomacy: The Example of Asante'. *International Journal of African Historical Studies* 8(1) (1975), 81–96; and Smith, Robert. 'Peace and Palaver: International Relations in Pre-Colonial West Africa'. *Journal of African History* 14(4) (1973), 599–621. See also Rajagopal who cites scholars such as Abdullahi An-Na'im, Richard Falk, V. S. Mani, Judge Weeramantry, Upendra Baxi, Bhupinder S. Chimni and Issa Shivji as some of the forerunners of the questions that this chapter is concerned with. See Rajagopal, Balakrishnan. 'International Law and Its Discontents: Rethinking the Global South'. *Proceedings of the Annual Meeting (American Society of International Law)* 106 (2012), 176–181, 177.

many on the African continent. Hence, the enquiry into the continent's contribution to the birth and development of international law is timely. These observations indicate that the calls for legal reform continue to be relevant for so many years after African states regained their independence. It should be recalled that upon regaining self-rule, African states reacted to the prevailing Eurocentric world outlook in a threefold way. They (i) rejected or resisted certain approaches of classical international law; (ii) they were ambivalent and eclectic towards some Eurocentric norms; and (iii) they pushed the agenda for a reform of international law's old rules, and the progressive development of new ones in light of prevailing needs of the international community.[18]

3 The Geographical Background of History, Standard Narratives and Excluded Traditions

There is plenty of literature on the subject of the origins of international law, and it is largely characterised by contestation regarding who developed what rules and when.[19] Race, religion, geographic location and political inclination are amongst the key ingredients that fuel this divergence of opinion amongst international legal scholars. Hence, from around the 19th century onwards, European jurists leaned more towards the worldview that saw Europe as the source of modern international law, to the total disregard of other contributors.[20] We must state at this juncture that by European jurists we also include writers from other parts of the Western world, who, in like fashion, follow that Eurocentric view of international law.

It is common cause that the evolution of international law is rooted in Judaeo-Christian tradition.[21] It is believed that until the fall of the Roman Empire, states were largely insular and regarded other states as barbarians and enemies;[22] and that following the fall of the Roman Empire, modern states began to evolve, gained some stability and independence and embraced the notion of sovereign equality. Grotius and the Peace of Westphalia have largely

---

18 Yusuf, Abdulqawi. *Pan-Africanism and International Law* (Leiden: Martinus Nijhoff, 2014), 101.

19 Gleider Hernandez acknowledges that there are diverging views on where and how international law began. See Hernandez, Gleider. *International Law* (Oxford: Oxford University Press, 2019), 5.

20 Orakhelashvili, Alexander. 'The Idea of European International Law'. *European Journal of International Law* 17(2) (2006), 315–347, 317.

21 Foster, John. 'The Evolution of International Law'. *Yale Law Journal* 18(3) (1909), 149–164, 152.

22 Ibid., 149.

been credited with situating international law squarely in its current form and mould. The prevailing narrative of the development and history of international law often cites Suarez and Gentili as some of the luminaries of their time, through whose industry and skill principles of the law of nations were being churned out in Europe.[23] Quite interestingly, what stands out from the above narrative on internationalisation is that this perceived overcoming of barbarism was not complete; the barbarian status was externalised and transferred to African states and other states of the Global South.[24]

3.1 *The Western Tradition: A Eurocentric View on International Law's History*

Although the above sentiments were held by scholars who wrote over one hundred years ago, the notion that Europe is the birthplace of international law remains pervasive in legal scholarship today. Literature as recent as 2017 still contain bold assertions that the foundations of international law 'lie firmly in the development of Western culture and political organisation'.[25]

Although such writings perceive international law as a European construct, they also proffer a postcolonial model of interaction with international law by the former colonies.[26] The quoted textbook concedes that recent developments, particularly within the 'developing countries' have served to destroy international law's Eurocentric hegemony, whilst at the same time affirming the universalist appeal of international law. Scholars of this inclination often try to support this view by highlighting the composition of the UN Security Council as an example of Africa's relevance in the international community. For them, the arrangement that the ten non-permanent members of the Security Council should go to Afro-Asian states (5 seats) and Latin American states (2 seats) is evidence that international law claims to take into account the viewpoints of all regions of the world.[27] This is as far as they are prepared to admit the participation of African states to international law. They do not

23 Ibid., 152.

24 Ikechi Mgbeoji argues that the *mission civilisatrice* was nothing more than cultural chauvinism, characterized by an assumed 'civilised self' and 'the barbaric other'. He notes that this phenomenon was also characterized by brutalization inflicted on the 'savage' by the 'civilised' in the name of enlightening and pacifying the former. See Mgbeoji, Ikechi. 'The Civilised Self and the Barbaric Other: Imperial Delusions of Order and the Challenges of Human Security', in International Law and the Third World, eds. Richard Falk, Balakrishnan Rajagopal and Jacqueline Stevens (Abingdon: Routledge, 2008), 151–166, 153.

25 Shaw, *International Law* 2017 (n 2), 10.

26 Ibid., 28.

27 Ibid., 29.

touch on the ways in which pre-colonial from African traditions and practices added value to the development of the subject as discussed below.

The claims that the 17th century was the period in which international law began is often accompanied by a disclaimer that this should not be interpreted to mean that 'there were no international rules before that date'.[28] This disclaimer, however, does not necessarily remedy the misconception that Africa and other regions did not contribute to the development of international law. The question that begs an answer is this: If international rules already existed elsewhere before the 17th century, then what entitles Europe to unilaterally pontificate about the date and place of origin of international law? The Eurocentric approach is compounded by mentioning only the Greek and Roman postulations prior to the European Renaissance. Scant reference is made to 'Chinese and Indian civilisations', without mention of African or other civilisations. Again, this could be attributed to the prevailing perception amongst Europeans that Africa was in need of civilisation hence the colonialist project. As such, the traditional understanding of international law unfortunately regards colonialism and non-European societies and their practices as peripheral to the discipline proper because international law originated in Europe.

Some European authors, whilst approaching the development of the subject using the Westphalian model, acknowledge that this approach is Eurocentric, but that it must nonetheless be taken as the starting point for modern international law in Europe.[29] Whilst this approach must be lauded for recognising Eurocentrism, criticism can be levelled at the uncritical acknowledgment that European colonialism and Christianisation spread the Westphalian system, and hence international law across the world.

Parallel with the perception that international law only came to Africa with the arrival of the first settlers is the notion that Africa's interaction with the outside world only started when the first colonialist set foot on African soil. This approach tends to see Africa as having had no law in general and no international law in particular, which is premised on the misperception that Africa

---

28 Klabbers, Jan. *International Law* (Cambridge: Cambridge University Press, 2013), 4. Klabbers cites the example of treaties regarding prisoners of war amongst the Greek city states and trade regulations amongst the Roman, as well as early incidents of diplomacy as evidence that international rules existed before the 17th century. Even though these, and more advanced rules existed in Africa way before those periods, Klabbers and other Eurocentric authors do not acknowledge that.

29 Hernandez, *International Law* 2019 (n 19), 5.

had no history prior to direct contact with Europe.[30] This worldview conflicts with historical evidence of external interactions between the African and the outside world. These interactions predate colonialism. Equally, African statehood predates colonialism by over 3000 years.[31]

For example, international treaties were entered into by Amenophis III and Akhenaten of Egypt as early as 1400 BC. Further, international trade took place between African traders on the East African coast and traders from India and the middle east as an example of African international legal history.[32] In 1870, most Africans lived in independent societies, most of which had had various forms of interactions both with each other and with other societies outside the continent. By 1915, all but two African states (Ethiopia and Liberia) had been conquered by Europeans.[33] For instance, there was trade between African states and others as early as the first century AD. A large economic network was established among African states and non-African states.[34] By the first century of AD, East Africa had formed trade relations with China, Middle East and India.[35] In 1482, Portugal established Elmina (modern day Ghana) as its first African trading post export.[36] There are historical records of the practice of sending a declaration of war before one kingdom attacked another; and of declarations of peace and ceasefire concluded via peace agreements. Instructive in this regard is the peace treaty (1600 and 1200 BCE) between King Ramses II of Egypt and King Ḫattušili III, the king of King Hatii.[37]

The Eurocentric view of the history of international law cannot be divorced from the imperialist notions that fuelled the subjugation of Africans by European powers.[38] It is common knowledge that the interactions between

30 Forji, Amin. 'International Law, the Civilizing Mission and the Ambivalence of Development in Africa: Conceptual Underpinnings'. *Journal of African and International Law* 6(1) (2013), 191–225, 195.

31 Levitt, Jeremy. 'African Origins of International Law: Myth or Reality?'. *UCLA Journal of International Law and Foreign Affairs* 113(19) (2015), 113–165, 118.

32 Zollmann, Jakob. 'African International Legal Histories – International Law in African: Perspectives and Possibilities'. *Leiden Journal of International* Law 31(4) (2018), 897–914, 910.

33 Maddox, Gregory. 'Introduction', in *Conquest and Resistance to Colonialism in Africa*, ed. Maddox Gregory (Abingdon: Routledge, 2018), xi–xv, xi.

34 Casley-Hayford, Gus. *The Lost Kingdoms of Africa*. (London: Bantam Press, 2012), 128.

35 Falola, Toyin. *Key Events in African History: A Reference Guide* (London: Greenwood Press, 2002).

36 Ibid.

37 Altman, Amnon. *Tracing the Earliest Recorded Concepts of International Law: The Ancient Near East (2500–330 BCE)* (Leiden: Brill, 2012), 99.

38 Walter Rodney argues that all the countries referred to as underdeveloped were exploited by others. He asserts that African and Asian societies were developing independently

Africans and the British was not a smooth affair. It was characterised by Victorian myths, which included prejudices such as perceived African inferiority, an active hostility towards the great independent kingdoms of Africa and a negation of the achievements and accomplishments of Africans.[39] Coupled with these was economic and cultural competition among African kingdoms.[40] The above partly explain the attitude of European powers to any political formation in Africa. The Europeans did not regard the actions and experiences of those formations as actions coming from states, and as a result, were not to be regarded as contributions to the growth of international law.[41] Indeed, the 18th century approach to Africa and similarly placed territories was coloured by the terms 'civilised' versus 'uncivilised'. Accordingly, only the civilised were recognised as proper subjects of international law, whilst those regarded as lacking civilisation were left outside the reach and ambit of international law.[42]

It is this perceived African inferiority that motivated Europeans to relegate African kings and queens to the status of 'chiefs' or 'paramount chiefs'.[43] Indeed, the idea of a queen in England, and a queen in Africa did not fit in well with

---

until such time that they were taken over by the capitalist, imperialist and colonialist powers. See Rodney, *How Europe Underdeveloped Africa* 1973 (n. 7), 19.

39 Examples of great kingdoms of Africa include: Sundiata Keita who ruled the western Sudanese empire of Mali in the 1200s; Osei Kofi Tutu (1660–1717) of the Ashanti Kingdom (current day Ghana). See Classical African Studies. 'The Greatest Rulers of Africa', available at: http://www.aceschools.online/the-greatest-rulers-of-africa/ (last accessed on 19 December 2019). Wallace-Bruce makes reference to the Kingdom of Ghana, which by the 1060s had become the largest and most powerful kingdom in the Western Sudan (present day Senegal, Mali and Mauritania). Ghana was ruled by a king with both central and provincial administrations. Ancient Mali was also established around 1240. The author lists further examples of pre-colonial political units, including Egypt, Nubia, Axum, Kush, Adal, Great Zimbabwe, Manyika, Mutapa, Kongo, Shongai, Zaghawa, Takru and Zaria. See Wallace-Bruce, Nii. 'Africa and International Law – The Emergence of Statehood'. *The Journal of Modern African Studies* 23(4) (1985), 575–602, 557.

40 Obichere, Boniface. 'African Critics of Victorian Imperialism: An Analysis', in *Conquest and Resistance to Colonialism in Africa*, ed. Maddox Gregory (Abingdon: Routledge, 2018), 31–50, 31.

41 Obrégon, Liliana. 'The Civilized and the Uncivilized', in *The Oxford Handbook of the History of International Law*, eds. Bardo Fassbender and Peters Anne (Oxford: Oxford University Press, 2012), 917–940, 918.

42 Ibid.

43 Mariane Ferme asserts that paramount chieftainship was an instrument of colonial administration and governance through various forms of indirect rule by the colonial power. See Ferme, Mariane. 'Flexible Sovereignty? Paramount Chiefs, Deterritorialization and Political Mediations in Sierra Leone'. *Cambridge Journal of Anthropology* 23(2) (2003), 21–35, 22.

the Euro worldview of an inferior Africa.[44] As a consequence, the colonialist project to purge Africa of barbarism and its uncivilised nature began with ensuring that all references to African institutions and systems were couched in demeaning terms.[45] These were terms quite dissimilar to European terms, such as references to the tribe, rather than the nation, a paramount chief rather than a king or queen, and the outright denial/denunciation of the existence of African states.

This is aptly captured in references to 'the end of colonisation and the birth of new states'.[46] African kingdoms that had existed for hundreds of years were regarded as new, having been born only at the date of 'granting of independence' by the colonial master.[47]

Even the birth of the UN, which is quite often hailed as a turning point in international law, was fraught with the above cited civilisationist approach. One of the key players in the drafting of the UN Charter was Jan Smuts, a key proponent of racial segregation.[48] Smuts is a former South African head of state, who was regarded as both a statesman and a symbol of world freedom.[49] He believed in national unity, but only for white people, as evidenced by his espousal of white supremacy.[50] He believed that Africans and Europeans were

44 For instance, when British colonialists subjugated African societies, they recognised the African king as a paramount chief, and not a king properly so called. The case of Swaziland, Lesotho and Botswana is illustrative in this regard. In Swaziland, King Sobhuza II was regarded as a paramount chief from 1921 up until the kingdom regained its independence in 1968. From there on he was officially referred to by the British as a king. Lesotho's Moshoeshoe II was also regarded as a paramount chief from until regaining independence in 1966.

45 Aime Cesaire attributes this to Christian pedantry, which laid down the dishonest equations *Christianity = civilization, non-Christian beliefs (or paganism) = savagery*. See Cesaire, Aime. *Discourse on Colonialism* (New York: Monthly Review Press, 2000), 33.

46 Shaw, *International Law* (n. 2), 27.

47 For instance, Maluwa, writing in the context of post-colonial Africa makes reference to 'newly independent states' and 'the participation of the new African states in the international legal order'. See Maluwa, Tiyanjana. 'International Law Making in Post-Colonial Africa: The Role of the Organisation of African Unity'. *Netherlands International Law Review* 49(1) (2002), 81–103, 81.

48 Indeed, Mahmood Mamdani asserts that the essence of colonialism is to be found in the practice of segregation, whether territorial or institutional. See in this regard Dirar, Uoldelul. 'Colonialism and the Construction of National Identities: The Case of Eritrea'. *Journal of Eastern African Studies* 1(2) (2007), 256–276, 258.

49 Dubow, Saul. 'Smuts, the United Nations and the Rhetoric of Race and Rights'. *Journal of Contemporary History* 43(1) (2008), 45–74, 45.

50 Ibid., 45.

not only different in colour but in minds and political capacity too.[51] Smuts' approach to human freedom at the global level was diametrically opposed to how he viewed the same subject domestically. He once opined, in reference to the indigenes of South Africa that:

> Natives have the simplest minds, understand only the simplest ideas or ideals, and are almost animal-like in the simplicity of their minds and ways … Instead of mixing up black and white in the old haphazard way, which instead of lifting up the black degraded the white, we are now trying to lay down a policy of keeping them apart as much as possible in our institutions.[52]

Leading South African international law scholars emphasise on the 'newness' of these post-colonial African states, and extol their willingness to embrace the Eurocentric version of international law, motivated by a desire to 'obtain the benefits of rules such as those governing diplomatic relations and the controlled use of force'.[53] These arguments presuppose that the African states had neither any rules of war (*ius ad bellum* and *ius in bello*) nor any diplomatic or trade relations amongst themselves and with other territories outside the continent. As will appear more fully below, these scholars lean towards the school of thought that perceives international law to flow out of Europe and pays little regard to the existence of rules amongst African socio-political formations.[54]

Most eminent international lawyers who embrace the mainstream Eurocentric view of the development of international often gloss over the contribution of Africa to this legal system. For example, most scholars limit their narrative to the period around colonisation and the so-called 'granting of independence', which supposedly led to the participation of 'third world countries' in the UN, and thereby allowed them to contribute to international law. It must be emphasised at this juncture, that such an outlook on global interactions ignores the fact that independence was not necessarily granted freely but was fought for by the very 'third world countries' that suffered immeasurable harm at the hands of a 'civilised Europe'. It also places Europe exclusively at the

51 Reynolds, John. 'Third World Approaches to International Law and the Ghosts of Apartheid', in *The Challenges of Human Rights: Past, Present and Future*, eds. David Keane and Yvonne McDermott (Cheltenham: Edward Elgar, 2012), 194–218, 197.

52 Ibid.

53 Shaw, *International Law* 2017 (n. 2), 29.

54 These authors include Shaw, Klabbers, Dugard, and Strydom.

centre of international legal development, whether in the sense of conceptualising the initial theories of international law during the so-called Renaissance, or in the sense of 'granting independence' to colonised states where the latter suddenly saw the benefits of embracing the European-inspired international legal order. All these perceptions are based on the superiority complex of the European coloniser and its misguided mission to 'civilise' the world.[55]

European history suggests that during this period, Europe birthed vigorous economic expansion, social, political and cultural transformation.[56] Most scholars refer to the Westphalian institutions or Westphalian states as being responsible for the coming into being of the modern state system which was epitomized by the Peace of Westphalia Treaty.[57]

The idea that Europe brought international law to a 'dark continent' is very reprehensible.[58] What is even more reprehensible, however, is the portrayal of history in which Europe simply descended on Africa and 'civilised it' much to Africa's benefit. Little, if at all, is said about the relentless fights and resistance by Africans, trying to prevent colonial subjugation. The eminent authors of international law, in tracing the history of international law in Africa, tend to portray a seamless introduction of the Eurocentric legal order by European saviours, and do not interrogate the resistance shown by, for example, the coastal forest people of Ivory Coast who fought for twenty seven years to preserve their independence.[59]

3.2 *Unheard Voices: How Do African Scholars Conceive of International Law?*

It is unsurprising that European and western scholars usually situate the birth of international law within their own local context. This is after all what their curriculum has taught for hundreds of years. Unfortunately, this same curriculum found its way to the halls of learning in African universities through the imposition of English and Roman-Dutch law. It is no wonder that African scholars would largely consume and redistribute this Eurocentric view of

55 Forji, 'Conceptual Underpinnings' 2013 (n. 30), 191–225, 197. Forji argues that Christianity and cultural differentiation motivated Europeans to see themselves as categorically superior to the 'others'.

56 Strydom, *International Law* (Oxford: Oxford University Press, 2017), 7.

57 Ibid., 4.

58 Ibid.

59 O'Sullian, John. 'The Franco-Baoule War, 1891–1911: The Struggle against the French Conquest of Central Ivory Coast', in *Conquest and Resistance to Colonialism in Africa*, ed. Maddox Gregory (Abingdon: Routledge, 2018), 73–100, 73.

international law. The leading scholars in the South African context also follow this approach. This could also be attributed to the fact that even though they are South Africans, they are products of the Eurocentric teaching of international law.

It is said that international relations began when states entered into external relations with each other or when they sought the formation of alliances between themselves for the protection of their own or collective interest.[60] Leading South African international law scholars are of the view that international law as we have come to know it today developed from Western culture. In tracing the historical development of international law, these contemporary South African scholars focus on the contributions of canonical scholars such as Cornelius van Bynkershoek, Francisco de Vitoria, Hugo Grotius, Alberico Gentili, and Jeremy Bentham.[61]

Although leaning more towards the idea international law was a product of the European state system called the European law of nations that came into being in the 16th century,[62] there is some acknowledgement that this system was rooted in convictions of European superiority which accorded little recognition to the political organisms in Africa. These convictions regarded territories occupied by non-European people as not constituting a social or political aggregation and were thus treated as *res nullius*.[63]

Such scholars attribute the establishment of international law in southern Africa to the arrival of the first European settlers. The prevailing idea is that South Africa only became a state when a Dutch man, Jan van Riebeeck settled and took possession of the Cape of Good Hope. He initially used the Cape

60 See generally Barnett, Michael and Sikkink, Kathryn. *From International Relations to Global Society*, in The Oxford Handbook of Political Science (Oxford: Oxford University Press, 2011), 748–768.

61 John Dugard emphasises the place of van Bynkershook in the birth and development of international law to the extent that he asserts that 'it is a disgrace not to know something about him'. See Dugard, John. 'Cornelius van Bynkershoek: A Treatise of the Law of War'. *Leiden Journal of International Law* 23(1) (2010), 269–276, 271.

62 Strydom, *International Law* 2017 (n. 57), 5.

63 The International Court of Justice held in the Western Sahara Advisory Opinion that state practice in the 1800s indicated that territories inhabited by peoples having a social and political organisation were not regarded as *terra nullius* (para. 80). It also found that in 1884 when Spain colonized Western Sahara it was inhabited by nomadic peoples who were socially and politically organised tribes under chiefs who represented them (para. 81). It concluded that due to the above, Western Sahara could not be regarded as terra nullius (para. 83).

of Good Hope as a refreshment station for the Dutch East Indian Company, which began an association between South Africa and the Roman-Dutch law.[64]

These views are extremely unfortunate, for they overlook a myriad of African systems and principles which regulated interstate relations, which far outdated the so-called European principles. Indeed, many international legal principles were developed, understood and practised by non-European states before the European presence in non-European areas intensified. Examples include the law of treaties and the law of war.[65] In 1483, the Kingdoms of Kongo and Ndongo (modern day northern Angola) recorded the first arrival of Europeans, as agents of their governments. King Nzinga formed a healthy relationship with the Portuguese and exchanged representatives. By 1568, the kingdom had expanded its diplomatic and political reach by establishing relations with Spain and the Vatican.[66] Nöthling cites instances of trade between Egypt and Crete, Palestine and Syria as early as 2000 BCE.[67] Ghana controlled trade routes and taxation between Sudan and the Mediterranean territories,[68] particularly trade in salt and gold around the year 800 BCE.[69]

In contrast to the authors cited so far, Viljoen is of the opinion that Africans played an active role in the development of international law.[70] His views corroborate those of Robert Smith, who argued that despite the unwritten nature of law in Africa, there existed plenty historical sources and other evidence of formal governmental relations between peoples of West Africa in the precolonial period.[71]

Viljoen condemns the negative view of anything African. He focuses on international human rights and humanitarian law, and argues that African issues have also given rise to solutions and thus played an active role in the

64 Dugard, John, Max Du Plessis, Anton Katz and Arnold Pronto. *Dugard's International Law: A South African Perspective* (Cape Town: Juta, 4th ed. 2012), 18.

65 Anghie, Antony. 'The Evolution of International Law: Colonial and Postcolonial Realities', in *International Law and the Third World*, eds. Richard Falk, Balakrishnan Rajagopal and Jacqueline Stevens (Abingdon: Routledge, 2008), 35–49, 38.

66 Heywood, Linda. *Njinga of Angola – Africa's Warrior Queen* (Cambridge: Harvard University Press, 2017), 7.

67 Nöthling, F. Johan. *Pre-Colonial Africa: Her Civilisations and Foreign Contacts* (Johannesburg: Southern Book Publishers, 1989), 35.

68 Smith, Ken and Nöthling, F. Johan. *North of the Limpopo: Africa since 1800* (Pretoria: University of South Africa, 1993), 14

69 Falola, *Key Events in African History* 2002 (n. 36), xv.

70 Viljoen, Frans. 'Africa's Contribution to the Development of International Human Rights and Humanitarian Law'. *Africa Human Rights Law Journal* 1(1) (2001), 18–39, 18.

71 Smith, Robert. 'Peace and Palaver' 1973 (n. 17), 599.

development of international human rights and humanitarian law, sometimes even initiating new paradigms.[72] Evidence of this positive contribution includes the role played by the Organisation of African Unity (OAU) in the adoption of the African Charter on Human and Peoples' Rights. Viljoen says that:

> Common wisdom has it that the African Charter is 'autochthonous' in its inclusion of the concept of 'peoples', its enumeration of individual duties, the non-justiciability of the dispute settlement procedure, its anti-colonial stance, its emphasis on morality, and its placing of first generation rights on a par with second and third generation rights. All these aspects represent the introduction of a series of ambiguities into the bipolar structural design of the international human rights discourse. The system, as it had developed by the 1970s, was premised on the dichotomies of 'individual vs community', 'rights vs duties', 'first vs second and third generation rights', 'enforceability vs non-enforceability'. In each instance, one of these polarities was privileged to construct the model or golden thread: what matters are individual rights, of the 'first generation', which are enforceable.[73]

Even though Viljoen leans more towards celebrating Africa's contribution to international law, he considers only the post-independence era. A majority of the other leading scholars on the subject from the region align themselves with the Eurocentric school of thought. What can be gleaned from the consulted literature is that an enquiry into the history and development of international law on the African continent requires a multi-disciplinary approach. In other words, the answers may not lie in the writings of legal scholars alone but in other fields as well, such as history and anthropology.

4 Africa's Pre-colonial Traditions in Selected Fields of International Law

The argument advanced above is that Africa did not only react to an imposition of international law after the arrival of European settlers, but that the continent already before meaningfully contributed to and embraced

72 Viljoen, 'Africa's Contribution' 2001 (n. 68), 18–39, 18.
73 Ibid., 20.

widely accepted principles of international law. What follows below is a brief treatment of selected instances indicating how various African states related with each other, and with other states from outside the continent. The list is not meant to be exhaustive. It simply gives some highlights that refute the Eurocentric view of international advanced above, as well as the assertion of international law being a purely post-colonial reality on the African continent.

4.1 *Diplomatic Relations*

Diplomacy is a central feature of international law. Relations between states are regulated through this core process, and it serves many purposes such as the prevention of war, the negotiation of policies and the well-functioning of international institutions. Diplomacy may be defined as the conduct of business between states by peaceful means.[74] The underlying goal in diplomacy is to provide the best means by civilisation for preventing international relations from being governed by force alone.[75]

Africa has a rightful claim to be the birthplace of this key institution of international society. Diplomacy began on the African continent way before the colonial powers arrived. There already existed diverse ways of settling differences among groups of peoples and these included alliances, compensatory means of dialogue, and cooperation. Other diplomatic methods of the time included consensus, compromise and coordination of efforts for development and peaceful coexistence.[76] Indeed, diplomatic relations are recorded in history between Egypt and its neighbours (Ethiopia and Sudan, and several states in the middle east) as early as 1100 BCE.[77]

Various pre-colonial African states maintained relationships with each other on a regular basis.[78] What was involved in the diplomatic arts in Africa was the same as what transpired elsewhere in the world, including in Europe. Treaties were negotiated, territorial and trade parameters were determined, dispute settlement mechanisms were established, and potential conflict was avoided through dialogue. Irwin makes the example of the Bunyoro in East

74 Irwin, Graham. 'Precolonial African Diplomacy: The Example of Asante'. *International Journal of African Historical Studies* 8(1) (1975), 81–96, 81.

75 Adegbulu, Femi. 'Pre-Colonial West African Diplomacy: Its Nature and Impact'. *The Journal of International Social Research* 4(18) (2010), 170–182, 171.

76 Spies, Yolanda. 'Africa and the Idea of International Society'. *Journal of Contemporary History* 41(1) (2016), 38–56, 42.

77 Ibid.

78 Irwin, 'Precolonial African Diplomacy' 1975 (n. 74), 82.

Africa where personal immunity for foreign emissaries travelling through the territory was assured. In the Asante kingdom, history records the reception of diplomatic officials from the coast, and one each from the territories of Dahomey, Salaga and Yendi.[79]

The unwritten nature of law in Africa does not necessarily mean that there was no practice of international law on the continent before the colonialists arrived. Indeed, plenty of historical records lend credence to this argument. For instance, in the 1500s, Idris Alooma (1570–1602) was noted for his prowess in the conduct of international relations. He led the Hanem-Bournu Empire, which created trade links between North Africa and West Africa known as Trans-Sahara Trade.[80] He designed boats for the lake Chad, cleared roads, and introduced standard units for measurements of grains.[81] He had agreements with North Africa to export grains in exchange with salt, kola nuts, ivory, slaves, animal hides, nitrate, cottons, ostrich feathers and perfumes.[82] He signed the first ever Cease Fire Treaty in Chadian History. He further made provision for foreigners in the empire as 200 emissaries from Tripoli, Cairo and Ottoman.[83]

Furthermore, the Kingdom of the Kongo had many connections with other central African states around the 1530s, including Matamba, which was located to the east of the Kingdoms of Kongo and Ndongo.[84] In pre-colonial Africa, formal relations existed at the highest levels of government between different peoples of West Africa.[85] There is evidence of exchange of ambassadors in around 1691 between the kingdoms of Benin and Warri.[86] Smith further records the exchange of diplomats between the Benin kingdom and Portugal in 1593.[87] Diplomatic engagements continued through the seventeenth and nineteenth centuries, between African states inter se, and between African states and Europeans states, although the latter form was more intrusive than voluntary.[88]

---

79 Ibid.

80 MiaPkum, Peter. 'Precolonial African International Relations: Kanem-Bournu External Relations under the Reign of Mia Idris Alooma (1517–1603)'. Lecture presented at the M.Sc International Relations and Strategic Studies at the University of Jos, Nigeria, 2015), 16.

81 Ibid.

82 Ibid., 17.

83 Ibid., 18.

84 Heywood, *Africa's Warrior Queen* 2017 (n. 66), 7.

85 Smith, 'Peace and Palaver' 1973 (n. 17), 599.

86 Ibid., 602.

87 Ibid., 601.

88 Ibid.

Closely intertwined with African diplomacy was the oath, the equivalent of modern day *pacta sunct servanda*. For instance, amongst the Asante, a huge premium was place on the *ntam* (oath) as a crucial element of the proper conduct of international affairs. The ratification of a peace treaty was accompanied by swearing an oath which involved all parties.

A legacy of African diplomacy that survives to this day is marriage as a diplomatic tool. Marriage for political unification was also used in European diplomacy, a famous example being the marriage 1469 between Queen Isabella of Castille and King Ferdinand II of Aragon.[89] There is evidence of such arranged marriages between royal households in southern Africa, as a means to establish cordial relations between two nations. For example, at the height of King Shaka Zulu's reign, the king of Swaziland, Sobhuza I married off two of his daughters to King Shaka, in the hope that this would prevent an attack from the Zulu king. The princesses were given in marriage after King Shaka asked for their hand, but relations soon soured when Shaka killed both of them for falling pregnant.[90] Hilda Kuper asserts that King Sobhuza's policy was to avoid conflict with militarily superior kings in the region, by establishing alliances such as through these marriages.[91] Although this marital arrangement did not yield much fruit, it is interesting to note that similar arrangements continues to this day between the Zulu nation in South Africa, and the Swati nation of Swaziland. The former Zulu monarch, King Goodwill Zwelithini was married to two wives from the Swaziland royal family.

The use of diplomacy to advance inter-kingdom relations in African, as seen above, predates the arrival of the colonialists in Africa. It adds credence to the claim that diplomacy and its rules were not merely received by African states through Christianisation or colonisation.

4.2 *Commercial Treaties between States or Similar Entities*

Trade often occurred between African kingdoms and at times this involved empires outside the African continent. The Mapungubwe area in South Africa contains interesting archaeological and anthropological facts, all pointing to trade in gold and ivory from as early as 1250 AD.[92] The kingdom at Mapungubwe

89 Strydom, *International Law* 2017 (n. 57), 6.

90 Eldredge, Elizabeth. *The Creation of a Zulu Kingdom, 1815–1828* (Cambridge: Cambridge University Press, 2014), 180.

91 Kuper, Hilda. *An African Aristocracy: Rank Among the Swazi.* (Abingdon: Routledge, 2018).

92 Huffman, Thomas. 'Mapungubwe and the Origin of the Zimbabwe Culture'. *South African Archaeological Society Goodwin Series* 8 (2000), 14–29, 21.

controlled trade through the east African ports to India and China, and throughout southern Africa. The kingdom managed to import Chinese porcelain and Persian beads in return.[93] There is anthropological and archaeological evidence that some of the beads that were traded in the Mapungubwe kingdom around the ninth century originated from the middle east. However, around the tenth century, scientific testing of these beads indicate that new imports originated from South Asia.[94] This indicates a diversification in the procurement of these products by the kingdom of Mapungubwe. Surely this inter-state trade which happened across continents was governed by some legal system agreed upon by the parties.

Furthermore, there exists evidence of inter-state and inter-continental trade amongst the Garamantes of the Libyan Sahara. This society consisted of indigenous Africans, who were formed into an advanced society in pre-Islamic Saharan Africa. Archaeological evidence suggests that this Garamantian society existed as a non-nomadic society with permanent villages from the first millennium BC. The Garamantian society traded with the Mediterranean and sub-Saharan Africa.[95] There is further evidence of international trade between the Garamantes and the Roman empire, as seen in Saharan rock art and paintings, which depict images of horses, warriors on horseback, horse-drawn chariots and camels.[96]

There also exists evidence that international trade between African states and European traders was regulated by elements of African customary law, albeit unwritten. Examples include protection of the law (flowing from unwritten contracts based on oaths and rituals) afforded to Portuguese traders. This

---

93 UNESCO, 'Mapungubwe Cultural Landscape' 2019, available at: https://whc.unesco.org/en/list/1099 (last accessed on 13 March 2019).

94 Dussubieux, Laure. 'Glass Beads in Trans-Saharan Trade', in *Trade in the Ancient Sahara and Beyond*, eds. David Mattingly, Victoria Leitch and Chloe Duckworth (Cambridge: Cambridge University Press, 2017), 414–432, 425.

95 Mattingly, David. 'The Garamantes and the Origins of Saharan Trade', in *Trade in the Ancient Sahara and Beyond*, eds. David Mattingly, Victoria Leitch and Chloe Duckworth (Cambridge: Cambridge University Press, 2017), 1–52, 2. Mattingly proceeds to discount the prevailing notion that trade between Sahara and sub-Saharan Africa was only made possible by the use of camels during Islamic times. He argues that there are studies supporting the position that these two regions traded way before the Islamic times, using inland routes in the desert that had existed from early historic times. All this is evidence of inter-state trade which occurred way before Europe colonised Africa, and which needed to be regulated by some form of international law between those trading entities.

96 Ibid., 22.

is evidence of a form of international law that regulated relations among West African states, as well as between West African states and European entities.[97]

All this demonstrates the existence of a pre-Islamic, pre-colonisation, pre-Christianisation system of inter-state trade governed by international rules.

4.3 *Sovereignty and Governance*

Although the Eurocentric view refuses to recognise African political organisms as states on an equal footing with European states, African kingdoms and empires existed and formulated rules for conducting their foreign relations. This, it can be argued was in pursuance of their sovereignty as supreme political entities. Sovereignty, being an evolving concept, cannot be understood solely by narrow focus on the Westphalian conception of sovereignty.[98] There is need to take stock of what sovereignty meant for those states that were subjugated by European powers. For this purpose, we understand sovereignty as the totality of rights and duties recognised by international law.[99]

The construction of sovereignty in pre-colonial Africa did not differ substantially from the European construct advanced by the likes of Grotius, Locke and Rousseau.[100] The theories advanced by these scholars recognised that sovereignty resided in the generality of the people. The people had to determine how a leader had to lead, and how and when to depose of a wayward leader. The pre-colonial African leader led at the pleasure and the behest of the people.[101] This is aptly captured in the African governance principle '*inkosi yinkosi ngabantu*', which literally means 'a king is a king through the people'. It is a form of checks and balances to ensure that the exercise of public power by a leader draws its legitimacy from the population he leads. Ironically, it is the colonialist powers that tried to corrupt this governance principle by mischievously asserting that 'the king can do no wrong'[102] and then importing this notion into Africa as part of their colonial project.[103] This phenomenon can be

97 Smith, 'Peace and Palaver' 1973 (n. 17), 600.

98 Deng, Biong. 'The Evolving Concept and Institution of Sovereignty: Challenges and Opportunities'. AISA Policy Brief No. 28 (June 2010), 2.

99 Ibid. 3.

100 Elias, Taslim O. *Africa and the Development of International Law* (Leiden: Martinus Nijhoff, 1988), 36.

101 Ibid.

102 *Nyathi v MEC for Health Gauteng* CCT 19/07; [2008] ZACC 8.

103 Dube, Angelo and Nhlabatsi, Sibusiso. 'The King Can Do No Wrong: The Impact of *The Law Society of Swaziland v Simelane NO and Others* on Constitutionalism'. *African Human Rights Law Journal* 16(1) (2016), 265–282, 275.

referred to as the 'present as colonialised past'. The present flows from the coloniser's act of transmuting the role that had previously been played by African kings and chiefs over thousands of years. This transmutation was effectuated by colonialists, and the role currently played by African leaders (especially after the Second World War) is not the original pre-colonial role but a product of this mutation.[104] The foregoing indeed aligns with the assertions above, namely that African leadership had taken cognisance of sovereignty and good governance until colonialism modified it.[105]

5 Towards an Inclusive Vision of International Law: Some Concluding Thoughts

Being authentically African does not mean closing the door on the Western model of knowledge creation. But it does mean that Africa needs to be placed at the centre of our thoughts, words and deeds. We have to acknowledge the perspectives of our immediate environment and use them to enrich our insights and outputs. It is not either/or, one or the other, but and/and, instead it involves using all models and perspectives. This is critical, given that even though several African principles existed prior to colonisation, they have not remained untainted by the received knowledge from the west. For example, the practice of the oath, *ntam*, which was practiced among the Asante in pre-colonial times, exists today in the form of *pacta sunt servanda*.[106] In one way or the other, the two systems have interacted and influenced each other. For instance, the idea that a king or a political leader is above the law did not find

104 Jaffe, Hosea. *A History of Africa*. (London: Zedbooks, 1985), 8.

105 For instance, the Swaziland case where the king still rules with absolute power derived from custom and decree, despite the existence of a supposedly 'supreme constitution' is instructive. The current king's late father, King Sobhuza II, used a royal decree to repeal Swaziland's independence constitution because it took away powers from him, and allowed the people to have political participation through political party politics. The African legal landscape prior to colonisation required that the king's decisions be ratified by a representative forum of elders and advisers. In fact, the reality was that the body of elders advised the king, and he simply endorsed their resolution. See generally in this regard Dube/Nhlabatsi, 'The King Can Do No Wrong' 2016 (n. 103), 265–282.

106 Irwin states that both Asante and foreign diplomats would partake in the drinking of water that had been infused with the bark of the *odum* tree as an indication that they would abide by the peace treaties they were ratifying. See Irwin, 'Precolonial African Diplomacy' 1975 (n. 74), 81–96, 91.

expression in African law prior to colonisation.[107] As discussed above, the king led at the pleasure of the people and could be subjected to correction in case he erred. However, the misguided belief that political leaders could not be subjected to the law has muddled international relations today. A striking illustration would be the strained relations between the African Union (AU) and its members on the one hand and the International Criminal Court (ICC) on the other, all of which flow from the desire by African state leaders to enjoy immunity before this international court. Whilst international law does not recognise the immunity of a head of state before an international court,[108] African leaders believe otherwise. Hence the conflict between the ICC and members of the AU. Further, the adoption of the Malabo Protocol in 2014 bears testimony to the belief amongst African state leaders that they are effectively above the law,[109] and as such enjoy immunity, even from an international tribunal. Hence, the Protocol's Article 46A *bis* provides for such immunity.[110] This is evidence of the mutual interaction of the two legal systems over time.

In light of the above arguments, it can be inferred that the claims that international law has been around for about four or five hundred years do not hold water. Further, placing Europe and Christianity at the centre of the birth and development of international law leads scholars, both north and south of the equator, to miss the rich, and diverse contributions of non-European states to the development of international law. What also emerges from the discussions above is that some of the key international law rules currently attributed to events in Europe were actually applied in Africa and other third world societies millennia before the so-called European Renaissance.

Whilst the attainment of independence and the end of colonialism in the 1960s and 1970s might have spurred some scholars to question the mainstream version on the history of international law; such interrogations in South Africa owe their existence to the student led movement, the #FeesMustFall movement. The movement's calls for decolonised, afro-centred education spurred

---

107 In *Nyathi v. MEC for Health Gauteng* (n. 102), the court held that this notion was a preconstitutional era.

108 *Prosecutor v Charles Taylor* SCSL 2003-01-I, para 53.

109 See the Protocol on Amendments to the Protocol on the Statute of the African Court of Justice and Human Rights adopted by the AU General Assembly, Malabo June 2014.

110 Article 46A *bis* provides that

> No charges shall be commenced or continued before the Court against any serving AU Head of State or Government, or anybody acting or entitled to act in such capacity, or other senior state officials based on their functions, during their tenure of office.

many a legal scholar to begin to engage with the subject matter of international law from an African perspective, and to question what hitherto was long accepted as a true reflection of this subject.

In conclusion, if international law is to shed itself off its colonial and prejudicial character, then its current assumptions about its origins need to be revisited. Positions taken by authors who emphatically insist that international law owes its current character to western culture and political organisation should be refuted and instead replaced with a more appealing explanation of the origins of international law. This universal approach should take into account the contributions of all of humankind to the development of this subject.

Bibliography

Adegbulu, Femi. 'Pre-Colonial West African Diplomacy: Its Nature and Impact'. *The Journal of International Social Research* 4(18) (2010), 170–182.

Altman, Amnon. *Tracing the Earliest Recorded Concepts of International Law: The Ancient Near East (2500–330 BCE)* (Leiden: Brill, 2012).

Anand, Ram P. 'The Influence of History on the Literature of International Law', in *The Structure and Process of International Law*, eds. Ronald Macdonald and Douglas Johnston (Leiden: Martinus Nijhoff, 1983), 341–380.

AOSIS Publishing. 'Transformation in Higher Education', available at: https://thejournal.org.za/index.php/thejournal/article/%20view/9%20/31 (last accessed on 16 December 2018).

Barnett, Michael and Sikkink, Kathryn. *From International Relations to Global Society* (2011), available at: http://www.oxfordhandbooks.com/view/10.1093/oxfordhb/9780199604456.001.0001/oxfordhb-9780199604456-e-035?print=pdf (last accessed on 2 February 2019).

Casley-Hayford, Gus. *The Lost Kingdoms of Africa* (London: Bantam Press, 2012).

Cesaire, Aime. *Discourse on Colonialism* (New York: Monthly Review Press, 2000).

Chesterman, Simon. 'Asia's Ambivalence about International Law and Institutions: Past, Present and Futures'. *European Journal of International Law* 24(4) (2017), 945–978.

Classical African Studies 'The Greatest Rulers of Africa', available at: http://www.aceschools.online/the-greatest-rulers-of-africa/ (last accessed on 19 December 2019).

Deng, Biong. 'The Evolving Concept and Institution of Sovereignty: Challenges and Opportunities'. AISA Policy Brief No. 28 (June 2010).

Dirar, Uoldelul. 'Colonialism and the Construction of National Identities: The Case of Eritrea'. *Journal of Eastern African Studies* 1(2) (2007), 256–276.

Du Preez, Petro, Simmonds, Shan and Chetty, John. 'Ethical Reflections on #MustFall Movements and Concomitant Gender-Based Violence'. *South African Journal of Higher Education* 31(6) (2017), 96–112.

Dube, Angelo and Nhlabatsi, Sibusiso. 'The King Can Do No Wrong: The Impact of *The Law Society of Swaziland v Simelane NO and Others* on Constitutionalism'. *African Human Rights Law Journal* 16 (2016), 265–282.

Dubow, Saul. 'Smuts, the United Nations and the Rhetoric of Race and Rights'. *Journal of Contemporary History* 43(1) (2008), 45–74.

Dugard, John, Max Du Plessis, Anton Katz and Arnold Pronto. *Dugard's International Law: A South African Perspective* (Cape Town: Juta, 4th ed. 2012).

Dugard, John. 'Cornelius van Bynkershoek: A Treatise of the Law of War'. *Leiden Journal of International Law* 23 (2010), 269–276.

Dussubieux, Laure. 'Glass Beads in Trans-Saharan Trade', in *Trade in the Ancient Sahara and Beyond*, eds. David Mattingly, Victoria Leitch and Chloe Duckworth (Cambridge: Cambridge University Press, 2017).

Eldredge, Elizabeth. *The Creation of a Zulu Kingdom, 1815–1828* (Cambridge: Cambridge University Press, 2014).

Elias, Taslim O. *Africa and the Development of International Law* (Leiden: Martinus Nijhoff, 1988).

Encyclopaedia Britannica. 'Thirty Years' War', available at: https://www.britannica.com/event/Thirty-Years-War (last accessed on 29 January 2019).

Falola, Toyin. *Key Events in African History: A Reference Guide* (London: Greenwood Press, 2002).

Fassbender, Bardo. 'Westphalia, Peace of (1648)', in *Max Planck Encyclopedia of Public International Law*, ed. Rüdiger Wolfrum (Oxford: Oxford University Press, 2011), available at: https://opil.ouplaw.com/view/10.1093/law:epil/9780199231690/law-9780199231690-e739?rskey=rwa8dV&result=1&prd=MPIL (last accessed on 10 May 2021).

Ferme, Mariane. 'Flexible Sovereignty? Paramount Chiefs, Deterritorialization and Political Mediations in Sierra Leone'. *Cambridge Journal of Anthropology* 23(2) (2003), 21–35.

Forji, Amin. 'International Law, the Civilizing Mission and the Ambivalence of Development in Africa: Conceptual Underpinnings'. *Journal of African and International Law* 6(1) (2013), 191–225.

Foster, John. 'The Evolution of International Law'. *Yale Law Journal* 18(3) (1909), 149–164.

Heleta, Savo 'Decolonising Knowledge in South Africa: Dismantling the "Pedagogy of Big Lies"'. *Ufahamu* 40(2) (2018), 47–65, 48.

Hernandez, Gleider. *International Law* (Oxford: Oxford University Press, 2019).

Heywood, Linda. *Njinga of Angola – Africa's Warrior Queen* (Cambridge: Harvard University Press, 2017).

Huffman, Thomas. 'Mapungubwe and the Origin of the Zimbabwe Culture'. *South African Archaeological Society Goodwin Series* 8 (2000), 14–29.

International Court of Justice. 'History', available at: https://www.icj-cij.org/en/history (last accessed on 14 February 2019).

Irwin, Graham. 'Precolonial African Diplomacy: The Example of Asante'. *International Journal of African Historical Studies* 8(1) (1975), 81–96.

Jaffe, Hosea. *A History of Africa* (London: Zedbooks, 1985).

Janis, Mark. *International Law* (Alphen aan den Rijn: Wolters Kluwer, 2016).

Klabbers, Jan. *International Law* (Cambridge: Cambridge University Press, 2013).

Kuper, Hilda. *An African Aristocracy: Rank Among the Swazi* (Abingdon: Routledge, 2018).

Levitt, Jeremy. 'African Origins of International Law: Myth or Reality?'. *UCLA Journal of International Law and Foreign Affairs* 113(19) (2015), 113–165.

Maddox, Gregory. 'Introduction', in *Conquest and Resistance to Colonialism in Africa*, ed. Maddox Gregory (Abingdon: Routledge, 2018), xi–xv.

Maluwa, Tiyanjana. 'International Law Making in Post-Colonial Africa: The Role of the Organisation of African Unity'. *Netherlands International Law Review* 49(1) (2002), 81–103.

Mattingly, David. 'The Garamantes and the Origins of Saharan Trade', in *Trade in the Ancient Sahara and Beyond*, eds. David Mattingly, Victoria Leitch and Chloe Duckworth (Cambridge: Cambridge University Press, 2017), 1–52.

Mgbeoji, Ikechi. 'The Civilised Self and the Barbaric Other: Imperial Delusions of Order and the Challenges of Human Security', in *International Law and the Third World*, eds. Richard Falk, Balakrishnan Rajagopal and Jacqueline Stevens (Abingdon: Routledge, 2008), 151–166.

MiaPkum, Peter. 'Precolonial African International Relations: Kanem-Bournu External Relations under the Reign of Mia Idris Alooma (1517–1603)'. Lecture presented at the M.Sc International Relations and Strategic Studies at the University of Jos, Nigeria, 2015), 16.

Newcomb, Steven. 'Theologian Francisco de Vitoria and International Law', available at: https://newsmaven.io/indiancountrytoday/archive/theologian-francisco-de-vitoria-and-international-law-blJ1kEeVhoK–vjumksAvFQ/ (last accessed on 1 December 2018).

Nöthling, F. Johan. *Pre-colonial Africa: Her Civilisations and Foreign Contacts* (Johannesburg: Southern Book Publishers, 1989).

O'Sullian, John. 'The Franco-Baoule War, 1891–1911: The Struggle against the French Conquest of Central Ivory Coast', in *Conquest and Resistance to Colonialism in Africa*, ed. Maddox Gregory (Abingdon: Routledge, 2018), 73–100.

Obichere, Boniface. 'African Critics of Victorian Imperialism: An Analysis', in *Conquest and Resistance to Colonialism in Africa*, ed. Maddox Gregory (Abingdon: Routledge, 2018), 31–50.

Obrégon, Liliana. 'The Civilized and the Uncivilized', in *The Oxford Handbook of the History of International Law*, eds. Bardo Fassbender and Anne Peters (Oxford: Oxford University Press, 2012), 917–940.

Orakhelashvili, Alexander. 'The Idea of European International Law'. *European Journal of International Law* 17(2) (2006), 315–347.

Rajagopal, Balakrishnan. 'International Law and Its Discontents: Rethinking the Global South'. *Proceedings of the Annual Meeting (American Society of International Law)* 106 (2012), 176–181.

Rekgotsofetse, Chikane. *Breaking a Rainbow, Building a Nation: The Politics Behind #MustFall Movements* (Johannesburg: Picador Africa, 2018).

Reynolds, John. 'Third World Approaches to International Law and the Ghosts of Apartheid', in *The Challenges of Human Rights: Past, Present and Future,* eds. David Keane and Yvonne McDermott (Edward Elgar: Cheltenham, 2012), 194–218.

Rodney, Walter. *How Europe Underdeveloped Africa* (London: Bogle-L'Ouverture Publications, 1973).

Shaw, Malcolm. *International Law* (Cambridge: Cambridge University Press, 2014).

Smith, Ken and Nöthling, F. Johan J. *North of the Limpopo: Africa since 1800* (Pretoria: University of South Africa, 1993).

Smith, Robert. 'Peace and Palaver: International Relations in Precolonial West Africa'. *Journal of African History* 14 (1973), 599–621.

South African History Online. 'Chumani Maxwele Ignites #RhodesMustFall Movement', available at: https://www.sahistory.org.za/dated-event/chumani-maxwele-ignites-rhodesmustfall-movement-uct (last accessed on 17 December 2018).

South African History Online. 'Student Protests in Democratic South Africa', available at: https://www.sahistory.org.za/article/student-protests-democratic-south-africa (last accessed on 16 December 2019).

Spies, Yolanda. 'Africa and the Idea of International Society'. *Journal of Contemporary History* 41(1) (2016), 38–56.

Strydom, Hennie. *International Law* (Cape Town: Oxford University Press, 2017).

UNESCO, 'Mapungubwe Cultural Landscape' 2019, available at https://whc.unesco.org/en/list/1099 (last accessed on 13 March 2019).

United Nations. 'Preceding Years – Forerunners of the United Nations', available at: http://www.un.org/en/sections/history/history-united-nations/ (last accessed on 20 January 2019).

Viljoen, Frans. 'Africa's Contribution to the Development of International Human Rights and Humanitarian Law'. *Africa Human Rights Law Journal* 1(1) (2001), 18–39.

Wallace-Bruce, Nii. 'Africa and International Law – The Emergence of Statehood'. *The Journal of Modern African Studies* 23(4) (1985), 575–602.

Yusuf, Abdulqawi. *Pan-Africanism and International Law* (Leiden: Martinus Nijhoff, 2014).

Zollmann, Jakob. 'African International Legal Histories – International Law in African: Perspectives and Possibilities'. *Leiden Journal of International* Law 31(4) (2018), 897–914.

CHAPTER 11

International Law and the European Court of Justice: The Politics of Avoiding History

Michel Erpelding

Abstract

Using the example of the European Court of Justice (ECJ), this chapter addresses the lack of historical contextualization which is prevalent in most general accounts of EU law and EU institutions. It argues that this narrative is the result of a tradition established by the founders of the discipline. For these early 'Euro-lawyers', distinguishing the practice of European institutions from earlier international institutions had important political implications. This was especially true with regard to the ECJ. By providing a selective and partly decontextualized narrative of this court and describing it as largely unprecedented in international law, early Euro-lawyers were not only able to bolster the 'supranational' and 'sui generis' character of their nascent discipline. They were also able to avoid comparisons between the ECJ and prior international courts and tribunals whose similarly wide-ranging powers and integrated nature had been considered as politically problematic.

Keywords

history of international adjudication – European Court of Justice – Mixed Arbitral Tribunals – Arbitral Tribunal for Upper Silesia – Mixed Courts of Egypt – Mixed Court of Tangier

The frequent use of history by international law scholars stands in contrast to its often cursory evocation by EU lawyers. Typically, international law manuals mention at least a few ancient arbitration awards and PCIJ decisions. They present the United Nations system as a response to the shortcomings of the League of Nations. Very often, they give an evolutionary account of the discipline's history since 1648, using an approach characterized

 | DOI:10.1163/9789004461802_013

as 'restatement-and-renewal'.[1] Conversely, EU law manuals tend to avoid elaborate historical references. Although they usually provide a short narrative of European integration since WWII, often revolving around Europe's 'founding fathers', they do not dwell on the antecedents of some of the legal techniques used by European institutions. In particular, they fall short of addressing the many continuities between the institutional heritage of the interwar period and the foundations of current EU law.[2] The failure to mention possible continuities between the institutions of the European Coal and Steel Community (ECSC) or the European Economic Community (EEC) and prior international institutions might partly be due to lack of archival materials.[3] However, the selective and partly decontextualized narrative of European integration prevalent in current EU law manuals can also be seen as merely following a tradition which dates back to the origins of the discipline. As a matter of

1 Berman, Nathaniel. 'In the Wake of Empire'. *American University International Law Review* 14(6) (1999), 1521–1554, 1523.

2 See, e.g., Blumann, Claude and Louis Dubouis. *Droit institutionnel de l'Union européenne* (Paris: LexisNexis, 5th ed. 2013), 2–3; Daniele, Luigi. *Diritto dell'Unione europea* (Milano: Giuffrè, 5th ed. 2014), 1–6; Haratsch, Andreas, Christian Koenig and Matthias Pechstein. *Europarecht* (Tübingen: Mohr Siebeck, 8th ed. 2012), 2–3; Isaac, Guy and Marc Blanquet. *Droit général de l'Union européenne* (Paris: Sirey, 10th ed. 2010), 2–3; Herdegen, Matthias. *Europarecht* (Munich: C.H. Beck, 19th ed. 2017) 54–55; Lenaerts, Koen and Piet Van Nuffel. *European Union Law* (London: Sweet & Maxwell, 3rd ed. 2011), 4–8; Mengozzi, Paolo. *Istituzioni di diritto comunitario e dell'Unione europea* (Padova: CEDAM, 2nd ed. 2006), 1–3; Rideau, Joël. *Droit institutionnel de l'Union européenne* (Paris: Librairie générale de droit et de jurisprudence, 6th ed. 2010), 32–33; Strozzi, Girolamo and Roberto Mastroianni. *Diritto dell'Unione europea: Parte istituzionale* (Torino: G. Giappichelli, 5th ed. 2011), 1–4; Tesauro, Giuseppe. *Diritto dell'Unione europea* (Padova: CEDAM, 7th ed. 2012), 4–8. Even handbooks comprising more elaborate chapters about the historical origins of European integration usually concentrate on the 'European idea', leaving aside concrete early experiments of international or regional integration. See, e.g., Chalmers, Damian, Gareth Davies and Giorgio Monti. *European Union Law: Text and Materials* (Cambridge: Cambridge University Press, 4th ed. 2019), 4–13; Van Raepenbusch, Sean. *Droit institutionnel de l'Union européenne* (Bruxelles: Larcier, 2nd ed. 2016), 11–16; Walker, Neil. 'The Philosophy of European Union Law', in *The Oxford Handbook of European Union Law*, eds. Anthony Arnull and Damian Chalmers (Oxford: Oxford University Press, 2015), 3–27.

3 For instance, the discussions around the Art. 41 ECSC preliminary reference procedure remain obscure, Boerger-De Smedt, Anne. 'La Cour de Justice dans les négociations du traité de Paris Instituant la CECA'. *Journal of European Integration History* 14(2) (2008), 30. The EEC Treaty's *travaux préparatoires* on the ECJ are similarly fragmentary: Pescatore, Pierre. 'Les travaux du "groupe juridique" dans la négociation des traités de Rome'. *Studia diplomatica* 24(1–4) (1981), 167.

fact, the very first EEC law manual,[4] Nicola Catalano's 1962 *Manuel de droit des Communautés européennes*, was just as selective in this regard.[5]

This might seem surprising at first. Like nearly all other members of the small circle of practitioners and scholars who created and promoted 'Community law' or 'European law' as an autonomous legal discipline between the 1950s and the mid-1960s,[6] thus forming the first generation of 'Euro-lawyers',[7] Nicola Catalano had been trained and socialized as a legal professional during the interwar period.[8] However, the tendency of early Euro-lawyers not to emphasize the continuities with the numerous international institutions of that period becomes less startling if one takes into account their will to establish the new concept of 'supranationalism'. This term, which the creators of the ECSC understood as a compromise between full federal integration and international cooperation,[9] accounted for the fact that member states had transferred sovereign powers to the Community and that the latter's institutions could enter into direct relations with private individuals and legal persons.[10]

4 Bailleux, Julie. *Penser l'Europe par le droit: L'invention du droit communautaire en France* (Paris: Dalloz, 2014), 296.

5 In his only paragraph on the historical precedents of the 'European idea', Catalano does not deny continuities with interwar efforts at European unification, but focusses entirely on individuals, mentioning the 'idealist' attempt to establish the United States of Europe made by 'prominent men, like Briand in France and Einaudi in Italy'. According to Catalano, the post-WWII process of European integration was a more 'realist' and 'cautious' continuation of these efforts by 'the most prominent and perspicacious politicians of our time': Adenauer (Germany), Spaak (Belgium), Schuman and Monnet (France), Bech (Luxembourg), de Gasperi and Sforza (Italy), Catalano, Nicola. *Manuel de droit des Communautés européennes* (Paris: Dalloz/Sirey, 1962), 8.

6 Bailleux, *Penser l'Europe* 2014 (n. 4) 9–10, 13–15.

7 Antoine Vauchez uses the term 'Euro-lawyer' to describe the legal professionals who actively contributed to European integration-through-law, which resulted in 'one unique transnational polity that constitutes a relatively stable order of practice and meaning', Vauchez, Antoine. *Brokering Europe: Euro-Lawyers and the Making of a Transnational Polity* (Cambridge: Cambridge University Press, 2015), 5.

8 Apart from Catalano, the most dynamic members of this group included Michel Gaudet (1915–2003), Maurice Lagrange (1900–1986), Robert Lecourt (1908–2004), Carl Friedrich Ophüls (1895–1970) and Pierre Pescatore (1919–2010). Ibid.

9 For Robert Schuman, 'the supranational is halfway between, one the one hand, international individualism which holds national sovereignty to be intangible and accepts only contractual, occasional and revocable limitations to it; on the other hand, the federalism of states that subject themselves to a super-state that enjoys its own territorial sovereignty'. Schuman, Robert. 'Préface', in *La Communauté européenne du charbon et de l'Acier*, ed. Paul Reuter (Paris: Librairie générale de droit et de jurisprudence, 1953), 7 (author's translation).

10 Ophüls, Carl F. 'Juristische Grundgedanken des Schumanplans'. *Neue Juristische Wochenschrift* 4(8) (1951), 289–292, 289; Reuter, Paul. 'Le Plan Schuman'. *Recueil des cours de l'académie de droit international de La Haye* 81 (1952), 523–634, 543–550.

From this, lawyers associated with the drafting of the Schuman-Plan such as Carl Friedrich Ophüls and Paul Reuter deduced that the relations between the Community and its member states had become partly federalized and were therefore subject to a specific form of public law distinct from international law.[11] After the failure of the European Defense Community (EDC) in 1954, Michel Gaudet, head of the ECSC High Authority's legal department, realized that the very idea of a specific Community law could be used to prevent the European integration process from reverting to classic international cooperation. With the support of the High Authority, the supranational and 'sui generis' character of Community law now became the rallying cry of the still nascent community of Euro-lawyers, who tried to have these features recognized by established international legal doctrine. However, during a congress organized at Stresa in 1957, it became clear that a majority of international lawyers were unwilling to heed this call.[12] The following year, the French Advocate General at the ECJ Maurice Lagrange concluded that a major doctrinal schism had taken place between the 'internationalists' and the 'supranationalists',[13] thereby heralding the birth of EC law as a new legal discipline whose representatives would eventually coalesce around the International Federation of European Law (FIDE) founded in October 1961.[14]

Apart from their doctrinal opposition with the 'internationalists', early Euro-lawyers had also more pragmatic incentives not to dwell on past international legal 'experiments'. Following WWII, the failure of interwar 'peace through law' schemes had partly discredited international law as a political tool. In this context, choosing 'supranationalism' over 'internationalism' was also a way for Euro-lawyers to demonstrate the dynamic character of the new European institutions, as opposed to the outdated and ineffective idealism of

11 Reuter noted that 'everything is as if, in regard to coal and steel, the six states had established, at least partially, a federal state; within the limitations of the Treaty, coal and steel have become "federal matters"'. Ibid., 550 (author's translation).

12 Bailleux, *Penser l'Europe* 2014 (n. 4), 172–220; see also Bailleux, Julie. 'How Europe became Law: The First International Academic Congress of the ECSC'. *Revue française de science politique* 60(2) (2010), 295–318.

13 Lagrange, Maurice. 'L'ordre juridique de la C.E.C.A. vu à travers la jurisprudence de sa cour de justice'. *Revue du droit public et de la science politique en France et à l'étranger* 64(5) (1958), 841–865, 841–842.

14 Bailleux, *Penser l'Europe* 2014 (n. 4) 213, 278–283. The founding members of FIDE included several members of the Luxembourg court (Nicola Catalano, Andreas Donner, Maurice Lagrange, Robert Lecourt, Riccardo Monaco, Massimo Pilotti, Karl Roemer, Otto Riese). They also included Carl-Friedrich Ophüls and Pierre Pescatore, but not Paul Reuter, who had abstained from supporting the autonomy of European law from international law at Stresa in 1957. Ibid., 209–210, 280–281.

the League of Nations.[15] Adopting a forward-looking approach was also more likely to foster a 'transnational esprit de corps'[16] within these institutions. Having been created in a post-conflict situation, the ECSC and the EEC brought together individuals with radically different backgrounds. This was especially true of the Court of Justice of the ECSC, desribed by the historian Vera Fritz as '*une drôle de Cour*'. As a matter of fact, the Luxembourg Court in its original composition comprised one former NSDAP-member (Otto Riese), one former deputy secretary-general of the League of Nations who had actively supported Italy's invasion of Ethiopia (Massimo Pilotti), one author and supervisor of Vichy France's anti-Jewish laws (Maurice Lagrange), one victim of these very laws (Jacques Rueff), one former defence counsel for Nazi war criminals (Karl Roemer), one former Nazi hunter (Charles-Léon Hammes), and one former trade unionist who had gone into hiding from the Nazi occupier (Petrus Serrarens).[17] This situation did not fundamentally change after the establishment of the EEC Court in 1958.[18] In these circumstances, frequent invocations of institutions created as part of the Treaty of Versailles or the League of Nations would hardly have bolstered unity within the ECSC and the EEC.

The avoidance of historical contextualization and the insistance on 'sui generis' qualifications also applied to early descriptions of the ECJ. Initially, the surpranationalists had placed more hopes in the High Authority than into the latter, which, despite its large procedural avenues,[19] had been conceived

15 Ibid., 197–198.

16 Vauchez, *Brokering Europe* 2015 (n. 7), 151.

17 Fritz, Vera. *Juges et Avocats Généraux de la Cour de Justice de l'Union européenne (1952–1972): Une approche biographique de l'histoire d'une révolution juridique* (Frankfurt am Main: Vittorio Klostermann, 2018), 53–54.

18 Of the ECSC Court's nine original members, six stayed on as members of the EEC Court (Delvaux, Hammes, Riese, Rueff, and the Advocates General Lagrange and Roemer). When Rueff left the Court in 1962, he was replaced by Robert Lecourt, a former resistant. One year later, just after *Van Gend & Loos*, Riese was succeeded by Walter Strauss who, like Rueff, had been a victim of anti-Jewish legislation. Ibid., 64–66.

19 For instance, in addition to actions between member states or between member states and the institutions, the Court could examine claims by companies and associations of companies for the annulment of certain High Authority measures affecting them (Art. 33 ECSC) and appeals on penalties imposed by the High Authority (Art. 36 ECSC). It could also grant compensation for wrongful acts by the Community or its agents (Art. 40 ECSC). Moreover, it had sole jurisdiction to give preliminary rulings on the validity of acts of the High Authority and of the Council where such validity was in issue before national courts (Art. 41 ECSC). Its decisions were immediately enforceable within all member states (Art. 44 and 92 ECSC).

as a check on the former.[20] As a matter of fact, before the creation of the EEC, the Court had remained rather cautious in its decisions. Although the High Authority's legal service had encouraged it to embrace a teleological and constitutional interpretation of the ECSC Treaty,[21] it had only rarely done so.[22] Euro-lawyers became more strategically interested in the Court after fierce public debates had led to the demise of EDC in 1954 and caused the member states to stop openly supporting supranational institutions. Under the 1957 Rome Treaty, the Council became the central institution, whereas the Community executive – not an 'Authority' but a 'Commission' – played a more subordinate role.[23] However, not only did the drafters of the Rome Treaty maintain the Court, they further judicialized it and endowed it with new powers, including the preliminary ruling procedure under Article 177 EEC.[24] After 1958, the ECJ replaced the High Authority as the symbol of supranationalism. Owing in part to sustained lobbying by the common legal service of the three Communities, it evolved into the most potent tool of European integration, with its preliminary rulings in *Van Gend & Loos* (1963)[25] and *Costa v. Enel* (1964)[26] eventually leading to the formal establishment of an autonomous European legal order and the redefinition of Europe as a 'community of law'.[27]

Most early commentators of the ECSC Court were reluctant to describe it as a new and more powerful type of international court that built on earlier precedents.[28] Instead, they insisted on the Court's double nature, establish-

20 Boerger-De Smedt, 'La Cour de Justice' 2008 (n. 3), 13; see also Boerger-De Smedt, Anne. 'Negotiating the Foundations of European Law, 1950–57: The Legal History of the Treaties of Paris and Rome'. *Contemporary European History* 21(3) (2012), 339–356, 341–343.

21 Rasmussen, Morten. 'Establishing a Constitutional Practice of European Law: The History of the Legal Service of the European Executive, 1952–65'. *Contemporary European History* 21(3) (2012), 375–397, 379–380; Bailleux, *Penser l'Europe* 2014 (n. 4), 232–233.

22 See notably Case 8/55, *Fédération charbonnière de Belgique v. High Authority*, 29 November 1956, ECR 245.

23 Pescatore, 'Les travaux du "groupe juridique"' 1981 (n. 3), 168–170.

24 Ibid., 172–174.

25 Case 26/62 NV, *Algemene Transport- en Expeditie Onderneming van Gend & Loos v. Netherlands Inland Revenue Administration*, 5 February 1963, ECR 1.

26 Case 6/64, *Costa v. ENEL*, 15 July 1964, ECR 585.

27 Bailleux, *Penser l'Europe par le droit* 2014 (n. 4), 221–223; Rasmussen, 'Constitutional Practice of European Law' 2012 (n. 21), 375–397; Vauchez, *Brokering Europe* 2015 (n. 7), 142.

28 One (slightly) contrasting example of a commentator with a more 'internationalist' perspective on the ECJ was Anik Antoine, legal adviser to the French diplomatic mission in the Saar. For Anik, the ECJ was 'proof that a real international court is possible'. While he also noted that the Court differed markedly from the ICJ and shared some features of the French *Conseil d'État*, this did not lead him to establish a strict separation between its 'international' and its 'administrative' functions, nor to call into question its international nature. For Antoine, the court was clearly 'an innovation, not a revolution', because it

ing a strict distinction between two types of disputes it dealt with. On the one hand, they described its jurisdiction over disputes between member states or between member states and Community institutions as specifically international. On the other hand, they labelled the annulment of High Authority decisions, appeals on sanctions, or claims for damages, as not international but administrative in nature, noting that it bore a domestic character.[29] Accounts made by Euro-lawyers on the ECJ following the adoption of the Rome Treaty further accentuated this tendency. For Nicola Catalano, the ECJ was only an international court when it resolved disputes between member states.[30] For Robert Lecourt, the French judge-rapporteur in *Costa v. Enel* and later a very activist president of the Court,[31] the ECJ could only partly be described as an international court. This was essentially due to the fact that it shared only very few features with the International Court of Justice (ICJ), notably its mission to resolve disputes between member states and the fact that its judges were appointed by the member states. However, the ECJ had also characteristics that distinguished it from the ICJ, and therefore from all other international courts: its members did not represent their member state or their legal system, it could examine claims by private persons, it could render preliminary rulings, and its decisions were immediately enforceable within the member states.[32] The Luxembourgish co-drafter of the EEC Treaty and later president of the ECJ Pierre Pescatore, whom Antoine Vauchez has decribed as the 'cosmopolitan Euro-lawyer *par excellence*',[33] used similar arguments when presenting the Court as marking the 'revelation' of 'unfettered' judicial power.[34] While Pescatore made brief references to international arbitration and the PCIJ, he immediately pointed out that the ECJ departed in three important

---

built on earlier institutions. However, the only international institution that he seems to have had in mind was the ICJ. Antoine, Anik. 'La Cour de Justice de la C.E.C.A. et la Cour Internationale de Justice'. *Revue générale de droit international public* 57(2) (1953), 210–261, 212, 259, 260 (author's translation).

29 Reuter, 'Le Plan Schuman' 1952 (n. 10), 549–550; Lagrange, Maurice. 'La Cour de Justice de la Communauté européenne du charbon et de l'acier'. *Revue du droit public et de la science politique en France et à l'étranger* 60(2) (1954), 419–420; Delvaux, Louis. *La Cour de Justice de la Communauté européenne du charbon et de l'acier* (Paris: R. Pichon & R. Durand-Auzias, 1956), 19–20.

30 Catalano, *Manuel* 1962 (n. 5), 73.

31 Vauchez, *Brokering Europe* 2015 (n. 7), 54–55.

32 Lecourt, Robert. 'Note sur la comparaison entre la Cour de Justice des Communautés européennes et les cours internationales', speech at the International Conference on World Peace through Law (Washington, DC, 14 Sep 1965), available at: http://aei.pitt.edu/13568 (last accessed on 1 April 2021).

33 Vauchez, *Brokering Europe* 2015 (n. 7), 78.

34 Pescatore, Pierre. *The Law of Integration: Emergence of a New Phenomenon in International Relations, Based on the Experience of the European Communities* (Leiden: Sijthoff, 1974), 83.

points from previous institutions. First, according to Pescatore the ECJ was the first court that had been really integrated within an international institutional system; second, the court's jurisdiction had been defined broadly enough to allow the judges to 'make law play its part fully'; third, its creators hade made sure to establish direct institutional ties between the ECJ and the domestic judiciaries.[35] More generally, Pescatore celebrated 'the deployment of the judicial element in the Community system' as a triumph of legal technique over politics, noting that '[it] is indeed the first time that, within the framework of a group of states, the judge has been allowed to play his part without having to submit to limitations arising either from the inadequacy of the substantive law, or from procedural deficiencies, or from political factors bringing into play the national interest of states.'[36]

The criteria used by early Euro-lawyers to distinguish the ECJ from previous international courts appear highly selective, as they relied on interstate arbitration, the PCIJ, and the ICJ as their only references. This was, of course, a very incomplete presentation, as international judicial or quasi-judicial bodies had proliferated during the interwar period, sometimes enjoying wide-ranging powers, jurisdiction over non-state actors, and integration with one or more domestic legal systems.[37] However, as this chapter will show, the architects of EC law had good reasons to ignore these precedents. By adopting a selective narrative, Euro-lawyers such as Maurice Lagrange, Michel Gaudet, Nicola Catalano, Robert Lecourt, and Pierre Pescatore were not only able to bolster their argument of the 'sui generis' nature of European institutions and their law. It also allowed them to avoid historical comparisons that might have fuelled criticism of the ECJ and its decisions.

Many early Euro-lawyers were indeed aware of prior models of international adjudication combining wide-ranging judicial powers and integration between the domestic and international spheres. Their awareness of these recent precedents was based either on their professional experience or on their training as lawyers during the interwar period. However, awareness of these earlier experiments also entailed knowledge of their limitations as meaningful

35 Ibid., 73.

36 Ibid., 84.

37 For a contemporary overview of the numerous international courts of the interwar period, see Schindler, Dietrich. 'Dritte Abteilung: Die Schiedsgerichtsbarkeit seit 1914: Entwicklung und heutiger Stand', in *Handbuch des Völkerrechts, Fünfter Band: Die internationale Streitbeilegung*, ed. Gustav Adolf Walz (Stuttgart: Kohlhammer, 1938). For a recent survey of early international tribunals with jurisdiction over individual claims, see Parlett, Kate. *The Individual in the International Legal System: Continuity and Change in International Law* (Cambridge: Cambridge University Press, 2011), 47–123.

precedents for postwar Europe. As a matter of fact, even during the interwar period, these precedents had been considered as highly problematic, as they seemed difficult to reconcile with the core international legal principles of sovereign equality and self-determination. Mentioning these precedents as direct or indirect sources of inspiration for the ECJ would likely have undermined rather than bolstered the legitimacy of the Court and the supranationalists' project of legal integration.

Many early Euro-lawyers were undoubtedly aware of three types of prior international institutions that shared some features usually described as distinctive of the ECJ. Just like the latter, all three had been established by a treaty, enjoyed wide-ranging powers, granted standing to private persons, and acted directly within one or several domestic legal systems. These courts, which I will successively address here, were the Mixed Arbitral Tribunals of the Peace Treaties of 1919–1923 (1), the Arbitral Tribunal for Upper Silesia established by the Geneva Convention of 15 May 1922 (2), and colonial-era mixed courts, especially the Mixed Courts of Egypt (1876–1949) and Tangier (1925–1952/56) (3).

1 International Adjudication of Private War Claims: The Mixed Arbitral Tribunals of the Post-WWI Peace Treaties (1919–1939)

The Mixed Arbitral Tribunals (MATs) created as a result of the Versailles and the other Peace Treaties of 1919–1923 were the only interwar courts that were mentioned during the Paris Treaty negotiations as an inspiration for the ECSC Court of Justice. During these negotiations, the German delegate Carl Friedrich Ophüls invoked the 'precedent' of individual complaints before the MATs to signal Germany's support for the right of private companies sanctioned by the High Authority to appeal these sanctions before the Court of Justice.[38] Ophüls had been commissary for the MATs at the German Ministry of Foreign Affairs in 1923–1930.[39] As such, he had an intimate knowledge of the procedural innovations introduced by the 40 MATs established on a bilateral basis between almost each former Allied and Central power after WWI.[40]

38 'Dokument 28: Kurzprotokoll des juristischen Sachverständigenausschusses, Sitzung vom 7. 8. 1950', in *Dokumente zum Europäischen Recht. Band 2: Justiz (bis 1957)*, eds. Reiner Schulze and Thomas Hoeren (Berlin: Springer, 2000) 45, 46.

39 Biographical note, Bundesarchiv, GND:11873637X [Ophüls, Carl Friedrich].

40 For contemporary publications, see, Niboyet, Jean Paulin. 'Les tribunaux arbitraux mixtes organisés en application des traités de paix'. *Bulletin de l'institut intermédiaire international* 7(2) (1922), 215–241; Schätzel, Walter. 'Die Gemischten Schiedsgerichte

He knew thus that the MATs did not only provide individuals with the possibility to file direct claims for compensation against a foreign state, but also that they enjoyed wide-ranging powers, such as the power to revise war-time judgments of domestic courts, suspend domestic laws, or even annul executive decisions.[41] Moreover, decisions rendered by the MATs were directly enforceable in the domestic legal systems of the signatories.[42] During the interwar period, the subject-matter jurisdiction of the MATs and their partial legal integration with their member states had led to debates about their more domestic or international nature.[43] The fact that the ECJ shared this distinctive feature with the MATs was clearly not lost on Paul Reuter. Remembering Anzilotti's characterization of the MATs as domestic courts common to several states,[44] he agreed that one might be tempted to analyze the ECJ in similar terms, especially from a dualist perspective, but did not further pursue this argument.[45]

However, despite their novel features, the discriminatory configuration of nearly all MATs[46] and the fragmentation of their case law had tarnished their image, as even those who viewed them in a positive light recognized.[47] After most of them had been closed down in the aftermath of the 1930 Young Plan, the MATs quickly fell into oblivion.[48] Even the proposal to establish a reformed (i.e. non-discriminatory and better organized) multilateral MAT on a regional basis and under the authority of an international organization did not

---

der Friedensverträge'. *Jahrbuch des öffentlichen Rechts der Gegenwart* 18 (1930), 378–454; Blühdorn, Rudolf. 'Le fonctionnement et la jurisprudence des tribunaux arbitraux mixtes créés par les traités de Paris'. *Recueil des cours de l'académie de droit international de La Haye* 41 (1932), 141–244; Carabiber, Charles. *Les juridictions internationales de droit privé* (Neuchâtel: La Baconnière, 1946). More recently, see, Zollmann, Jakob. 'Reparations, Claims for Damages, and the Delivery of Justice: Germany and the Mixed Arbitral Tribunals (1919–1933)', in *La grande guerre et son droit*, ed. David Deroussin (Paris: Librairie générale de droit et de jurisprudence, 2018), 379–394; Hess, Burkhard and Marta Requejo Isidro. 'International Adjudication of Private Rights: The Mixed Arbitral Tribunals in the Peace Treaties of 1919–1922', in *Peace through Law: The Versailles Peace Treaty and Dispute Settlement After World War I*, eds. Michel Erpelding, Burkhard Hess and Hélène Ruiz Fabri (Baden-Baden: Nomos, 2019), 239–276.

41 Hess/Requejo, 'International Adjudication 2019 (n. 40), 243–245.

42 Carabiber, *Les juridictions internationales* 1946 (n. 40), 200–201.

43 Hess/Requejo, 'International Adjudication 2019 (n. 40), 263–264.

44 Anzilotti, Dionisio. *Cours de droit international* (Paris: Sirey, 1929), 135.

45 Reuter, 'Le plan Schuman' 1952 (n. 10), 547–548.

46 Only before the MATs established by the 1923 Lausanne Treaty did the nationals of the vanquished state (i.e. Turkey) have the same standing as those of Allied states. Carabiber, *Les juridictions internationales* 1946 (n. 40), 192–194.

47 Ibid., 30, 53.

48 Hess/Requejo, 'International adjudication 2019 (n. 40), 275.

lead to any concrete realizations.[49] Perceived by many observers as inherently biased, the MATs were hardly suitable for integration within the official narrative of the ECJ. Many post-WWII publicists would likely have agreed with the statement made by the international legal scholar, war-time émigré and former member of the German–Italian MAT Ernst Rabel that 'International tribunals ought to be established totally different from the Mixed Arbitral Tribunals of the Versailles Treaty.'[50]

2 International Oversight of Provisional Regional Integration: The Arbitral Tribunal for Upper Silesia (1922–1937)

On 27 October 1951, Georges Kaeckenbeeck, a senior Belgian diplomat who had served as secretary-general of the International Authority of the Ruhr, spoke before the Grotius Society in London to comment on the recently adopted ECSC Treaty. Facing a rather sceptical audience, Kaeckenbeeck described the ECSC as 'a revolutionary scheme with an enormous political potential.'[51] In Kaeckenbeeck's eyes, the most extraordinary feature within that scheme was the Court of Justice: with its immediately executory judgments, it could be described as '[bearing] a federal character.'[52] Trained in Belgium and at Oxford, Kaeckenbeeck was one of Belgium's foremost international lawyers at the time, and also a seasoned international civil servant and judge.[53] It would not have come as a surprise to him that his government considered both him and the well-known publicist Charles de Visscher as candidates for the ECSC Court of Justice – although it ultimately decided to settle for the internationally rather inexperienced but politically well-connected Louis Delvaux.[54] Kaeckenbeeck would indeed have constituted a prime choice for this position, because his curriculum included something that both de Visscher and Delvaux lacked: during the interwar period, he had already worked as an international judge enforcing a 'revolutionary' treaty regime imagined by Jean Monnet.

49 For such a proposal, see, Carabiber, *Les juridictions internationales* 1946 (n. 40), 319–343.

50 Rabel, Ernst. 'International Tribunals for Private Matters'. *Arbitration Journal* 3(4) (1948), 209–212.

51 Kaeckenbeeck, Georges. 'The International Authority for the Ruhr and the Schuman Plan'. *Transactions of the Grotius Society* 37 (1951) 4–22, 5–6.

52 Ibid., 12–13.

53 Erpelding, Michel. 'Georges Kaeckenbeeck (1892–1973)'. 2018, available at: http://www.sfdi.org/internationalistes/kaeckenbeeck (last accessed on 14 September 2020).

54 Fritz, *Juges et Avocats Généraux* 2018 (n. 17), 82–83.

Pursuant to Article 88 Versailles Treaty, Upper Silesia, which before WWI had been Germany's second-largest industrial area, had been divided between Germany and the reborn Polish State following a plebiscite. The results of the referendum had suggested a border that cut in half the region's industrial core. As the Allies had been unable to solve this issue, they had sought the assistance of the new League of Nations. With the active participation of its deputy secretary-general Jean Monnet, the League had suggested to subject both parts of Upper Silesia to a treaty regime that would guarantee the continuation of its economic activities for a period of 15 years. With the active implication of Kaeckenbeeck, this suggestion eventually materialized in the Geneva Convention of 15 May 1922, a massive treaty of 606 articles.[55] In addition to a series of far-reaching bilateral obligations (e.g. protection of vested rights, right of residence of optants, freedom of movement of cross-border workers, freedom of movement of certain goods, extensive minority protection), the treaty also comprised two international monitoring bodies that would guarantee its implementation.[56] In addition to a Mixed Commission based in Katowice, whose President would play an important role in the protection of minority rights, including German Jews after 1933,[57] the Convention established an Arbitral Tribunal based in Beuthen (today Bytom). Kaeckenbeeck presided this Tribunal during the whole duration of its existence, namely between June 1922 and 15 July 1937.[58]

55 Convention between Germany and Poland Relating to Upper Silesia, signed 15 May 1922, entered into force 15 June 1922, 9 LNTS 465. For the full text of the Convention, see Kaeckenbeeck, Georges. *The International Experiment of Upper Silesia: A Study in the Working of the Upper Silesian Settlement, 1922–1937* (Oxford: Oxford University Press, 1942), 567–822.

56 Kaeckenbeeck's monograph remains the authoritative publication on this topic. See Kaeckenbeeck, *The International Experiment* 1942 (n. 55).

57 For contemporary publications, see Stone, Julius. *Regional Guarantees of Human Rights: A Study of Minorities Procedure in Upper Silesia* (London: Macmillan, 1933); Korowicz, Marc-Stanislas. *Une expérience de droit international: La protection des minorités de Haute-Silésie* (Paris: Pedone, 1946). More recently, see Erpelding, Michel. 'Mixed Commission for Upper Silesia', in *Max Planck Encyclopedia of International Procedural Law*, ed. Hélène Ruiz Fabri (Oxford: Oxford University Press, 2019).

58 Interwar publications this Tribunal include Kaeckenbeeck, Georges. 'The Character and Work of the Arbitral Tribunal of Upper Silesia'. *Transactions of the Grotius Society* 21 (1935), 27–44; Kaeckenbeeck, Georges. 'La protection internationale des droits acquis'. *Recueil des cours de l'académie de droit international de La Haye* 59 (1937), 317–419. More recently, see Conway, Gerard. 'The Arbitral Tribunal for Upper Silesia: An Early Success in International Adjudication', in *Experiments in International Adjudication: Historical Accounts*, eds. Ignacio de la Rasilla and Jorge E. Viñuales (Cambridge: Cambridge University Press, 2019), 98–124; Erpelding, Michel. 'Local International Adjudication: The Groundbreaking 'Experiment' of the Arbitral Tribunal for Upper Silesia', in *Peace through Law* 2019 (n. 40), 277–322.

Kaeckenbeeck's Tribunal had been planned as a more evolved MAT.[59] While its basic structure and its semi-permanent character closely mirrored the latter, it comprised several pioneering procedural tools. Its jurisdiction covered matters that could be labelled as 'administrative' within the meaning later used to describe the ECJ's jurisdiction over Community acts. For instance, individuals and companies could sue the States Parties (including their own state) before the Arbitral Tribunal for compensation as a result of the infringement of vested rights.[60] In addition, the Tribunal could review the decisions of national authorities regarding the nationality of individuals[61] or their right to free movement between both parts of Upper Silesia.[62] More importantly, the Tribunal had been endowed with the capacity to provide authoritative interpretations of the Geneva Convention in order to guarantee its harmonious implementation. This capacity manifested itself in two ways. First, once the Tribunal decided to publish one of its decisions, the legal principles proclaimed in that decision were not only binding upon the parties in the case at hand, but became the generally applicable law of the land in both parts of Upper Silesia.[63] Second, parties before a domestic court deciding on a case whose outcome depended on the interpretation of a provision of the Geneva Convention could ask that court to refer this question to the Tribunal in order to obtain an authoritative interpretation. This procedure, known as 'evocation', could be triggered at the request of one of the parties in a dispute.[64] Its resemblance with the preliminary question procedure later bestowed upon the ECJ by Article 177 EEC[65] (which had already been preceded by the less extensive Article 41 ECSC)[66] did not escape the Belgian international lawyer Henri Rolin,

59 Erpelding, 'Local International Adjudication' 2019 (n. 58), 289.

60 Art. 5 Geneva Convention. The Arbitral Tribunal expressly confirmed its jurisdiction over claims by private persons against their own state in: Case No. 1, C 7/27, *Steiner & Groß v. Poland*, 30 March 1928, *Amtliche Sammlung von Entscheidungen des Schiedsgerichts für Oberschlesien* 1 (1929) 8–10.

61 Arts. 58–62 Geneva Convention.

62 Arts. 296–300 Geneva Convention.

63 Art. 592 Geneva Convention.

64 Art. 588 Geneva Convention.

65 For a comparison, see Montoro, Fernando Irurzun. '¿La cuestión de interpretación ante el Tribunal arbitral de la Alta Silesia (1922–1937) como antecedente de la cuestión prejudicial europea?'. *Revista Española de Derecho Europeo* 63 (2017), 13–45.

66 Although preliminary references under Art. 41 ECSC were restricted to the validity of Acts of the High Authority, it is likely that the drafters of this provision understood it as conferring a power of authoritative interpretation upon the Court of Justice. Boerger-De Smedt, 'La cour de justice' 2008 (n. 3), 29.

who was clearly astonished that this important precedent had vanished from the collective memories of his contemporaries.[67]

It seems hardly surprising that Rolin, who had been a strong supporter of the League of Nations and always remained sceptical of supranationalism, would extol the precedent of the Tribunal presided by his former colleague Georges Kaeckenbeeck.[68] Conversely, is also clear that this precedent was hardly a good fit for the 'dynamic' narrative of the first Euro-lawyers. Although Jean Monnet had expressly mentioned Kaeckenbeeck's Tribunal as a model for the ECSC Court in exchanges with British diplomats in May 1950[69] and would later also recall it in his memoirs,[70] lawyers that worked with him preferred resorting to other comparisons. When describing the ECJ's novel procedures regarding the annulment of Community measures or claims for damages by private persons, they would make references to the French *Conseil d'État*.[71] When explaining its power to render authoritative interpretations of Community law, they would refer to the practice of domestic constitutional or supreme courts.[72] Apart from strengthening the supranational and hence sui generis

---

67 Rolin, Henri. 'Le contrôle international des juridictions nationales'. *Revue belge de droit international* 4(1) (1968), 165.

68 Salmon, Jean. 'Henri Rolin (1891–1973)', available at: http://www.sfdi.org/internationalistes/rolin (last accessed on 14 September 2020).

69 Monnet to Plowden, 25 May 1950, in *Documents on British Policy Overseas* (London: Her Majesty's Stationery Office, 1986), ser. 2, vol. 1, 94–96.

70 Monnet, Jean. *Mémoires* (Paris: Fayard, 1976), 102–106.

71 According to Maurice Lagrange, it was 'quite apparent that the judicial system set up under the Treaty draws directly on French administrative law. That was possible because, to some degree at least, the legal systems of the other Member States were familiar with it. This has also, with all due modesty, to be seen as a tribute to the historical activity of the French Conseil d'État.' Lagrange, Maurice. 'The Court of Justice of the European Communities from the Schuman Plan to the European Union', in *Mélanges Fernand Dehousse*, vol. 2 (Paris/Bruxelles: Fernand Nathan/Labor, 1979), 127–135, transl. CVCE.EU by UNI.LU, available at: http://www.cvce.eu (last accessed on 14 September 2020); see also Catalano, *Manuel* 1962 (n. 5), 66–68, 71. However, while Lagrange and French administrative law did indeed play a central role in shaping the ECSC Court, they do not account for all of its features. Boerger-De Smedt, 'La Cour de Justice' 2008 (n. 3), 24, see also Boerger-De Smedt, 'Negotiating the Foundations' 2012 (n. 20), 346.

72 For Nicola Catalano, owing to its wide-ranging 'federal' powers, the ECJ was best compared to the Constitutional Courts of Germany and Italy, see Catalano, *Manuel* 1962 (n. 5), 74–80. Robert Lecourt presented the ECJ less as an international court than as '*une Cour de justice suprême interne à un ensemble multinational*'. Lecourt, 'Note' 1965 (n. 32). Lagrange made references to the German and Italian Constitutional Courts, as well as to the United States Supreme Court, see Lagrange, Maurice. 'The Court of Justice as a Factor in European Integration'. *American Journal of Comparative Law* 15(4) (1967), 709–725, 711, 717. In a later publication specifically dedicated to Art. 177 EC, Pescatore noted that the historical origins were to be found in domestic law, especially constitutional law. Pescatore,

character of Community law, these references to the highest judiciary bodies of western democracies were politically much less problematic than the Upper Silesian precedent. Not unlike the Versailles Treaty, the Geneva Convention had not been freely negotiated by Germany and Poland, but had been more or less forced upon them by the Allies. As a result, neither party had ever fully embraced it, let alone suggested to make it permanent. Despite some positive effects, both States openly expressed their relief when it ended in 1937.[73]

3 International Judges as Guardians of Imperial Economic Freedoms: The Mixed Courts of Egypt (1876–1949) and Tangier (1925–1952/56)

Recent research suggests that colonial practices had a major impact on the law of international organizations.[74] Similar conclusions might also be drawn with regard to the ECJ. As a matter of fact, well before the ECJ's seminal rulings at the beginning of the 1960s, international judges had already used comparable techniques to protect treaty-based economic freedoms of Europeans. Between the late 19th century and the middle of the 20th century, western states had signed, either with non-western states or on their behalf, a certain number of agreements regarding the creation of 'mixed' – or 'hybrid' – courts as an alternative for consular courts. Since these colonial-era mixed courts were created within the legal system of the non-western country, they were not international courts in the classical sense. However, their international composition (which could or could not include 'native' judges) and their treaty-based origins also distinguished them from ordinary domestic courts.[75] Like other international bodies created within a colonial or semi-colonial context, they could be described, following an analysis by Paul Reuter, as a particular form of (unequal) international integration.[76]

Pierre. *References for Preliminary Rulings under Article 177 of the EEC Treaty and Cooperation between the Court and National Courts* (Luxembourg: Office for Official Publications of the European Communities, 1986), 7.

73 Erpelding, 'Local International Adjudication' 2019 (n. 58), 282–283, 310–313, 320–321.

74 See, in particular, Klabbers, Jan. 'The Emergence of Functionalism in International Institutional Law: Colonial Inspirations'. *European Journal of International Law* 25(3) (2014), 645–675.

75 Such mixed courts could be found in various locations, notably Egypt, the International Zone of Tangier, Chinese treaty ports, Siam, Ethiopia, the A Mandates, Indochina, and the New Hebrides.

76 Reuter, Paul. *Institutions internationales* (Paris: Presses Universitaires de France, 1955), 250.

Two colonial-era mixed courts seem particular likely to have had an impact upon the creators of the ECJ and its first members, namely the Mixed Courts of Egypt (1876–1949)[77] and the Mixed Court of Tangier (1925–1952/56).[78] Both had been widely discussed in the international legal literature.[79] Moreover, some of the ECJ's creators and early members had been in close contact with them. Thus, Nicola Catalano had occupied the strategic post of legal counsel to the International Zone of Tangier in 1951–1953. During his mandate, the local Mixed Court was transformed into the 'International Jurisdiction of Tangier'. Similarly, already in 1929, the future first President of the ECJ, Massimo Pilotti, had participated in efforts to reform the statute of the Tangier Mixed Court.[80] Another Italian judge appointed in 1958, Rino Rossi, had been a judge at the Italian capitulatory tribunal in Cairo between 1936 and 1940.[81] During this period, pursuant to the 1937 Montreux Convention,[82] the capitulatory tribunals were stripped of most of their prerogatives in favour of the Mixed Courts of Egypt.[83] Finally, in 1945–1948, one of the most influential Euro-lawyers, Michel Gaudet,

---

77 See, in particular, Yeates Brinton, Jasper. *The Mixed Courts of Egypt* (New Haven: Yale University Press, 2nd ed. 1968); Hoyle, Mark S. W. *Mixed Courts of Egypt* (London: Graham & Trotman, 1991).

78 See, in particular, Nefussy, Raymond. *Le Tribunal mixte de Tanger* (Lyon: Éditions de l'A.G.E.L., 1949), Tamburini, Francesco. 'Il "Tribunale Misto" di Tangeri (1925–1952): Balance of Power, Diritto e Mentalità Coloniale'. *Jura Gentium* 4(1) (2007), 55–86. Ceballos, Leopoldo. *Historia de Tánger: Memoria de la ciudad internacional* (Córdoba: Almuzara, 2nd ed. 2013), 115–122.

79 On the Mixed Courts of Egypt, see *les juridictions mixtes d'Égypte 1876–1926: livre d'or édité sous le patronage du conseil de l'ordre des avocats à l'occasion de cinquantenaire des tribunaux de la réforme, par le "Journal des tribunaux mixtes"* (Alexandria: Journal des Tribunaux Mixtes, 1926); Yeates Brinton, Jasper. 'The Mixed Courts of Egypt'. *American Journal of International Law* 20(4) (1926), 670–688; Heyligers, Théodore. 'L'organisation des tribunaux mixtes d'Égypte'. *Recueil des cours de l'académie de droit international de La Haye* 17 (1927), 1–107; Yeates Brinton, Jasper. *The Mixed Courts of Egypt* (New Haven: Yale University Press, 1930). On the Mixed Court of Tangier, see Rouard de Card, Edgard. *Le statut de Tanger d'après la convention du 18 décembre 1923* (Paris: Pedone and Gamber, 1925), 77–87; Weir, Brown R. 'Procedure under the Tangier Convention'. *Journal of Comparative Legislation and International Law* 7(1) (1925), 86–90; Fitzgerald, Robert G. 'L'organisation judiciaire de Tanger sous le régime international'. *Revue générale de droit international public* 34 (1927), 145–170; Hudson, Manley O. 'The International Mixed Court of Tangier'. *American Journal of International Law* 21(2) (1927), 231–237.

80 Tamburini, 'Il "Tribunale misto"' 2017 (n. 78), 67.

81 Fritz, *Juges et Avocats Généraux* 2018 (n. 17), 300.

82 Convention Regarding the Abolition of the Capitulations in Egypt and Rules Concerning Judicial Organisation Annexed Thereto, 8 May 1937, 182 LONTS 37.

83 On this 'transition period', see Brinton, *The Mixed Courts of Egypt* 1968 (n. 77), 200–207; Hoyle, *Mixed Courts of Egypt* 1991 (n. 77), 151–180.

had acted as legal counsel for the French Protectorate in Morocco, which exercised some oversight over the International Zone of Tangier. In Gaudet's own recollection, this episode 'very much shaped him as a person and a jurist'[84] and seems indeed to have influenced his understanding of European integration.[85]

Both the Mixed Courts of Egypt and Tangier shared features that Euro-lawyers would later present as unique to the ECJ. Even more than the post-WWI MATs and the Arbitral Tribunal for Upper Silesia, they were both international and fully integrated within the domestic legal system of their host countries. Thus, the 1875 Statute of the Mixed Courts of Egypt, although formally promulgated within the Egyptian legal system, had been adopted after intense international negotiations, acceded to by fourteen capitulatory powers, and published in the main treaty collections of that time.[86] Accordingly, it was

84 Boerger, Anne and Morten Rasmussen. 'The Making of European Law: Exploring the Life and Work of Michel Gaudet'. *American Journal of Legal History* 57(1) (2017), 51–82, 57.

85 Gauded used quite similar terms to describe the legal 'technique' (*'formule'*) of the Protectorate and those used as part of European integration. Gaudet described the French protectorate in Morocco as different from the unilateral 'integration techniques' (*'formules d'intégration'*) used by France in Algeria and its African colonies of French West and Equatorial Africa. He characterized it as a 'technique whose aim was not to transpose French institutions and techniques, but to find a way of cooperating between the institutions and techniques (and, above all, the economic development) of both France and other countries' (*'formule dans laquelle on n'entendait pas transposer des formules françaises, mais essayer de trouver une modalité de coopération entre les formules* (*et surtout le développement de l'économie*) *de la France et celles de pays différents*'). Anne Rasmussen, interview with Michel Gaudet (Paris, 23 September 1991, Interview No. 1), Interview No. 2, CD 1, Track 3. In Gaudet's view, the protectorate was essentially a form of intercultural cooperation: he characterized it as '*une forme extrêmement intéressante pour examiner comment on pouvait faire vivre ensemble des types de sociétés et de pouvoirs différents.*' Ibid. In other words, it was a form of 'institutional cooperation' ('*coopération institutionnelle*') whose mission was 'to reach some compromise or, more precisely, some common creation' ('*d'arriver à une espèce de compromis, plus exactement de création commune*'). Ibid., Track 6. Gaudet seems to have thought of this common French-Moroccan creation in quasi-federal terms, because he characterized Morocco's independence in 1956 as 'complete political secession' ('*sécession politique complète*'). Ibid., Track 7. Similarly, Gaudet described European integration (or, more accurately, '*la construction européenne*', since in his view the term '*intégration*' was reminiscent of assimilationist French colonial policies), as '*une entreprise fondée sur l'interculturalité*'. Interview No. 4, CD 1, Track 12. Therefore, it would have to rely on the harmonization, not the uniformization, of national rules. Ibid., Track 13.

86 Règlement d'organisation judiciaire pour les procés mixtes en égypte, 16 September 1875. Ibid., 680–690. For an English translation, see Brinton, *The Mixed Courts of Egypt* 1968 (n. 77), 232–241.

regarded by the Egyptian authorities themselves as an international treaty.[87] In the case of Tangier, the situation was even more straightforward. Although the Court's statute took the form of a Sherifian dahir (decree),[88] it was ultimately based on Articles 12 and 48 of the 1923 Paris Convention which had been negotiated and signed between France, the United Kingdom, and Spain, without any Moroccan participation.[89] Moreover, although they formally rendered justice in the name of the local sovereign, the mixed courts had a predominantly international composition.[90] These factors led many, including some of their members, to consider them also as international institutions. This was well known with regard to the Mixed Courts of Egypt, whose exact nature was at times hotly debated.[91] During his farewell address delivered in Alexandria on 25 March 1925, Maurice Sheldon Amos, the British Judicial Adviser to the Egyptian government, stated that 'next to the Church, the Mixed Courts are the most successful international institution in history. Even the august institution known as the League of Nations could see in it a favourable auspice for its future.'[92] In a similar vein, Théodore Heyligers (1882–1951), who served as a Dutch judge on the Mixed Courts, portrayed both as 'sui generis national courts' and predecessors of the PCIJ.[93] His Belgian colleague Firmin Van den Bosch (1864–1949), who served as *Procureur général* of the Mixed Courts, even claimed that these Courts had inspired the MATs.[94]

87 'This statute must be regarded as rather of the nature of a treaty than as a law emanating solely from the will of the legislator.' Court of Appeals, Native Courts, 10 December 1901. Quoted in ibid., 22, n. 4.

88 'Dahir chérifien sur l'organisation d'une juridiction mixte à Tanger' (16 February 1924), in *Textes organiques et codes de la zone de Tanger*, vol. 2 (Rabat: Imprimerie Officielle du Protectorat, 1925), 65–82. Quoted by Tamburini, 'Il "tribunale misto"' 2017 (n. 78), 76.

89 Convention regarding the Organisation of the Statute of the Tangier Zone, 18 December 1923, 28 LONTS 541.

90 The Mixed Courts of Egypt originally comprised 32 members. Of the 11 members of the Court of Appeals, four were Egyptians and seven were foreigners. The three District Courts each comprised seven members (three Egyptians and four foreigners). In 1949, the total number of judges had grown to 70, with the proportion of Egyptian judges having slightly increased. Brinton, *The Mixed Courts of Egypt* 1968 (n. 77), 44–45. Before its transformation in 1952, the Mixed Court of Tangier was exclusively composed of foreigners. Tamburini, 'Il "Tribunale Misto"' 2017 (n. 78).

91 Nuzzo, Luigi. *Origini di una scienza: Diritto internazionale e colonialismo nel XIX secolo* (Frankfurt am Main: Vittorio Klostermann, 2012), 187–201.

92 *Les juridictions mixtes d'Égypte* 1926 (n. 79), 26, 115; Brinton, 'The Mixed Courts of Egypt' 1926 (n. 79), 670 (author's translation).

93 Heyligers, 'L'organisation des tribunaux mixtes d'Égypte' 1927 (n. 79), 46, 102.

94 Bosch, Firmin van den. *Vingt années d'Égypte* (Paris: Perrin, 1932), 139. Van den Bosch did not cite any evidence to back up this claim. However, there are indications that, owing to their qualifications as members of a Francophone legal elite, several members of the

The Mixed Courts of Egypt and Tangier also had wide-ranging powers. Although they could not annul government acts, they could award compensation to private individuals and companies for damages caused by the host state.[95] Similarly, while both Mixed Courts usually applied 'mixed law' (i.e. rules based on European, mostly French, law which had been specifically drafted for and by foreigners),[96] they were given wide discretion in summoning other sources of law, or changing existing ones. Thus, 'in case of silence, insufficiency, and obscurity of the law', the Mixed Courts of Egypt could 'follow the principles of natural law and equity.'[97] In addition to this broad power of interpretation, they had been formally endowed with legislative powers. Pursuant to a 1889 decree, the General Assembly of the Mixed Court of Appeals in Alexandria was given the power to participate in the creation of police regulations by checking whether they did not discriminate against foreigners and were in keeping with Egypt's international obligations.[98] In 1911, a law decided that the General Assembly of the Mixed Court of Appeals could be enlarged to form a Legislative Assembly which would have to give its consent to any changes in the mixed legislation.[99]

Both Courts also used a teleological interpretation of their Statutes to develop a constitutional doctrine. Thus, they recognized themselves the power to set aside domestic laws infringing upon economic liberties guaranteed by their constitutive treaties. In 1876, invoking the purpose of the treaty by which it had just been established, the Mixed Court of Appeals at Alexandria refused to apply a decree postponing the repayment of Khedive Isma'il's debts to a

---

MATs later joined the Mixed Courts of Egypt. For instance, Rudolf Blühdorn (1887–1967), who had worked as an Austrian government agent with the MATs, was appointed in 1934 judge at Port Fouad, a position from which he had to resign in 1935 for reasons of health. Brinton, *The Mixed Courts of Egypt* 1968 (n. 77), 205, note 5.

95 In this respect, they somewhat resembled present-day investor-state arbitral tribunals, although they were clearly more institutionalized and transparent than these tribunals. See Brinton, *The Mixed Courts of Egypt* 1968 (n. 77), 125–134; Nefussy, *Le Tribunal mixte de Tanger* 1949 (n. 78), 179–194.

96 The Mixed Codes of Egypt were drafted during the summer of 1872 by Paul Manoury (1824–1899), an Alexandria based French lawyer who had been secretary to the international commission that had discussed the creation of the Mixed Courts. Hoyle, *Mixed Courts of Egypt* 1991 (n. 77), 15–21. The Tangier Codes were drafted between April and November 1924 by a committee of three jurists: Robert Geoffrey Fitzgerald, Joaquim Lacambra, and Maurice Gentil. Nefussy, *Le Tribunal mixte de Tanger* 1949 (n. 78), 219–220.

97 Statute (n. 86), Title I, Article 34.

98 Decree conferring legislative powers on General Assembly, 31 January 1889. Reproduced in ibid., 242.

99 Law creating Legislative Assembly of Court of Appeals, 11 November 1911. Reproduced in ibid., 243.

foreign creditor.[100] After this precedent, which ultimately led to the Khedive's deposition in 1879,[101] it was understood that the Mixed Courts would refuse to apply any laws that they considered in violation of the economic rights granted to foreigners as part of the local capitulations regime.[102] The Mixed Court of Tangier established a similar precedent on the eve of WWII. In 1938, after the (non-elected) legislative assembly of the Zone had adopted a legislative act prohibiting the use or operation of radio transmitters on grounds of national security, private individuals who had infringed the law were prosecuted before the Mixed Court which acquitted them. In the eyes of the Court, the 1938 law was contrary to the principles of the Zone's constitutional treaties, especially Article 105 of the Act of Algeciras guaranteeing 'the principle of economic liberty without any inequality'.[103] Consequently, and based on the general configuration of the international regime under which it had been created, the Mixed Court considered that it had the right to set aside the unconstitutional law.[104]

---

100 According to the Mixed Court of Appeals, 'if the Mixed Courts of Egypt, which were created to render justice in accordance with the Laws agreed upon by the creators of this institution [i.e. Egypt and the capitulatory powers], were obliged to use their authority to assist in the implementation of government ordinances which, being in contradiction with said Laws, infringe upon the vested rights of foreigners, Art. 11 of the Judicial Charter would be dead-letter and the Courts' independence merely illusory'. *Cesare Carpi v. Daira Sania* (Mixed Court of Appeals, 3 May 1876). Reprinted in: *Department of State Arbitration Series* 4 (4) (1932), 236 (author's translation).

101 Hoyle, *Mixed Courts of Egypt* 1991 (n. 77), 32–35.

102 Brinton, *The Mixed Courts of Egypt* 1968 (n. 77), 131.

103 General Act of the Conference of Algeciras, 7 April 1906, 34 Stat. 2905.

104 The Mixed Court noted that no explicit provision was necessary for it to enjoy this power. Indeed, 'although such a reasoning might apply vis-à-vis certain national courts in countries traditionally infused with the old and jealously maintained principles of the separation of powers, the same cannot be said with regard to an international Tribunal which holds its jurisdictional powers not by virtue of an actual delegation of sovereignty by H. M. the Sultan, who had already renounced his jurisdiction over the persons now subject to the Mixed Court by virtue of the capitulations, but by virtue of a collective transmission made for the appropriate purposes by both H. M. the Sultan and, especially, the various Powers – i.e. an international group – which had enjoyed these powers individually; those principles [of the separation of powers] cannot be an absolute in Tangier, the latter being an international zone of an unprecedented nature, born to normal life in 1923, where none of the restrictive traditions shared in these matters by countries with a constitutional tradition have become a part of local usage and local Laws.' *Ministerio Público v. Joseph Aerts and Alberto Azerraf* (Mixed Court of Tangier, Appeals Section, 10 March 1939) (author's translation). The official Spanish version of this decision can be found in *Tanger: Tratados, Códigos, Leyes y Jurisprudencia de la Zona Internacional*, ed. Manuel Díaz Merry (Tánger: Distribuciones Iberica, 1950), 2380–2391. For a discussion and a French translation of this decision, see Ménard, Alphonse. *La radio-diffusion à Tanger* (Paris: Sirey, 1939); see also Nefussy, *Le Tribunal mixte de Tanger* 1949 (n. 78), 203–217.

4 Conclusion

Mid-20th century publicists were clearly aware that international judicial bodies such as the MATs, the Tribunal for Upper Silesia, and colonial-era mixed courts provided a legacy was both technically interesting and politically problematic. For instance, in 1943, Scelle noted that institutions such as the MATs and the Mixed Courts of Egypt, despite their innovative features, had to be considered as politically outdated, adding that the Egyptians perceived the abolition of the Mixed Courts decided by the 1937 Montreux Convention[105] as a sign of their 'emancipation'.[106] As long as most people in Europe sought their emancipation through self-determination within the nation-state, using these courts as precedents would hardly have strengthened the ECJ.

Acknowledgement

I would like to thank Morten Rasmussen and Jakob Zollmann for their helpful remarks.

Bibliography

Antoine, Anik. 'La Cour de Justice de la C.E.C.A. et la Cour Internationale de Justice'. *Revue générale de droit international public* 57(2) (1953), 210–261.

Anzilotti, Dionisio. *Cours de droit international*, (Paris: Sirey, 1929).

Bailleux, Julie. 'How Europe Became Law: The First International Academic Congress of the ECSC'. *Revue française de science politique* 60(2) (2010), 295–318.

Bailleux, Julie. *Penser l'Europe par le droit: L'intervention du droit communautaire en France* (Paris: Dalloz, 2014).

105 Although this Convention maintained the Mixed Courts for a transitional period of 12 years, it stripped them of their legislative powers and prohibited them from making judgments on the validity or application to foreigners of Egyptian laws and regulations, thus putting an end to the precedent set in 1876. Montreux Convention (n. 82).

106 Scelle, Georges. *Manuel élémentaire de droit international public* (Paris: Domat-Montchrestien, 1943), 516–518. Like other major French publicists of his time, Scelle had been in direct contact with the Egyptian legal community. In March 1926, at the request of his mentor Léon Duguit, who had accepted a temporary appointment as the Egyptian Law Faculty's first dean, Scelle had given lectures in international law to graduate students in Cairo. Duguit, Léon. *Leçons de droit public général faites à la Faculté de droit de l'Université égyptienne pendant les mois de janvier, février et mars 1926* (Paris: E. de Boccard, 1926), 18.

Berman, Nathaniel. 'In the Wake of Empire'. *American University International Law Review* 14(6) (1999), 1521–1554.

Blühdorn, Rudolf. 'Le fonctionnement et la jurisprudence des tribunaux arbitraux mixtes créés par les traités de Paris'. *Recueil des cours de l'académie de droit international de La Haye* 41 (1932), 141–244.

Blumann, Claude and Louis Dubouis. *Droit institutionnel de l'Union européenne* (Paris: LexisNexis, 5th ed. 2013).

Boerger-De Smedt, Anne. 'La Cour de Justice dans les négociations du traité de Paris Instituant la CECA'. *Journal of European Integration History* 14(2) (2008), 7–33.

Boerger-De Smedt, Anne. 'Negotiating the Foundations of European Law, 1950–57: The Legal History of the Treaties of Paris and Rome'. *Contemporary European History* 21(3) (2012), 339–356.

Boerger-De Smedt, Anne and Morten Rasmussen. 'The Making of European Law: Exploring the Life and Work of Michel Gaudet'. *American Journal of Legal History* 57(1) (2017), 51–82.

Bosch, Firmin van den. *Vingt années d'Égypte* (Paris: Perrin, 1932).

Brinton, Jasper Yeates. 'The Mixed Courts of Egypt'. *American Journal of International Law* 20(4) (1926), 670–688.

Brinton, Jasper Yeates. *The Mixed Courts of Egypt* (New Haven: Yale University Press, 1930).

Brinton, Jasper Yeates. *The Mixed Courts of Egypt* (New Haven: Yale University Press, 2nd ed., 1968).

Brown, R. Weir. 'Procedure Under the Tangier Convention'. *Journal of Comparative Legislation and International Law* 7(1) (1925), 86–90.

Carabiber, Charles. *Les jurisdictions internationales de droit privé* (Neuchâtel: La Baconnière, 1946).

Catalano, Nicola. *Manuel de droit des Communautés européennes* (Paris: Dalloz/Sirey, 1962).

Ceballos, Leopoldo. *Historia de Tánger: Memoria de la ciudad internacional* (Córdoba, Almuzara, 2nd ed. 2013).

Chalmers, Damian, Gareth Davies and Giorgio Monti. *European Union Law: Text and Materials* (Cambridge: Cambridge University Press, 4th ed. 2019).

Conway, Gerard. 'The Arbitral Tribunal for Upper Silesia: An Early Success in International Adjudication', in *Experiments in International Adjudication: Historical Accounts*, eds. Ignacio de la Rasilla and Jorge E. Viñuales (Cambridge: Cambridge University Press, 2019), 98–124.

Daniele, Luigi. *Diritto dell'Unione europea* (Milano: Giuffrè, 5th ed. 2014).

Delvaux, Louis. *La Cour de Justice de la Communauté européenne du charbon et de l'acier* (Paris: R. Pichon & R. Durand-Auzias, 1956).

Duguit, Léon. *Leçons de droit public général faites à la Faculté de droit de l'Université égyptienne pendant le mois de janvier, février et mars 1926* (Paris: E. de Boccard, 1926).

Erpelding, Michel. 'Georges Kaeckenbeeck (1892–1973), available at: http://www.sfdi.org/internationalistes/kaeckenbeeck (last accessed on 14 September 2020).

Erpelding, Michel. 'Mixed Commission for Upper Silesia', in *Max Planck Encyclopedia of International Procedural Law*, ed. Hélène Ruiz Fabri (Oxford: Oxford University Press, 2019).

Erpelding, Michel. 'Local International Adjudication: The Groundbreaking 'Experiment' of the Arbitral Tribunal for Upper Silesia', in *Peace through Law: The Versailles Peace Treaty and Dispute Settlement after World War I*, eds. Michel Erpelding, Burkhard Hess and Hélène Ruiz Fabri (Baden-Baden: Nomos, 2019), 277–322.

Fitzgerald, Robert Geoffrey. 'L'organisation judiciaire de tanger sous le régime international'. *Revue générale de droit international public* 34 (1927), 145–170.

Fritz, Vera. *Juges et Avocats Généraux de la Cour de Justice de l'Union Européenne (1952–1972): Une approche biographique de l'histoire d'une révolution juridique* (Frankfurt am Main: Vittorio Klostermann, 2018).

Haratsch, Andreas, Christian Koenig and Matthias Pechstein. *Europarecht* (Tübingen: Mohr Siebeck, 8th ed. 2012).

Herdegen, Matthias. *Europarecht* (Munich: C.H. Beck, 19th ed., 2017).

Hess, Burkhard and Marta Requejo Isidro. 'International Adjudication of Private Rights: The Mixed Arbitral Tribunals in the Peace Treaties of 1919–1922', in *Peace through Law: The Versailles Peace Treaty and Dispute Settlement after World War I*, eds. Michel Erpelding, Burkhard Hess and Hélène Ruiz Fabri (Baden-Baden: Nomos, 2019), 239–276.

Heyligers, Théodore. 'L'organisation des tribunaux mixtes d'Égypte'. *Recueil des cours de l'académie de droit international de La Haye* 17 (1927), 1–107.

Hoyle, Mark S. W. *Mixed Courts of Egypt* (London: Graham & Trotman, 1991).

Hudson, Manley O. 'The International Mixed Court of Tangier'. *American Journal of International Law* 21(2) (1927), 231–237.

Isaac, Guy and Marc Blanquet. *Droit général de l'Union européenne* (Paris: Sirey, 10th ed. 2010).

Kaeckenbeeck, Georges. 'The Character and Work of the Arbitral Tribunal of Upper Silesia'. *Transactions of the Grotius Society* 21 (1935), 27–44.

Kaeckenbeeck, Georges. 'La protecion internationale des droits acquis'. *Recueil des cours de l'académie de droit international de La Haye* 59 (1937), 317–419.

Kaeckenbeeck, Georges. *The International Experiment of Upper Silesia: A Study in the Working of the Upper Silesian Settlement, 1922–1937* (Oxford: Oxford University Press, 1942).

Kaeckenbeeck, Georges. 'The International Authority for the Ruhr and the Schuman Plan'. *Transactions of the Grotius Society* 37 (1951), 4–22.

Klabbers, Jan. 'The Emergence of Functionalism in International Institutional Law: Colonial Inspirations'. *European Journal of International Law* 25(3) (2014), 645–675.

Korowicz, Marc Stanislas. *Une expérience de droit international: La protection des minorités de Haute-Silésie* (Paris: Pedone, 1946).

Lagrange, Maurice. 'La Cour de Justice de la Communauté européenne du charbon et de l'acier'. *Revue du droit public et de la science politique en france et à l'étranger* 60(2) (1954), 417–435.

Lagrange, Maurice. 'L'ordre juridique de la C.E.C.A. vu à travers la jurisprudence de sa cour de justice'. *Revue du droit public et la science politique en France et à l'étranger* 64(5) (1958), 841–865.

Lagrange, Maurice. 'The Court of Justice as a Factor in European Integration'. *American Journal of Comparative Law* 15(4) (1967), 709–725.

Lagrange, Maurice. 'The Court of Justice of the European Communities from the Schuman Plan to the European Union', in *Mélanges Fernand Dehousse*, vol. 2 (Paris/Bruxelles: Fernand Nathan/Labor, 1979), 127–135.

Lecourt, Robert. 'Note sur la comparaison entre la cour de justice des communautés européennes et les cours internationales', speech at the International Conference on World Peace through Law (Washington, DC, 14 Sep 1965), available at: http://aei.pitt.edu/13568 (last accessed on 14 September 2020).

Lenaerts, Koen and Piet Van Nuffel. *European Union Law* (London: Sweet & Maxwell, 3rd ed., 2011).

Les juridictions mixtes d'Égypte 1876–1926: livre d'or édité sous le patronage du conseil de l'ordre des avocats à l'occasion du cinquantenaire des tribunaus de la réforme par le « Journal des tribunaux mixtes » (Alexandria: Journal des Tribunaux Mixtes, 1926).

Ménard, Alphonse. *La radio-diffusion à Tanger* (Paris: Sirey, 1939).

Mengozzi, Paolo. *Istituzioni di diritto Comunitario e dell'Unione europea* (Padova: CEDAM, 2nd ed 2006).

Monnet, Jean. *Mémoires* (Paris: Fayard, 1976).

Montoro, Fernando Irurzun. 'La cuestión de interpretación ante el Tribunal arbitral de la Alta Silesia (1922–1937) como antecedente de la cuestion prejudicial europea?'. *Revista Española de Derecho Europeo* 63 (2017), 13–45.

Nefussy, Raymond. *Le Tribunal mixte de Tanger* (Lyon: Éditions de l'A.G.E.L., 1949).

Niboyet, Jean Paulin. 'Les tribunaux arbitraux mixtes organisés en application des traités de paix'. *Bulletin de l'institut intermédiaire international* 7(2) (1922), 215–241.

Nuzzo, Luigi. *Origini di una scienza: Diritto internazionale e colonialismo nel XIX secolo* (Frankfurt am Main: Vittorio Klostermann, 2012).

Ophüls, Carl Friedrich. 'Juristische Grundgedanken des Schumanplans'. *Neue Juristische Wochenschrift* 4(8) (1951), 289–292.

Parlett, Kate. *The Individual in the International Legal System: Continuity and Change in International Law* (Cambridge: Cambridge University Press, 2011).

Pescatore, Pierre. *The Law of Integration: Emergence of a New Phenomenon in International Relations, Based on the Experience of the European Communities* (Leiden: Sijthoff, 1974).

Pescatore, Pierre. 'Les travaux du "groupe juridique" dans la négociation des traités de Rome'. *Studia diplomatica* 24(1–4) (1981), 159–178.

Pescatore, Pierre. *References for Preliminary Rulings under Article 177 of the EEC Treaty and Cooperation between the Court and National Courts* (Luxembourg: Office for Official Publications of the European Communities, 1986).

Rabel, Ernst. 'International Tribunals for Private Matters'. *Arbitration Journal* 3(4) (1948) 209–212.

Rasmussen, Morten. 'Establishing a Constitutional Practice of European Law: The History of the Legal Service of the European Executive, 1952–65'. *Contemporary European History* 21(3) (2012), 375–397.

Reuter, Paul. 'Le plan Schuman'. *Recueil des cours de l'académie de droit international de La Haye* 81 (1952), 523–634.

Reuter, Paul. *Institutions internationales* (Paris: Presses Universitaires de France, 1955).

Rideau, Joël. *Droit institutionnel de l'union européenne* (Paris: Librairie générale de droit et de jurisprudence, 6th ed. 2010).

Roelofsen, Cornelis G. 'International Courts and Tribunals', in *The Oxford Handbook of the History of International Law*, eds. Bardo Fassbender and Anne Peters (Oxford: Oxford University Press, 2012).

Rolin, Henri. 'Le contrôle international des juridictions nationales'. *Revue belge de droit international* 4(1) (1968), 160–206.

Rouard de Card, Edgard. *Le statut de Tanger d'après la convention du 18 décembre 1923* (Paris: Pedone and Gamber, 1925).

Salmon, Jean. 'Henri Rolin (1891–1973)', available at: http://www.sfdi.org/internationalistes/rolin (last accessed on 14 September 2020).

Scelle, Georges. *Manuel élémentaire de droit international public* (Paris: Domat-Montchrestien, 1943).

Schätzel, Walter. 'Die Gemischten Schiedsgerichte der Friedensverträge'. *Jahrbuch des öffentlichen Rechts der Gegenwart* 18 (1930), 378–454.

Schindler, Dietrich. 'Dritte Abteilung: Die Schiedsgerichtsbarkeit seit 1914: Entwicklung und heutiger Stand', in *Handbuch des Völkerrechts, Fünfter Band: Die internationale Streitbeilegung*, ed. Gustav Adolf Walz (Stuttgart: W. Kohlhammer, 1938).

Schuman, Robert. 'Préface', in *La Communauté européenne du charbon et de l'acier*, ed. Paul Reuter (Paris: Librairie générale de droit et de jursiprudence, 1953).

Stone, Julius. *Regional Guarantees of Human Rights: A Study of Minorities Procedure in Upper Silesia* (New York: Macmillan, 1933).

Strozzi, Girolamo and Roberto Mastroianni. *Diritto dell'Unione europea: Parte Istituzionale* (Torino: G. Giappichelli, 5th ed. 2011).

Tamburini, Francesco. 'Il "Tribunale Misto" di Tangeri (1925–1952): Balance of Power, Diritto e Mentalità Coloniale'. *Jura Gentium* 4(1) (2007), 55–86.

Tesauro, Giuseppe. *Diritto dell'Unione europea* (Padova: CEDAM, 7th ed. 2012).

Van Raepenbusch, Sean. *Droit institutionnel de l'Union européenne* (Bruxelles: Larcier, 2nd ed. 2016).

Vauchez, Antoine. *Brokering Europe: Euro-Lawyers and the Making of a Transnational Polity* (Cambridge: Cambridge University Press, 2015).

Walker, Neil. 'The Philosophy of European Union Law', in *The Oxford Handbook of European Union Law*, eds. Anthony Arnull and Damian Chalmers (Oxford: Oxford University Press, 2015), 3–27.

Zollmann, Jakob. 'Reparations, Claims for Damages, and the Delivery of Justice: Germany and the Mixed Arbitral Tribunals (1919–1933)', in *La grande guerre et son droit*, ed. David Deroussin (Paris: Librairie générale de droit et de jurisprudence, 2018), 379–394.

PART 4

The Looming of the Past over the 20th Century

CHAPTER 12

Civilisation, Protection, Restitution: A Critical History of International Cultural Heritage Law in the 19th and 20th Century

Sebastian M. Spitra

Abstract

This chapter provides a new narrative for the history of cultural heritage law and seeks to contribute to current legal debates about the restitution of cultural objects. The modern protection laws for cultural objects in domestic and international law evolved in the 19th and 20th century. The chapter makes three new arguments regarding the emergence of this legal regime. First, 'civilisation' was a main concept and colonialism an integral part of the international legal system during the evolution of the regime. The Eurocentric concept of civilisation has so far been an ignored catalyst for the international development of cultural heritage norms. Second, different states and actors used cultural heritage laws and their inherent connection to the concept of civilisation for different purposes. Third, the international legal system of cultural heritage partly still reflects its colonial roots. The current restitution discussions are an outcome of this ongoing problematic legal constellation.

Keywords

cultural heritage – colonialism – restitution – third world approaches to international law (TWAIL) – UNESCO – cultural property protection

1 Introduction: The Quest for a New Narrative

'Civilisation' was an integral and major concept of international law in the 19th and early 20th century.[1] It was an attribute taken from history and other disciplines to characterise entities of international law and determine their

1 Notions, such as 'civilisation', 'civilised', 'standard of civilisation' or the German 'Kultur', 'Kulturstaat', 'Kulturstandard', are used in this chapter solely analytical and not affirmatively.

membership to the international community.[2] Only civilised states that fulfilled the standard were allowed to be full members of the *family of nations*.[3] During this era, also modern protection laws for cultural objects in domestic and international law evolved.

The aim of this chapter is to provide a new narrative for the history of the protection of cultural heritage. Such critical historiography shall revise the inherent politics of the often repeated, traditionally Eurocentric progress narrative to unveil the unjust structures of the past and their traces up to the present. The continuing discussions about the restitution of cultural heritage that has been 'translocated'[4] during colonial times demand a fresh, critical and systemic inquiry into the broader history and historiography of this field.

The notions of 'protection', 'cultural heritage' or 'cultural property' itself are historical concepts and evolved in certain theoretical and political contexts.[5] However, the scope and limitation of this chapter do not allow capturing all subtleties and complexities of the colonial contexts. It is necessary to make use of representative examples and to simplify some arguments, but further references are included in the footnotes to flag important debates or problematic issues.

The new approach of this chapter is to examine the role of the standard of civilisation in international law for the development of cultural heritage protection laws. The text proceeds by first, arguing based on three examples from international law that the concept of civilisation played a crucial role in the formation of cultural heritage norms that has been neglected so far. Second, it discusses how various actors used cultural heritage laws in different ways and how these norms fulfilled different purposes within the legal discourse of civilisation. Last, the chapter argues that today's discussions on returning cultural objects are not new but rather a reinvigoration of the decolonisation

---

In the following, these notions will be reproduced without quotation marks for an easier reading.

2 An important work was Guizot, François. *Histoire générale de la civilisation en Europe* (Paris: Pichon et Didier, 1828); see also Steiger, Heinhard. 'Völkerrecht', in *Geschichtliche Grundbegriffe*, vol. 7, eds. Otto Brunner, Werner Conze and Reinhart Koselleck (Stuttgart: Klett-Cotta, 1992), 97–140.

3 Anghie, Antony. 'Finding the Peripheries: Sovereignty and Colonialism in Nineteenth-Century International Law'. *Harvard International Law Journal* 40(1) (1999), 1–80.

4 Savoy, Bénédicte. *Die Provenienz der Kultur. Von der Trauer des Verlusts zum universalen Menschheitserbe* (Berlin: Matthes & Seitz, 2018).

5 For this argument, see, e.g., Prott, Lyndel V. and Patrick J. O'Keefe. "Cultural Heritage' or 'Cultural Property'?'. *International Journal of Cultural Property* 1(2) (1992), 307–320; Spitra, Sebastian M. *Die Verwaltung von Kultur im Völkerrecht. Eine postkoloniale Geschichte* (Baden-Baden: Nomos, forthcoming 2021).

movement as seen in the restitution debates at the UN General Assembly in the 1970s, which had been stagnated until the last few years.

2 The Neglected Role of 'Civilisation' in the History of International Cultural Heritage Law

This section identifies different examples in which the concept of civilisation manifested itself in international cultural heritage law. Several historic studies have already focused on the significance of the civilisation concept for international law in recent years.[6] Many fields of international law accordingly have revisited their founding narratives,[7] but such a critical reassessment is still pending for international cultural heritage law. Histories of international cultural heritage law tend to treat only the pre-history of legal instruments and not broader contexts of the discipline. Consequently, this chapter focuses on the neglected influences of the concept of civilisation on the development of cultural heritage laws. Nevertheless, not all colonial and imperial encounters in the history of international cultural heritage law were based on the patterns described in this text. Colonised peoples similarly had impact on the colonisers, their laws and culture.[8] Their contribution to this system deserves further research.

The historic understanding of the concept of civilisation in international law is best documented in the most widely used English and German international law textbooks at the end of the long 19th century.[9] One representative

---

6 Shahabuddin, Mohammad. 'The 'Standard of Civilization' in International Law: Intellectual Perspectives from Pre-War Japan'. *Leiden Journal of International Law* 32(1) (2018), 13–32; Becker Lorca, Arnulf. *Mestizo International Law. A Global Intellectual History 1842–1933* (Cambridge: Cambridge University Press, 2014); Obregón, Liliana. 'The Civilized and the Uncivilized', in *The Oxford Handbook of the History of International Law*, eds. Bardo Fassbender and Anne Peters (Oxford: Oxford University Press, 2012), 917–939; Pauka, Marc. *Kultur, Fortschritt und Reziprozität. Die Begriffsgeschichte des zivilisierten Staates im Völkerrecht* (Baden-Baden: Nomos, 2012); Anghie, Antony. *Imperialism, Sovereignty and the Making of International Law* (Cambridge: Cambridge University Press, 2005); Gong, Gerrit W. *The Standard of 'Civilisation' in International Society* (Oxford: Oxford University Press, 1984).

7 See, e.g., Miles, Kate. *The Origins of International Investment Law. Empire, Environment and the Safeguarding of Capital* (Cambridge: Cambridge University Press, 2013).

8 See, e.g., Schwartz, Bill. *The White Man's World* (Oxford: Oxford University Press, 2011).

9 Although international law always refers to a shared and sometimes universal understanding of the discipline, there are national differences, see, e.g., Roberts, Anthea. *Is International Law International?* (Oxford: Oxford University Press, 2017).

example is the standard treatise of the German law professor Franz von Liszt.[10] He already described on the first page the structure of international law and the role of the standard of civilisation:

> International Law ... contains the legal rules that determine the rights and duties of the states that belong to the community of *civilised states* ... . The community of the *civilised states* is delimited by the common shared convictions of law and the common culture and interests.[11]

The quote indicates that a state or legal entity has to be part of the community of civilised states (*Kulturstaaten*) in order to benefit from international legal rights. Liszt emphasised that a common culture and interests, which form the basis for the membership in this community, hold the community of civilised states together.

Another example is the authoritative English textbook of public international law written by the German émigré and legal positivist Lassa Francis Oppenheim.[12] He gave a definition comparable to Liszt's and only included civilised states in the legal sphere of international law: 'Law of Nations or International Law is the name for the body of customary and conventional rules which are considered legally binding by civilised States in their intercourse with each other'.[13] Oppenheim listed in his textbook the civilised states of his time and only counted, for instance, the Republic of Liberia as full member of the *family of nations* on the continent of Africa.[14]

These doctrinal explanations certainly did not reflect all subtleties of the colonial and imperial encounters on the ground; however, they present the intellectual framework and the legal justifications used in these contexts that also became important for shaping cultural heritage norms.[15] Considering this

---

10 Hermann, Florian. *Das Standardwerk. Franz von Liszt und das Völkerrecht* (Baden-Baden: Nomos, 2001).

11 Liszt, Franz von. *Das Völkerrecht systematisch dargestellt* (Berlin: Verlag von O. Haering, 1898), 1–4 (author's translation).

12 Schmoeckel, Mathias. 'The Internationalist as a Scientist and Herald: Lassa Oppenheim'. *European Journal of International Law* 11(3) (2000), 699–712.

13 Oppenheim, Lassa Francis Lawrence. *International Law. A Treatise*, vol. 1 (London: Longmans, Green, and Co., 1905), 1.

14 Oppenheim, Lassa Francis Lawrence. *International Law. A Treatise*, vol. 1 (London: Longmans, Green, and Co., 2nd ed. 1912), 164.

15 For such approaches, see, e.g., Benton, Lauren and Lisa Ford. *Rage for Order. The British Empire and the Origins of International Law, 1800–1850* (Cambridge: Harvard University Press, 2016); Rajagopal, Balakrishnan. *International Law from Below. Development, Social Movements and Third World Resistance* (Cambridge: Cambridge University Press, 2003).

problematic legacy of international law, it is surprising that these colonial and imperial contexts are hardly addressed in the histories of cultural heritage in international law.[16] This section intends to illustrate how the concept of civilisation has shaped the discourse on cultural heritage in international law based on three examples: the hegemonic patterns of cultural co-operations, the ambivalent implications of the 'civilising' narrative for the laws of war and the colonial bias of codification projects in the interwar period.

2.1 *Defining Hegemonic Interests: Cultural Co-operations in International Law*

The concept of civilisation was an important factor in organising international cultural co-operations, which was also acknowledged by international legal doctrine. The community of civilised states constituted for many international lawyers also a dogmatic construct carrying its own interests. The legal theories of 'common interests' and the 'solidarity of interests' built the background against which a common responsibility of civilised states for the cultural heritage in international law developed.[17] Those interests marked a point of origin and legitimised international regulations in the 19th and early 20th century.[18] Several influential international law textbooks focused on this 'community of interests' with regard to cultural matters.

One of them was authored by the Munich-based law professor Emanuel Ullmann. In his monograph, Ullmann acknowledged the collaboration in 'intellectual' issues to be an important area of the common activities of civilised states. Under this title, he discussed the international co-operation in the administration of cultural objects. Ullmann's (and also Liszt's)[19] main example for cultural co-operation was the so-called Olympia treaty between Germany and Greece.[20] Since 1874, this treaty has permitted Germany to conduct archaeological excavations and research on the ancient grounds of Olympia.[21]

16 For some exceptions, see, e.g., Gaudenzi, Bianca and Astrid Swenson. 'Looted Art and Restitution in the Twentieth Century – Towards a Global Perspective'. *Journal of Contemporary History* 52(3) (2017), 491–518; Greenfield, Jeanette. *The Return of Cultural Treasures* (Cambridge: Cambridge University Press, 2007); Vrdoljak, Ana Filipa. *International Law, Museums and the Return of Cultural Objects* (Cambridge: Cambridge University Press, 2006).

17 Liszt, *Völkerrecht* 1898 (n. 11), 2–3.

18 García-Salmones Rovira, Mónica. 'The Politics of Interest in International Law'. *European Journal of International Law* 25(3) (2014), 765–793.

19 Liszt, *Völkerrecht* 1898 (n. 11), 189 et seq.

20 Ullmann, Emanuel. *Völkerrecht* (Tübingen: J. C. B. Mohr, 1908), 412.

21 Vertrag zwischen Deutschland und Griechenland wegen Ausführung von archäologischen Ausgrabungen auf dem Boden des alten Olympia, 1.6.1875, Reichsgesetzblatt No. 19, 241–245.

The balanced treaty provisions demonstrate the co-operation between the two civilised states on an equal basis. For example, each state appointed a commissioner to supervise the compliance of the treaty (Article 2) and most importantly, the export of the proceeds of the excavations to Germany was prohibited (Article 6).

The comparison of the Olympia case with the cultural co-operation between France and Persia shows how the standard of civilisation mattered in these interactions among states. Unlike Greece, Persia was considered semi-civilized under international law.[22] Persia granted France a license to carry out archaeological research and excavations for the payment of 50,000 gold francs in 1895.[23] This licence was valid for the whole country and deferred to France the right to decide where to excavate.[24] In addition, France could also appropriate half of the excavation's proceeds and was allowed to export them. These exclusive rights were affirmed in a bilateral contract between France and Persia five years later on a visit of the Shah in Paris.[25]

Both legal documents that directed the conduct between France and Persia stood in sharp contrast to the Olympia treaty. To begin with, the permission to excavate in every region of the country and the license to appropriate and export half of the proceeds were regulated very differently in the Olympia treaty. Germany was prohibited from acquiring any antiquities and the excavations were carried out in close collaboration with Greek authorities. In contrast, France brought the Persian government to grant an unlimited extension of this exclusive right in a contract, in exchange France acknowledged Persia's international standing at the world exposition in Paris. The example shows that the status of civilisation, although not the only difference in these two cases, was an important factor with material consequences in the conception of cultural co-operations.

---

22 Liszt, *Völkerrecht* 1898 (n. 11), 3; Oppenheim, *International Law* 1905 (n. 13), 33.

23 Convention relative au privilège des fouilles à exécuter en Perse, 12 May 1985, France Archives, Ministère de l'Europe et des Affaires étrangères, Traités et accords de la France TRA18950049.

24 Chevalier, Nicole. 'France and Elam', in *The Elamite World*, ed. Javier Álvarez-Mon, Gian Pietro Basello and Yasmina Wicks (Abingdon: Routledge, 2018), 41–62.

25 Convention relative à la concession des antiquités de la Perse, 30 October 1900, France Archives, Ministère de l'Europe et des Affaires étrangères, Traités et accords de la France TRA19000021.

2.2 *Politics of Historiography: Challenging the Narrative of 'Civilising' the Laws of War*

It is a common narrative in the history of international law that the conduct of war and with it the laws of war became more civilised over the 19th and early 20th century.[26] A close study of the international legal doctrine gives evidence of a more diverse picture and the narrative of the ever more civilising laws of war appears to become a mere rhetorical metaphor of the long 19th century.[27] These norms only applied among civilised states and not to their relations with colonies.[28] For the purpose of this study, the prohibition to destroy cultural objects and the regulations on war booty are of interest.[29]

Most current historiographies on the development of international cultural heritage law tell a narrative by reproducing authors, such as Johann Caspar Bluntschli. The Heidelberg-based law professor was one of the leading international lawyers of his time.[30] In Bluntschli's public international law treatise, he emphasised the progress that international law made concerning the legal status of monuments and artworks in wartime in the 1870s.[31] Similarly, Richard Dana Jr., who edited the standard textbook of Henry Wheaton in its eighth edition some years earlier, stated that not only the destruction but also the seizure of such works would contradict liberal and civilised principles of warfare.[32] Antoine Pillet, one editor of the *Revue génèrale de droit international public*,

26 See, e.g., Greenwood, Christopher. 'Historical Development and Legal Basis', in *The Oxford Handbook of International Humanitarian Law*, ed. Dieter Fleck (Oxford: Oxford University Press, 2013), 1–44.

27 Jochnick, Chris and Roger Normand. 'The Legitimation of Violence: A Critical History of the Laws of War'. *Harvard International Law Journal* 35(1) (1994), 49–95; Vec, Miloš. 'All's Fair in Love and War or the Limits of the Limitations. Juridification of Warfare and its Revocation by Military Necessity', in *Civility, Barbarism and the Evolution of International Humanitarian Law: Who Do the Laws of War Protect?*, ed. Matt Killingsworth (Cambridge: Cambridge University Press, forthcoming).

28 See, e.g., Hull, Isabel V. *Absolute Destruction: Military Culture and the Practices of War in Imperial Germany* (Ithaca: Cornell University Press, 2005); Mégret, Frederic. 'From Savages to Unlawful Combatants: A Postcolonial Look at International Law's "Other"', in *International Law and Its Others*, ed. Anne Orford (Cambridge: Cambridge University Press, 2006), 265–317.

29 Sandholtz, Wayne. *Prohibiting Plunder: How Norms Change* (Oxford: Oxford University Press, 2007); O'Keefe, Roger. *The Protection of Cultural Property in Armed Conflict* (Cambridge: Cambridge University Press, 2006), 18–22.

30 See, e.g., Röben, Betsy. *Johann Caspar Bluntschli, Francis Lieber und das moderne Völkerrecht 1861–1881* (Baden-Baden: Nomos, 2003).

31 Bluntschli, Johann Caspar. *Das moderne Völkerrecht der civilisirten Staten als Rechtsbuch dargestellt* (Nördlingen: C. H. Beck, 1878), 364.

32 Wheaton, Henry. *Elements of International Law* (London: Sampson Low, Son and Comp., 8th ed. 1866), 449–450.

underlined the progress of international law regarding monuments and artworks in war since the art spoliations of Napoleon that filled the Louvre.[33]

The laws of war in the 19th and early 20th century did not necessarily reflect the 'enthusiasm'[34] of these international lawyers. The different codification drafts, such as the Brussels Declaration 1874,[35] the Oxford Manual 1880[36] and eventually the Hague Conventions of 1899 and 1907,[37] at least foresaw an exception for 'military necessity' that allowed the destruction of monuments and artworks in certain circumstances. The seizure of cultural objects was even allowed under Article 36 of the so-called U.S. Lieber Code 1863.[38]

While standard narratives stress the positive impact of the civilisation discourse on the laws of war, there actually existed a pluralism of geographically different opinions in international legal doctrine on this topic until the end of the 19th century.[39] The debates about the seizure of monuments and artworks in war times very instructively illustrate the ambivalent understanding of civilisation. Around the mid-19th century, two of the prominent proponents for the seizure of artworks were the German-U.S. jurist Francis Lieber and the U.S.-General and international lawyer Henry W. Halleck. In their view, the entire enemy's property could be appropriated because international law still did not include an obligation to spare cultural goods at the time.[40]

In the last quarter of the 19th century, interesting oppositions to the traditional civilising narrative developed. The two British scholars James Lorimer[41]

---

33 Pillet, Antoine. *Le droit de la guerre* (Paris: Arthur Rousseau, 1893), 339.

34 Koskenniemi, Martti. *The Gentle Civilizer of Nations: The Rise and Fall of International Law 1870–1960* (Cambridge: Cambridge University Press, 2001), 4.

35 'Project of an International Declaration Concerning the Laws and Customs of War, 27 August 1874', in *The Laws of Armed Conflicts. A Collection of Conventions, Resolutions and other Documents*, eds. Dietrich Schindler and Jiří Toman (Leiden: Martinus Nijhoff, 3rd ed. 2004), 21–28.

36 'The Laws of War on Land. Manual Published by the Institute of International Law, 9 September 1880', in Schindler/Toman, *The Laws of Armed Conflicts* 2004 (n. 35), 29–40.

37 Convention concerning the Laws and Customs of War on Land and its Annex: Regulations Respecting the Laws and Customs of War on Land, 18 October 1907, 205 CTS 277.

38 'Instructions for the Government of Armies of the United States in the Field. Promulgated as General Orders No. 100 by President Lincoln, 24 April 1863', in Schindler/Toman, *The Laws of Armed Conflicts* 2004 (n. 35), 3–20.

39 See also Vrdoljak, *International Law* 2006 (n. 16), 28.

40 Halleck, Henry W. *International Law; Or, Rules Regulating the Intercourse of States in Peace and War* (New York: D. Van Nostrand, 1861), 451; Lieber, Francis. *Manual of Political Ethics*, vol. 2 (Boston: Charles C. Little and James Brown, 1839), 663 et seq.

41 Koskenniemi, Martti. 'Race, Hierarchy and International Law: Lorimer's Legal Science'. *European Journal of International Law* 27(2) (2016), 415–29.

and Henry S. Maine[42] developed a remarkable approach using the concept of civilisation in relation with the laws of war to argue for the seizure of artworks in war times. James Lorimer stated that civilisation could benefit from the transfer of artworks to another country, because those cultural objects might become accessible for 'the public' for the first time.[43] This was his main argument why art plunders, such as the Napoleonic ones at around 1800, were principally justifiable under international law.[44] Such an argument undoubtedly corrupted the common narrative of civilisation as traditionally understood in relation to the laws of war.

In his writing about the seizure of artworks under international law, Henry S. Maine deliberated whether the accumulation of many masterpieces of art might actually promote civilisation. Maine concluded with reference to the art restitutions from Paris after Napoleon's defeat that the technological progress and the increased personal mobility since those times have made the cultural monuments of Europe just as accessible as if they were concentrated in one capital.[45] Maine is perhaps the only legal author considering technological innovations when evaluating the advantages of such art seizures.

The confrontation with the historical counter discourse of civilisation contests the traditional historiography of international cultural heritage law for the 19th and early 20th century. Despite the consensus that civilisation mattered as a concept for international law,[46] it becomes clear from these examples that the concrete understanding of civilisation varied among scholars and manifested itself differently in different places at different times.

2.3 *Codifying Inequalities: The Colonial Bias of* IMO*-Drafts in the League of Nations Era*

The world of cultural co-operation was newly organized after World War I. The League of Nations was founded and various institutions, such as the International Commissions for Intellectual Co-operation, the International Institute of Intellectual Co-operation and the International Museums Office

42 Mantena, Karuna. *Alibis of Empire: Henry Maine and the Ends of Liberal Imperialism* (Princeton: Princeton University Press, 2010).

43 Lorimer, James. *The Institutes of the Law of Nations. A Treatise of the Jural Relations of Separate Political Communities*, vol. 2 (Edinburgh: William Blackwood & Sons, 1884), 79.

44 Savoy, Bénédicte. *Kunstraub, Napoleons Konfiszierungen in Deutschland und die europäischen Folgen* (Vienna: Böhlau Verlag, 2011).

45 Maine, Henry S. *International Law* (London: John Murray, 1890), 195–197.

46 For a good elaboration of the historical argument, see, e.g., Pitts, Jennifer. *Boundaries of the International. Law and Empire* (Cambridge: Harvard University Press, 2018), 7.

(IMO), were established to address questions of cultural matters in a broad sense.[47] Despite the internationalisation, the concept of civilisation remained vital for this field. The General Assembly of the League of Nations made this explicit in its recommendation from 10 October 1932, which stated that the preservation of artistic and archaeological patrimony lies in the interest of the civilised states.[48]

This marked an important turn towards new international governance mechanisms for cultural objects.[49] Many states and individuals from different nations were involved in those efforts and particularly representatives of the peripheries actively shaped the discussions. However, when it came to the formulation of international legal instruments, the colonial bias of the civilisation discourse was still present.

The codification efforts of the International Museums Office to prepare multilateral instruments to protect cultural heritage in the 1930s give an instructive example of the lasting effect of the civilisation concept in international law. The IMO set up a drafting committee for this task headed by the Belgian international lawyer Charles de Visscher.[50] The aim was to compile two conventions on cultural objects, one for the conduct in times of peace and one for the times of war, but also to find a narrative to legitimise these proposals.

Visscher wrote a seminal article for the *Revue de Droit international*, which set the frame for these new regulatory fields in 1935.[51] To justify the convention on the *ius in bello*, he relied on a vast material of legal debates and codifications since the 19th century, but he also criticised other legal efforts to protect monuments in the course of war.[52] In a preliminary report to the IMO, Visscher particularly dismissed the so-called 'Roerich Pact', a treaty created on initiative of the Russian artist Nicolas Roerich for protecting monuments and signed

47 For an overview of the intellectual co-operation, see, e.g. Laqua, Daniel. 'Transnational Intellectual Cooperation, the League of Nations, and the Problem of Order'. *Journal of Global History* 6(2) (2011), 223–247; Brzeziński, Andrzej M. 'The Organization and Forms of International Intellectual Cooperation within the League of Nations (1922–1939)'. *Przegląd Zachodni* 1 (2017), 53–70.

48 'Recommandations de l'assemblée de la société des nations du 10 octobre 1932'. *Art et archéologie. Recueil de législation comparée et de droit international* 1 (1939), 114 et seq.

49 See also Vrdoljak, *International Law* 2006 (n. 16), 103–117.

50 Verhoeve, Joe. 'Charles de Visscher: Living and Thinking International Law'. *European Journal of International Law* 11(4) (2000), 887–904.

51 De Visscher, Charles. 'La protection internationale des objets d'art et des monuments historique'. *Revue de droit international et de législation comparée* 16 (1935), 32–74, 246–288.

52 De Visscher, Charles. 'Rapport préliminaire présenté au comité de direction de l'office international des musées, le 12 Octobre 1936'. *Art et archéologie. Recueil de législation comparée et de droit international* 2 (1940), 47–55.

by many American states in 1935.[53] Instead of giving credits to the initiative, Visscher polemicized against the Roerich Pact for not including a 'military necessity' exception to justify damages on monuments in war times.[54] This would make the treaty impractical for Europe. Its plurality of cultural treasures and historic cities would make, in contrast to the in this sense culturally short fallen American states, the conduct of war without a military exception clause impossible. Consequently, such a treaty might be sustainable there, but it would not be viable in Europe. With this argumentation, Visscher gave evidence of his and international law's Eurocentrism in the drafting of laws and how civilisation was used to argue for and against certain norms at the time.

Even more interesting than Visscher's remark about the convention on the laws of war was his narrative for the juridification of the norms in peace times. At this point, Visscher applied a comparative and historical point of view to legitimise the new legal regime of private international law.[55] He established that the opinion among the major civilised states in Europe was consistent in respect of the status of artworks in private international law by discussing domestic legal rules of European civilised states, such as France, Italy, Austria, Germany, and Spain.[56] In consequence, the understanding of European nation states was authoritative for international normative regimes. The final *Draft international convention for the protection of national collections of art and history* of 1939 also included openly discriminatory regulations for the colonies:

> Article 12. Any High Contracting Party may, at the time of its signature, ratification or accession, declare that in accepting the present Convention it assumes no obligation whatsoever in respect of the whole or part of its colonies, protectorates, overseas territories, territories placed under its sovereignty or territories for which a mandate has been entrusted to it.[57]

---

53 Treaty on the Protection of Artistic and Scientific Institutions and Historic Monuments (Roerich Pact), 15 April 1935, CLXVII LNTS 289; see also Roerich, Nicholas. *Roerich Banner of Peace* (New York: Roerich Museum Press, 1931).

54 De Visscher, 'Rapport préliminaire' 1940 (n. 52), 50.

55 For the entanglement between comparative law and private international law, see Reimann, Mathias. 'Comparative Law and Private International Law', in *The Oxford Handbook of Comparative Law*, eds. Mathias Reimann and Reinhard Zimmermann (Oxford: Oxford University Press, 2006), 1363–1396.

56 De Visscher, 'La protection internationale' 1935 (n. 51), 34–46.

57 Office International des Musées. 'Le projet définitif établi en 1939 en vue de la conférence diplomatique'. *Art et archéologie. Recueil de législation comparée et de droit international* 1 (1939), 78–87, art. 12.

According to this draft article, it would have been upon the empires to decide about the application of these normative regimes on their peripheries. This would have not only bypassed the question of restitution of colonial treasures and cultural objects back then, but, because of the intertemporal character of international law, might actually have this effect until today.[58] Although these drafts were never ratified, they indicate the continuing importance of the civilisation discourse for international cultural heritage law in the 20th century.

3 The Different Roles of the Law in the 'Civilisation' Discourse

The case studies of this section analyse various roles that cultural heritage laws played for different actors in diverse international settings. The standard of civilisation highly shaped these contexts; however, this does not mean that there was no agency on the part of the colonised. This section attempts to provide a more nuanced historic understanding by questioning the solely protective purposes of cultural heritage laws, but also to emphasise the different contexts in which such norms developed.

The focus of this section will be on interactions outside from armed conflicts and on cases that involve more controversial factual constellations regarding current questions of restitution. The fact patterns developed in this section are also intended to help evaluating restitution claims today. While the second section illustrated how the standard of civilisation was crucial for the evolution of the international legal discourse on cultural heritage, this section shall document how the discourse of civilisation impacted the development of regional and local cultural heritage laws in the 19th and 20th century.

Three different configurations shaped the development of these laws on a regional and national level: First, (semi-)peripheral states used cultural heritage laws with an emancipatory purpose. Second, empires used colonial laws to govern, appropriate and legitimise with reference to their civilising duty such interventions into the cultural heritage of other peoples. Third, laws also aimed to assure one's own national identity and political independence, particularly by excluding foreign nationals after a phase of colonization or foreign domination.

58 Shaw, Malcolm N. *International Law* (Cambridge: Cambridge University Press, 8th ed. 2017), 702.

3.1 *Using Culture as a Means of Emancipation in the International Community*

Some state actors intended to influence their standing in the international community by using domestic regulations on cultural objects and antiquities. These legislations were oriented towards western legal standards or were even drafted by European authors.[59] One aim of these norms was to participate in the discourse of civilisation by protecting what was regarded valuable among civilised states. A country with a contested position on the international level that used domestic cultural heritage laws in this sense was the Ottoman Empire.[60]

The German archaeologist Philipp Anton Déthier drafted the first 'antiquities law' in 1874 to meet the expectations of European excavators and favour their needs.[61] As a consequence of this regulation, Europeans could rather easily acquire cultural heritage on the territory of the Ottoman Empire. However, it was not before 1907 that Islamic artworks were considered worthy to protect under these laws.[62] This late consideration of Islamic artworks and the relaxed norms to obtain antiquities indicate that the laws were directed to enable international cultural co-operations and to gain recognition on the international plane.[63]

The Ottoman Empire also saw in the adoption of European institutions a way to demonstrate its international status as civilised empire. A telling example for this is the archaeological museum in Istanbul.[64] The Ottoman education minister and reformer of the *Tanzimat* period, Münif Pasha, held an instructive speech at the opening of the museum on 17 August 1880. Münif Pasha alluded to the acknowledgement that he expected for the new museum

---

59 See also the newly launched project *Decolonial Comparative Law* by Ralf Michaels and Lena Salaymeh, available at: https://www.mpipriv.de/en/pub/research/decolonial_comparative_law.cfm (last accessed on 14 September 2020).

60 Özsu, Umut. 'Ottoman Empire', in *The Oxford Handbook of the History of International Law*, eds. Bardo Fassbender and Anne Peters (Oxford: Oxford University Press, 2012), 429–448.

61 Khater, Antoine. *Le régime juridique des fouilles et des antiquités en Égypte* (Cairo: Imprimerie de l'institut français d'archéologie orientale, 1960), 275 et seq.

62 Hitzel, Frédéric. 'Osman Hamdi Bey et les débuts de l'archéologie ottomane', in *Turcica* 42 (2010), 167–190.

63 Marchand, Suzanne. 'Orientalism as Kulturpolitik. German Archeology and Cultural Imperialism in Asia Minor', in *Volksgeist as Method and Ethic. Essays on Boasian Ethnography and the German Anthropological Tradition*, ed. George W. Stocking (Madison: University of Wisconsin Press, 1996), 298–336.

64 For the role of museums, see, e.g., Meyer, Andrea and Bénédicte Savoy, eds. *The Museum Is Open. Towards a Transnational History of Museums 1750–1940* (Berlin: De Gruyter, 2014).

from European states. Consequently, the interest to protect these objects was not only a cultural, but also an emancipatory one:

> The opening of a museum in Istanbul similar to those in other civilised countries was the hope of our progressing nation … . There There is no need to go on at length about the benefits of such museums. They show the level of civilisation of past peoples and their step-by-step progress … . Everybody Everybody knows the great effects of archeology on European Civilisation … . Until now, Europeans have used various means to take the antiquities of our country away, and they did this because they did not see an inclination toward this in us.[65]

Other national legislation, institutions and cultural co-operations, such as in Latin American states, followed similar patterns. El Salvador established a national library to promote the education of its people with reference to institutions in other civilised states.[66] Honduras signed an excavation treaty with the Peabody Museum of Harvard University to ensure the appreciation of its historical remains by western archaeologists.[67]

The importance of domestic cultural heritage legislation for the international standard of civilisation is remarkably displayed by a repertory of the Prussian lawyer Alexander von Wussow. He collected the national cultural heritage legislation of the civilised states around the world and published them in 1885.[68] This collection included not only the heritage laws of European states, but also those of China, Japan, Brazil, Mexico and the Ottoman Empire. Being civilised meant for him having an historical conscience about the past and to protect its remains. As a result, passing legislation that protected monuments was an important element in the discourse of civilisation in international law at that time.

65 Shaw, Wendy. *Possessors and Possessed. Museum, Archaeology, and the Visualization of History in the Late Ottoman Empire* (Berkeley: University of California Press, 2003), 93 et seq.

66 El Salvador, Decreto de Fundacion de la Biblioteca Nacional, 1 July 1870, El Constitucional 4(40) (1870).

67 Honduras, Acuerdo por el traspaso de una concesion al Peabody Museum, 20 July 1891, UNESCO Database of National Cultural Heritage Laws, available at: https://en.unesco.org/cultnatlaws/list (last accessed on 14 September 2020).

68 Wussow, Alexander von. *Die Erhaltung der Denkmäler in den Kulturstaaten der Gegenwart* (Berlin: Carl Heymanns Verlag, 1885).

3.2 *'Colonial Protection': Justifying Interventions into Foreign Cultural Heritage*

Cultural heritage laws were used to appropriate and govern foreign cultural heritage under certain colonial contexts in the 19th and 20th century. Although the standard of civilisation contributed in various ways to a narrative of protection for these laws, it also legitimised the legal interventions in foreign cultural heritage. Some encounters in Asian countries provide insights into these practices and the construction of specific legislative aims.

The French École Française d'Extrême-Orient was one of the important European institutions in Asia that dealt with cultural heritage. In the French colony of Indochina, the colonial government imposed laws to regulate the administration of the 'cultural treasures' of the colony.[69] One site that received specific attention was Ângkôr, which was legally transformed into an archaeological park in 1925 to meet the interests of European tourists.[70] In a report to the French president, Édouard Daladier, the colonial minister of France, wrote about Indochina in the same year:

> Under reservation of the sovereign rights of the protected in French Indochina, the properties, which presents from an artistic and historic point of view a public interest for conservation, are classified as historic monuments by the governor general on proposition of the director of the École Française d'Extrême-Orient. The protection of these treasures is a task that imposes itself imperially on the French authority ...[71]

This report indicates that the protection of cultural monuments was considered a civilising responsibility. At the same time, it formed a justification narrative to enable legislation and a lawful acquisition of cultural artefacts.

The mandate system of the League of Nations legally and institutionally envisaged another more complex organization for the administration of cultural heritage. The league's covenant foresaw a distinction between the mandates according to their perceived 'civilisation stage'. Article 22 of the Covenant differed between communities formerly belonging to the 'Turkish Empire' (A), 'Central Africa' (B) and 'South-West Africa and certain of the South Pacific

---

69 Le Governeur général de l'Indochine, Arrête sur la conservation des monuments et objets ayant un intérêt historique ou artistique, 9 March 1900, UNESCO Database (n. 67).

70 Le Gouverneur général de l'Indochine, Arrêté créant le parc archéologique d'Angkor, 30 October 1925, *Bulletin de l'ecole française d'extrême-orient* 26, 677.

71 Le ministre des colonies. 'Rapport au président de la république française, December 23, 1924'. *Bulletin de l'ecole francaise d'extrême-orient* 26 (1926), 526–527 (author's translation).

Islands' (C).[72] Cultural heritages laws were put into place in the A-mandates Palestine, Syria-Lebanon, and Iraq by the mandate powers France and Great Britain.[73] These laws regulated the appropriation, the export, and the excavation of antiquities located in each one of these mandate territories. The Permanent Mandate Commission of the League of Nations acted as a type of supervisor in this system of foreign administration.[74]

Despite this supervisory function of the league, the different laws benefited the western archaeologists and the mandate powers with generous provisions for acquiring and exporting antiquities.[75] The exploitations went so far that the *Syro-Palestinian Congress* addressed in 1925 a petition to the Permanent Mandate Commission to complain inter alia about the careless treatment and appropriations of their cultural patrimony.[76] Despite the trusteeship relation of the mandate powers with their protégés and the international tutelages, the administration followed a pattern of domination and the laws just covered these hegemonic structures under the rhetoric of 'protection'.

3.3 *Reclaiming Cultural Heritage in the Struggles for National Independence*

The dominant discourse of civilisation also received backlash from former colonies or imperially dominated countries.[77] The resistance materialised also in cultural heritage norms, which had the purpose to reassure one's own independence and national identity.[78] Such constellations arose in Iraq, China

72 For the mandate system in general, see Pedersen, Susan. *The Guardians. The League of Nations and the Crisis of Empire* (Oxford: Oxford University Press, 2015) and for the A-Mandates Schayegh, Cyrus and Andrew Arsan, eds. *The Routledge Handbook of the History of the Middle East Mandates* (Abingdon: Routledge, 2015).

73 For an overview, see Goode, James F. *Negotiating for the Past. Archaeology, Nationalism, and Diplomacy in the Middle East, 1919–1941* (Austin: University of Texas Press, 2007).

74 Magee, Peter. 'The Foundations of Antiquities Departments', in *A Companion to the Archeology of the Ancient Near East*, ed. Daniel T. Potts (Malden: Blackwell Publishing, 2012), 70–86.

75 See, e.g., Israel/Palestine, Antiquities Ordinance 1920, 15 October 1920, Official Gazette of the Government of Palestine, Nr. 29/9, 4–16; Syria/Libanon, Arrête No. 207 Portant règlement sur les antiquités en Syrie et au Liban, 26 March 1926, Bulletin officiel des actes administratifs du Haut Commissariat 5, no. 8, 136–139.

76 League of Nations, Permanent Mandates Commission, Minutes of the 8th Session (Extraordinary) including the Report of the Commission to the Council, 8 March 1926, C.174.M.65.1926.VI., 174–186.

77 For the early 20th century, see also Vrdoljak, *International Law* 2006 (n. 16), 73–87.

78 A similar dynamic existed in Germany after World War I, see Obenaus, Maria. *Für die Nation gesichert? Das „Verzeichnis der national wertvollen Kunstwerke": Entstehung, Etablierung und Instrumentalisierung 1919–1945* (Berlin: De Gruyter, 2016), 22–44.

and Persia around the 1930s. International cultural co-operations with western powers became for these states a venue of opposition against perceived colonial and imperial policies.

Iraq gained independence from Great Britain's mandate rule and became a new member to the League of Nations in 1932. During this process, the Permanent Mandate Commission debated whether the Arabic state should be legally obliged to continue providing international access to its cultural treasures.[79] The proposal was finally refused with the argument that such a provision would prevent Iraq from showing a sign of generosity to its new co-members within the League of Nations by continuing the cultural co-operations. The members of the Permanent Mandate Commission were convinced that Iraq would seize this opportunity to obtain the respect of the civilised community for such a friendly act.[80] However, in contrast to their assumption, Iraq soon passed a new 'antiquity law'[81] that strictly regulated excavations and prohibited the acquisition of antiquities by foreign archaeological explorations.[82] The interests of the civilised world in continuing archaeological excavations in the country were neglected.

In a comparable way, China issued a new law to limit the entry of foreign archaeologists in its territory.[83] The French hegemony over the archaeological heritage of Persia came to an end in 1927.[84] Some years later, the administration of the country's cultural heritage was newly regulated in a revised law that was characterised by a more restrictive approach to the issue.[85] These cases

79 League of Nations, Permanent Mandates Commission, Minutes of the 21st Session, 29 December 1931, C.830.M.411.1931.VI., 118 et seq.

80 Ibid., 119.

81 For an overview, see Bernhardsson, Magnus T. *Reclaiming a Plundered Past: Archaeology and Nation Building in Modern Iraq* (Austin: Texas University Press, 2005).

82 Magee, 'The Foundations of Antiquities Departments' 2012 (n. 74), 70–86; for a biography of the director of the antiquities department at that time, see Cleveland, William L. *The Making of an Arab Nationalist. Ottomanism and Arabism in the Life and Thought of Sati' Al-Husri* (Princeton: Princeton University Press, 1971).

83 China, Executive Yuan, Rules Relating to the Participation of Foreign Academic Organization or Private Individuals in the Excavation of Relics, 16 March 1935, UNESCO Database (n. 67).

84 Accord de principe conclu entre le gouvernement de Sa Majesté Impériale le schah de Perse et le gouvernement de la République française au sujet de l'abolition de la convention franco-persane de 1900 relative au monopole des fouilles archéologiques, 18 October 1927, France Archives, Ministère de l'Europe et des Affaires étrangères, Traités et accords de la France, TRA19270050.

85 Iran, Règlement d'application de la Loi du 12 Aban – Mah 1309 relative à la conservation des antiquités de l'Iran, 3 November 1930, UNESCO Database (n. 67), arts. 38 and 47.

show that political independence materialised also in a re-appropriation of the own cultural heritage and the rejection of the dominant discourse of civilisation that demanded international cultural co-operation.

4 Conclusion: Resistance and the Continuities of a Problematic Structure

The momentum of decolonization and the new international venues established after World War II promised a change in international cultural heritage law towards the restitution of cultural heritage from colonial contexts of acquisition.[86] This section draws on the UN General Assembly resolutions as an example for the lasting effects of the civilisation discourse and the resistance against it by using international legal mechanisms.

The ambivalent history of cultural heritage in international law did not end with decolonization. The restitution of colonial plundered art nowadays is one of the most discussed aspects of international cultural law.[87] Restitution claims of African and Asian states have lately filled the headlines of several news media and are globally discussed among scholars.[88] An important cornerstone in the recent development is the report of Felwine Sarr and Bénédicte Savoy for the French government that argues for a return of more than 100 000 objects looted in Africa.[89] Today's debates thus are not new but rather continuing the discussion since decolonization in the 1970s.[90] The claims for

86 Vrdoljak, *International Law* 2006 (n. 16), 197–227.

87 Hauser-Schäublin, Brigitta and Lyndel V. Prott. 'Introduction: Changing Concepts of Ownership, Culture and Property', in *Cultural Property and Contested Ownership. The Trafficking of Artefacts and the Quest for Restitution*, ed. Brigitta Hauser-Schäublin and Lyndel V. Prott (Abingdon: Routledge, 2016), 1–20.

88 One of the latest successful restitution claims was brought by the Philippines against the U.S. concerning the Balangiga bells. See Gutierrez, Jason. 'U.S. Returns Bells Taken as War Booty From Philippines in 1901'. *The New York Times* (11 December 2018), available at: https://www.nytimes.com/2018/12/11/world/asia/balangiga-bells-united-states-philippines.html (last accessed on 14 September 2020).

89 Sarr, Felwine and Bénédicte Savoy. *The Restitution of African Cultural Heritage. Toward a New Relational Ethics* (2018), available at: http://restitutionreport2018.com/sarr_savoy_en.pdf (last accessed on 14 September 2020).

90 See also Fitschen, Thomas. '30 Jahre „Rückführung von Kulturgut"'. *Vereinte Nationen* 52(2) (2004), 46–51.

repatriation come together with the demand to acknowledge the colonial wrongs and sufferings of colonised peoples.[91]

The engagement of the UN General Assembly with the restitution of colonial plundered art already started soon after the adoption of the UNESCO Convention 1970 and the World Heritage Convention in 1972.[92] The government of Zaire, today's Democratic Republic of Congo, first proposed to the General Assembly a resolution that openly addressed the issue in 1973.[93] The condemning language of the draft resolution eventually entered the UN resolution: '*Deploring* the wholesale removal, virtually without payment, of *objets d'art* from one country to another, frequently as a result of colonial and foreign occupation'.[94] The resolution suggested restitution as a means to rectify the wrongs of the past.

As a consequence of this direct language, many states with a colonial or imperial past abstained from voting on the resolution, but still a majority of 113 of the then 135 UN member states voted in its favour. In the following years, the General Assembly regularly instructed the UN Secretary General to report on restitutions of cultural objects.[95] These reports indicate that the abstaining countries preferred bilateral negotiations and the forum of UNESCO to resolve the disputes instead of the UN General Assembly.[96] Subsequently, an own 'Intergovernmental Committee for promoting the return of cultural property to its countries of origin or its restitution in case of illicit appropriation'

---

91 Krueger, Anna. *Die Bindung der Dritten Welt an das postkoloniale Völkerrecht. Die Völkerrechtskommission, das Recht der Verträge und das Recht der Staatennachfolge in der Dekolonialisierung* (Berlin: Springer, 2018); Craven, Matthew. *The Decolonization of International Law. State Succession and the Law of Treaties* (Oxford: Oxford University Press, 2007).

92 Convention on the means of prohibiting and preventing the illicit import, export and transfer of ownership of cultural property, 14 November 1970, 823 UNTS 231; Convention concerning the Protection of the World Cultural and Natural Heritage, 16 November 1972, 1037 UNTS 151.

93 United Nations, Letter from the Permanent Representative of the government of Zaire to the United Nations addressed to the President of the General Assembly, A/9199, 6 November 1973.

94 United Nations, General Assembly, Restitution of works of arts to countries victims of expropriation, A/RES/3187(XXVIII), 18 December 1973 (italics in original).

95 See, e.g., United Nations, General Assembly, Restitution of works of arts to countries victims of expropriation, A/RES/3391 (XXX), 19 November 1975, para. 7.

96 See, e.g., United Nations, Secretary General, Report on the Restitution of works of art to countries victims of expropriations, A/32/203, 27 September 1977; or United Nations, General Assembly, 30th Session, 2410th Plenary Meeting, 30A/PV.2410, 19 November 1975, 928 et seq.

was set up by UNESCO to mediate in cases of conflicts in 1978.[97] Moreover, the second World Conference on Cultural Policies in 1982 formulated a set of recommendations for the return of cultural objects,[98] but the universality of cultural heritage was invoked by some delegations to refuse restitution claims at the same time.[99]

Neither the recommendations nor the new institutions were very successful in reconciling conflicts. The support for the still biannually proposed UN General Assembly resolutions on restitution diminished over time.[100] In 1997, the restitution resolution was only adopted by 87 votes (23 states abstaining, 75 states opposed), also because it contained a passage emphasising the positive value of restitutions for the relations between developed and developing countries.[101]

Further international initiatives, such as the UNIDROIT Convention,[102] refrained from addressing the questions of colonial plundered cultural heritage.[103] The intertemporal character of international law was often referred to for arguing against the formulation of legal claims to compensate or repatriate cultural property.[104] The existence of the UN General Assembly resolutions as 'narrative norms' about the colonial past of cultural heritage underline the urgency of the situation, but fail to provide legal rights as a remedy.[105]

The current constellation of most domestic and the international legal order are regularly perceived to obstruct restitution claims despite the long history of resistance. Such a history demonstrates not only the different ways in which the concept of civilisation in international law contributed

---

97 UNESCO, General Conference, Statutes of the Intergovernmental Committee for Promoting the Return of Cultural Property to its Countries of Origin or its Restitution in Case of Illicit Appropriation, 20C/Res. 4/7.6/5, 28 November 1978.

98 UNESCO, World Conference on Cultural Policies, Final Report, CLT/MD/1, November 1982, 94–97.

99 Ibid., 31.

100 See, e.g., United Nations, General Assembly, Return or restitution of cultural property to the countries of origin, A/RES/40/19, 21 November 1985.

101 United Nations, General Assembly, Return or restitution of cultural property to the countries of origin, A/RES/52/24, 18 December 1997, para. 2.

102 UNIDROIT Convention on Stolen or Illegally Exported Cultural Objects, 24 June 1995, 2421 UNTS 457.

103 See UNIDROIT Secretariat. 'UNIDROIT Convention on Stolen or Illegally Exported Cultural Objects: Explanatory Report', in *Uniform Law Review* 3 (2001), 476–564.

104 Taşdelen, Alper. *The Return of Cultural Artefacts. Hard and Soft Law Approaches* (Berlin: Springer, 2016), 91–93.

105 Jayme, Erik. 'Narrative Norms in Private International Law – The Example of Art Law'. *Recueil des cours de l'académie de droit international de La Haye* 375 (2014) 19–50.

to shape international cultural heritage law regimes, but also how different actors related to it. Embedding a critical narrative into the traditional historiography of international cultural heritage law emphasises the deficiencies of the contemporary legal order and might provide a perspective for future improvements.

Bibliography

Anghie, Antony. 'Finding the Peripheries: Sovereignty and Colonialism in Nineteenth-Century International Law'. *Harvard International Law Journal* 40(1) (1999), 1–80.

Anghie, Antony. *Imperialism, Sovereignty and the Making of International Law* (Cambridge: Cambridge University Press, 2005).

Becker Lorca, Arnulf. *Mestizo International Law. A Global Intellectual History 1842–1933* (Cambridge: Cambridge University Press, 2014).

Benton, Lauren and Lisa Ford. *Rage for Order. The British Empire and the Origins of International Law, 1800–1850* (Cambridge: Harvard University Press, 2016).

Bernhardsson, Magnus T. *Reclaiming a Plundered Past: Archaeology and Nation Building in Modern Iraq* (Austin: Texas University Press, 2005).

Bluntschli, Johann Caspar. *Das moderne Völkerrecht der civilisirten Staten als Rechtsbuch dargestellt* (Nördlingen: C. H. Beck, 1878).

Brzeziński, Andrzej M. 'The Organization and Forms of International Intellectual Cooperation within the League of Nations (1922–1939)'. *Przegląd Zachodni* 1 (2017), 53–70.

Chevalier, Nicole. 'France and Elam', in *The Elamite World*, ed. Javier Álvarez-Mon, Gian Pietro Basello, Yasmina Wicks (Abingdon: Routledge, 2018), 41–62.

Cleveland, William L. *The Making of an Arab Nationalist. Ottomanism and Arabism in the Life and Thought of Sati' Al-Husri* (Princeton: Princeton University Press, 1971).

Craven, Matthew. *The Decolonization of International Law. State Succession and the Law of Treaties* (Oxford: Oxford University Press, 2007).

De Visscher, Charles. 'La protection internationale des objets d'art et des monuments historique'. *Revue de droit international et de legislation comparee* 16 (1935), 32–74, 246–88.

De Visscher, Charles. 'Rapport preliminaire presente au comite de direction de l'office international des musees, le 12 octobre 1936'. *Art et archeologie. Recueil de legislation comparee et de droit international* 2 (1940), 47–55.

Fitschen, Thomas. '30 Jahre „Rückführung von Kulturgut"'. *Vereinte Nationen* 52(2) (2004), 46–51.

García-Salmones Rovira, Mónica. 'The Politics of Interest in International Law'. *European Journal of International Law* 25(3) (2014), 765–793.

Gaudenzi, Bianca and Astrid Swenson. 'Looted Art and Restitution in the Twentieth Century – Towards a Global Perspective'. *Journal of Contemporary History* 52(3) (2017), 491–518.

Gong, Gerrit W. *The Standard of 'Civilisation' in International Society* (Oxford: Oxford University Press, 1984).

Goode, James F. *Negotiating for the Past. Archaeology, Nationalism, and Diplomacy in the Middle East, 1919–1941* (Austin: University of Texas Press, 2007).

Greenfield, Jeanette. *The Return of Cultural Treasures* (Cambridge: Cambridge University Press, 2007).

Greenwood, Christopher. 'Historical Development and Legal Basis', in *The Oxford Handbook of International Humanitarian Law*, ed. Dieter Fleck (Oxford: Oxford University Press, 2013), 1–44.

Guizot, François. *Histoire générale de la civilisation en Europe* (Paris: Pichon et Didier, 1828).

Gutierrez, Jason. 'U.S. Returns Bells Taken as War Booty From Philippines in 1901'. *The New York Times* (11 December 2018), available at: https://www.nytimes.com/2018/12/11/world/asia/balangiga-bells-united-states-philippines.html (last accessed on 14 September 2020).

Halleck, Henry W. *International Law*; Or *Rules Regulating the Intercourse of States in Peace and War* (New York: D. Van Nostrand, 1861).

Hauser-Schäublin, Brigitta and Lyndel V. Prott. 'Introduction: Changing Concepts of Ownership, Culture and Property', in *Cultural Property and Contested Ownership. The Trafficking of Artefacts and the Quest for Restitution*, ed. Brigitta Hauser-Schäublin and Lyndel V. Prott (Abingdon: Routledge, 2016), 1–20.

Hermann, Florian. *Das Standardwerk. Franz von Liszt und das Völkerrecht* (Baden-Baden: Nomos, 2001).

Hitzel, Frédéric. 'Osman Hamdi Bey et les débuts de l'archéologie ottomane'. *Turcica* 42 (2010), 167–190.

Hull, Isabel V. *Absolute Destruction: Military Culture and the Practices of War in Imperial Germany* (Ithaca: Cornell University Press, 2005).

Jayme, Erik. 'Narrative Norms in Private International Law – The Example of Art Law'. *Recueil des cours de l'académie de droit international de La Haye* 375 (2014) 19–50.

Jochnick, Chris and Roger Normand. 'The Legitimation of Violence: A Critical History of the Laws of War'. *Harvard International Law Journal* 35(1) (1994), 49–95.

Khater, Antoine. *Le régime juridique des fouilles et des antiquités en Égypte* (Cairo: Imprimerie de l'institut français d'archéologie orientale, 1960).

Koskenniemi, Martti. 'Race, Hierarchy and International Law: Lorimer's Legal Science'. *European Journal of International Law* 27(2) (2016), 415–429.

Koskenniemi, Martti. *The Gentle Civilizer of Nations: The Rise and Fall of International Law 1870–1960* (Cambridge: Cambridge University Press, 2001).

Krueger, Anna. *Die Bindung der Dritten Welt an das postkoloniale Völkerrecht. Die Völkerrechtskommission, das Recht der Verträge und das Recht der Staatennachfolge in der Dekolonialisierung* (Berlin: Springer, 2018).

Laqua, Daniel. 'Transnational Intellectual Cooperation, the League of Nations, and the Problem of Order'. *Journal of Global History* 6(2) (2011), 223–247.

League of Nations, Permanent Mandates Commission, Minutes of the 8th Session (Extraordinary) including the Report of the Commission to the Council, 8 March 1926, C.174.M.65.1926.VI.

League of Nations, Permanent Mandates Commission, Minutes of the 21st Session, 29 December 1931, C.830.M.411.1931.VI.

Lieber, Francis. *Manual of Political Ethics*, vol. 2 (Boston: Charles C. Little and James Brown, 1839).

Liszt, Franz von. *Das Völkerrecht systematisch dargestellt* (Berlin: Verlag von O. Haering, 1898).

Lorimer, James. *The Institutes of the Law of Nations. A Treatise of the Jural Relations of Separate Political Communities*, vol. 2 (Edinburgh: William Blackwood & Sons, 1884).

Magee, Peter. 'The Foundations of Antiquities Departments', in *A Companion to the Archeology of the Ancient Near East*, ed. Daniel T. Potts (Malden: Blackwell Publishing, 2012), 70–86.

Maine, Henry S. *International Law* (London: John Murray, 1890).

Mantena, Karuna. *Alibis of Empire: Henry Maine and the Ends of Liberal Imperialism* (Princeton: Princeton University Press, 2010).

Marchand, Suzanne. 'Orientalism as Kulturpolitik. German Archeology and Cultural Imperialism in Asia Minor', in *Volksgeist as Method and Ethic. Essays on Boasian Ethnography and the German Anthropological Tradition*, ed. George W. Stocking (Madison: University of Wisconsin Press, 1996), 298–336.

Mégret, Frederic. 'From Savages to Unlawful Combatants: A Postcolonial Look at International Law's "Other"', in *International Law and Its Others*, ed. Anne Orford (Cambridge: Cambridge University Press, 2006), 265–317.

Meyer, Andrea and Bénédicte Savoy, eds. *The Museum Is Open. Towards a Transnational History of Museums 1750–1940* (Berlin: De Gruyter, 2014).

Miles, Kate. *The Origins of International Investment Law. Empire, Environment and the Safeguarding of Capital* (Cambridge: Cambridge University Press, 2013).

Ministre des Colonies. 'Rapport au président de la république française, December 23, 1924'. *Bulletin de l'ecole francaise d'extrême-orient* 26 (1926), 526–527.

Obenaus, Maria. *Für die Nation gesichert? Das „Verzeichnis der national wertvollen Kunstwerke": Entstehung, Etablierung und Instrumentalisierung 1919–1945* (Berlin: De Gruyter, 2016).

Obregón, Liliana. 'The Civilized and the Uncivilized', in *The Oxford Handbook of the History of International Law*, eds. Bardo Fassbender and Anne Peters (Oxford: Oxford University Press, 2012), 917–939.

Office International des Musées. 'Le projet définitif établi en 1939 en vue de la conférence diplomatique'. *Art et archéologie. Recueil de législation comparée et de droit international* 1 (1939), 78–87.

O'Keefe, Roger. *The Protection of Cultural Property in Armed Conflict* (Cambridge: Cambridge University Press, 2006).

Oppenheim, Lassa Francis Lawrence. *International Law. A Treatise*, vol. 1 (London: Longmans, Green, and Co., 1905).

Oppenheim, Lassa Francis Lawrence. *International Law. A Treatise*, vol. 1 (London: Longmans, Green, and Co., 2nd ed., 1912).

Özsu, Umut. 'Ottoman Empire', in *The Oxford Handbook of the History of International Law*, eds. Bardo Fassbender and Anne Peters (Oxford: Oxford University Press, 2012), 429–448.

Pauka, Marc. *Kultur, Fortschritt und Reziprozität. Die Begriffsgeschichte des zivilisierten Staates im Völkerrecht* (Baden-Baden: Nomos, 2012).

Pedersen, Susan. *The Guardians. The League of Nations and the Crisis of Empire* (Oxford: Oxford University Press, 2015).

Pillet, Antoine. *Le droit de la guerre* (Paris: Arthur Rousseau, 1893).

Pitts, Jennifer. *Boundaries of the International. Law and Empire* (Cambridge: Harvard University Press, 2018).

Prott, Lyndel V. and Patrick J. O'Keefe. "Cultural Heritage' or 'Cultural Property'?'. *International Journal of Cultural Property* 1(2) (1992), 307–320.

Rajagopal, Balakrishnan. *International Law from Below. Development, Social Movements and Third World Resistance* (Cambridge: Cambridge University Press, 2003).

'Recommandations de l'assemblée de la société des nations du 10 octobre 1932'. *Art et archéologie. Recueil de législation comparée et de droit international* 1 (1939), 114 et seq.

Reimann, Mathias. 'Comparative Law and Private International Law', in *The Oxford Handbook of Comparative Law*, eds. Mathias Reimann and Reinhard Zimmermann (Oxford: Oxford University Press, 2006), 1363–1396.

Roberts, Anthea. *Is International Law International?* (Oxford: Oxford University Press, 2017).

Röben, Betsy. *Johann Caspar Bluntschli, Francis Lieber und das moderne Völkerrecht 1861–1881* (Baden-Baden: Nomos, 2003).

Roerich, Nicholas. *Roerich Banner of Peace* (New York: Roerich Museum Press, 1931).

Sandholtz, Wayne. *Prohibiting Plunder: How Norms Change* (Oxford: Oxford University Press, 2007).

Sarr, Felwine and Bénédicte Savoy. *The Restitution of African Cultural Heritage. Toward a New Relational Ethics* (2018), available at: http://restitutionreport2018.com/sarr_savoy_en.pdf (last accessed on 14 September 2020).

Savoy, Bénédicte. *Die Provenienz der Kultur. Von der Trauer des Verlusts zum universalen Menschheitserbe* (Berlin: Matthes & Seitz, 2018).

Savoy, Bénédicte. *Kunstraub, Napoleons Konfiszierungen in Deutschland und die europäischen Folgen* (Vienna: Böhlau Verlag, 2011).

Schayegh, Cyrus and Andrew Arsan, eds. *The Routledge Handbook of the History of the Middle East Mandates* (Abingdon: Routledge, 2015).

Schindler, Dietrich and Jiří Toman, eds. *The Laws of Armed Conflicts. A Collection of Conventions, Resolutions and Other Documents* (Leiden: Martinus Nijhoff, 3rd ed. 2004).

Schmoeckel, Mathias. 'The Internationalist as a Scientist and Herald: Lassa Oppenheim'. *European Journal of International Law* 11(3) (2000), 699–712.

Schwartz, Bill. *The White Man's World* (Oxford: Oxford University Press, 2011).

Shahabuddin, Mohammad. 'The 'Standard of Civilization' in International Law: Intellectual Perspectives from Pre-war Japan'. *Leiden Journal of International Law* 32 (1) (2018), 13–32.

Shaw, Malcolm N. *International Law* (Cambridge: Cambridge University Press, 8th ed. 2017).

Shaw, Wendy. *Possessors and Possessed. Museum, Archaeology, and the Visualization of History in the Late Ottoman Empire* (Berkeley: University of California Press, 2003).

Spitra, Sebastian M. *Die Verwaltung von Kultur im Völkerrecht. Eine postkoloniale Geschichte* (Baden-Baden: Nomos, forthcoming 2021).

Steiger, Heinhard. 'Völkerrecht', in *Geschichtliche Grundbegriffe*, vol. 7, eds. Otto Brunner, Werner Conze and Reinhart Koselleck (Stuttgart: Klett-Cotta, 1992), 97–140.

Taşdelen, Alper. *The Return of Cultural Artefacts. Hard and Soft Law Approaches* (Berlin: Springer, 2016).

Ullmann, Emanuel. *Völkerrecht* (Tübingen: J. C. B. Mohr, 1908).

Vec, Miloš. 'All's Fair in Love and War or the Limits of the Limitations. Juridification of Warfare and Its Revocation by Military Necessity', in *Civility, Barbarism and the Evolution of International Humanitarian Law: Who Do the Laws of War Protect?*, ed. Matt Killingsworth (Cambridge: Cambridge University Press, forthcoming 2021).

Verhoeve, Joe. 'Charles de Visscher: Living and Thinking International Law'. *European Journal of International Law* 11(4) (2000), 887–904.

Vrdoljak, Ana F. *International Law, Museums and the Return of Cultural Objects* (Cambridge: Cambridge University Press, 2006).

Wheaton, Henry. *Elements of International Law*, ed. Richard Henry Dana (London: Sampson Low, Son and Co., 8th ed., 1866).

Wussow, Alexander von. *Die Erhaltung der Denkmäler in den Kulturstaaten der Gegenwart* (Berlin: Carl Heymanns, 1885).

CHAPTER 13

International Law, Science and Psychology in the New Haven School

Rían Derrig

Abstract

In the contemporary field of international law, the policy-oriented jurisprudence of Harold Lasswell and Myres McDougal, better known as the 'New Haven School', is widely understood as a post-war response to international relations realism and a methodological precursor of what some have called the 'empirical turn' in legal scholarship. This chapter draws on archival material, including sources previously unavailable for research, to challenge this contemporary understanding. The chapter argues for a re-reading of the New Haven School as an interwar, politically progressive project of engineering social order through law. It suggests the importance of a neglected dimension of early twentieth century and interwar legal theory – a widespread preoccupation with relations between psychological interiority, science and social order.

Keywords

New Haven School – psychoanalysis – philosophical pragmatism – legal science – policy-oriented – social order – microhistory – legal realism

1 Introduction

From the 1930s onwards, Harold Lasswell, a prominent political scientist, contributed to the introduction of psychological, and in that period specifically psychoanalytic theory to the American social sciences. Myres McDougal was a legal scholar who began his career in the 1930s as a specialist in property law, but achieved most prominence in the 1950s and 1960s as an international law scholar and practitioner. Collaborating together on teaching and in publications from 1935 onwards, Lasswell and McDougal developed a theoretical approach to law that became well-known in the post-war period as the 'New Haven School'. Drawing on archival sources in New Haven, New

 | DOI:10.1163/9789004461802_015

York and Chicago, including materials previously inaccessible to researchers, this chapter argues for a re-reading of the body of legal theory they created together – what Lasswell and McDougal themselves called 'policy-oriented jurisprudence'.

Emphasising the centrality and volume of psychoanalytic theory present in Lasswell and McDougal's collaborative work (particularly the 1950s seminar materials from which they taught at Yale Law School), this chapter suggests that the New Haven School draws attention to one facet of the intellectual atmosphere of interwar America and Europe – a widespread interest in projects of social and legal theory focused on connecting scientific enquiry to psychological interiority.[1] The chapter highlights the significance of this psychological mentality to conceptions of social order and value employed by legal theorists who, like Lasswell and McDougal, relied on ideas formed in important ways during the interwar period.

The widespread contemporary understanding of the New Haven School, on which this chapter seeks to cast doubt, runs as follows: In the 1940s American power rises. Shrugging the tired formalism of international law, Hans Morgenthau, George F. Kennan and other theorists of great power politics take the top table as advisors worthy of the moment. Myres McDougal senses the *zeitgeist* the realists have captured and leads a 'legal' response. Positivist social science is instrumentally refashioned as 'policy-science', the lawyer policy-scientist pitched as the anti-communist power behind the throne. The story tends to be completed by one of two alternative conclusions. For some critics this ends as a story of Cold Warrior lawyers hawking a method skewed to imperial American policy. A cautionary tale of lawyers losing sight of legality in a clash between 'realism' and 'legalism'.[2] A moral of this critical story

1 With the term 'psychological interiority', I follow Eli Zaretsky, who uses it to denote historically and culturally specific experiences of interiority: Zaretsky, Eli. *Political Freud a History* (New York: Columbia University Press, 2015), 20.

2 See, e.g., Koskenniemi, Martti. *The Gentle Civilizer of Nations: The Rise and Fall of International Law 1870–1960* (Cambridge: Cambridge University Press, 2001), 476 and more generally chapter 6; Koskenniemi, Martti. 'Law, Teleology and International Relations: An Essay in Counterdisciplinarity'. *International Relations* 26(1) (2012), 3–34, 14; Peters, Anne. 'There Is Nothing More Practical than a Good Theory: An Overview of Contemporary Approaches to International Law'. *German Yearbook of International Law* 44 (2001), 25–37, 31–32; García-Salmones Rovira, Mónica. 'Sources in the Anti-Formalist Tradition: A Prelude to Institutional Discourses in International Law', in *The Oxford Handbook of the Sources of International Law*, eds. Samantha Besson and Jean d'Aspremont (Oxford: Oxford University Press, 2017), 203–224; Chimni, Bhupinder S. *International Law and World Order: A Critique of Contemporary Approaches* (Cambridge: Cambridge University Press, 2nd ed. 2017), 107–109;

tends to be that policy-oriented lawyers were bought out of their vocation by hegemony and neoliberalism. In an alternative narrative, some interpreters distance themselves from McDougal's reputation as a strident Cold Warrior, but emphasise that the New Haven School bequeathed the field of international law a legacy of useful empirical methods and the admirable figure of the lawyer policy-maker. Many narrators of the second story claim the New Haven School as an intellectual ancestor of an American, post-1990s centre-left policy class.[3]

This chapter challenges three aspects of this contemporary understanding of the New Haven School. First, rather than a post-war reaction to international relations realism, Lasswell and McDougal's ideas need to be understood in the cultural context of 1920s and 1930s modernism. Re-periodising policy-oriented jurisprudence demonstrates the complexity of the project. It was motivated not by post-war American confidence and hegemony, but by interwar anxieties as international institutions lost support, mass political movements (such as socialism, communism, or fascism) seemed to many to offer the most likely prospects for social change, and old orders of value seemed inadequate to the moment.

Second, while foreign policy interventions McDougal made in the 1950s and 1960s in support of the US State Department (for example his 1963 defence of the naval blockade of Cuba; his 1955 assertion of the legality of hydrogen bomb tests on the Marshall Islands; and his defence of the June 1950 UN Security Council resolution that condemned North Korea for its 'armed attack' on South Korea) can seem to exemplify what we would now consider Cold War

---

Kratochwil, Friedrich V. *Rules, Norms, and Decisions: On the Conditions of Practical and Legal Reasoning in International Relations and Domestic Affairs* (Cambridge: Cambridge University Press, 1991), 104–199; and the sceptical reflections in Cassese, Antonio. *Five Masters of International Law: Conversations with R.-J. Dupuy, E. Jiménez de Arechaga, R. Jennings, L. Henkin and O. Schachter* (Oxford: Hart Publishing, 2011), 200–202.

3 See, e.g., Slaughter Burley, Anne-Marie. 'International Law and International Relations Theory: A Dual Agenda'. *American Journal of International Law* 87(2) (1993), 205–239, 209–213; Koh, Harold H. 'Is There a "New" New Haven School of International Law?'. *Yale Journal of International Law* 32(2) (2007), 559–573, 562; Hathaway, Oona A. 'The Continuing Influence of the New Haven School'. *Yale Journal of International Law* 32(2) (2007), 553–558, 555; Shaffer, Gregory and Tom Ginsburg. 'The Empirical Turn in International Legal Scholarship'. *American Journal of International Law* 106(1) (2012), 1–46, 2; Dunoff, Jeffrey L. and Mark A. Pollack. *Interdisciplinary Perspectives on International Law and International Relations: The State of the Art* (Cambridge: Cambridge University Press, 2013), chapter 1.

neoconservatism, the politics of the New Haven School are more complex.[4] The political arc of policy-oriented jurisprudence has its origins in New Deal redistributionism and European socialism. In the 1950s and 1960s, Lasswell and other colleagues maintained a view more critical than McDougal's of an increasingly hawkish, anti-communist American foreign policy establishment.[5]

Third, the two bodies of thought that can be described as the intellectual origins of the New Haven School – psychoanalysis and philosophical pragmatism – challenge the positivist empiricism and methodological objectivity often associated with the school.[6] Lasswell and McDougal sought to scientifically build social order by controlling politics and ideology through law, with ideas based on strong conceptions of the irrational, unconscious and emotional bases of social life. This chapter places Lasswell and McDougal's formative early scholarship and intellectual lives in an early twentieth century context of widespread interest in science's relation to psychological interiority. It argues that policy-oriented jurisprudence suggests the important influence this widespread interest in psychology had on early twentieth century and interwar legal theory.

A more complete story of the New Haven School's intellectual history cannot be told here.[7] Instead, this chapter identifies a cluster of core challenges to the dominant contemporary understanding of policy-oriented jurisprudence, and articulates a relationship between the aspects of McDougal and Lasswell's legal theory emphasised here, and a neglected but animating preoccupation of interwar legal theory – the idea that social order might be fashioned from psychological forces. In section 2, the chapter's methodological premises are

---

4 McDougal, Myres and Richard Gardner. 'The Veto and the Charter: An Interpretation for Survival'. *Yale Law Journal* 60(2) (1951), 258–292; McDougal, Myres and Norbert A. Schlei. 'The Hydrogen Bomb Tests in Perspective: Lawful Measures for Security'. *Yale Law Journal* 64(3) (1955), 648–710; and McDougal, Myres. 'The Soviet-Cuban Quarantine and Self-Defense'. *American Journal of International Law* 57(3) (1963), 597–604.

5 Lasswell rarely adopted public positions on such issues, possibly because the FBI maintained an open file on his suspected communist sympathies, but he expresses opposition to the Vietnam war and hopes for social change in American society in: Harrington Hall, Mary. 'A Conversation with Harold Lasswell: The Psychology of Politics'. *Psychology Today* 1 (October 1968), 56–64. For an example of a New Haven School adherent who frequently opposed McDougal's 'cold war partisanship', see Falk, Richard. 'International Law and the United States Role in the Viet Nam War'. *Yale Law Journal* 75(7) (1966), 1122–1160.

6 See, e.g., Shaffer/Ginsburg, 'The Empirical Turn' 2012 (n. 3) 1–46, 2.

7 This story is told in the author's doctoral thesis Derrig, Rián. *Educating American Modernists: The Origins of the New Haven School* (Florence: European University Institute, Department of Law, PhD Thesis, 2019).

outlined. I relate these methodological choices to what I identify as facets of policy-oriented jurisprudence overlooked by the contemporary field of international law. In section 3, these claims are illustrated through a condensed historical account of policy-oriented jurisprudence: developed by Lasswell in 1920s Europe; further adapted to law and embraced by McDougal in 1930s and 1940s America; and collaboratively taught somewhat after its period of inception in seminars at Yale Law School in the 1950s. Section 4 concludes.

2 A Microhistory of Forgotten Preoccupations

By placing McDougal and Lasswell's conception of a science of law in a context of late 19th and early 20th century ideas preoccupied with connecting scientific enquiry to psychological interiority, this chapter seeks to emphasise the extent to which the archival sources reflect this context and cultural moment. My aim is to understand the New Haven School as a cluster of ideas in a time and context, and at the same time to begin to understand that time and context through the New Haven School. I have drawn insights from Carlo Ginzburg's work in 'microhistory', which also attempts to explore presuppositions and preoccupations widely shared in particular historical moments and cultural contexts.

In his 1976 *The Cheese and the Worms: The Cosmos of a Sixteenth-Century Miller*, Ginzburg explores a set of cosmological and philosophical ideas held by Menocchio, a miller from Montereale in Northern Italy, through transcripts of his interrogations before officials of the Catholic Church as part of the Roman Inquisition.[8] While Ginzburg examines Menocchio's own ideas, he also uses them to access the cultural context in which Menocchio lived, by which he was shaped and to which he responded. Poorly understood currents of folk belief and dissident networks of critique that challenged Church orthodoxy are suggested and re-captured through the worldview of one person.

Engaging in a similar process of exploring a broader worldview in part through biographical case studies, and sharing Ginzburg's caution towards totalising narratives, I am interested in sketching what are sometimes called 'mentalities' or 'collective psychologies' of a particular historical moment.

8 Ginzburg, Carlo. *The Cheese and the Worms: The Cosmos of a Sixteenth-Century Miller* (Baltimore: Johns Hopkins University Press, 1976). See also Ginzburg, Carlo. *The Night Battles: Witchcraft & Agrarian Cults in the Sixteenth & Seventeenth Centuries* (Baltimore: Johns Hopkins University Press, 1992).

'Mentalities' can be understood as particular 'frameworks of inner experience', or experiences of the self and interiority.[9] In this sense, the chapter shares some emphases with a legal methodology suggested by Anthony Carty in 1994. Carty says of his objects of study, Hans Kelsen and Carl Schmitt: 'their works alone are taken as symbolic of the state of the culture to which they belonged – their pathologies are those of their culture.'[10] I suggest Lasswell and McDougal's policy-oriented jurisprudence can be read as symbolic of the psychological 'mentality' of interwar thought about law and science, as sharing cultural pathologies of that moment.

Lasswell and McDougal's writings about policy-oriented jurisprudence often indicated the extent to which their pursuit of a science of law was animated by insights, methods and problematics drawn from psychoanalysis. This was particularly true of their first collaborative publication in 1943, and the 1950s seminar materials from which they taught their legal theory.[11] Yet the

9 Vernant, Jean Pierre. *Myth and Thought among the Greeks* (New York: Zone Books, distributed by MIT Press, 2006), 19.

10 Carty, Anthony. 'Interwar German Theories of International Law: The Psychoanalytical and Phenomenologicial Perspectives of Hans Kelsen and Carl Schmitt'. *Cardozo Law Review* 16(3) (1994), 1235–1292, 1238.

11 For example, many references to different branches of research in social psychology can be found in their first collaborative publication: Lasswell, Harold and Myres McDougal. 'Legal Education and Public Policy: Professional Training in the Public Interest'. *Yale Law Journal* 52(2) (1943), 203–295, concerning new methods at 214–215, 286–287 (esp. n. 131), 291, and character and personality at 231, 279–282. Explicit explanation of the central role played by psychoanalytic theories of personality and culture (largely taken from Sigmund Freud's work) in policy-oriented jurisprudence can be found in the collaboratively written manuscript from which Lasswell and McDougal taught seminars from the late 1940s onwards. See Lasswell, Harold and Myres McDougal. *Law, Science and Policy* (1958) (unpublished working papers, copies on file with the author). In the present chapter references to these materials are to this original unpublished version, dated 1956–1958. However, a published edition that includes additions and edits made by Myres McDougal and Andrew Willard after Lasswell's death has been available since 1992: Lasswell, Harold and Myres McDougal. *Jurisprudence for a Free Society: Studies in Law, Science and Policy* (Alphen aan den Rijn/New Haven: Kluwer Law International/New Haven Press, 1992). On Freud and psychoanalysis in these materials see part II, chapter I 'The Social Process as a Whole' (compare 335–372 in the 1992 ed.); part II, chapter II 'Specific Value-Institution Processes' (375–587, 1992 ed.); part II, chapter III 'The Dynamics of Personality' (591–631, 1992 ed.); part II, chapter IV 'Political Personality' (631–669, 1992 ed.); part II, chapter V 'Political Culture' (theorising the continuity of social order through socially inherited generational psychologies by reading Plato's *The Republic* through Freud) (683–709, 1992 ed.); and part III, chapter 5 'The Projection of Future Developments' (relating the 'politically centered character' and 'anti-democratic character types' to childhood experiences that can affect the development of the ego, in particular the Oedipal phase) (compare

dominant contemporary narrative elides such notes, instead understanding their legal theory as a Cold War response to foreign policy realists, inspired by empirical social science.

With Ginzburg, this chapter argues that political and intellectual orthodoxies are supported in the present when dominant historiographies read particular cultural preoccupations out of the past because they cannot be articulated in familiar idioms or themes. I suggest that much of the contemporary field of international law pays scant attention to psychological theory. The interwar interest in conceptualising law, value and social order as phenomena constituted by psychological forces, of which the New Haven School is an example, is today a largely forgotten preoccupation.

3 Interwar Policy-Oriented Jurisprudence

3.1 *Harold Lasswell: Theorising Social Change in a Psychological Age*

During the 1930s, Lasswell established a national reputation as an authority on the relationship between psychology, politics and communication. His published work applied psychoanalytic ideas to social change, political elites and propaganda.[12] Recalling their development of policy-oriented jurisprudence after meeting in 1935, McDougal has said:

---

esp. 995–1002, 1992 ed.). Further development of these ideas can be found in other writings published by Lasswell in the same period, e.g. Lasswell, Harold. 'Democratic Character', in *The Political Writings of Harold D. Lasswell*, ed. Harold Lasswell (Glencoe: Free Press, 1951), noting the inclusion of material from his seminars with McDougal at 476 n. 22. For application of some of these ideas in the work of McDougal in this period see McDougal, Myres. 'The Law School of the Future: From Legal Realism to Policy Science in the World Community'. *Yale Law Journal* 56(8) (1947), 1345–1355, 1346 and 1349; and McDougal, Myres. 'The Role of Law in World Politics'. *Mississippi Law Journal* 20(3) (1949), 253–283, 254–257, 260–263, and 276. For examples in later, collaborative publications see McDougal, Myres, Harold Lasswell and James C. Miller. *The Interpretation of Agreements and World Public Order: Principles of Content and Procedure* (New Haven: Yale University Press, 1967), noting in particular the importance of Freud and later schools of psychology to their understanding of 'contextuality' at 50 n. 11; and McDougal, Myres and Harold Lasswell. 'Jurisprudence in Policy-Oriented Perspective'. *University of Florida Law Review* 19(3) (1967), 486–513, 489–490.

12 Lasswell, Harold. *Psychopathology and Politics* (New York: Viking Press, 1960 [1930]); Lasswell, Harold. 'The Triple-Appeal Principle: A Contribution of Psychoanalysis to Political and Social Science'. *American Journal of Sociology* 37(4) (1932), 523–538; Lasswell, Harold. *World Politics and Personal Insecurity* (Glencoe: Free Press, 1965 [1935]); Lasswell, Harold. 'What Psychiatrists and Political Scientists Can Learn From One Another'.

> Lasswell was primarily responsible for this [the theoretical framework of the jurisprudence], my role was to help him give it hands and feet. He had the map from the first day I met him there in the summer of nineteen and thirty-five but he didn't know enough about authority you see. He knew about effective power, he knew about the factors that affect human beings, the complexities of human being's perspectives … This first book on *World Politics and Personal Insecurity* has the germs of everything that I've said to you [describing policy-oriented jurisprudence] and our collaboration was just a slow process of working out this theory in a way that it could be applied to any subject.[13]

The 1935 monograph McDougal referenced, *World Politics and Personal Insecurity*, was Lasswell's most complete statement of his psychoanalytic social theory. Lasswell framed the book as an effort to inaugurate a shift in perspective 'in many respects parallel to the viewpoint introduced by Karl Marx and Friedrich Engels into modern social theory.'[14] Marx and Engels had considered as political aspects of society previously treated as depoliticised – the competitive market. In Lasswell's words, they 'marked the recovery of the political standpoint.' He also intended to recover a standpoint – 'the self-orientation which is the goal of analysis.'[15] Invoking unconscious psychological forces as determinants of social change alongside dialectical materialism, in *World Politics* Lasswell argued for the elite-led construction of a world society based on revolutionary socialism.[16]

As McDougal noted in the interview cited above and on other occasions, Lasswell's 1930s social theory would become the core of policy-oriented

---

Psychiatry 1(1) (1938), 33–39; Lasswell, Harold. 'The Contribution of Freud's Insight Interview to the Social Sciences'. *American Journal of Sociology* 45(3) (1939), 375–390.

13 Interview with Myres McDougal by Michael Reisman. *Reflections on the New Haven School* (New York: United Nations Audiovisual Library, 1982).

14 Lasswell, *World Politics* 1965 (n. 12), 17.

15 Ibid., 17–19.

16 Lasswell asked: 'Is there any way to disintegrate the middle classes as a whole more readily for the benefit of the proletarian mythology which might unite mankind? Certainly the present practice of insulting and intimidating them has strengthened fascism. Is it worth while to show that the revolutionary state of the socialists is the only one where able organizers and technicians are given security and scope, the only society in which the road to reward for effort is open, where it cannot be shut off by the erratic malcoordination of the capitalist economy?' Ibid., 201–202. For extensive discussion of the strengths of Marxist theory from a psychoanalytic perspective see ibid., 98–104.

jurisprudence.[17] It was the substructure of their first collaborative publication, a 1943 *Yale Law Journal* chapter, and of the seminars they taught together at Yale Law School in the 1950s.[18]

That theory was itself a product of extensive periods of research Lasswell had undertaken in Europe between 1923 and 1928, of his training at the University of Chicago, and to an extent of the reformist politics amidst which he grew up. His father was a Presbyterian minister, his mother a schoolteacher, and the family moved between a series of small towns in rural Illinois.[19] A teenager in the later years of the Progressive Movement, Lasswell's family holidays often included events on the Chautauqua speaking circuit, speeches delivered by politicians like William Jennings Bryan and Robert La Follette who railed against industrial monopolies and the railroad trusts, the stranglehold of corporate money in politics and the concentration of wealth and power in coastal cities. Lasswell was taken by these charismatic figures' rejection of 19th century liberal capitalism and their reformist visions of industrial society.

> On the platform under the great tent, La Follette would toss his great mane, pull off his coat, unloosen his tie, roll up his sleeves, and slay again the railroad dragon in four perspiring hours.[20]

Entering the University of Chicago in 1918, Lasswell found mentors who offered theoretical frameworks based on similar ideas. His supervisor, Charles Edward Merriam, was an important supporter, offering a research program with institutional and financial backing.[21] On a philosophical level, the pragmatism of

17 See, e.g., Interview with Rosalyn Higgins. *Oral History Discussion* (27 March 1993); Interview with Stephen Schwebel. *Oral History Discussion* (6 November 1992); Myres Smith McDougal Papers (MS 1636). Manuscripts and Archives, Yale University Library. Reproduction of these oral history materials was made possible with financial support from the Oscar M. Ruebhausen Fund at Yale Law School.

18 Lasswell/McDougal, *Legal Education* 1943 (n. 11); Lasswell/McDougal, *Law, Science and Policy* 1958 (n. 11).

19 Description of the careers of Linden Downey Lasswell and Anna Prather Lasswell, authored by Harold Lasswell (undated; partially handwritten). Harold Dwight Lasswell Papers (MS 1043). Manuscripts and Archives, Yale University Library, Series V.

20 Ibid.

21 Detailed correspondence between Lasswell and Merriam between 1923–1952: Merriam, Charles E. Papers (Box 34, Folder 4; Box 51 Folders 18–19; Box 64 Folder 22; Box 65 Folder 2). Special Collections Research Center, University of Chicago Library.

William James and John Dewey was a formative influence for Lasswell, as was the social psychology of George Herbert Mead.[22]

Between 1923 and 1928 Lasswell spent significant periods in Europe, conducting research in Geneva, London, Paris, Berlin and Vienna. Assisted by letters of introduction from Merriam's wealthy patrons, he evinced a Forrest Gump like ability to find himself amidst historically significant figures and events. Credentialed as League of Nations correspondent for the *Chicago Tribune*, he attended the press at meetings of the Council and the Assembly in Geneva's Hôtel National. Detailed correspondence with his parents sketches the fear and anxiety, the personalities and intrigues of summer 1923 at the League and among Geneva's cosmopolitan elite.[23]

In London he joined the intellectual networks of the London School of Economics, the Fabian Society and the Labour Party. Graham Wallas helped him to reflect on politics at the League. Wallas' writing on the social psychology of industrial civilisation prompted Lasswell to theorise means of manipulating social change in what he considered a 'psychological age'.[24] He was comfortable in the left-wing internationalism of the Fabian Society, attending meetings of the Fabian 'nursery', a discussion group for younger members, and campaigning for Bertrand Russell in his doomed bid for a parliamentary seat in the wealthy London constituency of Chelsea.[25]

---

22 Of his own development of 'policy science', Lasswell has said: 'The policy sciences are a contemporary adaption of the general approach to public policy that was recommended by John Dewey and his colleagues in the development of American pragmatism.' Lasswell, Harold. *A Pre-View of Policy Sciences* (New York: American Elsevier Publishing Co., 1971), xiv. See also Lasswell, Harold and Marvick Dwaine. *Harold D. Lasswell on Political Sociology* (Chicago: University of Chicago Press, 1977), 21–22; Smith, Mark C. *Social Science in the Crucible: The American Debate over Objectivity and Purpose, 1918–1941* (Durham: Duke University Press, 1994), 222; Lannes Smith, Bruce. 'The Mystifying Intellectual History of Harold D. Lasswell', in *Politics, Personality, and Social Science in the Twentieth Century: Essays in Honor of Harold D. Lasswell*, ed. Arnold A. Rogow (Chicago: University of Chicago Press, 1969), 49–52. Of particular help in reconstructing this period of Lasswell's intellectual life is a prospectus for an unrealised intellectual biography compiled by William Ascher and Ronald D. Brunner, who collaborated with Lasswell to develop his 'policy-science' framework: Ascher, William and Ronald D. Brunner. *Prospectus for an Intellectual Biography of Harold D. Lasswell* (unpublished manuscript, 1982); Harold Dwight Lasswell Papers (MS 1043), Manuscripts and Archives, Yale University Library, Box 4 Folder 13.

23 Letters from Harold Lasswell to Anna and Linden Lasswell, dated June 1923–July 1924. Harold Dwight Lasswell Papers (MS 1043), Manuscripts and Archives, Yale University Library, Series I. Box 56 Folders 775–780.

24 Ibid., Box 56 Folder 777. Letter from Harold Lasswell to Anna and Linden Lasswell, dated 28 November 1923.

25 Ibid.

Some of Lasswell's most formative experiences in this period came during his pursuit of psychoanalytic training in Vienna and Berlin in 1928. In Vienna, although he ultimately failed to see Sigmund Freud, Lasswell attended nightly meetings with the founder of the school of individual psychology and theorist of the inferiority complex, Alfred Adler, and his group in the cafes on the city's *Ringstraße*. He met Anna Freud, a prominent founder of the psychoanalytic field of child psychology, secretary to the Vienna Psychoanalytical Training Institute and gatekeeper to her father; attended meetings of the Vienna Psychoanalytic Society as a guest of the theorist of ego psychology Paul Federn, and discussed analyses of political personalities with Wilhelm Stekel, an important early collaborator of Sigmund Freud.[26] He was even more enamoured of the edgier political and cultural analytic circles in Berlin, and was analysed there by Theodor Reik, one of Sigmund Freud's first students who was prominently associated with the development of lay analysis.[27]

Lasswell discussed the personalities of politicians and the state of American jurisprudence with Hans Kelsen in Vienna. Kelsen was himself an important member of the Viennese psychoanalytic circles to which Lasswell had gained access. Lasswell knew that if he had any possibility of being granted an audience with Sigmund Freud, it would be on Kelsen's imprimatur.[28] Kelsen and Lasswell had much in common. As this context suggests, like Lasswell's social theory and later policy-oriented jurisprudence, Kelsen's own legal science can be understood as another answer to the moment's preoccupation with relationships between science, social order and psychological interiority.[29] As Judith Shklar has framed a similar point, a historically-aware reading of Kelsen's pure theory can understand it as one of a number of '... negative responses to the

---

26 Ibid., Box 56 Folder 782.

27 Ibid., Box 56 Folder 783.

28 Ibid., Box 56 Folder 782. Letter from Harold Lasswell to Anna and Linden Lasswell, dated 12 August 1928: 'If I am recommended by Kelsen and have a fixed list of questions to discuss at some length I may later see him [Sigmund Freud].'

29 The influence of psychoanalytic theory on Kelsen's scholarship in law has received little examination. A notable exception to this trend can be found in the work of Étienne Balibar: Balibar, Étienne. *Citoyen sujet et autres essais d'anthropologie philosophique* (Paris: Presses Universitaires de France, 2011), chapter 12. See also Reynolds, Bryan and Paul Celafu. *The Return of Theory in Early Modern English Studies: Tarrying with the Subjunctive* (London: Palgrave Macmillan, 2016), 121–143; and Carty, 'Interwar German Theories' 1994 (n. 10). For a brief contextual history, see Jabloner, Clemens. 'Kelsen and His Circle: The Viennese Years'. *European Journal of International Law* 9(2) (1998), 368–385, 382–384.

fanaticized consciousness and the distortions which it engenders.'[30] From this perspective, Kelsen's effort to scientifically 'purify' his legal theory of the state can be understood as another, contrasting reaction to the presence of the psychological unconscious as a driver of change in the social and cultural contexts to which he, like Lasswell, wanted to respond.

3.2 *Myres McDougal: After Legal Realism*

Myres McDougal grew up in Prentiss County, rural Mississippi. His mother managed the family farm and home, his father was a doctor and local politician. A doctor was a person of consequence in this farming community, but late in life McDougal recalled that his father wanted him to be a politician of more power, to be a senator.[31] Studying at the University of Mississippi in the early 1920s, he himself gravitated to politics, becoming a student leader and accumulating friends like James Eastland, later a powerful Democratic senator and opponent of desegregation.[32] McDougal's early political experiences suggest little engagement with race. Unlike Eastland and other 'Dixiecrats', he associated with an East Coast Democratic party elite that in the interwar period advocated redistribution of wealth, planned rural and urban development, and criticised Southern religious conservatism; and in the post-war period supported desegregation.[33]

Having studied classics at the University of Mississippi and law as a postgraduate at Oxford University, McDougal opened a career as a legal scholar after a doctorate at Yale Law School. His 1931 thesis applied a legal realist style of critique to contract law concepts, but he built a reputation as a teacher of land law.[34] Through the 1930s and 1940s, he approached the field as a strident realist critic and zealous advocate of New Deal community planning. With the French urban planner Maurice Rotival, he authored a report arguing for

30 Shklar, Judith N. *Legalism: Law, Morals, and Political Trials* (Cambridge: Harvard University Press, 1964), 41.

31 Interview with Eugene V. Rostow. *Oral History Discussion* (11 December 1992); Myres Smith McDougal Papers (MS 1636). Manuscripts and Archives, Yale University Library.

32 Interview with Frederick Tipson. *Oral History Discussion* (*1*) (11 September 1992); Interview with Elias Clark. *Oral History Discussion* (14 May 1993); Myres Smith McDougal Papers (MS 1636). Manuscripts and Archives, Yale University Library.

33 Interview with Nicholas Deb Katzenbach. *Oral History Discussion* (3 October 1992); Myres Smith McDougal Papers (MS 1636). Manuscripts and Archives, Yale University Library. Eastland said of McDougal: 'Mr. McDougal was a schoolmate of mine. He is a very distinguished professor at Yale University, and I think a very misguided liberal.' Cited in: Higgins, Rosalyn. 'Obituary: Professor Myres McDougal'. *The Independent* (9 May 1998).

34 McDougal, Myres. *Collateral Mistake in Contractual Relations* (New Haven: Yale University, School of Law, PhD Thesis, 1931) (unpublished PhD Thesis, copy on file with the author).

regional planning in New England.[35] Rotival was a prominent representative of modernist French urban planning. His adventurous work with McDougal was controversial in the conservative social circles that governed Yale University due to its being perceived as socialistic government intervention with property rights.[36] Similarly controversial was a 1948 casebook McDougal published with a student, David Haber.[37] The book's orientation towards land-use planning, at the time considered by some a controversial instrument of government intervention, coupled with an chapter on Russian property law, pushed legislators in Texas and Washington State to attempt to restrict its use in universities.[38]

During the Second World War McDougal worked in the Office of Lend-Lease Administration, the body that administered the aid and military hardware given by America to Allied countries in return for lease agreements permitting American military bases in those countries. He began to apply his community planning perspective to international affairs, a tendency that would become characteristic of his post-war scholarship in international law.[39] In this period McDougal also began to move from land law to international law. At the request of the State Department he co-wrote an article that sought to strengthen the president's ability to conclude international legal agreements.[40]

McDougal's 1930s publications almost entirely comprised book reviews bristling with criticism of the unwillingness of legal scholars to acknowledge value, politics or collective goals in law.[41] He thought 'legal realism' was a movement,

35 McDougal, Myres. *The Case for Regional Planning with Special Reference to New England* (New Haven: Yale University Press, 1947).

36 McDougal recalled an occasion when Rotival had a napkin thrown in his face by an enraged Yale alum at a formal dinner: Clark, 'Oral History Discussion' 1993 (n. 32).

37 McDougal, Myres and David Haber, eds. *Property, Wealth, Land; Allocation Planning and Development: Selected Cases and other Materials on the Law of Real Property* (Charlottesville: Michie, 1948).

38 Interview with Frederick Tipson. *Oral History Discussion* (2) (11 September 1992); Myres Smith McDougal Papers (MS 1636). Manuscripts and Archives, Yale University Library.

39 For examples of this tendency, see McDougal, Myres. 'Intervening'. *Proceedings of the American Society of International Law* 48 (1954), 113, 120–121; and McDougal, 'The Role of Law in World Politics' 1949 (n. 11), 282.

40 It was published in two parts: McDougal, Myres and Asher Lans. 'Treaties and Congressional-Executive or Presidential Agreements: Interchangeable Instruments of National Policy: I'. *Yale Law Journal* 54(2) (1945), 181–351; McDougal, Myres and Asher Lans. 'Treaties and Congressional-Executive or Presidential Agreements: Interchangeable Instruments of National Policy: II'. *Yale Law Journal* 54(3) (1945), 534–615.

41 For a representative example, see McDougal, Myres. 'Book Review: A Treatise on Mortgages. By William F. Walsh. Chicago: Callaghan. 1934 Pp. Xlv, 376'. *Yale Law Journal* 44(7) (1934), 1278–1282.

that it had energy and that most of its advocates were of the cultural moment in a way that charged them with progressive potential. He identified his ideas about law in society, less theorised than Lasswell's, with the 'left-wing' of this movement.[42] In this period McDougal's writing fell between a conservative, prediction-focused realism descending from the version of classical pragmatism applied to law by Oliver Wendell Holmes, and a tradition of radical, sometimes nihilistic social critique best represented by Nicholas St. John Green's more politically progressive application of pragmatism to legal doctrine.[43]

In this period he was looking for an intellectual apparatus he did not have. He did not have a scientific explanation for his belief in social values, for their character and relation to law. From 1937, his writings made it increasingly clear that he had found that apparatus in the work of Harold Lasswell. He adopted Lasswell's characteristic vocabulary, cited his psychoanalytic theories of communication, and employed his ideas about manipulating social change in industrial societies.[44]

---

42 McDougal, Myres. 'Book Review: The Law and Mr. Smith. By Max Radin. The Bobbs-Merrill Company, Indianapolis, 1938'. *University of Pennsylvania Law Review* 87(4) (1939), 495–496, identifying Radin with the 'right-wing' at 496.

43 For a reconstruction of the place of Holmes and Green in the intellectual history of philosophical pragmatism, see Menand, Louis. *The Metaphysical Club* (New York: Farrar, Straus & Giroux, 2001), 201–203. Holmes' writing is well-known, in particular: Holmes, Oliver Wendell. *The Common Law* (Basingstoke: Macmillan & Co., 1882). For examples of Green's writing, less extensive and less widely read due to his early death, see Green, Nicholas St. John. 'Proximate and Remote Cause'. *American Law Review* 4(2) (1870), 201–216 (critiquing ideas about causality in scientific inquiry from Aristotle, through Scholastic philosophy and into the ideas of Bacon and Descartes); Green, Nicholas St. John. 'Book Review: Commentaries on the Law of Married Women under the Statutes of the Several States and at Common Law and in Equity. By Joel Prentiss Bishop. Vol. I. Philadelphia: Kay and Brother. 1871'. *American Law Review* 6(1) (1871), 57–73 (attacking evangelical Christian sexism). For examples of McDougal's work drawing on these legal realist traditions see infra (n. 44).

44 For this progression, see McDougal, Myres. 'Book Review: The Promise of American Politics. By T. V. Smith. Chicago: University of Chicago Press, 1936. Pp. Xix, 308, $2.50'. *Yale Law Journal* 46(7) (1937), 1269–1272; McDougal, Myres. 'Book Review: Readings in Jurisprudence, Selected, Edited, and Arranged by Jerome Hall. Indianapolis: The Bobbs-Merrill Company. 1938. Pp. 1183. $7.50'. *Illinois Law Review of Northwestern University* 34(1) (1939), 109–111; McDougal, Myres. 'Fuller vs. the American Legal Realists: An Intervention. Review of The Law in Quest of Itself. By Lon L. Fuller, Professor of Law, Harvard Law School'. *Yale Law Journal* 50(5) (1941), 827–840; and McDougal, Myres. 'Book Review: Future Interests Restated: Tradition Versus Clarification and Reform. A Review of: Restatement of the Law of Property. Volume III. St. Paul: American Law Institute Publishers. 1940'. *Harvard Law Review* 55(7) (1942), 1078–1115.

3.3 *The Law, Science and Policy Seminars: Personal Character and Social Order*

Having collaboratively taught seminars at Yale Law School since 1939, Lasswell and McDougal composed their first statement of policy-oriented jurisprudence while working in government in wartime Washington – McDougal at Lend-Lease, Lasswell at the Library of Congress as 'Chief of the Experimental Division for the Study of War-Time Communications', a practicing propagandist.[45] In 1943, that statement was published in the *Yale Law Journal* as a call for reform of American legal education.[46] If we are to identify a thread of ideas in time that can be said to constitute the New Haven School, it would begin with this article and the seminars Lasswell and McDougal taught together. By the mid-1950s, they had expanded these ideas into a densely typed manuscript of several hundred pages, from which they taught seminars under the title *Law, Science and Policy*.[47]

Like Lasswell's *World Politics*, the seminars built a world outwards, from the human psyche to collectivities of people, to institutions, law and culture. Accordingly, by far the densest and largest portion of the materials developed a detailed theory of psychological interiority – what the self was, how it was constituted by relationships with other people, and how such relationships formed patterns of practises that constituted collective life.[48] Policy-oriented jurisprudence drew heavily on current anthropological research to relate this theory of psychology to social practises. Lasswell and McDougal deduced insights about what they thought were universal characteristics of human psychology from legal customs described in anthropological research widely

45 Memoranda, correspondence and materials from Lasswell's work at the Library of Congress can be found in Harold Dwight Lasswell Papers (MS 1043). Manuscripts and Archives, Yale University Library. Series I (n. 23), Boxes 53, 62, 81 and 95. For McDougal's reflections on his wartime work in government, see Collier, Bonnie. 'A Conversation with Myres S. McDougal', in *Yale Law School Oral History Series* (New Haven: Lillian Goldman Law Library, 2013), 14–17.

46 Lasswell/McDougal, *Legal Education* 1943 (n. 11).

47 Lasswell/McDougal, *Law, Science and Policy* 1958 (n. 11). The 1947 course description for these seminars can be found in McDougal, 'The Law School of the Future' 1947 (n. 11), 1353. These seminar materials constitute Lasswell and McDougal's most significant post-war collaborative work. Long after Lasswell's death, McDougal reflected that while they were teaching they published nothing explicitly setting out their framework of legal and social theory. Lasswell wished to do this but McDougal refused. Cf. Interview with Quintin Johnstone. *Oral History Discussion* (1 February 1993); Myres Smith McDougal Papers (MS 1636). Manuscripts and Archives, Yale University Library.

48 Lasswell/McDougal, *Law, Science and Policy* 1958 (n. 11). Concerning this theory of psychological interiority, see references supra (n. 11).

popular at the time, like Bronislaw Malinowski's study of the Tobriand islanders; Robert Lowie's writing on the state in 'primitive society'; Karl Llewelleyn and Edward Hoebel's study of the Cheyenne Indians; and Meyer Fortas and E. E. Evans-Pritchard's *African Political Systems*.[49]

At its core, *Law, Science and Policy* was concerned with what Lasswell and McDougal saw as the relationship between the personal characters of people, and the structures of social order they created and sustained. Building from Freud's critique of 'civilised' life, the seminars theorised the internal organisation of a personality that was 'democratic', examining influences in childhood and education that moulded such a personality.[50] In this quest for the 'democratic character', Lasswell and McDougal were themselves trying to fulfil the task their 1943 chapter had said was the preeminent one of their cultural moment – the cultivation of a rising American elite.

The New Haven School is today widely taken to refer to McDougal's 1950s foreign policy interventions, or the work of a group of younger international lawyers who began to self-identify as adherents of the school from 1968 onwards.[51]

49 Ibid. Part II, chapter II 'Specific Value-Institution Processes', citing Malinowski, Bronislaw. *Argonauts of the Western Pacific: An Account of Native Enterprise and Adventure in the Archipelagoes of Melanesian New Guinea* (London: George Routledge & Sons Ltd., 1932); Lowie, Robert H. *The Origin of the State* (London: Harcourt, Brace & Co., 1927); Llewellyn, Karl and Edward Adamson Hoebel. *The Cheyenne Way. Conflict and Case Law in Primitive Jurisprudence* (Norman: University of Oklahoma Press, 1941); and Fortes, Meyer and Evans-Pritchard, E. *African Political Systems* (Oxford: Oxford University Press, 1970). Late in his life, McDougal recalled being uncertain as to whether he should choose Bronislaw Malinowski, with whom he had begun to collaborate in the late 1930s, or Lasswell as his intellectual partner, cf. Tipson, 'Oral History Discussion (2)' 1992 (n. 38). On the fruitful relationship between American legal realism and anthropology in the interwar period, see Tuori, Kaius. 'American Legal Realism and Anthropology'. *Law & Social Inquiry* 42(3) (2017), 804–829.

50 Lasswell also wrote about this in some of his independent publications, while noting the close relationship between his ideas and the *Law, Science and Policy* seminar materials. See Lasswell, *Democratic Character* 1951 (n. 11), noting the seminars at 476 n. 22. In theorising the 'authoritarian personality', the seminar materials extensively employed Adorno, Theodor W., Else Frenkel-Brunswik, Daniel Levinson, and Nevitt Sanfor. *The Authoritarian Personality* (New York: Norton, 1969), cited in Lasswell/McDougal, *Law, Science and Policy* 1958 (n. 11), part II, chapter IV 'Political Personality'.

51 This began with Falk, Richard. 'On Treaty Interpretation and the New Haven Approach: Achievements and Prospects'. *Virginia Journal of International Law* 8(2) (1968), 323–355, 330 n. 11. Falk identifies the existence of what he christens the 'New Haven Approach': '[T]here exists a group of scholars that have self-consciously elected to guide their studies by an application of the framework of inquiry as it has been outlined in the principal methodological efforts of Professors McDougal and Lasswell.' Sediment was added to

But these are best understood as crystallisations of the phenomenon after the fact. The New Haven School must be understood through Lasswell and McDougal's sense of the necessity that a generation of modern American leaders be explained to themselves. Relying on ideas about law, science and psychology formed between the World Wars, Lasswell and McDougal thought that the extent to which societies would be democratic depended on the extent to which leaders of those societies had developed democratic characters. Their legal theory and teaching was an effort to understand and contribute to that development.

4 Conclusion

The condensed historical account presented above seeks to offer a broad outline of policy-oriented jurisprudence as an interwar, psychoanalytic project of engineering social order through education and law. This account claims we must re-read Lasswell and McDougal's work, advancing three main challenges to contemporary readings of their legal theory. First, connecting policy-oriented jurisprudence to its interwar intellectual origins identifies Lasswell and McDougal's motivating challenges, especially those prompted by experiences of modern industrial life, and doubt about orders of social value. Rather than an affectation of post-war American hubris, the New Haven School was a product of the difficult to characterise yet much-discussed modernist cultural moment. As such, it deeply reflected that moment's heady mix of insecurity, constructive possibility, and value-anxiety.

Second, paying attention to the interwar origins of Lasswell and McDougal's ideas about society and law changes our understanding of a central component of the contemporary narrative – the New Haven School's right-wing, Cold War politics. Through both McDougal and Lasswell, the account presented above emphasises the centrality of New Deal social planning and redistribution; psychoanalytically-inspired avant-garde culture and politics; and elite-led, collectivist politics, to the New Haven School story.

---

this inauguration of a 'school' by Higgins, Rosalyn. 'Policy and Impartiality: The Uneasy Relationship in International Law. Review of: Order in a Violent World by Richard A. Falk'. *International Organization* 23(4) (1969), 914–931, Higgins listed New Haven School members, including herself, and specified different orbits of association around Lasswell and McDougal at 920 n. 24. The same happened in: Weston, Burns. 'Review: The Interpretation of Agreements and World Public Order by Myres S. McDougal, Harold D. Lasswell and James C. Miller'. *University of Pennsylvania Law Review* 117(4) (1969), 647–664, 647 n. 1.

Third, by emphasising psychoanalysis and philosophical pragmatism as the movements of thought from which the New Haven School descends, the account seeks to challenge common associations of the school with contemporary positivist empirical social science. The conception of 'empiricism' underpinning policy-oriented jurisprudence was philosophically pragmatist and distinctly anti-positivist, while its reliance on psychoanalytic approaches to society and culture should place it closer to anthropological work in the American 'law and society' tradition than to contemporary political science.

Appreciating psychoanalysis and philosophical pragmatism as related parts of the substructure of policy-oriented jurisprudence also makes clear Lasswell and McDougal's commitment to a widespread early twentieth century interest in examining relationships between modern scientific knowledge, and experiences of psychological interiority. Like Sigmund Freud, the classical pragmatists critiqued inherited social orders they determined unsuited to modern life. Both Freud and the pragmatists did this by trying to relate their ideas about psychological interiority to the modern paradigm of scientific inquiry. They constructed this relation in different ways, but they all believed psychological forces were operating beneath the surface of social life.[52]

Through the New Haven School, this chapter seeks to suggest the significance of this preoccupation as an animating problematic in interwar legal theory. As the *Law, Science and Policy* seminars demonstrate, one manifestation of this epochal preoccupation with science and psychologies of social order was a close relationship between anthropology and psychoanalysis. Widely-reported anthropological accounts of 'primitive' societies were closely related to anxieties of life in industrialised societies, supporting analysis of the modern psyche, the 'civilised' self.[53]

In policy-oriented jurisprudence, this preoccupation manifested as a desire to use law as an instrument to scientifically control politics and ideology. Social order and value were understood as largely psychological realities – states of mind – that could be engineered through ever greater confrontation and

52 An illustrative example of this sentiment can be found in the work of John Dewey: 'Now the moment the complicity of the personal factor in our valuations is recognized, is recognized fully, frankly, and generally, that moment a new era in philosophy will begin.' Dewey, John. 'What Pragmatism Means by Practical', in *The Middle Works, 1899–1924*, vol. 4, ed. Jo Ann Bodyston (Carbondale: Southern Illinois University Press, 1977), 98–115, 113. In relation to Freud the seminal reference is Freud, Sigmund. *Civilization and Its Discontents* (London: Penguin Books, 2002).

53 A prominent example is Freud, Sigmund. *Totem and Taboo: Some Points of Agreement between the Mental Lives of Savages and Neurotics* (Abingdon: Routledge Classics, 2004).

control of unconscious psychological forces. Lasswell and McDougal believed it was possible and necessary to fashion scientific methods capable of productively using the unconscious, unreason and irrationality. The historical account developed above is an effort to suggest and re-understand the significance of these elements of a particular European and American cultural moment, through Lasswell and McDougal's engagement with them as problematics of law and social order.

Bibliography

Adorno, Theodor W., Else Frenkel-Brunswik, Betty Aron, Maria Hertz Levinson and William Morrow. *The Authoritarian Personality* (London: Norton, 1969).

Ascher, William and Ronald D. Brunner. *Prospectus for an Intellectual Biography of Harold D. Lasswell* (unpublished manuscript, 1982).

Reynolds, Bryan and Paul Cefalu. *The Return of Theory in Early Modern English Studies. Tarrying with the Subjunctive* (London: Palgrave Macmillan, 2016).

Balibar, Étienne. *Citoyen sujet et autres essais d'anthropologie philosophique* (Paris: Presses universitaires de France, 2011).

Carty, Anthony. 'Interwar German Theories of International Law: The Psychoanalytical and Phenomenologicial Perspectives of Hans Kelsen and Carl Schmitt Law and the Postmodern Mind'. *Cardozo Law Review* 16(3) (1994), 1235–1292.

Cassese, Antonio. *Five Masters of International Law: Conversations with R.-J. Dupuy, E. Jiménez de Arechaga, R. Jennings, L. Henkin and O. Schachter* (Oxford: Hart Publishing, 2011).

Chimni, Bhupinder S. *International Law and World Order: A Critique of Contemporary Approaches* (Cambridge: Cambridge University Press, 2nd ed. 2017).

Collier, Bonnie. 'A Conversation with Myres S. McDougal', in *Yale Law School Oral History Series* (New Haven: Lillian Goldman Law Library, 2013).

Derrig, Rián. *Educating American Modernists: The Origins of the New Haven School* (Florence: European University Institute, Department of Law, PhD Thesis, 2019).

Dewey, John. 'What Pragmatism Means by Practical', in *The Middle Works, 1899–1924*, vol. 4, ed. Jo Ann Bodyston (Carbondale: Southern Illinois University Press, 1977), 98–115.

Dunoff, Jeffrey L. and Mark A. Pollack. *Interdisciplinary Perspectives on International Law and International Relations: The State of the Art* (Cambridge: Cambridge University Press, 2013).

Falk, Richard. 'International Law and the United States Role in the Viet Nam War'. *The Yale Law Journal* 75(7) (1966), 1122–1160.

Falk, Richard. 'On Treaty Interpretation and the New Haven Approach: Achievements and Prospects'. *Virginia Journal of International Law* 8(2) (1968), 323–355.

Fortes, Meyer and Edward Evans-Pritchard. *African Political Systems* (Oxford: Published for the International African Institute by Oxford University Press, 1970).

Freud, Sigmund. *Civilization and Its Discontents* (London: Penguin Books, 2002).

Freud, Sigmund. *Totem and Taboo: Some Points of Agreement between the Mental Lives of Savages and Neurotics* (Abingdon: Routledge, 2004).

García-Salmones Rovira, Mónica. 'Sources in the Anti-Formalist Tradition: A Prelude to Institutional Discourses in International Law', in *The Oxford Handbook of the Sources of International Law,* eds. Samantha Besson and Jean d'Aspremont (Oxford: Oxford University Press, 2017), 203–224.

Ginzburg, Carlo. *The Cheese and the Worms: The Cosmos of a Sixteenth-Century Miller* (Baltimore: Johns Hopkins University Press, 1976).

Ginzburg, Carlo. *The Night Battles: Witchcraft & Agrarian Cults in the Sixteenth & Seventeenth Centuries* (Baltimore: Johns Hopkins University Press, 1992).

Green, Nicholas St. John. 'Proximate and Remote Cause'. *American Law Review* 4(2) (1870), 201–216.

Green, Nicholas St. John. 'Book Review: Commentaries on the Law of Married Women under the Statutes of the Several States and at Common Law and in Equity. By Joel Prentiss Bishop. Vol. I. Philadelphia: Kay and Brother. 1871'. *American Law Review* 6(1) (1871), 57–73.

Harold Dwight Lasswell Papers (MS 1043). Manuscripts and Archives, Yale University Library. Series I; Series V.

Harrington Hall, Mary. 'A Conversation with Harold Lasswell: The Psychology of Politics'. *Psychology Today* 1 (October 1968), 56–64.

Hathaway, Oona A. 'The Continuing Influence of the New Haven School'. *Yale Journal of International Law* 32(2) (2007), 553–558.

Higgins, Rosalyn. 'Policy and Impartiality: The Uneasy Relationship in International Law. Review of: Order in a Violent World. by Richard A. Falk'. *International Organization* 23(4) (1969), 914–931.

Higgins, Rosalyn. 'Obituary: Professor Myres McDougal'. *The Independent* (9 May 1998).

Holmes, Oliver W. *The Common Law* (Basingstoke: Macmillan & Co., 1882).

Interview with Myres McDougal by Michael Reisman. *Reflections on the New Haven School* (United National Audiovisual Library, 1982).

Jabloner, Clemens. 'Kelsen and His Circle: The Viennese Years'. *European Journal of International Law* 9(2) (1998), 368–385.

Koh, Harold H. 'Is There a "New" New Haven School of International Law?'. *Yale Journal of International Law* 32(2) (2007), 559–573.

Koskenniemi, Martti. *The Gentle Civilizer of Nations: The Rise and Fall of International Law 1870–1960* (Cambridge: Cambridge University Press, 2001).

Koskenniemi, Martti. 'Law, Teleology and International Relations: An Essay in Counterdisciplinarity'. *International Relations* 26(1) (2012), 3–34.

Kratochwil, Friedrich V. *Rules, Norms, and Decisions: On the Conditions of Practical and Legal Reasoning in International Relations and Domestic Affairs* (Cambridge: Cambridge University Press, 1991).

Lannes Smith, Bruce. 'The Mystifying Intellectual History of Harold D. Lasswell', in *Politics, Personality, and Social Science in the Twentieth Century: Essays in Honor of Harold D. Lasswell*, ed. Arnold A. Rogow (Chicago: University of Chicago Press, 1969), 49–52.

Lasswell, Harold. 'The Triple-Appeal Principle: A Contribution of Psychoanalysis to Political and Social Science'. *American Journal of Sociology* 37(4) (1932), 523–538.

Lasswell, Harold. 'What Psychiatrists and Political Scientists Can Learn from One Another'. *Psychiatry* 1(1) (1938), 33–39.

Lasswell, Harold. 'The Contribution of Freud's Insight Interview to the Social Sciences'. *American Journal of Sociology* 45(3) (1939), 375–390.

Lasswell, Harold. 'Democratic Character', in *The Political Writings of Harold D. Lasswell*, ed. Harold Lasswell (Glencoe: Free Press, 1951).

Lasswell, Harold. *Psychopathology and Politics* (New York: Viking Press, 1960).

Lasswell, Harold. *World Politics and Personal Insecurity* (Glencoe: Free Press, 1965).

Lasswell, Harold. *A Pre-View of Policy Sciences* (New York: American Elsevier Pub Co., 1971).

Lasswell, Harold and Dwaine Marvick. *Harold D. Lasswell on Political Sociology* (Chicago: University of Chicago Press, 1977).

Lasswell, Harold and Myres McDougal. 'Legal Education and Public Policy: Professional Training in the Public Interest'. *The Yale Law Journal* 52(2) (1943), 203–295.

Lasswell, Harold and Myres McDougal. *Law, Science and Policy* (1958) (unpublished working papers, copies on file with author).

Lasswell, Harold and Myres McDougal. *Jurisprudence for a Free Society: Studies in Law, Science and Policy* (Alphen aan den Rijn/New Haven: Kluwer Law International/New Haven Press 1992).

Llewellyn, Karl N. and Edward Adamson Hoebel. *The Cheyenne Way. Conflict and Case Law in Primitive Jurisprudence* (Norman: University of Oklahoma Press, 1941).

Lowie, Robert H. *The Origin of the State* (London: Harcourt, Brace & Co., 1927).

Malinowski, Bronislaw. *Argonauts of the Western Pacific: An Account of Native Enterprise and Adventure in the Archipelagoes of Melanesian New Guinea* (London: George Routledge & Sons Ltd., 1932).

McDougal, Myres. 'Collateral Mistake in Contractual Relations'. (New Haven: Yale University, School of Law, PhD Thesis, 1931).

McDougal, Myres. 'Book Review: A Treatise on Mortgages. By William F. Walsh. Chicago: Callaghan. 1934 Pp. Xlv, 376'. *Yale Law Journal* 44(7) (1934), 1278–1282.

McDougal, Myres. 'Book Review: The Promise of American Politics. By T. V. Smith. Chicago: University of Chicago Press, 1936. Pp. Xix, 308, $2.50'. *Yale Law Journal* 46(7) (1937), 1269–1272.

McDougal, Myres. 'Book Review: Readings in Jurisprudence, Selected, Edited, and Arranged by Jerome Hall. Indianapolis: The Bobbs-Merrill Company. 1938. Pp. 1183. $7.50'. *Illinois Law Review of Northwestern University* 34(1) (1939), 109–111.

McDougal, Myres. 'Book Review: The Law and Mr. Smith. By Max Radin. The Bobbs-Merrill Company, Indianapolis, 1938'. *University of Pennsylvania Law Review* 87(4) (1939), 495–496.

McDougal, Myres. 'Fuller vs. the American Legal Realists: An Intervention. Review of The Law in Quest of Itself. By Lon L. Fuller, Professor of Law, Harvard Law School'. *Yale Law Journal* 50(5) (1941), 827–840.

McDougal, Myres. 'Book Review: Future Interests Restated: Tradition Versus Clarification and Reform. A Review of: Restatement of the Law of Property. Volume III. St. Paul: American Law Institute Publishers. 1940'. *Harvard Law Review* 55(7) (1942), 1078–1115.

McDougal, Myres. *The Case for Regional Planning with Special Reference to New England* (New Haven: Yale University Press 1947).

McDougal, Myres. 'The Law School of the Future: From Legal Realism to Policy Science in the World Community'. *Yale Law Journal* 56(8) (1947), 1345–1355.

McDougal, Myres. 'The Role of Law in World Politics'. *Mississippi Law Journal* 20(3) (1949), 253–283.

McDougal, Myres. 'Intervening'. *Proceedings of the American Society of International Law* 48 (1954), 113.

McDougal, Myres. 'The Soviet-Cuban Quarantine and Self-Defense'. *American Journal of International Law* 57(3) (1963), 597–604.

McDougal, Myres and Richard Gardner. 'The Veto and the Charter: An Interpretation for Survival'. *Yale Law Journal* 60(2) (1951), 258–292.

McDougal, Myres and David Haber, eds. *Property, Wealth, Land; Allocation Planning and Development: Selected Cases and other Materials on the Law of Real Property* (Charlottesville: Michie, 1948).

McDougal, Myres and Harold Lasswell. 'Jurisprudence in Policy-Oriented Perspective'. *University of Florida Law Review* 19(3) (1967), 486–513.

McDougal, Myres, Harold Lasswell and James C. Miller. *The Interpretation of Agreements and World Public Order: Principles of Content and Procedure* (New Haven: Yale University Press, 1967).

McDougal, Myres and Norbert A. Schlei. 'The Hydrogen Bomb Tests in Perspective: Lawful Measures for Security'. *Yale Law Journal* 64(3) (1955), 648–710.

McDougal, Myres and Asher Lans. 'Treaties and Congressional-Executive or Presidential Agreements: Interchangeable Instruments of National Policy: I'. *Yale Law Journal* 54(2) (1945), 181–351.

McDougal, Myres and Asher Lans. 'Treaties and Congressional-Executive or Presidential Agreements: Interchangeable Instruments of National Policy: II'. *Yale Law Journal* 54(3) (1945), 534–615.

Menand, Louis. *The Metaphysical Club* (New York: Farrar, Straus & Giroux, 2001).

Peters, Anne. 'There Is Nothing More Practical than a Good Theory: An Overview of Contemporary Approaches to International Law'. *German Yearbook of International Law* 44 (2001), 25–37.

Rogow, Arnold A., ed. *Politics, Personality, and Social Science in the Twentieth Century: Essays in Honor of Harold D. Lasswell* (Chicago: University of Chicago Press, 1969).

Shaffer, Gregory and Tom Ginsburg. 'The Empirical Turn in International Legal Scholarship'. *American Journal of International Law* 106(1) (2012), 1–46.

Shklar, Judith N. *Legalism: Law, Morals, and Political Trials* (Cambridge: Harvard University Press, 1964).

Slaughter Burley, Anne-Marie. 'International Law and International Relations Theory: A Dual Agenda'. *American Journal of International Law* 87(2) (1993), 205–239.

Smith, Mark C. *Social Science in the Crucible: The American Debate over Objectivity and Purpose, 1918–1941* (Durham: Duke University Press, 1994).

Tuori, Kaius. 'American Legal Realism and Anthropology'. *Law & Social Inquiry* 42(3) (2017), 804–829.

Vernant, Jean Pierre. *Myth and Thought among the Greeks* (New York: Zone Books, distributed by MIT Press, 2006).

Weston, Burns. 'Review: The Interpretation of Agreements and World Public Order by Myres S. McDougal, Harold D. Lasswell and James C. Miller'. *University of Pennsylvania Law Review* 117(4) (1969), 647–664.

Zaretsky, Eli. *Political Freud a History* (New York: Columbia University Press, 2015).

Archival Sources

Harold Dwight Lasswell Papers (MS 1043). Manuscripts and Archives, Yale University Library.

Merriam, Charles E. Papers. Special Collections Research Center, University of Chicago Library.

Myres Smith McDougal Papers (MS 1636). Manuscripts and Archives, Yale University Library.

Myres Smith McDougal Papers (MS 1636), Interview with Elias Clark. *Oral History Discussion* (14 May 1993).

Myres Smith McDougal Papers (MS 1636), Interview with Rosalyn Higgins. *Oral History Discussion* (27 March 1993).

Myres Smith McDougal Papers (MS 1636), Interview with Quintin Johnstone. *Oral History Discussion* (1 February 1993).

Myres Smith McDougal Papers (MS 1636), Interview with Nicholas Deb Katzenbach. *Oral History Discussion* (3 October 1992).

Myres Smith McDougal Papers (MS 1636), Interview with Eugene V Rostow. *Oral History Discussion* (11 December 1992).

Myres Smith McDougal Papers (MS 1636), Interview with Frederick Tipson. *Oral History Discussion* (*1*) (11 September 1992).

Myres Smith McDougal Papers (MS 1636), Interview with Frederick Tipson. *Oral History Discussion* (*2*) (11 September 1992).

CHAPTER 14

Histories Hidden in the Shadow: Vitoria and the International Ostracism of Francoist Spain

Julia Bühner

Abstract

In recent years, interest in the historiography on the Dominican friar Francisco de Vitoria (1483–1546) has increased. Besides contributing to the current methodological discussions about the benefits of writing history of international law in context, the chapter focuses on the articles of a Spanish yearbook published by the *Asociación Francisco de Vitoria* and its political implications during the era of international ostracism of the Francoist regime. The authors, conception and composition of the yearbook are considered as well as the way in which the articles present and misuse the Dominican friar for propagandistic purposes.

Keywords

contextualism – historiography of international law – *Anuario de la Asociación Francisco de Vitoria* – politics – Francoist Spain – clerical fascism – Second World War – international ostracism

1 Introduction

The Dominican friar Francisco de Vitoria (1483–1546), a famous figure of sixteenth century's Spain, 'raised questions that equally preoccupy the minds of twenty-first century international lawyers'.[1] This is certainly one of the reasons why there has been continuous interest in the Dominican friar and his doctrine. Although the amount of research publications coming from various disciplines such as theology, philosophy or history could convey the impression that we already know everything about his life and work, there are still many aspects hidden in obscurity, waiting to be uncovered.

1 Niemela, Pekka. 'A Cosmopolitan World Order? Perspectives on Francisco de Vitoria and the United Nations'. *Max Planck Yearbook of United Nations Law* 12 (2018), 301–334, 333.

 | DOI:10.1163/9789004461802_016

Founder of the School of Salamanca, Vitoria is primarily known for his contributions to the debate on the legitimacy of the American conquest. This discussion also touched on fundamental questions of international law, inducing James Brown Scott (1866–1943), first chief-editor of the collection *Classics of International Law*, and Camilo Barcia Trelles (1888–1977) during the interwar period to reinforce Vitoria's position as the father of modern international law.[2] Disputing over the nature of the American Indians, dominion rights and missionary strategies, the scholarly discourse finally culminated in the Valladolid debate (1550–1551) between the adversaries Bartolomé de las Casas (1484/85–1566) and Juan Ginés de Sepúlveda (1490–1573).[3]

Whereas Las Casas is still characterised as the advocate of the Indians, Sepúlveda's as well as Vitoria's conventional portrayals were challenged during the past decades.[4] In the context of the rise of *post-colonial studies*, historians began to critically approach Vitoria's doctrine, leading to a radical transformation of the image of the Dominican in historiography: Before not only celebrated as the founder of international law but also as a courageous defender of the American Indians, post-colonial critics turned Vitoria into a legitimiser of colonial war who used international law as an 'instrument of empire'.[5] In the field of the history of international law this critical stance towards the Dominican friar and his oeuvre was introduced by Anthony Anghie's publication 'Imperialism, Sovereignty and the Making of International Law'.[6] Since

---

2 See Birr, Christiane and Wim Decock. *Recht und Moral in der Frühen Scholastik 1500–1750* (Berlin: De Gruyter, 2016), 77. For a detailed monography on the important role of James Brown Scott in the historiography on Vitoria, cf. Amorosa, Paolo. *Rewriting the History of the Law of Nations. How James Brown Scott Made Francisco de Vitoria the Founder of International Law* (Oxford: Oxford University Press, 2019).

3 See Bordat, Josef. *Annexion – Anbindung – Anerkennung. Globale Beziehungskulturen im frühen 16. Jahrhundert* (Hamburg: Tredition, 2008), 22–23.

4 Sepúlveda's position was often contrasted with that of Las Casas, ascribing him the 'role of devil's advocate', confer for example Fernández-Santamaria, José A. 'Juan Ginés de Sepúlveda on the Nature of the American Indians'. *The Americans* 31(4) (1975), 434–451, 450. Likewise, his role has been reconsidered in historical research since the 1980s, confer amongst others Abril-Castelló, Vidal. 'La bipolarización sepúlveda-las casas y sus consequencias. La revolución de la duodecima replica', in *Francisco de Vitoria y la Escuela de Salamanca. La etica en la conquista de América*, ed. Demetrio Ramos Pérez (Madrid: Consejo Superior de Investigaciones Científicas, 1984), 229–290.

5 See, inter alia, Todorov, Tzvetan. *Die Eroberung Amerikas. Das Problem des Anderen* (Frankfurt am Main: Suhrkamp, 1985), 182; and Williams, Robert A. *The American Indian in Western Legal Thought. The Discourses of Conquest* (Oxford: Oxford University Press, 1992), 108.

6 Anghie, Antony. *Imperialism, Sovereignty, and the Making of International Law* (Cambridge: Cambridge University Press, 2005).

then, historical studies on Vitoria have ranged between characterising 'his view of international order as one that either opposed o[r] justified Spanish imperialism in the New World'.[7]

Furthermore, debates on Vitoria's role in the history of international law have been inextricably interwoven with methodological questions. Framing the narrative of the common 'idealist intellectual approach'[8] to the history of international law as its starting point, thoughts on the founding father intermingled with methodological considerations based on the theories of the *Cambridge School of the History of Political Thought* or, more precisely, those of Quentin Skinner.[9] Adopting Skinner's criticism on the traditional *history of ideas'* approach, Martti Koskenniemi phrased in 2004 as a future task for the field to write contextualised, *intellectual histories* of international law.[10] Thereby, the extremely varying interpretations of Vitoria's intents were explained by different contextualisation.[11] But what is exactly meant by *context*?

In the discussions on Vitoria's role and the benefits of contextualism, three different qualities and meanings of *context* have appeared, requiring a clear distinction. First, in Skinner's theory *context* mainly means the linguistic

7 Valenzuela-Vermehren, Luis. 'Empire, Sovereignty, and Justice in Francisco de Vitoria's International Thought. A Reinterpretation of "De Indis" (1532)'. *Revista Chilena de Derecho* 40(1) (2013), 261–299, 261; important contributions in international legal history that rather stick to the traditional image of Vitoria are amongst others Cavallar, Georg. 'Vitoria, Grotius, Pufendorf, Wolff and Vattel: Accomplices of European Colonialism and Exploitation or True Cosmopolitans?'. *Journal of the History of International Law* 10(2) (2008), 181–209; Zapatero, Pablo. 'Francisco de Vitoria and the Postmodern Grand Critique of International law', in *At the Origins of Modernity. Francisco de Vitoria and the Discovery of International Law*, eds. José María Beneyto and Justo Corti Varela (Berlin: Springer, 2017), 177–195.

8 Rasilla del Moral, Ignacio de la. 'The Problem of Periodization in the History of International Law'. *Law and History Review* 37(1) (2019), 1–34, 11.

9 See Skinner, Quentin. 'Bedeutung und Verstehen in der Ideengeschichte (1969/2009)', in *Ideengeschichte*, ed. Barbara Stollberg-Rilinger (Stuttgart: Franz Steiner Verlag, 2010), 61–94.

10 See Koskenniemi, Martti. 'Why History of International Law Today?'. *Rechtsgeschichte – Legal History. Zeitschrift des Max-Planck-Instituts für europäische Rechtsgeschichte* 4 (2004), 61–66, 64.

11 See, inter alia, Koskenniemi, Martti. 'Vitoria and Us. Thoughts on Critical Histories of International Law'. *Rechtsgeschichte – Legal History. Zeitschrift des Max-Planck-Instituts für europäische Rechtsgeschichte* 22 (2014), 119–138; and Fitzmaurice, Andrew. 'The Problem of Eurocentrism in the Thought of Francisco de Vitoria', in *At the Origins of Modernity. Francisco de Vitoria and the Discovery of International Law*, eds. José Beneyto and Justo Corti Varela (Berlin: Springer, 2017), 77–93.

co-text.[12] In an article published in 2017, Pablo Zapatero for instance draws the conclusion that Vitoria was a 'moderate thinker' of his time.[13] Besides analysing the *Relectiones De Indis* and *De Justitia*, Pablo Zapatero supports his thesis by quoting Vitoria's letter to his friend Manuel de Arcos where he writes that the 'trickery and profiteering' in the New World would make the blood freeze in his veins. Or, he refers to the reprimand of Charles V to highlight that the Dominican's ideas were revolutionary, 'potentially dangerous … for the *status quo*'.[14] It is easy to counter this well-known evidence, favouring the conventional portrayal of Vitoria. Because, at the same time, the Dominican friar degraded the indigenous population, describing them in *De Indis* for instance as 'barbarians' and wild animals: *quam amentes, immo quam ipsae ferae et bestiae*.[15] That Vitoria's arguments could lead to two contrary interpretations is not least due to the general ambiguity of his statements. Some of his contemporaries, namely Las Casas and Melchor Cano, already made remarks about the numerous contradictions in and between Vitoria's works.[16] In this context, Andrew Fitzmaurice has argued that 'to a large degree, the different ways of reading Vitoria have depended upon which aspects of his thought were emphasised'.[17] When presented as a critic of Spanish conquest, Vitoria's statements concerning occupation and property would be highlighted. In contrast, interpretations seeking to condemn him as an apologist of Spanish imperialism would stress his thoughts on the natural right of communication and cultural differences.[18] Thereby mostly argued on the base of the same selection of source material,[19] the editors of the German translation of Vitoria's works have instead claimed that his doctrine could not be understood without taking all the *Relectiones*

12 See Mulsow, Martin and Andreas Mahler. 'Einleitung', in *Die Cambridge School der politischen Ideengeschichte*, eds. Martin Mulsow and Andreas Mahler (Berlin: Suhrkamp, 2010), 7–20, 14.

13 See Zapatero, 'Francisco de Vitoria' 2017 (n. 8), 177–179.

14 See ibid., 186–187.

15 Vitoria, Francisco de. 'De Indis', in *Vorlesungen II (Relectiones). Völkerrecht, Politik, Kirche*, eds. Ulrich Horst, Heinz-Gerhard Justenhoven and Joachim Stüben (Stuttgart: Kohlhammer, 1997), 370–541, 468 and 484.

16 See Brieskorn, Norbert. 'Die Kritik von Bartolomé de Las Casas an der Relectio de Indis', in *Francisco Vitorias >De Indis< in interdisziplinärer Perspektive*, eds. Norbert Brieskorn and Gideon Stiening (Stuttgart: frommann-holzboog, 2011), 219–250, 232–242. See also Delgado, Mariano. 'Die Zustimmung des Volkes in der politischen Theorie von Francisco de Vitoria, Bartolomé de las Casas and Francisco Suárez', in *Die Ordnung der Praxis. Neue Studien zur Spanischen Spätscholastik*, eds. Frank Grunert and Kurt Seelmann (Berlin: De Gruyter, 2001), 157–182, 175.

17 Fitzmaurice, 'The Problem of Eurocentrism' 2017 (n. 12), 77.

18 Ibid.

19 See Birr/Decock, *Recht und Moral in der Frühen Scholastik 1500–1750* 2016 (n. 3), 78.

and his comments on Thomas Aquinas, the *Lectiones*, into consideration.[20] Likewise, more effort should be put into comparing Vitoria's oeuvre with the rich *co-text*, the numerous works of other late scholastics, to escape the pitfalls of arguing with Vitoria against Vitoria.[21]

In the aftermath, Skinner's concept of *context* was criticised for its narrowness. Only focusing on texts and language, it would ignore the political, economic, social and cultural circumstances in which ideas arise.[22] This is the second, broader meaning of *context* which came up in the discussions on Vitoria when Pablo Zapatero for instance postulates: 'Thinkers of the past have to be read in their context, not ours'.[23] By taking the *co-text* as well as the *historical context* of Vitoria's lifetime into account, the hermeneutic circle of interpretation could be transformed into a spiral, hopefully offering new insights into the Dominican's argumentation also relevant for the present.[24]

The question of interpretation becomes even more complex when looking at the constant 'transformations and reinterpretations'[25] of Vitoria in historiography. Here, the third form of *context* interferes: political or other circumstances, position and mental set of the scholar writing about Vitoria. That we all look at the past from our own present perspectives, our political stance being a crucial part of it, was highlighted by Martti Koskenniemi when he

20 Stüben, Joachim. 'Die Relectiones des Francisco de Vitoria. Vorbemerkungen zum zweiten Band der lateinisch-deutschen Gesamtausgabe', in *Vorlesungen II (Relectiones). Völkerrecht, Politik, Kirche*, eds. Ulrich Horst, Heinz-Gerhard Justenhoven and Joachim Stüben (Stuttgart: Kohlhammer, 1997), 25. See also Deckers, Daniel. *Gerechtigkeit und Recht. Eine historisch-kritische Untersuchung der Gerechtigkeitslehre des Francisco de Vitoria (1483–1546)* (Freiburg: Herder, 1991), 344.

21 This situation is about change due to a large-scale project: Duve, Thomas, Matthias Lutz-Bachmann, Christiane Birr and Andreas Niederberger. 'The School of Salamanca: A Digital Collection of Sources and a Dictionary of Its Juridical-Political Language. The Basic Objectives and Structure of a Research Project'. *The Salamanca Working Paper Series* No. 2014(1) (2014), 1–29.

22 See Mulsow/Mahler, 'Einleitung' 2010 (n. 13), 14.

23 Zapatero, 'Francisco de Vitoria' 2017 (n. 8), 181.

24 In agreement with Andrew Fitzmaurice's argumentation, contextualism and relevance for the present are seen here not as mutually exclusive. On the contrary, by knowing what was expressible and thinkable in a specific historical moment can only bring us closer to the real meaning of past statements and thereby unfold their true relevance for the present. See also Stollberg-Rilinger, Barbara. 'Einleitung', in *Ideengeschichte*, ed. Barbara Stollberg-Rilinger (Stuttgart: Franz Steiner Verlag, 2010), 7–42, 40–41; cf. concerning this debate Fitzmaurice, 'The Problem of Eurocentrism' 2017 (n. 12), 88; Koskenniemi, 'Vitoria and Us' 2014 (n. 12), 127; Skinner, 'Bedeutung und Verstehen' 2010 (n. 10), 69–70 and 78–80.

25 Rasilla del Moral, Ignacio de la. 'Francisco de Vitoria's Unexpected Transformations and Reinterpretations for International Law'. *International Community Law Review* 15(3) (2013), 287–318.

characterised Anghie's as a postcolonial and Zapatero's as a liberal interpretation of Vitoria.[26] This perspectivity applies even more so to many of our ancestors of the twentieth century, not writing in a society of plural political opinions but under the dictate of a supposedly sole truth.

In the context of an increasing interest in the 'darker legacies of law in Europe',[27] do Ignacio de la Rasilla del Moral's publications, amongst others 'In the Shadow of Vitoria. A History of Law in Spain (1770–1953)'[28] cast light on the evolution and elevation of the Dominican friar in Spanish historiography. Using Rasilla del Moral's fundamental work as a 'historiographical backbone',[29] this chapter tries to add a small piece to the puzzle of the history of research into Francisco de Vitoria. In a first part, the chapter presents the concept and composition of a Spanish yearbook that summarised the works and lectures of the so-called *Asociación Francisco de Vitoria* and served as an official mouthpiece for studies on the Dominican friar. The second part shows how the members of the association exploited Vitoria and his doctrine to serve the ideological targets of Francoist Spain in the aftermath of the Second World War, the era of the regime's international ostracism.

2 The 'Asociación Francisco de Vitoria': Concept and Composition of Its Yearbook

Based on self-description and research literature briefly assessing the association and its activities, the general purpose of its foundation and main organ of publication, the *Anuario de la Asociación Francisco de Vitoria*, are discussed in the following. Intermingled with scientific motivations, we are going to see that the formation of Vitoria's portrayal was heavily influenced by cultural, religious and – above all – political interests. Moreover, not only international legal historians but also scholars from other fields took part in the international legal discourse on Vitoria, politically manipulating the Dominican friar against the backdrop of their own disciplines and professions.

---

26 See Koskenniemi, Martti. 'Empire and International Law: The Real Spanish Contribution'. *University of Toronto Law Journal* 61(1) (2011), 1–36, 10.

27 See Menéndez, Agustín José. 'From Republicanism to Fascist Ideology under the Early *Franquismo*', in *Darker Legacies of Law in Europe. The Shadow of National Socialism and Fascism over Europe and Its Legal Traditions*, eds. Christian Joerges and Navraj Singh Ghaleigh (Oxford: Hart, 2003), 337–360.

28 Rasilla del Moral, Ignacio de la. *In the Shadow of Vitoria: A History of International Law in Spain (1770–1953)* (Leiden: Brill, 2018).

29 Ibid., 20.

In the last third of the nineteenth century, Vitoria had experienced a revival in European historiography. In Spanish academia, interest in the Dominican friar and his oeuvre had arisen from the Dominican order (i.a. Beltrán de Heredia), in the context of an increasing nationalist historiography (i.a. Marcelino Menéndez y Pelayo) and in the field of legal history (i.a. Eduardo de Hinojosa y Naveros).[30]

In the interwar period, described by Ignacio de la Rasilla del Moral as the 'second and definitive "renaissance"'[31] of the Dominican, Vitoria's significance for the history of international law as its founding father was internationally consolidated. Under the banner of Vitoria, Spanish internationalists of that period tried to 'create a network of contacts that would allow Spain to expand, through *cultural diplomacy,* its weak international presence'.[32] The *Asociación Francisco de Vitoria*, founded in 1926 under the dictatorship of Primo de Rivera, contributed to the creation and consolidation of these international ties, characterised by Victor Manuel Egío García as a political mission with neo-colonial aspirations towards Latin America. As another argument favouring the political function of the association, he points out that the foundation's notice was not placed in the cultural but in the political news section of the *ABC*.[33] In the association's statutes, the members however emphasise the supposed 'exclusive scientific character' of the *Asociación Francisco de Vitoria*,[34] in this context also assigning their work to the field of studies in international law.[35]

Besides having – under the guise of science – also a political function, cultural memory and self-conception were driving forces of the association's members. In a short article published in *The American Journal of International Law*, James Brown Scott, association's member of honour, commented on

30 See Rasilla del Moral, Ignacio de la. 'The Study of International Law in the Spanish *Short* Nineteenth Century (1808–1898)'. *Chicago-Kent Journal of International and Comparative Law* 13(2) (2013), 122–150, 144–147.

31 See Rasilla del Moral, *Shadow of Vitoria* 2018 (n. 29), 3–4.

32 Gamarra, Yolanda. 'On the Spanish Founding Father of Modern International Law: Camilo Barcia Trelles (1888–1977)', in *At the Origins of Modernity. Francisco de Vitoria and the Discovery of International Law*, eds. José Beneyto and Justo Corti Varela (Berlin: Springer, 2017), 95–115, 103.

33 See Egío García, D. Victor Manuel. *El pensamiento republicano de Fernando Vázquez de Menchaca* (Universidad de Murcia, Departamento de Filosofìa, PhD Thesis, 2014), available at: https://tdx.cat/bitstream/handle/10803/287164/TVMEG.pdf?sequence=1, (last accessed on 14 September 2020), 147. See also ABC, Diario. 'La Asociación Francisco de Vitoria'. *Diario ABC, Noticias políticas* (16 November 1926), 18.

34 'Estatutos de la "Asociación Francisco de Vitoria"'. *Anuario de la Asociación Francisco de Vitoria* II (1929–1930), 7–16, 7.

35 See ibid., 8.

how the *Asociación Francisco de Vitoria* had 'come into being': celebrating the tercentenary of the publication of Hugo Grotius' work *De Iure Belli ac Pacis* in 1925, 'it occurred to the members of the committee in charge ... that the celebration would be incomplete unless a tribute were made in some way to Francisco de Vitoria, and Francisco Suárez. Therefore, the [Dutch Grotius Society] made a pilgrimage to Spain'. Fernandez Medina, Minister of Uruguay to Madrid, attending the celebrations as a guest, then suggested that 'an association in honor of Francisco de Vitoria should be formed'. The idea 'met with instant approval' and the association was founded.[36]

Similarly, the association's members emphasised in the Act of foundation that they intended to honour Vitoria as a figure of national pride and his doctrine as an exemplar of international justice, love of peace and respect to human rights. Moreover, the members sought to spread knowledge about and affirm the existence of a Spanish school of international law and, foremost, to foster an international recognition of the Spanish origins of international law.[37] Understanding themselves rather as grandsons of the great father than critical historians, the members of the association intended to embed their work into Vitoria's tradition and continue his search for a *ius inter gentes*, hopefully guaranteeing a peaceful and stable world order after the destructions of World War I.[38]

Whereas the Spanish journal *La Ciencia Tomista* had hitherto served as an official mouthpiece for studies on Vitoria, this role was now taken on by the association's yearbook, the *Anuario de la Asociación Francisco de Vitoria*.[39] Presided over by José María de Yanguas y Messía (1890–1974) who later became an influential supporter of Francisco Franco,[40] the yearbook was for the first time edited in Madrid, the association's domicile, in 1929.[41] After five successfully edited volumes, the yearbook's publication was for the first time disrupted with the outbreak of the Spanish Civil War (1936–1939). Nonetheless, the members of the association continued their activities, organising conferences and publishing works on the Dominican friar. Ignacio Forcada Barona,

---

36 Scott, James Brown. 'Asociación Francisco de Vitoria'. *American Journal of International Law* 22(1) (1928), 136–139, 138.

37 See 'Acta de la Fundación de la Asociación Francisco de Vitoria'. *Anuario de la Asociación Francisco de Vitoria* I (1927–1928), 43–49, 44 and 46.

38 See Fernández y Medina, Benjamín and Francisco Ramírez Montesinos. 'Nota preliminar'. *Anuario de la Asociación Francisco de Vitoria* I (1927–1928), 7–11, 8–9.

39 Castilla Urbano, Francisco. *El Pensamiento de Francisco de Vitora. Filosofía política e indio americano* (Barcelona: Anthropos Editorial del Hombre, 1992), 15.

40 See Rasilla del Moral, *Shadow of Vitoria* 2018 (n. 29), 199.

41 See Fernández y Medina/Ramírez Montesinos, 'Nota preliminar' 1927–1928 (n. 39), 7.

who investigated those activities, concluded that most of the members of the association turned into legitimators of the Francoist uprising, designating the Civil War as a crusade against the Anti-Spain.[42] But, not all of them had radicalised and voluntarily aligned themselves with Franco's dictatorship. Accused of spreading republican, Marxist or masonic ideas,[43] 'academia was among the professions where the impact of purges was the highest'.[44] This also strongly affected the association whose members opposing the Francoist uprising were either dead, in exile or forced, as Adolfo Miaja de la Muela (1908–1981) and Barcia Trelles for instance,[45] to conduct their university teaching and research in service of Christianity, fatherland and the ideals of the movement.[46] Strictly observed by the *Ministerio de Educación Nacional*, scholarship as well as law were dependent, both subordinate to the political policy of the regime, 'obstacle[s] on the way toward the realisation of certain political goals'.[47]

Consequently, one could assume that the association, having since its foundation also a political function, turned under the dictatorship of Francisco Franco into a mere instrument of political propaganda. But, on the contrary, in the 1940s the association maintained to a certain degree its functional diversity. By celebrating Vitoria's anniversary in 1946 and erecting monuments in his

---

42 Forcada Barona, Ignacio. 'La influencia de la religión católica en la doctrina internatcionalista espanola del período de entrguerras (1918–1939)', in *historia del pensamiento iusinternacionalista espanol des Siglo XX*, vol. 1, eds. Yolanda Gamarra and Ignacio de la Rasilla del Moral (Pamplona: Thomson Reuters Aranzadi, 2012), 253. See also concerning the activities of the members and especially their publications in *La ciencia tomista:* Carcedo Robles, Laureano. 'Primeros idéologos del Franquismo'. *Hispanística* XX 17 (1999), 359–378, 375–376.

43 See Miranda, Jaume Claret. *El atroz desmoche. La destrucción de la Universidad española por el Franquismo, 1936–1945* (Barcelona: Críteria, 2006), 23.

44 See Menéndez, 'From Republicanism' 2003 (n. 28), 344.

45 Miaja de la Muela was amongst other things indicted for misusing his university chair for teaching Marxist theories. Beside his brother Augusto having been Minister of the Second Republic, Barcia Trelles was blamed for criticising in conferences the imperialism of Charles V and the doctrine of Vitoria. See Serra, María Pilar Hernando. *Diccionario de catedráticos españoles de derecho* (1847–1943) (Madrid: Universidad Carlos III, 2011), available at: http://portal.uc3m.es/portal/page/portal/instituto_figuerola/programas/phu/diccionariode catedraticos/lcatedraticos, (last accessed on 14 September 2020); see ibid. and Peláez, Manuel J. Art. 'Camilo Barcia Trelles', in *Diccionario crítico de Juristas Españoles, Portugueses y Latinamericanos (Hispánicos, Brasilenos, Quebequenses y restantes francófones)*, vol. 1 (A–L) (Barcelona: Zaragoza, 2005), 134–135.

46 See Boletín Oficial del Estado, *Ley de 29 julio de 1943 sobre ordenación de la Universidad española*, 7406–7409.

47 See Cerar, Miro. 'The Relationship between Law and Politics'. *Annual Survey of International & Comparative Law* 15(1) (2009), 19–41, 23.

honour,[48] the members continued to enshrine Vitoria as a figure of national pride in cultural memory. Furthermore, in the articles of the yearbook, published again after eleven years of silence in the aftermath of the Second World War, the extent of direct political implications immensely differs. In volumes six (1943–45), seven (1946–47), eight (1947–1948) and nine (1948–49) of the yearbook, contributions that intermingle history, international politics and ideology – object of the subsequent analysis – are rather the exception than the rule. Vicente Beltrán de Heredia (1885–1973) amongst others makes no direct references to politics when arguing in favour of 1492 as the birthdate of the Dominican friar.[49]

A few of the articles of this period, addressing Vitoria and current international politics, are particularly striking in their polemic against the Anti-Spain. In his contribution Guillermo Fraile (1909–1970) for instance, who directed the publication of *La Ciencia Tomista* during the Civil War, presents the materialism of Bolshevism as well as the biological racism of Rosenberg as 'satanic' bodies of thought.[50] Understanding himself as part of a Christian, Thomistic-Aristotelian tradition, he generally draws clear lines in his works between right and wrong ways of thinking, expressing his sympathy or hatred towards certain philosophies, condemning scepticism for example as a 'tuberculosis of the human intelligence'.[51] The same applies to Venancio Diego Carro (1894–1972), founder and director of the *Instituto Histórico Dominicano,* and

48 See Arregui Barandiaran, Ana. 'El Monumento a Francisco de Vitoria. Historia de su construcción'. *Sancho el Sabio* 25 (2006), 165–179; García Arias, Luis. 'Crónica de la conmemoración del IV centenario de la muerte de Fray Francisco de Vitoria por la Asociación'. *Anuario de la Asociación Francisco de Vitoria* 7 (1946–47), 211–216.

49 Beltrán de Heredia, Vicente. '¿En qué año nació Francisco de Vitoria? Un documento revolucionario'. *Anuario de la Asociación Francisco de Vitoria* 6 (1943–45), 1–27; other articles without political references are: Beltrán de Heredia, Vicente. 'Orientación humanística de la teología vitoriana'. *Anuario de la Asociación Francisco de Vitoria* 7 (1946–47), 149–177; Miaja de la Muela, Adolfo. 'De la existencia de una escuela internacional española de los siglos XVI y XVII'. *Anuario de la Asociación Francisco de Vitoria* 9 (1948–49), 99–141; Lumbreras, Pedro. 'Cuando el salvaje illega al uso de razón'. *Anuario de la Asociación Francisco de Vitoria* 7 (1946–47), 85–128.

50 All direct quotes originally in Spanish were translated into English by the author. For the authentic version cf. Fraile, Fr. Guillermo. 'Vitoria y la orientación de la ciencia española en el siglo XVI'. *Anuario de la Asociación Francisco de Vitoria* 8 (1947–48), 55–100, 99–100; see the homage to him by Pintor-Ramos, Antonio. 'El Profesor Guillermo Fraile, historiador de la filosofía', *Cuadernos salmatinos de filosofía* 1 (1974), 259–271.

51 See Fraile, 'Vitoria' 1947–48 (n. 51), 67.

Ricardo García Villoslada (1900–1991), since 1940 professor at the *Universidad Pontificia* in Salamanca.[52]

In contrast to their ancestors of the nineteenth century these clerics – Villoslada was a Jesuit, the other two Dominicans – did not just celebrate a famous representative of their own holy order.[53] Especially considering the friend-enemy antagonisms in their texts,[54] these clerics also did not just study 'Spanish scholars under a National Catholicism approach',[55] as Yolanda Gamarra proposed as typical for this period, but clearly show a clerical fascist tendency; a phenomenon that had already spread throughout Europe in the interwar period, the Spanish Civil War being a milestone in its development.[56] In sum, Carro, Fraile and Villoslada seem to be striking examples not only of the first ideologists of the regime,[57] but also for clerical fascists writing about Vitoria, *ius gentium* and current international politics. Although no international legalist, they nonetheless contributed, as we are going to see in the following, to the 'formation of knowledge about the law of nations'.[58]

3 Francisco de Vitoria and International Legal Politics after the Second World War

In the first volume published under Franco's rule the members of the association declare that the study of Vitoria and the other classics of international law should mainly serve to face the political challenges of the moment, more

52 For more biographical details confer Velasco Sánchez, José Tomás. 'Real Academica de la Historia: Venancio Diego Carro', available at: http://dbe.rah.es/biografias/24359/venancio-diego-carro, (last accessed on 14 September 2020); Aldea Vaquero, Quintín. 'El historiador Ricardo García Villoslada en sus ochenta años de edad'. *Hispania Sacra* 34(70) (1982), 689–701; for other examples of this polemical writing style confer Villoslada, Ricardo G. 'La teología, norma del derecho a la luz de Suárez y de Vitoria'. *Anuario de la Asociación Francisco de Vitoria* 6 (1943–45), 191–232, 205–206.

53 See Forcada Barona, 'La influencia de la religión católica' 2012 (n. 43), 251–252.

54 See López García, José Antonio. 'La presencia de Carl Schmitt en España'. *Revista de estudios políticos (Nueva Epoca)* 91 (1996), 139–168, 143–149.

55 Gamarra, 'On the Spanish Founding Father' 2017 (n. 33), 102.

56 Pollard, John. 'Clerical Fascism: Context, Overview and Conclusion', in *Clerical Fascism in Interwar Europe*, eds. Matthew Feldman, Marius Turda and Tudor Georgescu (Abingdon: Routledge, 2013), 221–234, 229.

57 See Carcedo, 'Primeros ideólogos del Franquismo' 1999 (n. 43), 370–372.

58 Martti Koskenniemi declared himself in favour of an inclusion of other thinkers of international law in research, regardless of discipline and profession. See Koskenniemi, Martti. 'Law of Nations and the "Conflict of Faculties"'. *History of the Present. Law at the Intersection of Theory and History* 8(1) (2018), 4–28, 23.

concretely, those arising from the Second World War.[59] Tempted by the Axis powers and their imperialism, Spain's position at the beginning of the war can be described as 'non-belligerent'.[60] At the border station of Handaye in 1940, Francisco Franco and Adolf Hitler discussed the conditions of Spain's entry into the war. Later turned into the myth of the Caudillo's shrewdness in saying 'not yet' to Hitler, the Führer left, in fact angered by the exorbitant requests made by Franco as a condition of fighting alongside the Axis powers.[61] Nevertheless, Spanish volunteers were recruited to form the so-called Blue Division supporting the Wehrmacht on the Eastern Front. Thereby, the Spanish contingent was not just understood as a repayment for the help of German troops in the 'crusade' of 1936, but as an important participation in the crucial war between 'civilization' and Bolshevism.[62]

In 1943, the superiority of the Allies became more and more apparent. During an audience with the new US ambassador Carlton J. Hayes, Franco therefore tried to legitimate and defend the interference of the Blue Division in Leningrad with a theory of three wars, claiming that Spain had merely taken Germany's side in its war against Russia. However, in the eyes of the Anglo-Americans, Stalin was a faithful ally against fascism whereas Franco a comrade of Hitler and Mussolini.[63] This led to Spanish alienation from the Axis powers and a suppression of fascism, also perceptible in the articles of the association's yearbook, where the ideology of National Socialism is severely condemned.[64] However, Barcia Trelles for instance argues – without directly referring to, but likely meaning the Nuremberg trials – that the 'defeated waiting for sentence should not be ruined'; instead, the first and foremost purpose of the winners of war and the international community should be peace and stability.[65]

59 'Una nueva etapa' and 'In memoriam'. *Anuario de la Asociación Francisco de Vitoria* 6 (1943–45), v–vii.

60 See Bernecker, Walther L. *Geschichte Spaniens seit dem Bürgerkrieg* (Munich: C. H. Beck, 2018), 83.

61 Pecharromán, Julio Gil. *La política exterior del Franquismo. Entre Hendaya y El Aaiún* (Barcelona: Flor del Viento ediciones, 2008), 57–60.

62 See Bernecker, *Geschichte Spaniens* 2018 (n. 61), 84.

63 Pecharromán, *La política exterior del Franquismo* 2008 (n. 62), 109–110; 'Theory of three wars': (1) Germany vs. Great Britain and the United States, Spain neutral (2) Japan vs. United States, Spain on the side of North America (3) eastern Europe, Spain combatants with the Germans vs. communism.

64 See Fraile, 'Vitoria' 1947–48 (n. 51), 99–100.

65 See Barcia Trelles, Camilo. 'Francisco de Vitoria en 1946'. *Anuario de la Asociación Francisco de Vitoria* 7 (1946–47), 37.

This argumentation can probably be explained by Spain's precarious position in the aftermath of the Second World War. Public opinion of the western democracies as well as internal and external oppositions to the regime expected that a victory of the Allies should go hand in glove with an ouster of *franquismo*.[66] In the Potsdam Conference, the governments of the United States, the United Kingdom and the Soviet Union had already proclaimed their disapproval of a Spanish request for admission to the United Nations, followed by a recommendation of the General Assembly that 'the United Nations should act in accordance' with these statements.[67] Thereafter, the Security Council appointed a Sub-Committee to investigate the Spanish issue which came to the following appraisal:[68] Besides highlighting Spain's support given to the enemy powers in the course of the Second World War, the Sub-Committee asserted that in 'origin, nature, structure and general conduct, the Franco regime is a fascist regime patterned on, and established largely as a result of aid received from, Hitler's Nazi Germany and Mussolini's Fascist Italy'.[69] On that base, the General Assembly phrased the following recommendation in December 1946:

> The General Assembly ... recommends that the Franco Government of Spain be debarred from membership in international agencies established by or brought into relationship with the United Nations or by these agencies, until a new and acceptable government is formed in Spain ... . Recommends that if, within a reasonable time, there is not established a government which derives its authority form the consent of the governed ... , the Security Council consider the adequate measures to be taken in order to remedy the situation.[70]

As a third point, the General Assembly recommended the withdrawal of all ambassadors from Madrid. Except Portugal, Argentina and the Vatican, all

66 See Bernecker, *Geschichte Spaniens* 2018 (n. 61), 87–88.

67 See 'Mitteilung über die Dreimächtekonferenz von Berlin, 2. August 1945', in *Das Potsdamer Abkommen. Dokumentensammlung*, eds. Historische Gedenkstätte des Potsdamer Abkommens, Cecilienhof, Potsdam (Berlin: Staatsverlag der Deutschen Demokratischen Republik, 1980), 230; UNGA, *Relations of Members of the United Nations with Spain*, A/RES/32(I)/E, 9 February 1946.

68 See UNSC, *Resolution of 26 June 1946*, S/RES/7(1946)/E, 26 June 1946.

69 UNGA, *Relations of Members of the United Nations with Spain*, A/RES/39(I)/E, 12 December 1946.

70 UNGA, *Relations of Members of the United Nations with Spain*, A/RES/39(I)/E, 12 December 1946.

nations followed this last recommendation leaving Francoist Spain isolated, ostracised, therefore defensive and in fear of international sanction.[71]

Trying to change its colour like a 'chameleon' in the light of changing external circumstances,[72] Spain consequently presented itself more and more not as a fascist country with imperial ambitions, but as 'a natural-law oriented, ultra-catholic and anti-Marxist stronghold'.[73] Politically, the international ostracism left Franco only with one available tactic: to ride it out 'until the natural antagonism between the communist and capitalist blocs crystallised'.[74]

In his essay, 'The Fascist Mimesis of Spanish International Law and its Vitorian Aftermath, 1939–1953', Ignacio de la Rasilla del Moral postulates that 'the cultivation of the study of the Spanish friars who had "founded" international law was … perfectly consonant' with this 'preferred strategic portrayal'[75] of Francoist Spain.[76] Considering the articles in the *Anuario de la Asociación Francisco de Vitoria*, there are several parallels drawn to the lifetime of the Dominican friar. When the authors of the yearbook describe Russian communism for instance as more tyrannical as the despotic rule of the American Indians or present the accusations aimed at Francoist Spain as a revival of the Black Legend, they communicate aspects of the propagandistic image of ostracised Spain via these comparisons.[77]

Moreover, in Francoist propaganda the self-concept of sixteenth century's Spain as a catholic, colonial and militarist empire served not only as a source of identification, but also as a source of inspiration for the regime's preferred strategic portrayal. Whereas the idea of Spain as the last stronghold of Catholicism was already prominent in sixteenth century's Spanish empire,[78] Guillermo

71 See ibid. and Ahmad, Quasim. 'Britain and the Isolation of Franco, 1945–1950', in *Spain in an International Legal Context: 1936–1959*, eds. Christian Leitz and David J. Dunthron (New York: Berghahn Books, 1999), 219–243.

72 See Bernecker, Walther L. *Das Franco-Regime in Spanien. Der Streit um einen chamäleonhaften Systemtypus* (Frankfurt am Main: Peter Lang, 2016), 11 and 115.

73 Rasilla del Moral, Ignacio de la. 'The Fascist Mimesis of Spanish International Law and Its Vitorian Aftermath, 1939–1953'. *Journal of the History of International Law* 14(2) (2012), 207–236, 227.

74 Preston, Paul. 'Franco's Foreign Policy', in *Spain in an International Legal Context: 1936–1959*, eds. Christian Leitz and David J. Dunthron (New York: Berghahn Books, 1999), 1–13, 13.

75 Rasilla del Moral, *Shadow of Vitoria* 2018 (n. 29), 5.

76 See Rasilla del Moral, 'Fascist Mimesis' 2012 (n. 74), 227.

77 See Carro, Venancio D. 'Vitoria y los derechos del hombre'. *Anuario de la Asociación Francisco de Vitoria* 7 (1946–47), 76, 84 and 146; Carro, Venancio D. 'Los derechos del hombre de cáracter espiritual, ségun Vitoria y los teólogos salmantinos'. *Anuario de la Asociación Francisco de Vitoria* 9 (1948–49), 69–97, 70–71.

78 See Las Casas, Bartolomé de. *Apologética historia sumaria*, ed. Edmundo O'Gorman (Mexico: Universidad Nacional, Instituto de Investigaciones Históricas, 1967) chapter 163, 156–157; and see Sepúlveda, Juan Ginés de. 'Democrates secundus, sive de iustis bellis

Fraile for instance claims in his article, that compared to England, France and the United States, characterised as 'material powers', Spain's prosperity in the twentieth century would lie in still being the 'moral and spiritual reserve of Europe',[79] the last stronghold, so concluded by Ignacio de la Rasilla del Moral, against the 'spread of Russian imperialism and atheist Marxism'.[80]

Furthermore, Fraile reconstructs in his article the unique role ascribed to Spain as the last guardian of a great European-Christian tradition from its roots in the Golden Age to the 1940s.[81] He presents Spain as a country that had always followed, in contrast to other European nations, its own path, thereby giving the regime and its role a historical legitimation. Whereas in all other countries the new contagious intellectual and religious movements of the early modern period had taken roots, the Spanish empire supposedly retained its traditional medieval purity.[82] The consequences of the continual destruction of medieval Christian universalism by false ideas, from natural humanism and Protestantism to Kantian criticism and so forth, finally culminating in twentieth century communism, the epitome of Anti-Spain, could today be seen, so Fraile, on the 'bloody ruins of the battlefields'.[83]

In this propagandistic historical narrative, fostered by the *Asociación Francisco de Vitoria*, the Dominican friar and his works are presented, so already concluded by Ignacio de la Rasilla del Moral, as the 'essence of an intellectual uncontaminated Spanish thought'.[84] Above that, Vitoria was understood by the association's members as the incarnation of Spain's real nature and protector of Spanish traditional values, thereby marking the historical beginning of the unique role ascribed to Spain and its *caudillo*.

Moreover, the 'preferred strategic portrayal' of Spain, in the context of which Franco was presented as the watchman of the west,[85] aimed at three 'concrete foreign policy goals':[86] Even though having abandoned its imperial aspirations, Spain tried to optimise its precarious international position via diplomacy. Portraying itself as 'a moral supervisor and a cultural and religious guide to its ancient colonies', Francoist Spain tried to approach and gain

causis', in *Obras completas III*, ed. Coroleu A. Lletget (Pozoblanco: Ayuntamiento de Pozoblanco, 1997), 39–134, 65; Vitoria himself claimed that the Spaniards, in their prerogative to convert the Indians of the New World, granted by the papal bull *Inter ceterae*, were the 'chosen people', see Vitoria, 'De Indis'1997 (n. 16), 454.

79 See Fraile, 'Vitoria' 1947–48 (n. 51), 76–77.

80 Rasilla del Moral, 'Fascist Mimesis' 2012 (n. 74), 210.

81 See Rasilla del Moral, *Shadow of Vitoria* 2018 (n. 29), 5.

82 See Fraile, 'Vitoria' 1947–48 (n. 51), 56, 85–86 and 94.

83 See ibid., 83–84.

84 Rasilla del Moral, *Shadow of Vitoria* 2018 (n. 29), 8.

85 See Bernecker, *Das Franco-Regime in Spanien* 2016 (n. 73), 110.

86 Rasilla del Moral, 'Fascist Mimesis' 2012 (n. 74), 228.

sympathies in Latin America, so Ignacio de la Rasilla del Moral, 'under the fraternal cloak of the notion of *Hispanidad*';[87] a strategy also perceptible in the yearbook, when Miguel Arjona for instance characterises Spain as the country that turned 'the Indio a believer, a brother …' and created 'twenty nations that call Spain motherland'.[88]

Since the 'disaster of 1898',[89] the loss of the last Spanish colonial property in the Americas,[90] the decadence of the former empire had, in the eyes of the association's members, reached its peak with the condemnation and international isolation of the regime in 1946. Whereas in the time of the Dominican friar, so the current president of the association, José Gascón y Marín, the 'sun never set in the Spanish empire, today, we just don't want our truth, our spiritual greatness' and 'our love for social justice to be darkened'.[91] In this context, hoping for an international vindication, Vitoria was instrumentalised as the pride and joy of Spain to lobby for an international acceptance of the Francoist regime, reclaiming its rightful position in the international community as the cradle of international law.[92]

Besides contributing to the diplomatic ties between Spain and its former colonies and emphasising a Spanish paternity of international law, the association's members used Vitoria's concept of international order as an inspiration for their version of a new world order after the Second World War. In a lecture given in the context of the celebrations of the anniversary of the Dominican friar coinciding with Spain's exclusion from the United Nations, Barcia Trelles claimed that 'never before, humanity has followed trails that represented such a clear antithesis and regression of the Vitorian principles as in 1946'.[93] In the view of the association's members, the Second World War was followed by an era of moral disintegration. This moral-juridical vacuum, and in this point they

87 Ibid.

88 Arjona, Miguel. 'La crisis del sistema de Versalles y la comunidad internacional'. *Anuario de la Asociación Francisco de Vitoria* 8 (1947–48), 383–416, 390.

89 Rasilla del Moral, *Shadow of Vitoria* 2018 (n. 29), 171.

90 See Schwabe, Klaus. *Weltmacht und Weltordnung. Amerikanische Außenpolitik von 1898 bis zur Gegenwart* (Paderborn: Schöningh, 2007), 20–33.

91 Gascón y Marín, José. 'Discurso pronunciado en la sesión de clausura por el presidente de la Asociación Francisco de Vitoria'. *Anuario de la Asociación Francisco de Vitoria* 7 (1946–47), 203–209, 209.

92 See Arjona, 'La crisis del sistema de Versalles' 1947–48 (n. 89), 390.

93 Barcia Trelles, 'Francisco de Vitoria en 1946' 1946–47 (n. 66), 9.

agree,[94] could only be filled in one way:[95] 'In turning to the principles of the authentic founder of international law' could the world be saved from chaos, another use of nuclear weapons and the outbreak of a Third World War.[96] Just as Vitoria would had given law to the New World in form of the *Leyes Nuevas*,[97] the only path to permanent international peace would be, what the members call, the 'ruta vitoriana'.[98]

But what did they mean and intend by proclaiming that international politics should follow a 'Vitorian route'? Whereas they do not concretely explain how the principles of the Dominican friar could be used, one facet of their natural law-based concept becomes clear. In the eyes of the association's members, the Dominican friar was first a moralist and theologian and only secondarily a jurist and philosopher. Whereas one might agree on this aspect, they also underline that Vitoria's ideas only became as revolutionary as they are by approaching legal questions with the help of theology.[99] The same applies to the member's conception of a new world order, where Catholicism is also the crucial component: Only upon the fundament of the Catholic Church, an already existing grand family of peoples and nations, could a durable and universal international order be built.[100] Thus, following the 'Vitorian route' meant establishing an international order based on Catholic norms, or, more concretely, on the national values of Francoist Spain.[101]

94 See Gascón y Marín, 'Discurso pronunciado' 1946–47 (n. 92), 203–204; Carro, Venancio D. 'Las controversias de Indias y las ideas teológica jurídicas medievales que las preparan y explican'. *Anuario de la Asociación Francisco de Vitoria* 8 (1947–48), 13–53, 42.

95 See Barcia Trelles, 'Francisco de Vitoria en 1946' 1946–47 (n. 66), 17 and 37.

96 Ibid., 42.

97 See Gascón y Marín, 'Discurso pronunciado' 1946–47 (n. 92), 208.

98 Ibid.

99 See Villoslada, 'La teología, norma del derecho' 1943–45 (n. 53), 215; Beltrán de Heredia, 'Orientación humanística' 1946–47 (n. 50), 155; Castillo, Carlos Ruiz del. 'Las relaciones entre los derechos del hombre y el derecho internacional, según las inspiraciones de Francisco de Vitoria'. *Anuario de la Asociación Francisco de Vitoria* 9 (1948–49), 39–67, 46; Carro, 'Las controversias de indias' 1947–48 (n. 95), 20; Hamilton, Carlos D. 'Filosofía jurídica del maestro Fray Francisco de Vitoria'. *Anuario de la Asociación Francisco de Vitoria* 8 (1947–48), 103–259, 142.

100 See Villoslada, 'La teología' 1943–45 (n. 53), 231.

101 See ibid., 225; Carro, 'Vitoria' 1946–47 (n. 78), 146; Truyol y Serra, Antonio. 'Prémisses philosophiques et historiques du "totus orbis" de Vitoria'. *Anuario de la Asociación Francisco de Vitoria* 7 (1946–47), 179–201, 201; Gascón y Marín, 'Discurso pronunciado' 1946–47 (n. 92), 203–204.

4 Perspectives

'Although in the new international organisation absent from its peaceful duties, the day will come, once political passions have eased, when Spain will be recognised as a member state of the security council'.[102] What was in the yearbook merely expressed as a hope, became a real possibility in 1950. Where Churchill had recounted during the Potsdam Conference that he had written a frigid answer to Franco's letter, asking for a coalition of Western countries in view of the threat posed by the Soviet Union,[103] only five years later, with the beginning of the Cold War, the UN resolution was resolved, marking the end of Spain's international ostracism.[104] Whereas it was rather not the propagandising of Vitoria that led to a successful vindication of the regime,[105] the influence of his glorification on the historiography of international law as its authentic founder and father cannot be denied and should be object of further examination.

Already having lost its significance in the context of decolonization, the yearbook's publication was interrupted between 1949 and 1955. In 1964, the *Asociación Francisco de Vitoria* was absorbed by the state and restructured as an institute belonging to the *CSIC*.[106] The volumes were now printed under issue titles, such as 'Europeismo y universalismo' (XIV) or 'Perspectiva Historica del Pensamiento Clásico Español' (XV). The articles of these yearbook's editions still present the Dominican friar as the father of international law,[107] just as the defense against the Black Legend is still an argumentative context in which the Dominican friar is used.[108] Furthermore, the authors connect Vitoria's doctrine

102 Arjona, 'La crisis del sistema de Versalles' 1947–48 (n. 89), 390.

103 See 'Potsdamer Konferenz (Niederschrift der sowjetischen Delegation von den Verhandlungen) 17. Juli bis 2. August 1945', in *Das Potsdamer Abkommen. Dokumentensammlung*, eds. Historische Gedenkstätte des Potsdamer Abkommens, Cecilienhof, Potsdam (Berlin: Staatsverlag der Deutschen Demokratischen Republik, 1980), 75.

104 Confer UNGA, *Resolutions Adopted on the Reports of the AD HOC Political Committee, Relation of State Members and Specialized Agencies with Spain*, A/RES/386(V)/E, 4 November 1950.

105 See Hernández, José Luis Neila. 'The Foreign Policy Administration of Franco's Spain. From Isolation to International Realignment (1945–1957)', in *Spain in an International Legal Context: 1936–1959*, eds. Christian Leitz and David J. Dunthron (New York: Berghahn Books, 1999), 277–297, 280.

106 See Egío García, *El pensamiento Republicano* 2014 (n. 34), 142–147 and 153.

107 See Menéndez Pidal, Ramón. 'Prólogo'. *Anuario de la Asociación Francisco de Vitoria* XIII (1960–61), 1–10.

108 See Menéndez Pidal, 'Prólogo' 1960–61 (n. 108), 1–10.

to new questions of international relevance such as the nuclear threat.[109] In total having produced 18 volumes of the *Anuario*, the association edited its last one in 1972.[110]

Although the *Anuario de la Asociación Francisco de Vitoria* collects just a small part of the Spanish, and just a microscopic part of all the publications on the Dominican friar, one can hope that the endeavour and interest, mainly initiated by Ignacio de la Rasilla del Moral, in uncovering Vitoria's constant 'transformations and reinterpretations'[111] will remain. So that at last all the histories hidden in the shadow of his elevation will come to light: not only the evolutionary roots of his glorification, but also all the 'alternative histories of international law'[112] ignored or overlooked due to Vitoria's excessive presence and finally the histories about himself and his work that lie hidden in the shadow of his own glorification.

Acknowledgment

The author would like to thank the participants of the conference who discussed the chapter with her for their fruitful comments; an exchange that motivated her to spend more hours with Vitoria and the *Anuario*.

Bibliography

ABC, Diario. 'La Asociación Francisco de Vitoria', in *Diario ABC, Noticias políticas* (16 November 1926), 18.

Abril-Castelló, Vidal. 'La bipolarización sepúlveda-las casas y sus consequencias. La revolución de la duodocima replica', in *Francisco de Vitoria y la Escuela de Salamanca. La ética en la conquista de América*, ed. Demetrio Ramos Pérez (Madrid: Consejo Superior de Investigaciones Científicas, 1984), 229–290.

'Acta de la Fundación de la Asociación Francisco de Vitoria'. *Anuario de la Asociación Francisco de Vitoria* 1 (1927–1928), 43–49.

109 See Yanguas Messía, José. 'Prólogo'. *Anuario de la Asociación Francisco de Vitoria* XIV (1962–63), 15–20.

110 See Egío García, *El pensamiento republicano* 2014 (n. 34), 142–147 and 153.

111 Rasilla del Moral, 'Francisco de Vitoria's Unexpected Transformations' 2013 (n. 26), 287–318.

112 Kemmerer, Alexandra. 'Towards a Global History of International Law? Editor's Note'. *European Journal of International Law* 25(1) (2014), 287–295, 289.

Ahmad, Quasim. 'Britain and the Isolation of Franco, 1945–1950', in *Spain in an International Legal Context: 1936–1959*, eds. Christian Leitz and David J. Dunthron (New York: Berghahn Books, 1999), 219–243.

Aldea Vaquero, Quintín. 'El Historiador Ricardo García Villoslada en sus ochenta años de edad'. *Hispania Sacra* 34(70) (1982), 689–701.

Amorosa, Paolo. *Rewriting the History of the Law of Nations. How James Brown Scott Made Francisco de Vitoria the Founder of International Law* (Oxford: Oxford University Press, 2019).

Anghie, Antony. *Imperialism, Sovereignty, and the Making of International Law* (Cambridge: Cambridge University Press, 2005).

Arjona, Miguel. 'La Crisis del Sistema de Versalles y la Comunidad Internacional'. *Anuario de la Asociación Francisco de Vitoria* 8 (1947–48), 383–416.

Arregui Barandiaran, Ana. 'El Monumento a Francisco de Vitoria. Historia de su Construcción'. *Sancho el Sabio* 25 (2006), 165–179.

Barcia Trelles, Camilo. 'Francisco de Vitoria en 1946'. *Anuario de la Asociación Francisco de Vitoria* 7 (1946–47), 7–42.

Beltrán de Heredia, Vicente. '¿En qué año nació Francisco de Vitoria? Un documento revolucionario'. *Anuario de la Asociación Francisco de Vitoria* 6 (1943–45), 1–27.

Beltrán de Heredia, Vicente. 'Orientación Humanística de la Teología Vitoriana'. *Anuario de la Asociación Francisco de Vitoria* 7 (1946–47), 149–177.

Bernecker, Walther L. *Das Franco-Regime in Spanien. Der Streit um einen chamäleonhaften Systemtypus* (Frankfurt am Main: Peter Lang, 2016).

Bernecker, Walther L. *Geschichte Spaniens seit dem Bürgerkrieg* (Munich: C. H. Beck, 2018).

Birr, Christiane and Wim Decock. *Recht und Moral in der Frühen Scholastik 1500–1750* (Berlin: De Gruyter, 2016).

Boletín Oficial del Estado, *Ley de 29 julio de 1943 sobre ordenación de la Universidad española*, 7406–7431.

Bordat, Josef. *Annexion – Anbindung – Anerkennung. Globale Beziehungskulturen im frühen 16. Jahrhundert* (Hamburg: Tredition, 2008).

Brieskorn, Norbert. 'Die Kritik von Bartolomé de Las Casas an der Relectio de Indis', in *Francisco Vitorias >De Indis< in interdisziplinärer Perspektive*, eds. Norbert Brieskorn and Gideon Stiening (Stuttgart: frommann-holzboog, 2011), 219–250.

Carcedo, Laureano Robles. 'Primeros Ideólogos del Franquismo'. *Hispanística XX* 17 (1999), 359–378.

Carro, Venancio D. 'Los derechos del hombre de carácter espiritual, ségun Vitoria y los teólogos salmantinos'. *Anuario de la Asociación Francisco de Vitoria* 9 (1948–49), 69–97.

Carro, Venancio D. 'Vitoria y los derechos del hombre'. *Anuario de la Asociación Francisco de Vitoria* 7 (1946–47), 141–148.

Carro, Venancio D. 'Las controversias de Indias y las ideas teológico jurídicas medievales que las preparan y explican'. *Anuario de la Asociación Francisco de Vitoria* 8 (1947–48), 13–53.

Castilla Urbano, Francisco. *El pensamiento de Francisco de Vitoria. Filosofía política e indio americano* (Barcelona: Anthropos Editorial del Hombre, 1992).

Castillo, Carlos Ruiz del. 'Las relaciones entre los derechos del hombre y el derecho internacional, según las inspiraciones de Francisco de Vitoria'. *Anuario de la Asociación Francisco de Vitoria* 9 (1948–49), 39–67.

Cavallar, Georg. 'Vitoria, Grotius, Pufendorf, Wolff and Vattel: Accomplices of European Colonialism and Exploitation or True Cosmopolitans?'. *Journal of the History of International Law* 10(2) (2008), 181–209.

Cerar, Miro. 'The Relationship between Law and Politics'. *Annual Survey of International & Comparative Law* 15(1) (2009), 19–41.

Deckers, Daniel. *Gerechtigkeit und Recht. Eine historisch-kritische Untersuchung der Gerechtigkeitslehre des Francisco de Vitoria (1483–1546)* (Freiburg: Herder, 1991).

Delgado, Mariano. 'Die Zustimmung des Volkes in der politischen Theorie von Francisco de Vitoria, Bartolomé de las Casas and Francisco Suárez', in *Die Ordnung der Praxis. Neue Studien zur Spanischen Spätscholastik,* eds. Frank Grunert and Kurt Seelmann (Berlin: De Gruyter, 2001), 157–182.

Duve, Thomas, Matthias Lutz-Bachmann, Christiane Birr and Andreas Niederberger. 'The School of Salamanca: A Digital Collection of Sources and a Dictionary of Its Juridical-Political Language. The Basic Objectives and Structure of a Research Project'. *The Salamanca Working Paper Series* No. 2014(1) (2014), 1–29.

Egío García, D. Victor Manuel. *El pensamiento republicano de Fernando Vázquez de Menchaca* (Universidad de Murcia, Departamento de Filosofìa, PhD Thesis, 2014), available at: https://tdx.cat/bitstream/handle/10803/287164/TVMEG.pdf?sequence=1, (last accessed on 14 September 2020).

'Estatutos de la "Asociación Francisco de Vitoria"'. *Anuario de la Asociación Francisco de Vitoria* 2 (1929–1930), 7–16.

Fernández-Santamaria, José A. 'Juan Ginés de Sepúlveda on the Nature of the American Indians'. *The Americans* 31(4) (1975), 434–451.

Fernández y Medina, Benjamín and Francisco Ramírez Montesinos. 'Nota preliminar'. *Anuario de la Asociación Francisco de Vitoria* 1 (1927–1928), 7–11.

Fitzmaurice, Andrew. 'The Problem of Eurocentrism in the Thought of Francisco de Vitoria', in *At the Origins of Modernity. Francisco de Vitoria and the Discovery of International Law,* eds. José Beneyto and Justo Corti Varela (Berlin: Springer, 2017), 77–93.

Forcada Barona, Ignacio. 'La influencia de la religión católica en la doctrina internacionalista española del período de entreguerras (1918–1939)', in *Historia del pensamiento iusinternacionalista español del siglo* XX, vol. 1, eds. Yolanda Gamarra and Ignacio de la Rasilla del Moral (Pamplona: Thomson Reuters Aranzadi, 2012), 229–286.

Fraile, Fr. Guillermo. 'Vitoria y la orientación de la ciencia española en el siglo XVI'. *Anuario de la Asociación Francisco de Vitoria* 8 (1947–48), 55–100.

Gamarra, Yolanda. 'On the Spanish Founding Father of Modern International Law: Camilo Barcia Trelles (1888–1977)', in *At the Origins of Modernity. Francisco de Vitoria and the Discovery of International Law*, eds. José Beneyto and Justo Corti Varela (Berlin: Springer, 2017), 95–115.

García Arias, Luis. 'Crónica de la conmemoración del IV centenario de la muerte de Fray Francisco de Vitoria por la Asociación'. *Anuario de la Asociación Francisco de Vitoria* 7 (1946–47), 211–216.

Gascón y Marín, José. 'Discurso pronunciado en la sésio de clausura por el presidente de la Asociación Francisco de Vitoria'. *Anuario de la Asociación Francisco de Vitoria* 7 (1946–47), 203–209.

Hamilton, Carlos D. 'Filosofía jurídica del maestro Fray Francisco de Vitoria'. *Anuario de la Asociación Francisco de Vitoria* 8 (1947–48), 103–259.

Hernández, José Luis Neila. 'The Foreign Policy Administration of Franco's Spain. From Isolation to International Realignment (1945–1957)', in *Spain in an International Legal Context: 1936–1959*, eds. Christian Leitz and David J. Dunthron (New York: Berghahn Books, 1999), 277–297.

Kemmerer, Alexandra. 'Towards a Global History of International Law? Editor's Note'. *European Journal of International Law* 25(1) (2014), 287–295.

Koskenniemi, Martti. 'Empire and International Law: The Real Spanish Contribution'. *University of Toronto Law Journal* 61(1) (2011), 1–36.

Koskenniemi, Martti. 'Law of Nations and the "Conflict of Faculties"'. *History of the Present. Law at the Intersection of Theory and History* 8(1) (2018), 4–28.

Koskenniemi, Martti. 'Vitoria and Us. Thoughts on Critical Histories of International Law'. *Rechtsgeschichte – Legal History. Zeitschrift des Max-Planck-Instituts für europäische Rechtsgeschichte* 22 (2014), 119–138.

Koskenniemi, Martti. 'Why History of International Law Today?'. *Rechtsgeschichte – Legal History. Zeitschrift des Max-Planck-Instituts für europäische Rechtsgeschichte* 4 (2004), 61–66.

Las Casas, Bartolomé de. *Apologética Historia Sumaria*, ed. Edmundo O'Gorman (Mexico: Universidad Nacional, Instituto de Investigaciones Historicas, 1967).

López García, José Antonio. 'La Presencia de Carl Schmitt en España'. *Revista de Estudios Políticos (Nueva Epoca)* 91 (1996), 139–168.

Lumbreras, Pedro. 'Cuando el Salvaje Illega al Uso de Razón'. *Anuario de la Asociación Francisco de Vitoria* 7 (1946–47), 85–128.

Menéndez, Agustín José. 'From Republicanism to Fascist Ideology under the Early *Franquismo*', in *Darker Legacies of Law in Europe. The Shadow of National Socialism and Fascism over Europe and Its Legal Traditions*, eds. Christian Joerges and Navraj Singh Ghaleigh (Oxford: Hart, 2003), 337–360.

Menéndez Pidal, Ramón. 'Prólogo'. *Anuario de la Asociación Francisco de Vitoria* 13 (1960–61), 1–10.

Miaja de la Muela, Adolfo. 'De la existencia de una escuela internacional española de los siglos XVI y XVII'. *Anuario de la Asociación Francisco de Vitoria* 9 (1948–49), 99–141.

Miranda, Jaume Claret. *El atroz desmoche. La destrucción de la Univerisdad española por el Franquismo, 1936–1945* (Barcelona: Críteria, 2006).

'Mitteilung über die Dreimächtekonferenz von Berlin, 2. August 1945', in *Das Potsdamer Abkommen. Dokumentensammlung*, eds. Historische Gedenkstätte des Potsdamer Abkommens, Cecilienhof, Potsdam (Berlin: Staatsverlag der Deutschen Demokratischen Republik, 1980), 215–232.

Mulsow, Martin and Andreas Mahler. 'Einleitung', in *Die Cambridge School der politischen Ideengeschichte*, eds. Martin Mulsow and Andreas Mahler (Berlin: Suhrkamp, 2010), 7–20.

Niemela, Pekka. 'A Cosmopolitan World Order? Perspectives on Francisco de Vitoria and the United Nations'. *Max Planck Yearbook of United Nations Law* 12 (2018), 301–334.

Pecharromán, Julio Gil. *La Política Exterior del Franquismo. Entre Hendaya y El Aaiún* (Barcelona: Flor del Viento Ediciones, 2008).

Peláez, Manuel J. Art. 'Camilo Barcia Trelles', in *Diccionario crítico de Juristas Españoles, Portugueses y Latinamericano (Hispánicos, Brasilenos, Quebequenes y restantes francófonos)*, vol. 1 (A–L) (Barcelona: Zaragoza, 2005), 134–135.

Pintor-Ramos, Antonio. 'El Profesor Guillermo Fraile, historiador de la Filosofía'. *Cuadernos Salmatinos de Filosofía* 1 (1974), 259–271.

Pollard, John. 'Clerical Fascism: Context, Overview and Conclusion', in *Clerical Fascism in Interwar Europe*, eds. Matthew Feldman, Marius Turda and Tudor Georgescu (Abingdon: Routledge, 2013), 221–234.

'Potsdamer Konferenz (Niederschrift der sowjetischen Delegation von den Verhandlungen) 17. Juli bis 2. August 1945', in *Das Potsdamer Abkommen. Dokumentensammlung*, eds. Historische Gedenkstätte des Potsdamer Abkommens, Cecilienhof, Potsdam (Berlin: Staatsverlag der Deutschen Demokratischen Republik, 1980), 47–213.

Preston, Paul. 'Franco's Foreign Policy', in *Spain in an International Legal Context: 1936–1959*, eds. Christian Leitz and David J. Dunthron (New York: Berghahn Books, 1999), 1–13.

Rasilla del Moral, Ignacio de la. 'Francisco de Vitoria's Unexpected Transformations and Reinterpretations for International Law'. *International Community Law Review* 15(3) (2013), 287–318.

Rasilla del Moral, Ignacio de la. *In the Shadow of Vitoria: A History of International Law in Spain (1770–1953)* (Leiden: Brill, 2018).

Rasilla del Moral, Ignacio de la. 'The Fascist Mimesis of Spanish International Law and Its Vitorian Aftermath, 1939–1953'. *Journal of the History of International Law* 14(2) (2012), 207–236.

Rasilla del Moral, Ignacio de la. 'The Problem of Periodization in the History of International Law'. *Law and History Review* 37(1) (2019), 1–34.

Rasilla del Moral, Ignacio de la. 'The Study of International Law in the Spanish *Short* Nineteenth Century (1808–1898)'. *Chicago-Kent Journal of International and Comparative Law* 13(2) (2013), 122–150.

Schwabe, Klaus. *Weltmacht und Weltordnung. Amerikanische Außenpolitik von 1898 bis zur Gegenwart* (Paderborn: Schöningh, 2007).

Scott, James Brown. 'Asociación Francisco de Vitoria'. *American Journal of International Law* 22(1) (1928), 136–139.

Sepúlveda, Juan Ginés de. 'Democrates Secundus, Sive de Iustis Bellis Causis', in *Obras Completas*, vol. III, ed. Coroleu A. Lletget (Pozoblanco: Ayuntamiento de Pozoblanco, 1997), 39–134.

Serra, María Pilar Hernando. *Diccionario de catedráticos españoles de derecho (1847–1943)* (Madrid: Universidad Carlos III de Madrid, Instituto Figuerola de Historia y Ciencias Sociales, 2011) available at: http://portal.uc3m.es/portal/page/portal/instituto_figuerola/programas/phu/diccionariodecatedraticos/lcatedraticos, (last accessed on 14 September 2020).

Skinner, Quentin. 'Bedeutung und Verstehen in der Ideengeschichte (1969/2009)', in *Ideengeschichte*, ed. Barbara Stollberg-Rilinger (Stuttgart: Franz Steiner Verlag, 2010), 61–94.

Stollberg-Rilinger, Barbara. 'Einleitung', in *Ideengeschichte*, ed. Barbara Stollberg-Rilinger (Stuttgart: Franz Steiner Verlag, 2010), 7–42.

Stüben, Joachim. 'Die Relectiones des Francisco de Vitoria. Vorbemerkungen zum zweiten Band der lateinisch-deutschen Gesamtausgabe', in *Vorlesungen II (Relectiones). Völkerrecht, Politik, Kirche*, eds. Ulrich Horst, Heinz-Gerhard Justenhoven and Joachim Stüben (Stuttgart: Kohlhammer, 1997).

Todorov, Tzvetan. *Die Eroberung Amerikas. Das Problem des Anderen* (Frankfurt am Main: Suhrkamp Verlag, 1985).

Truyol y Serra, Antonio. 'Prémisses philosophiques et historiques du "Totus Orbis" de Vitoria'. *Anuario de la Asociación Francisco de Vitoria* 7 (1946–47), 179–201.

'Una nueva etapa' and 'In Memoriam'. *Anuario de la Asociación Francisco de Vitoria* 6 (1943–45), v–vii.

Valenzuela-Vermehren, Luis. 'Empire, Sovereignty, and Justice in Francisco de Vitoria's International Thought. A Reinterpretation of "De Indis" (1532)'. *Revista Chilena de Derecho* 40(1) (2013), 261–299.

Velasco Sánchez, José Tomás. 'Real Academica de la Historia: Venancio Diego Carro', available at: http://dbe.rah.es/biografias/24359/venancio-diego-carro (last accessed on 14 September 2020).

Villoslada, Ricardo G. 'La Teología, Norma del Derecho a la Luz de Suárez y de Vitoria'. *Anuario de la Asociación Francisco de Vitoria* 6 (1943–45), 191–232.

Vitoria, Francisco de. 'De Indis', in *Vorlesungen II (Relectiones). Völkerrecht, Politik, Kirche*, eds. Ulrich Horst, Heinz-Gerhard Justenhoven and Joachim Stüben (Stuttgart: Kohlhammer, 1997), 370–541.

Williams, Robert A. *The American Indian in Western Legal Thought. The Discourses of Conquest* (Oxford: Oxford University Press, 1992).

Yanguas Messía, José. 'Prólogo'. *Anuario de la Asociación Francisco de Vitoria* 14 (1962–63), 15–20.

Zapatero, Pablo. 'Francisco de Vitoria and the Postmodern Grand Critique of International law', in *At the Origins of Modernity. Francisco de Vitoria and the Discovery of International Law*, eds. José María Beneyto and Justo Corti Varela (Berlin: Springer, 2017), 177–195.

PART 5

New Methods and Approaches

CHAPTER 15

Turntablism in the History of International Law

Jean d'Aspremont

Abstract

This chapter uses the metaphor of turntablism to shed light on the confinement of international lawyers' engagement with history to the terms, vocabularies, and categories of the very historical narratives they seek to evaluate, disrupt, or displace. For the sake of this chapter, turntablism is understood here as the art of creating new music and sound effects by using one or several turntables on which a record is placed. This chapter argues that twenty-first century international lawyers engaging with the history of international law are talented turntablists in that the many historiographical works of international lawyers produced since the so-called 'historical turn' have remained confined to the very terms, categories, and vocabularies of the histories whose creation they have been discoursing and theorising. This chapter ultimately shows that turntablism is not the inevitable fate of international lawyers engaging with history, and that a radical historical critique is possible and should be promoted.

Keywords

international law – history – historiography – critique – critical legal studies – critical histories – colonialism – Eurocentricism

1 Introduction

Turntablism is the art of creating new music and sound effects by using one or several turntables on which a record is placed. The so-called turntablists – better known as DJs – manipulate records on turntables by moving them with their hand to cue the stylus to exact points thereon, and by touching or moving the record to stop, slow down, speed up, or spin the record backwards.[1] Using

1 On the notion of turntablism, see generally Holmes, Thom. *Electronic and Experimental Music: Technology, Music, and Culture* (Abingdon: Routledge, 2015), 476–483.

DOI:10.1163/9789004461802_017

the metaphor of turntablism for descriptive purposes, this chapter argues that twenty-first century international lawyers engaging in the history of international law are talented turntablists and that the much-celebrated invigoration of historical consciousness that has been constitutive of the 'historical turn' in international legal thought has been dominated by a turntablist attitude, restricting the critical potential of international lawyers' recent engagements with history.

This argument about the turntablism informing international legal studies on history proceeds as follows. After a few remarks on the 'historical turn', the chapter shows that the historical consciousness commonly associated with the 'historical turn' has long permeated the work of international lawyers and that the 'historical turn' should be better construed as a 'historiographical turn' (1). This chapter then uses the metaphor of turntablism to shed light on the confinement of international lawyers' engagement with history to the terms, vocabularies, and categories of the very historical narratives they seek to evaluate, disrupt, or displace, which it characterises as a turntablist attitude (2). It subsequently formulates a few remarks on the resilience of turntablism in international legal thought despite the critical mindset of many of the international lawyers nowadays engaging with history (3). In the final section, this chapter shows that turntablism is not the inevitable fate of international lawyers engaging with history, and that a radical historical critique is possible and should be promoted (4).

Before developing this claim about the dominant turntablist attitude in international lawyers' engagement with history, a preliminary caveat is necessary. It must be acknowledged that the discussion that unfolds in the following section is itself constitutive of a turntablist narrative that upholds the terms of markers, periodisation, and causal sequencing of dominant international lawyers' histories.[2] This is well illustrated by the articulation of the discussion

2 On the constitutive elements of historical narrativisation, see generally White, Hayden. 'Historical Discourse and Literary Writing', in *Tropes for the Past: Hayden White and the History/Literature Debate*, ed. Kuisma Korhonen (Amsterdam: Rodopi, 2006), 25–34, 30; White, Hayden. *Metahistory. The Historical Imagination in the 19th-Century Europe* (Baltimore: Johns Hopkins University Press, 2016), 7; Barthes, Roland. 'Le discours de l'histoire'. *Social Science Information* 63(4) (1967), 65–75, Southgate, Beverley. 'Postmodernism', in *A Companion to the Philosophy of History and Historiography*, ed. Aviezer Tucker (Hoboken: Wiley-Blackwell, 2011), 548; Surkis, Judith. 'When Was the Linguistic Turn? A Genealogy'. *American Historical Review* 700(3) (2012), 117; Certeau, Michel de. *L'écriture de l'histoire* (Paris: Gallimard, 1975); Carr, Edward H. H. *What is History?* (Cambridge: Cambridge University Press, 2nd ed., 1987), 11; In the international legal literature, see in particular Butler, William E. 'Periodization and International Law', in *Research Handbook on the Theory and History of International Law*, ed. Alexander Orakhelashvili (Cheltenham: Edward Elgar, 2011), 379; Diggelman, Oliver. 'The

that follows around the so-called 'historical turn'. The discussion that follows could thus be critically scrutinised in the very same way as it itself evaluates recent critical histories.

1 The 'Historical Turn' as a 'Historiographical Turn'

According to a common disciplinary narrative – for which the so-called 'historical turn' is a widespread shorthand[3] – international lawyers are said to have discovered, approximately two decades ago, the merits of robust engagement with the history of international law and emancipated themselves from the linear and one-dimensional historical accounts that had been dominating the field since the end of the nineteenth century. Before that, international lawyers, as this disciplinary narrative goes, were the complacent recipients of some linear disciplinary histories inherited from the late nineteenth and early twentieth centuries, and which they were trained to reproduce while refraining from critically engaging with them.[4]

It is submitted here that one can hardly deny that the end of the twentieth century witnessed a rise of interest by international lawyers in the study of history, as well as enhanced suspicion towards the linear mainstream disciplinary histories of international law that had been perpetuated throughout the twentieth century.[5] This change of attitude can be evidenced somewhat

Periodization of the History of International Law', in *The Oxford Handbook of the History of International Law*, eds. Bardo Fassbender and Anne Peters (Oxford: Oxford University Press, 2012), 996–1113, 996.

3 On the turn to history in contemporary international legal scholarship see Craven, Matthew. 'Theorizing the Turn to History in International Law', in *The Oxford Handbook of the Theory of International Law*, eds. Anne Orford and Florian Hoffmann (Oxford: Oxford University Press, 2016), 21–37; see also Galindo, George R. B. 'Martti Koskenniemi and the Historiographical Turn in International Law'. *European Journal of International Law* 16(3) (2005), 539–559, doi: 10.1093/ejil/chi130.

4 This watershed moment is often associated with the publication of Koskenniemi, Martti. *The Gentle Civilizer of Nations: The Rise and Fall of International Law* (Cambridge: Cambridge University Press, 2001).

5 See Orford, Anne. 'International Law and the Limits of History', in *The Law of International Lawyers: Reading Martti Koskenniemi*, eds. Wouter Werner, Marieke de Hoon and Alexis Galán (Cambridge: Cambridge University Press, 2015), 297–320, 297 ('... international law has always had a deep engagement with the past. Past text and concepts are constantly retrieved and taken up as a resource in international legal argumentation and scholarship. Thus the "turn to history" trope marks a turn to history as method, rather than a turn to history in terms of engaging with the past rather than the present', ibid. 297, 307). This growing interest in the history of international law is also witnessed in relation to private international law.

empirically, at least to the extent that the amount of scholarly publications that engage with the history of international law can plausibly constitute an indicator of greater engagement with the history of international law.[6] This change of attitude can also be institutionally illustrated by reference to the creation of new scholarly journals and book series specifically dedicated to the history of international law, which have themselves been the receptacle of a prolific body of scholarship on the subject. In this context, it seems difficult to deny the change in attitude and scholarly focus, as well as the much greater engagement with the history of international law, in the international legal literature over the last two decades.[7]

One important dimension of the disciplinary narrative about the 'historical turn' is the association of the latter with an invigoration of historical consciousness in the field. In fact, it is common for twenty-first century international lawyers to think of themselves as historically conscious and critically inclined in their engagement with history. It is true that, for instance, this 'historical turn' has brought with it unprecedented challenges to the classical linear histories inherited from the late nineteenth and early twentieth centuries in the form of counter-histories[8] and greater critical or methodological

See, e.g., Banu, Roxana. *Nineteenth-Century Perspectives on Private International Law* (Oxford: Oxford University Press, 2018). It has been said that a historical turn has similarly been witnessed in international relations. For an illustration about the current engagement with the history of international relations, see Bell, Duncan. 'International Relations: The Dawn of a Historiographical Turn?'. *British Journal of Politics and International Relations* 3(1) (2001), 115–126, doi:10.1111/1467-856X.00053; Armitage, David. 'The Fifty Years' Rift: Intellectual History and International Relations'. *Modern Intellectual History* 1(1) (2004), 97–109, doi:10.1017/S1479244303000027; Schmidt, Brian. *The Political Discourse of Anarchy: A Disciplinary History of International Relations* (Albany: State University of New York Press, 1998); Dunne, Tim. *Inventing International Society: A History of the English School* (London: Palgrave Macmillan, 1998); Brown, Chris, Terry Nardin and Nicholas Rengger, eds. *International Relations in Political Thought: Texts from the Ancient Greeks to the First World War* (Cambridge: Cambridge University Press, 2002).

6 On the idea that the 'historical turn' has attracted less attention in Germany, see Lange, Felix. 'The Dream of a völkisch Colonial Empire: International and Colonial Law during the National Scoialist Era'. *London Review of International Law* 5(3) (2017), 343–369, doi:10.1093/lril/lry004, 344.

7 In the same sense, and for some additional elements supporting this empirical claim, see Genin, Vincent. *Le laboratoire belge du droit international. Une communauté épistémique et international de juriste (1869–1914)* (Brussels: Académie Royale des sciences, des lettres et des beaux-arts de Belgique, 2018), 26–36.

8 Koskenniemi, *Gentle Civilizer* 2001 (n. 4); see Kennedy, David. 'International Law and the Nineteenth Century: History of an Illusion'. *Quinnipiac Law Review* 17(1) (1997), 99–138, 102–103.

scrutiny.[9] Some of the fundamental markers of the discipline have also come to be questioned. For instance, the fatherhood of Grotius,[10] the canonical status of his work,[11] and the cosmopolitan project associated therewith,[12] have

9 This has been one of the main purposes of those works falling under the so-called 'Third World Approaches to International Law' (TWAIL).

10 For a plea to study the precursors of Grotius as Grotius is the heir of a tradition, see Lesaffer, Randall. 'International Law and Its History: The Story of an Unrequited Love', in *Time, History and International Law*, eds. Matthew Craven, Malgosia Fitzmaurice and Maria Vogiatzi (Leiden: Brill, 2007), 27–42, 27, 40; see also Barreto, José-Manuel. 'Cerberus: Rethinking Grotius and the Westphalian System', in *International Law and Empire*, eds. Martti Koskenniemi, Walter Rech and Manuel Jiménez Fonseca (Oxford: Oxford University Press, 2017), 149–176, 154.

11 As was discussed by Simpson, the earlier works by Grotius, and especially *De Jure Praedae*, seem to point in the exact opposite direction of the twentieth century progressive narrative which it is supposed to have engendered. In *De Jure Praedae*, Grotius distinguishes between dates on the basis of their internal politics and moral characteristics. See Simpson, Gerry. *Great Powers and Outlaw States. Unequal Sovereigns in Their International Legal Order* (Cambridge: Cambridge University Press, 2004), 4. See also the idea that the modernity of international law started with the Spanish age, defended by Fassbender, Bardo. 'Peace of Westphalia (1648)', in *Max Planck Encyclopedia of Public International Law*, ed. Rüdiger Wolfrum (Oxford: Oxford University Press, 2011), para. 19. See also the remarks of John Haskell in Haskell, John. 'Hugo Grotius in the Contemporary Memory of International Law: Secularism, Liberalism, and the Politics of Restatement and Denial', in *New Approaches to International Law: The European and the American Experiences*, eds. José María Beneyto and David Kennedy (The Hague: T.M.C. Asser Press, 2012), 123–150.

12 On the idea of Dutch imperialism in the work of Grotius, see Barreto, 'Cerberus' 2017 (n. 11), 158 ('Grotius has not lost his place between the founding fathers of modern international law. He remains inhabiting such an Olympus, yet in another sense or for different reasons. It has been made clear that Grotius is not the founder of international law defined as a system that regulates the affairs between equal and sovereign states. Together with Vitoria, Grotius remains in the selected group of the "early parents of modern international law", a legal regime that is understood as emerging out of imperialism's needs for legitimation, and that regulated the relations between its subjects, including early modern companies'). On the idea that the writing of Grotius, like those of Gentili and Vattel, are construed as justifying 'imperial activities of their clients', see Koskenniemi, Martti. 'Introduction: International Law and Empire – Aspects and Approaches', in *International Law and Empire*, eds. Martti Koskenniemi, Walter Rech and Manuel Jiménez Fonseca (Oxford: Oxford University Press, 2017), 1–20, 4 (citing Israel, Jonathan. *Dutch Primacy in World Trade 1585–1740* (Oxford: Clarendon, 1989), 16–17 and 69–73). For some critique of Grotius as serving the VOC, see Straumann, Benjamin. '"Ancient Caesarean Lawyers" in a State of Nature: Roman Tradition and Natural Rights in Hugo Grotius's De iure praedae'. *Political Theory* 34(3) (2006), 328–350, doi:10.1177/0090591706286459; Jeffery, Renee. *Hugo Grotius in International Thought* (London: Palgrave Macmillan, 2006), 6–7; Kochi, Tarik. *The Other's War. Recognition and the Violence of Ethics* (London: Birkbeck Law Press, 2009), 59–60. On Grotius and Mercantile Capitalism, see Koskenniemi, Martti.

been severely questioned. Likewise, the very linear character of the common disciplinary histories similarly came under attack from claims that the history of international law should instead be seen as being 'pockmarked by a series of catastrophes and mutations'.[13]

It is submitted here, however, that the association of the 'historical turn' with an invigoration of historical consciousness is rather simplistic given the fact that the Enlightenment – which provided its dualistic patterns of thought and progress narratives to international law – itself came with an unprecedented historical consciousness.[14] For instance, when embarking on the creation of a disciplinary history during the professionalisation of the discipline,[15] nineteenth and twentieth century international lawyers understood and situated

---

'International Law and the Emergence of Mercantile Capitalism: Grotius to Smith', in *The Roots of International Law. Liber Amicorum Peter Haggenmacher*, eds. Pierre-Marie Dupuy and Vincent Chetail (Leiden: Martinus Nijhoff, 2014), 1–37, 3. On the criticisms of Grotius for his neo-liberalism, see García-Salmones Rovira, Mónica. *The Project of Positivism in International Law* (Oxford: Oxford University Press, 2013).

13 Berman, Nathaniel. 'In the Wake of Empire'. *American University International Law Review* 14(6) (1999), 1521–1554, 1523 ('The genealogical approach rejects this account of international legal history as an ever-advancing dialectic of restatement and renewal. It views international legal history as pockmarked by a series of catastrophes and mutations, as rocked by the countless forms of colonial conquest and anti-colonial resistance'). At page 1524 he writes: 'International legal genealogy rejects linear accounts of the origins and progress of the international community. It recounts the forging of that community through acts of unholy matrimony, through liaisons mostly asymmetrical, even when consensual, and all-too-often irreversibly coercive and massively violent – and usually constructing the power of some patriarch or other'. See also Haskell, John. 'The Traditions of Modernity within International Law and Governance: Christianity, Liberalism, and Marxism'. *Human Rights & Globalization Law Review* 6 (2015–2016), 29–50, 37 (discussing the kinship between modernity and linear history as well as the Christian heritage).

14 White, Hayden. *Metahistory. The Historical Imagination in the 19th-Century Europe* (Baltimore: Johns Hopkins University Press, 2014), 51 ('The Enlightenment's own posture vis-à-vis historical writing in general was Ironic ... [It] did so in full consciousness of the possibility of a choice between so using it and practicing it for its own sake or, as it is said, for itself alone'). See also Foucault, Michel. *L'archéologie de savoir* (Paris: Gallimard, 1969), 23. See also Sloterdijk, Peter. *Après nous le déluge* (Paris: Editions Payot & Rivages, 2016), 16; Gadamer, Hans-Georg. *Truth and Method* (London: Bloomsbury, 2013), xxiii; Certeau, Michel de. *L'Écriture de l'Histoire* (Paris: Gallimard, 1975), 15–17.

15 See Neff, Stephen. *Justice among Nations* (Cambridge: Harvard University Press, 2014), 304; d'Aspremont, Jean. 'The Professionalization of International Law', in *International Law as a Profession*, eds. Jean d'Aspremont, Tarcisio Gazzini, André Nollkaemper and Wouter Werner (Cambridge: Cambridge University Press, 2017), 19–37; Orford, Anne. 'Scientific Reason and the Discipline of International Law'. *European Journal of International Law* 25(2) (2014), 369–385, doi:10.1093/ejil/chu030.

themselves as agents of a disciplinary project, and demonstrated some remarkable historical consciousness.[16] Indeed, it is with international law becoming a self-standing object of study in university institutions which created professorships specifically dedicated to the teaching of international law,[17] as well as the primary focus of learned societies and scholarly periodicals,[18] that the perceived need to endow the field with a disciplinary history became very pressing.[19] For international lawyers of the time, providing a disciplinary history for international law[20] proved to be a way to confirm the maturity and

---

16 For instance, there seems to be no doubt that Lauterpacht wrote the 'Grotian Tradition' with an acute historical self-consciousness and the ambition of writing disciplinary history. Martti Koskenniemi writes: 'Lauterpacht's oeuvre and career constitute a striking illustration of an international legal consciousness that sought to resuscitate the rationalism of the nineteenth century in the aftermath of the First World War but used up its emancipatory potential in the doctrinal struggles of the 1930s.' Koskenniemi, Martti. 'Lauterpacht: The Victorian Tradition in International Law'. *European Journal of International Law* 8(2) (1997), 215–263, doi:10.1093/oxfordjournals.ejil.a015565, 261. In the same sense, see Hathaway, Oona A. and Scott J. Shapiro. *The Internationalists. How a Radical Plan to Outlaw War Remade the World* (New York: Simon & Schuster, 2017), 300.

17 For some general remarks on the professionalisation of international law see d'Aspremont, 'The Professionalization of International Law' 2017 (n. 16); Orford, 'Scientific Reason' 2014 (n. 16), 373; Coates, Benjamin. *Legalist Empire. International Law and American Foreign Relations in the Early Twentieth Century* (Oxford: Oxford University Press, 2016), 18–21, 61–68. Lapradelle, Albert G. de. *De la nationalité d'origine, droit compare, droit interne, droit international* (Paris: A. Giard & E. Brièr, 1893).

18 See, e. g., the creation of the *Revue générale de droit international et de legislation comparée* and later the *Revue générale de droit international public* in 1894. See generally Neff, *Justice among Nations* 2014 (n. 16), 300.

19 For a famous manifestation of this feeling of a need for a disciplinary history, see Oppenheim, Lassa. 'The Science of International Law: Its Task and Method'. *American Journal of International Law* 2(2) (1908), 313–356, doi:10.2307/2186595. For a discussion of Oppenheim's claim, see Perreau-Saussine, Amanda. 'A Case Study on Jurisprudence as a Source of International Law: Oppenheim's Influence', in *Time, History and International Law*, eds. Matthew Craven, Malgosia Fitzmaurice and Maria Vogiatzi (Leiden: Brill, 2007), 1–118, 100; see also García-Salmones, *The Project of Positivism* 2013 (n. 13).

20 Craven, Matthew. 'The Invention of a Tradition: Westlake, The Berlin Conference and the Historicisation of International Law', in *Constructing International Law: The Birth of a Discipline*, eds. Luigi Nuzzo and Miloš Vec (Frankfurt: Vittorio Klostermann, 2012), 363–402. Describing this historical self-consciousness is one of the main purposes of Koskenniemi's *Gentle Civilizer* 2001 (n. 5).

respectability,[21] identity,[22] and scientificity[23] of the field, entrench it in a tradition,[24] and make it a universal necessity.[25] It is in this context that the first systematic and comprehensive histories of international law[26] came to be produced with a great sense of historical consciousness.

For this reason, if the greater engagement with the history of international law over the last two decades, for which the 'historical turn' is a shorthand, were only 'historical', it would hardly be a turn but rather a perpetuation of the modern tradition of international law. It is argued here that the change of attitude witnessed two decades ago and dubbed the 'historical turn' marks not the historical self-consciousness of international lawyers or their historicising activities, but rather an upsurge of scholarly works discoursing and theorising about the specific forms and meanings given to the past by international lawyers and the way in which this past is written.[27] Whilst international lawyers' historical consciousness could be witnessed as early as the end of the nineteenth century, the gist of the change in the discipline of international law in the last two decades lies in their greater aptitude and inclination to discourse and theorise about the specific forms and meanings which their common histories of international law have provided to the past and the way in which such a past has been created. Discoursing and theorising about the specific forms

---

21 Obregón, Liliana. 'Writing International Legal History: An Overview'. *Monde(s)* 7(1) (2015), 95–112, doi:10.3917/mond1.151.0095, 110 (she argues that this was the avowed goal of Nys).

22 Kleinlein, Thomas. 'International Legal Thought: Creation of a Tradition and the Potential of Disciplinary Self-Reflection', in *The Global Community: Yearbook of International Law and Jurisprudence 2016*, ed. Giuliana Ziccardi Capaldo (Oxford: Oxford University Press, 2016), 811–830, 811, 812.

23 For some critical remarks, see Orford, 'Scientific Reason' 2014 (n. 16). See also Nuzzo, Luigi. 'The Birth of an Imperial Location: Comparative Perspectives on Western Colonialism in China'. *Leiden Journal of International Law* 31(3) (2018), 569–596, doi:10.1017/S0922156518000274, 596.

24 Kleinlein, 'International Legal Thought' 2016 (n. 23), 816. See also Orford, 'International Law and the Limits of History' 2015 (n. 6), 307 (on the notion of invention of tradition, see Hobsbawm, Eric. 'Introduction: Inventing Traditions', in *The Invention of Tradition*, eds. Eric Hobsbawm and Terence Ranger (Cambridge: Cambridge University Press, 1983), 1–14).

25 Chimini, Bhupinder S. 'The Past, Present, and Future of International Law: A Critical Third World Approach'. *Melbourne Journal of International Law* 8(2) (2007), 499–516, 502.

26 The work of Wheaton, Laurent, and Nys quickly acquired some referential status in this respect. In the United States, James Brown Scott also invested a lot in providing the field with a disciplinary history, albeit a slightly different variant of that prevalent in Europe at the time.

27 Cf. Janne Nijman, who has called it a turn to 'history as theory'. See Nijman, Janne. 'Seeking Change by Doing History'. 24 November 2017, available at: https://ssrn.com/abstract=316770, 9–10 (last accessed at 14 September 2020).

and the meanings provided to the past and the way in which such a past is created is characteristic of what is called *historiography*.[28] This is why the 'historical turn' is better understood as a 'historiographical turn'.[29] The reference to a 'historical turn' as a shorthand for such a change of attitude of international lawyers is a misnomer. Twenty years ago, international lawyers did not wake up with an invigorated historical consciousness but, more simply, with a greater historiographical appetite.

2 The 'Historical Turn' as Turntablism

This section uses the abovementioned metaphor of turntablism to shed light on one particular dimension of the historiographical attitude that has informed international lawyers' engagement with history over the last two decades, and which has been sketched out in the previous section. It is argued here that the 'historical turn', construed here as a 'historiographical turn', has been characterised by a very strong conservatism that makes engagement with history by international lawyers look like an exercise in turntablism. In other words, this section makes the argument that the historiographical works of international lawyers in the last two decades have remained confined to the very terms, categories, and vocabularies of the histories whose creation they have been discoursing and theorising. Using the metaphor of turntablism, it is thus argued here that, while undoubtedly creating new musical effects and melodies, international lawyers have simply not changed the records on their turntables and have used the same sounds. International lawyers' engagement

28 Cf. Jenkins, Keith. *On 'What is History'. From Carr and Elton to Rorty and White* (Abingdon: Routledge, 1995), 16. For Keith Jenkins, historiography 'theorises both the notion of "the past" and the "writing-up" of it'.

29 Jenkins notes the interchangeable use of history and historiography in the English language. He regrets the ambiguity of English because the term history does not sufficiently distinguish between history 'as that which has been written/recorded about the past' and the past history. In English, history covers both. Hence, it would be better to use 'historiography' to refer to the writing of historians about the past. See Jenkins, Keith. *Re-thinking History* (London: Routledge, 2003), 7. In contrast, Edward H. H. Carr promotes an approach to history that makes it primarily historiographical. See Carr, Edward H. H. *What is History?* (Cambridge: Cambridge University Press, 2nd ed. 1987), 22 ('when we take up a work of history, our first concern should be not with the facts which it contains but with the historian who wrote it'). Compare with the more generic uses of these notions as the one adopted in the *Companion to the Philosophy of History and Historiography*, see Tucker, Aviezer. 'Introduction', in *A Companion to the Philosophy of History and Historiography*, ed. Aviezer Tucker (Hoboken: Wiley-Blackwell, 2011), 1–6, 2.

with history over the last two decades has boiled down to spinning existing records differently.

The turntablism practised by those international lawyers engaging with history since the 'historical turn', and thus the confinement of international lawyers' engagement with history to the same categories, vocabularies, markers, events, texts, figures, periodisation, causalities, etc., can be illustrated as follows. Such turntablism expresses itself, for instance, in the fact that the historiographical imagination of international lawyers has continued to revolve around the same genealogical inquiries, namely whether Gentili, Vitoria, Grotius, Vattel, Lauterpacht, etc., are the spearheads, the heroes, the founding fathers, the (re-)inventers, or the heirs of the Western Enlightenment and (pre- or post-)modern international law. Although international lawyers today are prone to recognise that Gentili, Grotius, or Vattel may not have been the cosmopolitan humanitarians with which their status as fathers of international law endowed them, international lawyers' histories today continue to be historical narratives about Gentili, Vitoria, Grotius, Vattel, Lauterpacht, etc.[30] It could even be argued that the very critical discussions of some of these 'heroes' may well have contributed to their further canonisation, for critically engaging with those considered the 'fathers' only reinforces their fatherly place in disciplinary histories. A good example of this is provided by the numerous and well-known critical engagements with the legacy of Lauterpacht that have been witnessed in the literature. Indeed, while showing the limits and contradictions of Lauterpacht's scientific cosmopolitanism,[31] such studies have inevitably led to a further consolidation of Lauterpacht's stature in the linear disciplinary histories of the field.[32] It could even be ventured that Lauterpacht may not have been perceived to be as much a pivotal figure as he is today until the 'historical turn' and the critical engagement therewith.[33]

Turntablism is also found today in the restriction of international legal scholarship to the same periodisation as mainstream histories of international law: the scholastic, the pre-modern, Westphalia, the Enlightenment, the

30 See, e.g., Yasuaki, Onuma. *International Law in a Transcivilizational World* (Cambridge: Cambridge University Press, 2017), 11.

31 On Lauterpacht's liberalism and modernism, see the remarks of Koskenniemi in Koskenniemi, *Gentle Civilizer* 2001 (n. 5), 357.

32 For an example, see e.g. the introduction by Martti Koskenniemi in Lauterpacht, Hersch. *The Function of Law in the International Community* (Oxford: Oxford University Press, 2nd ed., 2011). Koskenniemi writes: 'The Function of Law is the most important English-language book on international law in the 20th century.' Ibid., xlvii. See also Koskenniemi, *Gentle Civilizer* 2001 (n. 4), 355–364.

33 Compare with the extent to which the discourse over the Orient is constitutive of the Occident; see Said, Edward. *Orientalism* (Abingdon: Routledge, 1978), 13.

modern, colonisation, the nineteenth century, the interwar period, the post-League of Nations, the post-Second World War, decolonisation, the cold war, the post-cold war, etc.[34] It could be contended that even the agendas debated in recent historiographical literature are identical to those in previous histories: humanism, cosmopolitanism, modernism, state-centrism, voluntarism, hegemony, capitalism, etc.

Albeit surprisingly, some similar turntablism can be witnessed in the many recent post-colonial histories that have very appropriately moved attention away from the writings of Western jurists and the practice of international law in Western locations, and opened new horizons.[35] Despite their immense merits and the refreshing disruption they offer, as well as all the work that still must be done in this respect, many of these studies have continued to resort to markers, periodisation, and causal sequencing all located in the West.[36] Turntablism can also be found in those works that seek to emphasise non-European

---

34 For an illustration of the use of 1648 in historical critique, see Kennedy, David. 'Primitive Legal Scholarship'. *Harvard International Law Journal* 27(1) (1986), 1–98, 1–2. See the remarks of Lesaffer, 'International Law and Its History' 2007 (n. 11), 40 (he writes that even if the myth of Westphalia has been debunked, it continues to be restated again and again). See also the remarks of Koskenniemi, Martti. 'Histories of International Law: Dealing with Eurocentrism'. 16 November 2011, 5, available at: https://dspace.library.uu.nl/bitstream/handle/1874/219007/Koskenniemi_Martti_oratie.pdf (last accessed on 14 September 2020).

35 See the remarks of Benton, Lauren. 'Made in Empire: Finding the History of International Law in Imperial Locations'. *Leiden Journal of International Law* 31(3) (2018), 473–478, doi: 10.1017/S0922156518000237.

36 This has been a criticism levelled by B. S. Chimni against the work of Koskenniemi. See Chimni, Bhupinder S. *International Law and World Order. A Critique of Contemporary Approaches* (Cambridge: Cambridge University Press, 2nd ed. 2017), 322, 327–339. See also Craven, Matthew. 'Introduction: International Law and Its Histories', in *Time, History and International Law*, eds. Matthew Craven, Malgosia Fitzmaurice and Maria Vogiatzi (Leiden: Brill, 2007), 1–26, 1, 12–13. This charge is not unheard of. It had already been raised against the first post-colonial histories of international law which, despite their attempt to provincialise Europe, have been criticised for reclaiming non-Western contributions within mainstream histories of international law. See, e.g., Alexandrowicz, Charles H. *An Introduction to the History of the Law of Nations in the East Indies* (Oxford: Clarendon Press, 1967); Alexandrowicz, Charles H. *The Law of Nations in Global History* (Oxford: Oxford University Press, 2017); Elias, Taslim Olawale. *Africa and the Development of International Law* (Leiden: Sijthoff, 1972); Anand, Ram P. *Origin and Development of the Law of the Sea: History of International Law Revisited* (Leiden: Martinus Nijhoff, 1983). For an overview of these works by the first generation of TWAIL scholars, see Becker Lorca, Arnulf. 'Eurocentrism in the History of International Law', in *The Oxford Handbook of the History of International Law*, eds. Bardo Fassbender and Anne Peters (Oxford: Oxford University Press, 2012), 1034–1048, 1034; Obregón, Liliana. 'Martti Koskenniemi's Critique of Eurocentrism in International Law', in *The Law of International Lawyers: Reading Martti*

perspectives,[37] for many of them re-centre non-Western locations and perspectives within a very Eurocentric history, and through European markers, periodisation, and causal sequencing.[38] When they do not seek a re-centring of non-Western locations and perspectives within a very Eurocentric history, these studies continue to treat non-Western contexts as 'peripheral',[39] or as a response to (or an encounter with) European or Western international law.[40] What is more, some of these histories, whilst rightly lamenting the resilience of the colonial project and the mirage of universality, still pursue the project of a universal international law according to a very European idea of universality.[41] By the same token, many of these histories, notwithstanding their very valuable disruptive insights, continue to rely on markers, periodisation, and causal sequencing of histories of international law built around, for instance, roman

Koskenniemi, eds. Wouter Werner, Marieke de Hoon and Alexis Galán (Cambridge: Cambridge University Press, 2015), 360–392, 360.

37 On this type of charge, see Liliana Obregón's comments on the occasion of her interview of Martti Koskenniemi, reproduced in Obregon, 'Martti Koskenniemi's Critique' 2015 (n. 37), 374–384 and esp. 378.

38 A good example thereof is provided by C. H. Alexandrowicz who sought to redeem non-Western practice by showing that Grotius had been influenced by Indian Ocean maritime traditions. See Alexandrowicz, Charles H. 'Grotius and India', reproduced in Alexandrowicz, Charles H. *The Law of Nations in Global History* (Oxford: Oxford University Press, 2017), 113–120. For a criticism of that claim, see Armitage, David and Jennifer Pitts. '"This Modern Grotius": An Introduction to the Life and Thought of C. H. Alexandrowicz', in *The Law of Nations in Global History*, eds. David Armitage and Jennifer Pitts (Oxford: Oxford University Press, 2017), 28–29.

39 In the same vein, see Becker Lorca, 'Eurocentrism in the History of International Law' 2012 (n. 37), 1054. It is interesting to note that Koskenniemi has tried to tone this down in Koskenniemi, Martti. 'The Case for Comparative International Law'. *Finnish Yearbook of International Law* 20 (2009), 1–8.

40 This is also a criticism made by Mohammad Shahabuddin: Shahabuddin, Mohammad. 'The "Standard of Civilization" in International Law: Intellectual Perspectives from Pre-War Japan'. *Leiden Journal of International Law* 32(1) (2019), 13–32, doi:10.1017/S0922156518000559. See also Meguro, Maiko. 'Backlash against International Law by the East? How the Concent of "Transplantation" Helps Us to Better Understand Reception Processes of International Law'. *Völkerrechtsblog*, 11 January 2019, available at: https://voelkerrechtsblog.org/backlash-against-international-law-by-the-east/ (last accessed on 14 September 2020).

41 Speaking of the work of Bedjaoui, Anand, and Elias, Liliana Obregon argues that this first generation of TWAIL scholars viewed the solution to international law's Eurocentrism as the need to make it 'truly universal'. See Obregon, 'Martti Koskenniemi's Critique' 2015 (n. 37), 373. See also the remarks of Pahuja, Sundhya. 'The Postcoloniality of International Law'. *Harvard International Law Journal* 46(2) (2005), 459–469, 464 (who argues that decolonisation can be construed as the granting of a formal legal status to entities to render them commensurable with the current forms of international law). See also the remarks of Koskenniemi, 'The Case for Comparative International Law' 2009 (n. 40), 4.

law, the scholastic, the *droit public de l'Europe*, the reformation, the Peace of Westphalia, the Enlightenment, the nineteenth and twentieth centuries, the encounter with European imperialism, etc.[42]

This being said, it would be simplistic to claim that international lawyers' engagement with history has been saturated by turntablism. Occasional critical histories that actually do away with Eurocentric markers, periodisation and causal sequencing have been witnessed.[43] Among the few actual departures from Eurocentric markers, periodisation and causal sequencing of dominant histories,[44] mention can be made, among others, of the recent Luis Eslava, Michael Fakhri, and Vasuki Nesiah's *Bandung, Global History and International Law. Critical Pasts and Pending Futures*,[45] Mohammad Shahabuddin's 'The "standard of civilization" in international law: Intellectual perspectives from pre-war Japan',[46] and, possibly, Robert Kolb's *Esquisse d'un droit international public des anciennes cultures extra européennes*.[47] Yet, subject to such

42 On this point, see the remarks of Koskenniemi, 'The Case for Comparative International Law' 2009 (n. 40), 4.

43 See, e.g., Hamamoto, Shotaro. 'A propos de deux clichés sur l'histoire du droit international en asie de l'est: Une reconsidération de l'ordre mondial chinois et du discours de traités inégaux', in *The Roots of International Law. Liber Amicorum Peter Haggenmacher*, eds. Pierre-Marie Dupuy and Vincent Chetail (Leiden: Martinus Nijhoff, 2014), 743–756, 743. See the few other examples mentioned by Becker Lorca, 'Eurocentricism in the History of International Law' 2012 (n. 37), 1034, 1044–1048.

44 Although still trying to redeem non-Western practice through Western heroes and concepts, C. H. Alexandrowicz has tried to propose a new periodisation in the history of international law that does away with the Peace of Westphalia and is centred on 1815, that is the time, not only of the Congress of Vienna but also the moment when the Kingdom of Poland was created. According to Alexandrowicz, this milestone is what allows the distinction between pre-nineteenth century law of nations based on natural law and universality and the positivist and European conception of international law. On this aspect of Alexandrowicz' work, see Armitage/Pitts '"Modern Grotius"' 2017 (n. 39), 19.

45 Eslava, Luis, Michael Fakhri and Vasuki Nesiah, eds. *Bandung, Global History, and International Law* (Cambridge: Cambridge University Press, 2017).

46 Shahabuddin, 'The "Standard of Civilization"' 2019 (n. 41), 13–32 (focusing on the pre-existing hierarchical order in the Far East and highlighting the relevance of non-European regional order in the discourse on international legal history). For a criticism of the use of sources by Shahabuddin, see Meguro, Maiko. 'Backlash against International Law by the East?' 2019 (n. 41).

47 Kolb, Robert. *Esquisse d'un droit international public des anciennes cultures extra européennes. Amérique précolombienne, Iles polynésiennes, Afrique noire, Sous-continent indien, Chine et régions Limitrophes* (Paris: Pedone, 2010). The work of Kolb is meant to continue the work on non-Western international law initiated by Wolfgang Preiser. On the ambition of such approach to history, see the remarks of Kolb, Robert. 'Considérations sur le droit international public des anciennes cultures extra-européennes', in *The Roots of International Law. Liber Amicorum Peter Haggenmacher*, eds. Pierre-Marie Dupuy and

exceptions, turntablism has been very resilient and most critical histories at work in the literature since the 'historical turn', notwithstanding their irrefutable insightfulness and sophistication, have commonly boiled down to variants of the very same markers, periodisation and causal sequencing as the ones on which dominant linear disciplinary narratives are built. They have provided very refreshing meaning-giving for mainstream linear disciplinary histories but have failed to liberate disciplinary imagination.

In the light of the foregoing, turntablism can be construed as a dominant attitude in international legal scholarship over the last two decades. The potential of the 'historical turn' does not seem to have been fully unlocked.

3 The Resilience of Turntablism after the 'Historical Turn'

At this stage of the discussion, it is important to highlight that the turntablism of international lawyers' engagement with the history of international law and, thus, the confinement of their recent historiographical studies to the very terms, categories, vocabularies, markers, events, texts, figures, periodisation, causalities, etc., of those narratives they are trying to question do not constitute a restriction that is unheard of. The critical historian Hayden White demonstrated how every discipline is made up of (and organised around) a set of restrictions on imagination.[48] From such a perspective, it could be said that historiography cannot be the home of critique as it is bound to be articulated around the very markers, causalities, and vocabularies of the historical narratives it engages with.

It is noteworthy that international lawyers interested in critical historical inquiries have shown some reasonable awareness for the abovementioned conservatism as well as of the Eurocentric character of their inquiries.[49] This is

Vincent Chetail (Leiden: Martinus Nijhoff, 2014), 673–709. It must however be stressed that the tone and presentation of this work remains very Eurocentric as those other experiences of international law are situated by reference to modern European international law.

48 White, Hayden. *Tropics of Discourse: Essays in Cultural Criticism* (Baltimore: Johns Hopkins University Press, 1978), 126–127.

49 Koskenniemi, Martti. 'Histories of International Law: Significance and Problems for a Critical View'. *Temple International and Comparative Law Journal* 27(2)(2013), 215–240, 223. See also Koskenniemi, 'The Case for Comparative International Law' 2009 (n. 40), 4; Chimni, *International Law and World Order* 2017 (n. 37), 322, 327–339; Becker Lorca, 'Eurocentrism in the History of International Law' 2012 (n. 37), 1044–1048; Tourme Jouannet, Emmanuelle. 'Des origines coloniales du droit international: A propos du droit des gens moderne au 18ème siècle', in *The Roots of International Law. Liber Amicorum Peter*

especially the case with Martti Koskenniemi.[50] For him, international lawyers cannot deny their debt to their predecessors in terms of histories.[51] He has also pointed out that a total rejection of the categories and vocabularies of preceding histories would be reductive[52] and that, as a result of such a rejection, international lawyers would deprive themselves of a tool to communicate 'by invoking widely shared historical associates' and building on 'shared imagination'.[53] According to him, the European pedigree of the vocabularies targeted by the new histories as well as the terms, categories, vocabularies, markers, events, texts, figures, periodisation, causalities, etc., of such histories cannot be unmade.[54] This is why he came to express some resignation as to the impossibility of avoiding some degree of Eurocentrism in those histories,[55] even acknowledging that a critique of Eurocentrism appears to arise from European preoccupations and political beliefs.[56]

4 The 'Historical Turn' 2.0: From Turntablism to Radical Historical Critique

As was shown in the previous section, there can be good reasons for international lawyers to satisfy themselves with the limits of their historiographical studies and their turntablist attitudes. After all, the historiographical works produced since the 'historical turn', and especially those works that focus on law and empire as well as non-Western contexts, locations, and practices, have very appropriately changed the way in which international lawyers engage with history. In that sense, it cannot be denied that international lawyers' engagement with history has been dramatically transformed in the last decades. And yet, the last part of this chapter argues that international lawyers should take their

---

Haggenmacher, eds. Pierre-Marie Dupuy and Vincent Chetail (Leiden: Martinus Nijhoff, 2014), 649–671, 648, 670.

50 For a thorough discussion of Martti Koskenniemi's take on Eurocentrism, see Obregón, 'Koskenniemi's Critique' 2015 (n. 37), esp. 374–384.

51 Koskenniemi, 'Histories of International Law' 2013 (n. 50), 216.

52 Ibid., 224.

53 Koskenniemi, Martti. 'A History of International Law Histories', in *The Oxford Handbook of the History of International Law*, eds. Bardo Fassbender and Anne Peters (Oxford: Oxford University Press, 2012), 945–971, 945.

54 Koskenniemi, 'The Case for Comparative International Law' 2009 (n. 40), 4. See also Martti Koskenniemi's remarks on the occasion of the interview conducted by Liliana Obregón and reproduced in Obregón, 'Koskenniemi's Critique' 2015 (n. 37), esp. 377–384.

55 Koskenniemi, 'The Case for Comparative International Law' 2009 (n. 40), 5.

56 Koskenniemi, 'Histories of International Law' 2013 (n. 50), 222.

cue from the few critical histories that actually do away with Eurocentric markers, periodisation and causal sequencing and which have been mentioned in the previous section with a view to limiting turntablist engagement with history. It is submitted here that there is room for a more systematic *radical historical critique* that consists of writing and rewriting historical narratives that consciously ignore the terms, categories, vocabularies, markers, events, texts, figures, periodisation, causalities, etc., of the dominant histories.[57] Such radical historical critique refers here to a critical engagement that moves beyond a mere historiographical attitude[58] and does away with the terms, categories, vocabularies, markers, events, texts, figures, periodisation, causalities, etc., of the dominant histories. From the perspective of the metaphor of turntablism used in this chapter, such radical historical critique corresponds to an engagement with history where music is created not only through a different spinning of the turntables but, more radically, through the use of new records.

The plea made here for a radical historical critique – and thus for a move away from the dominant turntablism of the discipline – requires that the very idea of radical historical critique be spelled out further. The radical historical critique envisaged here boils down to a conscious intervention to redraw the past and mobilise it to serve a present claim in a way that deliberately and consciously repudiates existing terms, categories, vocabularies, markers, events, texts, figures, periodisation, causalities, etc. In that sense, radical historical critique not only entails the production of counter-histories, but calls for new modes of thinking which register the terms, categories, vocabularies, markers, events, texts, figures, periodisation, causalities, etc., of the dominant histories with a view to consciously ignoring them in a new space of narrativisation.[59] Radical historical critique is thus interventionist: it registers accepted terms, categories, vocabularies, markers, events, texts, figures, periodisation, causalities, etc., and purposefully turns a blind eye to them. For that reason, using old

57 For another way to address the conservatism of counter-narratives, see Tourme Jouannet, 'Des origines coloniales du droit international' 2014 (n. 50), 670–671.

58 Foucault, *L'archéologie du savoir* 1969 (n. 15), 41 (who argues that once we are freed from immediate forms of continuity, we can start constructing new statements and narratives).

59 Cf. Frederic Jameson, speaking of Adorno: 'What needs to be invented therefore – and what in my opinion Adorno's dialectics proposes – is a new kind of stereoscopic thinking in which the concept continues to be thought philosophically and cashed at face value, while in some part of the mind a very different kind of intellectual regime reigns, a cruder and more sociological set of terms and categories, in which the form of that concept is noted and registered in shorthand and in which the existence of the financial and banking system thereby presupposed is somehow reckoned in'. See Jameson, Frederic. *Late Marxism. Adorno or the Persistence of the Dialectic* (London: Verso, 2007), 28.

materials in an innovative way[60] falls short of such radical historical critique. It is also important to highlight that such radical historical critique cannot seek to be scientific, truth-searching, or universalist in character.[61] Radical historical critique is better understood as what Rancière calls a 'poetry of knowledge' (*poétique du savoir*).[62] It does not aim at creating a new totality or intelligibility framework.[63] Radical historical critique pursues a rupture with the common historical referent of international lawyers' discourses.

Is it submitted that there is much to gain from a move towards such a radical historical critique. Such a move is about enabling the production of a wide range of new discourses about international law itself. The radical historical critique promoted here would allow international lawyers to imagine new contexts, new places, and new moments where legal claims and legal practices are made and unmade. In that sense, radical historical critique is about telling new stories filled with new actors, new turning points, new moments of rupture, new causations, new revolutionary moments, new agendas, new revolutions, new watershed moments, new crises, new infidelities, new milestones, new beginnings, new ends, new transitional periods, new genealogies, new pedigrees, new modes of liberation, new legal concepts, and new thoughts.

It must be acknowledged that embracing such a radical historical critique and discontinuing the turntablism of current legal scholarship does not constitute an easy posture. The route towards radical historical critique is not without pitfalls, some of which having been famously experienced in relation to the critique offered by those scholars affiliated with TWAIL.[64] Four obstacles to the radical historical critique envisaged here must be mentioned. First,

---

60 This is a plea made by Koskenniemi, 'Histories of International Law' 2013 (n. 50), 240.

61 See the remarks of Anne Orford against the writing of global history: Orford, Anne. 'On International Legal Method'. *London Review of International Law* 1(1) (2013), 166–197, doi: 10.1093/lril/lrt005. See also Orford, 'International Law and the Limits of History' 2015 (n. 6).

62 Rancière, Jacques. *Les mots de l'histoire. Essai de poétique du savoir* (Paris: Seuil, 1992), esp. 18–22.

63 Adorno, Theodor. *Negative Dialectics* (Abingdon: Routledge, 1973), 27.

64 Speaking of the work of Bedjaoui, Anand, and Elias, Liliana Obregón argues that this first general of TWAIL scholars viewed the solution to international law's Eurocentricism as the need to make it 'truly universal'. See Obregón, 'Martti Koskenniemi's Critique' 2015 (n. 37), 360, 373. See also the remarks of Pahuja, 'The Postcoloniality of International Law' 2005 (n. 41), 464 (who argues that decolonisation can be construed as the granting of a formal legal status to entities to render them commensurable with the current forms of international law). See also the remarks of Koskenniemi, 'The Case for Comparative International Law' 2009 (n. 40), 4. For an overview of these works by the first generation of TWAIL scholars, see Becker Lorca, 'Eurocentricism in the History of International Law' 2012 (n. 37), 1034.

there is the obstacle associated with the total loss of empirical rigour and, thus, the corresponding risk that radical historical critique veers into some disgusting revisionism. This is the risk that *anything goes*, which should be taken extremely seriously. In this respect, it must be pointed out that the radical historical critique envisaged here cannot be reduced to an exercise of literary creation. From the perspective of radical historical critique, engagements with history would still need to abide by some elementary empiricism and factual evidence when it comes to the materials that feed into the narrativisation concerned. It is true that the evidence and the empiricism informing the establishment of the facts populating the narrativisation would themselves be the object of discussion. Yet, those engaging with history would remain bound by those – admittedly fluctuating – constraints that apply to any argument for it to be plausible, intelligible, and acceptable for the audience that receives it. The foregoing does not mean, however, that the radical historical critique would be subject to any pre-defined methods or techniques. In particular, since such a radical critique ought to stop short of seeking to substitute one linear, progressive, scientific, true, and universal history for another, it shall certainly not espouse any pre-defined mode of investigation that is recognised as properly 'historical'.[65]

Secondly, there are important *linguistic barriers* that radical historical critique must reckon with. Indeed, writing historical narratives around new markers, new figures, new locations, new places, new empires, etc., would often necessitate international lawyers going beyond their usual linguistic and cultural communities and venturing into the study of locations, contexts, and practices possibly foreign to the author of the radical historical critique.[66] Such material and linguistic obstacles should not be played down or treated lightly. Yet, it is submitted here that they are not insurmountable.

Thirdly, there are important social and cultural obstacles, as those international lawyers engaging with history may simply not know other terms, categories, vocabularies, markers, events, texts, figures, periodisations, causalities, etc., than those found in the mainstream histories. It may be that they cannot think of their world outside those terms, categories, vocabularies, markers, events, texts, figures, periodisations, causalities, etc. Again, this should not sound insurmountable. If the discipline cannot have its turntablists change

65 In the same sense, see Anne Orford's plea against the idea that international lawyers should embrace 'historical methods'. See Orford, Anne. 'On International Legal Method' 2013 (n. 61), 166–197, doi:10.1093/lril/lrt005. See also Orford, 'International Law and the Limits of History' 2015 (n. 6), 302–303 and 312.

66 See the remarks of Maiko Meguro: Meguro, 'Backlash against International Law' 2019 (n. 41).

the records on their turntables, it is yet another reminder that new turntablists and new voices must constantly be invited to the arena. Radical historical critique necessitates a much greater opening of the stage to new voices, and especially to those trained outside the usual schools.

Finally, there is the risk of unintelligibility. In fact, the radical historical critique contemplated here, by disrupting common historical referents of international lawyers' discourses and by rejecting their terms, categories, vocabularies, markers, events, texts, figures, periodisation, causalities, etc., inevitably comes to distort intelligibility frameworks and, thus, bring about unintelligibility in historical discourses. This is the risk of cacophony. Yet, it is submitted here that such unintelligibility should not be feared or viewed in a dim light. Indeed, the intelligibility of current histories should not be exaggerated, for many of the histories found in the international legal literature rest on impressions of intelligibility. What is more, the loss of some degree of intelligibility of the historical discourses that would follow the radical historical critique advocated here constitutes a form of disobedience characteristic of critique.[67]

Because these obstacles, although very serious, are deemed here to be surmountable, it is argued at the ultimate stage of this chapter that the turntablism discussed in section 2, and notwithstanding the forces that make it so resilient and that were mentioned in section 3, ought not to constitute the dominant attitude of international lawyers engaging with history. Indeed, as is illustrated by the few works that depart from the Eurocentric terms, vocabularies, and categories of the dominant histories and which have been mentioned in section 2, there is room for a critical engagement with history that, as described in section 4, moves beyond a mere historiographical attitude[68] and does away with the terms, categories, vocabularies, markers, events, texts, figures, periodisation, causalities, etc., of the dominant histories. Such radical historical critique is not an end in itself but should arguably be pursued as a means to unlock the full potential of the 'historical turn' in international law. Said in terms of the metaphor of turntablism used in this chapter, exploiting the full potential of the 'historical turn' in international law requires that international lawyers engaging with history load new records on their turntables in order to start producing new sounds and new melodies, enabling the ravers in the arena to liberate their imagination, their discourses, and their worlds of possibilities.

---

67 On the idea of disobeying the totality, see Adorno, Theodor. *The Positivist Dispute in German Sociology* (New York: Harper Torchbooks, 1976), 12.

68 Foucault, *L'archéologie du savoir* 1969 (n. 15), 41 (who argues that once we are freed from immediate forms of continuity, we can start constructing new statements and narratives).

Acknowledgement

The author thanks Tim Clark for his assistance.

Bibliography

Adorno, Theodor. *Negative Dialectics* (Abingdon: Routledge, 1973).

Adorno, Theodor. *The Positivist Dispute in German Sociology* (New York: Harper Torchbooks, 1976).

Alexandrowicz, Charles H. *An Introduction to the History of the Law of Nations in the East Indies* (Oxford: Clarendon, 1967).

Alexandrowicz, Charles H. *The Law of Nations in Global History* (Oxford: Oxford University Press, 2017).

Anand, Ram R. P. *Origin and Development of the Law of the Sea: History of International Law Revisited* (Leiden: Martinus Nijhoff, 1983).

Armitage, David and Pitts, Jennifer. '"This Modern Grotius": An Introduction to the Life and Thought of C. H. Alexandrowicz', in *The Law of Nations in Global History*, eds. David Armitage and Jennifer Pitts (Oxford: Oxford University Press, 2017).

Armitage, David. 'The Fifty Years' Rift: Intellectual History and International Relations'. *Modern Intellectual History* 1(1) (2004), 97–109.

d'Aspremont, Jean. 'The Professionalization of International Law', in *International Law as a Profession*, eds. Jean d'Aspremont, Tarcisio Gazzini, André Nollkaemper and Wouter Werner (Cambridge: Cambridge University Press, 2017), 19–38.

Banu, Roxana. *Nineteenth-Century Perspectives on Private International Law* (Oxford: Oxford University Press, 2018).

Barreto, José-Manuel. 'Cerberus: Rethinking Grotius and the Westphalian System', in *International Law and Empire*, eds. Martti Koskenniemi, Walter Rech and Manuel Jimenez Fonseca (Oxford: Oxford University Press, 2017), 149–176.

Barthes, Roland. 'Le discours de l'histoire'. *Social Science Information* 63(4) (1967), 65–75.

Becker Lorca, Arnulf. 'Eurocentricism in the History of International Law', in *The Oxford Handbook of the History of International Law*, eds. Bardo Fassbender and Anne Peters (Oxford: Oxford University Press, 2012), 1034–1048.

Bell, Duncan. 'International Relations: The Dawn of a Historiographical Turn?'. *British Journal of Politics and International Relations* 3(1) (2001), 115–126.

Benton, Lauren. 'Made in Empire: Finding the History of International Law in Imperial Locations'. *Leiden Journal of International Law* 31(3) (2018), 473–478.

Berman, Nathaniel. 'In the Wake of Empire'. *American University International Law Review* 14(6) (1999), 1521–1554.

Brown, Chris, Terry Nardin and Nicholas Rengger, eds. *International Relations in Political Thought: Texts from the Ancient Greeks to the First World War* (Cambridge: Cambridge University Press, 2002).

Butler, William E. 'Periodization and International Law', in *Research Handbook on the Theory and History of International Law*, ed. Alexander Orakhelashvili (Cheltenham: Edward Elgar, 2011), 379–393.

Carr, Edward H. *What is History?* (Cambridge: Cambridge University Press, 2nd ed. 1987).

Certeau, Michel de. *L'écriture de l'histoire* (Paris: Gallimard, 1975).

Chimini, Bhupinder S. *International Law and World Order. A Critique of Contemporary Approaches* (Cambridge: Cambridge University Press, 2nd ed. 2017).

Chimini, Bhupinder S. 'The Past, Present, and Future of International Law: A Critical Third World Approach'. *Melbourne Journal of International Law* 8(2) (2007), 499–516.

Coates, Benjamin. *Legalist Empire. International Law and American Foreign Relations in the Early Twentieth Century* (Oxford: Oxford University Press, 2016).

Craven, Matthew. 'Introduction: International Law and Its Histories', in *Time, History and International Law*, eds. Matthew Craven, Malgosia Fitzmaurice and Maria Vogiatzi (Leiden: Brill, 2007), 1–26.

Craven, Matthew. 'The Invention of a Tradition: Westlake, The Berlin Conference and the Historicisation of International Law', in *Constructing International Law: The Birth of a Discipline*, eds. Luigi Nuzzo and Miloš Vec (Frankfurt am Main: Vittorio Klostermann, 2012), 363–402.

Craven, Matthew. 'Theorizing the Turn to History in International Law', in *The Oxford Handbook of the Theory of International Law*, eds. Anne Orford and Florian Hoffmann (Oxford: Oxford University Press, 2016), 21–37.

Diggelman, Oliver. 'The Periodization of the History of International Law', in *The Oxford Handbook of the History of International Law*, eds. Bardo Fassbender and Anne Peters (Oxford: Oxford University Press, 2012), 997–1113.

Dunne, Tim. *Inventing International Society: A History of the English School* (London: Macmillan, 1998).

Fassbender, Bardo. 'Peace of Westphalia (1648)', in *Max Planck Encyclopedia of Public International Law*, ed. Rüdiger Wolfrum (Oxford: Oxford University Press, 2011), available at: https://opil.ouplaw.com/view/10.1093/law:epil/9780199231690/law-9780199231690-e739?rskey=rwa8dV&result=1&prd=MPIL (last accessed on 14 September 2020).

Foucault, Michel. *L'archéologie du savoir* (Paris: Gallimard, 1969).

Gadamer, Hans-Georg. *Truth and Method* (London: Bloomsbury, 2013), xxiii.

Galindo, George R. B. 'Martti Koskenniemi and the Historiographical Turn in International Law'. *European Journal of International Law* 16(3) (2005), 539–559, doi: 10.1093/ejil/chi130.

García-Salmones Rovira, Mónica. *The Project of Positivism in International Law* (Oxford: Oxford University Press, 2013).

Genin, Vincent. *Le laboratoire belge du droit international. Une communauté épistémique et international de jurists (1869–1914)* (Brussels: Académie royale des sciences, des lettres et des beaux-arts de Belgique, 2018).

Hamamoto, Shotaro. 'A propos de deux clichés sur l'histoire du droit international en asie de l'est: Une reconsidération de l'ordre mondial chinois et du discours de traités inégaux', in *The Roots of International Law. Liber Amicorum Peter Haggenmacher*, eds. Pierre-Marie Dupuy, Vincent Chetail (Leiden: Martinus Nijhoff, 2014), 743–756.

Haskell, John. 'Hugo Grotius in the Contemporary Memory of International Law: Secularism, Liberalism, and the Politics of Restatement and Denial', in *New Approaches to International Law: The European and the American Experiences*, eds. José María Beneyto and David Kennedy (The Hague: T.M.C. Asser Press, 2012), 123–150.

Haskell, John. 'The Traditions of Modernity within International Law and Governance: Christianity, Liberalism, and Marxism'. *Human Rights & Globalization Law Review* 6 (2015–2016), 29–50.

Hathaway, Oona A. and Scott J. Shapiro. *The Internationalists. How a Radical Plan to Outlaw War Remade the World* (New York: Simon & Schuster, 2017).

Hobsbawm, Eric. 'Introduction: Inventing Traditions', in *The Invention of Tradition*, eds. Eric Hobsbawm and Terence Ranger (Cambridge: Cambridge University Press, 1983), 1–15.

Holmes, Thom. *Electronic and Experimental Music: Technology, Music, and Culture* (Abingdon: Routledge, 2015), 476–483.

Israel, Jonathan. *Dutch Primacy in World Trade 1585–1740* (Oxford: Clarendon Press, 1989).

Jameson, Frederic. *Late Marxism. Adorno or the Persistence of the Dialectic* (London: Verso, 2007).

Jeffery, Renee. *Hugo Grotius in International Thought* (London: Palgrave Macmillan, 2006).

Jenkins, Keith. *On 'What is History'. From Carr and Elton to Rorty and White* (London: Routledge, 1995).

Jenkins, Keith. *Re-thinking History* (Abingdon: Routledge, 2003).

Kennedy, David. 'Primitive Legal Scholarship'. *Harvard International Law Journal* 27(1) (1986), 1–98.

Kleinlein, Thomas. 'International Legal Thought: Creation of a Tradition and the Potential of Disciplinary Self-Reflection', in *The Global Community: Yearbook of International Law and Jurisprudence 2016*, ed. Giuliana Ziccardi Capaldo (Oxford: Oxford University Press, 2016), 811–830.

Kochi, Tarik. *The Other's War. Recognition and the Violence of Ethics* (London: Birkbeck Law Press, 2009).

Kolb, Robert. *Esquisse d'un droit international public des anciennes cultures extra européennes. Amérique précolombienne, Iles polynésiennes, Afrique noire, sous-continent indien, Chine et régions limitrophes* (Paris: Pedone, 2010).

Kolb, Robert. 'Considérations sur le droit international public des anciennes cultures extra-européennes', in *The Roots of International Law. Liber Amicorum Peter Haggenmacher*, eds. Pierre-Marie and Vincent Chetail (Leiden: Martinus Nijhoff, 2014), 673–709.

Koskenniemi, Martti. *The Gentle Civilizer of Nations. The Rise and Fall of International Law 1870–1960* (Cambridge: Cambridge University Press, 2001).

Koskenniemi, Martti. 'A History of International Law Histories', in *The Oxford Handbook of the History of International Law*, eds. Bardo Fassbender and Anne Peters (Oxford: Oxford University Press, 2012), 945–971.

Koskenniemi, Martti. 'Histories of International Law: Dealing with Eurocentrism'. 16 November 2011, available at: https://dspace.library.uu.nl/bitstream/handle/1874/219007/Koskenniemi_Martti_oratie.pdf (last accessed on 14 September 2020).

Koskenniemi, Martti. 'Histories of International Law: Significance and Problems for a Critical View'. *Temple International and Comparative Law Journal* 27(2) (2013), 215–240.

Koskenniemi, Martti. 'International Law and the Emergence of Mercantile Capitalism: Grotius To Smith', in *The Roots of International Law. Liber Amicorum Peter Haggenmacher*, eds. Pierre-Marie Dupuy and Vincent Chetail (Leiden: Martinus Nijhoff, 2014), 1–37.

Koskenniemi, Martti. 'Introduction: International Law and Empire – Aspects and Approaches', in *International Law and Empire*, eds. Martti Koskenniemi, Walter Rech and Manuel Jimenez Fonseca (Oxford: Oxford University Press, 2017), 1–20.

Koskenniemi, Martti. 'Lauterpacht: The Victorian Tradition in International Law'. *European Journal of International Law* 8(2) (1997), 215–263, doi:10.1093/oxfordjournals.ejil.a015565, 261.

Koskenniemi, Martti. 'The Case for Comparative International Law'. *Finnish Yearbook of International Law* 20 (2009), 1–8.

Lange, Felix. 'The Dream of a völkisch Colonial Empire: International Law and Colonial Law during the Nation Socialist Era'. *London Review of International Law* 5(3) (2017), 343–369, doi:10.1093/lril/lry004, 344.

Lapradelle, Albert G. de. *De la nationalité d'origine, droit compare, droit interne, droit international* (Paris: A. Giard & E. Brièr, 1893).

Lauterpacht, Hersch. *The Function of Law in the International Community* (Oxford: Oxford University Press, 2nd ed. 2011).

Lesaffer, Randall. 'International Law and Its History: The Story of an Unrequited Love', in *Time, History and International Law*, eds. Matthew Craven, Malgosia Fitzmaurice and Maria Vogiatzi (Leiden: Brill, 2007), 27–42.

Meguro, Maiko. 'Backlash against International Law by the East? How Concept of "Transplantation" Helps Us to Better Understand Reception Processes of International Law'. *Völkerrechtsblog*, 11 January 2019, available at: https://voelkerrechtsblog.org/backlash-against-international-law-by-the-east/ (last accessed on 14 September 2020).

Neff, Stephen. *Justice among Nations* (Cambridge: Harvard University Press, 2014).

Nijman, Janne. 'Seeking Change by Doing History'. 24 November 2017, available at: https://ssrn.com/abstract=316770 (last accessed on 14 September 2020).

Nuzzo, Luigi. 'The Birth of an Imperial Location: Comparative Perspectives on Western Colonialism in China'. *Leiden Journal of International Law* 31(3) (2018), 569–596, doi: 10.1017/S0922156518000274.

Obregón, Liliana. 'Martti Koskenniemi's Critique of Eurocentrism in International Law', in *The Law of International Lawyers: Reading Martti Koskenniemi*, eds. Wouter Werner, Marieke de Hoon and Alexis Galán (Cambridge: Cambridge University Press, 2015), 360–392.

Obregón, Liliana. 'Writing International Legal History: An Overview'. *Monde(s)* 7(1) (2015), 95–112, doi:10.3917/mond1.151.0095.

Oppenheim, Lassa. 'The Science of International Law: Its Task and Method'. *American Journal of International Law* 2(2) (1908), 313–356, doi:10.2307/2186595.

Orford, Anne. 'International Law and the Limits of History', in *The Law of International Lawyers: Reading Martti Koskenniemi*, eds. Wouter Werner, Marieke de Hoon and Alexis Galán (Cambridge: Cambridge University Press, 2015), 297–320.

Orford, Anne. 'On International Legal Method'. *London Review of International Law* 1(1) (2013), 166–197, doi:10.1093/lril/lrt005.

Orford, Anne. 'Scientific Reason and the Discipline of International Law'. *European Journal of International Law* 25(2) (2014), 369–385, doi:10.1093/ejil/chu030.

Pahuja, Sundhya. 'The Postcoloniality of International Law'. *Harvard International Law Journal* 46(2) (2005), 459–469.

Perreau-Saussine, Amanda. 'A Case Study on Jurisprudence as a Source of International Law: Oppenheim's Influence', in *Time, History and International Law*, eds. Matthew Craven, Malgosia Fitzmaurice and Maria Vogiatzi (Leiden: Brill, 2007), 91–118.

Rancière, Jacques. *Les mots de l'histoire. Essai de poétique du savoir* (Paris: Seuil, 1992).

Said, Edward. *Orientalism* (Abingdon: Routledge, 1978).

Schmidt, Brian. *The Political Discourse of Anarchy: A Disciplinary History of International Relations* (Albany: State University of New York Press, 1998).

Shahabuddin, Mohammad. 'The "Standard of Civilization" in International Law: Intellectual Perspectives from Pre-War Japan'. *Leiden Journal of International Law* 32(1) (2019), 13–32.

Simpson, Gerry. *Great Powers and Outlaw States. Unequal Sovereigns in Their International Legal Order* (Cambridge: Cambridge University Press, 2004).

Sloterdijk, Peter. *Après nous le déluge* (Paris: Editions Payot & Rivages, 2016).

Southgate, Beverley. 'Postmodernism', in *A Companion to the Philosophy of History and Historiography*, ed. Aviezer Tucker (Hoboken: Wiley-Blackwell, 2011), 540–549.

Straumann, Benjamin. '"Ancient Caesarean Lawyers" in a State of Nature: Roman Tradition and Natural Rights in Hugo Grotius's De iure praedae'. *Political Theory* 34(3) (2006), 328–350, doi:10.1177/0090591706286459.

Surkis, Judith. 'When Was the Linguistic Turn? A Genealogy'. *American Historical Review* 117(3) (2012), 700–723.

Taslim Olawale, Elias. *Africa and the Development of International Law* (Leiden: Sijthoff, 1972).

Tourme Jouannet, Emmanuelle. 'Des origines coloniales du droit international: A propos du droit des gens moderne au 18ème siècle', in *The Roots of International Law. Liber Amicorum Peter Haggenmacher*, eds. Pierre-Marie Dupuy and Vincent Chetail (Leiden: Martinus Nijhoff, 2014), 649–671.

Tucker, Aviezer. 'Introduction', in *A Companion to the Philosophy of History and Historiography*, ed. Aviezer Tucker (Hoboken: Wiley-Blackwell, 2011), 1–6.

White, Hayden. *Metahistory. The Historical Imagination in the 19th-Century Europe* (Baltimore: Johns Hopkins University Press, 2014).

White, Hayden. *Tropics of Discourse: Essays in Cultural Criticism* (Baltimore: Johns Hopkins University Press, 1978).

White, Hayden. 'Historical Discourse and Literary Writing', in *Tropes for the Past: Hayden White and the History/Literature Debate*, ed. Kuisma Korhonen (New York: Rodopi, 2006), 25–34.

Yasuaki, Onuma. *International Law in a Transcivilizational World* (Cambridge: Cambridge University Press, 2017).

CHAPTER 16

The Politics of Anti-Politics: Historiographies of International Law and the Paradox of Antiquity

Emiliano J. Buis

Abstract

For a long time, an emphatic denial of the existence of international legal rules in the pre-modern world has been a common landmark in the historiographies of international law. This chapter argues that such invisibility, motivated in the fact that in antiquity politics and law were conflated, is in fact a political move. By rejecting the ancient precedents in a diachronic study of international law, most historiographers of the discipline have been able to focus on a positive Westphalian model in which legal equality is seen as incompatible with hegemony and imperialism. By introducing sound references to ancient sources, international legal historiography should denounce the false rhetoric of anti-political 'objectivity' and unveil the real interests at stake that rest behind what we have been calling 'international law'.

Keywords

Historiographies of international law – antiquity – classics – ancient Greece – Rome – imperialism – Westphalia – critical studies

1 Introduction

An almost universal and emphatic denial of the existence of international legal rules in the pre-modern world has been a common landmark in the mainstream historiography of international law. Although a few authors, from Phillipson (1911) to Ténékidès (1956) and Bederman (2001), have argued for the need to revisit ancient sources for a more comprehensive study of international law and its origins, the truth remains that the inclusion of a chapter on antiquity in modern volumes on the subject is still rare, to say the least.

 | DOI:10.1163/9789004461802_018

The invisibility of the ancient era is allegedly the result of the preeminence of politics over law among ancient peoples. This widespread reading that undermines the role of law in antiquity, in my view, is not innocent and can be related to a very concrete agenda: the concealment of the political dimension of international law. This perception does not only misinterpret what we know about ancient cultures, but also draws a false relationship between modernity, sovereign equality and law, on the one side, and antiquity, hegemonic inequality and politics, on the other. The arguments to hold this position are of course varied, but there is a common ground in all of them that allows for the identification of some general features: the denial of the idea of ancient 'States', the omnipresence of war, and the lack of universality, among others.[1] In order to overcome that simplification, I will show that a legal-political *continuum* can be in fact identified, in spite of course of the different nature of applicable rules across the centuries. My claim is twofold. First, I will argue that, just as it happened in ancient times, modern international law is permanently conflated with politics and power but, as an independent realm, tries to ignore it in order to preserve its 'objective' nature. In the same breath, I will contend secondly that the regulation of international affairs in ancient times resorted to a legal fiction of equality, very similar to the fictional myth of sovereignty which we have today, to serve its purpose. Paradoxically, by replacing the importance of politics at its core, looking into antiquity might help to create an alternative history of international law that can describe better the legal order that we have today.

In order to advance my thesis, the first section of this chapter will briefly discuss the construction of modern international law and its premises. Placing the Peace of Westphalia in 1648 as the historical origin of contemporary international law has served to settle the impression of 'sovereign equality' as a necessary basis for a law presented as purged of political intentions. In this view, all other forms of regulation of international relations which cannot be read under the prism of equality – such as imperialism or hegemonic regimes – are conveniently deemed contrary to legality. As I will argue, this anti-political position is paradoxically a political move, which is interested in hiding the extra-legal sphere of power behind the appearance of a system which is falsely shown as a balanced order of coordination among equals.

In the second part of the chapter, I will argue that the fact that there was no universal balance among politically organized communities in the ancient

1 See, for instance, the line of continuity of some of these arguments from Laurent (1850–1851) to Eckstein (2006). We will explore these ideas in the first section of the chapter.

Greco-Roman world should not lead us to deny the existence of *inter potestates* relations or connections, which were expressed through diplomatic ties and were consistently translated into the negotiation of normative agreements on several issues. As I will develop in the following pages, denying this fact is, in my opinion, the consequence of an ideological stand, which attempts to undervalue the political side of international law in order to focus on a Westphalian 'authority'.

2 The Politics of Modern International Law: Upholding Sovereign Equality, Dismissing Hegemony, Ignoring Antiquity

Despite the existence of new actors who play very notable roles in international affairs, international law is frequently seen as a normative system that is created *primarily* by States. Such, ultimately, is the international legal order, a set of rules that States have created to regulate their own actions. In spite of heavy critiques that have been put forward to cast doubt on the legal nature of international law, it seems clear today in mainstream theories of international law that international law *is* law in the proper sense of the word (even if different in its nature from domestic legal systems), insofar as its rules create obligations and rights that are accepted by its subjects for the sake of their coexistence.[2]

In this effort to grant legal autonomy to international law, its relationship to international politics, economy, religion or other social regulations had to be sacrificed. This separation between international law and other dimensions of normativity has only recently been revisited by critical schools and theories which rely on more interdisciplinary foundations.[3] Nevertheless, for the most part yet, international law and international politics do not go hand in hand, and are in many occasions perceived as antithetic: power is of course at the very foundation of law, but is frequently kept separated from the legal dimension in

2 Henderson, Conway W. *Understanding International Law* (Hoboken: Wiley-Blackwell, 2010), 5, has demonstrated that it is possible to speak of a 'voluntary compliance' and thus to conceptualize international law as law in the true sense of the word. Now the discussion seems to have moved to the first element of the concept: Roberts, Anthea. *Is International Law International?* (Oxford: Oxford University Press, 2017) has opened the floor for a debate on the 'international' character of international law.

3 Higgins, Rosalyn. *Problems and Process: International Law and How We Use It* (Oxford: Oxford University Press, 1995), 2–4, has pointed out that, insofar as social construction cannot be independent of political reality, international law cannot be reduced to mere 'rules.' Rather, it is a process that is closely related to the exercise of authority.

order not to challenge its legal basis. The creation of a landmark for its 'historical origin' has been useful in order to support and consolidate this opposition.

It is generally contended in general monographs on international law that the first steps of its development were taken when a new political, legal, and religious order was gradually established in Europe during the 16th and 17th centuries. This assertion focuses on the recognition of 'sovereignty' as the basis for the creation of modern States. According to mainstream historiographies, international law found its opportunity to flourish in the mutual recognition of sovereignty as an essential characteristic of the State, and this did not occur before modernity.[4]

The so-called Peace of Westphalia of 1648, which ended the Thirty Years' War, is understood as a turning point since the treaties that conformed it (the Münster and Osnabrück agreements) set a regulatory mechanism based on the balance of power,[5] creating a system of European law shaped by the identification of an international community under the principle of the legal equality of its sovereigns.[6] States, according to this principle, are reciprocally recognized as equals in terms of law: each of them is sovereign over its own territory and, consequently, cannot be viewed as being dependent upon the other States, which also exercise their authority, respectively, each in its own zone of authority.[7]

The idea bequeathed by Westphalia is that the limitation of each State's desires for power and expansion somehow ensures that States will respect the integrity of foreign areas of sovereignty by creating a program for the peaceful coexistence of States which might have diverse interests and do not necessarily share common aims.[8]

Most historiographies usually place the origin of international law in this period because of the belief that the legal equality of States sets up a control on the hegemonic aspirations of the most powerful and provides a normative

---

4 Croxton, Derek. 'The Peace of Westphalia of 1648 and the Origins of Sovereignty'. *International History Review* 21(3) (1999), 569–852.

5 Moncayo, Guillermo, Raúl E. Vinuesa and Hortensia D. T. Gutiérrez Posse. *Derecho internacional público*, vol. I (Buenos Aires: Zavalia, 1977), 31.

6 Cf. Bull, Hedley. *Anarchical Society. A Study of Order in World Politics* (New York: Columbia University Press, 1977). On sovereign equality and its importance in the foundation of international law, see Dickinson, Edwin De Witt. *The Equality of States in International Law* (Cambridge: Harvard University Press, 1920) and Kooijmans, Pieter H. *The Doctrine of the Legal Equality of States: An Inquiry into the Foundations of International Law* (Leiden: Sijthoff, 1964).

7 Anand, Ram P. 'Sovereign Equality of States in International Law'. *Recueil des cours de l'académie de droit international de La Haye* 197 (1986), 9–228.

8 Oakeshott, Michael. *On Human Conduct* (Oxford: Oxford University Press, 1991).

framework that can only emerge from agreement among entities that find themselves in a legal equilibrium.[9] Endorsing Westphalia as the original charter of public international law implies a conception of the 'new' legal order as a decentralized,[10] horizontal[11] system in which States are subjects that create rules through free and voluntary agreement and in which there is no higher authority that can exercise control over them.[12] Thanks to the Westphalian myth of origin, the actual differences among States were concealed under a cover of equality that – along with the foundational idea of sovereignty – allowed for a successful fiction that would continue to characterize international law down to our own times.[13] In order to be born, international law required the exclusion of politics and the dismissal of imperial inequalities.[14] This theoretical move has interesting implications and gained fast track in the discipline: since 'equality' has been always perceived as a positive value, the insistence on the sovereign balance among States paved the way for the success of international law as an adequate tool for what was believed as a universal extension of its rules.

The *pax Westphalica* has created a useful rhetorical mechanism to preserve the *status quo* in international relations.[15] The model, however, seems

9 In truth, it is possible to regard the Peace of Westphalia as a foundation myth, as explained by Beaulac, Stéphanie. *The Power of Language in the Making of International Law. The Word 'Sovereignty' in Bodin and Vattel and the Myth of 'Westphalia'* (Leiden: Martinus Nijhoff, 2004).

10 Barboza, Julio. *Derecho internacional público* (Buenos Aires: Zavalía, 2008), 15–16.

11 Cheng, Bin. 'Introduction to the Subjects of International Law', in *International Law: Achievements and Prospects*, ed. Mohammed Bedjaoui (Paris/Leiden: UNESCO/Martinus Nijhoff, 1991), 23–40, 33.

12 Combacau, Jean and Serge Sur. *Droit international public* (Paris: Montchrestien, 1997), 2–3, identify a decentralized *interstate* law between state law (at the domestic level) and *suprastate* law (in which there exists a third party superior to the States).

13 On the limits of this theoretical construct, see Simpson, Gerry. *Great Powers and Outlaw States. Unequal Sovereigns in the International Legal Order* (Cambridge: Cambridge University Press, 2004).

14 Westphalia 'formalises a transition from Empire to sovereignty in the European political order ...', as stated by Simpson, Gerry. 'International Law in Diplomatic History', in *The Cambridge Companion to International Law*, eds. James Crawford and Martti Koskenniemi (Cambridge: Cambridge University Press, 2012), 25–46, 31.

15 On a revision of the Westphalian provisions from a historical perspective, cf. Lesaffer, Randall. 'The Westphalia Peace Treaties and the Development of the Tradition of Great European Peace Settlements prior to 1648'. *Grotiana* 18(1) (1997), 71–95; Cutler, A. Claire. 'Critical Reflections on the Westphalian Assumptions of International Law and Organization: A Crisis of Legitimacy'. *Review of International Studies* 27(2) (2001), 133–150; Osiander, Andreas. 'Sovereignty, International Relations, and the Westphalian Myth'. *International Organization* 55(2) (2001), 251–287; and Lesaffer, Randall. 'Peace Treaties

arbitrary from a diachronic perspective. In fact, beneath the supposed equality of sovereign States, there are hidden notorious inequalities that frequently determine the rules in the international arena. In spite of this clearly political background, sovereign equality still remains as an essential landmark of international law,[16] but it would be naive not to think that the international legal system has always been the outcome of interactions between entities that in practice prove notoriously different and relate to one another on a very unequal basis. Ultimately, in general terms the States with the greatest capabilities and opportunity to impose their view are those that succeed in shaping legal rules (and imposing them on the weakest or poorest States) to their advantage and according to their own interests.[17] Nevertheless, historiographies have mostly focused on issues regarding the content of the rules of international law or their application, instead of addressing the relevant questions, such as whom they empower, who stands behind the agenda and who decides on specific cases in accordance with that international law.[18] To deal with this awareness, counter-voices have arisen and new critical historical

---

from Lodi to Westphalia', in *Peace Treaties and International Law in European History: From the Late Middle Ages to World War One*, ed. Randall Lesaffer (Cambridge: Cambridge University Press, 2004), 9–44. According to Beaulac, *The Power of Language* 2004 (n. 9), 90, '... the principal objects and material provisions of the Osnabrück and Münster Treaties do not at all support the traditional position that the *Peace of Westphalia* constitutes a paradigm shift whereby the political entities involved gained exclusive power over their territories.' Similarly, Hurrell, Andrew. *On Global Order: Power, Values, and the Constitution of International Society* (Oxford: Oxford University Press, 2009), 54–55.

16 Concerning this feature of contemporary international law, cf. Pinto, Monica. *El derecho internacional. Vigencias y desafíos en un escenario globalizado* (Buenos Aires: Fondo de Cultura Económica, 2004), 55. Sovereign equality is the first principle stated in the Charter of the United Nations in its Article 2.1; see Fassbender, Bardo. 'Article 2(1)', in *The Charter of the United Nations. A Commentary*, vol. I, ed. Bruno Simma, Daniel-Erasmus Khan, Georg Nolte and Andreas Paulus (Oxford: Oxford University Press, 3rd ed. 2002), 68–91.

17 Krisch, Nico. 'International Law in Times of Hegemony: Unequal Power and the Shaping of the International Legal Order'. *European Journal of International Law* 16(3) (2005), 369–408.

18 When describing this 'mainstream' presentation of international law, Bianchi, Andrea. *International Law Theories: An Inquiry into Different Ways of Thinking* (Oxford: Oxford University Press, 2016), 21–23, suggests that it relies on the reproduction of a long-dated conception that pays almost no attention to extra-legal considerations: international law has been traditionally described as a system of objective principles and neutral rules that emanate from States' will, independently of political or cultural values and with little interest in its rooted intellectual constructions. He concludes that '[t]his attitude goes hand in hand with the denial that there might be hidden structures in the law, or values underlying its rules that may unveil the existence of policy choices or preferences.'

readings have been born to uncover the hegemonic tradition that has always existed in the law of nations.[19]

The basis for this theory is of course historical: it is believed that, since the earliest beginnings of the first politically organized communities, the most influential states tried to dominate the less fortunate through a series of legal rules that benefited themselves.[20] This political-realist model of international law, however, has been frequently criticized because it served to back a political view of the phenomenon by subordinating law to the decisions of States that exercise a greater power over the others. By constituting Westphalia as a starting point, mainstream international legal historiography has successfully endorsed law over other non-legal considerations in order to justify its object. Therefore, the Westphalian model managed to leave the political-realist model aside. And this was done by disregarding both the political realm and pre-modern experiences.

3 The Denial of Antiquity: Theoretical Reasons and Political Functionality

With the exception of a few specific monographs which have explained the importance of international law in antiquity and its legacy,[21] in the most recent

19 Thus Grewe, Wilhelm G. *Epochen der Völkerrechtsgeschichte* (Baden-Baden: Nomos, 1984), identifying historical periods based on different nations' hegemonies: a Spanish era (1494–1648), a French era (1648–1815), and a British era (1815–1919). These three periods represent the greatest degrees of imperialistic expansion by the respective nations. On this topic, see Cohen, Jean L. 'Whose Sovereignty? Empire vs. International Law'. *Ethics and International Affairs* 18(3) (2004), 1–24. For a complementary approach, the contribution by Eslava, Luis, Liliana Obregón and René Urueña. 'Imperialismo(s) y derecho(s) international(es): Ayer y hoy', in *Imperialismo y derecho internacional: Historia y legado*, eds. Antony Anghie, Martti Koskenniemi and Anne Orford (Bogotá: Universidad de Los Andes and Universidad Javeriana, 2016), 11–94, shows the role of third world countries in challenging this idea of excluding imperialism.

20 See Wolfke, Karol. *Great and Small Powers in International Law from 1814 to 1920 (From the Pre-History of the United Nations)* (Warsaw: Prace Wrociawskiego Towarzystwa Naukowego, 1961). As we shall see, the Greco-Roman world had the same political structure, likewise hidden beneath a fiction of legal equality.

21 See, for instance, Phillipson, Coleman. *The International Law and Custom of Ancient Greece and Rome* (London: Macmillan, 1911); Bickerman, Elias J. 'Remarques sur le droit des gens dans la Grèce classique'. *Revue international des droits de l'antiquité* 4 (1950), 99–127, and more recently Bederman, David J. *International Law in Antiquity* (Cambridge: Cambridge University Press, 2001). With some exceptions, these contributions do not come from the field of legal scholarship but rather from ancient history or classical philology. These authors, among others, managed to recognize in the Greco-Roman world the

literature on international law references to ancient civilizations are absent.[22] Some monographs even exclude ancient times explicitly when discussing the origins of international law.[23] In others, when the Greek and Roman experiences are mentioned, it is because these sources are believed to show the political basis for the emergence of international law, and nothing more.[24] In a last group of monographs, when a reference to the ancient world is made, it is generally not because it is considered international law as such, but rather because antiquity operates as a mere precedent.[25]

---

validity of certain institutions inherent to what today is known as 'public international law'. The volume directed by Bouineau, Jacques. *Droit international et antiquité: Aspects culturels* (Paris: L'Harmattan, 2011) only includes very limited works on classical antiquity. The main arguments for this position are clearly presented by Kaczorowska-Ireland, Alina. *Public International Law* (Abingdon: Routledge, 4th ed. 2002), 1: '[I]t is impossible to fix a precise date or a period in history to mark the beginning of international law as it predates recorded history.' This is of course not limited to the Greek and Roman experience: see Altman, Amnon. *Tracing the Earliest Recorded Concepts of International Law: The Ancient Near East (2500–330 BCE)* (Leiden: Martinus Nijhoff, 2012).

22 It is the case, for example, of several authors from different schools of thought. See Malanczuk, Peter. *Akekurst's Modern Introduction to International Law* (Abingdon: Routledge, 1997); Gardiner, Richard K. *International Law* (Essex: Pearson, 2003); Orford, Anne. *International Law and Its Others* (Cambridge: Cambridge University Press, 2006); Remiro Brotons, Antonio. *Derecho internacional: Curso general* (Valencia: Tirant Lo Blanch, 9th ed. 2010); Slomason, William R. *Fundamental Perspectives on International Law* (Boston: Wadsworth Cengage Learning, 2011); Vos, Jan A. *The Function of Public International Law* (The Hague/Berlin: T.M.C. Asser Press/Springer, 2013); and Chen, Lung-Chu. *An Introduction to Contemporary International Law* (Oxford: Oxford University Press, 3rd ed. 2015), who do not make any reference to antiquity.

23 For instance, Moncayo, Vinuesa and Gutiérrez Posse. *Derecho internacional público* 1997 (n. 5), 27; Wallace, Rebecca. M. M. *International Law* (London: Sweet & Maxwell, 4th ed. 2002), 4; Aust, Anthony. *Handbook of International Law* (Cambridge: Cambridge University Press, 2007), 3; and Henderson, *Understanding International Law* 2010 (n. 2), 22.

24 According to Shaw, Malcolm N. *International Law* (Cambridge: Cambridge University Press, 5th ed. 2003), 13, 'while the modern international system can be traced back some 400 years, certain of the basic concepts of international law can be discerned in political relationships thousands of years ago.' Only the political seed of international law can be traced back to ancient times. This is compatible with the proliferation of bibliography addressing the origin of international relations in antiquity, as recently suggested by Malchow, Howard LeRoy. *History and International Relations. From the Ancient World to the 21st Century* (London: Bloomsbury, 2015), 99–122, especially 121–122.

25 Hillier, Tim. *Sourcebook on Public International Law* (Singapore: Cavendish, 1998), 4, refers to the Middle Ages in order to show only the existence of the 'basic requirements for an international legal order'. Currie, John H. *Public International Law* (Toronto: Irwin Law, 2nd ed. 2008), 6, has explained that, in spite of its ancient foundations, 'the international legal system as we know it today has its origins in the sixteenth and seventeenth

In this sense, the classical period is subject to a dual treatment when examined: because of its ancient nature, it is normally perceived as a model, i.e. the weight of time has created a sense of respect toward this overvalued past, which is identified as the source of western civilization. At the same time, the ancients are considered aliens to us, since they lived in different conditions, i.e. we do not share a basic understanding of the reality that surrounds us precisely because of the time elapsed between their lives and our modern world. The phenomenon does not lack importance. The relationship to antiquity is torn between these two fictional ends, which operate as instrumental fantasies. Either because of the continuation of an uninterrupted tradition or because of the otherness that involves it, the truth remains in both cases that ancient cultures escape from a more critical and detailed analysis. These two poles are found in contemporary historiographies of international law: modern authors do not mention antiquity because they believe that it is the beginning of our present (as part of the 'Western" and 'European' origins of international law) and therefore does not deserve specific treatment (beyond an archeological interest) or, alternatively, because ancient peoples cannot be related to our modern culture (and therefore they do not represent any 'origin' to our social values).[26]

A closer examination of the reasons presented in most of these volumes in order to justify the exclusion of an ancient international law can be useful here. Pre-modern international law is generally discarded because of several motives, many of which can be traced to François Laurent, who authored three volumes entitled *Histoire du droit des gens et des relations internationales* (1850–1851), later compiled as part of his *Histoire de l'Humanité*. The importance of his contribution cannot be underestimated, since his arguments have been frequently quoted in order to justify the 'denial' theory. In his volumes – concerned with the East, Greece and Rome –, Laurent sustained the lack of

centuries, and that its birth-place was Europe'. Miéville, China. *Between Equal Rights. A Marxist Theory of International Law* (Leiden: Brill, 2005), 163, also suggests some ancient precedents but does not dare to talk about an ancient 'international law'. Similarly, Sørensen, Max. *Manual of Public International Law* (London/New York: Macmillan/St. Martin's Press, 1968), 14–26.

26 I am aware that, on the basis of the first pole, focusing on Greek and Roman sources could be criticized as upholding a Euro-centric perspective. However, it should be noted that ancient cultures cannot be ascribed to the modern opposition between Eastern and Western civilizations, as explained by Bederman, *Antiquity* 2001 (n. 21), 4. In fact I claim here that my attempt to revisit the classical past, instead of strengthening the arguments for Euro-centrism, serves the purpose of disclosing the arbitrary foundation of mainstream 'Western' doctrines, which have ignored antiquity to build a modern normative order based on rational a-political grounds.

international regulations in the ancient world. His arguments were aimed at showing that ancient peoples lived in a condition misleadingly called 'natural', where everyone was at war against everyone else and where power was in the hands of the strongest: that fact completely hindered the development of a true law of nations.[27] The lack of a concept about humanity (hence, of universal law)[28] and the non-recognition of equality and fraternity as ideas capable of founding a science of international law[29] were considered as sufficient reasons to believe that a regulatory framework to govern the relations among different 'primitive' peoples simply did not exist.[30]

What conceptions of international law (and what prejudices) lie behind these ideas? First of all, that 'States' as such did not exist in ancient times and that 'sovereignty' was absent in that context.[31] Concerning the first claim, it would suffice to say that the (politically) ambiguous concept of 'State' is still today under heavy debate, and that in any case ancient *póleis* –πόλεις–, *civitates* or *gentes* were organized entities possessing territory, population and governing bodies that made them independent, remaining close to the modern idea of statehood.[32] On the second criticism, it is true that attributing 'sovereignty' to pre-modern political entities is as such incorrect. Attempting to recognize the same sovereign equality in antiquity than the one which sustains current international relations is a failed attempt, since projecting a modern

27 Laurent, François. *Histoire du droit des gens et des relations internationales*, vol. 1 (Paris: Durand, 1850–1851), 15.

28 Ibid., 130.

29 Ibid., 328.

30 This skeptical or 'denial' position is still widely accepted in authoritative opinions. Eckstein, Arthur M. *Mediterranean Anarchy, Interstate War, and the Rise of Rome* (Berkeley: University of California Press, 2006), 37, for example, argues today that ancient Greek city-states existed in a world that basically lacked international law. The result, in his opinion, was a constellation of heavily militarized and diplomatically aggressive societies among which war was a commonplace.

31 On the arguments presented in order to deny the existence of international law in antiquity, see Gaurier, Dominique. *Histoire du droit international. De l'antiquité à la création de l'ONU* (Rennes: Presses Université de Rennes, 2014), 33–37, who considers that these statements are the two most important ones. He adds the lack of an autonomous corpus of rules, the ubiquitousness of war and the fact that *ius cogens* was inexistent, and he overcomes the criticism with a number of ideas that can be shared.

32 It is held, in fact, that in the Greek world the three elements of the city-state appear in some way in a consolidated hierarchy: first, the community of citizens, then, the political institutions, and, finally, the physical space; cf. Hansen, Morgens Herman. 'Introduction: The *Polis* as a Citizen-State', in *The Ancient Greek City State*, ed. Morgens Herman Hansen (Copenhagen: Det Kongelige Danske Videnskabernes Selskab, Munksgaard, 1993), 7–29, 7–9. In the case of Rome we find similar characteristics, which can be explained because of the common Indo-European background of these communities.

conceptualization of international law into other historical and cultural contexts is historically mistaken.[33] Nevertheless, the absence of balance among politically organized nations in the ancient world should not lead us to deny the existence of independent communities (characterized by *autonomía* – αὐτονομία – and *eleuthería* – ἐλευθερία – in Greece, or *libertas* in Rome) which established diplomatic or political ties among them, and which were capable of negotiating agreements without any sort of external interference.[34] An international law, conceived in this way, clearly existed in pre-modern times. In fact, the idea of *nómos koinós* (νόμος κοινός) in ancient Greece and *ius gentium* in Rome shows that the ancient world not only regulated international relations but also identified this regulation under a general normative framework which exceeded the limits of domestic legal systems.[35]

In the ancient world, this 'common' or international law presupposes a narrative which is useful for describing and justifying the actions of these political

33 These critical ideas have been recently sustained by an international 'Euro-centric' critique, which tries to reframe international standards based on new patterns that take into account different legal traditions. In that regard, see Becker Lorca, Arnulf. 'Eurocentrism in the History of International Law', in *The Oxford Handbook of the History of International Law*, eds. Bardo Fassbender and Anne Peters (Oxford: Oxford University Press, 2012), 1034–1057, for a general overview.

34 Hall, Jonathan M. 'International Relations', in *The Cambridge History of Greek and Roman Warfare*, vol. 1, eds. Philip Sabin, Hans van Wees and Michael Whitby (Cambridge: Cambridge University Press, 2007), 85–107, 85–88; Giovannini, Adalberto. *Les relations entre États dans la Grèce antique, du temps d'Homère à l'intervention romaine* (*ca.* 700–200 *av. J.-C.*) (Stuttgart: Franz Steiner Verlag, 2007), 14, argues that, unlike what happens in current society, the Greeks were united by a common language, religion and moral values, so that 'inter-national' relations in the classical Greece corresponded to ties among states within what could be conceived as a single nation. The relevant vocabulary to support this idea that 'sovereignty' was not a notion completely unknown to the mind of the ancient peoples will be discussed later in this chapter.

35 See Buis, Emiliano J. *Taming Ares. War, Interstate Law and Humanitarian Discourse in Classical Greece* (Leiden: Brill, 2018), 157 et seq. Interestingly enough, even legal historians working on international law find it difficult to approach *ius gentium* to international law; cf. Renaut, Marie-Hélène. *Histoire du droit international public* (Paris: Ellipses, 2007), 7, who nevertheless dedicates eight pages (13–20) to 'le droit des gens dans l'antiquité'. Neff, Stephen C. *Justice among Nations. A History of International Law* (Cambridge: Harvard University Press, 2014), 10, considers that international law existed in antiquity, even if 'our ancient ancestors did not apply that label': in this sense, he says that *ius gentium* 'would later metamorphose into international law' (44). Laghmani, Slim. *Histoire du droit des gens: Du* Jus Gentium *Impérial au* Jus Publicum Europaeum (Paris: Pedone, 2003), 7, considered that the notion of international law is not 'operational' in ancient times, and that international law then '*avait lieu* entre les peuples, il *ne naissait pas* des peuples.'

communities.[36] A subtle language, efficient because of its vagueness, endorsed the power of some allies over other parties to the negotiation. This tension between imposition and resistance reveals some of the earliest examples of a discourse on hegemonic supremacy and, thus, provides interesting historical insights on the rhetorical making of international law.

Far from being immersed in political anarchy, the ancient world frequently resorted to international rules in order to install a legal framework and justify the political action of relevant actors. I believe that this conflation of law (νόμος or *ius*) and concrete political agendas is precisely the main reason for the exclusion of antiquity in modern debates on the history of international law. A very succinct overview of some of the preserved Greek and Roman sources, as attempted in the next section of the chapter, will help explain the political move behind this exclusion. I expect that some few examples will show that, in spite of the notorious difference in power and strength among πόλεις, *civitates* or *gentes*, an archetype similar to that of the modern Westphalian model already existed in ancient times with the purpose of concealing a political-realist model based on inequality.

4 International Law and the Ancient Connection: The Coexistence of Models in Greece and Rome

Whatever theoretical support may undergird the foundations of modern international law, a quick look today at its practical dimension can show that the most powerful States, which in practice could obviously ignore international law given the absence of any means of enforcing it, have instead always tried to justify their behaviour by reinterpreting existing law and applying it.[37] Instead of openly violating the rules, States never acknowledge that they have committed actions in breach of its norms.[38] This is precisely because international law has always left ample room for States with greater political authority to seek legitimation for their own behaviour with respect to third parties.[39]

---

36 Goldsmith, Jack L. and Eric A. Posner. *The Limits of International Law* (Oxford: Oxford University Press, 2005), 167–172.

37 On the political importance of interpretation, see Venzke, Ingo. *How Interpretation Makes International Law. On Semantic Change and Normative Twists* (Oxford: Oxford University Press, 2012).

38 Pinto, *Derecho internacional* 2004 (n. 16), 163.

39 On the crisis of legitimacy in international law, produced in many instances by forced interpretations of the rules or the search for exceptions to explain a lack of compliance, see the chapters in Charlesworth, Hilary and Jean-Marc Coicaud, eds. *Fault Lines*

Taking into account such a view, some critics have challenged the mainstream historical trend that has traditionally regarded international law as a result of negotiations *inter pares.* Many scholars recently produced an opposing revisionist movement in order to generate spaces for contention based on a peripheral vision of international relations.[40] According to these critical readings, international law is best described pragmatically as an instrument of power, and thus adapts itself to diverse interests.[41] To them, the international legal system has validated a Euro-centric construction of the discipline (among civilized and sovereign States), and its rules have been set to ratify the values of the colonialist attempts in the dominated non-European world.[42]

The value of international legal history has thus been reaffirmed by this critical standpoint. Some authors have tried to explain that subordination has been a constant model in interstate affairs from its outset. Under this perspective, they speak of 'imperialism' in a broad sense, as a set of cultural, economic, institutional and legal mechanisms that have been efficient for the reproduction of power relations throughout time. Postcolonial studies, born in times of

---

of International Legitimacy (Cambridge: Cambridge University Press, 2010); Buchanan, Allen. 'The Legitimacy of International Law', in *The Philosophy of International Law*, eds. Samantha Besson and John Tasioulas (Oxford: Oxford University Press, 2010), 79–96, and Tasioulas's response in the same volume, 97–116.

40 See, for example, the seminal work by Rajagopal, Balakrishnan. *International Law from Below* (Cambridge: Cambridge University Press, 2003). These 'marginal' TWAIL theories of international law challenge previous advances instead of complementing them. The movement, in spite of internal differences among authors, mainly considers that international law is the result of the colonial encounter, and therefore has functioned as a tool to perpetuate and legitimate asymmetrical structures of power. Cf. Gathii, James Thuo. 'TWAIL: A Brief History of Its Origins, Its Decentralized Network, and a Tentative Bibliography'. *Trade Law and Development* 3(1) (2011), 26–48. For opposite ideas, see Müllerson, Rein A. *Ordering Anarchy: International Law in International Society* (Leiden: Martinus Nijhoff, 2000), 66–67, who claims that TWAIL does not contribute to the 'mainstream' development of the discipline.

41 Douzinas, Costas. *Human Rights and Empire: The Political Philosophy of Cosmopolitanism* (Abingdon: Routledge, 2007). A similar conclusion is reached from a Marxist perspective by Zolo, Danilo. *La giustizia dei vincitori. Da norimberga a Baghdad* (Rome: Laterza, 2006). Feminist readings of international law tend to see in this normative order the embodiment of a patriarchal regime, cf. Charlesworth, Hilary and Christine M. Chinkin. *The Boundaries of International Law. A Feminist Analysis* (Manchester: Manchester University Press, 2000). For a more revolutionary position reacting to the moral indignation produced by current international law and its manifest inequities, see Allott, Philip. *The Health of Nations. Society and Law beyond the State* (Cambridge: Cambridge University Press, 2004), 399–422.

42 This is one of the main claims in Anghie, Antony. *Imperialism, Sovereignty and the Making of International Law* (Cambridge: Cambridge University Press, 2005).

decolonization, have interpreted imperialism as a state-based exploitation of others, including the maintenance of control over other states' internal and external politics. Not surprisingly critical authors have tried to bring politics back to the legal debate around international law. According to these perspectives, imperialism and international law are not operating as antagonistic forces, as assumed so far by traditional interpretations. International law seems now to find a new *raison d'être*: offering legal foundations for imperialist projects.[43]

Historicizing the more traditional a-historical definition of imperialism requires the identification of those power-related models and narratives which have been constructed, in different places and times, to enforce domination. I suggest here that, precisely in this sense, the ancient experience is rich in endorsing and reproducing an 'imperialist' State-system which can be followed up to the modern and contemporary international reality. By resorting to a 'controlled use of anachronism' in order to address the past with categories that are useful for understanding it,[44] I feel inclined to endorse a flexible and historically wide-ranging conception of imperialism, which can be used in order to explain today's views from critical movements or to address several strategies of subjugation in the pre-modern era.[45]

By enlarging its historical scope, the critical view of international law, which now fights against the traditional narrative that has purposely avoided any reference to power, can find useful arguments in antiquity and can learn a lot from tracing modern political stakes in classical Greece or Rome. As explained below, ancient sources provide interesting testimonies about the production of international law and its underlying assumptions. They allow us to think about how international law has served, in such contexts, as an unmistakable tool of domination by the powerful. In these earliest examples, even if the law seems poorly systematized and is not universally valid, rules which πόλεις, *civitates* or *gentes* agreed upon did create rights and obligations between neighboring communities, generally by means of customary norms and bilateral treaties. The text of such ancient agreements, as shown in the examples that

43 Anghie, *Imperialism, Sovereignty* 2005 (n. 42). A narrow definition of 'imperialism' considers it a product of specific historical conditions related to modern capitalism (from the 16th to the 20th centuries). A wider concept, however, was developed during the sixties by the theoretical approaches to dependency, which criticized the ways in which developing nations were seen as primitive versions of civilized countries.

44 As suggested by Loraux, Nicole. 'Éloge de l'anachronisme en histoire'. *Le genre humain* 27(1) (1993), 23–39.

45 Such a broad definition can be found in Doyle, Michael W. *Empires* (Ithaca: Cornell University Press, 1987).

will be presented, clearly depended on the abilities of the involved parties to persuade, defend their interests, and promote their points of view in an international landscape.[46]

Looking carefully at the ancient experience in international treaty-making is a task that has not been performed in the historiographies of international law but which could provide illuminating insights into the field, especially regarding the interaction between the Westphalian model and the political-realist model. An analytical examination of a few Greek and Roman sources can reveal that the explicit appeal to a formal equality – supported by appeals to friendship, democratic equality, freedom, common interests and reciprocal obligations – was used to hide the traditional (implicit) dialectical scheme of 'powerful vs. weak' or 'hegemonic vs. subjugated' States.

In ancient Greece, for instance, the acknowledgment of independence in each *pólis* (πόλις) explained the creation of a notion of formal equality among them, conceived as parallel to internal *isonomía* (ἰσονομία).[47] In this sense, it represented a precedent to the Westphalian model, since the international relations among πόλεις were carefully described as the result of a delicate balance between even negotiators.[48] Appealing to equality helped to overcome the difficulty of dealing with the unfair distinction between dominant and subordinate city-states.[49] But even if most sources insist in a balance between city-states which were independent and did not allegedly depend on each other, in practical terms Greek international relations in classical times were determined by a notorious distinction between stronger and weaker πόλεις. In practice, war treaties (concerning alliances or friendship) relied on a pretended coordination among equals but tended to hide the unavoidable subordination

46 Cf. Buis, Emiliano J. 'Sobre gnomos y gigantes: Los tratados grecorromanos y la igualdad soberana de los Estados como ficción histórico-jurídica'. *Lecciones y ensayos* 89(1) (2011), 73–117.

47 Sheets, George A. 'Conceptualizing International Law in Thucydides'. *American Journal of Philology* 115(1) (1994), 51–73, 53.

48 Cf. Buis, Emiliano J. 'Ancient Entanglements: The Influence of Greek Treaties in Roman 'International Law' under the Framework of Narrative Transculturation', in *Entanglements in Legal History. Conceptual Approaches*, ed. Thomas Duve (Frankfurt am Main: Max Planck Institute for European Legal History, 2014), 151–185.

49 Boas, Gideon. *Public International Law: Contemporary Principles and Perspectives* (Cheltenham: Edward Elgar, 2012), 2, mentions Baron Korff's intervention in the first lecture delivered to the Academy of International Law at The Hague, where he asserted that, since ancient times, international relations have developed among and between relatively equally civilized peoples.

of subjects to the most powerful.[50] This is the case, for example, of the Spartans, who in 403 BCE imposed severe conditions against the Athenians in what would be called today an unequal treaty, forcing them to destroy their walls, to surrender almost all of their fleet and to 'have the same friends and enemies as the Spartans'; they were even obliged to follow the Spartans whenever needed.[51] Also in the context of interstate leagues or associations the role of these powerful πόλεις could not be underestimated. The effective supremacy of one of the πόλις in the group (the *hēgemón,* ἡγεμών) seemed to contradict in practice an image of balance among the cities.[52]

The opposition between the explicit expansion of *isonomía* (i.e. liberty, symmetry, cooperation) and the implicit will of *hēgemonía* (ἡγεμονία, i.e. enslavement, inequality, subordination) could explain the competing narratives present in the consolidation of a Hellenic 'international law'. This narrative shows the complex bases for endorsing the rationale behind the imposition of *nómoi* in bilateral or multilateral agreements. International law was used among the Greeks as a way to conceal a natural political inequality behind a façade of balance, reciprocity and mutual understanding.

As far as Rome is concerned, the institutional mechanism of promoting and signing unequal agreements was a common praxis for the Romans when interacting with the cities in the Italic peninsula during its first centuries as a Republic, as shown in the treaty with the Samnites in 354 BCE.[53] Nevertheless, not unlike the Greek examples, from the earliest of times the deep disparity of contracting parties was generally concealed behind an apparent – and extremely suspicious – equality. During the 2nd and 1st centuries BCE the few treaties between Rome and the eastern Greek cities that have been preserved

50 On war treaties, see Fernández Nieto, Francisco Javier. *Los acuerdos bélicos en la antigua grecia (Época arcaica y clásica)*, vol. I (Santiago de Compostela: Secretariado de Publicaciones de la Universidad de Santiago, 1975).

51 Xenophon, *Hellenika*, 2.2.20. An analogous obligation to have the same friends and enemies and to follow them as allies is included in the treaty imposed by the Spartans on the Olynthians in 379 BCE (Xenophon, *Hellenika*, 5.3.26). For the Athenians's supremacy over the Corcyraeans and the Thurians, see also Thucydides, 3.75.6 and 7.33.6, respectively.

52 Leagues and confederations used to be *de facto* under the guidance of a ἡγεμών or leader, which was able to decide on the common actions that the organization would take. In practical terms, a πόλις acting as ἡγεμών was granted some particular privileges which were very rarely disputed. See Bonk, Peter. *Defensiv- und Offensivklauseln in griechischen Symmakhieverträgen* (Bonn: Rheinische Friedrich-Wilhelms-Universität, PhD Thesis 1974), 67–68.

53 Neff, *Justice among Nations* 2014 (n. 36), 319. For a summary of these treaties, see Heitland, William Emerton. *A Short History of the Roman Republic* (Cambridge: Cambridge University Press, 1915), 84.

could be read under the political-realist model of international law.[54] Greek words such as 'supremacy' (*arkhé*, ἀρχή) or 'power' (*dynasteía*, δυναστεία) were essential in Roman diplomacy to understand the nature of the *foedera iniqua*: in these agreements the primacy of Rome was perceived, for instance, as long as its counterpart was obliged to identify the Roman enemies as their own.[55] This majesty clause (*maiestas*) allowed the Romans to ensure the respect of its own supremacy: the city that accepted the content of the agreement was therefore limited in its practical capacity of action and in its legal competence because of the existence of a duty of obedience and submission to Rome and its allies.[56]

However, these examples were not as common as those which concealed the inequality behind a disguise of 'legal' balance (*foedera aequa* or 'equal treaties'), such as the treaty with Maroneia (Thrace), from 167 or 166 BCE.[57] In its provisions, the greater relative authority of the Romans *vis-à-vis* their counterparts was hardly disclosed: a legal fiction was deployed to hide the dialectics of domination under a written statement that consecrated a sense of parallelism and sovereign equality.[58] Finally, in some 'mixed-type' treaties from the 1st Century BCE, the political-realist model and the Westphalian model seem to have coexisted.[59] Granting advantages to the local population was a frequent strategy to dissimulate the real legal intention of consolidating their subjection

54 According to Polybius (21.32.2–3) and Livy (38.11), in the treaty between Rome and Aetolia from 189 BCE, Romans imposed severe conditions and obligations: the Aetolians had to respect with loyalty the sovereignty and the power of the Roman people.

55 These *foedera iniqua* were essential to favour the position of Rome; on the nature of this expression, see Dahlheim, Werner. *Struktur und Entwicklung des römischen Völkerrechts im dritten und zweiten Jahrhundert v. Chr.* (Munich: C. H. Beck, 1968), 119–121; and Gruen, Erich S. *The Hellenistic World and the Coming of Rome* (Berkeley: University of California Press, 1984), 14.

56 The treaty signed by Rome and the Lycians in the 1st century BCE shows how Roman imperialism resorted to a diplomatic strategy in order to negotiate agreements enforcing its leadership. In the inscription the alleged *aequitas* vanished away when a majesty clause was introduced; cf. Mitchell, Stephen 'The Treaty between Rome and Lycia', in *Papyri Graecae Schøyen I*, ed. Rosario Pintaudi (Florence: Gonnelli, 2005), 163–258.

57 Ferrary, Jean-Louis. 'Traités et domination romaine dans le monde hellénistique', in *I trattati nel mondo antico. forma, ideologia, funzione*, eds. Luciano Canfora, Mario Liverani and Carlo Zaccagnini (Roma: L'Erma di Bretschneider, 1990), 217–235, 224, n. 18.

58 *SEG* 35 (1985), n° 823 (pp. 218–219); see Triantaphyllos, Diamantis. 'Symmakhia Romaion kai Maroniton'. *Thrakike Epeteris* 4 (1983), 419–449.

59 See Täubler, Eugen. *Imperium Romanum. Studien zur Entwickelungsgeschichte des römischen Reichs*, vol. I (Leipzig: Teubner, 1913).

to Roman hegemony. In the treaty with Aphrodisias[60] and Mytilene,[61] for instance, some benefits in favor of the local population were used to compensate the imposition of Roman *maiestas*.

5 Conclusion

It has been claimed that Classical Greece provides the best-documented case on record of small city-states trying to turn into large multicity states, and therefore its study should be of interest to comparative historians.[62] Rome, on the other side, has been seen as the first example in the West of an imperialist regime aiming to subdue foreign peoples under a common legal spirit. Nevertheless, both experiences are absent in contemporary mainstream historiographies of international law, precisely because of the widespread opinion that some of the aspects considered to be essential today (such as statehood, sovereignty or universality) were absent or, if they existed to a certain degree, could not in any case be compared to modern notions. The flaw in the reasoning is, in my opinion, obvious and suggests a troublesome misperception of ancient sources. In our current understanding of international law, nothing seems to point out that sovereign equality should stand as an essential element to the concept, and nevertheless the canonical historiography of the discipline seem to accept the idea, without further discussion, that international law can only occur when such political equality is reached.

In my view, what we call international law today has existed from ancient times since there has always been a need to regulate interstate behaviour. Not unlike what we experience today, these norms were used in favor of the most powerful political entities, but were described as created among equals in order to conceal the realities of power and to hide the fact that they represented a useful instrument for imperial supremacy.

The tension between the need to preserve balance and the realities of unequal power has set a framework for the conceptual construction of international law, both applicable in antiquity and elsewhere. The ancient experience

60 Reynolds, Joyce. *Aphrodisias and Rome* (London: The Society for the Promotion of Roman Studies, 1982), n. 9; and Canali de Rossi, Filippo. *Le ambascerie del mondo greco a Roma in età repubblicana* (Roma: Istituto Italiano per la Storia Antica, 1997), 374, n. 438.

61 Sherk, Robert K., ed. *Roman Documents from the Greek East* (Baltimore: The Johns Hopkins Press, 1969), n. 26.

62 Morris, Ian. 'Greek Multicity States', in *The Oxford Handbook of the State in the Ancient Near East and Mediterranean*, eds. Peter Fibiger Bang and Walter Scheidel (Oxford: Oxford University Press, 2013), 279–303, 300.

might well provide one of the earliest examples of an efficient technique created for the justification of different sorts of imperial endeavours under an acceptable disguise (i.e. a Westphalian model *avant la lettre*) that can provide a fictional but efficient idea of strong equality between the parties. Revisiting these classical sources can therefore pave the way to the possibility of rethinking the complexities of hegemonic narratives today.

As already advocated, Westphalia is a myth that helped to establish a fabricated historical starting point: by rejecting the existence of an interstate legal framework in pre-modern times, scholars have managed to create a biased (but very efficient) paradigm in which, in order to exist, international law ought to be built upon legal coordination.[63] This is a highly politicized manner of endorsing what is in fact an unequal arena, in which only a few States are fully able to use international law to their own benefit. Thus, the consideration that the ancient Greco-Roman world falls outside the scope of 'international law' is a political move, since its inclusion in the mainstream historiographies of international law would imply accepting the unequal nature of States and acknowledging that the authority of imperialist control has always been a common landmark of foreign affairs and that law exists there in order to preserve it. This is something that most States would not be ready to accept, but which could well explain the obvious disparities that are present today in bilateral treaties such as the North-South foreign investment agreements. Bringing back politics through the example of antiquity and speaking of international law as an efficient technique of power can shed light on the false equality that seems to characterize the economic legal order.

By rejecting the ancient precedents in a diachronic study of international law, deemed to show politics instead of law, most historiographers of the discipline have been able to focus on a positive Westphalian model in which legal equality is incompatible with hegemony and nationalist exceptionalism. In sum, placing international law as opposed to imperialist politics is a highly political (conscious or unconscious) bet that needs to be disclosed.

The paradox of antiquity is therefore clear: remote in time, ancient treaties provide perhaps the best comparative example to reveal the nature of international law today, its political meaning and its tension between a system based superficially on equality and an underlying political-realist model. We have to go back to the distant past to be aware of the present we live in. In short, it

63 This idea of a 'pedigree history' of international law that could explain European expansion as the fulfillment of universalism based on Westphalian legal equality is presented by Koskenniemi, Martti. *The Gentle Civilizer of Nations: The Rise and Fall of International Law 1870–1960* (Cambridge: Cambridge University Press, 2001), 101–102.

becomes indispensable to plunge into very different civilizations, away in time, to see the political continuities in international law that helped reproduce a network of empowerment which seems naturalized and escapes scrutiny. By introducing sound references to ancient sources, international legal historiography should denounce the false rhetoric of anti-political 'objectivity' and unveil the real interests at stake that rest behind what we have been calling 'international law'.

Acknowledgments

I want to express my deepest gratitude to all the participants and engaged listeners at the International Conference *Politics and the Histories of International Law* (Heidelberg, February 2019), who commented on my draft. In addition, special thanks are owed to the editors of this volume for providing me with sharp observations to improve some of my arguments. Needless to say, all remaining mistakes throughout the chapter are my own.

Bibliography

Allott, Philip. *The Health of Nations. Society and Law beyond the State* (Cambridge: Cambridge University Press, 2004).

Altman, Amnon. *Tracing the Earliest Recorded Concepts of International Law: The Ancient Near East (2500–330 BCE)* (Leiden: Martinus Nijhoff, 2012).

Anand, Ram P. 'Sovereign Equality of States in International Law', *Recueil des cours de l'académie de droit international de La Haye* 197 (1986), 9–228.

Anghie, Antony. *Imperialism, Sovereignty and the Making of International Law* (Cambridge: Cambridge University Press, 2005).

Aust, Anthony. *Handbook of International Law* (Cambridge: Cambridge University Press, 2007).

Barboza, Julio. *Derecho internacional público* (Buenos Aires: Zavalía, 2008).

Beaulac, Stéphanie. *The Power of Language in the Making of International Law. The Word* Sovereignty *in Bodin and Vattel and the Myth of Westphalia* (Leiden: Martinus Nijhoff, 2004).

Becker Lorca, Arnulf. 'Eurocentrism in the History of International Law', in *The Oxford Handbook of the History of International Law*, eds. Bardo Fassbender and Anne Peters, Oxford: Oxford University Press, 2012), 1034–1057.

Bederman, David J. *International Law in Antiquity* (Cambridge: Cambridge University Press, 2001).

Bianchi, Andrea. *International Law Theories. An Inquiry into Different Ways of Thinking* (Oxford: Oxford University Press, 2016).

Bickerman, Elias J. 'Remarques sur le droit des gens dans la Grèce classique'. *Revue international des droits de l'antiquité* 4 (1950), 99–127.

Boas, Gideon. *Public International Law: Contemporary Principles and Perspectives* (Cheltenham: Edward Elgar, 2012).

Bonk, Peter. *Defensiv- und Offensivklauseln in griechischen Symmakhieverträgen* (Bonn: Rheinische Friedrich-Wilhelms-Universität, PhD Thesis 1974), 67–68.

Bouineau, Jacques. *Droit international et antiquité: Aspects culturels* (Paris: L'Harmattan, 2011).

Buchanan, Allen. 'The Legitimacy of International Law', in *The Philosophy of International Law*, eds. Samantha Besson and John Tasioulas (Oxford: Oxford University Press, 2010), 79–96.

Buis, Emiliano J. 'Ancient Entanglements: The Influence of Greek Treaties in Roman 'International Law' under the Framework of Narrative Transculturation', in *Entanglements in Legal History. Conceptual Approaches*, ed. Thomas Duve (Frankfurt am Main: Max Planck Institute for European Legal History, 2014), 151–185.

Buis, Emiliano J. 'Sobre gnomos y gigantes: Los tratados grecorromanos y la igualdad soberana de los Estados como ficción histórico-jurídica'. *Lecciones y ensayos* 89(1) (2011), 73–117.

Buis, Emiliano J. *Taming Ares. War, Interstate Law and Humanitarian Discourse in Classical Greece* (Leiden: Brill, 2018).

Bull, Hedley. *Anarchical Society. A Study of Order in World Politics* (New York: Columbia University Press, 1977).

Canali de Rossi, Filippo. *Le ambascerie del mondo greco a Roma in età repubblicana* (Roma: Istituto italiano per la storia antica, 1997).

Charlesworth, Hilary and Christine M. Chinkin. *The Boundaries of International Law. A Feminist Analysis* (Manchester: Manchester University Press, 2000).

Charlesworth, Hilary and Jean-Marc Coicaud, eds. *Fault Lines of International Legitimacy* (Cambridge: Cambridge University Press, 2010).

Chen, Lung-Chu. *An Introduction to Contemporary International Law* (Oxford: Oxford University Press, 3rd ed. 2015).

Cheng, Bin. 'Introduction to the Subjects of International Law', in *International Law: Achievements and Prospects*, ed. Mohammed Bedjaoui (Paris/Leiden: UNESCO/Martinus Nijhoff, 1991), 23–40.

Cohen, Jean L. 'Whose Sovereignty? Empire vs. International Law'. *Ethics and International Affairs* 18(3) (2004), 1–24.

Combacau, Jean and Serge Sur. *Droit international public* (Paris: Montchrestien, 1997).

Croxton, Derek. 'The Peace of Westphalia of 1648 and the Origins of Sovereignty'. *International History Review* 21(3) (1999), 569–852.

Currie, John H. *Public International Law* (Toronto: Irwin Law, 2nd ed. 2008).

Cutler, A. Claire. 'Critical Reflections on the Westphalian Assumptions of International Law and Organization: A Crisis of Legitimacy'. *Review of International Studies* 27(2) (2001), 133–150.

Dahlheim, Werner. *Struktur und Entwicklung des römischen Völkerrechts im dritten und zweiten Jahrhundert v. Chr.* (Munich: C. H. Beck, 1968).

Dickinson, Edwin De Witt. *The Equality of States in International Law* (Cambridge: Harvard University Press, 1920).

Douzinas, Costa. *Human Rights and Empire: The Political Philosophy of Cosmopolitanism* (Abingdon/New York: Routledge/Cavendish, 2007).

Doyle, Michael W. *Empires* (Ithaca: Cornell University Press, 1987).

Eckstein, Arthur M. *Mediterranean Anarchy, Interstate War, and the Rise of Rome* (Berkeley: University of California Press, 2006).

Eslava, Luis, Liliana Obregón and René Urueña. 'Imperialismo(s) y derecho(s) international(es): Ayer y hoy', in *Imperialismo y derecho internacional: Historia y legado*, eds. Antony Anghie, Martti Koskenniemi and Anne Orford (Bogotá: Universidad de Los Andes and Universidad Javeriana, 2016), 11–94.

Fassbender, Bardo. 'Article 2 (1)', in *The Charter of the United Nations. A Commentary*, vol. 1, ed. Bruno Simma, Daniel-Erasmus Khan, Georg Nolte and Andreas Paulus (Oxford: Oxford University Press, 3rd ed. 2002), 68–91.

Fernández Nieto, Fracisco Javier. *Los acuerdos bélicos en la antigua Grecia (Época arcaica y clásica)*, vol. 1 (Santiago de Compostela: Secretariado de publicaciones de la Universidad de Santiago, 1975).

Ferrary, Jean-Louis. 'Traités et domination romaine dans le monde hellénistique', in *I trattati nel mondo antico. forma, ideologia, funzione*, eds. Luciano Canfora, Mario Liverani and Carlo Zaccagnini (Rome: L'Erma di Bretschneider, 1990), 217–235.

Gardiner, Richard K. *International Law* (Essex: Pearson, 2003).

Gathii, James Thuo. 'TWAIL: A Brief History of its Origins, Its Decentralized Network, and a Tentative Bibliography'. *Trade Law and Development* 3(1) (2011), 26–48.

Gaurier, Dominique. *Histoire du droit international. De l'antiquité à la création de l'ONU* (Rennes: Presses Université de Rennes, 2014).

Giovannini, Adalberto. *Les relations entre États dans la Grèce antique, du temps d'Homère à l'intervention romaine (ca. 700–200 av. J.-C.)* (Stuttgart: Franz Steiner Verlag, 2007).

Goldsmith, Jack L. and Eric A. Posner. *The Limits of International Law* (Oxford: Oxford University Press, 2005).

Grewe, Wilhelm G. *Epochen der Völkerrechtsgeschichte* (Baden-Baden: Nomos, 1984).

Gruen, Erich S. *The Hellenistic World and the Coming of Rome* (Berkeley: University of California Press, 1984).

Hall, Jonathan M. 'International Relations', in *The Cambridge History of Greek and Roman Warfare*, vol. 1, eds. Philip Sabin, Hans van Wees and Michael Whitby (Cambridge: Cambridge University Press, 2007), 85–107.

Hansen, Morgens Herman. 'Introduction: The *Polis* as a Citizen-State', in *The Ancient Greek City State*. Symposium on the Occasion of the 250th Anniversary of the Royal Danish Academy of Science and Letters (1–4 July, 1992), ed. Morgens Herman Hansen (Copenhagen: Det Kongelige Danske Videnskabernes Selskab, Munksgaard, 1993), 7–29.

Heitland, William Emerton. *A Short History of the Roman Republic* (Cambridge: Cambridge University Press, 1915).

Henderson, Conway W. *Understanding International Law* (Hoboken: Wiley-Blackwell, 2010).

Higgins, Rosalyn. *Problems and Process: International Law and How We Use It* (Oxford: Oxford University Press, 1995).

Hurrell, Andrew. *On Global Order: Power, Values, and the Constitution of International Society* (Oxford: Oxford University Press, 2009).

Kaczorowska- Ireland, Alina. *Public International Law* (Abingdon: Routledge, 4th ed. 2002).

Kooijmans, Pieter Hendrik. *The Doctrine of the Legal Equality of States: An Inquiry into the Foundations of International Law* (Leiden: Sijthoff, 1964).

Koskenniemi, Martti. *The Gentle Civilizer of Nations: The Rise and Fall of International Law 1870–1960* (Cambridge: Cambridge University Press, 2001).

Krisch, Nico. 'International Law in Times of Hegemony: Unequal Power and the Shaping of the International Legal Order'. *European Journal of International Law* 16(3) (2005), 369–408.

Laghmani, Slim. *Histoire du droit des gens: Du* Jus Gentium *impérial* au Jus Publicum Europaeum (Paris: Pedone, 2003).

Laurent, François. *Histoire du droit des gens et des relations internationales*, vol. 1 (Paris: Durand, 1850–1851)

Lesaffer, R. 'Peace Treaties from Lodi to Westphalia', in *Peace Treaties and International Law in European History: from the Late Middle Ages to World War One*, ed. Randall Lesaffer (Cambridge: Cambridge University Press, 2004), 9–44.

Lesaffer, R. 'The Westphalia Peace Treaties and the Development of the Tradition of Great European Peace Settlements prior to 1648'. *Grotiana* 18(1) (1997), 71–95.

Loraux, Nicole. 'Éloge de l'anachronisme en histoire'. *Le genre humain* 27(1) (1993), 23–39.

Malanczuk, Peter. *Akekurst's Modern Introduction to International Law* (Abingdon: Routledge, 1997).

Malchow, Howard LeRoy. *History and International Relations. From the Ancient World to the 21st Century* (London: Bloomsbury, 2015).

Miéville, China. *Between Equal Rights. A Marxist Theory of International Law* (Leiden: Brill, 2005).

Mitchell, Stephen. 'The Treaty between Rome and Lycia', in *Papyri Graecae Schøyen I* (Papyrologica Florentina, 35), ed. Rosario Pintaudi (Florence: Gonnelli, 2005), 163–258.

Moncayo, Guillermo, Raúl E. Vinuesa and Hortensia D.T. Gutiérrez Posse. *Derecho internacional público*, vol. 1 (Buenos Aires: Zavalia, 1997).

Morris, Iian. 'Greek Multicity States', in *The Oxford Handbook of the State in the Ancient Near East and Mediterranean*, eds. Peter Fibiger Bang and Walter Scheidel (Oxford: Oxford University Press, 2013), 279–303.

Müllerson, Rein A. *Ordering Anarchy: International Law in International Society* (Leiden: Martinus Nijhoff, 2000).

Neff, Stephen C. *Justice among Nations. A History of International Law* (Cambridge: Harvard University Press, 2014).

Oakeshott, Michael. *On Human Conduct* (Oxford: Oxford University Press, 1991).

Orford, Anne. *International Law and Its Others* (Cambridge: Cambridge University Press, 2006).

Osiander, Andreas. 'Sovereignty, International Relations, and the Westphalian Myth'. *International Organization* 55(2) (2001), 251–287.

Phillipson, Coleman. *The International Law and Custom of Ancient Greece and Rome* (London: Macmillan, 1911).

Pinto, Monica. *El derecho internacional. Vigencias y desafíos en un escenario globalizado* (Buenos Aires: Fondo de Cultura Económica, 2004).

Rajagopal, Balakrishnan. *International Law from Below* (Cambridge: Cambridge University Press, 2003).

Remiro Brotons, Antonio. *Derecho internacional: Curso general* (Valencia: Tirant Lo Blanch, 9th ed. 2010).

Renaut, Marie-Hélène. *Histoire du droit international public* (Paris: Ellipses, 2007).

Reynolds, Joyce. *Aphrodisias and Rome* (London: The Society for the Promotion of Roman Studies, 1982).

Roberts, Anthea. *Is International Law International?* (Oxford: Oxford University Press, 2017).

Shaw, Malcolm N. *International Law* (Cambridge: Cambridge University Press, 5th ed. 2003).

Sheets, George A. 'Conceptualizing International Law in Thucydides'. *American Journal of Philology* 115(1) (1994), 51–73.

Sherk, Robert K., ed. *Roman Documents from the Greek East* (Baltimore: Johns Hopkins Press, 1969).

Simpson, Gerry. *Great Powers and Outlaw States. Unequal Sovereigns in the International Legal Order* (Cambridge: Cambridge University Press, 2004).

Simpson, Gerry. 'International Law in Diplomatic History', in *The Cambridge Companion to International Law*, eds. James Crawford and Martti Koskenniemi (Cambridge: Cambridge University Press, 2012), 25–46.

Slomason, William R. *Fundamental Perspectives on International Law* (Boston: Wadsworth Cengage Learning, 2011).

Sørensen, Max. *Manual of Public International Law* (London/New York: Macmillan/St. Martin's Press, 1968).

Tasioulas, John. 'The Legitimacy of International Law', in *The Philosophy of International Law*, eds. Samantha Besson and John Tasioulas (Oxford: Oxford University Press, 2010), 97–116.

Täubler, Eugen. *Imperium Romanum. Studien zur Entwickelungsgeschichte des römischen Reichs*, vol. 1 (Leipzig: Teubner, 1913).

Triantaphyllos, Diamantis. 'Symmakhia Romaion kai Maroniton', *Thrakike Epeteris* 4 (1983), 419–449.

Venzke, Ingo. *How Interpretation Makes International Law. On Semantic Change and Normative Twists* (Oxford: Oxford University Press, 2012).

Vos, Jan Anne. *The Function of Public International Law* (The Hague/Berlin: T.M.C. Asser Press/Springer, 2013).

Wallace, Rebecca M. M. *International Law* (London: Sweet & Maxwell, 4th ed. 2002).

Wolfke, Karol. *Great and Small Powers in International Law from 1814 to 1920 (From the Pre-History of the United Nations)* (Warsaw: Prace Wrociawskiego Towarzystwa Naukowego, 1961).

Zolo, Danilo. *La giustizia dei vincitori. Da norimberga a Baghdad* (Rome: Laterza, 2006).

CHAPTER 17

Taming Politics or Naïveté of Positivism in International Law?: Lassa Oppenheim and His Ascertainment of Customary International Law

Hirofumi Oguri

Abstract

Along with the 'turn to historiography' in international law, there has been a growing number of studies on the interaction between international law and history and its methodology as well as ongoing debate regarding the need to balance contextualism and anachronism. This chapter suggests that this dispute over methods (*Methodenstreit*) only concerns epistemic beliefs about the historical past, while all sides the share the understanding that positivistic methods of international law are marred by a naïve faith in the trajectories of state practices and treatises without due regard for their sources. With a case study of the identification of customary international law, it is argued that a well-equipped source criticism (*Quellenkritik*) is a possible way to reduce such 'naïveté'. Because the 'positivist' but *critical* focus on the sources are not inevitably naïve, there is no need to resort to an untamed 'politics' of history writing.

Keywords

Methodenstreit in international legal historiography – naïve positivism – Lassa Oppenheim – customary international law

1 Introduction: International Legal Historiography and Its Inevitable 'Political' Bias?

The so-called 'turn to historiography'[1] has inspired many international lawyers to engage in historiographies to intervene in the present by mobilising the

1 E.g., Galindo, George R. B. 'Martti Koskenniemi and the Historiographical Turn in International Law'. *European Journal of International Law* 16(3) (2005), 539–559; Craven, Matthew. 'Theorizing the Turn to History in International Law', in *The Oxford Handbook*

 | DOI:10.1163/9789004461802_019

knowledge of the past.[2] Along with this turn, international lawyers have begun to discuss how they should engage in historiographies.[3] Although the methodological debate has been presented that between contextualism and anachronism, as briefly summarised below, this chapter argues that these two strands of dispute over methods (*Methodenstreit*) ultimately come from researchers' *epistemic beliefs* about the historical past itself. The main objective of this chapter is to show that source criticism can tame 'politics' in doing history. It introduces a case study on custom-ascertainment in treatises and demonstrates that well-equipped source criticism is a possible way to tame politics in the historiographies of international law, irrespective of one's epistemic belief.

In terms of the 'methodology' addressing how scholars think about the historical past and thus about what and how they read,[4] there are mainly two strands of methodology. Janne Nijman, for instance, recently recalled that there is a '*Methodenstreit*' in terms of the interaction between history and theory. What Nijman sketched as a disagreement between 'history for history's sake' and 'history *as* mere theory' echoes a critique against anachronism as lacking a contextual reading of the past.[5] This presents a dichotomy between anachronism and contextualism in the methodological debate on international legal history.[6] Since 'doing history of thought is a profoundly hermeneutic exercise', it 'necessarily has a *subjective* element'.[7] In so far as historical knowledge as 'a usable past' is brought to bear in ongoing present controversies, history is necessarily 'political'.[8] Along this line, some international lawyers take the critical viewpoint that international legal history is a discourse, a particular

---

of the Theory of International Law, eds. Anne Orford and Florian Hoffman (Oxford: Oxford University Press, 2016), 21–37.

2 E.g., Dhondt, Frederik. 'Recent Research in the History of International Law'. *Tijdschrift voor Rechtsgeschiedenis* 84(1–2) (2016), 313–334, 313. Monographs published as part of the series 'The History and Theory of International Law' (Oxford University Press) are also a good example.

3 Craven, Matthew. 'Introduction: International Law and Its Histories', in *Time, History and International Law*, eds. Matthew Craven, Malgosia Fitzmaurice and Maria Vogiatzi (Leiden: Martinus Nijhoff, 2007), 1–25, 7.

4 Orford, Anne. 'On International Legal Method'. *London Review of International Law* 1 (2013), 166–197, 167.

5 Nijman, Janne. *Seeking Change by Doing History* (Amsterdam: Amsterdam University Press, 2018), 7–10.

6 Fitzmaurice, Andrew. 'Context in the History of International Law'. *Journal of the History of International Law* 20(1) (2018), 5–30; Benton, Lauren. 'Beyond Anachronism: Histories of International Law and Global Legal Politics'. *Journal of the History of International Law* 21(1) (2019), 1–34.

7 Nijman, *Seeking Change* 2018 (n. 5), 6.

8 Moyn, Samuel. 'Legal History as a Source of International Law: The Politics of Knowledge', in *The Oxford Handbook of the Sources of International Law*, eds. Samantha Besson and Jean d'Aspremont (Oxford: Oxford University Press, 2017), 301–319, 301–302.

way of understanding the world based on scholars' subjective and thus political choices. This is a typical example of anachronism, famously supported by Martti Koskenniemi[9] and Anne Orford.[10] Based on his standpoint that the past is indeterminate and thus historical narratives are aimed at 'a political act', Koskenniemi articulates that 'historical narrative liberates the political imagination to move more freely in the world of alternative choices, illuminating both its false necessities and false contingencies'.[11] Furthermore, Koskenniemi endorses anachronism when he argues about the limits of contextualism and proposes that we should choose and evaluate the past to develop a better understanding of today's world.[12]

This attitude originates from the intentions and objectives of international lawyers who aim to 'look at history because they need it to better understand current issues and trends'. As Randall Lesaffer summarises, the aim of this type of historiography 'is clearly not to understand what happened, but to give current ideas or practices roots in the distant past', and it can be evaluated in 'functional relation' to history.[13] Lesaffer, on the part of so-called contextualists, criticises this type of historiography as 'sins against methodology' and submits that this type 'describes history in terms of similarities with or differences from the present, and not in terms of what it was'.[14]

Against this critique by contextualists, anachronists respond that contextualists use 'the idea of "context" as a proxy for policing anachronism',[15] and the debate on methodology continues. As it is clear from the arguments of defenders of anachronism, they claim that international legal history is a discourse

---

9 Koskenniemi, Martti. *The Gentle Civilizer of Nations: The Rise and Fall of International Law 1870–1960* (Cambridge: Cambridge University Press, 2001), 10.

10 Orford, Anne. 'International Law and the Limits of History', in *The Law of International Lawyers: Reading Martti Koskenniemi*, eds. Wouter Werner, Marieke de Hoon and Alexis Galán (Cambridge: Cambridge University Press, 2017), 297–320, 302–303. See also, Orford, 'International Legal Method' 2013 (n. 4), 170–177. On Orford's defence of anachronism, see further Fitzmaurice, 'Context in the History' 2018 (n. 6), 8–12; Benton, 'Beyond Anachronism' 2019 (n. 6), 3–11.

11 Koskenniemi, Martti. 'The Politics of International Law – 20 Years Later'. *European Journal of International Law* 20(1) (2009), 7–19, 18.

12 Koskenniemi, Martti. 'Histories of International Law: Significance and Problems for a Critical View'. *Temple International and Comparative Law Journal* 27(2) (2013), 215–240, 230–232. On Koskenniemi's defence of anachronism, see also Fitzmaurice, 'Context in the History' 2018 (n. 6), 10–12.

13 Lesaffer, Randall. 'International Law and Its History: The Story of an Unrequited Love', in Craven/Fitzmaurice/Vogiatzi, *Time, History and International Law* 2007 (n. 3), 27–41, 33.

14 Ibid., 34–35.

15 Orford's own words, borrowing from the following article: Kemmerer, Alexandra. '"We Do Not Need to Always Look to Westphalia ...": A Conversation with Martti Koskenniemi and Anne Orford'. *Journal of the History of International Law* 17(1) (2015), 1–14, 10.

hinged on scholars' subjective and political choices. I refer to them as 'agnostics' who believe that the historical past is unknown and unknowable.[16] They are agnostics because they avoid seeking a neutral description of the past 'as it actually was' on the grounds that 'that sort of knowledge is not open to us'.[17] However, importantly, agnostics are criticised not for their intentions to use the historical past for the sake of present controversies but for their lack of proper respect for the past. Lesaffer describes this as follows:

> [W]hatever the intentions and purposes of the scholar studying the history of international law, he should approach the past with proper respect. This means that he should make use of the basic rules of historical methodology. In itself, there is nothing wrong with the desire to learn something useful for the present from the past, nor with evolutional history. But before one can learn something from the past other than what one knows from the present, one first has to let the past be the past – at least as far as this is humanly possible.[18]

What he argues here is an orthodox position that is widely shared by (legal) historians, which is based on the belief that one can approach the historical past through a careful reading of historical sources. However, as Lesaffer clearly states, scholars 'should make use of the basic rules of historical methodology' to approach the past. The rules are known as source criticism (*Quellenkritik*), and their origin is said to be in the German Historical School of the 19th century.[19] This approach is generally employed to verify the reliability of sources in terms of the authorship and the authenticity or corruption of the text.[20] Its principal aim is to evaluate the process by which sources are made and then to reveal the subjectivity of the observers. To uncover political intentions and context of the authors of the sources helps the observers espouse their less political meta-position; therefore *Quellenkritik* can serve to tame politics in historiographies in general. In terms of the establishment of the meanings

16 I owe this label of 'agnostics' to the following book: Akashi, Kinji. *Fukashi no 'kokusaihō': Hobbuzu, Raipunittsu, Rusō no kanōsei* [*Doctrinae invisibiles juris gentium: Hobbes, Leibniz et Rousseau*] (Tokyo: Keio University Press, 2019), 17–18, fn. 6.

17 Koskenniemi, *Gentle Civilizer* 2001 (n. 9), 10.

18 Lesaffer, 'International Law and Its History' 2007 (n. 13), 37.

19 See, e.g., Lorenz, Chris. 'History: Theories and Methods', in *International Encyclopedia of the Social & Behavioral Sciences*, vol. 11, ed. James Wright (Amsterdam: Elsevier Science, 2nd ed. 2015), 132–133.

20 See, e.g., Müller, Philipp. 'Understanding History: Hermeneutics and Source-Criticism', in *Reading Primary Sources: The Interpretation of Texts from Nineteenth- and Twentieth-Century History*, eds. Miriam Dobson and Benjamin Ziemann (Abingdon: Routledge, 2009), 21–36.

of historical sources, source criticism amounts to what Lesaffer calls 'the textual and contextual analysis', by which historians should 'see to it that their sources are as authentic as possible, try to read them as the contemporaries of the authors would' and 'relate them to the contexts and the concerns of the authors'.[21]

It should be noted, however, that historical works will simply follow a path based on 'naïve faith' in state practices and doctrines embedded in treatises without due regard for their context if they lack the 'proper respect' for the past.[22] This chapter identifies such an epistemic belief in the historical past as 'naïve positivism', which lies at the opposite end of the spectrum from agnosticism. Such a perspective is 'naïve' because those who fail to give due regard to contexts ignore the basic rules of historical methodology with which they can verify the reliability of sources. In other words, they are 'naïve' by not utilising the basic rules to analyse primary sources. They are then subject to 'politics'. 'Politics' here refers to the idea that historiography is inevitably subjective because of the observer's choice of events he or she analyses and the way in which he or she narrates them. This understanding of 'politics' typically underlies the agnostics' statements as shown above,[23] and is also shared by those who do not consider themselves agnostics.[24]

Although the merit of labelling these observers' bias as 'politics' per se deserves further discussion, for the sake of argument here, both strands of the *Methodenstreit* admit that doing history is subject to the observer's choice, or, put differently, the observer's 'naïveté'. The point of disagreement between the two strands is that one side accepts the subjectivism of agents as a given and calls for anachronism with an agnostic attitude towards the past, while the other side utilises certain procedures to minimise subjectivism and for exploring a more neutral understanding of the past.

Against these backdrops, this chapter aims to show that well-equipped *Quellenkritik* is a possible way to tame politics in the historiographies of international law. Political bias has been omnipresent in international law, and it has appeared specifically when treatise-writers identify customary rules of

21 Lesaffer, 'International Law and Its History' 2007 (n. 13), 38.

22 Yanagihara, Masaharu. *Vorufu no kokusaihō riron* [*The Theory of International Law of Christian Wolff*] (Tokyo: Yūhikaku, 1998), 4–5. See also Yanagihara, Masaharu. 'Significance of the History of the Law of Nations in Europe and East Asia'. *Recueil des cours de l'academie de droit international de La Haye* 371 (2015), 273–435, 419.

23 Orford, 'Limits of History' 2017 (n. 10), 311.

24 E.g., Skouteris, Thomas. 'Engaging History in International Law', in *New Approaches to International Law*, eds. José María Beneyto and David Kennedy (The Hague: T.M.C. Asser Press, 2012), 99–121, 106; Craven, 'Theorizing the Turn to History' 2016 (n. 1), 35.

international law from the relevant practices of states. Early in the last century, Lassa Oppenheim was aware of this when he articulated the tasks and methods of international lawyers, although he has been considered to have political bias in favour of Great Britain.[25] Section 2 of this chapter revisits early takes by Oppenheim to facilitate the understanding that positivism includes the risk of 'naïveté' and explains why this paper deems Oppenheim a good example for a case study. Then, section 3 introduces a case study regarding whether there was a general custom that coastal fishing boats enjoyed immunity from attack and seizure, which Great Britain did not recognise. The case study shows that description of the past as what it really was easily fails without analyses of primary sources in light of textual and contextual meaning. Finally, section 4 provides concluding thoughts.

2 Oppenheim and His 'Wholly Positive and Impartial' Method of the Science of International Law

As it is well known, Lassa Oppenheim, one of the eminent international lawyers at the beginning of the 20th century, contributed to the establishment of the tasks that international lawyers should address and noted the necessity of historical research in the 'science' of international law.[26] Oppenheim called attention to mistakes by treatise-writers that are influenced by their political preferences and reiterated the importance of ideal impartiality, specifically in case of custom-ascertainment. Some studies, however, have attempted to uncover his political bias in the description of customary law pursuant to English practices. Before introducing a case study, this section outlines what Oppenheim deemed as the ideal for the ascertainment of custom (**2.1**), then reviews some critics against Oppenheim (**2.2**).

2.1 *The Role of Historical Studies in International Legal Scholarship*

In an article published in 1908, Oppenheim illustrates the first and chief task for international lawyers: the exposition of the existing recognised rules of international law. However, Oppenheim admits that there is a historical task for scholarship because this task 'is often to a certain extent impossible

25 For details, see infra 2.2.

26 'Science' as used here means a department of systematised knowledge as an object of study. For Oppenheim, to establish international legal scholarship as 'science (Wissenschaft)', it must become wholly positive, impartial and international. Oppenheim, Lassa. 'Die Zukunft des Völkerrechts', in *Festschrift für Karl Binding zum 4. Juni 1911*, vol. 1 (Leipzig: Verlag von Wilhelm Engelmann, 1911), 140–201, 192.

without a knowledge of the history of the rules concerned'.[27] After he identifies the role of history in the science of international law, Oppenheim argues for the need to establish a 'wholly positive and impartial (ganz positiv und unparteiisch)' method to be adopted by international lawyers.[28] In introducing what constitutes 'positive' methods of international law, Oppenheim questions 'what appreciation is due to authoritative writers on international law', and he emphasises that 'it is quite common to make improper use of so-called authorities and to overestimate the value and importance of the mass of the literature on international law'.[29] Because of the absence of international courts at that time, as Oppenheim puts it, the roles played by publicists are important 'with regard to the question whether a certain rule of international law is or is not in existence, and what is its scope, its extent, and its proper meaning'.[30]

Oppenheim notes, however, that 'ultimately it is not the authoritative assertion of a writer which decides the question, but the fact that it can be proved that the rule is really recognized and followed in practice to the extent and with the scope and meaning as asserted by the writer concerned'.[31] For him, even great authorities make mistakes because they 'are influenced by their political fancies' and 'confound their own opinion with what is generally recognized', and some rules are 'mere book-rules, fancies of their authors, but not recognized rules of international law'.[32]

Oppenheim also submits that, regardless of what authorities assert about the existing customary international law, 'great care is necessary in positively verifying its existence, contents, scope, and real meaning'. In this process, customs must be carefully distinguished from mere usage, and the question of whether a custom is universal or only general should be considered with great care.[33] Oppenheim then maintains the following:

> [t]ext-book writers mostly overlook that there are scores of rules which are customarily recognized, although one or more individual states refuse to recognize them. The fact is that these rules are based upon a *general* custom only, whereas others are based on a *universal* custom and

---

27 Oppenheim, Lassa. 'The Science of International Law: Its Task and Method'. *American Journal of International Law* 2(2) (1908), 313–356, 315–316.

28 Oppenheim, 'Zukunft' 1911 (n. 26), 192. For an English translation, see Oppenheim, Lassa. *The Future of International Law* (Oxford: Clarendon Press, 1921), 56.

29 Oppenheim, 'The Science of International Law' 1908 (n. 27), 344.

30 Ibid., 345.

31 Ibid.

32 Ibid., 345–346.

33 Ibid., 346.

> are therefore recognized by every member of the family of nations. Take, for instance, the rule that fishing boats belonging to enemy subjects can not be attacked and seized by a belligerent. That this rule is based on a general custom, there is no doubt. But the custom is not universal. *The fact that Great Britain has never recognized it prevented the rule from being universally recognized before the Second Hague Peace Conference.*[34]

The same remark is included in his treatise on the laws of war, which was first published in 1906. Here, Oppenheim describes historical development of the rule as follows:

> Already in the sixteenth century treaties were concluded between single States stipulating such immunity to each other's fishing-boats for the time of war. But throughout the seventeenth and eighteenth centuries there are instances enough of a contrary practice, and Lord Stowell refused to recognise in strict law any such exemption, although he recognised a rule of comity to that extent. Great Britain has hitherto always taken the standpoint that any immunity granted by her to fishing-boats was a relaxation of strict right in the interest of humanity, but revocable at any moment, and that her cruisers were justified in seizing enemy fishing boats unless prevented therefrom by special instructions on the part of the Admiralty.[35]

Although Oppenheim declared in the preface of the treatise that he 'tried to write this volume in a truly international spirit, neither taking any one nation's part nor denouncing any other',[36] this passage shows the historical development of the alleged customary rules with a great emphasis on British practice.

2.2 *Oppenheim's Politics: Biased in Favour of Britain?*

With regard to this prima facie contradiction between his ideal impartiality and his description of customary law, some studies have questioned whether Oppenheim had a political bias or, to put it more precisely, whether he emphasised English practices when he explained customary rules. A recent statement that 'the political Oppenheim [is identified] as British'[37] is a good example,

34 Ibid. (emphasis added).

35 Oppenheim, Lassa. *International Law: A Treatise*, vol. 2 (London: Longmans, Green and Co., 1906), 193 (citations omitted).

36 Ibid., vii.

37 García-Salmones Rovira, Mónica. *The Project of Positivism in International Law* (Oxford: Oxford University Press, 2013), 51. Her evaluation seems to be based on studies by Kingsbury and Schmoeckel.

but this view was already expressed by Benedict Kingsbury, who identifies Oppenheim's bias in favour of Britain in the treatment of the question of the balance of power that constituted one of his five 'morals'.[38] For Oppenheim, these morals were deduced from his observation of the history of international law, but Kingsbury considers them what Oppenheim believed to be 'political conditions for the effective international law'.[39] In a similar vein, Amanda Perreau-Saussine identifies Oppenheim's morals with his utopian ideals and calls him a 'noble liar' who makes 'a *political* claim which he knows is untrue'.[40] The argument that these two commentators have in common is that Oppenheim, as one of the inaugurators of international legal positivism with a strong insistence on the separation of legal claims from moral ones, offered his accounts of international law based on what he believed were ideals for international law. Although these are important interventions in light of what 'positivism' means in the international legal scholarship, for the sake of argument in this chapter, it is more helpful to elaborate an historical study to which both critiques refer.

An article by Mathias Schmoeckel analyses in depth Oppenheim's interpretation of the rules of naval warfare 'to test Oppenheim's national partiality'.[41] Schmoeckel notes the destruction of enemy private vessels and the problem of armed merchantman and then describes how Oppenheim supported the position of Britain when he wrote about these customs. After showing how Oppenheim supported the British view on these rules, however, Schmoeckel rather expresses the modest opinion that Oppenheim's bias was 'faint' and even concludes that 'it cannot be denied that Oppenheim tried hard to be true to his ideal of impartiality, and therein was fairly successful'.[42] To support his

38 Oppenheim, Lassa. *International Law: A Treatise*, vol. 1 (London: Longmans, Green and Co., 1905), 73–76.

39 Kingsbury, Benedict. 'Legal Positivism as Normative Politics: International Society, Balance of Power and Lassa Oppenheim's Positive International Law'. *European Journal of International Law* 13(2) (2002), 401–436, 403.

40 Perreau-Saussine, Amanda. 'Three Ways of Writing a Treatise on Public International Law', in *The Nature of Customary Law*, eds. Amanda Perreau-Saussine and James Bernard Murphy (Cambridge: Cambridge University Press, 2007), 228–255, 250. See also Perreau-Saussine, Amanda. 'A Case Study on Jurisprudence as a Source of International Law: Oppenheim's Influence', in Craven/Fitzmaurice/Vogiatzi, *Time, History and International Law* 2007 (n. 3), 91–117.

41 Schmoeckel, Mathias. 'The Story of Success: Lassa Oppenheim and his "International Law"', in *East Asian and European Perspectives on International Law*, eds. Michael Stolleis and Masaharu Yanagihara (Baden-Baden: Nomos, 2004), 57–138, 75.

42 Ibid., 81.

conclusion, Schmoeckel notes that Oppenheim was 'rather cautious' in his treatise compared with the 'one-sidedness' he clearly showed in other articles. Schmoeckel also mentions the impossibility 'to remain indifferent and impartial in all respects' in the field of law of warfare.[43] However, these two reasons apparently do not fully support his opinion that Oppenheim's bias was faint; moreover, the second reason spoils his initial aim 'to test Oppenheim's national partiality'. This is why there remains room for elaborating the alleged partiality of Oppenheim, even though Schmoeckel submits that Oppenheim *did* support the position of Britain for certain rules of customary international law.

If we recall the epistemic beliefs on the past shown in the previous section, it can be argued that Oppenheim's political bias reflects his naïveté.[44] These critiques against the naïveté of positivism drive agnostics to develop their belief that doing history always involves the subjective and thus political viewpoint of observers. For the sake of argument developed here, we should take these doubts seriously and persuade agnostics to take part in 'a circle' in which all participants attempt to reach an intersubjective understanding about the historical past *correctly*, if not *truly*.[45] However, before we pursue the analysis of Oppenheim further, it should be mentioned that the identification of specific customary rules involves the past[46] and entails 'politics' because the process always involves the selectivity of state practices.[47] This political character remains the same regardless of whether the (non-)existence of customs is judged by judicial organs, state authorities or publicists. This chapter does not propose that there is a certain approach to apolitically identify customs. Rather, it submits that a well-equipped source criticism can make the historiography more neutral. To put it differently, it is argued here that there is a way to tame the politics of the historiography that is shown as Oppenheim's naïveté. Next, a case study is introduced to elaborate whether source criticism is useful to tame politics and naïveté in the historiography of international law.

---

43 Ibid.

44 This 'naïveté' is not the case only with Oppenheim but with positivist international lawyers in general because it is difficult to establish 'the purely positivist method in international Law'. Akashi, Kinji. *Cornelius van Bynkershoek: His Role in the History of International Law* (Alphen aan den Rijn: Kluwer Law International, 1998), 176–177.

45 Bevir, Mark. 'Objectivity in History'. *History and Theory* 33(3) (1994), 328–344, 332. Cf. Skouteris, 'Engaging History' 2012 (n. 24), 117.

46 Lesaffer, 'International Law and Its History' 2007 (n. 13), 29.

47 Cf. Carty, Anthony. *The Decay of International Law: A Reappraisal of the Limits of Legal Imagination in International Affairs* (Manchester: Manchester University Press, 1986), 30–35.

3 The Exemption from Seizure of Vessels Used Exclusively for Fishing along the Coast: A Case Study

As noted above, this chapter takes the following example from Oppenheim's statement: there was a general custom that coastal fishing boats enjoyed immunity from attack and seizure; however, Great Britain did not recognise it.[48] In his treatise, Oppenheim showed the opposing view of Great Britain against immunity by employing the following three statements: (i) a judgement of Lord Stowell in *Young Jacob and Joanna* that immunity is not a rule but a comity; (ii) citing William Edward Hall's treatise, Great Britain's view is that immunity is granted by a relaxation of a strict right in the interest of humanity and is thus revocable at any moment; and (iii) referring to some practices of government, citing a monograph of Thomas Erskine Holland. Here, apart from the authenticity of the text, Oppenheim's statements are examined.[49] In light of source criticism, two steps should be followed: (i) to examine the contents of the sources to which Oppenheim referred and their relevance to his arguments (**3.1**) and (ii) to see how Oppenheim's contemporaries described immunity and to identify the contexts (**3.2**).

3.1 *Textual Analysis*

We should examine three statements employed by Oppenheim to support the British view of immunity. First, with regard to a judgement of Lord Stowell in *Young Jacob and Joanna* in November 1798, this was the case of a small Dutch fishing vessel that was taken in April 1798, during the French Revolutionary Wars, on her return from the Dogger Bank to Holland. Lord Stowell opened his verdict by stating that immunity was 'a rule of comity only, and not of legal decision'.[50] According to Stowell, 'it has prevailed from views of mutual accommodation between neighbouring countries, and from tenderness to a poor and industrious order of people'.[51]

As Stowell continued, however, he presumed that there had been sufficient reason for changing this mode of treatment in that war, and the vessel should be captured because such boats were 'constantly and exclusively employed in the enemy's trade'.[52] Obviously, Oppenheim was right to cite this decision to

48 Oppenheim, 'The Science of International Law' 1908 (n. 27), 346.

49 Oppenheim, *International Law* 1906 (n. 35), 193.

50 Robinson, Christopher. *Reports of Cases Argued and Determined in the High Court of Admiralty: Commencing with the Judgments of the Right Hon. Sir William Scott, Michaelmas Term 1798*, vol. 1 (London: Strahan, 1799), 20–21.

51 Ibid., 21.

52 Ibid.

establish that immunity was a rule of comity rather than a rule of law, and indeed, some treatises also invoked Lord Stowell's opinion.[53] It can be argued, however, whether a single legal case suffices to formulate the government's view on immunity. It is so argued not only because nearly one hundred years had passed since the judgement was handed down when Oppenheim cited it in his treatise, but an English publicist cast doubt on the judgement, as is considered below.

Second, we must examine the nature of immunity. Oppenheim alleged that immunity was a rule of comity, which was 'a relaxation of strict right in the interest of humanity'. Here, Oppenheim cites the following passage from Hall's treatise:

> Throughout that war [the War of American Independence] and in the beginning of the revolutionary wars both parties [France and England] refrained from disturbing the home fisheries, but the English government in 1800 distinctly stated that in its view the liberty of fishing was a relaxation of strict right made in the interests of humanity, and revocable at any moment for sufficient reasons of war.[54]

Although Hall did not present the primary source that supported his statement, the evidence seems to have been found in a series of correspondence between Great Britain and France collected by Georg Friedrich von Martens, called the 'Actes entre la Gr. Bretagne et la France, touchant l'exemption de saisie pour les vaisseaux pêcheurs', among which one passage reported as follows:

> Je dois vous faire part, citoyen, d'un avis que le ministre a transmis en ce port d'après une explication qui a eu lieu avec le gouvernement anglois, au sujet de la liberté de la pêche, par l'entremise du citoyen Otto, commissaire françois à Londres pour l'échange des prisonniers de guerre. Il paroit que le gouvernement anglois entend: 1) Que *la liberté de la pêche n'est aucunement fondée sur une convention, mais sur une simple concession de sa part*, qui fut provoquée par l'appel fait en dernier lieu à l'humanité du ministère britannique et de la nation entière, et que cette concession sera toujours subordonnée à la convenance du moment.[55]

53 See infra notes 63, 65, 71–73.

54 Hall, William Edward. *A Treatise on International Law* (Oxford: Clarendon Press, 3rd ed. 1890), 449.

55 'Le chef d'administration au sous-commissaire de marine aux sables'. *Recueil des principaux traités d'alliance, de paix, de trêve, de neutralité, de commerce, de limites, d'échange etc.: Conclus par les puissances de l'Europe tant entre elles qu'avec les puissances et etats*

It can be observed from the source that Great Britain expressed the same opinion as Lord Stowell, although the direct evidence for 'a relaxation of strict right' is not found.[56]

The third proposition was that the cruisers of the British government were justified in seizing enemy fishing boats unless prevented from doing so by special instructions from the Admiralty. Here, Oppenheim referred to Holland's monograph on prize law, which provided that '[s]hips engaged exclusively on a voyage of Scientific Discovery are usually exempt from Detention; as may be, though only under special instructions, boats engaged in coast fisheries'.[57] Holland cited the last part of this quote, in which reference was made to *Young Jacob and Joanna*. Therefore, the same conclusions were drawn from the third proposition as were drawn from the first.

3.2 *Contextual Analysis*

Now and finally, let us move on to the second stage to compare what Oppenheim wrote regarding its context. It is of great use to refer to Oppenheim's contemporary elaborations and to contextualise his statement about the customary status of immunity. In his treatise, Oppenheim listed many textbooks as well as articles and monographs on the matter. In referencing the treatises (approximately 20),[58] it is first observed that British writers[59] such as Hall[60] and Thomas Joseph Lawrence[61] were of the opinion that the immunity enjoyed by coastal fishing vessels was not a legal obligation but merely a rule of comity based on humanity.

---

dans d'autres parties du monde depuis 1761 jusqu'à present, vol. VI, ed. Georg Friedrich von Martens (Gottingue: Dieterich, 2nd ed. 1829), 514 (emphasis added).

56 For confirmation of the relevance of the source cited here for Hall's argument about 'the relaxation of strict right', see Ortolan, Théodore. *Règles internationales et diplomatie de la mer*, vol. II (Paris: Plon, 4th ed. 1856), 53–54. Both Ortolan's text and Martens's *Recueil* were cited in the opinion of the United States Supreme Court in *The Paquete Habana*, 175 U.S. 677 (1900), 692–693.

57 Holland, Thomas Erskine. *A Manual of Naval Prize Law* (London: Darling & Son, 1888), 12.

58 Oppenheim, *International Law* 1906 (n. 35), 187.

59 Oppenheim referred to the treatises of Robert Phillimore and Travers Twiss; however, to the best of the author's knowledge, they wrote nothing about immunity. Phillimore, Robert. *Commentaries upon International Law*, vol. III (London: Butterworths, 3rd ed. 1885), para. 347; Twiss, Travers. *The Law of Nations Considered as Independent Political Communities: On the Rights and Duties of Nations in Time of War* (Oxford/London: Clarendon Press/Longmans, Green and Co., 2nd ed. 1875), para. 73.

60 Hall, *A Treatise* 1890 (n. 54), 450.

61 Lawrence, Thomas Joseph. *The Principles of International Law* (Boston: D. C. Heath & Co., Publishers, 3rd ed. 1904), 383–385.

To understand the context, the following points should be noted. First, soon after having made the assertions presented in the above quote, Hall continued as follows:

> England does not seem to have been unwilling to spare fishing-vessels so long as they are harmless, and it does not appear that any state has accorded them immunity under circumstances of inconvenience to itself. It is likely that all nations would now refrain from molesting them as a general rule, and would capture them as soon as any danger arose that they or their crews might be of military use to the enemy; and it is also likely that it is impossible to grant them a more distinct exemption.[62]

Lawrence expressed the same view as Hall after stating that immunity is a comity only by reference to the opinion of Lord Stowell.[63] Second, even in Britain, there were two exceptions to the view that immunity was not a rule of international law. One was by Thomas Alfred Walker, who admitted that immunity was established as *a rule of international law* by the general consent of states.[64] Another exception was John Westlake, whose treatise was published in 1907, which means that Oppenheim could not have read it when he prepared his textbook. However, this exception helps us assess the judgement made by Lord Stowell because Westlake cautioned about 'the extreme sensitiveness which he [Lord Stowell] always showed about his position relatively to the government'. Westlake held a sceptical view against immunity as a mere comity and therefore maintained that immunity is a rule 'of international law in the only true sense, namely, that the conscience of our international society demands it and that it is observed'.[65]

By consulting the rest of the treatises, it is easily observed that almost all the writers from other states were of the opinion that immunity was established as a customary rule of international law, which we can find, for instance, in

62 Hall, *A Treatise* 1890 (n. 54), 450.

63 Lawrence, *The Principles* 1904 (n. 61), 383.

64 Walker, Thomas Alfred. *A Manual of Public International Law* (Cambridge: Cambridge University Press, 1895), 147.

65 Westlake, John. *International Law*, vol. 2 (Cambridge: Cambridge University Press, 1907), 137–138.

American,[66] German,[67] French[68] and other writers, such as Alphonse Rivier[69] and Charles Calvo.[70] Among them, Scherston Baker,[71] Hannis Taylor[72] and Calvo[73] paid attention to Great Britain's opposition to immunity and described its legal status in well-balanced ways. Regarding other monographs on prize law, the same attitude can be seen, for instance, in Ferdinand von Perels's monograph.[74]

Furthermore, in terms of the diverse conceptions of the nature of custom in that period,[75] it is observed that some treatise writers did not regard immunity as a rule of international law in light of their conceptual apparatus of custom and international law itself. To provide a few examples, Ortolan submitted that immunity was not so general as to create 'une règle internationale absolue'.[76]

66 Wharton, Francis. *A Digest of the International Law of the United States: Taken from Documents Issued by Presidents and Secretaries of State, and from Decisions of Federal Courts and Opinions of Attorneys-General*, vol. III (Washington: Government Printing Office, 2nd ed. 1887), 316–317; Baker, Scherston. *Halleck's International Law or Rules Regulating the Intercourse of States in Peace and War*, vol. II (London: K. Paul, Trench, Trübner & Co., 3rd ed. 1893), 106–107; Taylor, Hannis. *A Treatise on International Public Law* (Chicago: Callaghan & Company, 1901), 558–559.

67 Bluntschli, Johann Caspar. *Das moderne Völkerrecht der civilisirten Staten als Rechtsbuch dargestellt* (Nördlingen: C. H. Beck, 1878), 377; Heffter, August Wilhelm. *Europäische Völkerrecht der Gegenwart* (Berlin: H. W. Müller, 8th ed. 1888), 299.

68 Despagnet, Frantz. *Cours de droit international public* (Paris: L. Larose, 2nd ed. 1899), 672–673; Nys, Ernest. *Le droit international: Les principes, les théories, les faits*, vol. 3 (Bruxelles/Paris: A. Castaigne/A. Fontemoing, 1906), 467–473; Bonfils, Henry. *Manuel de droit international public* (Paris: Librairie Arthur Rousseau, 4th ed. 1905), 735–737; Pradier-Fodéré, Paul. *Traité de droit international public Européen et Américain: Suivant les progrès de la science et de la pratique contemporaines*, vol. 8 (Paris: A. Pedone, 1906), 520–524.

69 Rivier, Alphonse. *Principes du Droit des Gens*, vol. 2 (Paris: Librairie Nouvelle de Droit et de Jurisprudence, 1896), 338.

70 Calvo, Charles. *Le droit international: Théorique et pratique, précédé d'un exposé historique des progrès de la science du droit des gens*, vol. IV (Paris: Librairie nouvelle de droit et de jurisprudence, 5th ed. 1896), 325–327.

71 Baker, *Halleck's International Law* 1893 (n. 66), 107.

72 Taylor, *A Treatise* 1901 (n. 66), 559.

73 Calvo, *Le droit international* 1896 (n. 70), 325–327.

74 Perels, Ferdinand von. *Das internationale öffentliche Seerecht der Gegenwart* (Berlin: Ernst Mittler, 2nd ed. 1903), 201–202.

75 For detailed observations on a variety of understandings of custom in general, see Mokre, Hans. *Theorie des Gewohnheitsrechts: Problementwicklung und System* (Berlin: Springer, 1932); Guggenheim, Paul. 'Contribution à l'histoire des sources du droit des gens'. *Recueil des cours de l'academie de droit international de La Haye* 94 (1958), 37–53.

76 Ortolan, *Règles Internationales* 1856 (n. 56), 55. The same remark can be found in Paul Pradier-Fodéré, who argued that immunity was not universal but mere custom 'inspirée

In the same vein, Charles de Boeck argued that immunity was a mere custom that was not established as a rule of positive international law because Great Britain did not endorse it, which means that de Boeck presupposed the rules of international law as universally applicable.[77]

As can be clearly understood from the arguments outlined above, whilst some British jurists, apparently based on the opinion of Lord Stowell, regarded immunity as a rule of comity and denied its legal character, in Oppenheim's contemporaneous views, immunity was identified as a custom, although it depended on the underlying conceptual presuppositions of customs and international law itself. What about the state practices that are relevant for immunity? Hall and Lawrence, who were of the opinion that immunity was not a legal obligation, noted that Great Britain indeed granted immunity, and it can be observed that the immunity of coastal fisheries vessels was *general* in practice. This was the exact reason why many publicists stated that immunity was established as a customary rule of international law, not as a mere comity.

This is also observed in the following case law. In *The Paquete Habana and The Lora*, which was filed in the US Supreme Court seven years before Oppenheim published his treatise, Justice Gray scrutinised many relevant state practices to identify whether immunity was established as a rule of international law, such as French custom, English conduct in the Crimean War and Japanese policy during the Sino-Japanese War.[78] With a detailed examination of the writings of contemporary jurists, Justice Gray decided that the 'the review of the precedents and the authorities on the subject appears to us abundantly to demonstrate' that immunity was 'an established rule of international law' 'by the general consent of the civilized nations of the world'.[79] In his opinion, Justice Gray reviewed Hall and Lawrence, extracted from the same pages cited by Oppenheim, and he took note that those two English text writers admitted 'little real difference in the views, or in practice, of England and of other maritime nations'.[80] Justice Gray thereby came to the opposite conclusion from that set forth by Oppenheim in his treatise: immunity was established as a rule of international law, not of comity.

---

par des raisons d'humanité'. Pradier-Fodéré, *Traité de droit international public* 1906 (n. 68), 522–524. Antoine Pillet, in contrast, admitted that Great Britain was not in conformity with immunity but claimed that immunity was a 'veritable coutume internationale'. Pillet, Antoine. *Les lois actuelles de la guerre* (Paris: A. Rousseau, 2nd ed. 1901), 128.

77 Boeck, Charles de. *De la propriété privée ennemie sous pavillon ennemi* (Paris: Durand et Pedone-Lauriel, 1882), 216–224.

78 US Supreme Court, *The Paquete Habana* (n. 56), 694–700.

79 Ibid., 708.

80 Ibid., 705.

It should further be noted that the opinion of Justice Gray was dissented by Chief Justice Fuller together with Justices John Marshall Harlan and Joseph McKenna. The dissenting opinion, by reference to the judgement of Lord Stowell and Hall's treatise, held that 'it is difficult to conceive of a law of the sea of universal obligation to which Great Britain has not acceded'.[81] In addition, Justice Fuller argued that 'it is needless to review the speculations and repetitions of the writers on international law', simply mentioning Ortolan and de Boeck, who considered immunity not to be an absolute international rule, in addition to Heffter and Calvo, who regarded it as a rule of international law, and with the following reason alone: '[t]heir lucubrations may be persuasive, but are not authoritative'.[82] Here, it is observed that Chief Justice Fuller responded in the same vein engaged by Oppenheim.

4 Concluding Remarks

Although the different judges consulted approximately the same materials, what divided their conclusions about immunity? It can be answered that it was their *Quellenkritik*, by which they analysed their sources textually and contextually. Justice Gray devoted nearly two-thirds of the opinion to the review of the precedents and the teachings of publicists and therefore aimed to verify the rational understanding of the legal status of immunity. Chief Justice Fuller, in contrast, did not develop his arguments using authorities, let alone in convincing manners. For Oppenheim, he failed to mention what Hall and Lawrence wrote about immunity, and in this regard, he *did* make the 'improper use of the authority' against which he cautioned. As Justice Gray held by reference to Hall and Lawrence that there was little real difference between England and other maritime states, immunity was finally codified at the Second Peace Conference held in The Hague in 1907, without an objection from the British government.[83] Accordingly, Oppenheim followed his government's approval

81 Ibid., 719.

82 Ibid., 720.

83 At the conference, immunity was proposed by the Belgian delegate, and this proposal was further elaborated by the Portuguese delegate. According to Henri Fromageot, who served as a Rapporteur at the committee in charge of the matter, 'cette pratique est universellement approuvée'. 'Rapport de M. Fromageot, Rapport général à la conférence sur les travaux de la quatrième commission', in *Deuxième Conférence Internationale de la Paix. La Haye, 15 Juin – 18 Octobre 1907. Actes et documents*, vol. 1, ed. Le Ministère des Affaires Étrangères des Pays-Bas (La Haye: Imprimerie Nationale, 1907), 269–270.

of immunity in his second edition published in 1912[84] and admitted it as 'a universal custom' in his later article[85] in accordance with his 'positive' method, which clearly shows his naïveté.

At the same time, it should be noted that these differences have much to do with the linkage between the methods adopted by international lawyers and their conceptions of custom (and international law). With positivistic methods such as those adopted by Oppenheim, some jurists have theorised customs in different ways. For instance, there was a presupposition that customs are general or universal international law based on objective constructions that facilitate comprehension of the world and that proceed not only from the will of states but also from transcendental elements, such as natural law, reason and the international community.[86] Others, still pursuing natural law with an objectivist foundation, constructed customs in the same manner as Oppenheim and refused their general / universal validity because there was no need to invoke customs to establish the general / universal validity of rules that could be supported by natural law in their conceptual apparatus. These examples illustrate that customs were not considered rules of international law for some international lawyers.[87] For Oppenheim, the immunity is not a *universal* but a *general* custom except for Britain. In light of their conceptual settings, it should be highlighted that Oppenheim endorsed the legal character of immunity irrespective of the fact that the immunity was initially developed as a mere comity, whilst Chief Justice Fuller denied its legal nature at all.

---

84 Oppenheim, Lassa. *International Law: A Treatise*, vol. 2 (London: Longmans, Green and Co., 2nd ed. 1912), 234.

85 Oppenheim, Lassa. 'Zur Lehre vom internationalen Gewohnheitsrecht'. *Niemeyers Zeitschrift für internationales Recht* 25 (1915), 6.

86 On the dichotomy between objectivism and subjectivism here, see Weil, Prosper. 'Le droit international en quête de son identité'. *Recueil des cours de l'academie de droit international de La Haye* 237 (1992), 66–81; Bernstorff, Jochen von. *Der Glaube an das universale Recht. Zur Völkerrechtstheorie Hans Kelsens und seiner Schüler* (Baden-Baden: Nomos, 2001), 13–37.

87 This shows the need to reappraise the doctrines and theories of customs in that period. It is observed here that a dichotomy between law and comity, which in this context originated from Lord Stowell's opinion at the end of the 18th century, was mirrored in Oppenheim's positivism, which rigorously discerned the legal from the moral. There were, in contrast, many publicists who identified immunity as customary *law*, although immunity was based on *humanity* rather than legal conscience. These facts illustrate the 'multinormativity' in international law. It also explains the 'judicial absolutism' in the 19th century. See Vec, Miloš. 'Principles in 19th Century International Law Doctrines', in *Constructing International Law: The Birth of a Discipline*, eds. Luigi Nuzzo and Miloš Vec (Frankfurt am Main: Vittorio Klostermann, 2012), 209–227, 227.

Nevertheless, as shown above, source criticism by which (legal) historians analyse historical sources textually and contextually with proper respect to the past itself reminds us of the existence of the rich context in which the source was placed. Just like the cases of Oppenheim and Chief Justice Fuller, primary materials such as treatises and evidence of state practices convey the naïveté of their authors, which we should bear in mind when utilising them as primary sources to engage the international legal historiography. As seen in the case study above, a selection of materials such as state practice and treatises indeed reflects treatise writers' views of what customary rules are. Without analyses of such primary sources in light of textual and contextual meaning, description of the past as what it really was easily fails. In this sense, source criticism can tame subjective and thus political viewpoint of observers, as well as the naïveté of positivism in international law specifically in case of the custom-ascertainment. This approach should be taken irrespective of one's epistemic belief. Even the 'agnostics' attempts to better understand the present by mobilising historical pasts ultimately fail where they naïvely rely on sources. Without source criticism, agnostics cannot really use the historical past to legitimise their argument on present controversies 'to make our present situation clearer to us'[88] because the past does not offer any persuasive argument if used naïvely. It is undeniable that historical research is motivated by diverse intentions. However, as Lesaffer advised,[89] diversity is assured only when historical studies are conducted with the professional procedures by which we first seek to understand (as best as we can) the past on its own terms, instead of speculating about it to better understand the present. Even accepting agnostics' views that we can never access the past as it was, this does not mean we must abandon this professional approach to the past; it is all the more essential for their objectives to ensure the legitimacy of their interpretations of the past. Doing history is a dynamic process to acquire a more persuasive comprehension of the past, and through constant communication among those who are involved in historical studies, the historiographical turn in our scholarship will be enriched, instead of a confrontation of methods, a mere *Methodenstreit*.

Acknowledgements

I would like to thank Professor Anne Peters and Raphael Schäfer for useful feedback on earlier versions of this chapter. For giving me the opportunity to

88 Koskenniemi, *Gentle Civilizer* 2001 (n. 9), 10.

89 Lesaffer, 'International Law and Its History' 2007 (n. 13), 37.

present and discuss some parts of this chapter during research stays, I would like to gratefully acknowledge Professor Miloš Vec and the members of the Department for Legal and Constitutional History, University of Vienna. I am also pleased to acknowledge my debt to Professors Kinji Akashi and Masaharu Yanagihara for keeping me consciously aware of *Methodenstreit* in international legal historiography. All errors and omissions that remain are, of course, my own.

Bibliography

Akashi, Kinji. *Cornelius van Bynkershoek: His Role in the History of International Law* (Alphen aan den Rijn: Kluwer Law International, 1998).

Akashi, Kinji. *Fukashi no 'kokusaihō': Hobbuzu, Raipunittsu, Rusō no kanōsei* [*Doctrinae invisibiles juris gentium: Hobbes, Leibniz et Rousseau*] (Tokyo: Keio University Press, 2019).

Baker, Scherston. *Halleck's International Law or Rules Regulating the Intercourse of States in Peace and War*, vol. II (London: K. Paul, Trench, Trübner & Co., 3rd ed. 1893).

Benton, Lauren. 'Beyond Anachronism: Histories of International Law and Global Legal Politics'. *Journal of the History of International Law* 21(1) (2019), 1–34.

Bernstorff, Jochen von. *Der Glaube an das universale Recht. Zur Völkerrechtstheorie Hans Kelsens und seiner Schüler* (Baden-Baden: Nomos, 2001).

Bevir, Mark. 'Objectivity in History'. *History and Theory* 33(3) (1994), 328–344.

Bluntschli, Johann Caspar. *Das moderne Völkerrecht der civilisirten Staten als Rechtsbuch dargestellt* (Nördlingen: C. H. Beck, 1878).

Boeck, Charles de. *De la propriété privée ennemie sous pavillon ennemi* (Paris: Durand et Pedone-Lauriel, 1882).

Bonfils, Henry. *Manuel de droit international public* (Paris: Librairie Arthur Rousseau, 4th ed. 1905).

Calvo, Charles. *Le droit international: théorique et pratique, précédé d'un exposé Historique des progrès de la science du droit des gens*, vol. IV (Paris: Librairie nouvelle de droit et de jurisprudence, 5th ed. 1896).

Carty, Anthony. *The Decay of International Law: A Reappraisal of the Limits of Legal Imagination in International Affairs* (Manchester: Manchester University Press, 1986).

Craven, Matthew. 'Introduction: International Law and Its Histories', in *Time, History and International Law*, eds. Matthew Craven, Malgosia Fitzmaurice and Maria Vogiatzi (Leiden: Martinus Nijhoff, 2007), 1–25.

Craven, Matthew. 'Theorizing the Turn to History in International Law', in *The Oxford Handbook of the Theory of International Law*, eds. Anne Orford and Florian Hoffman (Oxford: Oxford University Press, 2016), 21–37.

Despagnet, Frantz. *Cours de droit international public* (Paris: L. Larose, 2nd ed. 1899).

Dhondt, Frederik. 'Recent Research in the History of International Law'. *Tijdschrift voor Rechtsgeschiedenis* 84 (2016), 313–334.

Fitzmaurice, Andrew. 'Context in the History of International Law'. *Journal of the History of International Law* 20(1) (2018), 5–30.

Galindo, George R. B. 'Martti Koskenniemi and the Historiographical Turn in International Law'. *European Journal of International Law* 16(3) (2005), 539–559.

García-Salmones Rovira, Mónica. *The Project of Positivism in International Law* (Oxford: Oxford University Press, 2013).

Guggenheim, Paul. 'Contribution à l'histoire des sources du droit des gens'. *Recueil des cours de l'academie de droit international de La Haye* 94 (1958), 1–84.

Hall, William Edward. *A Treatise on International Law* (Oxford: Clarendon Press, 3rd ed. 1890).

Heffter, August Wilhelm. *Europäische Völkerrecht der Gegenwart* (Berlin: H. W. Müller, 8th ed. 1888).

Holland, Thomas Erskine. *A Manual of Naval Prize Law* (London: Darling & Son, 1888).

Kemmerer, Alexandra. '"We Do Not Need to Always Look to Westphalia ...": A Conversation with Martti Koskenniemi and Anne Orford'. *Journal of the History of International Law* 17(1) (2015), 1–14.

Kingsbury, Benedict. 'Legal Positivism as Normative Politics: International Society, Balance of Power and Lassa Oppenheim's Positive International Law'. *European Journal of International Law* 13(2) (2002), 401–436.

Koskenniemi, Martti. *The Gentle Civilizer of Nations: The Rise and Fall of International Law 1870–1960* (Cambridge: Cambridge University Press, 2001).

Koskenniemi, Martti. 'The Politics of International Law – 20 Years Later'. *European Journal of International Law* 20(1) (2009), 7–19.

Koskenniemi, Martti. 'Histories of International Law: Significance and Problems for a Critical View'. *Temple International and Comparative Law Journal* 27(2) (2013), 215–240.

Lawrence, Thomas Joseph. *The Principles of International Law* (Boston: D. C. Heath & Co., 3rd ed. 1904).

Le Ministère des Affaires Étrangères des Pays-Bas, ed. *Deuxième Conférence Internationale de la Paix. La Haye, 15 Juin–18 Octobre 1907. Actes et documents*, vol. 1 (La Haye: Imprimerie Nationale, 1907).

Lesaffer, Randall. 'International Law and Its History: The Story of an Unrequited Love', in *Time, History and International Law*, eds. Matthew Craven, Malgosia Fitzmaurice and Maria Vogiatzi (Leiden: Martinus Nijhoff, 2007), 27–41.

Lorenz, Chris. 'History: Theories and Methods', in *International Encyclopedia of the Social & Behavioral Sciences*, vol. 11, ed. James Wright (Amsterdam: Elsevier Science, 2nd ed. 2015), 131–137.

Martens, Georg Friedrich von, ed. *Recueil des principaux traités d'alliance, de paix, de trêve, de neutralité, de commerce, de limites, d'échange etc.: Conclus par les puissances de l'europe tant entre elles qu'avec les puissances et etats dans d'autres parties du monde depuis 1761 jusqu'à Present*, vol. VI (Gottingue: Dieterich, 2nd ed. 1829).

Mokre, Hans. *Theorie des Gewohnheitsrechts: Problementwicklung und System* (Berlin: Springer, 1932).

Moyn, Samuel. 'Legal History as a Source of International Law: The Politics of Knowledge', in *The Oxford Handbook of the Sources of International Law*, eds. Samantha Besson and Jean d'Aspremont (Oxford: Oxford University Press, 2017), 301–318.

Müller, Philipp. 'Understanding History: Hermeneutics and Source-Criticism', in *Reading Primary Sources: The Interpretation of Texts from Nineteenth- and Twentieth-Century History*, eds. Miriam Dobson and Benjamin Ziemann (Abingdon: Routledge, 2009), 21–36.

Nijman, Janne. *Seeking Change by Doing History* (Amsterdam: Amsterdam University Press, 2018).

Nys, Ernest. *Le droit international: Les principes, les théories, les faits*, vol. 3 (Bruxelles/Paris: A. Castaigne/A. Fontemoing, 1906).

Oppenheim, Lassa. *International Law: A Treatise*, vol. 1 (London: Longmans, Green and Co., 1905).

Oppenheim, Lassa. *International Law: A Treatise*, vol. 2 (London: Longmans, Green and Co., 1906).

Oppenheim, Lassa. 'The Science of International Law: Its Task and Method'. *American Journal of International Law* 2(2) (1908), 313–356.

Oppenheim, Lassa. 'Die Zukunft des Völkerrechts', in *Festschrift für Karl Binding zum 4. Juni 1911*, vol. I (Leipzig: Verlag von Wilhelm Engelmann, 1911), 140–201.

Oppenheim, Lassa. *International Law: A Treatise*, vol. 2 (London: Longmans, Green and Co., 2nd ed. 1912).

Oppenheim, Lassa. 'Zur Lehre vom internationalen Gewohnheitsrecht'. *Niemeyers Zeitschrift für internationales Recht* 25 (1915), 1–13.

Oppenheim, Lassa. *The Future of International Law* (Oxford: Clarendon Press, 1921).

Orford, Anne. 'On International Legal Method'. *London Review of International Law* 1 (2013), 166–197.

Orford, Anne. 'International Law and the Limits of History', in *The Law of International Lawyers: Reading Martti Koskenniemi*, eds. Wouter Werner, Marieke de Hoon and Alexis Galán (Cambridge: Cambridge University Press, 2017), 297–320.

Ortolan, Théodore. *Règles internationales et diplomatie de la mer*, vol. II (Paris: Plon, 4th ed. 1856).

Perels, Ferdinand von. *Das internationale öffentliche Seerecht der Gegenwart* (Berlin: Ernst Mittler, 2nd ed. 1903).

Perreau-Saussine, Amanda. 'A Case Study on Jurisprudence as a Source of International Law: Oppenheim's Influence', in *Time, History and International Law*, eds. Matthew Craven, Malgosia Fitzmaurice and Maria Vogiatzi (Leiden: Martinus Nijhoff, 2007), 91–117.

Perreau-Saussine, Amanda. 'Three Ways of Writing a Treatise on Public International Law', in *The Nature of Customary Law*, eds. Amanda Perreau-Saussine and James Bernard Murphy (Cambridge: Cambridge University Press, 2007), 228–255.

Phillimore, Robert. *Commentaries upon International Law*, vol. III (London: Butterworths, 3rd ed. 1885).

Pillet, Antoine. *Les lois actuelles de la guerre* (Paris: A. Rousseau, 2nd ed. 1901).

Pradier-Fodéré, Paul. *Traité de droit international public européen et américain: Suivant les progrès de la science et de la pratique contemporaines*, vol. 8 (Paris: A. Pedone, 1906).

Rivier, Alphonse. *Principes du droit des gens*, vol. 2 (Paris: Librairie Nouvelle de Droit et de Jurisprudence, 1896).

Robinson, Christopher. *Reports of Cases Argued and Determined in the High Court of Admiralty: Commencing with the Judgments of the Right Hon. Sir William Scott, Michaelmas Term 1798*, vol. 1 (London: Strahan, 1799).

Schmoeckel, Mathias. 'The Story of Success: Lassa Oppenheim and His "International Law"', in *East Asian and European Perspectives on International Law*, eds. Michael Stolleis and Masaharu Yanagihara (Baden-Baden: Nomos, 2004), 57–138.

Skouteris, Thomas. 'Engaging History in International Law', in *New Approaches to International Law*, eds. José María Beneyto and David Kennedy (The Hague: T.M.C. Asser Press, 2012), 99–121.

Taylor, Hannis. *A Treatise on International Public Law* (Chicago: Callaghan & Company, 1901).

Twiss, Travers. *The Law of Nations Considered as Independent Political Communities: On the Rights and Duties of Nations in Time of War* (Oxford/London: Clarendon Press/Longmans, Green and Co., 2nd ed. 1875).

Vec, Miloš. 'Principles in 19th Century International Law Doctrines', in *Constructing International Law: The Birth of a Discipline*, eds. Luigi Nuzzo and Miloš Vec (Frankfurt am Main: Vittorio Klostermann, 2012), 209–227.

Walker, Thomas Alfred. *A Manual of Public International Law* (Cambridge: Cambridge University Press, 1895).

Weil, Prosper. 'Le droit international en quête de son identité'. *Recueil des cours de l'academie de droit international de La Haye* 237 (1992), 9–370.

Westlake, John. *International Law*, vol. 2 (Cambridge: Cambridge University Press, 1907).

Wharton, Francis. *A Digest of the International Law of the United States: Taken from Documents Issued by Presidents and Secretaries of State, and from Decisions of Federal Courts and Opinions of Attorneys-General*, vol. III (Washington: Government Printing Office, 2nd ed. 1887).

Yanagihara, Masaharu. *Vorufu no kokusaihō riron* [*The Theory of International Law of Christian Wolff*] (Tokyo: Yūhikaku, 1998).

Yanagihara, Masaharu. 'Significance of the History of the Law of Nations in Europe and East Asia'. *Recueil des cours de l'academie de droit international de La Haye* 371 (2015), 273–435.

CHAPTER 18

A History of International Law in the Vernacular

Jacob Katz Cogan

Abstract

Histories of international law have typically focused on the origins of legal rules and doctrines, the decisions of courts and other formal tribunals, the views of professors and legal theorists and diplomats, and the evolution of the legal profession. That is, international legal histories have centered on the concerns of lawyers and states and have reflected a positivist vision of international lawmaking. We need a history of international law that focuses more on international law in action – the invocation, elaboration, and contestation of rules in and through their everyday application, not just by states, high-level state actors, legal theorists, and state-organized domestic and international institutions, but also by individuals, low-level officials, private groups, and nongovernmental actors and in places outside of the usual fora where 'international law' is said to be found. We need a history of international law in the vernacular.

Keywords

legal history – international law – vernacular

Introduction

Histories of international law have typically focused on the origins of legal rules and doctrines, the decisions of courts and other formal tribunals, the views of professors and legal theorists and diplomats, and the evolution of the legal profession.[1] That is, international legal histories have centered on the concerns of lawyers and states and have reflected a positivist vision of international lawmaking. Given this internalist motivation and formalistic predisposition, international legal histories, even those that seek to incorporate

1 For example, Koskenniemi, Martti. *The Gentle Civilizer of Nations: The Rise and Fall of International Law 1870–1960* (Cambridge: Cambridge University Press, 2001); Pitts, Jennifer. *Boundaries of the International: Law and Empire* (Cambridge: Harvard University Press, 2018).

 | DOI:10.1163/9789004461802_020

non-Western perspectives and experiences,[2] are generally hierarchical, top-down enterprises, disregarding the encounters of low-level players and regular persons with the law, and instead preferring investigations of the spaces and processes where law is officially said to be made and articulated and prioritizing the writings and actions of top government officials, 'key jurists', and other elite actors.[3] While there is much to be learned, and still to be learned, from studying international law's history in this manner, and indeed there have been many important studies within this tradition, the ways in which international law is made, claimed, and enforced are much broader, and its histories need to better reflect that.

We need a history of international law that focuses more on international law in action – the invocation, elaboration, and contestation of rules in and through their everyday application, not just by states, high-level state actors, legal theorists, and state-organized domestic and international institutions, but also by individuals, low-level officials, private groups, and nongovernmental actors and in places outside of the usual fora where 'international law' is said to be found. What's needed is a more inclusive history of international law, one that focuses on everyday practice and recognizes that law can be generated and used through lived experience and conflict and articulated outside of formal arenas and the 'normal' places and by persons who may not be lawyers or officials.[4]

At the most general level, what's required is a social history of international law. But, as Martti Koskenniemi noted a few years ago, 'Social history … [has]

2 See, for example, Becker Lorca, Arnulf. *Mestizo International Law: A Global Intellectual History, 1842–1933* (Cambridge: Cambridge University Press, 2015); Pahuja, Sundhya. 'Letters from Bandung: Encounters with another International Law', in *Bandung, Global History, and International Law: Critical Pasts and Pending Futures*, eds. Luis Eslava, Michael Fakhri and Vasuki Nesiah (Cambridge: Cambridge University Press, 2017), 552–573, doi: 10.1017/9781316414880.036. The same might be said for histories that seek to incorporate other perspectives, such as those of women, that have often been omitted. See, for example, Amann, Diane Marie. 'Cecelia Goetz, Woman at Nuremberg'. *International Criminal Law Review* 11(3) (2011), 607–620, doi: 10.1163/157181211X576456.

3 Benton, Lauren. 'Beyond Anachronism: Histories of International Law and Global Legal Politics'. *Journal of the History of International Law* 21(1) (2019), 7–40, 7, 12, doi: 10.1163/15718050-12340100; see also Hanley, Will. 'Statelessness: An Invisible Theme in the History of International Law'. *European Journal of International Law* 25(1) (2014), 321–327, 321, doi: 10.1093/ejil/chu015 ('the history of international law is dominated by Europe, by states, and by ideas (especially the ideas of great men)').

4 Compare Hanley, 'Statelessness' 2014 (n. 3), 326 ('those who do not speak for states rarely meet the threshold of inclusion in conventional histories of international law, despite their evident participation in the world of international law').

yet to penetrate international law'.[5] Similarly, Valentina Vadi has recently concluded that '[Law and Society] approaches remain underused' by historians of international law.[6] This is odd because socio-legal approaches to the history of law have dominated the legal history field since the 1970s. Though Lauren Benton has noted the recent 'influence of socio-legal approaches ... to global history', especially in imperial legal history and histories of global ordering, the preoccupations of most historians of international law, remain fixated on the internalist concerns of lawyers or the subversive analysis of international law's critics.[7] While it may now be harsh to say that 'the history of international law ... seems to be about where the history of law of other fields was about a half-century ago', as John Witt did in 2011,[8] it is not too far off the mark.

But if a social history of international law is concerned most broadly with 'making sense of the social and political significance of international law', my intervention here is more specific.[9] We need a history of international law in the vernacular. The absence of such a history has led to omissions, to an incompleteness. People are left out, subjects are omitted, and our understanding of how international law is made, operates, and functions is skewed.

1 The Allegiances of Lawyers and Historians

Why do historians of international law focus primarily on conventional legal actors and conventional legal sources, searching for the origins of a particular

5 Koskenniemi, Martti. 'Expanding Histories of International Law'. *American Journal of Legal History* 56(1) (2016), 104–112, 104, 107, doi: 10.1093/ajlh/njv011.

6 Vadi, Valentina. 'International Law and Its Histories: Methodological Risks and Opportunities'. *Harvard International Law Journal* 58(2) (2017), 311–352, 311, 339.

7 Benton, 'Beyond Anachronism' 2019 (n. 3), 20, 26; see also Benton, Lauren. 'Made in Empire: Finding the History of International Law in Imperial Locations'. *Leiden Journal of International Law* 31(3) (2018), 473–478, doi: 10.1017/S0922156518000237.

8 Witt, John F. 'A Social History of International Law: Historical Commentary, 1861–1900', in *International Law in the U.S. Supreme Court: Continuity and Change*, eds. David L. Sloss, Michael D. Ramsey and Williams S. Dodge (Cambridge: Cambridge University Press, 2011), 164–187, 164, 177, doi: 10.1017/CBO9780511977121.006.

9 Witt, 'Social History' 2011 (n. 8), 179. For excellent histories in the social history tradition, see, for example, Hirsch, Francine. *Soviet Judgment at Nuremberg: A New History of the International Military Tribunal after World War II* (Oxford: Oxford University Press, 2020); Moyn, Samuel. *The Last Utopia: Human Rights in History* (Cambridge: Harvard University Press, 2010); Whitman, James Q. *The Verdict of Battle* (Cambridge: Harvard University Press, 2012); Witt, John F. *Lincoln's Code: The Laws of War in American History* (New York: Free Press, 2012).

rule or the field or the profession itself? Why has a socio-legal approach been largely absent from the history of international law?

The starting point for understanding why this is begins with the fact that most historians of international law are not historians first but lawyers, by which I simply mean that they have not been trained as historians in a history department. Instead, they are lawyers by training and socialization, and their doctoral studies, even if focused on the history of international law, were in a law faculty and not a history department. I generalize, and I don't want to rehash a long-ago stale debate about 'lawyer's history' and 'historian's history' and claim that it is only the latter that matters. I simply mean that, with regard to the type of history one writes, it matters whether you were trained in a history department or alternatively some other department within the university, whether that other department is law, political science, sociology, or something else.

The location of one's university training matters in many ways, but one stands out: historians and lawyers, because of the disparate sites of their training, have different allegiances. The allegiances of legal historians trained in law faculties is to the law and taking law seriously *as law* and to determining what the law is and what its origins are. I don't mean an uncritical allegiance. But that allegiance explains the focus on jurists, judges, cases, and negotiating histories, to the exclusion of almost everything outside the confines of 'the law'. The people, places, sources, and questions under study flow from a fairly rigid and formalistic conceptualization of law and lawmaking, one that is attenuated, if not detached, from the outside world and real life, and one which indeed is wary of recognizing the import of acts outside of recognized legal processes. Such a commitment seems to be even more important for international lawyers, and therefore the history that they write.

Those who have trained in history departments learn not just to think of the past as a different place, but, more importantly, legal historians who are trained in history departments take for granted the basic insight that law and legal actors are not independent variables unconnected to the world that surrounds them. As John Witt has noted, 'for at least a half-century ..., historians have adopted one or more variations on the basic legal realist observation that law is embedded in society and is inescapably a way of accomplishing policy ends inexplicable outside that context'.[10] Law reacts to or is a product of political and social pressures while at the same time constructing the world that surrounds it. For those trained in history departments, law 'cannot be explained

10 Witt, 'Social History' 2011 (n. 8), 176.

apart from the social movements and political transformations outside of the domain of formal' law and institutions.[11] Law for legal historians is understood capaciously.[12] It is 'rooted ... in lived experience'.[13] It is only when you have these inclinations and this perspective that you can be, and would be, inclined to undertake a social history of international law, examining law outside of the usual places, as applied or articulated by persons beyond the legal mainstream.

But such an approach can be very difficult for many international lawyers. Subject to (and defensive about) the claim that international law is not law at all but simply power, it is no wonder that international lawyers would avoid a type of history that concedes, which is in fact premised on, the inseparability of law and society.[14] The history of international law as written by international lawyers therefore typically eschews sources and stories in which international law is not found through established mechanisms of lawmaking, law interpretation, and law application. It instead is committed to formalism as the baseline for inquiry and to states and institutions and their representatives as the basis for international law and its history.[15] Even critical and postcolonial historians of international law, who write skeptically and subversively about the international law project, have not taken advantage of the social history perspective, perhaps because the premise of their critique – law as power – limits the scope of their inquiry. It is a great irony that international law, which along with domestic constitutional law is that domain of law that is most connected with political and social pressures, has a history, thus far, that is not fully reflective of that fact.

11 Ibid.

12 See Edwards, Laura F. 'Law as Social History', in *The Oxford Handbook of Legal History*, eds. Markus D. Dubber and Christopher Tomlins (Oxford: Oxford University Press, 2018), 119–134, 119, 120, doi: 10.1093/oxfordhb/9780198794356.013.7.

13 Benton, 'Beyond Anachronism' 2019 (n. 3), 32.

14 On related themes, see Koskenniemi, Martti. 'Between Commitment and Cynicism: Outline for a Theory of International Law as Practice', in *The Politics of International Law* (Oxford: Hart Publishing, 2011), 271–293, doi: 10.5040/9781472565587.ch-011.

15 See Kahn, Paul W. *The Cultural Study of Law: Reconstructing Legal Scholarship* (Chicago: University of Chicago Press, 1999), 109–110; Lustig, Doreen. 'Governance Histories of International Law', in *The Oxford Handbook of Legal History*, eds. Markus D. Dubber and Christopher Tomlins (Oxford: Oxford University Press, 2018), 859–882, 865, doi: 10.1093/oxfordhb/9780198794356.013.46.

2 History beyond the Usual People and Places

I don't mean to suggest that other types of history are of no value. There are plenty of wonderful international legal histories outside of the social history genre. And, indeed, training in a history department does not guarantee the use of a social history method, let alone a history in the vernacular. But I am interested here in what the history of international law currently leaves out and the benefits of thinking about history in another way. The way one writes history reflects choices (about what law is, how law is made, and who makes law), and such choices have a politics.

If conventional international legal histories focus on the people and places of the formal legal system, then those who are not in those places or who are not lawyers or high government officials are those who are left out, their concerns and ideas excluded. A history in the vernacular recognizes that law is found in the claims of low-level officials, non-lawyers, and regular people and outside the usual places where law is said to reside, and that such law may contest or simply be different from the law of the formal legal system. There have been correctives in recent years to the Eurocentrism of the history of international law, expanding the geographic scope of the enterprise to include officials and lawyers from non-Western countries. A global history approach may be helpful since, as Anne Peters and Bardo Fassbender wrote, 'Global history no longer takes the nation-state as the traditional object of historical analysis. Instead, to global historians, the major actors or subjects of a global history are movements … and business … .'[16] Similarly, the greater inclusion of women in international legal history may move us in this direction, so too might micro-histories, as they both have the potential to bring us to 'unusual' spaces and participants.[17] But not necessarily. The move to global history has mostly not yet led to the type of history I am describing here (though that may be changing). A history of international law in the vernacular is not about non-Western understandings of international law, per se, no matter how much such studies unsettle our preconceptions of international law and its histories. A history from the perspective of the elite recognizes no boundaries.

---

16 Fassbender, Bardo and Anne Peters. 'Introduction: Towards a Global History of International Law', in *The Oxford Handbook of the History of International Law*, eds. Bardo Fassbender and Anne Peters (Oxford: Oxford University Press, 2012), 1–24, 9, doi: 10.1093/law/9780199599752.003.0001.

17 On micro-histories, see Vadi, Valentina. 'The Power of Scale: International Law and Its Microhistories'. *Denver Journal of International Law and Policy* 46(4) (2018), 315–348; Vadi, Valentina. 'Perspective and Scale in the Architecture of International Legal History'. *European Journal of International Law* 30(1) (2019), 53–71, doi: 10.1093/ejil/chz001.

3 What Is a History of International Law in the Vernacular?

A history of international law in the vernacular has four characteristics: First, and most distinctively, it extends the history of international law to include people other than jurists and judges, high-level officials and legal theorists and incorporate places beyond those of high-level diplomacy. Second, it is concerned with the relationship, at a particular moment in time, between international law and the social and political world in which law is embedded. This type of history, as Paul Kahn has written, seeks to 'study international law as a social practice and system of belief'.[18] Third, vernacular history allows us to view international law in action, how it works – the operative law as it is used and contested, not the law as it appears in the books. Fourth, it 'challenges the singularities that mainstream legal scholarship insist on as what it means to "do" or think about "law"'.[19] A vernacular history of international law, in other words, broadens what and how we think about international law. It extends our conceptualization of international law's participants, it expands our notions of what influences international law, it enlarges our understanding of how international law is made, applied, and used, and it recognizes that there are different purposes, functions, and 'dialects' of international law. Consequently, a vernacular history of international law requires us to accept the idea, contrary to the formalist inclinations of most international lawyers, of a vernacular international law.

The historian who has best exemplified this type of work is Lauren Benton. For example, in her book *A Search for Sovereignty*, the chapter on 'Sovereignty at Sea' emphasizes the role of non-lawyers, specifically navy captains and pirates, in participating in the construction of the international maritime legal order.[20] The legality of the sea captains' actions depended on their commissions, which (if authentic and applicable) authorized them to seize other vessels and reap the proceeds from their sale. 'Not surprisingly', Benton writes, 'both captains and common sailors cultivated a certain expertise in representing their commissions as legitimate and the assets they seized as legal prizes'.[21] Indeed, she continues, 'as a consequence, [captains] actively engaged in imaginative legal posturing, rehearsing stories that might serve to establish actions as legal in

18 Kahn, *Cultural Study of Law* 1999 (n. 15), 109.

19 Hartog, Hendrik. 'Response: A Muddle in the Middle'. *Law & Social Inquiry* 44(2) (2019), 534–547, 545, doi: 10.1017/lsi.2019.21.

20 Benton, Lauren. *A Search for Sovereignty: Law and Geography in European Empires, 1400–1900* (Cambridge: Cambridge University Press, 2010).

21 Ibid., 113.

judicial forums'.[22] Not to be outdone, pirates sought to obtain commissions and represent those as valid. At trial for piracy or unlawful seizures, both pirates and navy captains would make creative arguments about the validity of their commissions. These arguments and disputes, as they arose around the globe, Benton writes, 'enter[ed] metropolitan politics and prompted early modern jurists to begin to define the law of the sea as a particular strand within the ius gentium'.[23] 'The international regulation of privateering', she explains, 'was emerging more out of a replication of administrative legal orders [stemming from the claims of sea captains and pirates] than as a result of adherence to a settled understanding of the law of nations'.[24]

In their book *Rage for Order: The British Empire and the Origins of International Law*, Benton and Lisa Ford make an even more interesting claim.[25] In place of the 'tendency to place the history of international law solely within the framework of intellectual history', they write, 'We propose a different approach marked by a paradox: the history of international law advances by receding as a topic'.[26] 'To make sense of the early nineteenth century as a phase within the history of international law', they say, 'we must look away from international law and international lawyers and toward processes of imperial legal change'.[27] The history of international law, they claim, describing what they call a 'vernacular constitution', 'sits in unusual places … [in] the correspondence of middling officials …, records showing the legal strategies of the empire's most vulnerable subjects, the reports of commissions of inquiry, notes on colonial scandals, communications … by merchants and sojourners'.[28] These documents might occasionally refer to Vattel and 'draw [vaguely]' on the writings of high-level jurists, but they 'also produced new and powerful frameworks' that were not readily connected with that jurisprudence.[29] In Benton and Ford's history, international law is found in unusual places and is constructed or instigated by 'unlikely juridical thinkers'[30] as they negotiated the

22 Ibid.

23 Ibid., 120.

24 Ibid., 156.

25 Benton, Lauren and Lisa Ford. *Rage for Order: The British Empire and the Origins of International Law* (Cambridge: Harvard University Press, 2016).

26 Ibid., 20–21.

27 Ibid., 21.

28 Ibid.

29 Ibid.

30 Ibid., 17.

world in which they lived, opportunistically and creatively using and adapting elite ideas and doctrines, establishing their own 'vernacular' law.[31]

The challenge of a history of international law in the vernacular is similar to that of all history from below. As Rohit De explained in his *A People's Constitution: The Everyday Life of Law in the Indian Republic*, 'To understand how constitutional law works in India, ... it is necessary to understand what people (whether legal officials or ordinary citizens) believe law is and what they do with this knowledge as they make decisions in their daily lives'.[32] In a recent paper, De criticized 'The new histories of [human] rights [which he says] have broadly fallen into two genres, intellectual history (where thinkers, politicians and philosophers have articulated claims) and diplomatic history (which has focused on negotiations between states and the creation of international instruments)'.[33] 'Significant as these histories have been', De argues, 'the[ir] focus [is] on the creation of norms above rather than their articulation and assertion [of norms] by ordinary people in their everyday interactions'.[34] But, he asks, 'how does one write and explain global legal transformations at the scale of the local rather the international?'[35]

The answer, as De suggests, and as Benton and Ford's work shows, is to look at the use of and people's interaction with 'international law'. What is needed is a practice-oriented approach. Will Hanley contends in a recent article on late-Ottoman Egypt, that 'a practical approach would emphasise the everyday business of the ordinary workers in the international legal edifice that included the West but – critically – extended far beyond it'.[36] He explains, as an example, that 'Lawyers in the Legal Bureau of the Ottoman foreign ministry ... worked with treaty texts but rarely composed them. Instead, they applied

31 Benton, 'Beyond Anachronism' 2019 (n. 3), 26; see also Benton/Ford, *Rage for Order* 2016 (n. 25), 14 ('Powerful vernacular varieties of political theory developed out of the empire's legal politics'.); see also Merry, Sally Engle and Peggy Levitt. 'The Vernacularization of Women's Human Rights', in *Human Rights Futures*, eds. Stephen Hopgood, Jack Snyder and Leslie Vinjamuri (Cambridge: Cambridge University Press, 2017), 213–236, 213, doi: 10.1017/9781108147767.009.

32 De, Rohit. *A People's Constitution: The Everyday Life of Law in the Indian Republic* (New Haven: Yale University Press, 2018), 21.

33 De, Rohit. 'Representing the other Race: Indian African Lawyers and the Local Histories of Universal Rights'. Paper Presented at the Conference 'Between Public and Private: A Celebration of Dirk Hartog', Princeton University, 12–13 October 2018.

34 Ibid.

35 Ibid.

36 Hanley, Will. 'International Lawyers without Public International Law: The Case of Late Ottoman Egypt'. *Journal of the History of International Law* 18(1) (2016), 98–119, 98, 113, doi: 10.1163/15718050-12340053.

them to specific situations that arose. In this way, they built the jurisprudence of international law, case by case, largely through administrative opinions'.[37] Natasha Wheatley's article on petitions to the League of Nations and Kalyani Ramnath's on how 'ordinary litigants' utilized 'legal language to capture how places, ideas, and things were connected' provide additional examples of international legal history in the vernacular.[38]

4 Varieties of Vernacular Legal History and Its Promise

While all vernacular history extends the scope and scale of international legal history to new people and places, and in so doing recognizes a broader understanding of what law is and how law is made and enforced, as these examples suggest, there are different varieties. One kind focuses on the interaction of legal ideas and interpretations between the local and the global. This can take the form of iterative exchanges that stem from the decisions of low-level actors who, in the course of implementing policies, revise authoritative rules or principles that they are tasked with applying or from the arguments made by those who, when confronted with the enforcement of such rules or authority seek, to revise them to their benefit. This 'interactive' type of vernacular history can also take the form of local actors reimagining existing rules as a means of reshaping international policy through engagement with international institutions and other authoritative governmental bodies. A second type is unidirectional and looks at the appropriation and localization of the international. Merry and Levitt have described this form of 'vernacularisation' as 'the extraction of ideas and practices from the universal sphere of international organizations, and their translation into ideas and practices that resonate with the values and ways of doing things in local contexts'.[39] A third vernacular genre examines an 'international law' that is entirely locally generated through the articulation of ideas and rules based on people's everyday interaction with the issues and problems of global society. It's what a formalist might describe as local custom. The distinctions between these categories does not imply categorical

37 Hanley, 'International Lawyers' 2016 (n. 36), 113–114.

38 See Wheatley, Natasha. 'Mandatory Interpretation: Legal Hermeneutics and the New International Order in Arab and Jewish Petitions to the League of Nations'. *Past & Present* 227 (2015), 205–248, 205, doi: 10.1093/pastj/gtv020; Ramnath, Kalyani. 'Intertwined Itineraries: Debt, Decolonization, and International Law in Post-World War II South Asia'. *Law & History Review* 38(1) (2020), 1–24, 1, 23, doi: 10.1017/S0738248020000012.

39 Merry/Levitt, 'Vernacularization' 2017 (n. 31), 213.

separation, however, as locally generated ideas, for example, may be used to contest rules imposed from above.

Regardless of the type, a history of international law in the vernacular has the promise of making the story of international law more capacious, expanding its purview to include more participants and more places, going 'beyond the rarified domains ... [into] wider circles of engagement and debate'.[40] It also provides an opportunity to see international law as contested, 'as an arena of struggle between contending and changing normative orders'.[41] The exclusivity of much of the history of international law as it has been written has a politics, since through its narrow conceptualization of law it limits the participants and contents of that history, and so bringing more people into international law and its history is a political move as well, one that is well worth pursuing.

Bibliography

Amann, Diane Marie. 'Cecelia Goetz, Woman at Nuremberg'. *International Criminal Law Review* 11(3) (2011), 607–620, doi: 10.1163/157181211X576456.

Becker Lorca, Arnulf. *Mestizo International Law: A Global Intellectual History, 1842–1933* (Cambridge: Cambridge University Press, 2015).

Benton, Lauren. *A Search for Sovereignty: Law and Geography in European Empires, 1400–1900* (Cambridge: Cambridge University Press, 2010).

Benton, Lauren. 'Made in Empire: Finding the History of International Law in Imperial Locations'. *Leiden Journal of International Law* 31(3) (2018), 473–478, doi: 10.1017/S0922156518000237.

Benton, Lauren. 'Beyond Anachronism: Histories of International Law and Global Legal Politics'. *Journal of the History of International Law* 21(1) (2019), 7–40, doi: 10.1163/15718050-12340100.

Benton, Lauren and Lisa Ford. *Rage for Order: The British Empire and the Origins of International Law* (Cambridge: Harvard University Press, 2016).

De, Rohit. *A People's Constitution: The Everyday Life of Law in the Indian Republic* (New Haven: Yale University Press, 2018).

De, Rohit. 'Representing the other Race: Indian African Lawyers and the Local Histories of Universal Rights'. Paper Presented at the Conference 'Between Public and Private: A Celebration of Dirk Hartog' Princeton University, 12–13 October 2018.

40 Sartori, Andrew. *Liberalism in Empire: An Alternative History* (Oakland: University of California Press, 2014), 7.

41 Hartog, Hendrik. 'The Constitution of Aspiration and "The Rights That Belong to Us All"'. *Journal of American History* 74(3) (1987), 1013–1034, 1032, doi: 10.2307/1902163.

Edwards, Laura F. 'Law as Social History', in *The Oxford Handbook of Legal History*, eds. Markus D. Dubber and Christopher Tomlins (Oxford: Oxford University Press, 2018), 119–134, doi: 10.1093/oxfordhb/9780198794356.013.7.

Fassbender, Bardo and Anne Peters. 'Introduction: Towards a Global History of International Law', in *The Oxford Handbook of the History of International Law*, eds. Bardo Fassbender and Anne Peters (Oxford: Oxford University Press, 2012), 1–24, doi: 10.1093/law/9780199599752.003.0001.

Hanley, Will. 'Statelessness: An Invisible Theme in the History of International Law'. *European Journal of International Law* 25(1) (2014), 321–327, doi: 10.1093/ejil/chu015.

Hanley, Will. 'International Lawyers without Public International Law: The Case of Late Ottoman Egypt'. *Journal of the History of International Law* 18(1) (2016), 98–119, doi: 10.1163/15718050-12340053, 98–119.

Hartog, Hendrik. 'The Constitution of Aspiration and "The Rights That Belong to Us All"'. *Journal of American History* 74(3) (1987), 1013–1034, doi: 10.2307/1902163.

Hartog, Hendrik. 'Response: A Muddle in the Middle'. *Law & Social Inquiry* 44(2) (2019), 534–547, doi: 10.1017/lsi.2019.21.

Hirsch, Francine. *Soviet Judgment at Nuremberg: A New History of the International Military Tribunal after World War II* (Oxford: Oxford University Press, 2020).

Kahn, Paul W. *The Cultural Study of Law: Reconstructing Legal Scholarship* (Chicago: University of Chicago Press, 1999).

Koskenniemi, Martti. *The Gentle Civilizer of Nations: The Rise and Fall of International Law 1870–1960* (Cambridge: Cambridge University Press, 2001).

Koskenniemi, Martti. 'Between Commitment and Cynicism: Outline for a Theory of International Law as Practice', in *The Politics of International Law* (Oxford: Hart, 2011), 271–293, doi: 10.5040/9781472565587.ch-011.

Koskenniemi, Martti. 'Expanding Histories of International Law'. *American Journal of Legal History* 56(1) (2016), 104–112, doi: 10.1093/ajlh/njv011.

Lustig, Doreen. 'Governance Histories of International Law', in *The Oxford Handbook of Legal History*, eds. Markus D. Dubber and Christopher Tomlins (Oxford: Oxford University Press, 2018), 859–882, doi: 10.1093/oxfordhb/9780198794356.013.46.

Merry, Sally Engle and Peggy Levitt. 'The Vernacularization of Women's Human Rights', in *Human Rights Futures*, eds. Stephen Hopgood, Jack Snyder and Leslie Vinjamuri (Cambridge: Cambridge University Press, 2017), 213–236, doi: 10.1017/9781108147767.009.

Moyn, Samuel. *The Last Utopia: Human Rights in History* (Cambridge: Harvard University Press, 2010).

Pahuja, Sundhya. 'Letters from Bandung: Encounters with another International Law', in *Bandung, Global History, and International Law: Critical Pasts and Pending*

Futures, eds. Luis Eslava, Michael Fakhri and Vasuki Nesiah (Cambridge: Cambridge University Press, 2017), 552–573, doi: 10.1017/9781316414880.036.

Pitts, Jennifer. *Boundaries of the International: Law and Empire* (Cambridge: Harvard University Press, 2018).

Ramnath, Kalyani. 'Intertwined Itineraries: Debt, Decolonization, and International Law in Post-World War II South Asia'. *Law & History Review* 38(1) (2020), 1–24, doi: 10.1017/S0738248020000012.

Sartori, Andrew. *Liberalism in Empire: An Alternative History* (Oakland: University of California Press, 2014).

Vadi, Valentina. 'International Law and Its Histories: Methodological Risks and Opportunities'. *Harvard International Law Journal* 58(2) (2017), 311–352.

Vadi, Valentina. 'The Power of Scale: International Law and Its Microhistories'. *Denver Journal of International Law and Policy* 46(4) (2018), 315–348.

Vadi, Valentina. 'Perspective and Scale in the Architecture of International Legal History'. *European Journal of International Law* 30(1) (2019), 53–71, doi: 10.1093/ejil/chz001.

Wheatley, Natasha. 'Mandatory Interpretation: Legal Hermeneutics and the New International Order in Arab and Jewish Petitions to the League of Nations'. *Past & Present* 227 (2015), 205–248, doi: 10.1093/pastj/gtv020.

Whitman, James Q. *The Verdict of Battle* (Cambridge: Harvard University Press, 2012).

Witt, John F. 'A Social History of International Law: Historical Commentary, 1861–1900', in *International Law in the U.S. Supreme Court: Continuity and Change*, eds. David L. Sloss, Michael D. Ramsey and Williams S. Dodge (Cambridge: Cambridge University Press, 2011), 164–187, doi: 10.1017/CBO9780511977121.006.

Witt, John F. *Lincoln's Code: The Laws of War in American History* (New York: Free Press, 2012).

Index

www.ingramcontent.com/pod-product-compliance
Lightning Source LLC
LaVergne TN
LVHW010636300926
849161LV00005B/959